TOWARD WHAT BRIGHT GLORY?

TOWARD WHAT BRIGHT GLORY?

A NOVEL

ALLEN DRURY

William Morrow and Company, Inc.   New York

Recognizing the importance of preserving what has been written, it is the policy of William Morrow and Company, Inc., and its imprints and affiliates to have the books it publishes printed on acid-free paper, and we exert our best efforts to that end.

Library of Congress Cataloging-in-Publication Data

Drury, Allen.
    Toward what bright glory? : a novel / Allen Drury.
        p.   cm.
    ISBN 0-688-07713-7
    I. Title.
    PS3554.R8T6   1990
    813'.54—dc20   89-13756
                                                    CIP

Printed in the United States of America

First Edition

1 2 3 4 5 6 7 8 9 10

BOOK DESIGN BY MANUELA PAUL

To

STANFORD

which nurtured us
and sent us forth to war
and troubled peace

"Hitler's armies struck today without warning deep into the heart of Poland," the announcer's tense voice boomed out into the serene quiet of the friendly hills. "In London, Prime Minister Chamberlain will make a radio address shortly to the British people. He is expected to announce that Great Britain and her Empire are once again at war with Germany."

Wilson turned off the radio and, for some reason he could not have explained, stood up.

"Well," he said in a voice that shook more than he knew, "I guess that does it."

They stared at one another blankly. Donn started to cry.

A sudden melancholy touched his heart. He reached down and rested his hand gently on her head.

Forever after part of him would always be standing on the lovely hill above the lovely valley, his hand on her head, the gentle haze of summer, summer, summer lying on the world.

Tears came into his eyes and all the happy days rushed through his heart going somewhere, somewhere, lost, gone, irretrievable, leaving him stranded on this distant hill while far below the red-tiled roofs of the University shimmered in the sun.

Ah, you wonderful place, he thought, you good times and dear friends! What will they do to us, in their pride and their anger? Where will they send us drifting, on the darkening flood of the years? Toward what bright glory? Into what far harbor?

He could only wonder, in fear and apprehension, on this golden afternoon while far away the hounds of hell were running free and would, he knew now beyond all escaping, come closer.

Perhaps if he and his friends were lucky they might, in time, achieve a fragile peace and so come home, in a different season.

But of that there was no surety.

NOTE

"The University" of course is Stanford. Why not call it so?

The reasons are auctorial and have to do with a certain freeing-up of narrative flow, a certain ease of reference. Basically the physical descriptions are exact, the time frame is exact, the capture of spirit, mood and atmosphere within that time frame is, I hope, exact.

Here and there, a minor revision of detail, whether for purposes of story or because of that passage through an author's mind of people, places and events that transforms them into things suggested by, distantly related to, yet definitely distinct and different from, actuality.

Any resemblance to any person living or dead is, as they say, entirely coincidental. Bits and pieces may here and there remotely exceed coincidence but the amalgam is all mine.

The only really arbitrary interference with facts is that I have conferred victory in the Big Game of 1938 upon the University whereas in historical reality it belongs to the University of California at Berkeley. But I could not deny Moose his triumph, and all but the most exacting of Cal alumni will, I hope, forgive me once they know that bumbling but likeable character. I think he deserves what Franky Miller calls his "F.A.T." So I have given it to him.

One serious historical note. The world in general did not know, at that time, exactly what was happening to the Jews in Germany. In the United States we got only sporadic and fragmentary reports, received only occasional sinister rumors. The truth, when it got through at all, was consistently downplayed by our leaders for reasons of state that at the time seemed valid to them. Consequently, with little accepted proof available, what we heard was frequently ridiculed by major figures in our press, radio and academic worlds as "just Allied war propaganda." The tensions and arguments that arise between characters in this novel are based upon what we knew then— the half-knowledge that was not knowledge, the deliberate minimizing or ridiculing of facts, for which those who were responsible should always, by history, be held accountable.

To good friend Richard M. Blois, associate staff legal counsel for Stanford's Office of Development, and to the always able and cooperative staff of the University archives, my thanks for most generous help with the detailed research necessary to complement memory.

A.D.

Members of the House, 1938–39, and Friends

Seniors

RAYMOND BAKER, Arvin, California. Pre-legal. RAY

TIMOTHY MERRILL BATES, Baltimore, Maryland. Political science–journalism. TIM

GILBERT GULBRANSEN, Minneapolis, Minnesota. Pre-medical. GIL

> KAREN ANN WATERHOUSE, La Jolla, California. Sociology. KAREN ANN

EDWARD PAUL HAGGERTY, Springfield, Illinois. Economics. HACK

> FRANCINE HELEN MAGRUDER, Houston, Texas. Pre-legal. FRAN

WILLIAM LATTIMER, Fargo, North Dakota. History. LATT

> KATHERINE ELLSWORTH, Seattle, Washington. English. KAY

NORTH McALLISTER, Los Angeles, California. Pre-medical. NORTH

> BETTY JUNE LETTERMAN, Salt Lake City, Utah. History. B.J.

FRANCIS ALLEN MILLER, San Leandro, California. Sociology. FRANKY

MARY KATHERINE SULLIVAN, Medford, Oregon. Graphic arts. KATIE

THEODORE KRASNIK MUSAVICH, Chicago, Illinois. Physical education. MOOSE

SUZANNE WAGGONER, Piedmont, California. Sociology. SUZY; "WELCOME"

ARTHUR JOHN RICHARDSON III, Montclair, New Jersey. Social sciences. BUFF

CLYDE GAIUS UNRUH, Honolulu, Hawaii. Pre-medical. GUY

MARGUERITE JOHNSON, Trenton, New Jersey. Economics. MAGGIE

RICHARD EMMETT WILSON, Terra Bella, California. Political science–public administration. WILLIE

DONNAMARIA VAN DYKE, West Park, New York. Social sciences. DONN; DONNA

Juniors

ANTONIO ANDRADE, Brooklyn, New York. Engineering. TONY

ANGELINA D'ALESSANDRO, San Francisco, California. Economics. ANGIE

LOUISE GIANFALCO, St. Helena, California., Economics. LOU

GALEN BRYCE, Burlingame, California. Psychology. GALE

SMITH CARRIGER, Gwynned Valley, Pennsylvania. Business administration. SMITTY

LOREN DAVIS, Long Beach, California. Engineering. LOR

ROBERT GODWIN, St. Louis, Missouri. Political science. BOB; "GOD"

JOHN THOMAS HERBERT, Philadelphia, Pennsylvania. History. JOHNNY

ALAN FREDERICK OFFENBERG, Cleveland, Ohio. Education. DUKE

RACHEL SHAHNA EPSTEIN, Hollywood, California. History. SHAHNA

RENÉ SURATT, Hillsborough, California. Economics. RENNY

Sophomores

JEFFERSON DAVIS BARNETT, Charleston, South Carolina. Social sciences. JEFF

RANDOLPH RAMIREZ CARRERO, Albuquerque, New Mexico. Political science. RANDY

 BEVERLY RAE STEVENS, Butte, Montana. Social sciences. FLUFF

RUDOLPH JOHN KROHL, Ridgewood, New Jersey. Business administration. RUDY

ROGER LEIGHTON, Phoenix, Arizona. Physics. RODGE

HENRY ELLIS MOORE, Gaithersburg, Maryland. Education. HANK

MARCUS ANDREW TAYLOR, Pittsburgh, Pennsylvania. Engineering. MARC

WILLIAM HENRY WILSON, Terra Bella, California. Education–dramatic arts. BILLY

 ELIZABETH JANE MONTGOMERY, Portland, Oregon. English. JANIE

BAYARD WHITTINGTON JOHNSON, Chicago, Illinois. Mechanical engineering. BY

 MARYETTA BRADFORD, Berkeley, California. Sociology. MARYETTA

ARAM KATANIAN, Fresno, California. Pre-legal. ARI

YOSUHIRO NAGATANI, Fresno, California. Political science–business administration. BILL

1

His heart was full of dreams, his head was full of schemes.

He was twenty-one years old and the world, or so his particular corner of it believed, was his oyster.

Late in September of a year long ago, while Adolf Hitler raved in Europe and in America an uneasy nation argued whether he really meant it, Richard Emmett Wilson—"Willie"—sometime lover, ofttime philosopher, student of human nature and, as his friends often wryly told him, P.B.P. (Perfect Boy Politician) and S.M.O.C. (Superman on Campus), drove north through the lingering summer heat of California's Central Valley toward the red-tiled roofs, youth-filled colonnades and well-loved meadows, groves and sandstone buildings of the University.

He was happy.

And why not?

First and most importantly, he was incoming president of the student body, having been elected by a handsome majority just before close of school in June, in a contest with his former freshman roommate, Aram Katanian.

Ari at the time had been president of Interclub Conference, Willie president of Interfraternity Council. Willie had been, inevitably, the candidate of what was known enviously as "the Row Machine." Aided by the fact that at the time he was also president of the junior class, chairman of Rally Committee, president of Cardinals, former president of his fraternity house and, with a few exceptions, the darling of almost everybody, he had swept to an easy victory.

Ari had known from the start that he didn't have a prayer. But there was more to it than Wilson's prominence and popularity. Their other roommate, now his fraternity brother, Clyde Gaius Unruh, had tried to analyze it soon after they all met for the first time in freshman dorm.

"Willie's mystique," Guy Unruh called it, shaking his head with a certain friendly bafflement, as people often did when discussing Richard Emmett Wilson. "He's got something."

And so he appeared to have, as his highly successful years at the University unfolded and nearly everyone came to recognize his abilities with a respect that in many cases bordered on awe.

On election night when Ari called to offer congratulations, he too paid tribute.

After admitting that his defeat "hurts like hell but I expected it," he added, "But then, everything has always been easy for you, Willie. You don't have to worry about life. You can't lose."

"Don't tell me that!" Wilson retorted, surprising himself with his own vehemence. "You scare me!"

"I know," Ari agreed soberly. "It isn't easy, carrying the burden of people's belief in you."

"Tell me about it," Willie said in an odd, almost bitter tone; and then, as always afraid of revealing himself too much, pulled back and made light of it. "Thanks for your understanding, Ari. I appreciate it." Adding with characteristic wryness, "I'll do my damnedest to be worthy of this great public trust in me."

"Don't knock it, pal," Ari said, refusing to be put off. "You have it. You certainly have all *my* support, too, you know that. Call on me when there's anything I can do to help."

"There will be," Wilson said with undisguised gratitude, Ari being one of the very few whose uncomplicated honesty could usually bring him out from behind his many careful barricades. "I *do* appreciate it. Stand by."

But who, he thought now as he drove at a steady sixty-five up Highway 99 through the groves of oranges and olives—the peaches, pears, plums, grapes, figs and apricots—the cantaloupes, honeydews, casabas and watermelons—the apples, cherries, walnuts and pomegranates—the cattle, cotton, wheat, alfalfa and who-knew-what-all of the endlessly fertile San Joaquin Valley—who could *really* "help" Richard Emmett Wilson?

Instantly the self-irony that was one of his most appealing saving graces came to his rescue and he thought:

Christ, what a pathetic idea!

Poor old nobody-loves-him Willie! Poor abandoned child! Who can help poor Willie, football of the universe!

Knock it off, he suggested to himself as he swung out around a truck loaded with cotton and was almost broadsided by a truckload of Mexican farmhands he hadn't seen, roaring onto the highway from an orchard road, occupants screaming invective.

"Fuck *su* madre too!" he shouted back with some exuberance and then reflected more soberly that taking chances like that wasn't really like him, particularly when driving this $150 secondhand 1934 Chevy convertible he had tooled around in ever since early sophomore year. Now, if it was his Dad's Studebaker, in which he could step on the gas and really take off—

The thought of Henry Wilson brought everything back to an abruptly more practical view of life. Dear old Dad. Thank goodness *that* was all receding for a while. Parents didn't really count too much, at the University. They paid the bills, in varying degrees, but once you were on campus, they sort of faded out into the background somewhere. You never really knew much about your friends' parents unless they appeared, either too loud or too self-effacing, at athletic contests or other special occasions. It was only your own who retained much reality when you were in the University's world; and they, mercifully, were in most cases comfortably far away.

He put the thought of Dad and his ideas, Mom and her earnest attempts to act as buffer, behind him as much as he could as he passed through Fresno and Madera, turned off toward Los Banos and returned to that sober but on the whole satisfied appraisal of his life which was known in the house as "Willie contemplating his navel again." He supposed "again" was the pejorative word. They all felt he did it too much, even though he was never very outward about it—or about much of anything really personal, for that matter. And, as he sometimes rather acridly pointed out, they did the same thing.

Everybody in their age group contemplated his or her own navel.

What, after all, was more fascinating and more worthy of study in this world? And some world it was, too.

He frowned.

God damned Hitler in Germany, and what did that mean? Winds of intimation were already blowing pretty hard around his generation. He couldn't see them going away anytime soon. Willie was a pessimist in foreign affairs, which made people like Renny Suratt and Rudy Krohl tend to scoff at him in the increasingly bitter house bullsessions that were beginning to rage on the subject. Already the house was getting pretty divided about it; hell, the whole country was getting divided about it. There was a sizable group, led by Tim Bates, who felt that war might be coming and that it might eventually drag in the United States. There was a smaller but equally vocal group led by Suratt and Krohl who were convinced, or professed to be, that there wasn't any real danger, that the whole thing would eventually blow over "after Hitler gets what he wants."

"Which is *what?*" Bates would demand.

Then the argument would go off into personalities and wind up with charges that people who didn't accept the probabilities didn't want to because they were afraid they might have to go to war themselves someday.

At least that was the way the final argument, just before school ended in June, had gone. It had begun about eleven on the last night of exams and had raged on until about two in the morning, as Wilson remembered it. Nobody

had won but eventually a lot of personal animosities had been exchanged.
He hoped everybody had cooled down over the summer, but he doubted it.
The screaming little jerk with the mustache was still throwing his weight
around Europe. In fact, as 1938 moved toward autumn, he now sounded
damned serious about it. It was easy to become gloomy, if one let one's
imagination run.

For a few minutes his did, blighting the hot but pleasant day. Even with
the windows rolled down to create a flow of air and try to beat the heat, it
was still suffocating, as the San Joaquin Valley can be when it tries. He could
stand it, though. After all, he had grown up in it, in the big old ranch house
south of town where the orange groves marched up the flanks of the foothills
of the Sierras and he could ride his horse whenever he pleased over the
rolling contours of the land as it lay before him like a sprawled-out giant.
This was home, this great brown valley, green only briefly for three or four
weeks of spring, then dry and stark, with a golden sheen, for the rest of the
year. It was filled with a subtle beauty of its own. It grew on you. He loved
it, though he wasn't sure he would stay there after he finished his schooling.

Which led him back to his father and rapidly away again. He wasn't going
to think about that now, when he was on his way to school and all the
challenges and triumphs and good times that awaited him there. When he
made his decision he would make it, and that would be that. He hadn't the
slightest doubt that his father would accept it, whatever it was. Didn't
everybody?

And again his little man inside came to his rescue, to inquire scornfully:
Now, what the hell kind of arrogant remark is that? Who is this cocky bastard
Willie who thinks he runs the world? He's not so much, just a crazy, mixed-
up kid—though not, he told the little man forcefully, as mixed up as nine-
tenths of the people he knew. Willie was *steady*, so most of his fraternity
brothers often admiringly remarked. The conviction made him central to
their affairs and, translated campus-wide, had brought him this final grati-
fying prominence in his senior year.

So: what did he intend to do with it?

Guy had written him a letter during the summer from his parents' home
near Diamond Head in Honolulu, where, he said, he was "busy chasing surf
and girls." His advice had been to "just coast along, don't stir up Prexy or the
trustees, put it on your job applications later on, and have a ball. I would."

Yes, Wilson thought dryly, thinking of Unruh, who managed to be a
brilliant pre-med student and star basketball player and still found time to
chase the girls with notable success, *you* would. Representing the other side
was Tim Bates, who had been on a walking tour of Europe with Buff Richardson for the summer, prior to coming back to assume the editorship of the
Daily. Bates was as full of ideals as he himself was, Willie reflected, the only
difference being that Bates wore his on his sleeve and Willie had long ago

developed the knack of keeping his under wraps until needed. Tim knew how to appeal to him.

"Things look ominous over here," he had written. "The damned Germans are sieg-heiling like mad and the rest of Europe is quaking and shaking and seems almost anxious to give in: at least it would stop the noise. But they can't afford to and we can't afford to. . . . You'd better get into it, Willie. You've got a pulpit, now, you can have some influence on the damned pacifists like Rudy Krohl and Suratt and that bunch. I'll back you with the *Daily*, you know that. I also think there are a lot of things you can do as president, completely aside from any world-politics stuff. You have the brains and you have the ability to lead people. Get in there and stir up the dear old University! We could stand a shaking up!"

Tim hadn't been specific about what he had in mind, though Wilson knew generally from all their many talks over the two years they had been in the house together. They would be quite a formidable team, he president of the student body, Bates editor of the *Daily*. He knew they could raise hell if they wanted to. They really could "stir up Prexy and the trustees," as Unruh had put it. But toward what purpose?

His campaign last June had been confined to the sort of generalities campus campaigns were usually confined to: "We will work for a better university . . . defend student rights against unwarranted encroachment by the administration and the board of trustees." (The president, Dr. Chalmers, had smiled at that one: it happened every time.) ". . . will seek a more equitable distribution of tickets to athletic games and other campus events . . . will seek more emphasis on constructive education." (Again Prexy smiled.)

Generally big stuff, Wilson had remarked dryly to Bill Lattimer, who chuckled in his usual quiet way and advised, "Don't knock it, Willie. All you have to do is be yourself. Nobody expects you to offer anything dramatic. After all, there isn't anything very dramatic."

And here in America, on these generally placid campuses in this particular year, he reflected, Latt was right. Things might look increasingly ominous overseas and maybe here, too, but aside from social issues left over from the dying Depression, such as the rights of labor unions, particularly the longshoremen who were striking in San Francisco, and some agitation about expanding voting rights for Negroes in the South, what was there for him to get involved in?

There were some people on campus, the usual small group who could always be counted on to agitate about anything, who could be relied upon to make a fuss over these things. He thought he might very likely join them: that would be a sensation. He knew it would surprise them mightily, because their number included the few students who were inclined to be contemptuous, rather than adoring, of Richard Emmett Wilson.

I may, he thought wryly, have a surprise or two for *you*.

But other than that, what was there? You couldn't tie up the University for nothing—tying up the University for *anything* was virtually unthinkable in this day and age, anyway—and at the moment he couldn't see any great cause to which he should devote himself. Maybe in the end it would all turn out just as Guy Unruh suggested: he might just drift along, preside over the usually peaceful flow of student affairs, meet whatever challenges might come from conflict of personalities and ambitions, which was the only place they usually came from at school, and let it go at that. It would, as Guy suggested, look great on his job application.

Still, that wasn't what he wanted to do. He shouldn't take himself or the student-body presidency *too* seriously, even though a hell of a lot of people would have liked very much to have the prestige of it. It was, after all, just a college campus. But he was always aware, rather more than most, that college was a preview and a preparation for life—or was it LIFE?—and so what you did there *was* important later on.

And *he* was important, to his friends in the house and to a lot of other people. But still, he felt restlessly, not in a way that might really matter in the ultimate scheme of things.

He told himself impatiently that he was certainly getting into a hell of a state of mind over nothing. He couldn't go out and create some big challenge just to make himself feel good. He was too level-headed for that. He had already overcome most of the challenges of his college career, just by holding all the offices he had, and by making as many good friends as he had, and by being certain Phi Beta Kappa and potential Rhodes scholar as he was, and by keeping himself on a reasonably steady emotional keel, as he had. So what more was there? There must be something. But what was it?

He supposed all this was just being twenty-one and in your senior year, with college soon to end and a war maybe waiting in the wings for him and his generation if Hitler kept it up and the world wasn't lucky. Maybe it was the adolescent crap they gave German names to and talked about in psych and philosophy classes. Maybe it was just growing up. And maybe he was an example that growing up was just as tough for Willie the all-successful as it was for the less skilled, less adept and less popular.

And maybe he was a pompous, self-conscious ass, too.

There was always, he told himself with the sudden inner smile that often occurred but that nobody saw, that possibility.

Anyway. Contrary to what Guy Unruh obviously expected, he *was* going to have a ball in his senior year whether his presidency was full of surprises or just "drifting along." He suspected the surprises might come, both in dealing with the school administration and in the house and other areas of campus life. Things sometimes turned up, he had found out in his twenty-one years, when you least expected them. They could scare hell out of you.

You just had to meet them and keep plugging. He could not imagine, at this moment, what they might be but he felt he could handle them. Particularly with the good friends he had in the house, with good old Dr. Chalmers as president of the University—a presidency rather more important than his, he conceded with a repeat of the inner amusement—and with Donnamaria Van Dyke bubbling cheerfully and efficiently along at his side.

She had written him two or three letters during the summer from her home in upper New York State. They had been busy, bright and full of that half-joking lightness that he was beginning to notice more and more as she tried to move into his life. At least, that was how he saw it; and he didn't know whether to feel pleased or irritated.

He had dated Donn Van Dyke quite often since they had met in a history class freshman year, and he still didn't really know what he thought about her. She was always so *cheerful*, as Franky Miller remarked whenever her name came up. She was also blond, pretty, charming, dynamic, appealing, intelligent, competent, smart, determined, ambitious and—he could go on and on, but that was probably enough for Donn Van Dyke. She knew everybody, was into everything, had been nominated by her sorority to be his running mate last June and now was incoming vice-president of the student body and destined to be his close colleague for the next nine months.

He had sometimes thought idly about marrying Donna, but he rather resented the fact that now he was probably going to have to think about it more often. He wasn't ready yet. But a tacit understanding seemed to be creeping into her letters: they would do such *great* things for the student body, and in the course of it be *really* close. This made him uneasy. Nobody moved in on Richard Emmett Wilson like that. He didn't smother and he didn't intend to be smothered. The problem was that Donna, in her absolutely honest, eager and straightforward way, didn't seem to realize this or admit that such hesitations could even be understandable.

She would just have to learn to see it his way, that's all. He was a guy who might be facing a war—and he had always been an independent soul—and he didn't like to be pushed around—and he didn't like people who took him for granted, especially women—and—and—and there was Donna Van Dyke.

He sighed as he started up the narrow, winding, dangerous road over Pacheco Pass that would take him across the hills into the Santa Clara Valley, its carpet of groves and orchards now dreaming peacefully in the autumn sun. Why did life have to be so complicated? It hadn't been a few minutes ago. It had been a little puzzling, maybe, as to what the hell it all added up to, the student-body presidency and everything; but it hadn't been *complicated*. What was there about women that created all these difficulties, anyway? Sometimes you'd think they were all there was in the world.

This had never particularly been his problem, he told himself with reviving confidence. He had always dated a fair amount but not obsessively like

Guy Unruh or Gil Gulbransen, both of whom just had to walk down the
Quad to find it suddenly strewn with recumbent, palpitating female bodies.
Or so they told it, anyway— he and the rest of the house were not always so
convinced by their tall tales of sexual triumphs. But probably a good many
of them were true; some of them sounded pretty authentic. He was glad he
wasn't that sex-mad. He could take it or leave it, he told himself with
satisfaction, the bright insistent image of Donn Van Dyke retreating a little
from his mind—until the next time it burbled in.

As for Dr. Chalmers, he had heard from him, too, during the summer: a
terse and typical note in mid-August which yet gleamed a bit with the shy,
gentle humanity and wry, unsuspected humor of that unusual and interesting man.

"Dear Willie," he had written. "Things are pretty quiet right now. Summer quarter, as always, is a drowsy time. Not many here to enjoy our
beautiful Quad and walk our tree-shaded lanes. I miss the sound of all those
young voices and I miss those, like yours, that are always full of sound advice
for us old fogies who run the place.

"I just wanted you to know that we're getting ready for your administration. I only hope there's a tiny little corner in it somewhere for mine!

"Come and see me when you get back. We'll have a lot to talk about."

Signed, as always, with a formal "Yours most sincerely, Edward H.
Chalmers."

Funny guy, Wilson mused; extremely intelligent, extremely competent—
and extremely shy, a fact that not many recognized; stalking the Quad like
some tall, forbidding replica of Abraham Lincoln, nodding with the slightest
of smiles to teachers and students as he walked along, wrapped in the
invincible armor of his office, which was practically God on campus, so
dignified and seemingly so forbidding in his gaunt presence and innate
courtly reticence that hardly anyone, faculty or student, ever really dared to
relax in his presence. Yet wanting desperately, and often sadly, Willie suspected, to be able to relax and just be one of the boys. Funny guy, but very
fair-minded and just. On that, Wilson told himself, he was counting if any
conflicts did arise with the administration or the trustees. He did not know
any of the trustees. He would have to rely on Dr. Chalmers to be a buffer
there, if necessary. He never considered the possibility that they might
unite against him, because he couldn't imagine any reason for them to.

So he drove on through the seemingly unending fruit trees and peaceful
farmlands that stretched, unbroken by commerce or industry, from San Jose
north to the University. He began to feel a rising happy anticipation. He
would arrive in time for the first dinner of the year.

His kid brother, Billy, would be waiting when he got there—he had been
visiting his best girl, Janie, for a few days in Oregon and was driving down
with her. And everybody else would be coming steadily in over the week-

end, if they weren't already there: his old friends, his dear friends, his brothers in the house who, for these brief fleeting years, knew him better than anyone else except his family, and perhaps in some ways even better than they . . . and all his campus pals and acquaintances, all the amalgam of students and faculty whose perceptions, impressions and knowledge, intimate or general, comprised that public thing known as Willie Wilson . . . behind whose amiable facade lived and dreamed, hoped and schemed, endured hurt and looked for happiness, welcomed triumph and tried to avoid adversity, grew and with luck matured, that likeable and intelligent youth who knew, more than anyone else ever could, who Willy Wilson really was.

He began to pass, on his right, the outskirts of the beautiful little tree-shaded city where most of the University's faculty lived. Off to his left near the highway the enormous bulk of the stadium loomed above the oaks and eucalyptus.

He came to the two huge sandstone columns, replicas of medieval castle guard towers, that flanked the entrance—paused for oncoming traffic—turned left and started down the drive.

Far down at the end of the mile-long avenue of palms that insulated the University from the hurrying world, he saw the green Oval and the squat, familiar sandstone bulk and brightly muraled front of Memorial Church.

A sudden singing excitement filled his heart and mind. Surprisingly or not so surprisingly, for Willie was more of a sentimentalist than most of his compatriots understood, he felt the sting of tears.

He was home.

Cutting sharply across the drowsy peace of the golden afternoon, seeming as though it must shatter the very composure of the campus itself, came the shrill imperious jangle of the first bell for dinner. As though rent by a major convulsion of nature, the house sprang to life from top to bottom.

Doors began to slam, feet hit the floor with a thud and began to pound on the stairs, hot water started to run furiously in the upstairs washrooms, the radio went on with a roar downstairs. On the third floor Wilson stopped unpacking, dropped his half-empty suitcase in the middle of the room, stretched to his full six feet and shouted, "Oh, God *damn* it!" for no particular reason. Next door Baker threw down the magazine he was reading, shucked off his clothes, put on a pair of slippers, took a towel from the rack on his closet door and started slowly for the showers. In the room just beyond, Richardson got up from the studio couch on which he had been lying absentmindedly playing with himself while dreamily surveying the enormous blowup of Rita Hayworth on the wall, adjusted his pants and began to run a comb slowly through his permanently tousled blond hair. In his room at the end of the hall, Godwin crumpled up the piece of paper on which he had been methodically writing "Things to Accomplish This Year (Junior)" and threw it toward the wastebasket, which it missed, before he too stood up to get ready to go downstairs.

Down the hall in the big west room that overlooked the sun porch, Gulbransen finished telling Bryce and Carriger about his adventures with the redhead he had met on the plane coming out from Minneapolis and they piled into the hall, laughing, just in time to pick up Suratt and Offenberg, coming out of Suratt's room, where they had been debating the merits of their respective dates for the Registration Dance.

By that time, Wilson had already begun his characteristic lunge down the stairs, leaning heavily on the rail, taking them three and four at a time and accompanying his cometlike progress with a formless and profane war-cry.

Disturbed by this ungodly sound out of a reverie on the cares of the world, a form of mental frustration in which he often trapped himself, Bates jumped up from his easy chair in the little room off the head of the stairs, stuck his head out the door, and shouted in no uncertain terms for that loudmouthed bastard of a Wilson to stop making so much God damned noise. Willie's scatological reply was lost as he hit the landing and raced along the second-floor hallway.

As Wilson thundered on, Bates too stripped down, picked up a towel and started for the showers, humming snatches of the "The Bastard King of England" to himself in a preoccupied tone until he came to Andrade's door, which he banged upon, effectively disrupting the bridge game in which McAllister and Andrade were soundly trouncing Miller and Krohl. In the west washroom a moment later, Herbert remarked to Musavich that it was just like old times, and Moose said, yeah, it sure was. Lattimer emerged from one of the stalls to remark dryly that things never changed, particularly the noise around here, to which Bates upon entering retorted that only a stiff-necked dry-ball would object to youthful exuberance brought on by the sheer joy of living. A debate at once began in which Lattimer and Bates contended while Herbert and Musavich impartially applauded.

Meanwhile on the floor below, Wilson's noisy progress had effectively awakened Davis, just off the train from L.A., who shouted to Willie to for God's sake stop making so much frigging noise and let a guy rest. Again Wilson's reply was lost in the clatter of his lunge down the stairs, and next door Unruh, lazily putting on a frayed shirt and tattered shorts, shouted through the wall to Davis that he knew nobody could control Wilson when Wilson didn't want to be controlled, so why try?

Two doors away, Barnett and Carrero, comparing notes on summer vacation, Barnett's spent working on a Mississippi barge and Carrero's running cattle for his dad on their ranch south of Santa Fe, looked at one another, grinned and shrugged. In Taylor's room he and Leighton, slowly unpacking as they discussed class schedules and tried to decide what to take, put them aside to begin what they hoped, as new members, would be a dignified, if self-conscious, progress along the hall to the stairs. Billy Wilson, staring bemusedly at the 8 × 11 color photograph of Janie which she had given him half an hour ago when he dropped her off at the main women's dorm, hardly heard his brother or anyone else and had to be physically jogged on the elbow by Moore before he came to with a start and realized it was time to go to dinner.

Ten minutes later most of them were downstairs in varying degrees of dress and readiness, the living room beginning to fill up with their excited chatter about summer and their plans for the school year ahead. Carrero, Barnett and Billy Wilson had started a game in the poolroom. Off in a corner of the living room the radio was mumbling something about Hitler again, and somebody snapped it off impatiently. Haggerty, surrounded at the piano by a covey of awed sophomores, began to play "What Is This Thing Called Love?" in a moody and ominous fashion that made them all shiver, pleasantly. Josephine, the house cat, surveyed all this placidly from the top of the piano. Napoleon, the house Great Dane, rushed around barking excitedly and slobbering affection upon everyone.

At this moment Wilson, Bates, Richardson and Miller entered the room together and converged at once upon the evening paper, strewing it from one end of the room to the other in a running battle to gain control of the comics. Bates broke away to hold up the front page and cry in disgust, "Look at *that!*"—which was a headline reading HITLER DEMANDS INSTANT RETURN OF SUDETENLAND TO GERMANY. Nobody paid much attention as he sank down thoughtfully on one of the sofas and began to read.

The second bell for dinner jangled out along a Row in which some thirty other houses were similarly engaged.

It was September 24, 1938.

So began, in "the best God damned fraternity at the best God damned university in the whole God damned world," the first meal of the first quarter of what for many of them would be the last year.

And so began, although they could not know it then, the great unraveling of the world that would continue all their days, and whose ending is not yet.

2

In the season that breaks the heart the golden haze of autumn lay upon the Santa Clara Valley. On the campus the school year that was beginning marched side by side with the physical year that was dying. A clearer light touched fields and buildings, a cooler and more searching wind blew through the arches of the Quad. An underlying sense of nature going quietly to rest even as the school year sprang to life heightened their emotions and encouraged their moods. "California has no seasons," the cliché goes, but for those who know her, California does. Subtle but inexorable the changes come. In young hearts equally with old—sometimes, for the sensitive, even more sharply—a bittersweet melancholy of dear times passing, of precious things that must be grasped and savored before they go, underlies the surge of campus life. In spring all things are possible. In autumn they are gifts that may not come again, if indeed they come at all.

At the University, sprawled on its nine thousand acres rising gently toward the foothills of the Santa Cruz coastal range, the dualism of life resuming and nature in decline has always moved the hearts and minds of those fortunate enough to study or teach there. The University is at once the embodiment of present hopes and dreams and the guardian of all hopes and dreams that have gone before; at once an educational machine and an emotional repository. It is mother, father—teacher, mentor—guide, disciplinarian (this last not always successfully)—home away from home for four years (in many cases more)—home bigger, and often more real, in many ways, than home itself.

It is its own world, founded on idealism, moated about with practicality, seeking to help its students grow up and prepare themselves for the world outside even as it seeks, through educational product, gifts, endowments, careful leases of land and carefully structured investments, to consolidate and perpetuate itself in an age of constant change.

Over it all preside the spirit and vision, the foresight and idealism, of its founders—the railroad-building Senator, into whose financial practices the University's legend-makers do not search too diligently, and his gentle, iron-willed, indomitable wife, who carried on alone successfully after his death to secure the establishment of a great university in memory of their only child, dead of typhoid just short of age sixteen.

"The children of California shall be our children," legend has the Senator saying.

Now children from the wide world over walk the Quad, in a long continuing cavalcade that began with the first classes in 1891, wound on through World War I, on through the troubled times of Richard Emmett Wilson and his contemporaries, on through World War II, on through the tense, chaotic decades since, and still goes on, into the unknowable future. Many have been the changes in physical plant and many the shifts in faculty and student attitudes, but stubborn and unyielding as the founders themselves remain the vision and dream they set forth in the University's charter, which Dr. Chalmers, like many another before and since, quotes proudly and often.

It was to be, they said, "A University of high degree . . . [for] the cultivation and enlargement of the mind; its object, to qualify students for personal success and direct usefulness in life; its purpose, to promote the public welfare by exercising an influence in behalf of humanity and civilization, teaching the blessings of liberty regulated by law, and inculcating love and reverence for the great principles of government as derived from the inalienable rights of man to life, liberty and the pursuit of happiness."

"It's enough," Franky Miller remarked lightly to Willie one time as they paused to read the document when it was on display in the main library, "to make you think the old place has some purpose after all."

"Do you think any of us lives up to it?" Wilson inquired.

"I think a lot of us try," Franky said seriously. "I think we really do."

Wilson nodded.

"I think so too."

They had stood in silent reverie for several moments, until Musavich came along, with the usual worried frown he wore every time he stepped into the library, and asked plaintively, "Can you guys help me with this damned English theme? I don't know what the hell I'm supposed to write about ethics and morality in the major poets of Elizabethan England."

So after bawling him out, but affectionately, for being such a jerk as to take a course he couldn't possibly pass, they abandoned the founders to try to help Moose qualify himself "for personal success and direct usefulness in life." Then they all went to the Cellar in the basement of the Student Union and had a Coke and went on back to the house and played a couple of fast games of pool before going to bed. A month later, just as they had predicted, Moose flunked the course. But maybe, they told each other wryly, giving him some suggestions for his theme had been their share in the University's general purpose of "exercising an influence in behalf of humanity."

"I think we were *very* humane," Wilson said.

"We always are, to Moose," Franky grinned.

"I assume they did, after all, want us to be good human beings," Willie remarked.

"The best," Franky said, and added cheerfully, "And so we are."

But now in autumn they were tending to be rather moody ones, as the first day drew to a close and everybody gradually got unpacked and settled in and the tales of summer began to circulate through the house. Most of them turned in rather early, though Wilson stayed up until almost one o'clock talking to Bates and Richardson about their hiking trip through Germany. When he finally did get to bed, he fell asleep like a log until . . .

Somebody bellowing, and a light too bright upon his eyelids: "Telephone for WILSON!" After a moment of silent protest he came up on one elbow and stared blearily down the length of the sleeping porch. The self-sufficient face of Smith Carriger peered across the bunks, many of them still occupied by twisted forms with blankets and pillows drawn over their heads, some beginning to shift uneasily at the noise.

"Smitty!" he said, in a loud whisper, coming awake with a cordial yawn and holding out his hand. "How the hell are you, boy? When did you get in?"

"About an hour ago," Carriger whispered back.

"Drive from Philly?"

"Yeah. Prexy's on the phone."

"Dr. Chalmers? What time is it?"

"Ten-thirty. Want me to tell him you'll call back?"

"I do not." He galvanized out of bed. "Tell him I'll be right there."

A minute later he was sitting in the upstairs phone booth, stark naked.

"Yes, sir?" he said politely. The president's calm tones came over.

"Welcome back, Willie. It's good to hear your voice."

"Good to hear yours, too, sir," Wilson said. "At your service."

"I thought perhaps we should have a little talk about the program for the year," Dr. Chalmers said. "I'm sorry I got you out of bed."

"Who said you did, sir?"

The president chuckled.

"I've been dealing with the young for thirty years: I know Sunday mornings. Can you come down to the administration building at eleven-thirty tomorrow? Then we can have lunch after."

"Yes, sir."

"Tell Tim Bates, too, if you will. Shall I call Donna Van Dyke or would you like to?"

Wilson's heart stopped for a second and went on again.

"You may."

"Oh? I thought perhaps since she's your vice-president—"

"I said you may, sir."

"Very well," Dr. Chalmers said. "See you both tomorrow at eleven-thirty."

"Right, sir," Wilson said. After he hung up he noticed that his heart was functioning all right, and also that he was the possessor of a stout erection.

Donna in absentia often had this effect on him. Donna in person aroused so many conflicting reactions as to paralyze him in that department. He waited a couple of minutes for the thing to subside and then walked sedately back to the showers, which he found himself sharing with Leighton and Moose, both also slightly groggy-eyed; went to his room, got dressed, and went downstairs to join them on a slow walk through the fresh bright morning to the Cellar for a "snail," that gooey confection, and a cup of coffee.

On his way out he yelled to Bates to join them. Bates yelled back that he was busy, he'd see him later.

"Not studying *already?*" Wilson demanded with exaggerated disgust and disbelief.

"Only human nature," Bates hollered back.

"Well, get you," Willie retorted. "Don't you sound precious."

"I am," Tim replied, as Unruh shouted from the sleeping porch in a muffled voice, "For Christ's *sake*, people are still asleep around here!"

"Hell with you too, Unruh," Wilson yelled back cheerfully. "See you later, children."

And walked out into the brilliant sunshine, a little cooler already than it had been yesterday, to join Moose and Rodge Leighton. As he did so, Bates leaned over the balcony railing above the door and called down, "Exactly how old are you, Willie?"

"Twenty-one and never been done," he called back. Several fellows appeared in various stages of undress at windows of the houses that flanked them on both sides to respond with derisive hoots.

"Come," he said grandly to Moose and Rodge. "Ignore the lowlife sons of bitches. What do you want to know for, Tim?"

"I'll tell you someday," Tim said, going back inside. "Maybe."

"Now what the hell does that mean?" he asked Moose, who shook his head and said, "I don't *know*," in the tone of great earnestness that often got him through difficult conversations with housemates he felt—hell, *knew*—were a lot brighter than he.

"Me either," Rodge said loyally. "Isn't it a beautiful morning?"

"Gorgeous," Wilson agreed as they started down the Quad. He stretched his arms above his head, turned his face up to the sun with an unself-conscious, animal grace and uttered a shout of happiness.

"What have we done," he inquired, "to deserve being alive in a place like this?"

Which was what Tim Bates was trying to put on paper as he returned to his room and shut the door firmly against possible intruders who he knew would soon be wandering around now that Willie had successfully awakened them. He was hoping for relative privacy as he took a small, locked iron strongbox from his top closet shelf and placed it on his desk. He was probably going to be so busy editing the *Daily* this quarter that he wouldn't have the time to glance at its contents. But it made him feel good to have it around even though the mere sight of it often frustrated him greatly. It wasn't getting done. Nothing was happening. It just *sat*.

What he had in the box was the scattered and disjointed beginning of what he referred to in his own mind as My Novel. It consisted at this point principally of brief character sketches of members of the house, himself included, along with their generally recognized girlfriends, where applicable. He knew he would probably be shot for some of his comments if anyone saw them, but he didn't intend to let that happen.

He had begun the seniors alphabetically with Ray Baker—Raymond Baker, from Arvin, California, pre-legal. Good, honest, likeable Ray, with his earnest, amiable, nice-guy appearance and his steady, dependable personality that had resulted in his being permanent-by-acclamation house manager for the past two years.

As Tim saw him, Ray was "a little sober, a little slow, a little humorless, but always reliably on the solid side as befits one whose father is principal of a small high school in the southern San Joaquin Valley and whose upbringing has been by the book. The sort who will one day be a very good small-town lawyer, of the type that rises slowly but steadily to an unchallengeable place in the community because he is competent, thorough, scrupulously honest, making up in hard work and integrity what he may lack of the flash and dash that smooth the way for some others."

Short, Tim thought, and sweet. Next down the alphabet, what did Bates the All-Knowing think of himself?

He wasn't altogether satisfied with what he had written. He had tried to be objective but, reading it over, he had to admit that he came across as a pretty noble being. He frowned: that wasn't really the way he wanted people to think of him. On the other hand, if you couldn't blow your own horn once in a while, especially in the privacy of your own thoughts, who would?

He had described Timothy Merrill Bates from Baltimore, Maryland,

journalism–political science major, as "the philosopher of the house, idealistic tilter with windmills and fighter of great battles in the *Daily*, of which
he is about to become editor. Sardonic, cynical, and impatient as only the
idealistic can be, yet with an unending faith and hope in humankind and a
constant devotion to what he believes to be the public good. Never lacking
in causes to back or campaigns to launch." Here he paused and added two
new sentences. "Has just returned from summer vacation in Europe. Re-
joins the campus determined to arouse it to the implications of what is going
on in Germany."

And he would, too, he told himself grimly. He was scared to death of what
might be coming, and he fully intended to scare the University too. The
Daily staff would be meeting in the Shack at two that afternoon to put
together the first paper of the school year for distribution tomorrow morning. He already had in mind a front-page editorial and accompanying headlines. Many would probably object to their urgency but he didn't give a
damn. He was editor now and he was going to use the paper as he saw fit.
One little voice on the West Coast of the United States would be speaking
out against that bastard in Berlin, anyway.

Memories of the vast stadium, the massed troops, the hushed, worshiping
hundreds of thousands, the flaring torches and wind-whipped swastika flags,
the lifted arm, the mad, hypnotic voice and the responding animal roar of
"*Sieg heil! Sieg heil! Sieg heil!*" suddenly overwhelmed him.

By God, you bastard, he thought, *stay away*.

But he wouldn't and Tim knew it. He only hoped he could make his
contemporaries know it too, as deeply and irrevocably as he did.

He told himself to snap out of it. There'd be plenty of chance for that kind
of argument in coming months.

More than enough.

Tim shrugged impatiently and returned to his notes. The self-confident
face of the brother whom Unruh, who didn't do so badly himself, called "our
resident sex symbol" came to mind.

Gilbert Gulbransen, from Minneapolis, Minnesota, pre-med, was "tall,
blond, extremely good-looking, with a constant gleam in his eye. Thrives on
sex in a way that might be offensive were it not so natural to him. Appeals
to women and men alike because his success is so completely masculine in
nature. The woman isn't born who can resist the temptation to at least
consider being one of his conquests, and there isn't a man born who can
resist envying him for it. Very well liked by everyone who knows him,
though his reputation as a Don Juan on campus is egregious. A damned good
man, in every way."

Tim became aware that Haggerty was running over something on the
piano downstairs. The notes came up clearly and pleasantly in the bright fall
morning, perfectly apropos, of course, to the next entry, Edward Paul Hag-

gerty, from Springfield, Illinois, economics major. His description of Hack, Tim thought, was particularly good. But then, Hack and a piano could inspire anyone, because "the piano talks for Haggerty as it does for few others, professional or nonprofessional. The tales it tells are not of classic themes or stately chords delivered with exquisite technique, but of dance floors on crowded nights, of sentimental tunes played by superb bands through the babble of talk, of the fleeting broken loves of youth laughing and playing straight toward threatening darkness, unaware, yet poignantly half aware, of the heartbreak that lies ahead.

"Haggerty is one of the authentic voices of his generation, a fact not altogether perceived by his fellows, partly because there are few more solidly built citizens—he looks like a good-natured wrestler until he starts to play the piano—and also because he tends to deprecate his talent. Despite his self-sarcasm, however, and despite their difficulty in believing that such a thing as genius actually exists in a form to be recognized and lived with, all he has to do to fascinate the house into rapt silence is sit down and begin to transform one of their favorites into a thing of profoundly moving melody in which laughter and melancholy are inextricably mixed.

"Claims to be unmoved by the events of the world and unconcerned by its infinite tragedies but, as Wilson sometimes remarks, he could never play the way he does if he didn't ache inside. Aside from his music he is a pragmatic, good-humored Good Joe.

"To his music, in a way which his fellows don't always understand but respect, he is dedicated with an inner purpose from which nothing deflects him."

His next entry, Bates realized with a sudden guilty start—though he shouldn't worry, he only had to fold his notes and pretend they were something else, if interrupted—was at the moment walking past his door with Randy Carrero. Randy was saying in an embarrassed tone, "Well, you see, Latt, I only cashed twenty bucks on Friday, but I have a date with Fluff Stevens tonight and I was just wondering if you could loan me ten until Monday?"

And good old Latt, with never a hesitation or murmur, was saying matter-of-factly, as he did to every one of his never-ending string of debtors in the house, "Why, of course, Randy."

"You're sure it won't strap you too much—?" Randy asked hesitantly.

"Don't worry," Latt said with mock but kind fatherliness. "If it were going to, I'd put you in your place."

"Golly," Randy said as they passed on down the hall to the stairs and out of earshot, "you are the *nicest* guy, Latt."

And so he was, Bates reflected as he read over his notes on Latt. The nicest guy—the brainiest guy—the steadiest guy—you could say so much about Latt that he really had said very little:

William Lattimer from Fargo, North Dakota, history major, was "dignified, gentle, kindly, considerate and good, possessed of a mind like a diamond and a sense of humor friendly and never hurtful. Has the highest grade average in school and is the first to kid himself about it. Shares with Wilson and Unruh, though in a different way, control of the house. Latt roomed next door to them in freshman dorm—'our next-door roommate,' they call him. The balance wheel, unperturbed and unshaken, standing firm by Christian principles which he quietly and unhesitatingly exercises. Not so apparent a leader as Wilson, lacking a certain ability to mix in the marketplace which Wilson has, yet possessing, as Wilson long since recognized, a basic worth of enormous value. A friend who would contribute to one's life still, were one to know him a hundred years."

How relatively simple he seemed, Bates reflected, compared to the next entry—"the enigma of the house" as Willie called him, sometimes to his face.

"My dear boy!" North McAllister cried on one such occasion. "I? By what foul and devious means do you arrive at such a withering appraisal of such an innocent as I? Why do you pour out your bile and bitter scorn upon little old me? Why, I ask you, lord and master of us all! Why?"

"Oh, for Christ's sake, North," Wilson had said, laughing in spite of himself. "You must admit you're a mysterious sort of guy. I've known you for three years and I'm damned if *I* know what makes you tick."

"Ah, *ha!*" North exclaimed triumphantly. "Aye, there's the rub! Willie the invincible can't figure me out! It's a matter of pride, is it? Well, poor thing! I feel sorry for you!"

"Just so long as you don't feel sorry for yourself," Wilson shot back, and for just a second a strange little expression—pain, almost, though why pain? had come into North's eyes. But it had gone in a flash as he picked up a pillow and threw it at Willie, who promptly threw it back. And so the whole thing dissolved in a few moments of laughing volley and countervolley.

But there *was* something. Maybe he was being too dramatic about North, Tim thought, but on the other hand there *was* something no one could quite put a finger on. North McAllister, from Los Angeles, pre-med, was "a bit of a mystery, sometimes—a complex character. Regarded with liking and the respect a really excellent mind entitles him to, but in many ways unknown . . . unknown and, when all is said, quite likely unknowable."

Which, of course, Tim reflected, was his privilege, and who was he, or anybody, to try to break down barriers and probe where probing wasn't wanted—or excusable?

And so to Franky Miller, and from Tim the fond and affectionate smile that was almost everyone's reaction to that rotund and witty gentleman.

Franky too was unique, in a different way. What a houseful of characters they had, really! Tim wondered how they had all happened to get together.

Thinking back to his own pledge days three years ago he couldn't recognize any dominant strain of eccentricity in those then in charge that might have accounted for the eccentric mix of himself and his classmates—if indeed they were as eccentric as they sometimes liked to think they were.

Maybe they were just young and lively and a little wacky, like most kids.

The important thing was that they all—or almost all—liked one another with varying degrees of approval and/or sufferance, from Suratt the sharp-tongued skeptic to Musavich the humbly grateful. That was all that mattered when you came right down to it: they had to get along and most of them did. It was good for them. They had their ups and downs, and he knew there would be a few unexpected things this year as there always were. But on the whole, they managed.

"That's because the inmates are running the asylum," Willie characterized it.

"And who better?" Franky demanded.

Francis Allen Miller, from San Leandro, California, social sciences major, had, in Tim's estimation, "an excellent mind equipped for nothing in particular but to enjoy the sort of easygoing, good-natured, catch-as-catch-can existence its owner leads. A dabbler in this and that, earnestly 'liberal' without much conception of the real issues involved. Fat, sloppy but surprisingly graceful. Enjoys living and lives to live. Funny, clever and original. Likes virtually everyone he meets with a few notable exceptions whom he characterizes with sometimes acrid but usually jocular wit. Looks older than his contemporaries, though only twenty-one."

Out on the lawn Tim could hear the snap of a football, the sound of pounding feet, Napoleon's excited barking, voices shouting in the bright fall air. Moose, Rodge Leighton and Wilson must be back from their quick breakfast in the Cellar. He could hear shouts from McAllister and Buff Richardson as they clattered down the front steps to join them. Such health nuts, he thought: touch football wasn't for him. The sound of their voices was pleasant, though, and up the Row on the two communal tennis courts he could hear other voices calling, the sharp ping! of rackets and the solid thunk! of balls. Campus was coming alive all over. The rising excitement of the new quarter was everywhere.

Moose gave a happy shout of triumph and yelled, "Touchdown!" Poor guy, Bates thought, it was probably the only touchdown he'd make all year, for all his time in the stadium in the view of thousands. What a dope—what a dumbbell—what a big, shaggy, lovable guy.

Theodore Krasnik Musavich, from Chicago, Illinois, majoring in physical education, "is big, slow, awkward, except in a game. Passionately interested in just one thing—football, in which he has not, aside from the occasional fluke, shown anything more than dependably average ability. He still hopes to find in it a final triumph, an ultimate justification, before leaving college;

this, he earnestly believes, is the only way to repay the Chicago alumni group that persuaded the University to give him an athletic scholarship. Adopted long ago in freshman dorm by Wilson, Bates, Lattimer and Unruh, and taken care of ever since: tutored when hard exams are coming up, interceded for with faculty members when it becomes necessary; humbly grateful for the friendship which is always given him unquestioningly by his self-appointed protectors, who regard him with a special affection because he is so big, so naive, so helpless and so sincerely desirous of doing the right thing. He has attempted from time to time to do things for them to show his gratitude, but somehow they always go wrong and misfire, whereupon Willie or somebody suggests something else to do and they all go do it and have a swell time anyway and he doesn't feel so bad.

"Moose's current girlfriend is a campus character, but fun—Suzy Waggoner, known, for reasons generally assumed to be valid, as 'Welcome' Waggoner. Her decision to go after Moose puzzles everybody, not least Moose. He hasn't hesitated to take advantage of it, however, 'But,' he often inquires, 'why me?' 'Brains,' Unruh suggests, and Renny Suratt agrees without missing a beat, 'Yes, all eight inches of them.' Moose does think sometimes that he ought to find someone with less of a reputation, but it *is* nice to have one's brains respected for a change. And Welcome Waggoner certainly does take care of them."

Down on the lawn Tim heard his next subject utter an anguished "Oh, God *damn* it!" as he missed a catch. In mind's eye he could see his big, lumbering frame, as bulky as Moose's, and his amiable, always-smiling face as he lunged unsuccessfully for the ball. Buff Richardson—Arthur John, III, from Montclair, New Jersey, social sciences—"is everybody's pal, even-tempered as the day is long, always ready for a game, a beer, a meal or a girl—in about that order. The sun always shines on Buff Richardson, even in the stormiest weather. Even as they firmly mark 'F' on his papers, his professors feel fond of him. Nothing ever fazes him, which probably comes from several million dollars in the family coffers. Friendly, uncritical, always good-natured and easygoing. Spends money like a drunken sailor but never thinks of himself as prodigal because he is usually spending it on his girls, his car or his friends. Unaffectedly modest about himself and his wealth. Likes humanity with a large, brotherly love and expects it to like him. It does. Fall-quarter president and the best rusher on the Row."

Tim heard him shout again, this time triumphantly. Pretty soon he'd be ready for his beer, which of course was illegal on campus but somehow Buff always managed to secrete some somewhere. "Our official happy," Wilson called him.

Not far behind in general amicability was the next-to-last senior—alphabetically, although Tim knew he was far from next to last in importance in the house and on campus. He could hear him now down the hall, singing

in the shower as he often liked to do, in his clear, pleasant tenor: "*I wandered today to the hill, Maggie, to see the fields below—*"

Moving and pure, his voice caressed the old sentimental ballad and suddenly it rang true and was no longer just an old sentimental ballad but a
yearning recall of days gone by and dear love remembered. It was things like
that, Tim thought, that made you realize that there was much more to Guy
Unruh than sometimes appeared on the surface. It also made you realize that
he was probably more in love with his own Maggie than he was ready to
acknowledge, even to himself. Tim listened to him finish the song before he
returned to his notes, which began by describing Clyde Gaius Unruh, from
Honolulu, Hawaii, pre-med, as a youth "who gives strangers meeting him
for the first time the impression that they ought to address him by his full
name. He is a young man with the air of arrogance that goes with six feet,
four inches, a magnificently trained body, the abilities of a natural athlete
and the legend of the best basketball player on the Coast. A delight of
instinctive physical coordination to watch on the court, he is a self-assured
and more than a little impressive specimen off it. His effect on most girls is
immense, and with a casual air of taking what is his obvious due from an
admiring world he often makes the most of it.

"Despite these qualities, particularly the arrogance which sometimes sur-
faces when it shouldn't, few men in the house or on campus are better liked,
for underneath his sometimes annoying exterior he possesses a good, hard,
practical head and a determination to make the most of his education. Something of the idealism which must in the long run be found in all good doctors
is to be found in him; in addition to which, he can be very kind to those in
trouble and sometimes has done so at considerable cost, in time and effort,
to himself. Unruh is one of the most worthwhile people in school, even
though his morals are sometimes casual and his self-esteem occasionally
profound."

After hearing Guy sing that song, Tim felt, there wasn't much doubt about
the validity of his own conclusions about Maggie Johnson, either. If Unruh
in his heart didn't really want her, then Tim was a pretty poor observer. He
thought he was a pretty good one.

He became conscious of a stirring below, voices, laughter, people tramp-
ing up the stairs. The lawn had fallen silent, the game was over. It was time
to raid the icebox for the cold cuts Dewey the cook had left to tide them over
the weekend when he was off and no formal meals were served. A peremp-
tory rapping told Tim he would soon have to abandon his private pursuits
and join the mob. The voice of the final senior, the senior of seniors, the
ultimate senior, he told himself wryly, began the process of dislodging him.

"Timmy!" Wilson called. "Are you still in there?"

And he began to rattle the door.

"Not so hard, damn it!" Tim said. "You'll break the latch."

"What's it doing on the latch?" Willie demanded. "Didn't your mother tell you not to lock the door when you're in your room? It leads to bad habits."

"Up yours, Willie," Bates retorted. "I told you I was thinking."

"There *is* an odd humming noise out here," Wilson admitted. "And a distinct smell. That must be it. How about dropping it for a while and joining us for lunch?"

"I'll be down in a minute," Tim said. "You run along. I'll get there."

"Moose and I are going to eat on the balcony," Willie said. "Join us."

"In a *minute*," Bates repeated. "*Jesus*."

"Thank you, sunshine," Wilson said cheerfully, and went on up the stairs, where Bates could hear him joshing with Haggerty, who lived up there in the nether regions alongside him.

Willie was certainly riding high, Bates thought: but then, he had a right to, being the new president of the student body. As did he, he reminded himself with satisfaction, being the new editor of the *Daily*.

His notes on Wilson were quite subjective and intimate, more so than on most of his brethren. But they had talked a lot, particularly in the last year or so when it was becoming apparent that they were probably going to wind up in tandem influencing University affairs. Willie hadn't really unburdened himself a great deal—he was a hell of a cautious soul when it came to anything personal and revealing—but Tim thought he understood him well enough to make some educated guesses. At least his notes reflected what he thought were the most intriguing aspects of Willie, who was probably the most interesting guy he knew on campus. Maybe he had oversentimentalized him a little, made him larger than life. But he didn't think so.

Richard Emmett Wilson, from Terra Bella, California, political science major and potential lawyer or maybe public administrator or even politician, "is the pivot of the house. A mind as sharp as a razor, keen, understanding and perceptive, its smooth functioning concealed beneath a hard-hitting humor that is always perfectly frank but rarely hurtful. Enjoys an enormous respect and liking in the house and on campus. The man everyone always depends upon when things go wrong. The man who subtly, not always unobtrusively but often quite unconsciously, sets the tune to which the whole house moves.

"Destined to rise and aware of it, aware also that this to some degree sets him apart, for all the affection others feel for him. Realizes that in the last analysis he does not need other people, that he makes his own security, his own world, his own way, realizes that this places him always just a little outside looking in. Suspects that while he probably won't ever really need anyone, perhaps by the same token no one will every really need him—an intimation that accounts for much in a highly complex character that runs its world with what appears to be complete mastery and complete success, rarely revealing the strain of melancholy that occasionally underlies it.

"A constant interest in the necessities of politics, even in so small a world as the campus; a constant concern with his own position as an honest man forced sometimes to compromise to gain his own ends. How much can a man compromise and remain honest?—one of his principal philosophical and personal preoccupations. Always aware that this campus world is full of many, many implications for later living."

Two final characters, Tim thought with amused affection, and then *he'd* be off to lunch. "Our permanent seniors," as they were often referred to—

"Josephine, cat of unknown ancestry, probably aged eight or nine, possessor of a glossy black coat, a beautiful plume of tail and eyeglass markings that give her the aspect of an amiably inquisitive owl. Adopted the house when a kitten, one frosty morning when she appeared out of the mist to take up residence, and a fixture ever since. Because no one ever took the time to have her spayed, she produces a regular stream of kittens, many of which now grace other fraternities and sororities. In late afternoons she waits atop the piano for Haggerty, one of her favorites. At night she sleeps at random on the sleeping porch, moving from bed to bed to the accompaniment of protesting curses as she lands on a stomach, sinks softly and suffocatingly down on an unsuspecting nose, or decides to give her claws a last sharpening on some convenient leg. Nobody would ever dream of getting rid of her, though. Josephine years ago decided that this was where she wanted to live and, being a cat and serene in her convictions, never doubts the wisdom of her choice.

"Her friend, companion and competitor for kitchen scraps is—

"Napoleon, Harlequin Great Dane, age probably about eight, brought to the house as a puppy by some long-gone brother and handed down from class to class. A fixture during the academic year, taken care of during the summers by Dewey the cook, who works that season at a restaurant in Berkeley and likes the prestige and 'protection' of having Napoleon in his little house there. A huge, ungainly animal with a tail, according to Wilson, that can sweep books off a desk at ten paces. Loves everybody, slobbers on everybody, tries without success to get into everybody's lap under the impression that he is a toy poodle. Always underfoot, either romping on the lawn and with great goodwill tripping people up in the midst of a touch football game, or sprawling sound asleep in the midst of some main thoroughfare, snoring at one end and emitting awful smells at the other with a gently rhythmic Fhuht . . . Fhuht . . . FhuhtFhuhtFhuhtFhuhtFhuht Fhuht*Fhuht!* . . . Fhuht . . . Fhuht . . . Fhuht-FHUHT!!!

"The dog is a God damned fucking fart-machine!" exclaims Franky, and so he is. But nobody can conceive of the house without Napoleon and Josephine. They are set for life and know it, being friends of all, including each other, and enemies of none."

He heard Willie clatter down the stairs again and an enormous shout of, "BATES! ARE YOU GOD DAMNED COMING TO LUNCH!"

"YES!" he shouted back, gathering his notes quickly and placing them in the box. "I AM GOD DAMNED COMING TO LUNCH!"

He locked the box and returned it to the closet shelf under a pile of shirts. It had given him the familiar excitement and urge to get going: he planned to review "Juniors" and "Sophomores" as soon as he could. But he knew that, as usual, the life of the house and the *Daily* would intervene. He promised himself determinedly that he *would* get at it soon, though.

He went down to the kitchen, which he found full of housemates, filled a plate and went out on the balcony to join Willie, Moose and Ray Baker, who had happened along. They began speculating about the meeting with Dr. Chalmers tomorrow.

"He's going to beard us both at the same time," Tim said, biting into the enormous salami sandwich he had made for himself.

"I'm ready for him," Wilson said with relish, taking a gulp of Coke.

"Me, too," Tim agreed.

"Gosh," Moose said. "You guys aren't scared of *anything*."

"Only great big football heroes like you, Mooser," Wilson said, reaching over to ruffle his hair affectionately.

"Shucks," Moose said. "I don't scare *anybody*."

3

At registration that year there were, according to statistics published a couple of weeks later in the University register ("the Bawlout"), a total of 4,200 students admitted, of whom 1,123 were graduate, 3,007 undergraduate. Of the total, approximately 40 percent, or 1,680, were women, their number decided principally by the amount of housing available. An arbitrary limitation of five hundred women stipulated by the founders had finally been abandoned a couple of years previously. "The last of the five hundred" were moving on toward graduation and disappearance into history.

Of the total at that time, residents of California were, as always, in the majority: 3,752. Oregon came next with 164, then Washington with 155. Far in the future were the days when New York would rank second in the number of entering freshmen, followed by Texas, Illinois, Washington and New Jersey. Far in the future also were the days when applicants for the freshmen class would number as high as 17,652 from all over the United States and more than seventy countries. In Willie's day foreign representation was very thin—105 students from twenty-two countries, including eighteen from Canada, thirteen from China, eleven from the Philippines, nine from Japan, seven from South America, on down to one each from such as France, Hungary, India, Ireland, Madagascar, Spain, Sweden.

To house the 4,200 of Willie's time, the University provided a freshmen dormitory and three other dorms for men, a freshmen dormitory and three other dorms for women. Fraternities and sororities, in varying states of good grace with the school administration, provided housing for their members, chosen each year in a series of rushing periods. Residents of the Row told themselves not to be smug but generally considered themselves superior to the rest. The rest, and the administration, were not always so sure.

To instruct what Dr. Stafford, the English professor who dazzled the campus with her piercing wit and scathing tongue, referred to as "these busy little sperm bags running around trying to gain entry into unsuspecting maidens"—and to instruct the sometimes not so unsuspecting maidens themselves—the university had a faculty of 1,422. This figure included 280 professors, full, associate, and assistant; 605 others, in declining rank, clinical professors, lecturers, associates and assistants; and 110 administration personnel, plus miscellaneous clerical help. They pontificated, performed and often genuinely taught in a fluctuating number of dusty classrooms, worn and battered by forty-five college generations, scattered through the Quad and in what would eventually prove to be only the first of a constantly proliferating number of outlying buildings devoted to separate schools and departments, each erected when some alumnus who had struck it rich decided he wanted to immortalize himself on campus. Fortunately most of these—not all, but most—would be done with an architectural taste and style that would blend smoothly into the comfortable sandstone beauty of the original buildings.

Happily for Willie and his contemporaries, this inexorable growth had scarcely begun when they were there. The University was still a relatively small, quiet, rambling, pleasant, old-shoe sort of place. It was still possible to talk of "the University family" and have it mean something. They did not realize then how fortunate they were.

For this privilege, and the privilege of that education envisioned by the founders that would "qualify students for personal success and direct usefulness in life," they paid somewhere between $319 and $460 a quarter, plus various special fees: a grand total of $957 on the average, or $1,380 at the most opulent, for the usual three-quarter academic year.

This was not within the capabilities of many parents, a large number of whom were gradually emerging from the grip of the Great Depression. Then as now, two-thirds of the student body either were aided by scholarships, deferred tuition notes or student loans, or held down part-time jobs either on the teaching or administrative sides of the University, or in private homes and businesses, or in specialized activities such as the combo (drums, saxophone, bass, trumpet, trombone, clarinet and piano) that Hack Haggerty organized and led. Although the University then, as now, was considered by its critics to be "a rich man's school," "a country club," "a rich kids' playground," because of what was presumed to be the boundless wealth of every one of its students, it was then, as now, a university "of high degree" and generally modest individual budgets.

In the house, for instance, fifteen of the twenty-six were either on scholarships or had part-time jobs. Ray Baker received free board and meals for serving as house manager. Tim Bates was on a journalism scholarship established by the publisher of one of Southern California's more stridently conservative newspapers, which made Tim somewhat uneasy but was undeniably a big help. Franky Miller was beneficiary of one of the University's many commemorative scholarships, his benefactor "somewhere in the sweet by-and-by," as he put it. Guy Unruh and Moose Musavich held athletic scholarships established by former team members in the alumni association. Bill Lattimer, the outstanding scholar, held a scholarship in the history department and also served as assistant to the head of the department. Tony Andrade, Randy Carrero, Jeff Barnett and Hank Moore worked as dinnertime waiters, or "hashers," Tony and Jeff at the house, Randy at Donna Van Dyke's sorority, Hank at the Thetas. Galen Bryce had a job as a teaching assistant in the psychology department, Willie Wilson the same in the political science department, Duke Offenberg the same in education. Johnny Herbert and Bob Godwin worked as part-time clerks in the main library, which Bob considered an excellent position from which to further his political ambitions since, as he said, "sooner or later you see everybody, in the Libe."

The rest were supported by parental wealth that ranged from modest but adequate to the very substantial family fortunes of Buff Richardson and Smith Carriger.

The great majority on campus didn't think of themselves as being enormously rich, Franky frequently pointed out with some annoyance, and actually they weren't. So why the hell did everyone say they were?

"Just our innate superiority, I guess," Willie suggested wryly.

"Innate bullshit," Franky snorted.

He really got quite indignant about it.

In any event, the University ignored its detractors and did its good work, and its students, as they often told one another thankfully, were damned lucky to be there. On Registration Day, particularly, they came together in excitement and self-congratulation, and it was then that they began spinning the wheels and cooking the deals which, along with the substantial academic load most of them carried, made up the rounds of their busy days and pushed them inexorably toward a maturity that would eventually take them—where?

"Boy!" Lattimer exclaimed to Willie as they sat in Memorial Hall completing their registration forms and watching the milling crowd that filled the room with constant movement and high excited chatter of Have-a-good-summer? and How've-you-been? and Whatcha-taking? "Bates really let us have it, didn't he?"

And he held up the *Daily:*

In the right-hand top two columns, the usual opening-day story and its big headline: SCHOOL'S IN! CAMPUS SURGES TO LIFE AS FALL QUARTER BEGINS. And on the left, in type equally big above a two-column picture of an angry

face, a thrusting arm and little black mustache that were all too familiar to
the world—

THIS MAN MAY DECIDE YOUR FUTURE.

DOES HITLER WANT *YOU?*

"It's always nice to come back to school," the boxed editorial just beneath
began casually, "and find out how remote we are from everything. But if
you've been to Europe last summer, as the editor has, you're aware that
somebody is looking over our carefree shoulders. His name is Adolf Hitler,
and if he is not checked by the massed powers of Europe, he may very well
turn most of our plans for the future into pipe dreams.

"It is true, of course, that an isolationist America might just possibly
escape the consequences of Nazi domination in Europe. However, the
chances are overwhelming that . . ."

And it went on to advocate in no uncertain terms that America join with
"the forces of civilization" to oppose Hitler's ambitions.

In an almost equally prominent spot in the center of the page were the
headline and news story:

HITLER MAKES FINAL DEMAND FOR SUDETENLAND.

"Berlin—Reichsfuehrer Hitler today told a massive throng of chanting
Germans that if President Eduard Beneš of Czechoslovakia will not return
the Sudetenland to Germany by Saturday, he will take it by force.

"Britain, France and Russia have pledged to aid the tiny Central European republic if the German Fuehrer sends his troops across the border.
European capitals were tense awaiting Hitler's next move. . . ."

"Pretty strong stuff," Willie agreed. "But he feels very deeply about it.
Particularly having just been there."

"I think a lot of us feel deeply," Latt said. "But I don't know that we want
to go around screaming about it, exactly. There's such a thing as proportion."

"Well, maybe he's right. Maybe that jerk Hitler really is a threat to this
country. Eventually."

"Lots of people can't see 'eventually,' " Lattimer remarked. "I'm not sure
I can myself. I know a lot here"— he gestured around the big, busy room—
"can't. I think Tim may be swimming upstream."

"Oh, yes. He'll get plenty of hell for it, I'm sure. I know Dr. Chalmers will
be upset. He told him yesterday he didn't think it was wise for him to do it."

"But he didn't tell him not to."

"Oh, no. You know Chalmers. He takes the University's motto seriously:
Die Luft der Freiheit weht—'The winds of freedom blow.' He believes
in it—most of the time. Plus he's got his own standard of ethics to live
up to."

"Some of the trustees may not like it," Latt suggested. Wilson shrugged.

"They probably won't notice. And if they do—well, Tim has his standards, too."

He turned to stand and shake hands as Ari Katanian stopped by, dark and engaging, teeth gleaming in his usual broad smile.

"Willie!" he said. "How the hell are you? Hi, Latt. I don't think this guy looks very presidential, just sitting there. Make him do something presidential."

"I can't make him do anything," Latt said, shaking hands. "You know Willie."

"Alas, too well," Ari said with a rueful grin. "There but for the grace of God and several thousand votes go I. What new directions have you got for us, pal?"

"Nary a one," Wilson said, sitting back down again. "You're all on your own. I'm just going to preside benevolently while you ruin your young lives any way you damned please."

"I'm going to do brilliantly in all my exams and go on to law school and have one hell of a career," Ari said cheerfully.

"And by God, he means it, too," Wilson said to Latt.

"Insufferable egomaniac," Latt said to Wilson.

"O.K., you guys," Ari said with a grin. "Waste yourselves and see if I care. Nothing's going to stop me. You'll be thankful someday when you need my legal assistance. Oops!" he said suddenly. "There's Welcome Waggoner. I've got to go see if she'll be on Rally Committee this year."

"You know she will," Wilson said. "How can you keep her off—and get anybody else to go on, if she's there?"

"A good question," Ari said. "They asked me to ask her, so here goes." And off he went.

"And what did Dr. Chalmers say to *you*?" Latt inquired as they resumed their seats, only to rise again quickly as they saw Donnamaria Van Dyke and Betty June Letterman approaching together.

"I'll tell you later," Wilson said. "It wasn't much."

"Willie!" Donn said, looking healthy as all get-out in an expensive pink blouse with matching skirt that had probably set her back as much as twenty dollars at Roos-Atkins downtown. "Dr. Chalmers really gave us a talking-to, didn't he?"

"She's been telling me all about it," B.J. said with a chuckle. "Sounds as though he thinks you might be a real troublemaker, Willie."

" 'Not much,' " Lattimer echoed dryly. "What a faithless churl thou art, President Wilson."

"Why?" Donn demanded brightly. "Was he trying to give you some story about it?"

"Not really," Latt said with a smile. "He's just too modest, that's all. You gals through registering?"

"Just about," B.J. said. "Have you seen North around anywhere?"

"He was here a little while ago," Latt said. "I think with that football player from the Zete house he palled around with spring quarter. Bradley, isn't it? Bob?"

"He was supposed to meet *me!*" B.J. said, making a joke of it, but they could see it upset her. "Well, I guess he'll show up. We're supposed to have a date at the Cellar for lunch."

"He'll be there," Willie promised. "We'll boot him along when we see him."

"Do that," she said, dismissing it, sunny again. "Boy, am I going to be working hard this quarter!"

"Me, too," Donn said. "Sixteen units. Plus"—she twinkled suddenly at Willie—"my official duties. I don't think," she said to Lattimer, "that he's going to let me do *anything.*"

"Keeping Donn Van Dyke from doing *anything,*" Wilson said with a laugh, "is just like keeping B.J. Letterman from doing *anything.* The man doesn't exist on this planet who can do that, with either of you. Plus you're going to get mostly straight A's, Donn. B.J. and Latt here are going to lead the pack as usual with those disgusting, impossible grade averages. The rest of us can only hide and try to conceal our shame."

"You'll manage," Lattimer said. "At least two A's and two B's this quarter or I miss my guess."

"I don't know about that English course," Willie said. "Armpits McGee has had it in for me for three years. This may be the year she finally gets her revenge."

"Professor McGee is one of the brighter ornaments of our faculty," Donna said solemnly. She uttered a sudden gurgle of laughter. "I hear this year she's switched to Arrid."

The mental picture this evoked dissolved them all into happy laughter as the girls said goodbye—Donn saying cheerfully to Willie, "See you at the Cellar!"—and took off to turn in their registration forms at the front desk. Wilson and Latt sat down again but immediately stood up once more as Welcome Waggoner appeared out of the crowd and stopped by to say hello and tell them what fun it would be to be on Rally Committee. After that they made no attempt to settle down again as the crowd grew and more and more friends from all over campus stopped to greet Wilson and wish him luck.

In the next hour he must have said hello to at least two hundred friends of varying degrees of intimacy, some of them just wanting to speak to the new president, some, like Bob Godwin, with more specific favor-seeking missions in mind.

Bob Godwin, from St. Louis, Missouri, political science major, was occasionally referred to (Tim had noted) as "God" by his less impressed fraternity brothers. "He is one of the most ambitious men on campus and for three years has been running for student-body president. Whether he will make it over Wilson's opposition, if Wilson decides to oppose him, is one of those questions which torture him constantly, for he is not at all sure that he has endeared himself to Wilson even though he has tried faithfully for a long time. A likeable kid, his main fault is the only one that might arouse various people against him—he *is* ambitious, and he is not enough of a dissembler to keep it from showing. Accomplishes a great deal of good, rather incidentally, on charity drives and other things of an eleemosynary nature in his search for votes. Will be terribly hurt if his ambitions don't work out, but probably a sadder and wiser man. Wiry, dark and good-looking, with an engaging smile and an attractive manner, he has every chance of getting ahead successfully in anything he tries if he just won't nag his luck too hard."

"Oh, Lord," Willie murmured to Latt as they saw Bob approach. "Here comes God."

"The house's second Perfect Boy Politician," Lattimer murmured back. "He's your creation, Willie. Don't let him down now."

"But he *tries* so hard," Wilson objected. "If only he'd *relax*."

But Bob never would relax, Willie knew that. He had seen him at breakfast but once again he held out his hand and gave him a cordial shake. He felt that Bob's morale, which he sensed was really rather shaky underneath, needed bolstering.

"Bob, friend!" he exclaimed. "All through registering?"

"Oh, a couple of hours ago," Godwin said. "But you know how it is. Have to hang around and greet the voters."

"Thank God *that's* over with," Wilson said. Godwin looked envious.

"For you, yes. Not for me, damn it. That is, if I still want to go anywhere."

"And where might that be?" Wilson asked. Bob poked him in the arm.

"Stop being coy with me, you bastard," he said, but careful to keep it light.

"At least you're honest about it," Lattimer said with a smile. Godwin nodded seriously.

"I am, and why not? I mean—if you don't let people know, then they won't be able to vote for you, will they?"

"They'll vote for you, Bob," Wilson said, "if you just won't push it too hard. Let it grow a little. You'll get there."

"But will I have your support?" Bob asked frankly. "That's what worries me. I can't make it without that."

"Oh, hell you can't!" Wilson said. "After all, you're president of the junior class, you're on half a dozen committees, you're a letter man in tennis, everybody knows you—"

"If you backed somebody else," Bob said solemnly, "I'd die."

"Who is there?" Wilson asked. "I don't know anybody."

"Oh," Bob said with a frown. "I keep worrying you'll think of someone."

"I'm not aware of him yet," Wilson said.

"Sure?" Godwin inquired, giving him the intense yet supplicating look that made Wilson feel uncomfortably that he was looking into someone's soul; and at once, of course, made him feel perversely unhelpful.

"I'll let you know if I do," he said, and for just a second Bob looked quite openly despairing.

"You see?" he said to Latt. "A guy can't depend on *anything.*"

"Oh, now," Lattimer said in his kindly way. "Don't let him bug you, Bob, he's just doing it to tease."

"Do you think so?" Godwin asked wistfully. "I'd like to think so, but I never know with Willie."

"I know Willie," Latt said firmly, "and I'm telling him to stop this. O.K., Willie?"

"O.K.," Willie said meekly. "Don't worry, Bob. It'll all work out. . . . There's a couple of Rally Committee guys over there. Shouldn't you go talk to them?"

"I guess I should," Bob said, turning to stare across the room. "Yes—yes, I think I'd better. See you back at the house, you guys. Thanks, Willie."

"Now, what," Wilson inquired, as Bob took his earnest, worried face busily away, "is he thanking me for? You're the one who was kind to him, I'm the one who teased him."

"Why?" Latt inquired, sounding genuinely curious. Wilson looked a little shamefaced.

"I don't know, really. It *isn't* kind, you're right. He's just so—so *anxious,* that's all."

"Lucky Willie," Latt said. "Never had to be anxious."

"Well, no, as a matter of fact, I never really have," Wilson said. "And maybe," he added soberly, "that's not been a good thing for me. . . . O.K., I'll try to be nice to him from now on. For your sake. We do a lot of things for your sake, Latt, did you know that? You'd be surprised at how much we think of you."

"I know," Lattimer said gravely. "And we think a lot of you, too. Which is why I don't like to see you demeaning yourself by mocking another guy's hopes. He has a right to them. We all do."

"Yes," Willie said with equal gravity. "I will be good. . . . I . . . *will* . . . be . . . good."

"I hope so," Latt said calmly. "It's more becoming."

"Yes, sir," Wilson said. Then he smiled. "Who said you couldn't make me do·anything?"

After that they lingered for a while as many others came by to say hello. Around the noisy room they could see their housemates going through the same rituals of greeting. Registration was a time for renewing old ties, starting new ones. This was an obviously happy process for some. For others, Latt and Willie were sensitive enough, and by this time mature enough, to perceive, it was less so.

Of the less happy, the episode that struck them most as they watched from the rim of the stage where they had gone to perch after turning in their registration forms was occurring below, to their right and about fifteen feet over. A short, dark, chunkily good-looking youth was talking to a short, blond, vivaciously pretty girl. The boy had a warm, engaging smile that lighted up his face, an appealing and attractive manner that endeared him to most people. It was obviously not endearing him very much to his girl, whose eyes were here, there, and everywhere and who seemingly didn't care whether he remained talking to her or wandered away. This was making him look desperately unhappy and, unfortunately, very obvious.

"Why," Unruh demanded as he hoisted himself up beside Willie and Latt, "does Carrero hang around that little bitch? She's just leading him on."

"I don't know," Wilson said. "I think he likes her."

"Of course he does," Latt said. "He's crazy about her."

"More fool he," Unruh said with the certainty of an old campaigner. "She isn't worth his little finger."

"Maybe he can't help himself," Wilson remarked. Unruh snorted.

"Anybody can help himself in that kind of situation," he said scornfully.

"Not everybody," Latt said quietly. "Sometimes it really hurts. Sometimes people really care."

"And I don't?" Guy demanded. "You're so superior, Latt. How would you know?"

"All it takes is a little sensitivity to others."

"I think I'll go down and help him out," Unruh said. "I'll break it up." And he started to shift himself off the proscenium.

"Don't you dare," Wilson said quietly, but his hand on Guy's arm was firm. "You stay right where you are, pal, and don't you get into that at all. Hear me?"

For a moment Unruh studied his unyielding face. Then he grinned and relaxed.

"All right, Daddy. It might be fun, though. From what I hear, she's a hot little—"

"I don't care what you hear, Brother Unruh," Willie said, "*you* stay out of it. O.K.?"

Again Unruh studied him, again he grinned.

"I said I would."

"All right," Wilson said, "do that. I'm not going to have you hurting Randy. He's hurt enough, at the moment."

And so, indeed, he appeared to be. His face, honest and open, looked crushed—particularly so when the girl suddenly gave him a vague little smile, turned away and started through the crowd toward a tall, blond, strikingly handsome older student, surrounded by three other attentive females. She immediately became the center of the conversation as the blond student abruptly and very obviously concentrated all his considerable charm upon her.

"Damn!" Unruh said. "You see? You've made me lose out to Gulbransen again. Why do you do things like that to me, Willie?"

"It's for your own good," Wilson said. "And in this case, Randy's."

"Hell," Guy said. "Anything that would really break that up would be the best thing that ever happened to him."

"He's seen us and is coming over," Lattimer reported, "so keep it down to a low roar, if you don't mind."

"Hi," Randy Carrero said, managing a pretty good replica of his normally open and sunny smile. "How're you guys getting along? All registered?"

They told him they were, but were just killing time until lunch.

"Nothing like Reg Day," Guy said brightly. "It's the best chance in the world to look over the merchandise."

Wilson and Lattimer gave him a disgusted glance as Randy looked a little shaken but responded gamely, "It looks pretty good to me."

"It always does on Reg Day," Unruh agreed. "It begins to fade rapidly after that. Well," he said cheerily as his classmates gave him another disapproving glance, "guess I'll be shoving along."

A sudden bitter expression crossed Randy's face as Unruh moved confidently away. "I guess I am pretty obvious, at that," he said, "but I just can't help it." He looked suddenly very young, very bleak and very alone. "I can't—" he said. "I can't—" He gave up.

"Well," Lattimer said, "anytime you want to talk about it, Willie and I are here."

"Thanks, you guys," Randy said, managing a shred of smile. "I may take you up on that one of these days. But I expect—" Again he looked bleak and alone— "I expect I'll just have to work it out on my own. But I'll let you know."

And he moved off toward the registration desks, carefully not looking over toward the conversational group which had now miraculously reduced itself to just Fluff Stevens and Gil Gulbransen, the other girls having somehow been pleasantly and efficiently dismissed.

"Dear, dear," Wilson murmured. "Young love."

"He's got too much going for him to waste it on that little flibbertigibbet," Latt said.

"He'll get over it," Willie said. Latt frowned.

"I'm not so sure. Sometimes when you have as much on the ball as he has, you can get too intense, all around. . . . Well," he added, easing himself off the proscenium and stretching, "it's almost eleven and I think I'd better be running along. I have a date with Kay to go over to the beach for a picnic. Ray's lending me his car. Want to come along?"

"No, thanks. I think I'll go back to the house and just relax for a while. I'll see you later. If the house meeting ends in time tonight maybe we can take in a movie. I see there're a couple of good ones in town—Fred Astaire and Ginger Rogers in *Carefree* and Alice Faye, Tyrone Power, and Don Ameche in *Alexander's Ragtime Band*. Both designed to take the harried scholar's mind off the new academic year."

Latt smiled. "Thanks. We'll think about it. In the meantime, take care and have a good rest—" He paused abruptly. His voice took on an interested, disbelieving tone. "Now, what's that?"

"Who's that, is more like it," Wilson said, his voice changing too as he saw what Latt saw.

Down the aisle from the back of the auditorium there was a little stir, a movement, a tall, lanky figure, a hesitant but dogged face; and following close behind, a sudden, obvious hushing all around.

Because the face was black, and in 1938 that was not at all a usual thing, at this university or at many another. It was so unusual and startling, in fact, that within a minute virtually all conversation had ceased and a curious, watchful silence had settled on the room. It was not hostile, but it was intent; and the world, for the moment, seemed curiously suspended.

Into the silence the owner of the figure and the face came bravely down the aisle toward the registration desks. He was accompanied by the assistant dean of men. Both looked tense and uneasy. Some among their audience such as Wilson and Lattimer were sensitive enough to realize what that walk down the aisle under all those surprised and intently watching white eyes must be costing the owner of the figure and the face, and what a brave thing he was doing in the context of the place and time. More were struck by the presence of the assistant dean of men, and what this indicated regarding the administration's expectation of trouble.

Most of them were decent enough, and tolerant enough, and proud enough of their university's traditions, that they instinctively rejected the idea that any trouble could happen. But that certainty could not keep them from staring, in a way the owner of the figure and the face would always remember.

The two came down the aisle and approached the registration desks. The Negro asked for the registration forms in a low, almost inaudible voice, received them and turned to look for a seat. A couple of students in the first row jumped up as if shot and gestured to theirs. He smiled tentatively—and they smiled tentatively—but the hush continued as he sat down and they backed away, almost as though seeking protection in the crowd.

The assistant dean asked clearly, "You're sure you're all right?"

The black boy said, "I'm fine, thanks," in a low but pleasantly modulated voice.

"O.K., then, I'll leave you," the assistant dean said. "Call on me if you need anything."

"Thanks," the boy said. "I will."

The assistant dean left, the room began to relax. The babble of conversation resumed and within seconds had risen to its former level.

But their eyes did not leave the boy as he turned to the forms and began slowly and patiently filling them out.

He knew, and they knew, that something new had been added and that somehow nothing would ever be quite the same again.

"Well, well," Wilson said softly. "What do you know."

"Yes, indeed," Latt said.

"I like his looks," Wilson said with a sudden calm decisiveness, knowing full well the impact his actions would have on his fellow students. "Let's go meet him."

Lattimer gave him a quick, affectionate smile.

"You know," he said, "you're quite a guy, Willie. Let's."

And they walked across the open space that seemed to have grown around the boy; stood beside him for a second while he kept his head down, aware of their presence but apparently not quite daring to look up; and then simultaneously held out their hands.

"I'm Willie Wilson," Wilson said, "and this is Bill Lattimer. Welcome to the University."

The boy gave them a great big smile they never forgot, rose to tower over them, tall as they both were, and shook their hands with grateful pressure.

His name, he said, was Bayard Johnson. He came from Richmond, Virginia, he was a sophomore transfer from Howard University in Washington, D.C., majoring in mechanical engineering, he played basketball, he was an above-average student—which he didn't want to tell them until Willie pressed and he admitted with a shy smile that he had "done pretty well so far. I'm not one of the A's, though, I'm just one of the brighter B's," which Willie said was good enough for them. He had always wanted to come west to the University, and finally his father, who owned a small department store, had agreed, provided he could get a scholarship. He had, based upon his basketball record, he believed, though he hoped his grades had had something to do with it too. And here he was.

"It's good to have you," Willie told him as they prepared to leave. "We'll be seeing you around. If you need any help on anything, just give us a ring at the Alpha Zete house. In fact, we'll have you up for a meal sometime soon. We'd like all the members to meet you."

"Thank you so much, Mr. Wil—Willie," Bayard Johnson said. "I'd like that. And thank you both for coming over. It really means a lot to me. You're very kind."

"We're absolute bastards, really," Wilson said with a smile, "but we like to fool people once in a while. Good luck with everything, Bayard. We'll see you."

"Willie . . ." Latt said tentatively, as they left him to the rapidly growing crowd of students who suddenly seemed to want to shake his hand and walked out of Memorial Hall and started up the Quad in the sparkling autumn day.

"Yes?" Willie said sharply, because he knew what was coming.

"Aren't you moving a little fast, maybe? After all, we really don't know much about him—"

"Only way to find out. Just go at it. Right?"

"Well, yes. But there may be some people in the house who might feel they're being pressured—"

"I'm not pressuring anybody," Willie said blandly. "Just moving things along. Have a good picnic."

"We will," Latt said as they parted. "Let me know if you do anything else sensational today."

"I will," Wilson said with a grin, hitting him on the arm. "You can count on me, Latt."

"Always," Lattimer said, hitting him back. "Always."

It was only when he looked back a few days later that Wilson realized that he had done something else sensational that day, although he had not recognized it at the time.

He came out of the Cellar with Donna after a hamburger-and-Coke lunch and accidentally bumped into a girl who was just coming in. He had a quick impression that she was blond, rather tall, pretty but not overwhelmingly so. She wore a green-gold dress, or something green with a gold note in it anyway, and her voice was soft and pleasant as she exclaimed, "Oh, I'm sorry!" and he said, "No, I'm sorry," and they passed and went on their respective ways.

"Who was that?" he asked Donn, but Donn didn't know. And after a while, as he returned to the house and stretched out for a nap, she slipped from his thoughts as he began to drift off, deciding that the incident wasn't even notable, let alone sensational.

Shortly after three he was roused by the ringing of the house phone. Johnny Herbert got it and yelled for him. Once again he found Dr. Chalmers on the line.

"I just wanted to congratulate you and Bill Lattimer," the president said. "That was a fine thing you did today."

"Thank you, sir," Wilson said. "It seemed like a good idea."

"It was," Dr. Chalmers said. "It will make things a lot easier for him, I think."

"I hope so," Wilson said. "Latt and I really liked him."

"He's a good boy," the president said, not being patronizing as Jeff Barnett, for instance, with his South Carolina background might have been, just stating a fact: Bayard *was* a good boy.

"Sir—" Willie said.

"Yes?"

"Is this a trend? I mean—are you breaking new ground? I don't think I've ever seen a Negro here before. Have we ever had any?"

"Not to my knowledge," Dr. Chalmers said. "I thought I'd try it out. You've already been an enormous help."

"I think we should have more," Wilson said—an idea he had never really thought about before. Suddenly it seemed a good one.

"In time, possibly," the president said, his voice becoming a shade reserved. "Let's see how young Johnson works out. One can't get too far ahead of the parade, can one?"

"No, sir," Willie said, knowing the tone and thinking he had better drop the subject before it turned into an argument. "Well, thank you, sir. I'll tell Latt you called. We'll do everything we can to make the experiment successful."

"It really depends on Bayard," the president said. "If any place could be receptive to that line of development, it's us, as you know."

"We'll give him a hand up in every way we can," Wilson promised.

"Good," the president said. "I'll count on you."

For a split second Wilson hesitated. Then he pressed again. "Let's think about it more, sir."

"In time, possibly," Dr. Chalmers repeated, his tone now quite firm. "Give it time, Willie. Let's just do the best we can with what we have, first."

"Yes, sir," Wilson said obediently. "Thank you for calling."

"I felt you and Latt deserved it," the president said. "You've got this off to a fine start."

And said goodbye politely and rang off, leaving Wilson to return to the sagging old sofa in his room and lie for a while longer staring up at the ceiling, doing a lot of thinking. He had known as he made his decision in Memorial Hall that he was helping to start a revolution. He wondered whether it would continue, and where it would end. Or would it?

He decided that he would not raise the matter in the first house meeting of the year that night, which turned out to be a wise decision. The meeting was loud, raucous, irreverent and filled with the happy excitement of being back together again—"a damned disorderly bunch," Buff Richardson remarked in mild protest after they had confirmed by acclamation his election as president, Tony Andrade's as secretary-treasurer and Ray Baker's, once again, as house manager.

"If you guys don't settle down and maintain a little order," Buff added, trying hard to sound stern, "I'm going to have to start imposing fines."

The threat was uttered with such a disarming expression and such an amiable air, however, that no one paid any attention. Whereupon he suddenly said, "Oh, the hell with it!," picked up a pillow and threw it at Unruh, who snagged it gracefully and pegged it at Wilson. From then on there was a general melee as others plucked pillows from chairs and sofas and hurled them about with happy abandon.

"Mr. President!" North McAllister finally shouted. "I move we adjourn!"

"The meeting is adjourned!" Buff shouted back from his prudent presidential position lying behind one of the sofas. "All I can say," he added with dignity as he stood up, still fending off flying pillows, "is that this is a damned childish way to start the year."

And no time, Wilson reflected as several members happily told Buff, with further pillows, where he could go and what he could do, to introduce the subject of Bayard Johnson. Or any other serious subject. Life would turn serious enough tomorrow morning when classes began. And when the world, now so happily shut out and kept away, came rushing back with the impact he knew they all at heart uneasily anticipated.

And so of course it did, as students, laughing, chattering, calling out to one another in the cool, foggy morning, streamed down from the Row and over from the halls, pausing only briefly to snatch up copies of the *Daily* from the stands scattered about the Quad as they hurried to their first eight-o'clock classes.

Bates had again given it full treatment. The headlines and stories leaped with an angry clamor off the page:

WAR CRISIS GROWS.

"Berlin—Reichsfuehrer Adolf Hitler today readied Germany's armed forces for a strike into Czechoslovakia in the wake of his 'final demand' for the return of the Sudetenland to Germany.

"Prime Minister Neville Chamberlain announced that Great Britain would consider guaranteeing the Sudetenland's return to Germany if Germany promised to refrain from war. . . ."

F.D.R. MAY SEEK EUROPEAN CONFAB.

The student body read, exclaimed, shook heads, exchanged worried speculations.

Willie thought wistfully: The future seems less and less friendly every time you turn around.

Not only the morning was cool.

Not only the fog made them shiver and seek the protective warmth of being together in classrooms.

There were intimations of winter.

Suddenly it seemed it might be the winter of the world.

School, not impervious but nonetheless inexorable, went on.

4

All around the Quad, Willie and his friends and fellow students began to apply themselves to the work of the academic year as it now unfolded in earnest in all the buildings and facilities that comprised the University.

"The central group of University buildings," the Bawlout described them, "containing two quadrangles, the one surrounding the other, is an adaptation of the mission architecture and reproduces on an imposing scale the open arches, long colonnades and red-tile roofing of the old Spanish missions of California. The inner Quadrangle consists of twelve one-story buildings and the Memorial Church, connected by a continuous open arcade, and surrounding a court 586 feet long by 264 wide, or three and a half acres. The buildings are of buff sandstone, somewhat varied in color, the stonework of broken ashlar, with rough rock face, and the roofs covered with red tile.

"The extreme length of the Outer Quadrangle is 894 feet . . ."

And it went on to describe in some detail the buildings that soon after one entered the University came to comprise the landscape of the mind:

The funny, musty little old museum out along Palm Drive toward the town, filled in those days with the odds and ends and few miscellaneous antiquities the founders had collected in their travels . . . the chemistry building and laboratories between the Quad and the museum . . . the school of engineering workshops and labs to the south . . . the freshman men's dorm east of the Quad, and the three other men's dorms . . . the four women's dorms . . . the Row southeast of the quad . . . Memorial Hall, northeast of the Quad . . . Memorial Amphitheater, set in a sunken wooded vale behind Memorial Hall . . . the men's gym out toward the stadium, the women's gym near the main women's dorms . . . the basketball pavilion . . .

the stadium, a quarter mile northwest of the Quad near the highway and the town . . . the art gallery, hidden in trees along the walk from the Quad to the freshman men's dorm . . . the library ("the Libe"), a couple of hundred feet east of the Quad, containing 736,000 volumes . . . the school of education building, first of the gifts that were to proliferate over the years, immediately southwest of the Libe . . . the Union, south of the Quad, comprising three ivy-covered buildings connected by arcades, containing rooms for sixty-five women, public dining rooms including the basement "Cellar," an ever-popular rendezvous, and offices for student organizations . . .

And to put it all in geographical perspective some thirty miles south of San Francisco:

"The Bay of San Francisco is about three miles east of the University grounds. The Santa Clara Valley is one of the most attractive portions of the state in fertility, in natural beauty, and in the excellence of its climate. In winter the mercury rarely falls below 30 degrees, with an average midday temperature of about 55 degrees. In summer the midday temperature ranges between 60 degrees and 80 degrees, occasionally higher and lower, the average being about 70 degrees; the nights are cool, the usual range being from 50 degrees to 58 degrees. The rainfall, normally about eighteen inches, is chiefly confined to the months from December to April, inclusive.

"Perhaps no university in America," the official description concluded proudly, "has a more beautiful setting, a more salubrious climate or an atmosphere more conducive to the acquiring of that quality of education desired by the Founders."

And that, a forlorn and shaggy-haired figure wearing fashionably dirty cor-duroy pants and a fashionably tattered old wool sweater thought to himself as he trudged along beside his small, bouncy companion, was where he came in.

Theodore Krasnick Musavich was about to meet the educational system for the fourth year running, and while it had not succeeded in entirely conquering him, he had very definitely not conquered it. Aided by several interested alumni, the Board of Athletic Control, the scholarship office, and many devoted housemates and quite a few lenient teachers, he had managed to keep the system at bay—barely.

Just barely.

"I wish I weren't so dumb," he said now, morosely, to Rodge Leighton, and Rodge said loyally, "Nonsense!"

"Well, I *am*," Moose said. "I'm just a plain damned dumbbell and I'll never be anything else. I start each year with all sorts of hopes and plans and I know the minute I step onto the Quad again that I'm going to go right straight down the drain where I've always been. It's discouraging."

"Maybe you won't this year," Rodge said, trying to sound both comforting and convinced, which was hard because he wanted to be comforting but he really wasn't any more convinced than Moose was. "I mean, I'm not so bright, either—"

"Oh, hell," Moose said as they climbed the steps and started down the raised stone floor of the east colonnade toward English Corner. "Oh, *hi!*" he added with a pleased smile to several cute girls and half a dozen fellows who hailed him as they hurried by. "*Hi,* there!"

"You see?" Rodge demanded. "You have all *sorts* of friends. Everybody likes you. They're real glad to see you, Moose. I wish I had as many good friends as you do."

"That's not what I'm talking about," Moose said, again morose, "and you know it. You're only a sophomore, you'll have all the friends you need by the time you're my age. What I mean is, I'm dumb. And you're not. And that's all there is to it."

"I can't play football," Rodge Leighton said, casting about rather desperately for something to alleviate the gloom. "I sure can't do that, Mooser!"

"And who said *I* could?" Moose inquired forlornly. Rodge stopped so abruptly he almost got them run down by the hurrying throng.

"Oh, now, Moose, that is *really* dumb!" he exclaimed. "That is *really* dumb. Why, what would the coach do without you—"

"Get somebody else," Moose said wanly. "He's always threatening to."

"He'd better not!" Rodge said fiercely. "Or I'll . . . I'll . . ."

"You won't do anything," Moose said, "and you know it." He did, however, begin to look more cheerful, and indeed almost began to laugh at the sight of Rodge's earnest young face. "You're a good pal," he said, giving him an affectionate poke that almost sent Rodge, five feet four and 126 pounds, spinning off the edge of the Quad into the bushes below. "I like you."

"Well, I *hope* so," Rodge said, recovering his balance and coming back gamely. "Jeez! You wear me to a frazzle with that Gloomy Gus act of yours, Mooser. I'll have to talk to Willie and the others about you."

"They know me," Moose said. "They know me. Well, I'm going to break off here and go to that damned Methods and Techniques of Officiating Athletic Contests. I also have a Problems of Physical Education class at eleven. They're starting me off busy this year. How about you?"

"Atomic Physics."

"You physics guys," Moose said admiringly. "What brains! I wish I had them."

"Now," Rodge said firmly, "don't get into that again. Anyway, don't I see Welcome Waggoner—Suzy—down the Quad, there? That ought to give you something happy to think about."

"Enjoyable," Moose said, relaxing into a grin. "Not necessarily happy. See you later, Rodge."

"Sure, take care," Rodge said, and swung away toward Engineering Cor-

ner. He hoped he was going to see that little girl he had met Reg Day who
had just decided to major in physics, too. There was a brain—a damned
sweet-looking one, too. He wanted to cultivate that. He sure hoped he had
managed to shake Moose out of his mood. He worried about him. It was no
way to start the school year. He really liked Moose, they were getting to be
real pals. But then, as Bates had noted in his little locked box, Rodge liked
everybody and everybody liked Rodge. He came from Phoenix and was
going to major in atomic physics, which was an interesting if somewhat
obscure and relatively unused science. While he wasn't one of the more
sensational people in the school, there were a lot of fine things about Roger
Leighton, physics major, from Phoenix, Arizona, "one of those nice, amiable, average-guy characters who form the backbone of many a fraternal
organization and are particularly valuable as balance wheels. Academically,
he falls somewhere near the exact University mean of brains, ability, and
likeability, and with this he is quite content. He comes from a modest
family, has modest dreams, conducts himself without blemish in a modest
life. He has already decided the kind of girl he wants to marry, and with that
settled is able to concentrate without distraction on the physics he loves and
in which he hopes to find himself a suitable financial niche when he leaves
school. He can always be relied upon to speak well of everyone and, perhaps
most importantly, openly admire and support people whose egos need it,
particularly Musavich.

" 'Just wait till Moose fumbles one of those passes in the first game of the
season and *that* love affair will be over fast,' " Suratt predicts acidly, but
probably it won't, because somehow between the big, awkward linesman
and the cheerful, bright little scholar a real trust and affection seems to be
developing. In a world in which he generally feels that people are looking
down on him, Moose, who considers himself no hero, has apparently found
a hero-worshiper.

"In grateful return he has several times assured Roger, 'If anybody gives
you any trouble, you just let me know and I'll knock his block off.' Rodge,
who likes everybody and finds it quite inconceivable that anyone would ever
want to give him trouble or that he in turn would ever want Moose to knock
somebody's block off, is nonetheless touched and flattered by an offer of
support he can't help but appreciate. It is one of those relationships, quite
innocent but quite genuine, that sometimes develops between friends who
to the world seem mismatched."

Moose's other relationship, not at all innocent, was even more baffling
these days, as was evident from the general tone of Tim's notes. In this he
reflected the general view of the campus and of Moose's housemates, who
felt protectively that their feckless child was in a league too fast for him when
he dated Suzy Waggoner.

"There is one on every campus," Tim had written. "In fact, quite a few.

Suzy is rich, smart, pretty, selfish, implacably determined to have her own way, and as loose-moraled as the house cat, Josephine. Always one of the principal topics of gossip on campus—she is known generally as 'Welcome Waggoner'—she is aware of it and doesn't give a damn. 'Have you ever done it with a member of the football team?' one of her wide-eyed younger sorority sisters once asked her. 'All of them,' she answered crisply. 'And she meant it, too!' her sorority sister told the rest in an awed tone. They looked amused. 'We know Suzy,' they said: 'Maybe yes, maybe no. She loves to kid about it.' It is true that *everybody* knows Suzy—which doesn't mean, of course, that she isn't accepted, popular, a Big Woman on Campus and generally considered a 'student leader.'

"She can no more avoid calculating her chances and approaching any handsome male than Josephine can; the only difference, as Franky Miller remarked, 'is that Suzy is *always* in heat.' 'There are only so many hours in the day,' Unruh objects; 'I don't know how she does it.' 'She managed it with you, didn't she?' Miller responds, and Unruh chuckles, 'Several times.' 'Me, too,' Franky says with an answering chuckle. 'Three Dekes, a Beta, four Zetes and a Phi Delt were waiting in line.'

"Whether all of this is entirely true, nobody knows for certain; a lot of it, they suspect, is self-promotion. But enough of it is true that her reputation is high, wide and handsome. 'Have a date with Welcome Waggoner' is one of the charges often given to pledges in certain houses during Hell Week. Some of them take the order seriously and try. At least two or three times each fall their success is heralded with shouts of brotherly commendation heard up and down the Row."

And now here she was, surrounded, as Franky put it, by "three Dekes, a Beta, four Zetes and a Phi Delt"—or at least four other guys, at whom Moose scowled in his amiable and not very forbidding fashion as he came alongside.

"Oh, *hi*," Suzy said brightly. "*There* you are!"

"Hi," he said; and "Hi" to the guys; and then stood there with an expression they took to be inscrutable and faintly menacing, although it was really just that he was trying to decide what to offer in the way of small talk. Before he could make up his mind, one or two of them nervously muttered something about "Better hurry or I'll be late for that history class," and they all mumbled unintelligible things in hasty agreement, smiled nervously, and faded away.

"Well," Moose said. "When did you get back? I thought you'd call me."

"I tried to," Suzy said virtuously, placing a hand on his arm in a proprietary way.

"I saw you across the room on Reg Day," Moose said accusingly. "You didn't come over."

"Neither did you," she pointed out calmly.

"I was busy."

"So was I. Shall we walk along together for a bit? I'll be late for that history class, too, if I don't hurry."

"I'm going the other way," Moose said.

"O.K.," she said cheerfully, and started to turn away. "See you later sometime."

"Now, wait a minute!" he said anxiously. "I didn't mean—"

"What are you doing tonight?" she interrupted as the ten-minute warning bell rang loudly through the Quad and all the other buildings.

"What do you want to do?" he asked.

She gave him a wry smile.

"Talk about physical education."

"I have football practice at three o'clock," he said. "We probably won't be through until almost six."

"Come as you are," she suggested and turned on the full power of her smile, which, as Unruh put it, "could make a group of stone statues get a hard-on." She uttered a little laugh that did exactly that to Mooser. "Don't shower. I *love* it when you're all sweaty."

"Well—" he said. "Well—"

"Pick me up at the house," she directed, "and we'll get a bite to eat and then go out west of campus off Sand Hill Road someplace."

"O.K.," he said numbly, as usual quite paralyzed by her directness. "See you later."

"You bet," she said cheerfully and swept away, catching up as she did so with that tall dark guy from the halls that Moose had noticed Reg Day with a mild stirring of jealousy—linking her arm intimately into his, then turning back for a last brilliant smile at Moose as they disappeared around a corner.

Oh, Christ, he told himself as he plodded off toward the men's gym, here we go again. He couldn't claim to be exactly upset, though. She was good, there was no doubt of that; and they both understood: no strings. He only got upset half a minute later when everybody's most unfavorite fraternity brother yelled at him to slow down and wait for a guy.

"I saw you with Welcome," Renny Suratt said. "You great big romantic character, you."

"Hi, Renny," he said. "Are you going my way?"

"I know you can't stand it," Renny said cheerfully, falling into step, "but for a few hundred feet, I am. Are you and Welcome resuming this quarter? Or did you ever stop?"

"I didn't hear from her all summer, if that's what you mean," Moose said. "She was at Tahoe with her folks."

"Probably screwing all the lifeguards," Suratt said briskly. "What did *you* do all summer, whang it off in the shower?"

"I worked," Moose said with dignity. "In a hamburger joint."

"A hamburger joint!" Renny cried, and Moose said flatly, "Yeah, a hamburger joint. What did you do? Anything?"

"I was at Tahoe too, but we were on the Nevada side of the lake. I never saw Our Lady of the Rubbers. I just sailed and swam and played tennis and had fun."

Moose snorted.

"Well, rub it in. I can take it if your dad's rich and mine's poor. So what the fuck what?"

"What *what*?" Suratt inquired. "Your English is getting too tangled for me, Moose."

"Shove on, then," Moose suggested. "I can stand it."

"You can?" Suratt asked, dark eyes amused and dark clever face peering intently at his. "You really can stand the loss of my company, Moose? Now, that isn't a very nice thing to say!"

"You're the one who doesn't say nice things," Moose said. "Why don't *you* shove off?"

"Because I'm going in the same direction as one of my favorite fraternity brothers and I want his company."

"Well, you're not one of *my* favorites, and I don't want yours," Moose said, "so I repeat, why don't you just run along? I have to see enough of you at the house."

"Now you're really being nasty," Renny said with a pleased smile. "People think you're such a pussycat, but you're really a tiger underneath, aren't you?"

"Oh—!" Moose exclaimed in complete frustration, whereupon Suratt burst into genuine laughter and started to attempt everybody's favorite gesture of ruffling Moose's hair. Moose drew back instantly and sounded really angry.

"God damn it, leave my hair alone!" he said, so loudly that several passing students looked at them curiously. "I don't like to be touched. At least by you."

"Willie and the rest are a different matter, right?" Suratt asked with a sudden switch to bitterness. "You *like* them to paw you."

"They don't 'paw' me!" Moose exclaimed angrily and raised his arm almost threateningly. Renny danced back a step but continued to tease.

"Yes, you really *enjoy* it when Wilson and Bates make love to you. And as for Rodge Leighton, that little hero-worshiper—"

Moose stopped dead, grabbed Renny's arm, and held him forcibly still.

"Listen!" he said, tone low but at last filled with a very real, and very rare, annoyance. "Don't you talk to me about Rodge Leighton, or Willie, or Bates, or *anybody*, understand? Just *knock it off*."

For a moment Renny studied his face carefully. Then he said mildly, "Would you mind letting me go, Moose? We really do have to get to class, you know."

"Well, all right," Moose said after a second, breathing heavily. "But you be careful what you say about things, Renny, or you and I are *really* going to have trouble this year. And I mean it!"

"O.K.," Renny said in a resigned tone. "If I can't kid around without you getting all—"

"You don't kid," Moose said. "You hurt. Now I'm going to class. Goodbye!"

"All right," Renny said; and in some strange way and for some strange reason, he really did feel unhappy and bereft as Moose put his head down and lumbered away. "If that's the way you feel."

And yet, God damn it, as Franky Miller often said, Suratt brought it on himself. Why did he always have to dig, dig, dig? Why couldn't he just relax?

Bates' notes indicated that he thought he had the answer. Renny Suratt from Hillsborough, California, junior, economics major, "is a person whom many people don't like, and he doesn't like many people. Slight, dark and somewhat exotic in appearance, he is possessed of an infinite inferiority complex which expresses itself in delusions of persecution, extremely ironic remarks, and a witty but hurtful sense of humor resulting in sometimes funny, usually unkind statements, often amusing but not always tolerant or charitable. Sometimes he can be a good companion, his humor pleasant and unhurtful; but he is always apt to turn suddenly with some cutting statement, and so spoil the friendliness by putting his companion at once on the defensive.

"Suratt is extremely jealous of Wilson, and, to a slightly lesser degree, of Bates, but doesn't dare oppose them, criticize them or antagonize them openly; this provides him with much self-torture and appetite for revenge— for what, he would be at a loss to say.

"The world would get along all right with him and he would get along all right with it if he would only relax and 'act like a human being,' as Unruh often puts it. Since he won't, there are many who dislike him, and some, some of them in the house, who dislike him intensely."

Now Suratt paused, irresolute. For just a moment he seemed to himself to be out there somewhere where he couldn't quite touch the ground, staring after Moose until he disappeared across the meadows to the athletic facilities. Then a disdainful smile crossed his face, he laughed shortly, shook his head impatiently, turned and started back toward the Quad. Moose couldn't take a joke if it came up and hit him, he was that dumb. He'd done one good thing for Renny, though, as he always did: made him feel superior, which Renny knew he was. It was nice to have it reaffirmed, though. He needed that. At regular intervals Moose, and indeed most of his other brethren, did that for Renny Suratt.

He was just thinking of turning back to English Corner when a flying figure overtook him and he recognized one of the house sophomores whom he particularly wanted to cultivate, since he was about as close to headquarters as you could get: Billy Wilson, running to a theater class in Memorial Hall.

"Hey, Billy!" he called. Billy, shorter and blonder than his older brother, slightly plump, open-faced, nice-looking, decent, earnest, honest (and all those other good things, Renny told himself dryly), focused on him abruptly, said, "Oh, hi, Renny," and slowed to a walk.

"You don't have to run," Suratt pointed out with a smile. "It isn't a track meet. How's Janie?"

"Oh, she's just fine," Billy said, beaming. "I've just been up to Oregon visiting her, you know. We drove down to school together."

"Yes, I know," Renny said. "You told us."

Billy smiled shyly.

"I guess I do talk about her an awful lot."

"No more than any healthy, normal, red-blooded all-American boy," Suratt said. "She's a sweet girl," he added, having only last night described her to Marc Taylor as "one hundred and ten percent sugar."

"Thank you," Billy said, still shyly. "I think she's pretty nice."

"First rate," Suratt agreed heartily. "No doubt about that."

"Don't you have an eight o'clock?" Billy asked, starting to step up the pace again.

"At English Corner," Renny said. "I'm practically there. Just thought I'd get a little fresh air before going in. Glad I did, because I saw you."

"Oh, well," Billy said. "I'm not much." He stopped and asked politely, "What can I do for you?"

"Just be friendly." Suratt said, which struck Billy as a little odd. He smiled.

"I always am," he said, accurately.

"I know," Renny said, "and I appreciate it. Good luck with theater class. I'll see you at the house."

"Why, sure," Billy said, still a little puzzled. "I guess you will, all right. Good luck with your class, too."

"Dr. Stafford," Renny said. "But she likes me, the old bat. I think she fancies me as a Tudor lad in tights with enormous delights under the codpiece. If she only knew. It's minuscule."

"Oh, I wouldn't say that," Billy said with a rather uncertain laugh. He didn't know what this sudden turn was supposed to be all about, if anything.

"Oh, you noticed!" Suratt said. "How nice of you!"

"Not really," Billy said, looking more flustered. "I just meant as a general principle, one shouldn't say that."

"Oh," Renny said, and fixed him with a grin that made Billy, to his horror, start to blush. "*That's* what you meant!"

"Yes, that's it. I've really got to run, now, Renny. I'll see you at the house."

And he turned hurriedly and ran off, leaving Suratt thinking, What the *hell?* Don't tell me—? He gave a satisfied smile and filed the conversation away for whatever it meant, which, he recognized, probably wasn't much. Billy really was an all-American boy. But at least Renny had embarrassed little brother. And in some obscure way he couldn't define, that made him feel that he had scored off big brother.

He liked that.

Out of breath and still flustered, Billy sat in Memorial Hall thinking: Gosh! What do you suppose he meant by that?

Now it was dead on eight and all across campus the long, jangling bell rang out again as it did every hour on the hour, all day long, to mark the start of classes. Everybody was supposed to be tucked away in his or her seat, mind alert and wits at the ready, prepared to imbibe Education. With only a handful of exceptions among the house's twenty-six members, they were; and so were most of the more than three thousand who had eight-o'clocks. Legs crossed or stretched out, eyes bright or glazed over, dresses carefully neat and pants carefully sloppy, brains fully awake or still half rooted in bed, they stared up expectantly, or dully, or eagerly, or halfheartedly, or cordially, or resentfully, at the men and women who were supposed to fill them full of knowledge. It was the beginning, as Willie expressed it, of the annual warfare.

For himself and his ten fellow seniors, it was rounding into the home stretch on an old familiar track. They were settled into their majors now, they had taken classes already from most of the professors who were to address them this morning, there weren't many surprises left on the academic side of things—except, as Franky said, it was just harder this year. You really had to bear down, he said, in the slightly aggrieved tone of one who had always managed not to in his passage through the University. With varying degrees of application, they were beginning.

Ray Baker was seated in Administrative Law after a brief and pleasant chat on the Quad with Haggerty's gracious Fran McGruder, who was on her way to see her law adviser about a directed research project in immigration law that she wanted to pursue this quarter. Tim Bates was settling into a journalism class on Reporting of Public Affairs which was banal, obvious, and unnecessary except to fulfill requirements. On the other side of the Quad the three pre-meds were getting to work, Gulbransen and McAllister side by side in Special Procedures in Diagnosis and Treatment. A few doors away Unruh was beginning Oncology.

Over at History Corner, Lattimer and his principal scholastic competition, B. J. Letterman, were exchanging private jokes as the august silver-haired head of the department began his popular series of lectures on The Westward Movement in America: Present Days. He disapproved of their relaxed attitude but told himself, What can you do, they're such brilliant students they don't *have* to pay attention. In another room close by, Welcome Waggoner, though seated in the back row of History of American Democracy, was deliberately and successfully disconcerting her rather stuffy young professor with a slow, secretive smile. Over in Social Sciences, Franky was studying *his* professor with a lazy and practiced eye as the fellow, new to the University, stumbled a bit in his opening remarks on Personal Problems in Modern Society. ("Christ," Franky murmured behind his hand to Buff Richardson, seated behind him, "don't we have enough already?" Buff laughed silently and obligingly.) Over at English Corner three recognized girlfriends were taking notes, Latt's dignified Kay Ellsworth and Unruh's quiet Maggie Johnson in Types of Poetry, Donna Van Dyke in Short Story Writing. In Sociology, Gulbransen's Karen Ann Waterhouse was dutifully transcribing information on Social Organizations with her customary slightly superior and disdainful air.

Promptly at eight-fifty the bell rang again. Students poured out into the huge, graveled central courtyard of the Inner Quad and broke up into laughing, chatting groups as they compared notes on the first class of the year and prepared to move on to the next.

The fog had burned off, the temperature was up 15 degrees, it was suddenly a clear, warm, lovely autumn day. Franky announced loudly in the center of the Quad that it was an absolute crime to keep healthy young men and women indoors on a day like this, and got a big hand for it. Then the bell rang again and all those who had class went dutifully back inside.

Willie did not, being free until eleven when he was due in Modern Germany—to be followed at two P.M. by Modern Russia—he was really piling it on this quarter, his kid brother had told him admiringly. He said he thought the times required it.

He found himself walking slowly around Engineering Corner, thinking for the moment about nothing much except the glorious Indian-summer weather, when his eye caught a sudden splash of green turning off into the central Quad a hundred feet ahead. Moved by a sudden impulse he couldn't understand but which nonetheless impelled him, he broke into a run and took after it as it disappeared around one of the circles of palms planted at intervals in the central courtyard. Slightly out of breath, he ran around the circle and slowed abruptly as he came upon his quarry. Alerted by his noisy approach over the gravel, she swung around with a tentative smile. He saw mousy brown hair, big horn-rimmed glasses, a plain, studious face, a tentatively friendly expression prepared, from much experience, to be disappointed. He favored her with his most brilliant and overwhelming smile and passed by: he was disappointed too.

He hadn't seen his green-gold girl of Reg Day in almost twenty-four hours.

That suddenly seemed like a very long time.

He shook his head with a wry little smile and reminded himself that there had been a purpose originally in his going to the vicinity of Engineering

Corner. There was someone else he wanted to see. He had planned the encounter with some care, after exercising a little executive privilege and checking with the registrar's office yesterday afternoon to ascertain where his quarry might be at this hour. He would have just come out of one of his engineering classes.

Sure enough, there he was, sitting on one of the stone benches in one of the circles of palms, all by himself, studiously turning the pages of his textbook—determinedly casual but, as Wilson accurately surmised, quite miserably self-conscious.

He watched him for a moment as a group of fellows walked past him on their way to the Quad. They did speak to him, but it was quickly and almost furtively, and that wasn't enough, Willie told himself firmly. That just wasn't enough. We've all got to do better than that.

He was alongside and seated on the bench before Bayard Johnson even knew it. When Bayard sensed another presence he glanced up quickly with a smile, prepared to be hurt and go quickly and obediently away. But when he saw who it was, it broadened and became animated—and painfully grateful, too, Willie thought, and that wasn't right, either. But, he told himself, as Dr. Chalmers said: one step at a time.

"Bayard!" he said, holding out his hand cordially. "How nice to run into you. What's up?"

"Oh," Bayard Johnson said, sounding more forlorn than he knew, "I'm just sitting here."

"Can I sit with you?"

At this Bayard did relax a bit and his smile, while still a little cautious, became amused.

"Can't stop you, can I? Not the big student-body president."

"With all his honors and glories," Wilson agreed. "Forget them!" he ordered with mock sternness. "Underneath this golden exterior, hung about and weighted down with jewel-studded chains of office, beats the heart of a mortal man. Even as you and I, he sits beneath the palms of this beautiful place on this beautiful day and thinks: What the hell, what crap, why do sensible youths and maidens have to waste their precious hours that will never come again in some fusty-dusty damned old classroom, having their brains belabored by elderly, decrepit men and women, most of them at least thirty years old, who are utterly, infinitely, *shamefully* their inferiors in every conceivable way?"

"Is that what he thinks?" Bayard asked, really relaxed and laughing now. "I wouldn't have guessed all that from the way you look."

"I hope I look as grungy as everybody else," Willie said. "It's the image we all work so hard to project. You, for instance, are much too neat. Get those corduroys dirty, brother! Rip a few holes in that nice new sweater! Scuff your shoes in the mud a few hundred times! Forget to shave once in a while, preferably when you've got some class like Dr. Stafford's or Armpits Mc-Gee's. Be a sludge! Be a jerk! Be a lousy crumb-bum collitch kid! That's what your folks sent you here for. *Don't let them down!*"

Bayard, he was pleased to note, was quite convulsed with laughter now. Willie did feel rather pleased with himself, at that: it had been one of his better efforts. And the cause was very worthy.

"Now," he said, more calmly. "How are things going, really?"

Bayard's face—and it was, Willie realized, a very handsome face, sculptured, classic, with deep-set eyes and a quick, ready, appealing smile and laugh that were very young and very vulnerable—became sober and his expression far away. He sighed, too heavily.

"Oh," he said. "Things are going pretty well, I guess."

"What's wrong with them?" Willie asked in a tone that assumed he would be told the truth. He was.

"You've made them accept me," Bayard said, turning to look at him with complete and hurting candor. "But you haven't made them like me."

"Oh, for Christ's sake!" Willie said with a show of anger. "You've only been here a couple of days, for Christ's sake! How do you know how people feel about you? How do you know about this 'they' you're so spooked about?"

"Because," Bayard said simply, "I'm a Negro. And I know when it's wise for me to be spooked."

"Well," Wilson said—telling himself: O.K., miracle man, answer *that* one if you can—"it isn't wise to be spooked here, Bayard. This place is different— no, wait," as Bayard made a movement of protest. "It *is* different. This is a civilized place and a decent place. I expect it always has been and I pray it always will be. You're judged for what you are inside, here, not for what you look like outside. You're judged—"

"I don't think," Bayard interrupted, quietly but in a tone of finality, "that a Negro is judged for what's inside him or her, here or anywhere else in America today. That's how *I* feel about it."

"Then I don't think you feel right," Wilson said.

"How do you know?" asked Bayard simply; and they were silent for a while in the gorgeous morning, because there was no answer to that. But presently Willie told himself: *No answer as far as it goes.* And resumed.

"I still think," he said, "that you're not giving us a fair chance. We're trying to give you a fair chance—"

"Oh, that sounds so patronizing!" Bayard said bitterly.

"All right!" Wilson snapped. "*I'm* trying to give you a fair chance. Am *I* patronizing you? Am *I* spooking you? Was *I* just indulging myself in some— some—*publicity* stunt yesterday when Latt and I came over? Was Latt? Is that how little you think of us? Because if you do, buddy, you aren't worthy of the friendship we freely and genuinely offered to you. And to hell with you!"

And he made as if to stand up. Bayard, as he knew he would, put a hand
on his arm and pulled him back.

"No," he said, voice trembling. "No. sit down. Sit down. I'm terribly,
terribly grateful for what you did yesterday. I'm more grateful than I could
ever"—his voice broke for a second— "than I can ever say to you, for what
you and Latt did for me. You'll always be my friends. Always!"

"Then on behalf of the University," Willie said, and to his great surprise
he found that his voice was threatening to break, too, "may I kindly invite
you to give us all a chance? That's all we ask of you. Will you do that for us?"
He hesitated a split second and then put it on the basis he knew now that he
had successfully established: "Will you do that for *me*?"

For several seconds Bayard stared straight ahead. More students passed.
Some glanced at him shyly and did not speak. Some uttered a tentative "Hi!"
and hurried on, when, lost in his thoughts, he did not respond.

And there were some, whom only Willie saw—and whose reality he
accepted—whose eyes slid over Bayard with an obvious annoyance, disdain
and dislike.

Bayard fortunately did not see them. When Wilson did, and caught their
eyes, he responded in kind; and they had the grace to blush, and look away,
and move swiftly on.

Overall, though, he congratulated himself that the friendly far outnum-
bered the hostile. He knew then that he was right: that there was a solid
foundation to build upon and that, at least in this time and in this place, all
would in due course come right.

He was suddenly no longer afraid of the future. And he bent his energies
and his charm to guaranteeing that his new young friend would no longer be
afraid either.

"Will you give us all a chance—for me?" he repeated gently; and after a
moment Bayard finally came back from wherever he had gone and began to
relax, gave him a sidelong glance and, presently, a tentative but genuine
smile.

"It won't be easy," he said.

Wilson shook his head impatiently.

"Hell!" he said. "Whatever is, that one really wants to achieve? Of course
it won't be easy. Nobody guarantees you that. But we'll just go about it
patiently and steadily and fearlessly—and it will happen. O.K.?"

Again Bayard hesitated for what seemed like a quite a long time before he
said at last, "O.K."

"Good," Wilson said, and quickly made his voice businesslike. "Now: Are
they treating you all right in the dorm?"

But that seemed to touch a chord—maybe *the* chord, Willie suspected, for
Bayard's expression again turned uncertain and unhappy.

"Well," he said, and hesitated. "There's a couple of guys right next door to me that aren't very nice. And my roommates aren't—very nice—either."

"You're sure of this, now?" Willie asked, fixing him with a steady and unwavering look. "I'm not going to go to bat for you over there if this is just nerves. They really *are* hostile, you think? It isn't something you can overcome with a little patience and goodwill?"

Again Bayard spoke with the chilling, simple certainty he had before.

"I *know*. You can't be a Negro and not know."

"All right," Willie said. "Then I'll talk to Aram Katanian and we'll get you moved."

"Who's Aram Katanian?"

"He's head of Interclub Council. He's also one of the nicest human beings *you'll* ever meet. I'll talk to him. The guys in the halls can shift things around in ways they never even dream about in the dean of men's office. Ari will take care of it."

"Thank you," Bayard said. He smiled wistfully. "I seem to be saying a lot of thank-yous to you. What next?"

"That depends on how the fast-breaking saga of Young Bayard Johnson at the Great Big University unfolds," Willie said with a smile. "Pretty soon I expect you'll be doing all right on your own. In fact, I'm sure of it." He stood up and again held out his hand. Bayard gripped it as tightly as he had yesterday in Memorial Hall. Willie returned the pressure and then let it go. "I mentioned coming up to dinner at the house, yesterday; I'm not forgetting it. Meanwhile, keep in touch, will you? I'll reach Ari sometime today or tonight. Let me know what happens. And anything else that you want fatherly advice on." He grinned suddenly. "I regard it as part of my presidential duties."

"You're going to be a good one," Bayard said with genuine admiration. "I can sure tell that already."

"Call me," Willie ordered. "If you don't, I'll call you. You can't escape."

"Who said I want to?" Bayard inquired with, finally, a genuinely relaxed and happy grin.

"Take care," Willie said, and walked away in what, to Bayard, seemed a halo of golden and wonderful light.

And so it goes, Wilson told himself. He decided he would take a ramble to the bookstore, the post office and the Union before coming back to the Quad for his eleven o'clock. Have to see what the constituents were up to. Have to see who else, of his many charges, he could be of assistance to.

And maybe, with a little luck, run into what he was already, almost in spite of himself, thinking of as "his" green-gold girl.

5

The juniors of the house were all in the midst of ten o'clocks, endur-
ing them with varying degrees of attention and interest.

Having successfully survived Dr. Stafford's Tudormania for an hour,
Renny Suratt was sitting now beside Johnny Herbert in Armpit McGee's
Prose Style, which both felt would be a good thing to know something about,
Johnny because it would be helpful in pursuing his ambition to teach and
write American constitutional history, Renny because he felt that a powerful
prose style was good equipment for whatever battles he might have to fight
in his life. He suspected there would be a few. He did not know of what
nature exactly, but since he was not one to suffer fools gladly (he often told
himself with pride), he was certain there would be some. An effective style
would be a good weapon.

"Do you ever wonder," he whispered to Johnny as their earnest, rather
dowdy pedagogue droned on, "what someone like Armpits does for sex? I
mean, do teachers like her *really* have a life? Is it possible?"

"You're awfully hard on her," Johnny whispered back with his usual live-
and-let-live good nature, result of much conquering of much physical pain.
"You just think that she's rather awkward and helpless and maybe slightly
laughable, and that makes her an easy target, so you're going to say unpleasant things. You wouldn't do it if she were the type who would fight back."

"You amateur psychologists about me disgust me!" Suratt said as sharply
as a whisper would permit: Armpits was becoming conscious of their conversation and might get up nerve to utter a reprimand, or take reprisals in
her grading. "You don't understand me at all."

"Can't say as I do," Johnny agreed as the exchange ended. "I'll have to talk
with Gale Bryce. I'm sure he does. Or thinks he does."

Galen Bryce at that moment was, in fact, thinking about Renny Suratt and Johnny Herbert: their paths had crossed in mid-Quad half an hour ago on the way to class. He was not particularly fond of them—Galen Bryce, like Suratt, was not particularly fond of many people and, in similar fashion, considered himself superior to most of them. But he found them interesting, and now, as he sat in the Psychology of Personality class and with a few knowing winks and chuckles at his professor's sallies began laying the groundwork for the straight A he intended to get, he was thinking that each seemed to have been conditioned heavily by his background and experiences.

As who was not? But Galen Bryce, preparing to become a psychiatrist and either teach or go into the private practice that was becoming increasingly popular and lucrative in America, felt lucky. He had his own private laboratory. Each of his fraternity brothers was a study from whose close observation he felt he profited greatly.

He would have been astounded and furiously angry if he had known that he had been dissected himself every bit as sharply and unkindly as he had ever dissected one of them. In Tim Bates' little box there was a special acid in his account of Galen Bryce from Burlingame, California, psychology major:

"Galen Bryce is one of those people destined always to project an air of slight but unmistakable superiority to all with whom he comes in contact. That this superiority is assumed by him and not conferred by others he apparently really does not realize. Buff Richardson, normally the most good-natured of souls, once called him to his face, in a rare moment of annoyance, 'Your Damned Self-Appointed Highness.' Franky Miller refers to him consistently as 'that smug, superior snot.' Gale always attributes these rumblings of disenchantment to simple jealousy. That is what his teachers tell him usually prompts the irritation of others, and it makes it so much easier to handle, and, indeed, a sort of triumph: it can only be because he really *is* superior. He feels he knows more about his brethren than they know themselves, a belief in which he is also fortified by his studies, which tell him that a psychiatrist is privy to everyone's secrets if he will just take a deep breath and gamble on it with sufficient assurance and gall. He has rarely been known to utter an honest guffaw, an uncontrolled burst of resentment, a spontaneous expression of like or dislike. Everything is carefully calculated, carefully expressed.

" 'I'm damned if I know why we ever pledged the damned guy,' Bates once exploded to Wilson. Wilson shrugged. 'His father's an alum. It's just one of those things.' And, in fairness, they have to admit that Gale is highly intelligent, can be amusing and witty when he wants to be, and underneath the pompous pretense is probably a pretty good guy. But many find him a burden to be around, and civility becomes strained. 'If only he didn't act so damned knowing all the time,' Haggerty says. 'I feel as though I'm constantly under a damned microscope.' His teachers assure him he is going to know an awful lot about human nature, and he thinks he already does. Secure in this, he doesn't really give a damn what his housemates think. He doesn't think so much of most of them, either."

And he did not think much of Suratt; but he did find him an interesting specimen. He was sure that Renny was conditioned by his family's considerable wealth and by the inferiority complex this seemed to have given him toward those, like Wilson and Bates, whose backgrounds were more modest but who nonetheless seemed to have personal attributes and abilities that drew a lot of people willingly into their orbits. At the University, money didn't matter much: things were on a different level here. Wealth was something some had and some didn't but it wasn't the overriding criterion of anything. You were judged on a lot of factors above and beyond money. By those standards, Suratt fell behind. He would probably never, Gale Bryce thought with the comfortable self-assurance that was his own insulation against the world, get over it as long as he lived.

Poor Renny, he thought with a complacent pity. How sad to be inherently foredoomed to be forever second best.

Johnny Herbert, he conceded, was a different matter. By any standard except that of money, which his folks had little of, Johnny measured up as a notable human being. He was, in fact, one of the few on campus for whom Gale felt a genuine (but carefully never expressed) admiration. It wouldn't do to let Johnny know he felt this way: as Gale interpreted his teachers, to do so would be to give Johnny some emotional hold, possibly even dominance, over him; and he was not about to *ever* let anybody do that. To utter a genuine and uncalculated compliment to a fellow human being would be in some irretrievable way to bring him, Gale, off his pedestal of superior perception and put him on the same level; and no psychiatrist, his teachers had already convinced him, could ever afford to do that.

It would be entirely too human.

Like everyone in the house, Gale had heard the story of Johnny soon after he became a member. Johnny was often held up, in the house and on campus, as an example of character, strength and fortitude; and Johnny was. It was all so ironic, but there it was. He handled it in a way few of them were sure they could have. No wonder an admiring note had crept into Tim's notes on John Thomas Herbert from Philadelphia, Pennsylvania, history major:

"Johnny Herbert has had a great deal of pain in his life, and it has left him with an odd combination of Christian patience and human protest, so that he often suffers his burden with a smiling courage that tears the heart, but at the same time is apt to switch suddenly to most profound bitterness and despair. This latter, out of consideration for his friends, he does not reveal to any but a select few, but others suspect its presence: they don't see how it would be possible for him not to feel it, in fact.

"On Big Game Night in freshman year he was stripped and tied to a bed, which was then pushed through a window and lowered carefully onto the roof of the floor just below. The original plan had been to bring him in shortly, but everyone goes a little wild on Big Game Night and people get forgetful. Something came up, several of the fellows left, something else distracted the others, and he was forgotten for several hours, during which it clouded over and rained. Out of that night he contracted pneumonia, from which he eventually recovered, only to suffer a relapse which turned into tuberculosis and forced him to drop out and spend a year in Arizona. The experience left him with weak lungs, subject to bronchial infections that carry with them terrific headaches, and a weak heart. Since then he has never been really well and indeed is often in considerable pain. All his activity, his plans and his life have been curtailed by the recurring illnesses which carry with them so many unexpected and unpredictable complications.

"The fortitude of Job would have been necessary to take the bitter blasting of his college career and his life without an inward protest searing in its depth. The irony of it all, he often says, is that it wasn't as though anyone had wanted to do him harm: it was just one of those kid tricks everyone does— only, in this case, it went wrong. He can see little ahead for himself and has often considered suicide; despite his pain, however, life is still too pleasant on the campus to desert it just yet. Indeed, he will probably never do so, for he is possessed of a really excellent mind and an instinctive talent for historical research, plus the ability to write forceful and dramatic English, which seems to show promise of great things ahead for him in his particular field. But life is an unyielding struggle to keep hope and faith alive and not give in to the complete despair which circumstances would make so easy— and perhaps so justified—for him."

When the bell rang at eleven and the center of the Quad erupted into noisy life again, Loren Davis, making his way from Geology of Oil and Coal to the bookstore, overtook the short, slim, dark-haired figure of Tony Andrade. Tony insisted, rightly enough, on the pronunciation "Ahn-*drah*-dee," and if anything was going to disturb his usually sunny disposition, it was to have some unwitting stranger call him "Ann-drade." For this reason, Lor Davis, with his customary well-meaning but slightly off-center humor, called out cheerily, "Hi, there, Ann-drade!" and slapped him heartily on the back.

Tony swung around, his normally friendly expression wiped out in a sudden scowl until he saw who it was. Then he relaxed into a grin.

"Bastard," he said as Lor fell into step. "I might have known it was someone like you. How's it going so far?"

"Tough as a son of a bitch," Lor said, shaking his head in a way that made his loose-cropped straw-colored hair swirl about until he looked like one of the younger Roman emperors, not yet dissipated by life and privilege. "I've got a couple of real ass-pluggers this quarter. I tell you, if I didn't think I was going to make a million in oil someday, I'd drop my geology major and take up something like social sciences the way Buff does. He says he never has to study as long as he picks the right courses. He told me it's tailor-made for dumbbells if you play it right."

"Well," Tony said with a chuckle as they walked along greeting friends, "he ought to know."

"Oh, hell, yes," Lor said. "And I'm not much better. If my family didn't own a couple of oil wells down south at Seal Beach I really would do something else. But as it is I'm stuck. What does your dad do, anyway? I never thought to ask you."

"You're not very curious," Tony agreed with a smile. "We've only been fraternity brothers for two years. He owns a restaurant in Brooklyn."

"Well," Lor said stoutly. "Nothing wrong with that."

"I didn't say there was, did I?" Tony inquired, grinning again at his usually carefree companion's sudden look of discomfiture. "It's all right, Lor," he added with an exaggerated kindness, "I don't care if you think I am a poor peasant from Brooklyn while you're a sleek seal from Seal Beach. I *am* a poor peasant from Brooklyn." He looked suddenly so fierce that Lor didn't know for a second whether he meant it or not. "*Want to make something of it?*"

"No," Lor said hastily. "No! I just—" Then he saw Tony laughing and began to laugh too. "You son of a bitch. Don't scare me like that. Are you going to Reg Dance tonight?"

"Oh, sure. Have to see who's who and what's what. Are you?"

Lor hesitated for a moment, then decided to be truthful.

"I haven't got a date."

"A Greek god like you?" Tony exclaimed with a smile. "Wha' hoppen? I thought you were a junior edition of Guy Gulbransen."

Lor responded with a surprisingly humble smile.

"I'm shy, boy. I don't score all the time."

"Well, *good*," Tony said with an exaggeratedly relieved sigh. "I'm glad I'm not the only one. Come with me and the girls. We can always use one more in our group."

"Do you think they'd mind?" Lor asked hesitantly. Tony laughed.

"Oh, hell no. It isn't as though anybody's *engaged*, you know. We're just friends. In fact"—he paused and looked far across the inner Quad—"if I'm not mistaken, I see them now. Talking to Donna Van Dyke, I think. Let's see if they have eleven o'clocks, and if they don't, let's take them to the Union for coffee. Quick!" he ordered. "Donna's leaving and they're moving on." He tore off through the crowd with Lor close behind, shouting, "*Angie! Lou!*"

Just under the arches on the opposite side, two striking brunettes stopped, turned around, broke into smiles and waved and gestured to them to slow down, they'd wait. Puffing, the boys caught up.

"Hi," Tony said, out of breath. "You know Lor Davis—Angie D'Alessandro—Louise Gianfalco."

"Sure," the cousins said together, and Lor nodded and smiled, too out of breath himself to reply for a moment.

"Wow!" Angie said, "Are we ever flattered!"

"First time I ever had anybody run after *me* all the way across the Quad in front of God and everybody," Louise said. "I wonder what we've done?"

"Aside from being our usual beautiful and irresistible selves," Angie suggested.

"That's quite enough," Lor said, having finally recovered breath and relative composure.

"You do say the *nicest* things," Angie told him with the sudden sunny smile that lighted up her darkly pretty, clever face.

"He looks nice, too," her cousin said, her own smile slower, more reflective, somehow more reserved, though as always perfectly friendly. "I remember you from the poli sci course last year, Loren. You were the brightest guy in the class."

"That's cr—that's hooey and you know it," Lor said with a grin. "But lay it on. I love it."

"How are you doing, honorary cousin?" Angie asked.

Tony smiled, "O.K. Civil engineering is no breeze, but I think I'll be able to manage."

"Why don't you get your degree in mining engineering?" Lor suggested. "Then we could combine forces, prospect for oil, strike it big and live happily ever after."

"I've thought about it," Tony said lightly. "I might yet. Keep a place open for me in your company."

"It's not much of a company," Lor said. "Just a couple of wells."

"But surely you won't stop there," Louise Gianfalco suggested. Lor looked at her thoughtfully.

"No," he said. "Probably not." He grinned. "If I can survive my geology courses."

"This handsome gentleman," Tony said, "and let's face it, he *is*. God, *yes*. This handsome gentleman—"

"All right," Lor said. "Knock it off."

"—is really a miserable little wallflower who doesn't have a date for tonight, poor thing."

"Hey!" Lor protested, not entirely amused, as the girls laughed again. "I didn't mean knock it off like *that*."

"Anyway, he wants to know—"

"I do *not*!" Lor said indignantly. "It was your idea."

"Anyway," Angie said soothingly, "it's a good one. Of course you can join us. We'd love it. Right, Lou?"

"Of course," her cousin agreed. "I think Johnny Herbert will be with us, too."

"Oh," Lor said quickly. "I didn't know. In that case—"

"Think nothing of it," Tony said. "Come with us anyway. What the hell, Johnny won't mind, either."

"Well—" Lor said.

"Good," Louise said calmly, "then it's settled. Were you guys going to the Cellar for coffee?"

"Certainly," Tony said. "Come with us."

"My treat," Lor said firmly. He looked at Tony and shook his head with a rather shamefaced smile. "You're something else. You really are."

"It's nothing," Tony said with an answering smile. "You just have to like people. Life works out."

"I guess so," Lor said as they walked up toward the Union in the bright crisp morning. The bell rang and the quiet of classes in session settled again upon the Quad.

So far, for him anyway, thought Antonio Ahn-*drah*-dee, peasant from Brooklyn, life *had* worked out; not always easily—sometimes, he thought bleakly, as tough as a son of a bitch—but *had*, that was what counted. He had his battles with himself, but up to now he always seemed to win them and hardly anybody even suspected they were there. His perennial quick smile, his always outgoing manner, his air of liking the world and being at ease in it seemed to fool everybody—or almost everybody. He wasn't always sure about Louise; but he was finding that propinquity, custom and habit seemed to be pushing him closer and closer toward some sort of relationship with Angie. Louise was a friend, but he was always just a little wary with her: she was one sharp girl, as everyone recognized. Angie was a little softer, a little gentler, a little more willing to accept things: less judgmental and therefore easier to contemplate as a wife.

Bates had them all pegged pretty well, though he, too, concentrated on what Franky Miller called "the happy threesome" aspects and perhaps missed some deeper channels that ran beneath sunny waters. Like everyone, however, he thought very highly of them all. A generally admiring tone ran though his notes on:

"Tony, small, dark, quick, and usually laughing, possessed of abundant energy and a friendliness which he bestows generously upon a flattered world. Everyone likes Tony and he likes everyone with a resilient good humor and a certain innate, bred-in-the-bone tolerance, verging close upon cynicism at times, which permits him to take the occasional human foibles he runs into in his friends. Something of a very old, very disillusioned and very sophisticated people has been passed along to this descendant in a foreign land; and now and again behind his outward and apparently unchanging demeanor, the wry knowledge that people, no matter how you play them, are going to act like people gives him a secret and sardonic amusement and buoys him up when some friend or idol turns out to be not quite so fine as he had supposed.

"He accepts it with a shrug: that's how people are, and so what? He doesn't turn a hair, and why should he? It isn't his worry. It is this quality of having no desire whatsoever to judge others, plus his unfailing grin and the sincere and generally joking greeting which he has for everyone, that makes him so popular and so well-liked in the house and on the campus. No one ever feels ill at ease with Tony Andrade."

And since Tony had told him quite a bit about the cousins, he had also been able to put together a reasonably accurate picture of:

Angelina D'Alessandro from San Francisco, California, economics major, and her cousin, Louise Gianfalco from St. Helena, California, majoring in business administration.

"Angie D'Alessandro comes from an enterprising San Francisco North Beach family three of whose brothers, her father and two uncles, operate a small 'fishing fleet' of three boats. But it's growing, and their wives have already opened a small seafood restaurant on Fisherman's Wharf and they have plans in due time to increase both the fleet and the number of restaurants. Farther north in Napa Valley Mario Gianfalco, the fourth brother, owns a hundred acres of vineyards and he, too, has plans. The families are doing very well and, with native determination, thrift, enterprise and imagination, intend to do much better. Angie and her cousin Lou Gianfalco are two of the prettiest, brightest, most likeable and most popular girls on campus; and it is not surprising that Tony Andrade in particular should have gravitated to them the very first day all reached the campus as freshmen.

"Since then he has dated them both, sometimes one, sometimes the other, sometimes taking the two of them out together for a picnic or a movie. They call him their 'honorary cousin' and kid around together a lot. Quite often he and Johnny Herbert double-date with them; and little by little it is beginning to be accepted that Angie is Tony's girl, Louise Johnny's. They are settling into an implicit family foursome, with which the parents seem to be quite pleased; except that Mario worries quite a bit about Johnny's fragile health and sometimes asks Louise if she knows what she's doing. He doesn't dare ask this too often, because behind the dark and smiling beauty there lies a good deal of his own quick temper and he is secretly quite afraid of this lovely creature he helped to create, particularly since her mother died when she was very young, and there were no other children. Mario never remarried and she is all he has.

"If Johnny is what Louise wants in order to be happy, that's what she shall have. He is already thinking in terms of bringing Johnny into the vineyard operations. He has not consulted Johnny about this, but reflects comfortably that if Louise wants it, Johnny will agree.

"Angie, a little less intense and determined than her cousin, thinks quite often about marriage with Tony but isn't ready yet to become serious about it; nor is he. They have never had a quarrel, never had any friction of any kind. Sometimes Angie wonders, a little troubled by it, whether they are going to; but then Tony makes some joke or proposes some fun thing, and she forgets all about it in the sheer pleasure of his laughing, exuberant company. It is only later that she sometimes pauses to reflect, somewhat uneasily, that he might just possibly be using this as a shield to hold her off. But then she thinks that, no, she's Tony's girl and they probably are going to get married someday, and then whatever the subtle barrier may be, it will go away."

Lor Davis, Tony reflected as the four of them sat laughing and talking in the sparsely populated between-classes Cellar and slowly drank their coffee, was everybody's good guy—not very brainy, but easygoing and likeable. And, of course, there were those good looks, by which everybody—and, he reflected wryly, he did mean everybody—was mesmerized. Tony wasn't jealous, he was just content to look and enjoy: particularly when he reflected on the mental capacity. He would have been amused, could he have read Tim's notes, by the tone of actual envy that seemed to have crept into them concerning Loren Davis from Glendale, California, geology major:

"The Loren Davises of this world are a somewhat select group but most fraternity houses have at least one of them. Their chief attribute is physical: they are stunningly handsome, with curly hair, close-set ears and clear large eyes set beneath level brows, above a full, slightly sensuous mouth and a classic chin. Aside from that, they are rather vacuous characters, knockouts with the girls, good friends with most of the men, but rarely the sort who achieve much or are considered very important. It is hard to avoid being impressed with them, for they are undeniably striking; but when one goes further and inquires into the qualities of mind which go with this natural bounty, an average mentality is revealed, hitting close to the norm and occasionally even slipping over into the not-so-sharp. Yet such is the ubiquitous impact of their physical presence that they achieve a considerable fame for it—the sort of fame which is understood very well by the young and given by them a place of undeniable importance in the world.

"Lor Davis is the dream-god of a thousand palpitating females, many of whom have been out with him and assess him with a sure knowledge for the amiable lightweight he is. Most of them nonetheless continue to be moved by his physique and are almost always willing to accept him for a date.

"Franky Miller once referred to his progress down the Row as 'Lady Godiva in pants.' He is impossible to dislike sincerely, however, and his friendship is flattering and freely distributed. A good man—a good average man, save for his classic face and figure. He would probably be quite impossible to live with if his mind measured up to them. Or if he gave it a second thought."

Over in the economics department in the eleven o'clock Capital and Interest class, the small, compact, self-assured figure of Smith Carriger, tidy of person, mind, approach and achievement, was beginning the process of sopping up facts and figures like a human sponge which had won him the admiration and highly favorable grades of all his teachers since the day he had hit the campus in the fall of 1936. Of all the juniors in the house, he was probably the most consistently good student. Add to that his record in extracurricular activities, which was not exceeded by even Bob Godwin, and you had a pretty effective campus leader, even if he did say so himself, which he sometimes did with a complacency that would have offended more than it did had it not been supported by the facts. Nobody could really get too annoyed with him, because, like Godwin, he really did do a lot of good, heading committees, chairing charity drives, working on special projects devoted to the general betterment of student life and the greater glory of the University, giving freely of time and energy because, as he put it simply, "the Carrigers always do."

"A very fine young man," Dr. Chalmers, not given to effusion, had called him publicly at the conclusion of last year's highly successful Convalescent Home drive, which he had co-chaired as a sophomore class representative.

Smitty agreed.

Now he was making notes with about half his mind, which he felt was quite sufficient for the uninspired soul who was trying to make an important subject come to life for students already distracted by the increasing pangs of noontime hunger. With the other half he was busily planning what he would do this quarter in what he referred to as "the public area." He knew he would be expected to do a lot and he intended to. Looking back years later he would wonder how he and the other active ones on campus ever found time to study, there were so many extracurricular things going on all the time.

That, he supposed, was youth, and he had come to the University determined to make the most of it, as he had been determined from a very early age to make the most of everything. That had been his inborn instinct and it had been the conditioning of his family, whose members in Pennsylvania had a great deal of money derived from oil and coal, and felt, with a certain never clearly expressed but nonetheless implicit guilt, that they owed public service to society in return for the riches they had been lucky and enterprising enough to take out of the ground. So he had hummed along through life from his earliest years, small, brisk, organized, competent, contributive;

not always fully understood, but satisfied in his own mind that what he did was for the general good of everybody.

Misinterpretations were something he shrugged off; his father had told him a long time ago that these were the occasional price one paid for wealth and prominence.

Smith Carriger from Gwynned Valley, Pennsylvania, business administration major, "carries (as Bates puts it) an indefinable glitter that goes with his rather unlikely name. Small, wealthy, efficient, brisk, a sort of slick finish lies over him and everything he does. More than anyone else, even Bob Godwin, he is the activity boy of the house. Dates heavily with the best girls, whom he buys the best orchids and takes to the best places, where he is seen by all the best people. He is on everything and in everything in campus affairs—'Ask Smitty Carriger'—'Have you seen Smitty Carriger about that?'—'Smitty Carriger is chairman and you'd better check with him'— these are among the stock phrases of the campus, a tribute to his organizational genius.

"A roaring success as a Big Man on Campus, he has gathered power, influence and authority with a bland air that refuses to be intimidated by the sometimes half-admiring, half-impatient jibes of his friends. Only great wealth and years of knowing that the Carrigers are unsurpassed could have given him the indefinable glitter, coming close to glamour at times, with which he moves about the campus and the well-ordered business of living the life of Smith Carriger."

When class was over and the noon bell rang, Smitty decided he would go to the Cellar and get a hamburger and a milkshake and take them over to the library and sit under the trees. It was one of his favorite spots in good weather, because sooner or later everybody passed by: he could transact a lot of business just by being there. Ahead of him in the crowd streaming out of the Quad he saw Alan Offenberg and Shahna Epstein, her arm linked in his—their customary lovey-dovey pose, but oh well. They didn't have to make such a big deal of it; everybody knew they'd been inseparable ever since they met as freshmen in the Western Civilization class, but if they had to they *had* to, he supposed.

"Duke!" he shouted. "Shahna! Lovebirds! Hey!"

Alan Offenberg—"Duke" to everyone—swung his six-foot-three frame around and smiled. Shahna, about Smitty's height, laughed as he hurried toward them.

"Don't rush," she called. "You'll lose weight."

"I could stand it," he said as he caught up.

Duke smiled.

"Hi, pal, what's up? Going to lunch?"

"In a little bit," he said. "I have to see some people. I'm glad I saw you, because I was wondering if you'd like to be on Executive Committee this year. I know Willie'd like you to be."

"He hasn't mentioned it to *me*," Duke said, a little huffily. "When did he get the idea? I saw him at breakfast and he didn't mention it then."

"I think he just decided on it," Smitty said, thinking: Lord, Duke's touchier than usual. He can often be a pain in the ass but he usually doesn't start this early in the year. "I ran into him in the bookstore around ten-thirty and he said he'd been planning a few things."

"Well," Duke said, still sounding a little miffed, "I suppose I can do it if he really wants me to. But I hope he'll ask me himself. After all, we are in the same house."

"I'm sure he will," Shahna said soothingly—it seemed to Smitty that she was always interceding for Duke, who was a generally nice guy but certainly had a thin skin. "He probably didn't even ask Smitty to mention it."

"Well, no," Smitty admitted. "But it's something I've got to help him get organized, so I thought I'd just go right ahead with it."

"I don't know how this campus would run without you, Mr. Carriger," Duke said, sounding more amiable but still with a little sting. "You aren't about to drop in on Dr. Chalmers and give him a few pointers, are you?"

For a second Smitty debated whether it would be worth it to flare up, but then, as usual, decided against it. He didn't need that kind of stuff: it only interfered with the things he wanted to do.

"I may," he said cheerfully. "He could probably use it. Good, then, Duke, thanks so much. There'll be a lot to do this year."

"I've got enough with my education major as it is," Duke said. "But I guess I can give some time to it."

"Of course you can," Shahna said. "You're going to practically coast home in those courses this year, anyway. He's going to make Phi Bete," she added proudly. "Dean Dobbs just told him this morning."

"I think I may, too," Smitty said, more casually than he felt: actually he was damned pleased. "Things look pretty good. You still planning to be president of the University, Duke?"

At this reference to an ambition long held and once inadvertently admitted in the midst of a late-night bullsession in the house, Duke Offenberg started to scowl, then thought better of it and grinned.

"Move on, Chalmers," he said. "Here I come."

"I expect to be chairman of the board of trustees," Smith Carriger said, not entirely kidding either. "So watch out!"

"That wouldn't be so bad," Duke said. "We might make a pretty good team."

"If there isn't a damned war to throw us all off schedule first," Smitty said more soberly. Instantly, it seemed to him, both his companions were staring at him with sudden sharp attention. Duke's normally open expression had clouded over. Shahna's smiling, shrewd little face was abruptly shadowed.

"Do you think there will be?" she asked anxiously. He shrugged and tried to get things back on a lighter plane.

"Look, I don't know. It doesn't look very good over there today. But maybe it'll work out."

"Rudy Krohl says: 'When Hitler has what he wants,' " Duke said; and added thoughtfully, "I don't like that bastard."

"Which one?" Smitty asked, half-smiling. Duke was entirely serious when he responded: "Both."

"Rudy's a jerk," Smitty said, dismissing perhaps the most difficult of the house's sophomores with the dislike he, too, had come to feel for him in their few contacts last spring. Now that Rudy and the rest of his pledge class had moved in, he wondered with some misgivings how they were all going to get along. "As for Hitler—well, he's no jerk but he's a menace, all right."

"He's a monster," Shahna said with feeling.

"And a smart one," Duke observed. "He scares the hell out of me." He gave Smith a sudden nakedly candid look. "Out of us."

"Yes," Shahna said softly. "Out of us."

"Oh, I don't know," Smitty said, feeling suddenly very uncomfortable at this unexpected and—he felt almost resentfully—uninvited and uncalled-for confidence. "You're way over here and he's over there. He can't hurt you."

"He's hurting a lot of people," Duke said. "He's always attacking the Jews in his speeches. And persecuting them, too."

"I still have distant cousins in Munich," Shahna said. "not close, but they *are* relatives. We haven't heard from them for two years."

"He's just making a noise," Smitty said uncomfortably. "He just wants a scapegoat."

"Why the Jews?" Duke inquired with a frown.

"Because they're—" Smith said, and stopped.

"Because they're what?" Shahna asked instantly.

"Nothing," he said lamely. Why the hell did they always push you into these corners and force you to defend yourself over even the most passing of thoughts? "Just because they're *there*, I guess. They're an obvious target, I guess."

"Why?" Duke asked again, completely concentrated now, ignoring the curious students who walked past them as they stood in the alcove in the corner of the Quad to which they had instinctively withdrawn as their discussion became more intense.

"I don't *know*," Smith said desperately. "They wouldn't be to me, but I guess they are to Hitler."

"I don't see it," Duke said flatly. "To think that if Shahna and I went over there we'd be scorned just because—just because we are what we are. That seems terrible to me."

"It *is* terrible," Smitty said. "I'm not defending it, Duke. For God's sake, don't put me in *that* league."

"We're not," Shahna said, touching his arm placatingly. "It's just that when people like you—fine people—seem to condone it—"

"I'm not con—"

"No, of course you're not," she said hastily. "But—accept it, maybe that's the better word—"

"And I don't do that, either," he said, beginning to feel, finally, protest and the start of anger. "Look: don't get yourselves in the state of mind where you judge everybody by Hitler. This isn't Germany."

"He gets a lot of sympathy on that over here, though," Duke observed unhappily. "A lot of people agree with him, whether they admit it or not."

"Rudy Krohl," Smith said scornfully.

"Not just Rudy Krohl," Duke said. "A *lot* of people."

"Not here at the University," Smith Carriger said. "Surely not here!"

"How would you know?" Shahna asked softly; and Smitty for once was at a loss for the efficient word, the constructive thought that would move things along.

"Well," he said lamely. "I just don't think so, that's all."

"I'm glad you live in a gentile paradise," Duke told him bitterly. "There are a lot of little things you don't have to see. But they all add up," he said bleakly. "They all add up."

"Well," Smitty said, again lamely, "maybe they'll be able to stop him in Czechoslovakia this time."

"And maybe they won't," Duke said.

"And that will mean war," Shahna said. "What then?"

"Then he'll have to be beaten," Smitty said simply. "What else?"

"By whom?" Duke inquired. "Us? You and me?"

"Maybe," Smith said. "Maybe it'll come to that."

Duke stared at him for a long moment.

"Maybe it will," he said finally.

"Well, why not?" Smitty demanded. "You don't want him over here, do you? We've just been discussing that, haven't we?"

"He's here already," Shahna said softly. "That's what's so frightening."

"Well," Smith said, suddenly brisk. "We aren't going to settle it right here, anyway, that's for sure. We'll count on you for Excom then, Duke. See you at the house. Take care, Shahna. Try not to worry too much."

"I'll try," she said, and for a second looked a thousand years old with the immemorial tiredness of her heritage. "Take care, Smitty."

They watched his small, trim figure move briskly off up the street toward the Union, laughing, smiling, waving, pausing now and then to shake hands and exchange a quick word, calling out to others as he passed. Smith Carriger was back in business.

But the bright day was shadowed and darkened over for them. In that moment of their deep instinctive worry, Tim Bates, could he have realized

how profoundly it affected them, might have revised his comments on Alan
Frederick Offenberg from Cleveland, Ohio, education major, to end on an
even more foreboding note than they did already:

"Tall, dark, possessed of arrogant, aristocratic good looks, the impression
he gives is of completely self-assured, completely self-centered self-control.
This may or may not be entirely true: but it is the impression. Consequently,
while the campus as a whole has great respect for a mind that consistently
pulls down straight A's in most things, it does not regard him with overwhelming affection. He can, from long practice and experience, enter into
the easygoing chaff of the house with the best of them, but there is always
the possibility that he will grow bored and go away upon some pursuit of his
own which he considers more worthwhile.

"The nickname 'Duke,' given him by Musavich long ago in a moment of
rare sarcastic annoyance, expresses what most of his contemporaries feel
towards him. He is capable of great charm but he doesn't waste his goodwill,
as Unruh puts it."

That Bates saw through some of this bravado in this present moment,
however, was apparent in his notes on Rachel Shahna Epstein, from Hollywood, California, majoring in history:

"Duke has dated Shahna steadily since they met as freshmen in a Western
Civilization class. Her sense of humor never fails him or, more importantly,
herself. She is able, when necessary, to inject just the right note of humorous deflation to bring Duke back to steady ground. Daughter of one of
Hollywood's most noted and longest-running producers, she never had to
worry about a thing until injected into an environment where she was faced
with a certain reserve and the knowledge, for the first time in her life, that
there were people in the world who were going to place a barrier between
her and themselves for no other reason than race. This was her first great
hurt in life, and it took a while for even her indomitable spirit and sense of
humor to come to her rescue. Duke underwent the same thing, and it was
not until Wilson, Unruh, Lattimer, and Hack Haggerty joined forces to
shame the house into accepting him as a member that his initial feeling of
being crushed—which possibly accounted for the overcompensation later—
began to dissipate a little.

"Shahna was not so lucky. A couple of sororities approached her tentatively but did not follow through; her sponsors did not possess the strength
of character or the vocabularies of Duke's. They were unable to successfully
overcome prejudice, even though there are few girls on campus with more
personality and more attractiveness—or more money, which is usually the
final operative item with sororities. So she resides in the main women's
dorm and has found campus activities—the *Daily*, the student council, the
Convalescent Home drive, theater, etc.—more than adequate compensation
for not being on the Row. It is only in recent months that events in Europe

have begun to shake Shahna's humor and confidence. Duke is being forced out of his usual confident self-absorption by Rudy Krohl's jibes and the state of mind in some segments of America which he represents. They *think* things will be all right in their own country, but as the war nears, it seems to them that even here the future may be shadowed by dark and terrible things: the instincts of five thousand years of history bid them beware."

Now as they watched Smitty moving up the street, working the crowd in his efficient, effective way, their frightening sense of isolation deepened.

Outwardly there was no reason why it should. They were a handsome couple, popular, accepted, not overtly threatened by anything or anyone on campus. But—it just did.

"He doesn't really want to think about it," Duke remarked. "He's a nice guy and he means well. But he doesn't want to think."

"Few of them do," Shahna said.

They looked at each other for a long moment.

Then he put his arm around her shoulders and gave her a tight, protective hug as they too went along to the Union.

In the dirty, dusty, tumbledown old *Daily* Shack west of the Quad, filled with the detritus—and the ambitious imaginings and romantic dreams of glory—of the hundreds of would-be journalists who had passed through its splintered portals and trod its sagging floor over the campus generations, Tim was consuming a hamburger and Coke at the editor's desk.

He was not haunted by five thousand years of automatic inherited apprehension.

But he was under the prod of a lively, well-informed and perceptive mind which had told him some months ago that he and his generation were probably living in a fool's paradise if they thought they were going to escape the consequences of Adolf Hitler.

His European summer with Buff Richardson had moved this beyond hunch into settled conviction. Well before the question would throw his country into bitterly divisive debate, Tim had taken sides. What he and Buff had seen on their hike through Germany a month ago had left him with vivid memories and a chilling certainty that no amount of hopeful rationalizing could shake. A lot of things had contributed to the process, starting with the rosy-cheeked uniformed little kids in their schoolyard formations shouting, "Heil Hitler!" in their shrill, piping voices—going on through the goose-stepping squadrons of uniformed soldiers, very little older, clanking ominously through the cities—culminating in the massive rally he and Buff had seen in Munich, with its seemingly endless ranks of military, its hundreds of thousands of hysterical civilians chanting in one great animal roar, "*Sieg heil! Sieg heil! Sieg heil!*"

Buff, who operated on a much-easier-going, more casual, pleasure-centered view of life, had told him he was taking it all too seriously.

"Relax, Timmy. It isn't the way we'd do things," he said comfortably, "but it seems to suit the Germans. Anyway, it's Europe's problem. How can it possibly affect us?"

"The President thinks it may," Tim said, meaning, as one did in those days when one said the word in a certain tone, the President who really *was* the President—of the United States; the glittering, glamorous figure with the confident grin and the hypnotic voice, about whom students had furious arguments with their parents and each other.

That President.

"I don't agree with him," Buff said simply. "Why should we get involved? As long as Hitler stays in his own backyard—"

"He won't," Tim said flatly. "He's getting ready to move."

And now he was beginning to, and the wire service copy that came over Tim's desk was carrying almost hourly bulletins as the tension mounted in Europe and the days moved toward Saturday and the expiration of the ultimatum Hitler had given President Beneš of Czechoslovakia demanding return of the Sudetenland to Germany.

Bates sighed as he read the bulletins. Without realizing it, he must have done so quite loudly. A familiar face appeared around the edge of the door and grinned at him.

"Boy!" its owner said. "Are we ever into heavy stuff today! Tim Bates is carrying the world on his shoulders again, everybody! Watch out!"

"Hi, Bill," he said relaxing into a somewhat sheepish smile. "Go to hell, O.K.?"

"I don't think so," Bill Nagatani said with a chuckle. "I think I'll bring in my Coke and hamburger and eat with you while we discuss the makeup of tomorrow morning's paper. How about that?"

"Since you're associate editor," Tim said, "I guess I can't stop you." He shoved papers around, exposing an inch or two of desktop. "Here, put your stuff there."

"That's generous of you," Bill said, amused. Bill Nagatani, Tim thought, seemed always to be amused, about everything—except on the few occasions when he was not. Tim had seen some of them and had found them, for reasons that again had to do with his instincts about things, quite disturbing.

Like most of the campus, Tim found Bill Nagatani—Yosuhiro in fact, the "Bill" being his own choice, adopted by everyone—to be somewhat of an enigma. He was Nisei, second-generation Japanese, short, stocky, black-haired, almond-eyed, impassive of expression except when he was smiling or laughing, which seemed to be almost always—an automatic defense and protection, Tim believed. Son of immigrant farming parents in the San Joaquin Valley, straight-A student, smart, shrewd, pleasant, friendly, sociable, very well liked, very popular—and, Tim had concluded after a friendship and association on the *Daily* going back three years, enigmatic and probably destined to remain so.

"Now," Bill said, after he had put his hamburger, fries and Coke in the designated space, enlarging it somewhat by knocking a few sheets of crumpled copypaper off on the rutted, almost never swept floor. "What's the problem?"

"Germany," Tim said. "Germany's the problem."

"Ah," Bill said slowly. "Yes."

"Don't play the Inscrutable East with me," Bates told him, but amicably. "Say something!"

"I *am* the Inscrutable East," Bill said with another chuckle. "East Fresno. What am I supposed to say?"

"What do your folks think about it?" Tim asked, thinking he probably wouldn't get an answer. He didn't.

"Oh," Bill said lightly, pausing to take a gulp of Coke before replying, "I suppose they read the papers, like everybody."

"Yeah, I know," Tim said, deciding for once to press it further just for the hell of it, "but they must get some papers from home. What do they think about the things they read there?"

Bill shrugged.

"We don't talk about it much. They're pretty old-fashioned. They don't interest themselves much in what's going on. And I can't read the papers myself, at least not very well. I'm an Amurrican, boy!" And he smiled amicably at Tim.

"But the Japs—Japanese," Tim corrected himself hastily, but not before the slightest little glint had come into Bill's eyes, "are in so deep in China— and with the Axis pact with Germany, and all—and with what Hitler's apparently trying to do to Czechoslovakia right now—I mean, they must have *some* ideas about it, don't they? Don't you ever discuss it at home?"

"I came up to campus a week ago," Bill said, "because I wanted to get an early start on my reading for business administration. I've got some son-of-a-bitching courses this quarter. My parents didn't seem very agitated when I left. I haven't talked to them since things began to heat up over there, so I really don't know, Tim. Want me to call them and ask them? I'd be glad to if you think it would help."

"Oh, no," Tim said. "No need to do anything special, I just thought maybe they'd said something. Or you had some feelings about it yourself. It would just help clarify my own thinking to get some ideas from the other side, that's all."

"Other side of what?" Bill Nagatani asked, pausing in his consumption to give him an innocently interested stare. Bates was annoyed with himself for putting it that way but he was damned if he was going to apologize.

"I thought there might be," he said calmly, "particularly on the part of your folks, a Japanese point of view on these things—at least one a little different from what we're getting from Roosevelt and the Administration."

"Nope," Bill Nagatani said flatly. "Not so far as I know. They're Amurrican too, you know," he added, giving it the same exaggerated pronunciation and smiling amiably the while. "Thirty years as of July. So—there we are."

"That's right," Tim said, and decided to respond with a smile equally broad. "There we are. So what do you think about it yourself? I mean *really* think?"

"I'm supporting you on it, aren't I?" Bill inquired rather blankly. "I seem to recall the staff was up in arms over the first issue and our headlines and editorial, but little old Bill N. was right there backing you up, wasn't I? I thought I was."

"You were," Tim agreed, "and I appreciate it."

"And I will be, right along." Bill said. He grinned with a sudden candor. "After all, you know, I want to be editor next volume. I'm not going to make you mad at me."

"Oh, if that's all it is," Tim said, deciding to sound offended and see what happened, "then I'm not sure I want that kind of support. If you have objections to the way I'm handling it, Bill, speak up. That's the honest thing to do."

"I am honest," Bill Nagatani said mildly. "I think Hitler's a bastard. I think he's going to drag us all into this before he's through."

"He's certainly going to drag Japan in if he can, that's for sure. What do you think about the way *they're* behaving?"

"I suppose," Bill Nagatani said, "that I think what most people think. They're bloody invaders of China, they're brutal, they're ruthless, they're— well, they're bastards too, aren't they?"

Tim gave him an interested look.

"Is that what you think?"

Bill put aside his hamburger and leaned forward earnestly, eyes wide and candid.

"Look," he said reasonably, "slow down, Tim. Don't forget I'm an American, too. I'd be the first one to squawk if I thought those bastards in Tokyo were trying to put anything over on us."

"They sank the gunboat *Panay* in the Yangtze River last year," Tim said. "They must have something in mind. That was a test, I think."

"Well, I—don't—know," Bill said flatly. "How the hell could I?"

Tim shrugged.

"I don't know. I just thought maybe—"

"Yes," Nagatani said with a sudden bitter edge in his voice, kicking the door shut even though the Shack was deserted at that hour. "I know what you thought: He's a Jap, he must know what they think. He must be in on all their shitty plans, he must be leading a secret subversive underground of slant-eyed little yellow bastards, right?"

"I didn't think that at all," Tim said angrily. "I'm not that kind and you know it."

"I don't know what kind anybody is when he gets hysterical," Bill said with equal anger. "I know there are a lot of suspicions on this campus—"

"There are *not*," Tim retorted, anger increasing. "How many Japanese— Japanese and Japanese-*Americans*," he amended as Bill made a movement of protest, "are there here, anyway? You must know. A hundred? A hundred and fifty? Two hundred?"

"I haven't checked this year's registration yet," Bill said. "Probably close to a hundred and fifty."

"Yes, and you have your Japanese Students' Association and you have your clubhouse and you have your meetings and nobody interferes with you at all. And everybody likes you and *you're* associate editor of the *Daily*. So what the hell right do you have to say—"

"You almost took me into your house sophomore year, didn't you?" Bill interrupted, so abruptly that Tim started and for a second looked openly dismayed.

"Who told you that?"

Bill shrugged.

"I don't remember, it was such a long time ago. I wouldn't tell you anyway. The point is, you almost did—and then you didn't." He looked squarely at Bates. "Why not?"

Thinking back over that furious wrangle two years ago, Tim said, "If it were only that simple, Bill."

For just a moment something both pained and disturbing came into Nagatani's eyes as his voice turned flat and unamused: "It was that simple for me."

And that, Tim thought, pretty well wraps up *that*.

They were silent for a moment. Then, not meeting one another's eyes, they resumed eating.

Outside in the main room of the Shack, where the sagging desks and the antique Underwoods were, they heard the noisy voices of the first staffers drifting in to start work on tomorrow's stories.

Presently Bates spoke in a matter-of-fact voice.

"We've got to keep right on giving the Hitler story a big play until something's decided one way or the other. How about this layout?"

And he handed over his clipboard with the piece of copypaper on which he had been sketching out tomorrow's front page.

Bill studied it carefully for a moment and then handed it back.

"Looks good to me," he said, in an equally businesslike voice. "I think your formula of local stuff on the right, Hitler et al on the left, is the logical and most effective one. I think we ought to follow that right on through. Any indication yet on the wire as to what's going to happen?"

"There are hints of some sort of meeting but nothing definite so far. Want to do the editorial on it today?"

"Sure," Bill said, sounding pleased. "Thank you. Do you want The-world-today-teetered-on-the-brink-of? Or do you like In-this-crisis-America-for-the-sake-of-her-own-honor-cannot-hold-aloof-from? Or would you rather have America-must-exercise-the-utmost-caution-and-statesmanship-in-the-face-of? I'm your all-purpose editorial writer. Punch the button and out it comes."

"Aren't we all," Tim said with a smile as they began to relax back into their usual amicable groove. "How about a mix of all three?"

"With emphasis on America-cannot-refrain-from," Bill suggested with a smile. Tim smiled back.

"That's how I feel. Which is no secret." He sighed, suddenly grim. "But maybe we'd better play it a little more gently at the moment. After all, war would be a terrible thing."

"Yes," Bill said soberly. "It sure as hell would."

He stood up, tossed his luncheon leavings into the nearest of three waste-baskets Bates kept around his desk to catch the failed expressions of his busy thoughts. He started to open the door; paused.

"I was wondering," he said slowly. "You don't think we should say anything about what Willie did with the colored kid yesterday?"

"Oh, I think so," Tim said. "In fact, I'm thinking about doing my column on it. Or maybe have Randy Carrero do it, if he wants to."

"Good," Bill said emphatically. "I think we should. Willie deserves a lot of credit."

"Just for being human?" Bates inquired, a trifle dryly. Bill's response was perfectly amicable, but clear.

"Not everybody," he said, "can make that claim." And then, quickly, "Are you going to the Reg Dance tonight?"

"Yeah," Tim said, deciding to let it go. "Haven't got a date yet, but maybe something will turn up. Anyway, I'll be there."

"Good," Bill said.

He opened the door and the rising bustle of the Shack flooded in. In another four hours or so, they'd have a paper.

Somewhere in midafternoon, the Quad almost deserted, the campus lying somnolent in the lazy sun, a figure his fraternity brothers would have recognized had they seen him—but he was pretty sure they were all in afternoon classes, in the library studying, or otherwise occupied elsewhere—walked casually along under the arches until he came to a certain corner. He turned casually in, walked casually along the empty corridor to the men's room; disappeared casually into it, after a few minutes came casually out; re-emerged into the Quad and walked casually off toward the Libe; never looking back, but knowing that behind him someone else was casually, in the opposite direction, doing the same.

"So Ah said to him, Ah said, Sir, *you*-all know what y'all's talkin' about! He di'n lahk it"—a delighted, and delightful, burst of laughter—"but he took it lahk the li'l ole gemmun he *ee*-uz!"

So spoke Jefferson Davis Barnett, standing in the second-floor shower stark naked, his swimmer's body glistening with soap and water, his tousled hair wet and dripping, his laughing mischievous eyes twinkling with amusement and the sheer joy of being alive at age nineteen. Next to him Guy Unruh, basketball star and no mean physical specimen himself, listened with an amused smile as he vigorously soaped himself and rinsed off. Next to Guy, Franky Miller, "roly-poly, fat and holy," as his grammar-school mates used to jeer to his great annoyance, struck a pose under the gushing water and exclaimed proudly, "See that? One hundred eighty-five, *and not an ounce muscle!*"

Now as the house—or most of it—prepared for the Registration Dance after a reasonably good dinner consumed in high spirits and customary haste, Jeff had been holding forth, to his elders' amusement, about his interview with his faculty adviser, an earnest gentleman who was torn between wanting to lecture Jeff about the need for more attention to his studies this year and a great urge to express abject adoration for his physical attributes. Since he was certain Jeff would dismiss this with a well-bred tolerance that would be much more devastating than scorn, the interview had been quite an agony for him. Jeff, who was as aware of his physical attributes as the next man, had turned it into a rollicking tale for his fraternity brothers. Meanwhile the poor adviser was safely home with his wife and kiddies in his snug house in the hills behind the campus, all unsuspecting that his innocent, or not so innocent, impulses were undoubtedly known to a sizable portion of the male population on campus.

Lattimer, apprised of all this, was not so amused as some others as he stepped into the shower vacated by Franky.

"Be kind, Jeff," he advised. "Be kind. Everybody's human. You might need some sympathy yourself someday."

"Not about *that*," Jeff said, sobering down as he began vigorously toweling himself to dry. "But you're right, Latt. I suppose it isn't so funny, after all." He looked genuinely regretful. "I guess I *am* a little snot sometimes."

"Lovable," Lattimer agreed, giving him an appraising glance, "but in need of seasoning. And don't look so downcast. You don't do it often. You're kind to everybody, most of the time."

"I try," Jeff said, his accent by now so familiar that most times they hardly noticed it at all. "I appreciate you calling me on it. These guys"—and he snapped his towel at Franky—"just lead me on to express the worst in me."

"Really ruin you, don't we, boy?" Franky said, jumping out of reach with an agility that always surprised. "Well, hang in there, Reb. You'll survive. The South *will* rise again."

"If I weren't a Southern gentleman," Jeff said cheerfully, "I'd suggest you perform a physical impossibility on yourself, Brother Miller. But your weight would get in the way, anyway."

"Be KIND, he said, God damn it!" Miller roared, threatening with his towel again. Jeff laughed delightedly, fending him off, and finally, laughing, Franky departed to get ready for the dance. Jeff started to leave too but paused as Wilson came in.

"Here, child," he said grandly, stripping the towel from his loins and tossing it. "Hold this and keep me company. Unless you're in a tearing hurry to go get your hot date."

"I don't have a date," Jeff said, sitting down on the bench along the wall. "This Reg Dance always comes too soon for me. I'm a slow worker, man. I need time to sort of ease in there."

"You're going, though," Willie said.

"Oh, sure," Jeff said with a grin. "Never know what might turn up."

Willie nodded approvingly.

"Good. We need your smiling face if nothing else. Latt, isn't Unruh through *yet?*"

"You may address me directly, my good man," Guy said, stepping out of the shower with dignity. "No need for intermediaries between us old campaigners."

"*You're* the campaigner," Willie said as he began soaping up. "Who is it tonight, Maggie Johnson?"

"Yep," Unruh said.

"Going at it again this quarter, eh?" Willie said. "*She'll* never fall."

"I don't really want her to," Unruh said thoughtfully. "I'm getting quite romantic in my old age."

"Getting quite marriage-minded, *I* think," Lattimer observed.

"And why not?" Guy demanded, surprising them and himself with his sudden seriousness.

"No reason at all," Latt said. "I think it's great, myself. You could go a lot farther and do a lot worse."

"She's a *nice* girl," Unruh announced, almost defiantly.

"She *is*," Latt concurred solemnly. "*Go to it!*"

"I *will!*" Guy said.

"*Good!*" Willie said.

"Hot dog, *everybody!*" Jeff exclaimed with a grin and they all began to laugh.

"Come meet her, sport," Unruh suggested, mussing his hair affectionately as he went out. "You'll like her. And she'll like you."

"I'm honored," Jeff said, and meant it. "Have you had a good day, Willie?"

"Can't—talk—soap—hair," Wilson mumbled, then ducked his head, rinsed and spat. "Damn, you made me get a mouthful anyway. So much for sophomore kids who can't see when the old folks are busy. *I* had a good day, yes. Did you?"

"Oh, first-rate," Jeff said—no one, really, had ever heard him answer anything else concerning his day at the University. "A couple of tough courses in history, but you know how that is, Latt—they're very interesting too. And a real good practice session with the swimming team. We're going to break some records this year, I'll bet."

"I'll bet you are too," Wilson said. "Water sprites like you. . . . And how was your day, Latt?"

"Fine," Lattimer said, stepping out and beginning to towel down. "B.J. and I went to class and then spent the rest of the morning in our independent study course. We only have the one class this quarter, the rest is all independent."

"I saw our colored friend this morning," Willie said casually, and was aware of Jeff's quick interest.

"Oh?" Latt said. "How's he getting along?"

"Pretty well, I think. Having a little trouble in the hall, apparently, but I talked to Hank and he's going to take care of it."

"Is that y'all's nigrah friend?" Jeff asked, accent suddenly sounding much more pronounced to them—or was it only the subject matter that made them think so?

"Yeah," Willie said matter-of-factly. "Have you met him?"

"No, not yet," Jeff said. "Why? Should I?"

"No," Wilson said, stepping out of the shower and accepting the towel Jeff automatically handed him. "I just thought you might have."

"I'm not going out of my way, if that's what you mean," Jeff said. "He looked like a nice boy from where I sat, but he's hardly what I think of as a bosom buddy."

"He might be someday," Wilson said lightly. "Never know what's going to happen when you get away from the South."

"Yes," Jeff said, not conceding anything. "Well. It isn't going to happen with *me*, Willie, so don't get any ideas, hear? They're fine in their place but their place isn't my place, and that's that."

"My goodness," Willie said mildly, and with a smile. "Hear that, Latt? We've been warned."

"I'm not 'warning' you," Jeff said, handsome young face genuinely dismayed at the thought. "I don't 'warn' people. I'm just sayin' he's not for me, that's all. You-all do what you want, that's your business. But don't try to get me in on it, 'cause I'm not interested. Anyway, you wouldn't be really interested in whether we really liked each other. You'd just be trying to prove somethin'."

"Yes," Wilson said gravely, "maybe I would. Prove to you that it wouldn't kill you."

"It wouldn't kill me, man!" Jeff said with a note close to desperation in his voice. "I *like* nigrahs. I *grew up* with nigrahs. Two or three of 'em back home *are* my best friends. But they're *my* nigrahs, can you understand that? They're not something you just—just dragged in and threw in my face and said, 'Love him!' I don't operate like that! I can't!"

"That's right," Lattimer said firmly, "and I think we should respect that, Willie, and drop it."

"But—" Wilson began.

"D-r-o-p it, I said," Lattimer repeated. He gave Jeff a kindly smile and touched him lightly on the shoulder. "You relax, kid. Nobody's going to force you to do anything. You may not even see him all year, who knows. No reason why you should."

Jeff gave them both a shrewd look.

"Not unless Willie brings him up here to the house," he said, *"Then* I will."

"Who said anything about bringing him up to the house?" Wilson demanded with an innocent air—so innocent that Jeff couldn't resist a smile.

"I know you, Willie," he said with considerable affection. "You don't rest when you get one of these ideas in your head. It's the logical next step, isn't it?"

"You'll be the first to know," Wilson said with more dryness in his voice than he intended. "You can arrange to eat somewhere else that night if you want to. You won't be missed."

Jeff looked as if he had been struck in the face and Latt said in dismay, "Oh, now, Willie, *come on!* You don't mean that!"

"No," Wilson said, instantly contrite, "I do not. I apologize, Jeff. That wasn't called for."

"I hope not," Jeff said, eyes wide, looking about ten years old, and stricken. "I sure hope not!"

"No, it wasn't, and I *am* sorry," Willie repeated. "Shake on it?"

"Sure," Jeff said, taking his hand but still somewhat uncertainly. He looked for a split second as though he might cry. "I wouldn't want you mad at me, Willie. But I just—I just—you have to understand that some things I just can't—"

"I know," Willie said with true regret. "I *am* a son of a bitch sometimes. But sometimes—" His eyes widened, he sighed. "Sometimes I just—just want things to happen for the best, that's all. And I overdo it."

"Yes," Latt said, voice deliberately reserved. "You do."

"And don't *you* make it hard on me, either," Willie said with a rueful smile. "Latt's my conscience," he said to Jeff. "I guess I deserve him."

"He's a good one to have, I'll bet," Jeff said, relaxing a little but still cautiously. "I probably need one, too."

"No, you don't," Wilson said. "You have a good heart, Jeff, and that's sufficient."

"Well," Jeff said, still a bit uncertain. "I *hope* I do."

"You do," Wilson said. "And," he added with an inner relief he really felt, having let a too-quick tongue get him in this tangle, "so does *this* orphan of the storm. Where the hell have *you* been, buster? You look as though you've been through the wringer."

"I," Moose said in a sepulchral voice, "have been having a date with Welcome Waggoner."

"My God," Willie said, bending down and examining his naked body with exaggerated attention. "No wonder it's dragging right—down—to—the ground. It won't come alive for a week!"

"Maybe not," Moose admitted, morosely turning on a shower and stepping under it. "I wouldn't be surprised. But"—he brightened—"it was worth it."

"Good as ever, hmm?" Willie inquired.

"Better." And suddenly, startling them all, he threw his head back, turned on both shower handles full blast and shouted, "Yaaaa—*hoooo!*"

"And I suppose," Willie said as they all burst out laughing, "you're going to take her to the dance and more of the same."

"You *bet!*" Moose said happily. "And it isn't going to take any *week* either! See there?" and he pointed proudly. And unnecessarily.

"Disgusting," Lattimer exclaimed. "Positively disgusting."

"Impressive, too," Wilson admitted.

"I never saw the likes of that in the *whole South!*" Jeff said in an elaborately awestruck tone, and broke again into his delighted and infectious laugh.

Thank God for that, Wilson thought: I guess we're over that one, thanks to Moose.

"Let's get dressed, you guys," he said to Jeff and Lattimer. "And Mooser," he added sternly, "I want you to keep your hands where they belong after we leave, understand? Don't get anxious. Welcome's waiting."

"I think I can safely say," Moose replied with dignity, "that she will not be disappointed."

"He's some guy," Jeff said to Wilson as they came to the turn in the hall and parted to their respective rooms.

"The best," he said. "See you at the dance."

"Sure thing," Jeff said, and hesitated. "Willie—I'm sorry I blew up at you."

"Good Lord, man, you didn't blow up," Wilson said. "You never blow up at anybody. It was my fault entirely. Try to forget and forgive, if you can."

"I don't hold grudges," Jeff said. "You're forgiven. Just—just don't blame me for the way I was brought up. I can't help it."

Wilson smiled.

"It's difficult for everybody," he admitted. "But with a little luck, I guess it will all work out."

"Maybe," Jeff said as he turned away. "I wouldn't really know."

But his tone was amicable enough and he had apparently returned to his usual sunny, even-tempered disposition. It was another lesson, though, Willie reflected as he went thoughtfully about his dressing, that Jeff was not your average student on campus. As Tim acknowledged in his notes, Jefferson Davis Barnett from Charleston, South Carolina, history major, was something almost exotic, for that place and that time:

"Jeff, often called 'Reb' for obvious reasons, is something of a rarity in the house and on campus: not too many Southerners get this far west. His accent couldn't be more Southern nor could his basic beliefs, which, supported by some of his less tolerant brethren, give rise to many a heated argument when it comes to racial matters. Nigrahs are fine in their place, and as far as Jeff and his family are concerned, that place has been a mighty good one and Jeff deeply resents the charge that it hasn't been. He's grown up with 'em, been reared by 'em, knows 'em like his own kinfolk. That doesn't mean he wants to go to bed with 'em, though he's honest enough to admit that over time many have.

"The Barnetts, Jeff points out, had already freed their slaves some twenty years before the War Between the States, and if it hadn't been for the damned Yankees tryin' to push the South around, the Barnetts wouldn't probably have ever fired a shot in anger. After the war ended they treated their people about as perfect as you can get, takin' care of 'em in every phase of life and never once betrayin' or undercuttin' or doing anythin' bad to 'em. And most real gentlefolks in the South, they've always done the same, and Jeff can't see why you damned Yankees can't get that through your thick skulls.

"These views come as something of a shock to his housemates, because they really thought Jeff was one of the prizes of his pledge class. There is continuing frustration about Jeff because as Willie says to Latt, 'Anybody who looks that normal ought to *be* normal.' Latt snorts and says, 'If by normal you mean somebody whose ideas agree with yours, Willie, then the kid's a real weirdo. Obviously he isn't, so how do you handle that?' Willie and most of Jeff's brethren aren't really quite sure. Somebody that likeable just *must* see things the way sensible people do. But he doesn't—and *he* thinks he's quite sensible.

"Meanwhile, things are further complicated by the fact that he is the best man on the swimming team, and headed straight for the next Olympics (which rumor says may not be held because of 'the situation in Europe'); and that makes him a real asset for the house, which is not noted for its athletic prowess except for Unruh and Moose."

In his little room at the top, under the eaves—"Willie's throne room," Latt called it, from which he could survey his world like king-on-the-mountain—Wilson was beginning to feel ashamed of himself for being sarcastic to Jeff. Why did he do things like that? Normally he was the friendliest and most decent of people, but every once in a while some little devil inside would creep out and lash out. He didn't understand it, it wasn't a major aspect of his personality as it was with Suratt or Bryce . . . but he knew he had to watch it. He sighed and thought bleakly that he really was a son of a bitch sometimes.

Then he told himself to snap out of it, he wasn't *that* bad; and after a moment, felt better. But it bothered him, sometimes. He liked to understand himself and sometimes he didn't. It hurt him more, sometimes, than anyone, probably, would ever know.

In the third-floor shower room, across the house on the other side, a lonesome and forlorn little figure was standing under a gentle spray of water doing more thinking, really, than showering. Not everybody at college, he was thinking resentfully, was a sex expert like Unruh and Gulbransen; not everybody found it easy to command everything he wanted, like Smith Carriger or Bob Godwin; not everybody could be Phi Beta Kappa like Latt or a sports hero like Musavich.

It wasn't so easy for some people to fall into bed with every girl they met. Some people, in fact, had never fallen into bed with a girl at all. It took some people a long, long time, if ever, to become sure of themselves in the college environment and mature into it, as everybody said you were supposed to do, and expected you to do.

Not everybody was outgoing, comfortable and popular with house and campus.

Some people in fact, were young, uncertain, desperately shy, afraid and unhappy.

To some people, the world of the University was a difficult and frightening thing.

Marcus Andrew Taylor from Pittsburgh, Pennsylvania, business administration major, was, as Renny Suratt had put it with typical cutting unkindness at a rushing party last spring when he knew Marc would overhear, "one of the dimmer stars in our sophomore galaxy."

They had pledged him, as Bates put it in his notes, because he appeared "sober, solid, industrious and agreeable; not 'a real grind,' but presumably possessing qualities of steadiness and application that were supposed, as

Lattimer put it, 'to leaven the loaf.' Instead he is already proving to be, in Guy Unruh's estimation, 'pretty dull.' Lattimer says he's too hard on the kid, but give him time: 'If this house doesn't relax him, nothing will.'

"Many feel that Marc is the classic Rushing Mistake. For one thing, he can't get over the fact that his father made a lot of money in manufacturing (adding-machines and similar heavy office equipment), which he began in Pittsburgh with a two-thousand-dollar bank loan and 'the honest toil of an honest man.' That is really the way Marc refers to it, with perfect solemnity and an absolute lack of humor; and of course he's absolutely right, it isn't funny and it *is* something to be proud of. It's just that people in this college generation don't often utter such platitudes with such a straight face.

"Marc looks forward with pride, anticipation—and considerable apprehension, they can sense—to the day when he will graduate and return home to help his father, and, eventually, take over the firm. His future has been planned for him from the day he was born, an only child, and ever since he was old enough to realize what it was, he has cooperated. 'Such dedication is worthy of some respect,' Lattimer says, and Guy agrees—'but it still doesn't make him the Laughing Boy of Salvatierra Street.'

"Unfortunately, while apparently not the most sensitive of beings, Marc is sensitive enough to realize that a lot of his brethren regard him with a patience more devastating than dislike."

Right now he was thinking desperately, as he seemed to be doing increasingly these days, that perhaps he should resign from the house and go live in one of the relatively anonymous mens' dorms. He certainly didn't seem to be getting anywhere here.

And, he reflected darkly, he wasn't getting anywhere much in the University, either. He had made very few friends in freshman dorm, very few in freshman classes. Now in the opening days of his sophomore year he hadn't found anyone so far who seemed likely to become a real friend. And since he was weighted down by his feeling of inferiority, his grades to date weren't very good, either.

As for girls—*ha*.

Nobody would look at *him* twice, that's for sure.

With a moroseness that he seemed to be feeling increasingly these days, he closed his eyes and held his face up to the hot water, letting it fall gently over him, soothing, comforting, helpful—undemanding.

There were too many demands, for eighteen.

Too many things.

He did not know how long he stood there in the deserted shower room, but suddenly a shower splattered into life alongside him and one of the classmates he most liked and admired—though he was sure neither sentiment was reciprocated—spoke to him. He came out of himself with a start as he realized that the greeting was not the usual ebullient one from that source. Randy Carrero, in fact, sounded as down as Marc felt. What was the matter with *him*?

The question was a valid one, because no one ever expected anything to be wrong with Randy Carrero. Randy Carrero was a golden boy. It wasn't just the fact that he was to a large extent Bates' protégé that filled Bates' notes on him with such a tone of respect and admiration. Randy was *great*. So thought Marc and everybody. Tim had set forth the reasons with obvious approval when he wrote about Randolph Ramirez Carrero from Albuquerque, New Mexico, political science major:

"Randy Carrero is an extremely bright kid who is already on his way to the inevitable Phi Beta Kappa key and quite possibly a Rhodes Scholarship. He comes from a moderately wealthy background in New Mexico, where his grandfather arrived sixty years ago as an illegal immigrant and where his father owns a successful department store and a sizable cattle ranch.

"In addition to getting straight A's in all his freshman subjects, he followed up on his career as No. 1 state tennis champion by moving to the top of the University freshman team. He made a notable debut on the *Daily* with a cleverly written, highly popular series of feature articles that began with a three-part series, 'First Days on Campus,' and went on through the year with occasional humorously deft and sometimes ironic reports on the adventures of 'Anxious Arnie,' the typical freshman. This success brought him a promise from Bates that he will have an occasional crack at Bates' own column, 'On the Quad,' in his sophomore year. In addition to that he has decided to go out for the swimming team with Jeff Barnett and is already giving Jeff a few thoughtful moments. And in addition to *that*, he has already applied for and received appointment as a part-time clerical helper in the office of the president. This places him directly under the eye of Dr. Chalmers and guarantees him the fatherly support of that influential gentleman.

" 'And in addition to all *that*,' Gulbransen remarks with a somewhat baffled grin, 'he's actually one hell of a nice guy and not a bit spoiled.' 'He just happens to be damned good in ev'thang,' Jeff concedes somewhat ruefully. 'You can't fault a guy for that.'

"Willie says he fully expects Randy to make president of the student body, Phi Bete, Rhodes scholar, governor of New Mexico— 'Why not President of the United States?' Unruh inquires, not entirely in jest. 'That, too,' Willie says."

But the Randy who spoke to Marc now appeared, at the moment, to be far from the self-assured character Bates had portrayed.

"Hi," he said almost shyly, which in itself was unusual for one normally so ebullient. "Mind if I join you?"

"Why, sure, Randy," Marc said, trying to sound upbeat and welcoming. But Randy, whatever his own inner devils, was always sensitive to the moods of others, and it didn't work.

"What's the matter?" he asked with genuine concern. A rather wistful smile crossed his dark engaging face. "You sound as gloomy as I feel."

"Do I?" Marc inquired with an awkward attempt at a smile. "I didn't mean to."

"I know you didn't *mean* to," Randy said, stepping to one side to adjust his shower, "but you do. Tell me about it. Maybe we can make each other feel better. Maybe it will make *me* feel better. Misery loves company, you know."

"I'm not sure," Marc said, not meeting his eyes. "I just feel—feel blue, I guess. Is that how it is with you?"

"Without any reason, you mean?" Randy asked, finding the temperature he wanted and stepping back under. "That's not good." He sighed. "*I* have a reason."

"What's that?" Marc asked—hesitantly, because surely this glamorous campus dynamo was not really going to confide anything of any importance to *him*. But Randy obviously needed to talk.

"My reason," he said with a sudden frown whose unhappiness Marc could tell was genuine, "is a bitch."

"You mean—"

"A bitch," Randy interrupted. "A bitch bitch. A girl. You know how that is."

"Well, no," Marc admitted with forlorn honesty. "I don't, really. At least, not yet."

"Then be thankful," Randy said, soaping himself as though he were going to take the skin off. "Stay away from it. Don't *ever* get involved with a bitch. They aren't worth it."

"Well," Marc said, awkward again because he didn't know what demands of intimacy this conversation was going to impose upon him and he wasn't sure he wanted any, even from this bedazzling figure, "I mean, that's too bad, Randy."

"It's worse than that," Randy Carrero said, peering from under a hat of soapsuds to give him a somber look.

"I mean, I *am* sorry," Marc said hastily. "It's really bad. I mean, it *is*." He applied some soap himself while Randy seemed to relax and enjoy the water for a moment. He tensed up again as soon as Marc got up the courage to ask, "Who is it? I mean, if—if you want to tell me, that is."

"You may know her," Randy said, turning up the water a notch and beginning to rinse off. "Her name is Beverly Stevens. They call her Fluff," he added with a sudden savagery, "and by God, *she is*."

"I—I think I know her," Marc said obligingly. "Is she rather tall and dark? There was one in freshmen English class last year—"

"No, that's Joanne Stevens," Randy said. "No relation. She comes right after Fluff in the Bawlout. I dialed her by mistake one time." He kicked the wall angrily, clutched his toe and said, "Oh, *Christ!*" in a tone of agony. "I should have followed through and forgotten all about Fluff. That was my chance. I missed it." He stepped out of the shower, turned on the cold water full blast, soaked a towel, wrapped it around his foot and sat down on the bench which, as in the other shower room, lined the wall. "Fluff was supposed to call me right after dinner about going to the dance, but she didn't." He looked suddenly very young, very bleak and not at all the self-sufficient and secure character he was generally believed to be.

"Oh, I'm sure she will," Marc said earnestly. "It isn't even eight o'clock yet, and the dance doesn't start until nine, does it?"

"That's right," Randy said. He looked even gloomier. "But I know her. She's going to stand me up. And I know who with, too." He tensed again as they heard the sound of voices down the hall, the closing of a door, the slap-slap of sandals on their way to the shower. "God *damn* it," he said in a fierce whisper, "here comes the son of a bitch now."

"Do you want me to leave?" Marc asked hurriedly and Randy snapped, "Christ, no! I need reinforcements. Stand by!"

"Well—" Marc said. "I wouldn't want to—"

"SHHH!" Randy ordered in the same fierce way. "Shut up!" And he bent down and examined his foot carefully as the slap-slap drew nearer and stopped in the doorway.

"Hi, guys," Gil Gulbransen said, stripping the towel off his belly to reveal himself with what Marc could only feel was an insolent satisfaction; warranted, he could see, but still obviously meant to annoy someone. The someone did not look up but kept on examining his toe, by now slightly swollen.

"Hi," he said in a noncommittal voice, and "Hi, Gil, how are you?" Marc said in a voice that rose a little from sheer nervousness.

Gulbransen laughed comfortably and moved to a shower. He turned the faucets, testing for temperature, and asked casually, "Everybody going to the dance tonight?"

Randy said nothing.

"I'm not," Marc said, feeling that somebody had to say something.

"Why not?" Gulbransen demanded. "No date?"

"I'm afraid not," Marc said apologetically. Gil gave him a fatherly glance.

"You should have one," he said. "Why don't you come with me? Maybe I can fix you up with somebody. Lots of sophomore and freshman women running around loose at Reg Dance."

"Do you have a date?" Marc asked and immediately cursed himself for stupidity as Randy made an ominous movement.

"Sure thing," Gil said. "Hey, Randy!" he added, turning around to face him as he soaped himself with prolonged and loving care. "Do you have one?"

"I may or I may not," Randy said evenly, finally looking up and studying him with an exaggerated interest. "Is there a sheep alive that can take that?" he inquired. "I don't think any ordinary female could." ·

"You should be so lucky, boy," Gil said with a chuckle, channeling the water over his shoulder with one hand to rinse himself off with the other hand with as much care as he had soaped up. "I've never had any complaints yet. Nor," he added complacently, "do I expect to have any tonight. If you don't have a date, Randy," he added kindly, "why don't you come along with me too. I'm sure she wouldn't mind."

Oh my God, Marc thought frantically. *Now they're going to fight.*

"Guys!" he exclaimed hastily. "Say, guys!"

"What?" they asked, and it seemed to him that they turned upon him fiercely in unison.

"Well," he said hastily, thinking: *Oh, Lord, what'll I say now?* "Well, I mean, it ought to be fun, shouldn't it?"

"I'm planning on it," Gil assured him, laughing heartily as he turned off the shower and rubbed himself down vigorously. "Hurry it along if you want to go, though. And you too, Randy. Fluff's expecting me in half an hour."

Marc hesitated and looked at Randy, who shrugged.

"Why don't we meet you at the dance?" Marc suggested.

"O.K.," Gil said cheerfully. "See you there, slugger," he said, hitting Randy lightly on the shoulder as he went out.

"Son of a bitch," Randy said in a strangled voice. "Lousy fucking big-cocked son of bitch."

"Yes, he is, rather," Marc said with a nervous little laugh that made Randy glower at him.

"Don't sound like a moron, Taylor," he ordered. "Are you going with that arrogant son of a bitch, or not?"

"I thought I might," Marc said. "He really does know a lot of girls, I guess, and maybe he *can*—" his voice faltered at Randy's forbidding expression— "fix me up."

"I'm sure of it," Randy said dryly.

Marc hesitated, and then asked, "Are you?"

For a moment Randy looked utterly bleak and abandoned.

"I suppose so," he said finally in a low voice. He gave Marc a nakedly helpless look. "I've got to see her, I can't help myself." He drove his right fist into his left palm. "God damn it," he said in a desperate and agonized tone, "I can't help myself."

Marc thought: Golly, if only I could feel that deeply about someone! And then he thought: But boy, am I glad I don't!

"Shall we meet downstairs?" he asked.

Randy nodded, again looking down at his feet.

"Quarter to nine," he said. He uttered a bitter little laugh. "We don't want to miss anything."

"No," Marc said nervously. "No, that's right."

"Hey, Marc!" Randy said, as he started out. "You stop worrying, O.K.? You haven't a thing to worry about."

"Well—" Marc said doubtfully. "Maybe not."

"Believe me," Randy said, "not a thing. So snap out of it, O.K.? Enjoy life. You don't know how lucky you are."

"Well," Marc said lamely, "maybe I am." An increasing melancholy seemed to be revived by Randy's genuine kindness in the midst of his own trouble. "I guess."

"Sure you are," Randy said firmly. "Meet you downstairs at a quarter to nine. And chin up!'

"Yes, Randy," Marc said humbly. "I guess so."

After Marc had gone down the hall and climbed slowly up the stairs to the room he shared with Rodge Leighton next to Wilson under the eaves, Randy sat for a few moments longer contemplating his rapidly swelling big toe. Of all the God damned things to do, he thought bitterly, get himself in this kind of a fix when he wanted to be in good shape to take Fluff away from Gulbransen if he could manage it during the dance. Now he probably wouldn't be able to—assuming she gave him the chance, which he very much doubted. She was going to be extra-bitchy tonight. He was sure of it.

Randy Carrero had enjoyed a lot of girlfriends in high school, two of them quite intensely: intense was his nature, under an almost always smiling exterior. But, like all those things in high school that suddenly seemed far away and unimportant when you got to college, none had been as important or all-consuming as Fluff Stevens. He was damned if he knew why, or why this blight should have fallen across his life just as he was starting what should be a highly successful second year on campus.

Because it *was* a blight, he told himself: that was the only word for it. It had begun as a casual sort of fun thing, but before he knew it he was genuinely and deeply in love—with someone whom he knew, both instinctively and analytically, to be his inferior. Fluff didn't have many brains, she wasn't interested in any of the things he was, and she was capable of hurts and cruelties that were so foreign to his nature that his first reaction had been complete bafflement. Nobody had ever been deliberately unkind or hurtful to him before and he wasn't prepared for it. The date made and deliberately broken—the phone call promised and never made—the sudden abandonment in the middle of what he had thought to be a pleasant occasion in order to go openly and flauntingly away with someone else— the sort of feckless and haphazard uncaring that apparently underlay all this—none of these had been his experience. At first he had thought they were done deliberately to be provocative, and to a certain extent some of them were; but he had finally concluded, angrily and sadly, that they were part of a nature that just didn't know any better because it wasn't equipped to know any better. A basic insensitivity was allied to an incurably flirtatious habit, and the combination was hell for him, who was absolutely honest in his emotions and his actions. He never deliberately hurt anyone, why should anyone deliberately hurt him? It seemed a question that answered itself, except that it didn't, where Fluff Stevens was concerned.

And the damnable thing about it, he thought now as his toe really began to throb and he started to hobble slowly along the hall to the room he was to share this quarter with Billy Wilson, was that along with what he recognized to be a nature essentially destructive of genuine emotions, there went a body to which he was overpoweringly attracted. So much so, in fact, that it completely wiped out all his natural caution and his conscious thoughts that he really must get away from this for the sake of his own sanity and peace of mind.

Not that he felt that it was seriously threatening his sanity, of course, that was old-fashioned dime-novel stuff; but it certainly was smashing his peace of mind all to hell, that was for sure. And now, with what he thought of bitterly as "this little show with Gulbransen" which had begun on Reg Day, it was putting him into a mental state that he felt might really threaten his studies, his work on the *Daily*, and all those other activities that were already part of the entity "Randy Carrero."

He couldn't blame Gil Gulbransen for this—Gil was basically an amicable and likeable soul who just happened to be your genuine ever-ready tomcat. Randy was certain he had no real interest in Fluff except as a target of opportunity and maybe a chance to tease a little a too-serious younger fraternity brother whom Gil really liked.

Randy was convinced there wasn't any malice in it as far as Gil was concerned, however he may have teased in the shower.

He wasn't so sure about Fluff.

Or rather, he was damned sure.

He had written her often during the summer, telling her about his life on the cattle ranch in southern New Mexico. Maybe one time in four, she had replied, always very briefly, very sketchily—very hurtfully, that was the word he kept coming back to, simply because her replies were so offhand and basically uninterested, either in what he was doing or in being polite enough to keep from bruising his feelings.

It was all very well to brood about this under the endless skies of New Mexico, where all you had to do was help run cattle. It was quite another to sit at a typewriter in the *Daily* Shack, as he had this afternoon, and find the image of Fluff putting you into such a turmoil that you really couldn't think and finally had to turn a prized editorial assignment back to Tim Bates with some mumbled excuse he couldn't even remember now. He did remember that Tim had given him a real funny look, as he had every right to, and asked with genuine concern, "Are you all right, Randy?" And then, not waiting for an answer, had shouted across to Bill Nagatani and asked him to take on the project along with the lead editorial he was writing. Bill had looked at Randy funny too, and that was very bad, to get both the editor and his likely successor upset with you.

He really didn't know how it had happened, he only knew that for a few important minutes there, he couldn't seem to think straight. And that was *really* bad.

He sighed heavily as he reached the room and entered it to find Billy Wilson examining his new jacket and pants critically in the full-length mirror some long-ago fraternity brother had nailed to the wall. Randy rallied enough—because he had to, he couldn't afford to get *everybody* worried about him—to give Billy a pretty good grin and a joshing comment.

"You look beautiful," he said. "Janie will be absolutely overcome."

Billy responded with his characteristic shy smile and said in his gentle voice, "Oh, she knows me pretty well by this time. I don't think she will be."

"But look at that tie," Randy said, turning to the closet to select his own outfit for the evening—not that it really mattered, he thought glumly, because Fluff sure wouldn't be impressed, either, though not for the same reason. "You're sensational."

"And *you're* a kidder," Billy said. "I think," he added thoughtfully, "that we're going to get along together pretty well, don't you?"

"Absolutely," Randy said, adding with mock solemnity, "as long as you don't get too drunk and rowdy all the time."

"I never get drunk!" Billy said in a shocked voice, and then relaxed. "See, you are a kidder. You know I don't drink."

"Me either," Randy said, beginning to dress. "Or very little, anyway. A few beers now and then, hard stuff once in a great while. I don't like to feel I'm out of control of my mind, you know? It isn't me."

"Good for you," Billy said. "I don't either."

"Willie doesn't drink much either, does he?" Randy asked. Willie's brother shook his head.

"A little bit. I think he and Unruh and some of the older guys go to the City once in a while and have a bash someplace, but not very often. He never drinks at home. Our dad wouldn't let him."

"You mean somebody actually exercises some discipline over Willie?" Randy asked with a smile. "I didn't think anyone could."

"That's what Willie wants people to think," Billy said with an answering smile. "Dad does. It isn't always easy, but he does. Willie *is* pretty special, I guess."

"Is he a good brother?" Randy asked as he moved to the mirror and tied his tie. Billy looked positively reverential.

"He's fought my battles all my life," he said simply. "I don't know what I'd do without Willie. Do you have any brothers and sisters?"

"Both," Randy said. "Two brothers above, two sisters below. Lucky Randy, always in the middle. We're very close-knit, too. I come," he said with a sudden emphatic defensiveness that puzzled Billy, "from a *very nice* family."

"I can tell that," Billy agreed, smiling again. "Are you taking Fluff Stevens to the dance?"

"Maybe," Randy began, and then thought: Oh, to hell with it, what's the point in false pride? "I had planned to," he said honestly. "But Gil Gulbransen beat me to it."

Billy looked surprised. "I didn't know she knew him."

"She didn't until yesterday morning," Randy said; and added bitterly, "But that's long enough for her to get started."

"Why do you—" Billy began, and hesitated.

"Waste my time on her?" Randy completed for him. He stared at himself in the mirror. "I don't really know, to tell you the truth." He gave a wry little smile. "I wish I could break the habit, but it doesn't seem to be possible. So, I guess I'll just suffer." And he struck a pose of self-mockery and cried out, "Suffer, suffer, *suffer*! God, do I ever *suffer*! Isn't it romantic?"

Billy looked at him for a moment. Then he said quietly, "I think you really do."

"Well," said Randy, suddenly bleak, "I shouldn't let it get me down. I'm only eighteen, for Christ's sake. I shouldn't let Fluff Stevens mess up my whole life. You're damned lucky. You have Janie."

"Yes," Billy said softly, "I have Janie. And I am very lucky. I don't quite know what I've done to deserve her, but I seem to have her."

"What would you do if somebody like Gulbransen moved in on her?"

"I've never thought about it," Billy said simply, "because nobody's going to. She wouldn't cooperate."

Confronted by this serene conviction, Randy was momentarily at a loss; yet it was, as he had recognized in their few brief talks during rushing periods last year, entirely characteristic of Billy. And of Janie as well, he suspected. Bates could have confirmed this. He sometimes told himself that his notes on these two came as near to being plain gooey as anything he had ever written about anybody. And yet—that was the way they were.

William Wilson from Terra Bella, California, majoring in dramatic arts, "is one of those rare people who seem to exist just to make other people satisfied with the human race. Not because he goes out of his way to do things for them, necessarily, but just because he is always honest, always open, always friendly and forthright and sympathetic and interested in everything and everyone around him. Probably as long as he lives he will continue to carry in his eyes, his face and his smile something of the generous candor of a singularly decent and honest child. Almost everyone is very fond of Billy. Enormously idealistic, he has great plans for his years as a teacher of drama, being one of those increasing rarities, a youth who sees in teaching the challenge of a great crusade. He is going to be both greatly hurt and greatly strengthened by the shortcomings of humankind."

And Janie? Bates told himself he was equally saccharine. But what could you do, in the face of these two kids:

Elizabeth Jane Montgomery from Portland, Oregon, English major, "is the perfect match for Billy Wilson, and that is what, in sophomore year, they have already agreed she is going to be. 'The ideal mating of treacle and syrup,' Suratt remarks, but everyone knows Suratt is just jealous because his own prickly personality puts off all but the most willfully self-deluded and desperate young ladies. Janie is the only child of a devoted couple to whom she was born when they were in their late thirties, and as such has received the most careful and cosseted of upbringings. Surprisingly this has not made her spoiled, willful, or otherwise obnoxious; like Billy, she is a genuinely sweet person. They met on Reg Day when they were freshmen and have been inseparable ever since. On the rare occasions when Billy runs into obstacles or suffers hurts, she is there with staunch support to make him feel better. He does the same for her. 'God, she's insipid' Suratt exclaims, but he is very careful not to exclaim it to the Wilson brothers or to anyone who might carry it back to them."

"So, if somebody moved in on her she wouldn't cooperate," Randy repeated in a tone that sounded both envious and bemused. Billy's response was flat and final:

"She wouldn't cooperate."

"Unlike some," Randy said bitterly. "What would you do if you were me?"

"I don't know," Billy said thoughtfully. "Ride it out, I guess. If I could . . . and if I felt she was worth it."

Randy again looked bleak and far away.

"That's what I have to decide, I guess," he said at last. "And I just don't know . . . I *just don't know*."

There was a hesitant knock on the door. Marc peered in.

"I was going to meet you downstairs as you said," he told Randy, "but I was just coming by, so I thought I'd look in to see if—"

"Quite right," Randy said, pulling himself back to a fair semblance of his usual incisive manner. "I'm ready. Let's go." He took a deep breath. "See you there, Billy."

"Sure," Billy said. "Good luck."

Randy sighed heavily.

"I'll need it. Come along, Marc." His expression turned wry. "Misery has company tonight, all right."

Marc wanted to respond with something humorous and upbeat but for the life of him he couldn't think of anything. So he just responded in a vaguely commiserating way.

They started down the stairs, both looking glum.

There were just too many demands, for eighteen.

Too many things.

In the crowded lobby of the Union, the remaining sophomores, Hank Moore and Rudy Krohl, were waiting along with some twenty or thirty other fellows for their dates. Hank as always looked pleasant and self-effacing, which, Gale Bryce once remarked, was about all you could say for Hank Moore. Rudy Krohl looked big, blond and overbearing, which, Franky Miller had retorted, was about all you could say for Rudy Krohl. Rudy and Hank didn't like one another particularly, but the luck of the draw had thrown them together as roommates, so Hank, at least, was making the best of it. Hank was a quiet, easygoing, tolerant soul who could stand almost anybody for a reasonable period of time, and Rudy was usually oblivious to his effect upon others, so they were getting along quite amicably now as they waited.

Rudy was holding forth, as he did frequently these days, on the situation in Europe. Hank from time to time was injecting a note of mild demur that did not please, but did not inhibit, his roommate.

A rather unlikely pair, Bates had commented when Ray Baker said he was going to put them in the same room. Tim's notes reflected the general uneasiness the house felt about Rudy and the friendly but slightly patronizing attitude its members had toward Hank:

Rudolph John Krohl from Ridgewood, New Jersey, economics major, "has for father a very successful and very wealthy auto dealer whose parents brought him to this country from Bavaria at age three. Ties to the old country have never really slackened much (trips 'home' every two years keep them strong), and it is no wonder young Rudy has grown up with a considerable feeling that things German are still much to be admired and defended. With the rise of Hitler and the growing tensions in Europe he has followed his father's lead and become increasingly pro-German and anti-Jewish; between Rudy and Duke Offenberg a really serious tension has arisen. Rudy is big, beefy, German-looking; his mind is also German, rigid, stubborn, literally unable to see or accept an opposing point of view. 'We never should have pledged him,' Wilson often remarks. 'He's trouble,' Latt agrees—the only time he has ever been known to utter a critical word about anyone.

"So far the trouble has not exploded into anything really serious. Duke makes no secret of the fact that he voted against pledging Rudy, and Rudy growls threats from time to time, but it has not yet come to actual blows. The potential is there, however. At the time Rudy was pledged he was at his most ingratiating and the majority saw no reason to keep him out, particularly since many felt that Duke was 'prejudiced' in his vote. However, a certain imperiousness has entered Rudy's manner with the successes of Hitler in revitalizing Germany, a certain arrogance that brooks no argument.

"He suffers from asthma, which he is smugly confident will protect him from military service if, as he puts it with relish, knowing it will infuriate, 'that damned Jew-lover Rosenfelt lets Britain drag us into a war with Germany.' Everybody assures him angrily that this will never happen, that the U.S. simply *isn't going* to war, so forget it. There are a few who are beginning to question Rudy's loyalty, though that seems too exaggerated and extreme to most."

No one could be a greater contrast to big, blustering Rudy than mild-mannered Henry Ellis Moore of Gaithersburg, Maryland, education major:

"Friendly, amicable, quiet, good-natured, without possessing any very definite characteristics that permit him to stand out from the hundreds of similar good-students-and-good-friends on the campus, Hank Moore lives a life of undeviating normalcy, has the proper reactions to all the proper things and fills his niche without fuss or circumstance. He is one of those youths who make up 'well-rounded' in the phrase, 'A well-rounded house.' He isn't a neutral character, neither is he an outstanding one. He's just a nice decent kid, not particularly strong of personality, not particularly weak. In a house that has its full share of dominant egos, his is a nice, medium-sized one which never hurts anybody or gets underfoot in the scrimmages. Not strong and not weak—just normal. That's Hank Moore."

Rudy had just stated emphatically once again, for perhaps the hundredth time in the hearing of his fraternity brothers, that everything would calm down over there "as soon as Hitler gets what he wants," and Hank for the third time this evening had murmured, "And what might that be?" when the door opened with a characteristic flourish and Duke appeared. Rudy made no attempt to look welcoming. Instead he murmured, "I'd forgotten she lives here. There's a real nest of them in the Union."

"Yes," Hank said pleasantly. "I'm waiting for Sally Ahrends, myself."

"Pardon *me*," Rudy said elaborately. "I didn't know you liked them, too."

"Oh, knock it off!" Hank said with a sudden quite uncharacteristic annoyance as Duke came toward them. "You make me tired!"

"Not as tired as *I* am," Rudy said in a fierce whisper. "Of *them*. Hi, Duke," he added, tone carrying the near-insolence it always did when he addressed him. "Picking up Shahna?"

"Who else?" Duke inquired with a friendliness that sounded quite natural, though as always he was fighting himself inside to remain civil to Rudy. "And you guys?"

"I'm waiting for Helga Berger," Rudy said with a note of defiance so obvious that in spite of himself Duke had to laugh.

"Well, all right," he said. "So, good for you. Who's Helga Berger?"

"She comes from Trenton, New Jersey," Rudy said. "She's *good American stock*."

"Aren't we all?" Hank inquired calmly, as Duke for a second looked ready to take the bait. "I'm waiting for Sally Ahrends, myself. You probably know her, Duke. She's an education major, too."

"Yeah, I do," Duke said, deciding to let it go, and smiling. "Very nice girl indeed. Congratulations on your good taste, Hank. How about swapping dances sometime during the evening?"

"Sure," Hank said. "I'll be pleased and so will she."

"Good," Duke said. "Always fun to do that. With friends."

"Helga and I will probably exchange a few ourselves," Rudy said. His tone became mimicking. "With friends."

"That's good," Duke said. "Always good to do things with friends. If," he gave a sudden bland smile, "one has some."

"Yes!" Rudy snapped. "One has some."

"Who's the band tonight?" Hank asked, deciding the best thing to do was ignore the exchange, if possible. "Is Hack's group playing?"

"Yes, I think so," Duke said. "They're always damned good. He's so terrific."

"And a very nice guy to boot," Hank observed.

"And I'm not?" Rudy demanded.

Hank gave him a look of mild surprise.

"Nobody was talking about you, Rudy," he said. "Don't be so self-conscious."

"I'm not being self-conscious!" Rudy said. "I know when people are saying things!"

"So do I," Duke said evenly. "I guess if I can take it, you can. In fact, nobody would say anything about you if you didn't go around saying things about other people."

"Listen, you guys," Hank said hastily, as several in the lobby began to look at them with some curiosity. "Confine that to the house if you have to do it, will you? Let's don't spoil a nice evening with a public row."

"Oh!" Rudy said in a disgusted tone. "You're always so namby-pamby, Moore!"

"No, I'm not," Hank said. "I'm just trying to be a gentleman. I suggest you do the same."

"How can anyone be a gentleman with people like—like—" Rudy began, and hesitated. Duke seemed suddenly taller. Rudy was big but Duke was bigger.

"Like what?" Duke inquired with an ominous softness.

"Like *you!*" Rudy said defiantly, and just at that moment when it seemed civility might disappear completely, Shahna appeared at the front desk. Hank said in a relieved voice, *"There* she is!" He grabbed Duke's arm, which felt like iron as it tensed against his hand, and swung him around.

"Great!" Duke said, giving him a quick smile as he stepped forward to meet her. "Let's get out of here," he said, not giving her time to do more than smile at them, Hank returning it, Rudy frowning. "See you at the dance, Hank."

"Right," Hank said.

He and Rudy resumed their seats. Interest in them dissipated. They were silent for several minutes.

"I don't see," Rudy said finally, "how you can enjoy being with that— that—"

"What?" Hank inquired, sounding as ominous as Duke.

"Kike," Rudy said defiantly.

"That doesn't deserve an answer," Hank said sharply. "All I can say is, you'd just better watch it, Rudy. We don't like that kind of talk around here."

"*Everybody* likes that kind of talk, only they won't admit it," Rudy asserted, unabashed. "Why do you think Hitler is—"

"You and your God damned Hitler!" Hank said with an anger very rare for one normally so mild. And he repeated it: "You and your *God damned* Hitler!"

"That's all right," Rudy said with a sort of smug superiority that seemed to indicate he had some secret knowledge less favored mortals didn't. "I can make trouble for some people. A *lot* of trouble!"

Hank gave him a look of disgust as Sally Ahrends appeared and he stood up to go and meet her.

"You're absurd," he said. "Just plain absurd."

"You'll see," Rudy said darkly as Hank turned his back on him and at the door, a blond Brunhildic vision, Helga Berger strode into view. "*You'll* see!"

"What was that all about?" Sally inquired as they went out. Hank shrugged.

"Oh, just Krohl," he said. "He's a jerk."

But he wasn't, entirely, Hank thought as he began asking about her classes and making small talk while they walked over to the women's gym, where the dance was beginning. Rudy represented something, and it was something that made Hank and a lot of people uneasy. He decided he'd talk to Willie about it when he got the chance. He hadn't had much opportunity, as a new member, to talk to Willie, but he had the impression that Willie was a pretty sound and savvy citizen. A lot of things, Hank had already concluded, revolved around Willie.

At that moment, waiting at her sorority for Donn Van Dyke to come swirling down the stairs in her usual eager, healthy rush, the paragon of Hank's—and many another's—respectfully admiring thoughts was wondering what the hell he was doing there, really. For the first time he was beginning to realize that he was getting a little restive about the general assumption that he was always to be paired with his ebullient vice-president. He was an independent being, damn it. Other people's assumptions shouldn't be controlling his life. *Nobody* controlled *his* life.

Yet here he was, dutifully waiting, right where everybody expected him to be. A knowing acceptance, a secretly amused (or so it seemed to him) lack of surprise, an arch air of you-can't-fool-us-girls, seemed to him to be present in the greetings he got from Donna's sorority sisters as they passed him on the way out. He suddenly found this quite annoying. He was tempted to shatter their complacent assumption by saying loudly, "Look, girls, this was her idea." But that wouldn't be gentlemanly. And also, it wouldn't answer the retort, "You're a big boy. Then why are you here, if you don't like it?"

For that, he had to admit honestly, he didn't have much answer. Nor could he honestly say that Donna had actually asked him to the dance. Again, it was just sort of an assumption. She had just said brightly, "You'll come by about a quarter to nine, then?" and without really thinking, he had replied, "O.K." And he was signed, sealed and delivered.

This could be said, if any of her very few critics on campus had known about it, to be quite characteristic of Donnamaria Van Dyke, West Park, New York, English major. In Tim Bates's brief but admiring analysis, Donn Van Dyke "is one of those awesome girls who manage to combine beauty, many brains, complete femininity and the most practical executive ability all in one attractive personality. Product of an old Hudson Valley Dutch-Spanish family whose ancestry has been paid romantic tribute in the selection of her name, she combines considerable hardheadedness with a sex appeal composed of sheer good health and good spirits, which has most of the campus male population at her feet and gave her the largest vote ever cast for a vice-presidential candidate. She is virtually without enemies, although the apparently inexhaustible store of energy with which she organizes drives, chairs committees, and supervises charities occasionally provokes good-humored kidding on the campus. Her distinctive appeal was once summed up by Unruh, who remarked that she looked sexy coming toward you and executive going away, so that you didn't realize until after she left that she had been after something all the time—and had usually achieved it."

Franky Miller had warned Wilson cheerfully last year when Willie had begun dating her during the campaign.

"More marriages," Franky said with a grin, "have been based on society's *assumptions* than on any other single thing, old buddy. So watch out!"

"How did you get to be such an expert?" he asked dryly.

"It's just a hunch of mine," Franky said. "Proceed at your own peril."

"It's no peril," he said firmly. "In the first place, I like Donna. And in the second place, I'm certainly not going to marry her."

However, he was beginning to feel that this might be easier said than not done. There was a sort of drift you began to get into as you entered senior year. It was easier to fall into patterns and habits. The field narrowed down. Time began to push you toward the perpetuation of the race. Society's assumptions began to take over. A sort of automatic pilot went on. The organ played in Memorial Church and dozens of graduates bowed to the inexorable will of Mother Nature.

Well, in due course, he fully intended to. But not yet, and not, he found himself insisting to himself more and more often, with Donnamaria Van Dyke.

And yet—he also found himself thinking—why not? She was everything a man could want—pretty, intelligent, active (Lord, how active), public-spirited, good-natured, decent, popular with everyone—loving—lovable—I mean, he found himself asking himself with some exasperation, what more do you want?

Why not just give in to the assumptions and take the easy way out? His parents would be delighted, her parents would be delighted, the house would be delighted, the campus would be delighted, and so, no doubt, would be he and Donna. But was all that enough, for such a fundamental decision? Was it really what he wanted? Was she, to quote a dozen popular songs of the day, the one and only?

Or was he really hoping that he would see his green-gold girl at the dance tonight, find out who she was, and get to know her better?

Here Donna came now, tripping down the stairs, bright-eyed, rosy-cheeked, exuding good health, good nature and, he thought dryly, all those other good things. Before he knew it she had kissed him lightly on the cheek, linked her arm in his and was steering him gently but firmly toward the door. Before he knew it they were outside walking briskly along in the crisp autumn night.

"Well!" he said with some amusement in his voice. "You're a masterful one! How are your classes shaping up?"

She smiled brightly. "Not too badly. I decided to cut back the units a bit this quarter so I could give more time to helping you."

"Oh," he said, rather lamely, "that's nice. I hope you didn't short-change yourself in some way, though. I mean, we don't have *that* big a job to do."

"If we do it right," she said firmly, "we do! And I intend to do it right!"

"So do I," he said, "but I don't really think we have to knock ourselves out for the student body. I mean, I intend to do a good job—I'm not going to sit around and slough things off—I plan on being really involved in a lot of things. But I don't think the University is going to collapse if we aren't frantic about it."

She stopped abruptly and stared at him, wide-eyed.

"Am I frantic?" she asked, sounding genuinely hurt.

"Oh, no!" he said quickly, thinking: *Oh, Lord, now I've done it.* "No, no, no! You're about the best and most public-spirited citizen we have around here. No kidding. You really make this campus function. You're the one who ought to be president."

"That would be the day!" she said, amused at the thought and apparently mollified somewhat as they resumed walking. But she still sounded upset as she added, "I hope I'm not 'frantic.' It's just my nature to be involved in things, I guess. I just want to do them *right*. And I do like to help people." She looked very earnest. "I really do."

"I know you do," he said, tucking her hand more firmly under his arm. "I'm sorry I said that. I didn't mean to sound critical. It's a wonderful trait to have. The way you participate in things is just great, and believe me, everybody on campus appreciates it. Where would we *be* without Donn Van Dyke?"

She laughed, sounding more like herself, to his relief.

"Nine more months," she pointed out, "and the campus will have to get along without both of us. Do you think it possibly can?"

"I expect it will manage," he said as they began to be overtaken by others walking quickly along. "But," he added ruefully, "it isn't really a happy thought, is it?"

"No," she agreed, suddenly sobered, clinging more tightly to his arm. "Oh, Willie! What is going to happen to the world?"

"I don't know," he said gravely. "We just have to hope that whatever it is passes us by, I guess."

"But if it doesn't?"

"Then we have to meet it as best we can, and hope we come through all right."

"It scares me."

He sighed.

"Me, too . . . all of us, I guess. But," he said firmly, "we've got to keep hoping. There isn't a lot we can do about it out here, so—"

"That's right," she agreed, forcing herself to become determinedly cheerful again. "So let's go to the dance!"

"Right!" he exclaimed, slipping her hand into his and breaking into a half-run as they neared the brightly lighted doorway of the women's gym and the jostling, laughing crowd that was working its way in.

Immediately he saw the one he was looking for, again dressed in something green flecked with gold. She was with some guy he didn't know, but knew immediately he didn't like.

He thought she saw him, but her glance was so fleeting he couldn't be sure.

Inside, balloons, banners, streamers and confetti had transformed the room into a scene rather far from the austere room in which sweating young women exercised during the week. B. J. Letterman and Smith Carriger had been in charge of the volunteer decorating committee and the job had been done with the speed, efficiency and taste characteristic of them. Between four and six P.M. the gym had been transformed into a local version of the Paradise Ballroom. Promptly at nine its excited and happy occupants began to swing, sway and jitterbug to the smoothly pulsating rhythm of "Hack's Hacks."

Looking out across the floor jammed with wall-to-wall students, the leader of this small but highly popular aggregation told himself that this was going to be a good night. Registration was over, classes were settling in, the school year with all its renewed hopes and tantalizing promises was under way. It was good to be young and alive and enjoying life. At least, he hoped most of them were enjoying life.

He was playing the piano, and that was enjoyment, and more than enjoyment, for him.

Opening, as he always did, with "Stardust," Hack, as always, made of its opening bar a statement commanding instant attention:

And now the purple dusk of twilight time—rather like the opening notes of Beethoven's Fifth in his slow, deliberate, powerful rendition—

Steals across the meadows of my heart—slipping gently, attention now secured, into a much softer, more subtle, more insinuating line—

At the end he had them standing quite still, riveted and enrapt by the power of the music and the powerful personality behind it.

The usual great burst of applause, cheers, shouts of approval. And so, with scarcely a two-second break, into "Come On, Come On, Get Happy!"—and the dance was on.

Studying the crowd as its members danced with varying degrees of skill, enthusiasm and competence, Hack saw that the house was well represented.

Shortly before the end of the first set, he turned command over to his drummer, a fast-living, hard-drinking (but damned good-drumming) senior from the Deke house, and made his way across the floor to one of the tables along the wall. There he sank into a seat beside the gracious, dark-haired, obviously intelligent girl who had been patiently waiting for him, took her hand and said, "Well, hi, lady. How are you?"

"I'm fine," Fran Magruder said with a smile. "And you?"

"Good," he said. "It's going well."

"Oh, very," she said. "It always does."

He shrugged.

"Nyah," he said, making a face. "Sometimes."

"Always," she said. "And you know it. So stop being modest."

"Somebody has to be," he said with a smile. "I don't expect it from my legal eagle here."

"Why, Hack Haggerty!" she protested, half amused, half indignant. "You know perfectly well I'm modest. You've never heard me utter a boastful word in your life!"

"No, that's true," he conceded, squeezing her hand affectionately. "I'm just being my usual ornery self. What are you drinking, lemonade?"

"It's punch," she said. "Basically gingerale, I think."

"My God!" he said. "Does the dean of women know about this? The campus is going to hell in a handbasket." At this, provoking as it did the thought of the dumpy, motherly-looking, ever-hovering, old-fashioned little lady who presided over the lives of "my girls" with a whim more iron than Queen Victoria's, they both laughed.

"Don't tell her," Fran said. "She'll cancel all our two o'clock passes for the next three months."

"Might be a good thing," he remarked, taking a swallow from her paper cup. "Stop all this dissipated helling around that's wearing you to a frazzle."

"Me?" she said. "Law is what's wearing me to a frazzle, buster, as you know very well."

"You don't *have* to go into law," he said, as he had often said before, and she made the same answer she often had before.

"Sure I do. I love it. I love it, and there are things I want to do in it. Anyway," she added, "it's too late now, I'm committed. So why reopen the subject? And at a time and place like this?"

"I thought I'd give it another try."

"Oh?" she said with a wry smile. "Why don't *you* give up music?"

He gave her a long look, eyes half closed.

"Are you kidding?"

"Sure," she said. "Are you?"

He gave her a smile equally wry.

"I guess I'd better be. Want to dance a quick one before I have to go back?"

"With pleasure," she said, and stood up, tall, graceful—gracious. It was the key word for Fran Magruder. Along, he thought with a profound pride that she belonged to him, with words like intelligent, idealistic, determined, capable, decent and kind.

She'd have to be kind, he thought as they swung easily into the rhythm, to put up with a prickly bastard like me.

Noting the perfect blend of their bodies and the ease of their being together as they danced past him in the midst of the floor, Tim Bates thought with satisfaction that his own observations, and a long talk with Hack late one night last spring, had enabled him to capture Francine Helen Magruder, Houston, Texas, pre-legal, very well. Everybody was agreed that Fran "is a Real Brain and it was as one Real Brain recognizing another that she first became attracted to Hack Haggerty. It did not take long after their initial meeting in Dr. Stafford's Shakespeare and Marlowe class before she realized that there might be much more to it than that. The same conviction simultaneously struck Haggerty. Since then they have been inseparable. She is possessed of a wry sense of humor that matches his; her mind seems to meet his on every level. The only thing that could possibly be a problem, she often reflects, is Haggerty's devotion to his music; because even though he is majoring in economics and maintains doggedly that he's going to go into his father's stockbrokerage 'because, hell, music's fun but I've got to make a living,' Fran isn't convinced—any more than he is, really. She knows where his heart lies and she knows him well enough to know that it would be broken if he really couldn't pursue the life that his great talent impels him toward. Yet she, too, knows that there is a practical side: if they are to marry, have an established home, raise a family, there has got to be a stable basis, not, it seems to her, the sometimes uncertain chances of a musical career, brilliant though it may be. The only thing they ever really quarrel about is this. She reflects, with an almost wistful determination, that they will work it out somehow, though it may not always be easy."

Watching him proudly as he made his way back to the bandstand after handing her over to Buff Richardson, who had stepped into their path with a grin and an easy "May I?" she was more than ever determined that they would.

"The thing is," Franky Miller was saying to Katie Sullivan as Hack gave them a grin and a nod on his way back to the piano, "this is really too much like exercise."

He was puffing a bit, sweating a bit, and looked genuinely relieved when the combo played one more set and then took a break, during which Hack returned to Fran and at various tables around the room other members of the house came to rest temporarily.

"A little exercise," Katie said severely, "is good for you."

She was wearing a pert little dress, a pert little cap, and looked, as always, her pert little self. Cute as a button, people said, and so she was. Smart, too, as Franky often told her approvingly. Which she responded was a good thing, as he probably wouldn't hang around otherwise. He said, "Oh, I don't know." But she did.

"A *little* exercise, yes," he said now, "but not galloping all over the floor all night. I've probably dropped ten pounds if I've dropped an ounce."

"You probably haven't dropped an ounce," she said with a giggle, "let alone ten pounds. Why don't you just stop eating?"

"And give up life's principal pleasure?" he demanded. "Woman, you're crazy!"

"I thought I was your principal pleasure," she remarked, waving to Buff and Tim as they looked around for a table. They saw her and started over.

"You are," he said. "I was hyperbolizing. You're first. Food comes next. Doing nothing comes third."

"A sensible list, I'd say," she remarked. "So are we just going to sit out all the rest of the dances?"

He uttered a martyred sigh.

"Oh, no. I'll manage a few more. If I don't," he added as the brethren sat down beside them, "these kindly old gentlemen will oblige, I'm sure."

"I'm kindly," Buff said with his lazy I-love-everybody smile. "I don't know about this one, though. I suspect he may bite sometimes."

"That comes from carrying the world on his shoulders," Franky said. "How is it tonight, Timmy? Pretty grim and getting grimmer?"

"Getting grimmer," Bates said, looking grim himself. "When I left the Shack the late wires were saying that Great Britain and France are mobilizing, Italy's partially mobilizing, and of course Germany is mobilized already. I don't know what the hell is going to happen."

"Eat, drink and be merry," Franky suggested wryly, "for tomorrow we die."

"Oh, I hope not!" Katie said with a shiver. "Not us."

"Well, no," Franky agreed, more soberly, "I don't think so. We'll stay out—even if people like Tim here want us to get in."

"That's not quite fair," Tim said. "I just don't see how we can stay out, that's all—ultimately. So maybe we ought to get in early rather than wait until we get dragged in at some later time without being really prepared for it."

"We're prepared right now?" Franky inquired.

"I know," Tim said stubbornly, "but it would be better to let everybody know where we stand, I think. That might make the bastard stop before he does even more damage."

"That's what Roosevelt thinks," Franky said, "except he hasn't got the guts to tell us."

"He's got a problem," Tim said. "The country doesn't want to go, that's all there is to it."

"Listen!" Franky said, leaning forward, completely serious, usual jesting forgotten for the moment. "I have a lot of faith in the American people, myself. I think if F.D.R. laid it on the line, they'd follow him. There'd be some noisy ones who wouldn't, but the majority would. Why doesn't he trust us?"

"He can't do that," Buff said with a grin. "He has a third-term election to win."

"He hasn't said he's running," Tim said. Buff snorted.

"I'm not sitting here, either. But don't try to use my chair, please."

"He obviously isn't going to do what you want, Franky," Katie said, "so let's don't get into an argument here. This is a fun night!" She looked about at them brightly. "I mean, isn't it?!"

"You're cute," Franky said, giving her hand a squeeze.

"I know," she said. "But everybody's getting so *tensed up* these days. It spoils things."

"These are tense times," Tim said, stating something he believed but sounding a little more pretentious than he meant to.

"I heard that!" North McAllister said as he and B. J. Letterman, each precariously carrying three full paper cups, approached the table. "Have a drink of this wild stuff, you guys, and relax. You too, Timmy."

"Can't," Tim said with a smile, getting up and borrowing two empty chairs from an adjoining table. "Can't, can't, can't. It's too serious."

"You'd better, O sagacious scribe," North told him as they sat down, "or you'll pop. And where would our flatulent local organ of public opinion be then? Leaderless, lost, adrift, bereft. No, no, I say, no, no!"

"Is this guy all right?" Buff asked B.J. She smiled.

"He *is* a little keyed-up this evening, but probably no more than usual. Isn't this a nice dance? Are you folks enjoying it?"

"Immensely," Buff said. "I've met at least three smashing freshmen women already. This seems to be my night for freshmen."

"Cradle-robber," North told him. Buff gave his amiable grin.

"Anywhere I can find it, Dad," he said. "Anywhere I can find it. I see our gallant leader, Brother Wilson, is doing his duty by Miss Van Dyke. Trust Willie to perform as we all expect him to. I wonder if his heart is in it."

"Of course it is!" Katie and B.J. said simultaneously, and everyone laughed.

Franky said, "You girls do stick together, I've always said it. Woe to the man who fails to conform!"

"I hope we aren't *that* bad!" B.J. protested. North chuckled.

"She keeps *me* on a tight rein," he remarked. She hit him lightly on the arm.

"I do *not!*" she said. "I don't know where you are half the time. How could I possibly keep you on a tight rein?"

"Well," he conceded. "Tight enough."

"I really *don't* know where he is half the time," she said to Katie. "He can be very mysterious sometimes."

"Oh, come *on*," North said, sounding for a second just a little edgy, but quickly changing it. "I'm not mysterious at all. Gadzooks! Ask anybody, 'Have you seen North?' 'Oh, yes, he's in the lab.' Or, 'Oh, yes, he's at the Libe right now.' Or, 'Have you thought of calling the house? He's usually right there studying.' "

"Not always," she said in a tone that for a second made the others feel uncomfortable.

"Anyway," Franky said quickly, "he's here right now. And we *do* know he studies a lot at the house. Do you want us to keep a time clock on him?"

"No," she said, laughing and apparently deciding to let it drop. "Talk about girls sticking together! I think you fellows would cover for each other if one of you—if—"

"Oh, no!" North cried with exaggerated drama. "Dearest Lady of Shalott or some other frabjous place, not *that!*"

"Men!" Katie said. "We can't win, B.J. Might as well give up."

"Any—*way*," North said, finishing his cup of punch, standing up and holding his hand out to B.J., who obediently took it and stood up too. "I think we ought to table-hop a little more before the maestro gets us back on the floor. Let's go see Moose and Welcome. They're always good for a barrelful of laughs."

"Take care, you guys," she said. "See you later."

"I'm glad *you're* not the suspicious type," Franky said to Katie as they watched them cross the floor to the table where Moose and Suzy were talking to Randy Carrero and Marc Taylor. "It would drive me mad." He mimicked North's exaggerated delivery. "Mad, mad, *mad!*"

"She's got a problem, evidently," Buff remarked. "But I'm damned if I know what it is."

"Me either," Franky said, genuinely puzzled. "I thought they were getting along just great."

"Probably just a passing thing," Buff said.

Tim took a thoughtful swallow from his cup.

"I'm sure of it," he said, but he wasn't at all, really. The really solid ones, he thought, were Franky and Katie. B.J. and North, he felt, had always been on slightly slippery ground. If the one relationship that was solid was due largely to the shrewd and sunny personality of the girl involved, was the other due to some tension in B.J.'s character? He hadn't noticed it. They both seemed lovely girls to him. He only wished he would be so lucky one of these days.

Katie, he had written—Mary Katherine Sullivan from Medford, Oregon, graphic arts major—"is known generally as 'that little Irish cutie of Miller's.' She has been going steadily with that gentleman for three years, and something in her seems to complement exactly the spirit of easygoing eccentricity in him. She understands Miller as instinctively as he understands her. One of the rare couples of which it is said, with some envy, 'they were meant for each other.' 'Sullivan and Miller are always doing some damned thing' is a stock comment around the house. So they are, and always in perfect agreement.

"Katie has considerable talent for painting, and a great subsurface reservoir of ambition and determination to do something with it. This extends to Miller and his future, too. When he grins and tells her, 'Hell, you might as well know now that you'll be marrying a broken-down good-for-nothing no'count who will never do nothin' nohow,' she just laughs and agrees, knowing perfectly well that she will take care of that when the time comes. This one quality alone is enough to make Miller, who knows his own shortcomings, humbly grateful to her. As for her interests aside from him and her painting, she is president of her house and secretary of Pan-Hellenic. These two have a great deal of fun together and will probably still be having it in their seventies."

And of B.J., Tim had written with equal admiration, for B.J., even more than Katie, he considered a quite remarkable citizen:

"Betty June Letterman from Salt Lake City, history major, is one of those activity girls who are already set in college upon a future course of A.A.U.W., women's clubs, charity drives, P.T.A., school board, political fund raisers, and whatever else comes to hand, overcoming all obstacles fate and man can put in their paths. Before she knows it she will be the mother of four and the first name that comes to mind every time there is something that needs to be done in her community. She and Donna Van Dyke are a pair; in fact, they ran against each other last June for vice-president of the student body. Despite this, they are the closest of friends and frequently confer on what needs to be done to improve campus life in general and their own immediate circle of friends in particular.

" 'Between the two of them,' Franky remarks, 'they take care of everything that Willie and God don't have time to.' Along with it, both have excellent grades, B.J.'s especially brilliant. Lattimer's fraternity brothers think he ought to marry her and breed a flock of little geniuses—'You'd give a whole new meaning to the term I.Q.,' Franky says. 'Impossibly Quaint,' Unruh suggests. 'Incwedibly Qwever,' Wilson offers, and ducks.

"But that perfect union of I.Q.'s is not to be. B.J. has broached the possibility of marriage tentatively on a few occasions to North, but so far has detected resistance. But she does like him, and he does seem to like her, and so she continues to hope, somewhat nervously, that it will come about."

Across the room at Wilson's table his would-be successor wondered nervously what Willie was thinking as he sat, rather absentmindedly Bob Godwin thought, surveying the room while Donn Van Dyke rattled on happily beside him. Bob wondered if Willie was thinking about him. Bob always wondered if anybody in his vicinity was thinking about him. In his outwardly bright and go-getter way Bob was as self-conscious as Marc Taylor, though for a different reason. Bob was self-conscious because he wanted to *go places* and *do things*, as his fellow junior Renny Suratt put it with sarcastic emphasis. He felt that everybody must be studying him all the time, reaching conclusions and making up minds against the day toward the end of the school year when Bob, he fervently and anxiously hoped, would run for the office that Wilson now held with such nonchalant aplomb.

God, if he could only have one-half of Willie's inner certainties!

But then, he thought enviously, all Willie's battles were won. He didn't have anything more to worry about.

To which Willie, had this been articulated, would probably have responded, "That's what *you* think." He was debating at the moment how in the world he could gracefully and unnoticed cross the hundred feet that separated them and speak to the girl of whose presence he was so overwhelmingly and, yes, annoyingly conscious. He didn't want to be conscious of her, he didn't want to be so fascinated that he could barely maintain the air of disinterest he knew he must maintain when his eyes inevitably strayed in her direction. He was like some—some *school* kid, he thought with magnificent self-disgust. Things like that simply didn't happen to Richard Emmett Wilson anymore. He was too mature and grown-up for it. He was twenty-one years old, for God's sake.

Nonetheless, it did seem to be happening. In and out and through and around it, he was vaguely aware that Donna was bubbling on in her happily enthusiastic way about what the two of *them* were going to do during the year, the great plans *they* had for the year's activities, the unity with which *they* were approaching the jobs entrusted to *them* by the student body. He realized with half an ear that she was wrapping them in a cocoon of intimate exclusiveness. He knew he ought to at least make a mild attempt to break out of it, particularly since Lattimer and Kay Ellsworth and Guy Unruh and Maggie Johnson had joined them and were listening with amiable interest to this discourse. They were fond of Donna, as everyone was, and used to her enthusiasm; it was obvious that they also rather enjoyed Willie's not quite concealed restiveness as she painted her typically exuberant word-picture of their unity of purpose and singleness of mind. They had also been secretly amused by the way Godwin had eased himself into their close-knit circle.

The whole thing, in fact, prompted Latt at one point to wink at Guy, whose lips twitched in the start of a carefully suppressed smile as he winked back. It was—so *school*, somehow. It made them know they were back on campus. It was fun.

"Bob," Willie said, turning on Godwin so abruptly he visibly jumped. "How are things going?"

Bob gave him his characteristically bright and concentrated look.

"Oh, fine!" he said enthusiastically. "Really *fine*! I think it's going to be a great year, don't you?"

"Sure do," Wilson said. "I just hope you're getting started right, that's all. I mean, we all hope you are."

"Oh, yes," Bob said. "I *really* think I am."

"Everything pretty well lined up?" Unruh inquired, not without some gentle malice: poor God tried *so* hard.

"I'm doing my best," Bob said. "I have quite a bit of work left to do in the halls, though. I've got to talk to Ari Katanian just as soon as I can arrange it."

"He's coming up to the house for dinner sometime next week," Wilson offered. "Maybe that would be a good time."

"Say!" Bob exclaimed with an eager smile. "That *would* be great! Thank you, Willie. I really appreciate it!"

"I can't promise he'll do anything for you," Wilson said, "but he does have a lot of clout in the halls. He can swing a lot of votes if he's in your corner."

"I *know*," Bob said. "Could you—" He hesitated. "Could you say something—to him—for me?"

"I might," Willie said thoughtfully. "I might . . . but—" He almost stopped the teasing, poor Bob's face fell so instantaneously at his seeming hesitation. "But Ari's his own man, you know. Guy and I roomed with him in freshman dorm, and Latt was right across the hall, and we're all close, but I don't know whether he'd listen to any of us or not. Let me think about it, O.K.? I'll have to approach him pretty carefully . . . if I do."

"Well," Bob said with an awkward little laugh. "Anything you can do, Willie, I'd sure appreciate it. You know that."

"He'll talk to him," Lattimer said with a stop-pulling-wings-off-butterflies glance at Willie. "It's the least he can do for a fraternity brother. Right, Willie?"

"Well—" Wilson said, and then decided he had teased poor Bob long enough; but God was *so* intense. "Probably. Sure. I'll say something to him, Bob, don't worry. But you're the one who's going to have to do the real convincing. Ari's the kind who has to make up his own mind on things."

"Oh, I'll work on him!" Bob promised with a smile so willing it almost hurt. "I'll really work on him. You'll see!"

"Good luck," Unruh said more kindly. "He'll be a real assist if you get him."

"I'll sure try!" Bob promised again. He stood up as his date returned from the restroom and Ari and the group resumed playing. "See you guys later."

"You bet," Wilson said. "Glad you stopped by."

"You shouldn't tease him so," Donn said with a chuckle. "He wants it so badly. And so did you."

"Was I ever that obvious?" Wilson demanded. "I don't believe it."

"There was a sort of inner fire," Latt said. "Just beneath the surface."

"Yes," Guy agreed. "Volcanic forces. We all knew you'd kill to get it."

"That's always been the way with Willie," Latt observed. "You can always tell when he really wants something."

"Who *is* that at the table over there, anyway?" Unruh inquired casually, and before he could stop himself Willie had swung around to look; and then, trying to cover, asked innocently, "Where?" Fortunately familiar figures were at the table adjoining theirs and he was able to add quickly, "That's Carriger and his date. And Billy and Janie. You aren't getting blind, are you, Guy?"

"No, I meant the other table," Guy said in the same innocent way, which indicated that despite his best efforts Willie's careful casualness had been noted by those who knew him best. "Who's the babe? She looks nice."

"Yes," Latt agreed, as the girls gave her a quick appraising glance. "Worth meeting, don't you think, Willie?"

"I don't know," he said with a shrug, turning back. "She might be. I don't know who she is."

"I do," Kay Ellsworth said unexpectedly. "Her name is Marian Emerson and she's a junior transfer from Mills College. She sits beside me in one of my English classes. She's very nice."

Oh, great, Willie thought. *Now it really will be in the family.*

"Pretty girl," he remarked in an offhand way that he hoped would damp down further discussion.

"Worth meeting, wouldn't you say?" Lattimer repeated blandly.

"I suppose we will sooner or later," he said indifferently, trying in vain to reach Latt's foot under the table and give him a good kick. "How about a dance, Maggie?"

"Why, thanks," Maggie Johnson said as Hack swung the group into "I've Got You Under My Skin." "I'd love to."

"Excuse us," Willie said firmly, ignoring Guys' wink and Latt's amused look. "Get moving, you guys. Don't let these lovely ladies just sit there."

"This is always such a nice affair," Maggie remarked in a voice as comfortable as her plump little person, as they all swung out into the now slowly moving crowd. The dance was getting older, the more hectic early stages were over, things were getting dreamier. He and Maggie negotiated the floor with pleasant ease and talked of this and that. He found himself thinking that Guy was very fortunate and very wise to be concentrating more and more upon this calm, steady little character. She was what Guy needed. As for himself . . . he found he was following Marian with his eyes as she and her date danced near and then away. He was positive she must be aware of him. How could she not be, when he was so aware of her?

"I think they go so well together, don't you?" Maggie said, and just in time he realized that she was talking about Latt and Kay Ellsworth, who were dancing nearby.

"Yes, they do," he agreed. "I think they're lucky to have each other. I think Guy is lucky to have you."

"Well, I don't know about that," she said, sounding pleased. "I think he does need somebody to help him in his medical career. He needs somebody to sort of—sort of—"

"Steady him down?" he suggested, thinking: I didn't know you'd noticed, little Maggie. You're shrewder than I thought. "Yes, I think he does. And you're just right for him."

"You're too nice," she said, blushing slightly. "And what about you and Donna?"

"She's a great girl," he said seriously.

"That isn't exactly my question," she said with a little smile.

He laughed in the noncommittal way he had learned to use in about the second year of high school: a laugh could successfully obfuscate the answer to almost anything; almost anything, you could hide behind a laugh.

"Oh, she's great," he repeated. "We're going to have a good year together."

"And afterward?"she pressed, and again he gave the seemingly candid, smoothly uninformative laugh.

"Time will tell, Maggie," he said. "Time will tell."

A little later, dancing with Kay Ellsworth, he found himself subjected to much the same kind of gentle but persistent feminine cross-examination. That was the trouble with old friends and their girls, he thought, amused but a little annoyed too: they felt they had a license to pry. He could fend off the girls all right, but the old friends knew him too well. There had been a moment when they were slyly calling attention to his green-gold girl—using the name "Marian" seemed a little awkward to him, but no doubt it would soon come easy—when he could cheerfully have shot Unruh and Lattimer. Fortunately the girls hadn't really caught on; they were all too direct and uncomplicated in their approach to things. Somebody like Fran Magruder, for instance, would have gotten it instantly. And as for Suzy Waggoner, if she'd been at their table, she would have hooted with happily raucous relish and destroyed all his carefully constructed pretense of disinterest.

He decided to go on the offensive when Kay began probing, as Maggie had, about his future plans with Donna.

"I really couldn't say at the moment," he said blandly. "The thing that interests me is, when is Latt going to make an honest woman of *you?*"

"I *am* an honest woman," Kay said, her always pleasantly cordial expression widening into a laugh. "Maybe that's the trouble. The poor boy doesn't have anywhere to go."

"Does he want to?" Wilson asked, deciding that two could play at the prying game.

"We have a good friendship," Kay said. "A *very* good friendship. I think it's going to be all right." For a second she looked a little forlorn. "I hope so, anyway."

"So do I," he said seriously, regretting the impulse to probe. "I know he cares for you a very great deal."

"He does?" she asked. "Sometimes I wonder, Willie. We don't really date a great deal—I mean something like this. We eat at the Cellar quite often, and study together a good deal, and often chat when we run into each other on the Quad. But as for being really *serious*, in the way that you and Donna are serious—"

"Wait a minute," he interrupted.

"Well, all right," she said with a smile, "you're not. But anyway, as for being really *serious*, I just don't know about Latt. I think he's afraid maybe he doesn't—measure up, somehow—or won't have the money—or something . . . I don't know." She sighed. "Here he is, the brightest guy in school—"

"And nice to boot," he interjected with a smile.

"Nice to boot," she agreed. "*I'm* the one who's not worthy."

"Listen," he said, as the concluding note of "That Old Feeling" indicated the end of the set, "you're worthy of anybody, Kay, and don't you ever say you're not. Or feel you're not. He's damned lucky to have you, and you can tell him I said so. *I'll* tell him I said so. I *have* told him, dozens of times. I'll have to tell him to get off the dime and get moving. Time's a-wastin'. Right?"

"Well," she said with a rueful little smile, "it's moving on, anyway."

Two of the luckiest guys, he thought, as they returned to the table to find Guy and Donn, happily flushed, and Maggie and Latt, dignified and un-winded, just arrived.

Rejoining Franky Miller and Katie Sullivan after a fast round with another of the timid but cute little freshmen girls who seemed to be inundating the place, Bates glanced over and told himself somewhat ruefully that all three were the luckiest guys. Not having been present for the teasing about Wilson's mysterious unknown, he adhered to the general assumption that Willie and Donna were a marriage made in heaven. Like everyone else, he expected that it would occur at graduation. The others too, he felt, were all set except for walking down the aisle in Memorial Church. They were three nice girls and he was fond of them all, even though they didn't have quite the same high rating on campus as Donn and B.J., who always came first in everyone's mind when in a congratulatory mood about the generally high quality of women at the University.

Maggie Johnson and Kay Ellsworth were quieter, but to them too he paid respectful tribute in his notes—Marguerite Johnson from Trenton, New Jersey, romance languages major, "at first blush seems an unlikely girl for Unruh to end up with, but those who know them both are not surprised. Maggie is, as Donn Van Dyke says, 'a very careful girl'; and a very careful girl, his fraternity brothers agree, is just what Unruh needs. 'Not that I ever thought he'd have sense enough to know that,' Wilson remarks, 'but once again, he's fooled me.' This does not mean that Unruh does not seek femi-nine companionship where he can, but he is reasonably faithful to Maggie. They date quite frequently; the number of times is increasing as his senior year moves on. He is no fool and realizes that Maggie is genuinely in love with him; little by little he is beginning to realize he probably is with her, too. Her 'careful' qualities, the intense care and attention with which she looks after him, worries about him, tries to make sure that he feels he has support and is happy in his studies and his plans for the future, indicate to him that she will undoubtedly be a very good wife. 'A little overprotective,' as he remarks thoughtfully to Willie, 'but she isn't domineering about it.' 'Not yet,' Suratt remarks to Smith Carriger, 'but wait until she has him hooked for a while.'

"This may or may not prove in the long run to be true; at the moment the jury is still out. Unruh is getting ready to gamble on it, although they both know that with medical school they have a long and grinding row ahead. She is quite prepared, as she has told him, to go to work to support them both if necessary. Renny, who does not approve of very many women, considers her 'sticky sweet,' but underneath there is a firm determination that promises well for her as a doctor's wife. What it promises for Unruh's continued existence as a moderately freewheeling young soul, and the possibility that he may ultimately be a very dominated husband, is off there in the future where he doesn't worry about it very much. Maggie has her own program and with her characteristic quiet determination intends to proceed with it. For the time being her steady support and approval are coming to mean more and more to Clyde Gaius Unruh."

The relationship between Kay and Lattimer, Tim recognized, was a little more complex. He and Latt had been studying late one night and had knocked off about eleven-thirty to go down to the kitchen and put together a couple of sandwiches. Somehow this had led into a discussion of women—most things, Tim thought wryly, eventually seemed to lead into a discussion of women, no matter how remote the original topic of the talk might have been. Inevitably Kay had rapidly become the focus of it. Latt had unburdened himself quite a lot, which made Tim feel flattered because Latt usually didn't confide much in any of his fraternity brothers except for Wilson and Unruh. Based on that, Tim thought he had a reasonably good handle on the Lattimer-Ellsworth situation.

He described Katherine Ellsworth from Seattle, Washington, education major, as "a tall, dignified, bright and attractive girl who possesses a quiet good humor and cordiality toward the world that endears her to Lattimer.

"He is not quite ready to think about marriage yet, because aside from brains he sometimes wonders what else he has to offer her—just the chance to be the wife of a college professor somewhere, maybe Harvard, maybe the University, specializing in the American frontier and its reflection in the present-day West. Kay seems perfectly adaptable, professes no hesitations about the academic life when he mentions the possibility, but he feels unworthy of her apparent unquestioning compliance and develops feelings of inferiority he feels toward no one else. She can't understand this and it hurts her, but she remains loyal, gentle, pleasant, supportive, even though he goes for days at a time without seeing her except for an occasional Coke after class at the Cellar. Even Latt, most stable and well-grounded of personalities, has his Achilles' heel, a feeling of guilt and uncertainty that he can't possibly live up to her unflinching optimistic faith in him.

"Kay keeps busy, goes out for a lot of campus activities, keeps her grade average up to a steady B-plus, and is just what Latt ought to have, everybody agrees. He just won't permit himself to think that she might not wait for him."

Nor could he imagine it either, Tim thought now, watching them laugh together as they got up for another dance, because it just wouldn't happen. They might have a few rough passages, but she'd be there for him. Tim had a great faith in the determination of most of the women on campus. It was a formidable thing, really. He just wished wistfully that he could get one of them to focus it on him.

The music came gracefully to an end, the dancers began to leave the floor, Hack ran though his usual concluding arpeggio to signify intermission. Then he segued the combo into a fanfare. There was a swift end to chatter, everyone turned and looked, surprised, at the bandstand. A tall, dignified, completely unexpected figure had appeared quietly upon it, accompanied by his spare, gray-haired, keen-eyed wife. Not even the seniors could remember a time when the president had come to a Reg Dance. Or any dance, for that matter; as Franky murmured to Katie, "He just ain't the dancin' type."

"Fellow students," Hack said into the microphone, "we're honored to have with us the president of the University, Dr. Chalmers."

The president took the mike and looked out upon them with a shyly pleased expression. The applause died down into a hushed and respectful silence.

"Thank you, Hack," he said, "and thank you, ladies and gentlemen. . . . As you know, I will address you more formally Friday afternoon for the first general assembly of the academic year, but tonight Mrs. Chalmers and I were coming home from a dinner with the trustees in the City and on a sudden impulse we thought we'd swing by and give you an informal hello." He paused and then added with a twinkle, "As many of you know, I am not one given to much impulse. But sometimes dinner with the trustees can produce strange effects!"

At this humorous irreverence from so august a source, delighted laughter and even a rebel yell from Jeff Barnett, quickly suppressed and causing even more laughter, filled the room.

"Thank you, Mr. Barnett," the president said with a chuckle, and there was another burst of laughter and applause during which Unruh said admiringly to Wilson, "By God, he knows *everybody*," and Wilson responded, "Not a sparrow shall fall—"

"Tomorrow I shall discuss the challenges that will meet you here at the University," Dr. Chalmers said. "Tonight I thought I would mention, very briefly, the challenges that are meeting everyone in the broader world." He paused. They were suddenly very quiet. Nobody stirred. "I debated as I came in here whether this was the time and the place; but perhaps it is. Perhaps the contrast between this always pleasant occasion and the elements outside which may ultimately threaten all that it represents to you and to the

University, makes this a particularly significant, and perhaps a particularly suitable, time and place in which to speak.

"Mrs. Chalmers and I were listening to the radio as we drove down Palm Drive. Things are very serious tonight in Europe." The room became more quiet, if possible. "As you all know, the Chancellor of Germany is threatening to plunge Europe into war if he is not given the Sudetenland in Czechoslovakia. In the past five years he has rearmed Germany, retaken the Rhineland, and invaded and conquered Austria, and now stands poised to seize major portions of the Continent's sturdiest and most independent democracy. Against him are arrayed the might of the British Empire, the strength of France, the hearts and spirits and determination of much of the western world. The question is, will they be enough to make him halt or will he continue on his way, risking possible major war in Europe and perhaps, in time, its extension to many other areas, with consequences we cannot now foresee?

"Will it come, in time, even to this remote and pleasant world which we have here, this lovely world of youth and striving and hopefulness which we know as the University?

"Ladies and gentlemen," he said gravely as they sat, utterly stilled, uneasy and spellbound, "no one at this moment knows the answer. All we know is that sometime in the next few days, possibly the next few hours, the answer will have to be given. Let us hope and pray that it is an answer of peace. Let us hold constantly in our hearts, as we go about the daily round of classes—the march of activities and athletic events, all the things that compose the busy and happy life of the campus—the hope and prayer that somehow sanity may prevail so that Europe, and perhaps many other areas, may be spared the devastations of another war.

"And let us live our lives here to the fullest, getting the most we can from our studies, being kind and decent and helpful to one another, doing our best to so live that, no matter what comes, we shall be equipped with the inner strength and certainty to meet it."

He paused and there was not a sound save for a few tense breaths here and there and, at Tim Bates' and Bill Nagatani's tables, the rapid scratching of pens on paper as they raced to take down, in Bates' broad generous scrawl and Bill's rapid shorthand, these stunning and powerfully moving words of a man who rarely spoke directly from the heart but obviously was now.

"I must apologize, perhaps," Dr. Chalmers concluded quietly, "for using so carefree an occasion for so somber a message. But our hearts are full, as I know yours are, too. The future rises dim and indiscernible before us. But I believe in the University family. I hope you do, too. I think we can take whatever comes. Have a good year. God bless you all."

And with a suddenly shy little bow and wave, he took Mrs. Chalmers' arm and they made their way off the bandstand and out of the room, leaving

behind a growing roar of voices as everyone began to talk at once, and across
the excited room Bates gestured to Bill Nagatani and they jumped up and
raced to the *Daily* Shack to stop the presses and remake the front page of
tomorrow morning's paper.

Wilson looked at Latt and Unruh.

They looked at him.

All he could say was: "Wow!"

And *"Wow!"* was all they could find to respond.

After that, as Suratt remarked to Carriger, who happened to be standing
near him as the president spoke, the mood was not exactly hysterically
joyful. But, since they were young and resilient, it did not take long for them
to bring it back to a reasonable approximation of what it had been. Many
were sobered and deeply troubled, but you couldn't go on feeling that way
for long without some kind of break. Reg Dance was supposed to be fun,
after all. It *was* fun, and while they respected Dr. Chalmers and his concerns, which many of them shared, there had to be some lightening of the
load. The future *was* dim and indiscernible, and it very likely *would* be
decided in the next few days or even hours, but meanwhile it was not only
good to relax again after the tensions brought to the surface by his remarks,
it was a psychological necessity.

Hack thought for a split second and then led the combo into a driving
rendition of "Boogie Woogie." The dance was on again.

For the remaining hour, however, it was not quite the carefree occasion
it had been—not that it had been carefree for all of them, even without open
forebodings of war. Some, like Rudy Krohl and Helga Berger, held solemn
discussions between numbers about how unjust it was that Great Britain and
France seemed to want to thwart Hitler's perfectly justified desire to bring
all Germans back together under one Reich. Others, like Duke Offenberg
and Shahna Epstein, murmured tense worries to one another about her
relatives and, perhaps oversensitively but they couldn't help it, about what
they saw as growing anti-Semitism at home. Marc Taylor was ending the
evening twice as depressed as before, because Gil Gulbransen had indeed
spotted an unattached and attractive sophomore woman, swiftly bedazzled
her with his tall blond charm into joining their party, turned her over to
Marc—and Marc, awkward and shy, had unhappily been tongue-tied and
struck out, much to Gil's obvious, though manfully suppressed, impatience.
Randy Carrero also was ending the evening more depressed then before.
His toe was swollen, it hurt, he couldn't dance, he could barely hobble, he
didn't quite dare challenge Gil too openly, and Fluff, flattered by the contest
for her attentions, was, as he had anticipated, even bitchier than usual.

Not that Gil had been obstreperous about it—Randy was still convinced he didn't give a damn, and only wished Fluff could realize what a self-centered lightweight he was—but, as witness her obvious pleasure at being the center of attention, he had been effective.

After the first couple of dances, in which he had whirled her around the floor in great style while she peered around his shoulder from time to time to make sure Randy was watching, he had swung her back to the table with a flourish and practically twirled her into Randy's lap with a cheerful, "Here you go, Randy! Take her away!"

Randy had reached for her but she skillfully wriggled out of his hands. This made him sound extra-grumpy when he growled, "You know I can't dance. I hurt my foot."

"Poor guy!" Gulbransen said, sounding sympathetic but really mocking him, Randy thought. "How did that happen?"

"I stubbed it in the shower," Randy said, giving Marc a warning look. Marc was too busy agonizing about the general lack of attention he was getting from his "date" to even notice.

"Stubbed it?" Gil asked, puzzled. "I didn't notice. How come?"

"I don't know!" Randy snapped. "I just did!"

"What's the matter?" Gil asked in what seemed to Randy an unnecessarily amused tone. "Have a bad class today? Or somebody do something to you, or something? You aren't usually such a grouch. Carrero's the bright light of the campus, isn't he? A real dynamo. You don't sound like it now."

"Gil," he demanded, "do I always have to be on stage? I mean, can't *I* have a down day once in a while, too? Must I always keep everybody in laughs?"

"Come on!" Gulbransen said, apparently making a sincere effort to kid him out of it. "Don't be so serious, pal. I know your foot hurts but that's no excuse for spoiling the party. Relax. We're having a good time—it's a good dance—good company. Isn't that right, Fluff? O.K., Marc?"

"I'm having a *great* time," Fluff said, snuggling up to his arm, which he obligingly put around her shoulders, pulling her close.

"Yeah," Marc said in a rather bemused tone as his "date" suddenly cried, "Oh, I think I see someone I know over there!" jumped up and disappeared. He looked absolutely desolate for a moment. "At least," he said carefully, "I think I am."

"Got to be more aggressive, boy," Gulbransen said in a tone between disappointment and annoyance. "Got to get in there and *pitch*. I'll take you aside some night at the house when we're through studying and really tell you all about it. I mean, it's an art. Isn't it, Randy? Fluff knows!"

"Yeah," Randy said dourly. "She sure does."

This provoked a merry peal of laughter from Fluff, who reached over and hit him coyly on the arm.

"Oh, *you!*" she said. "You're always so *serious*, Randy. Loosen up!"

"That's right," Gulbransen said. He stood up, six feet three of gorgeous golden male, and stretched with obvious satisfaction, not even having to look to know that half the females in the room were watching him. "If you'll excuse me for a few minutes, I think I'll go cut in on North and B.J. She looks a little glum this evening. You two be good while I'm gone, now. And Marc—get in there and cut in on somebody, boy. You have to go after 'em! You can't just sit there."

"I can't?" Marc inquired. "Oh—all right." He stood up uncertainly and took a tentative step toward the churning crowd. He would have turned back except that at that point Gil seized him firmly by the arm and propelled him into the fray.

"Now!" he ordered sternly. "Go to it!"

Marc gave him a wild backward glance, but he did step forward and, after a moment, got up enough courage to tap someone on the shoulder. The fellow gave him an obliging smile, the girl did likewise, and in a moment he was dancing her away, still looking a little like a startled colt, but, Gil noted with an amused smile as he headed toward McAllister and B.J., doing his best. Reluctantly. But doing it.

"Well," Randy said as Fluff moved demurely away to sit in the exact center of her seat. "I guess you're satisfied."

"You rascal, you!" she completed the song tag with a happy giggle. "What am I supposed to be satisfied about?"

"Standing me up tonight."

"Why, Randy Carrero," she exclaimed. "I did no such thing!"

"You did too! After you promised."

She looked very patient and, unhappily for him, very blond and very cute.

"I said *maybe* I would and check with me later. You never did."

"I did, too!" he said hotly. "I called your house at four o'clock this afternoon and you wouldn't come to the phone. I heard you in the background. I know you were there!" He looked even more bitter. "You were laughing. At me, no doubt."

"Well," she said with another little giggle, "you must admit you *are* funny."

"I'm not funny when somebody doesn't keep her word," he said. "I believe in keeping mine and I like people who do the same."

"Well, Mr. Pompous," she said, "then maybe we'd better just forget about it and don't call me again. Because I can't be tied down all the time! Why don't you just go somewhere else and *leave me alone?*"

"Because," he said with a heavy sigh that sounded far older than eighteen, "I don't think I can. I—just—don't—think—I—can."

She sniffed.

"You're just a plain pest, Randy Carrero, and I don't care if you're the campus big shot or not. You're just a bore, to me. Just a plain, jealous, bothersome bore! Why don't you go away! Am I ever tired of *you!*"

"It's mutual," he snapped. "It's damned well mutual!"

"Well, well," Gil Gulbransen said, coming breezily back to reclaim his chair, and Fluff. He gave them a shrewd look. "Everybody having a great time?"

"No!" Randy said.

"I am now *you're* back," Fluff said sweetly, cuddling into the curve of his arm again. "*Now* everything's all right!"

"That's good," Gil said, suppressing a smile which was really directed at her, though Randy, who saw it, instantly misinterpreted it as being directed at him and became even more upset. "Where's my boy Marc? Still plugging away in there?"

Randy decided it was best to be distracted and turned away to scan the crowd.

"I guess he must have gone back to the house," he said finally. "I don't see him anywhere."

"That's too bad," Gil said. "I don't think he had a very good time. I really will have a talk with him. He needs instruction."

"Well, you're the man to give it to him, Gil," Randy said wryly. He stood up, grimacing as the pain in his toe hit again. "I think I'll go back too. See you there. Thanks for including me."

And he turned and limped away, leaving Fluff looking slightly ridiculous as she found herself foreclosed from delivering the final retort she had been preparing for him.

"What was that all about?" Gil asked. "You have a fight?"

"Oh!" she said. "He's such a pain!"

"He's a good man," Gil said. "I like him." He stood up. "Come on, I'll walk you back to the Row. I've got some heavy medical stuff tomorrow morning. I don't think I can stay for the whole thing."

"But it's only another half hour!" she protested with dismay. "And then I thought we could—"

"Not tonight," he said with a smile he made deliberately fatherly. "Little girls have to get their beauty sleep."

"But you'll call me, won't you?" she asked anxiously as he took her arm and walked her firmly to the door.

"I'll try," he said. "But you know how it is. We get awfully busy in pre-med."

"But—" she protested again.

"I'll call you," he said in a cheerfully offhand tone as they emerged into the clear night air. "Don't worry. I will."

"Well," she said, sounding quite forlorn. "I sure hope so."

"Come on," he said. "It's cold out here. Let's step lively."

And so they did, half running, and when they reached her house and she asked anxiously, "You *will* call, won't you?" he chuckled and gave her a quick fatherly kiss on the cheek.

"Sure thing," he said, sounding about as sincere as she often did. "You bet I will."

I bet you won't, she thought in frustration. But once inside the door and facing the questions of the little group of sisters who had not gone to the dance, she said brightly and breathlessly, "Oh, he's *wonderful*. He's just *great*. He's *marvelous*."

He went up to the third floor when he got home and rapped quietly on Randy's door.

"Yes?" Randy said, sounding tired and unhappy.

"Are you all right, buddy?"

"Oh, sure," Randy said, tone instantly reserved as he recognized the voice. "I'm all right."

"That's good," Gil said. "Don't worry about me, pal. She's cute but I'm not really interested. She's all yours if you think you can handle her."

The door opened and Randy stood there, looking as tired as he sounded. His eyes were actually red, which Gil noted and ignored: he felt really flattered that Randy wasn't trying to conceal the fact from him.

For just a second Randy considered telling him he was being damned patronizing. He rejected it because he realized that Gil was so sure of himself with girls that he probably wasn't even aware of how it sounded. He really was sincerely trying to be helpful.

"Thanks, Gil," he said quietly. "I don't know that I *can* handle her, but—thanks."

"Sure thing," Gil said, smiling into his eyes. "Now go to bed and get some sleep. It will look better tomorrow."

"Yeah, I will," Randy said. He gave a wan little smile, some of his natural humor returning. "I doubt *that*, however."

"Give it a try," Gil suggested. He chuckled. "Take two aspirin and call me in the morning."

At that Randy did genuinely laugh, and they said good night, and parted friends.

And all that, Gil thought wryly, as he undressed in his room and surveyed himself with satisfaction in the mirror, over a frivolous little chit he didn't really give two hoots about. He shouldn't have had his fun with Randy: the kid obviously was hurting like hell. But why, he couldn't analyze. She was cute, sure; but worth anybody's peace of mind? He couldn't see it. Any more than Randy's other fraternity brothers could. Most of them agreed with Tim that Beverly Rae Stevens from St. Louis, Missouri, social sciences major, was, "in her own carefree way, a younger version of Welcome Waggoner; or at least so her reputation goes on campus. Medium-bright, attractive, cheerful—her manner seems to promise almost anything to the many beaus who escort her to dances, campus functions, evenings in the City. To hear them tell it, the promise is often fulfilled, though this may be just boasting.

She goes her own merry way, happily irresponsible with Randy's feelings. Some of his brethren suspect that she may be more intrigued by him than he thinks she is. She manages to keep them both in a state of tension that she finds very enjoyable. He sometimes wonders where it will all end. His older brethren, worried, wonder too."

One last little detail, Gil thought as he came out onto the second-floor sleeping porch and passed Marc Taylor's bed. A small lump with a pillow over its head was huddled forlornly under the blankets, its rigid outline indicating clearly that its owner was the farthest thing from sleep.

He squeezed its foot as he went by.

"Hang in there, pal," he said softly. "Things will be O.K."

As he expected, there was no response. He clambered into bed, amused at himself. By God, he thought, I really am everybody's Old Dad tonight.

His own concerns, Gil reflected, were considerably deeper than anything Fluff Stevens had to offer at this stage of the game. He and Karen Ann were having another of their fights, which is why he had not taken her to the dance (they had only glared at one another across the room) and had decided to give little Miss Overeager a thrill instead.

Karen Ann, he often said, was something else. So was their relationship, which, like Randy's and Fluff's, had its tensions. It was very off-and-on and in-and-out. But they kept coming back to each other, just the same.

That, he suspected, might be the key to it, as he had told Bates, who had set it down with a few added perceptions of his own on Karen Ann Waterhouse from La Jolla, California, sociology major:

"Karen Ann 'goes with' Gulbransen, as much as any girl can; and she's a match for him. Perfectly groomed product of an extremely wealthy family, she is cool, calm, collected and not about to be patronized or taken for granted by anyone, although she herself can be very patronizing. Her technique with Gil is simple, the old hard-to-get; when he does capture her from time to time, she is as passionate and determined a lover as he is. This gives her a certain advantage—momentary, because he always slips out of her grasp and goes after someone else, sometimes in the same evening. Having gone together and battled off and on for three years, they are beginning to come to the conclusion that they probably deserve each other, could probably work out a pretty good relationship 'based on mutual mistrust,' as Suratt puts it with dry relish, and that probably they had better consider the idea of getting married when school is over.

"Although this is still an era in which it is the general assumption that marriages are made to last, both have the mental reservation that theirs may not. But without ever articulating it too much they are coming to the conclusion that they might as well go through with it: he is handsome and very personable, she is pretty and attractive; he can be the perfect 'society doctor' and she can be his perfect wife. She is not particularly well liked but no one can fault her style. Probable marriage to Gil is just one of those accepted things—not a recipe for the happiest of lives ahead, but a recipe for a smooth, surface-good, acceptable, socially and economically effective pairing. Neither expects to have any kids, both expect to wander just as they have before. Both may find life surprising them considerably, when all is said and done."

At the dance, Hack led the group into his standard closing signature, the brief final movement of his most recent composition, "Walk on the Quad," a syncopated passage that combined quick snatches of the University hymn, the fight song, a couple of campus songs and a special coda all his own. Then into "Good Night, Ladies," and the final dance began.

Across the swaying bodies the two who had met that afternoon on the Quad winked at one another over the dreamily snuggling heads of their dates. A lot of games had been played that night at Reg Dance, most innocent and most reasonably happy. Theirs was not at all innocent. It was in fact very dangerous. And "happy," in their experience so far, was not the word either would ever have chosen to describe it.

The dance ended, the last arpeggio faded out. With a smile and wave Hack closed the piano, the others began putting away their instruments. Students began streaming out of the gym. As they walked back across campus to their respective dorms and houses, they noted that it had grown colder outside. Many looked up at the diamond-clear infinitude of the cloudless sky and shivered a little as they wondered what was going on under it in Germany tonight.

6

A decent, weak, stubbornly righteous, arrogantly well-meaning old man, tired and gaunt and gray, prepared to fly to Munich.

A monstrous megalomaniac, at the height of his mental and physical powers, in the full flood of his evil genius, ranted and raved.

For forty-eight hours, while the old man, who was Prime Minister of Great Britain, sadly and helplessly surrendered to the megalomaniac, who was Chancellor of Nazi Germany, the world stood still; not for the first time and, unhappily, not for the last.

On a campus far away about which he knew nothing (to paraphrase the old man's description of Czechoslovakia), the somber days of the crisis played themselves out in the pages of the *Daily* and in many a worried bullsession around radios that stayed almost constantly tuned to the news bulletins that came in with frantic regularity from the capitals of Europe.

The abyss appeared to be opening again after twenty years of tenuous and uneasy peace.

The World War was ancient history to Wilson and his friends, something their parents had been involved in in their youth—an event already long ago—an object of opinionated analysis and discussion at home and in history classes—too ancient already, in the vast chronologies of adolescence, to be a living reality.

Now it seemed that its child was about to be born, in pain and potential terrible agony, to launch itself upon humanity with terrifying consequences no one could foretell.

There was an awful feeling that everything was about to fly apart—that soon there would be no certainties, no anchors, no ordered framework left for civilization—that everything would change, never to be put back together again in the recognizable order the world had known before.

At Munich it was to be guaranteed that all of this would soon be so. Only the timetable was a little premature.

The day was not yet, but indeed was coming.

The second war indeed was being born.

Riding herd on the *Daily* during the rising tensions of those days, Bates took his cue from Dr. Chalmers and concluded that his journalistic approach to the crisis had been the right one. He had not been entirely sure, at first: there had seemed to be some indication that the president wanted to calm the emotions of the campus as much as possible. His brief talk at Reg Dance had seemed to reverse all that. Tim proceeded accordingly. The headlines were big and bold and black. His front-page editorial when the crisis "ended" did not join the relieved chorus that greeted the event in many other places. It was dark and ominous and full of harsh anticipation.

The headlines said:

CHAMBERLAIN PROMISES SUDETENLAND TO GERMANY IF HITLER GIVES NO-WAR PLEDGE . . .

BRITAIN PLEDGES AID TO CZECHS IF HITLER INVADES . . .

TOURISTS ADVISED TO LEAVE FRANCE . . .

HITLER DELIVERS FINAL ULTIMATUM . . .

MUSSOLINI READIES ITALY FOR WAR . . .

ANGRY HITLER READY TO MOVE ON CZECHOSLOVAKIA . . .

GREAT BRITAIN MOBILIZES FLEET . . .

EUROPE ON BRINK OF WAR . . .

F.D.R. URGES POWERS CONFER ON CRISIS . . .

HITLER, CHAMBERLAIN, DALADIER, MUSSOLINI MEET IN MUNICH . . .

CRISIS ENDS AS POWERS GIVE HITLER GO-AHEAD. CZECHOSLOVAKIA ABANDONED, NAZI TROOPS MARCH IN. CHAMBERLAIN HAILS "PEACE FOR OUR TIME " . . .

"A tired old man," Tim's editorial said, "almost broken by the strain of recent days, came home from Munich to hold up a piece of paper with Adolf Hitler's signature on it and describe it as 'peace for our time.'

"If the signature is worth what it has been for the past few years, the paper is nothing more than paper and peace will not last for a year, let alone 'for our time.'

"Hitler ranted, raved, bluffed—and won.

"The democracies wavered, waffled, panicked—and lost.

"The outcome perhaps was inevitable from the first, for one simple reason: Hitler had the guns, the courage and the will, and his opponents did not. Given his gambler's instincts, which so far have brought him the Ruhr and Austria, and now a chunk of Czechoslovakia which includes its strongest defenses and paves the way for a complete conquest of the country, it was no wonder he moved with supreme confidence to get what he wanted.

"It may, in the eyes of many, have been an insane gamble.

"But it has to be judged by the only standard that ultimately prevails in international affairs:

"It worked.

"And it will continue to work unless there is a united, concerted, determined and unrelenting buildup of military forces by the democracies. Plus a unity of thought and purpose centered on the one thought: *This thing must be stopped.*

"If it is not, then soon its leader will be back again with more demands, more bluffs, more conquests. And then he and his Axis partners, the bombastic Mussolini and the imperialistic Japanese, will be able to turn to the one great power that will still remain to oppose him—us.

"And in places far from this lovely campus, you and I will have to stand and pay the price of European weakness and lack of will this week in Munich."

When he read the editorial to the staff before sending it to the backshop to have it set into type, Tim received what he was honest enough to recognize as a very mixed response. A slim majority appeared to be with him, though uncertain and uneasy; a sizable minority was visibly and vocally upset. Bill Nagatani, appealed to by this group, refused to say more than, "He's the editor"; and, under continued pressure, finally protested, "Can't you see I can't say anything?"

"I *am* the editor," Tim said, much more quietly and confidently than he felt, because he realized he was doing what Willie often warned against, "getting ahead of the constituency." But damn it, that was how he saw it—he knew he was right—couldn't imagine how anyone could *not* see it—and he didn't believe in leaders who followed instead of led.

"So in it goes," he added; and, with a little smile, "If any of you disagree sufficiently, write a letter to the editor. We'll print it."

It was already obvious at the hour of ten A.M. that this was a promise incapable of being fulfilled, because by then the Shack was flooded with at least two hundred hastily written responses on all kinds of paper, some formally addressed in envelopes, other scrawled on pages torn from notebooks, most from students but a surprising number of faculty letterheads.

He asked Nagatani to help him, and after lunch they went through the approximately four hundred received by then. The pro pile, he noted with some secret dismay, was quite a bit smaller than the anti. Nagatani was noticeably polite about this but Tim had the distinct impression he was pleased.

"Pick out fifteen of the best critical ones," Tim said, "and ten that support me, and we'll use the whole edit page, if necessary. I'll write a short front-page editorial conceding that the balance is against me and that we'll run some more on Monday. But," he added grimly, "I'm going to say what I think unless Chalmers stops me."

"I don't see how he could," Bill remarked. "After what he said last night he's probably applauding all the way."

The president, however, made only the briefest of references, when the student body gathered to hear him in Memorial Hall at two-thirty. Most of his talk was the usual one he delivered every year: how pleased the University was to see them all, the newcomers, the old-timers, the great opportunities here for the good citizens, the diligent students, the hope that they would all give much and get much and go forth at the end of senior year better, more educated, more mature and worthy men and women . . . a passing reference to "difficult times" . . . the need for application . . . the need to be prepared for whatever the future might bring . . . the wish that they might find the campus hospitable, the faculty helpful, their time in this beautiful place well spent . . . the invitation to come see him if there was a major problem others couldn't take care of . . . God bless, good luck, goodbye.

They streamed out into a world so serene and calm and peaceful in the hazy golden autumn afternoon that it seemed impossible that it could also hold Munich and the terrible travail of hapless states and helpless peoples.

It all erupted that night at dinner, however, into one of the sharpest arguments anyone could remember—an argument no one could win because it dealt in future hopes and fears, in assertions and denials no one could support at that moment with facts.

It was a microcosm of all the millions of arguments going on across America and the world that night.

It was, as Willie and many of them suspected, a harbinger and a foretaste of agonizing days and years to come, until the time when a decision would finally be made for them and they would indeed stand in places far from their lovely campus to help their country pay the price that history's endless replay of weakness and lack of will versus strength and ruthless determination had made inevitable that week in Munich.

7

"Dear Folks," Willie began his dutiful semimonthly letter home. "Things here seem to be shaping up very well for the new quarter. I've already had a couple of good talks with Dr. Chalmers and my vice-president, Donnamaria Van Dyke, and tomorrow I'm going to be holding the first meeting of my Executive Committee, or 'Excom,' which is sort of our overall legislative body, you might say. There don't seem to be any very pressing issues ahead of us at the moment, though everybody has been quite worried about the situation in Europe, as I guess you have too. A lot of people seem to think war may come yet, thanks to Hitler, but the tension seems to have died down a lot since the meeting at Munich and now we're all concentrating on getting through this quarter with reasonably good grades.

"Life in the house seems to be settling down well, too, with a good group of new sophomore members and old hands like myself, Guy Unruh and Bill Lattimer to ride herd on them with sage advice. (Ha!) We have a lot of good guys among the juniors, too, so all in all, it looks like a good year for the house, too.

"Thanks for the cookies, Mom, they were a great hit with everybody and didn't last more than ten minutes. Any further contributions gratefully received. Dad, I hope all goes well at the bank and with the ranch. Tell all the guys hello for me and particularly Ranger. I miss him. Is his right foreleg still bothering him? Tell him the first thing I'm going to do when I come home for Christmas is saddle him up and take him up into the foothills on one of our favorite trails. I really miss the ranch and the Valley and the foothills. They clear my mind. Not that it's getting too cluttered here, you understand—I think my profs are already beginning to think it isn't cluttered enough with serious subjects! But don't worry, I'm buckling down to my studies in spite of all the campus activities, which are now getting into full swing. I don't know where we find time to do all the things we do, but somehow it all falls into place.

"Well, must close now. It's almost time for dinner and I have a couple of guests coming up. One of them is Aram Katanian, who you remember was my freshman roommate and came down to spend spring vacation with us that year. Also, as you know, my distinguished opponent last spring. No hard feelings, though. He didn't really expect to win and we're too good friends to let the election get in the way. It just means I have the headaches and he doesn't, although he's still so involved in everything that he's almost as busy as I am. My other guest is a sophomore transfer from the East named Bayard Johnson. A real nice guy, I think, whom Latt and I met on Registration Day and took a liking to. We're thinking about him as a possible member here, although that of course is up to the house. And he may not even want to, as far as I know. Anyway, they'll be coming along in just a few minutes, so I'd better wind this up.

"I'll call next week on the usual schedule. Meanwhile I hope you're both feeling great. Billy, incidentally, is doing just fine. He and Janie are as thick as ever. Really Young Love in Bloom! I assume he's writing, too. Let me know if he isn't and I'll paddle his bottom.

"Take care of yourselves. Much love from

Your 'presidential' son,
Willie"

And that, he thought as he addressed the letter and put it in his binder to drop off at the post office tomorrow morning, was that, for another two weeks. In the weeks between he and Billy alternated in telephoning them, collect, and they had a chat. Dad didn't believe in running up too many phone bills even if he was president of the bank and the ranch was beginning to do quite well as the economy gradually pulled out of the depths of the Depression. He said it was enough maintaining two sons at the University without a lot of frills. But Mom insisted on vocal contact with "my babies," as she had called them as recently as last summer in the presence of company, which embarrassed them intensely though their only response had been, "Oh, *Mom!*" from Billy and "*Really*" from him. They agreed later that mothers were incorrigible, but what could you do? "They seem to think they have some rights over us," he had remarked with a chuckle, and Billy had laughed and agreed. "I guess they've earned it," he said, and they agreed that theirs was pretty wonderful, and had indeed.

One thing they could never claim, he reflected as he ran a comb quickly through hair disarranged from unconscious cogitative mussing while he carefully framed his letter, was an unhappy childhood or an unsupportive family.

Dad was a little starchy now and then when Willie indicated that no, he probably wasn't going to come home and start in at the bank, even if he did love the ranch and the Valley and the foothills. But Dad didn't object very strongly, and Mom was always on Willie's side. Billy made it easier, too, because he wanted to be an actor and a teacher and maybe write plays, and they could both see that Dad—although shrewd enough not to object too much to that, either—was absolutely convinced that it was a pipe dream whose failure was inevitable, and that the younger son would soon be back, even if the older strayed.

And he wasn't planning on straying too far, after all. Only to San Francisco, which wasn't exactly the moon or Mars. He'd be around.

That was still a way off, though, and right now he had his dinner guests, and the reaction of the house, to worry about.

He and Latt had discussed it at some length yesterday before he had issued the invitation. Latt in his calm and steady way had finally said, "Now, look, Willie, you led the parade on Reg Day. Did you mean it or didn't you?"

"Sure I meant it."

"Well, so did I. So—"

Willie grinned.

"I just wanted you to tell me to do what I was going to do anyway."

"You're a character," Latt said. "Want me to call one of 'em, or do you want to call 'em both?"

"Why don't you call Hank?" he suggested. "Remind him I said we wanted him to come up, and tell him we want his help with Bayard Johnson."

"He'll love it," Latt predicted. "You know Hank and matters of principle. There's nothing he loves better than to get into a big battle over them."

"I guess that applies to the three of us, doesn't it?" he asked, and it was Latt's turn to smile.

But it wasn't really all that easy, he reflected as he took a deep breath and prepared to go downstairs to face the thundering herd in the living room. It wasn't easy in any context. He was acutely aware of how carefully he had refrained in his letter from giving his parents any inkling that Bayard was a Negro. His parents were people of high principle, too, but it was in areas they had been brought up with and were accustomed to. As a general rule they would have opposed anybody being rude or unkind to "a decent young man who is a fellow student of our sons at the university." In practical effect, it would have stopped there. Like millions of their fellow countrymen, they would have drawn the line.

The line, Willie told himself now, was what he was interested in removing. And it warn't goin' to be easy, as their chief cowhand on the ranch always remarked when confronted with some task he finally performed with perfect calm and perfect success.

So, take a lesson from Rodrigo, he told himself firmly, and sail into it.

But again, it wasn't that easy because Bayard himself hadn't made it that easy. It was clear, in fact, that he was scared to death and not at all convinced that he should be involved in what he finally referred to as "your experiment." His whole approach had been cautious and reluctant.

Wilson tried three times without success to reach him at his hall before he was finally rewarded with a tentative "Hello?" after several people had bellowed "JOHNSON!" up and down corridors.

"Hi," he said comfortably. "I didn't see you at Reg Dance."

"Who is—" Bayard began; then, with a pleased recognition, "Oh, it's you. No, I didn't go."

"Why not?" Wilson demanded. "Latt and I were looking for you."

"You were the only ones," Bayard said, sounding bleak.

"Now what the hell," Wilson said, "do you mean by that? What kind of poor-mouth crap is that?"

"You don't have to bully me," Bayard said, but sounding, to his credit, more wistfully amused than antagonistic. "I know when I'm not wanted."

"I *said* Latt and I were looking for you," Wilson said. "I even had a girl picked out."

"White?" Bayard asked, and he added quickly, "But of course. What else would she be?"

"Yes," Willie said calmly, "white. What's the matter, are you prejudiced or something?"

At this Bayard actually did laugh. It didn't last long.

"I'm sure she was great—is great," he said. "But I'm also sure she wouldn't want to be seen with me."

"You underestimate yourself," Willie said. "You're a handsome guy, Bayard. Lots of girls would like to be seen with you."

"Lots have," Bayard said. "But they were all one color." He could not, however, keep himself from sounding interested. "Who is this girl, anyway?"

"Her name," Wilson said, and would ever after remember the moment he got Bayard interested in her, "is Maryetta Bradford. She's a sophomore transfer, too. An old family friend. Her mother and mine were best friends at the University of California at Berkeley a long time ago. I'm supposed to look her up, haven't yet, but thought the dance would be a good time."

"To kill two birds with one stone," Bayard suggested wryly. "One white bird and one—"

"Oh, shut up," Willie said. "You make me tired. Are you coming up to the house to dinner, or not?"

There was a silence for a moment. Finally Bayard said, "You really meant it, then."

"Of course I meant it, jerk. What do you think I do, go around passing out invitations like some—some campus party boy, or something?"

"Will you have to pay for me?" Bayard asked.

"That's a strange question. Yes. But if it will make you feel better, little Bayard, I'll let you reimburse me. How's that?"

"I'd feel better about it," Bayard said. Willie snorted.

"Well, bless your heart, you do that. Are you coming, then?"

Again there was hesitation.

"What will your fraternity brothers say?"

Wilson uttered a disgusted sound.

"Who gives a damn?"

"Oh, Willie," Bayard said. "Now *you're* sounding like the jerk."

"They won't say anything to my face," Willie said, "and behind my back I really *don't* give a damn. And you shouldn't either."

"Oh, but I do," Bayard said softly. "Oh, but I do."

"Well, don't," Wilson ordered. "I'll be with you, Latt will be with you, all our decent guys will be with you."

"Not all," Bayard said, as one who knew. "Plenty of decent ones can't bring themselves to go that—that far . . . yet. Maybe they will someday. But not yet."

"I'll tell you who else will be along," Wilson said. "In fact, I'll ask him to stop by for you and bring you with him. And that's Ari Katanian."

"Oh," Bayard said, sounding less cautious and more pleased. "I like Ari. He's being very good to me, over here in the hall."

"All right, then," Wilson said triumphantly. "I'm providing you with a convoy and you'll be met by a welcoming committee. What more do you want?"

"I want your experiment to work out," Bayard said with a wistful little laugh. "But I'm not sure I can participate as wholeheartedly as you'd like."

"You'll have to, to make it succeed," Willie said. "Otherwise you'll fail us both. And you don't want that, do you?"

Again the hesitation and the silence. And, finally, gravely, "No, I don't want that."

"O.K.," Willie said briskly. "Dinner's at six. Hank will pick you up at five and walk you over and we'll round up the brethren to meet you. They're a motley crew but I don't think they'll bite. If they do, they'll hear from me."

"All right," Bayard said, still with obvious reluctance. "I'll be there. And thank you, Willie. You know I appreciate what you're trying to do. Personally I think they're going to give both of us fits. But if it's what you want of me"—he sighed again—"then I'll do it."

"Thank you," Wilson said. "And don't worry. It will go just fine."

But of that, of course, he was not at all sure. When he had announced at dinner last night that he would have guests tonight, several had asked who. When he said Ari Katanian there had been general sounds of approval.

"And who else?" Renny Suratt inquired as he apparently concluded.

"A mystery guest," he said.

"Rita Hayworth?" Buff Richardson asked, and since they all knew Buff's fixation on Rita, everybody laughed. Across the big U-shaped table, however, Jeff Barnett put down his fork and fixed Willie with a quizzical expression somewhere between amusement and disapproval.

"Ah know who it is!" he exclaimed. "Ah know you, Willie! You got that li'l ole bee buzzin' in your bonnet and you're not goin' to be satisfied until you get it out. It's that boy By'rd, Ah'll bet mah ass!"

"Well," Wilson said dryly, "that's a very valuable commodity to throw into the pot, Jeff, and no doubt there are many who would gladly toss you for it. But I wouldn't want you to risk it, so I'll say yes, it is. Anybody want to make anything of it?"

And he looked around the table with an innocent-but-not-to-be-challenged air.

"It won't work, Willie," Jeff said quietly. "Ah *will* bet you mah ass, it won't work."

"We'll see," Willie said, and from down the table Rudy Krohl said, in a tone oddly and unnecessarily defiant, "Yes, we will!"

Suratt laughed.

"Yes," he agreed. "We sure will."

And on into the night, and all day today, Wilson supposed, they had been thinking about it and buzzing about it, wherever they ran into each other on campus or in the house. And now the occasion was here, and he and that boy By'rd and Latt and Ari Katanian and everyone who agreed with them must rise to it.

At the front door he heard Hank Moore say cordially, "Aram Katanian? I'm Hank Moore. And this is Bayard Johnson? Hi, I'm Hank Moore."

Willie uttered his customary whoop and began his usual clatter down the stairs.

For the first few moments, all seemed to be going well. Ari Katanian couldn't have been more at ease—but then, Ari was at ease anywhere. Hank Moore stuck encouragingly close, Haggerty played the piano, waved cordially and called, "Come over here," which Bayard did, self-consciously but looking shyly pleased as Hack continued to play the bass while reaching across with his right hand with a welcoming smile. Franky Miller appeared in the doorway, fat and grinning as he came forward. Moose lumbered in and stuck out a paw. Unruh arrived, followed closely by McAllister, Andrade, Smith Carriger, Billy and Randy. In twos and threes the rest of the house gradually drifted in.

Most were as self-conscious as Bayard but doing their best, Willie noted with approval, doing their best. It was one of the many times when he wished University rules permitted at least a small amount of tension-breaking liquor, but they didn't, so that was that. Natural friendliness combined with good intentions took its place for most of them. He supposed it was patronizing to be proud of them, but he was—and doubly proud of

Bayard, the one who was really on the spot, trying hard to respond as naturally and unself-consciously as he could.

Sincerely, earnestly, perhaps a little mixed and confused in motivation but full of goodwill, most were behaving very well.

This had been going on for some fifteen minutes when Jeff, Rudy, Renny Suratt and Galen Bryce appeared together in the doorway, smiled vaguely in their general direction and started right on through to the adjoining poolroom.

"Hey!" Wilson said in a tone that did not brook ignoring. "Jeff! Come over and meet a couple of friends of mine."

Jeff paused and turned to Ari Katanian with a sudden charming smile.

"Hi, Aram," he said. "Ah think Ah've already met you."

"Yes, you have," Ari said, smiling and pulling him firmly forward as they shook hands. "And this is Bayard Johnson. Jeff Barnett."

Willie had been conscious from the instant Bayard had seen the foursome's ostentatious ignoring that he was tensing up. The moment Jeff opened his mouth, the accent tensed him further. He was practically rigid now. Willie took his other arm and stepped forward with Ari. He could feel that the poor kid was actually trembling. He tightened his grip on Bayard's arm to encourage him—and also, he thought wryly, so he won't turn tail and run right out the door this very minute.

"Yes, Jeff," he said easily. "*I'd* like you to meet my friend Bayard, too."

For just a moment Jeff looked at him with a beseeching expression and Willie thought: This poor kid is having trouble too. It's as hard for him as it is for Bayard. But he wasn't going to relent.

"Come on, Jeff," he said quietly. "Say hello and shake hands."

"Well—" Jeff said, while all around the room grew very still. "Well, I—"

"Might as well," Bayard said with a shaky little laugh and voice that trembled. "You know Willie."

In spite of himself Jeff did smile a little at that; and suddenly his defenses appeared to crumble.

He held out his hand. There was an audible release of breath around the room.

"Hi, By'rd," he said. "It's—" He paused and then forced it out. But he did say it, Willie thought triumphantly: he did say it. "It's nice to have you here."

"Thank you, Jeff," Bayard said in a tone that sounded more awed than he knew. "I appreciate that."

"Rudy," Willie said quietly, but calling the roll in a tone not to be denied. "Renny—Gale—come say hello."

"I'm going to play pool," Rudy announced loudly and started to turn away. "Coming, Renny? Gale?"

"Why don't you come meet Bayard first?" Willie suggested, softly, but, as

Ari Katanian had remarked years ago, "When Willie gets really quiet, it's a good time to pay attention."

Suratt, no man's fool, stepped forward and, with a wry smile, held out his hand.

"Hi, Bayard," he said. "I'm Renny Suratt. I hope you can stand the food."

"I'll try," Bayard said with a still uncertain little laugh.

"And I'm Galen Bryce," Gale said, following suit. "The gentleman in the poolroom," he added dryly, "is Rudy Krohl."

"Gale and Renny probably encouraged this just to see what would happen," Franky Miller whispered indignantly to Gulbransen. "Damned snotty sons of bitches."

"Gale's going to write it up as an experiment for one of his psych classes," Gil whispered back, and they laughed in a way that made Gale look at them sharply.

"I'm not in the poolroom!" Rudy snapped. He came forward and stuck out his hand belligerently, "I'm Rudy Krohl!" Bayard reached for his hand just as Rudy pulled it away again. "I won't be eating with you, though. I'm going to eat at the Cellar. Coming, Jeff?"

Again the room quieted down abruptly. Jeff looked at him, looked at Willie, looked, finally, at Bayard.

"I think," he said carefully, "I think—I'll eat here, Rudy. If you don't mind."

Rudy gave him an indignant and scornful look.

"But I thought you said you wouldn't put your feet under the same table with that pushy—"

"*You shut up!*" Jeff interrupted loudly. "I'll make my own decisions on what I do, damn it! You eat wherever you damned like and leave me out of it!"

"Unruh!" Haggerty called blandly from the piano. "Come give us a lead here!"

And he swung with great gusto, and a certain ironic touch, into the University fight song. Unruh came over, others began to gather around the piano. Willie and Ari propelled Bayard toward it. Singing began. Rudy, looking disgruntled, finally did disappear into the poolroom. After a moment Gale and Renny did too. No one followed them. Jeff picked up the evening paper and began to read it. Others broke into groups and began to talk, very conscious of Bayard's presence but carefully avoiding the subject. Presently the bell rang for dinner and they all trailed in.

Wilson thought for a split second of asking Jeff to sit beside Bayard but decided he'd gone far enough with Jeff for one evening. He seated Bayard between himself and Buff Richardson, whose inner reactions were concealed behind the charming persona he put on with friends, strangers, professors, the young, the old, men, women, children, dogs, cats and indeed the whole wide world. He was the perfect host, Buff was, Willie told himself with inner amusement.

In ten seconds he was chatting with Bayard about his classes, apparently fascinated by everything Bayard said. In less than half a minute, Willie could see, he had the kid relaxed and at ease. Thank God for Buff.

On his right he had put Ari Katanian, and then had called casually across the room to Godwin, "Bob, why don't you join us next to Ari?"

Bob gave him a worshipful look and came over so fast he practically knocked down Lor Davis and Smitty Carriger in his rush to take his seat. Hank gave Willie a quick wink, reached over and pulled out Bob's chair for him. "If Bob was a woman," Franky murmured to McAllister, "I swear on the bones of my dear Aunt Fanny he'd swoon dead away."

"I didn't know you had an Aunt Fanny!" North exclaimed loudly and then cried, "Ouch, you bastard!" as Franky elbowed him sharply in the ribs. North picked up a glass of water and held it over Franky's head. Buff, hardly missing a beat in his conversation with Bayard, said firmly, "All *right*, you guys!" and, laughing, they subsided.

"This is a hell of a crew to ride herd on," Buff confided to Bayard with a whimsical laugh. "I don't know why I ever agreed to be president." Bayard, much flattered, laughed too and said, "Oh, they seem pretty nice to me."

"Well," Buff said comfortably, "they're not *too* bad. So you like Professor Babcock?" And their friendly talk resumed.

"Bob's wondering about things over in the halls, Ari," Willie said easily as the big heavy plates filled with bread, butter, meat, vegetables, salad, flew up and down around the table almost faster than the eye could see, sped by young hands and voracious appetites on their rapidly diminishing way. "He's wondering if you think it might be a good idea for him to talk to a few people over there."

"Yes," Bob said, leaning forward to give him another grateful look across Ari's lanky body and amicably impassive face. "Anything you could suggest would be very helpful, Ari. That is, if—if you want to."

"Well, of course, you know," Ari said, snagging the bread as it came by and skillfully serving Willie, Bob and himself before speeding it on its way, "that I'm going to be obligated to support the hall candidate. I mean, you know I can't very well break ranks for a Row guy."

"Oh, we know that," Wilson said as one of the meat platters reached them and he returned the favor, "but we just thought that maybe, just as a matter of fairness, you guys might at least give Bob a hearing over there. After all, you know, I did arrange for you to be invited up here for dinner just before election last spring so you could talk to the whole house."

"And all the time I thought that was Latt's doing!" Ari exclaimed with exaggerated surprise. "I thought you were in the City that weekend and didn't know a thing about it. So *that's* how it all came about! Well, what-yah know!"

"So I didn't fool you?" Willie inquired with a grin. His ex-roommate grinned back.

"I knew you were hiding under the pool table all the time," he said. "You didn't fool me for one minute. So now it's time to call in the chits, right?"

"Well," Willie said with mock gravity, "I *did* think that in simple *fairness* you *might* consider giving my pal here equal time. How about it?"

"You're a ruthless politician, Richard Emmett Wilson, you know that?" Ari said. "Have you ever thought of running for public office when you leave this benighted place?"

"If you don't beat me to it," Willie said. Ari chuckled.

"We'll see."

He turned to Bob, who knew his cause was being advanced under the easy chitchat and was almost literally holding his breath for the outcome. "Why don't we start by having you two come over and have dinner with me some night soon?"

Willie held up a cautionary hand before Bob could rush in with an obviously ready agreement. "I don't think it's such a good idea for me to be along," he remarked. "That would be too obvious, don't you think? Bob's got to do it for himself when all's said and done. Why don't you two work it out without me?"

"Good thinking," Ari agreed. "O.K., Bob?"

"Perfect," Bob said fervently. "Just *perfect*."

"Good," Ari said. "I'll get back to you soon. It may be a week or two, but don't worry. I won't forget."

"The guy's a damned elephant," Willie observed. He turned his head away from Bayard on his left and directly toward Ari, dropping his voice to a near-murmur even though the roar of conversation and cutlery that filled the dining room made it unnecessary. Godwin got the signal and obediently turned his back on Ari and began talking busily to Duke Offenberg on his right.

"Incidentally," Willie said, "I want to thank you for what you're doing for our boy here."

Ari gave a deprecatory shrug.

"It's nothing. I investigated and found it was true what he told you. A few were giving him a bit of a hard time, including his two roommates." He grinned. "I split them up and they're in Siberia with other fringe cases. I fixed your boy up with a couple of really nice fellows from North Dakota." He chuckled. "They don't even know what a Negro *is* in North Dakota. I think it's going to work out fine. What I want to know is, how's it going to work out *here*?"

"What do you mean?" Wilson asked innocently. But Ari wasn't having any.

His dark eyes sparkled, his mouth widened in the lively grin that could turn his pleasant face into a handsome one in a second.

"Come on, you crafty son of a bitch. What's happening?"

"Nothing," Willie protested. "Really, nothing. At least," he added with a grin, "not yet."

Ari's expression sobered and became thoughtful.

"You're going to have quite a problem, boy. It isn't going to be all that easy. You know, Willie can't *always* have everything he wants."

Wilson too looked sober and even, thought Ari, who knew him so well, a little bleak.

"Well I know," he said gravely. "Well I know."

"Well, good luck, anyway," Hank said. "I'll observe the experiment from afar with great interest. And so, I suspect, will many others."

"Keep your fingers crossed," Willie suggested, turning away to speak to Bayard just as Buff, observing the end of his talk with Ari, turned to Moose on his left to agree about the dessert, which tonight was a pretty gruesome compote of canned fruit and graham crackers.

There was just time, before Unruh started the general exodus from the table, for Willie to ask, "What do you think?" and for Bayard to reply gratefully, "It's been great, Willie. They're a nice bunch of guys." His eyes darkened for a second but then he repeated firmly, "A nice bunch of guys."

"Not too many exceptions?" Willie inquired quietly as he walked him out of the dining room.

"No," said Bayard seriously. "Not too many."

"That's good," Willie said. "They'll improve with time. You'll see."

"Oh, I don't expect I'll be back very often," Bayard said quickly. "Will I?"

Willie stepped deliberately to a window giving onto the front lawn, turning his back on the few who still lingered before departing for the Libe, or upstairs, to study. He lowered his voice again.

"Do you want to?"

He glanced sideways at Bayard and could see a lot of thinking was going on.

"I don't know just yet," Bayard confessed at last. "I really just don't know."

"Well, think about it," Willie said. "Think about it, and let me know. I'm ready to go to bat for you if you want me to. But I can't do it without your wholehearted support, that's for sure."

"I know," Bayard said with a painful honesty. "And that's what I'm not sure I can give you—yet, anyway." His expression changed, he smiled shyly.

"One thing, though," he said. "What did you say that girl's name was?"

Wilson gave a delighted whoop of laughter.

"You son of gun!" he exclaimed. "Maryetta Bradford. I'll tell her to expect your call."

"Oh, now, wait!" Bayard protested, genuinely alarmed. "You can't go too fast with *everything*, Willie. Give me a *little* time. *Please*."

"We'll see," Wilson said with a comfortable smile as loyal little Hank

Moore came over with Tony Andrade, Johnny Herbert and several others to say good night to Bayard. "We'll see."

But later, around eleven when most were through studying and the house was gradually quieting for the night, the whole thing became serious again when there was a very soft knock on the attic door he had decorated with skull and crossbones and a huge DEATH, INVADERS! banner across it.

He opened the door to find Jeff Barnett in bathrobe and slippers. He had a finger to his lips.

"Can I come in for a minute?" he whispered.

"Sure," Willie whispered back and carefully closed the door behind him. "What's up?"

"Well, Willie," Jeff said, still half whispering, looking very young, very solemn and, Wilson could see, very tense. "I just wanted to tell you that—that I went along with it tonight because I like you and respect you and hope we'll be real good friends this year—and you wanted me to. But I want you to know that if you try to carry it any further in this house, I'm goin' to fight you, Willie. A lot of us are. There's a lot of feelin' about it; you just don't know. And we're going to lick you, Willie, if you force us to. We're just goin' to downright lick you. I thought you should know that."

Wilson looked at him for a long, steady moment.

"I don't know what I'm going to do yet—"

"Oh, Willie!" Jeff said with a smile half protesting, half fond. "We know you. We know what you have in mind. And we're ready for it."

"Well," Wilson said wryly, "let's make it a fair fight, O.K.? Let's don't burn any crosses on the lawn, all right?"

And for the second time he felt that he had almost made Jeff cry, because his face contorted and he started to protest. Then a sort of mask went down.

"I'm not that sort, Willie," he said with dignity, "and I wish you'd stop hurtin' me by implyin' I am. I just can't help how I feel and I just wanted to warn you, that's all. And I wanted you to know I've got company. Is that fair enough?"

Wilson sighed and held out his hand, which Jeff, after a moment's hesitation, accepted.

"Again, I apologize," he said. "I mustn't—mustn't—*mustn't* say things like that. You *are* fair and I'm not, and I'll try to be. But I can't help how I feel, either. So if I finally decide to push this, we'll just have to battle it out, I guess. I hope we can still be friends."

"I hope so," Jeff said gravely. "And I hope you *can* restrain that tongue of yours, Willie. You're too good and too great to let yourself hurt people like that."

"I know," Wilson said, finding himself, amazingly, on the verge of a reaction much more emotional than he had expected. "You'd better go, Jeff. I appreciate it. Good night."

"Good night, Willie," Jeff said quietly as he turned and stepped out into the silent hallway. "See you in the mornin'."

For a long time Willie sat in his battered old rocker, hand-me-down from several past fraternity brothers, and stared unseeing at the wall.

Probably not even his closest friends would have believed it of the great Richard Emmett Wilson, he thought wryly, but he really was very upset with himself and just—just things in general. In fact, he really felt almost like crying, for some reason, elusive but oppressive, that he couldn't define.

But that didn't mean, he told himself grimly, that he wasn't going to keep on doing what he thought was right, in this as in other things.

8

The golden days of Indian summer settled in, for how long a time no one knew but wonderful while they lasted. A little fog, early, burning off fast. Mornings a little crisper. Afternoons a little cooler. Nights now consistently sharp. A few trees shedding. A few turning color. The great majority, eucalyptus and live oaks, showing little change except for a dusty, bedraggled look that would remain until the rains of winter washed them clean. The hills behind campus more sharply defined, against a bluer sky. The year passing. Time passing. Youth, so imperceptibly that its stealthy departure was scarcely noticed save by the sentimental, passing. . . .

A dreamy drowsiness suffused the air.

Under its gentle cover the busy activities of the campus year raced forward just as always.

Hurrying down to the sports pavilion in his brisk and businesslike fashion, Smith Carriger was bound for a meeting of the intramural sports committee which supervised the innumerable contests between the various teams of hall and Row. Hall played hall; fraternity played fraternity; fraternity played hall; hall played fraternity; eating clubs within the halls played each other and the fraternities. Women's groups, fewer and less athletic, engaged in the occasional contest of volleyball, ping-pong or something equally ladylike. Males, it seemed to Smitty, were all over the place all the time, shouting, grunting, groaning, sweating, swearing, playing volleyball, soccer, touch football, ping-pong, tennis, sandlot baseball and any other kind of organized athletic activity that provided an excuse for exercise.

In addition to the constant intramural contests, the formal athletic schedule of the University included football, basketball, swimming, tennis, soccer, track, wrestling, rugby, polo, fencing, the rifle team, equestrian contests, golf, javelin-throwing, water polo, badminton, boxing. Most of these had both varsity and freshman teams. Most, thanks to the climate of the Santa Clara Valley, were played year 'round. Some of the teams were referred to informally as "the Prune Valley Boys," this being fifty years before silicon and developers wiped out the orchards and destroyed most of the valley's gentle charm.

All of this ceaseless and determined physical activity was benignly smiled upon and encouraged by Dr. Chalmers and the administration—"The theory apparently being," Franky Miller remarked, "that if we expend all our energies on sportin' we won't have any energies left for sportin', if you know what I mean. It's like putting saltpeter in the milk in freshman dorm"—that ancient and never verified legend of all universities. "Somebody ought to tell Chalmers it doesn't work."

Sports did, however, provide arenas for ambition, satisfy the desire for glory, and release many tensions in a vigorous and healthy way. Like almost everyone, Smitty considered them a good thing even though he often joined Franky in pointing out that "somebody has to do the applauding, after all." He was surprised to find himself suddenly involved in it. Ari Katanian, who was chairman of intramural sports, had asked him to be on the committee the other night when he was up to dinner.

"Why me?" Smitty had inquired with a laugh. "You know me and sports—give me a front-row seat and a pretty girl and I'm the best little audience you ever saw. But that's it. Anyway, where would I find the time?"

"Where we all find it," Ari had responded with a smile. "At the other end of the clock. Stop procrastinating. When did Smith Carriger ever say no?"

"That's Smith Carriger's trouble," Smitty said wryly. "He never does say no."

"Backbone of the campus, boy," Ari assured him, "backbone of the campus. I'll be at the gym at two P.M. tomorrow. Be there."

"Yes, sir," Smitty said. "You're impossible to argue with."

"Tell that to my dates," Ari said with his engaging grin, white teeth gleaming in his thin, high-cheekboned face. "Are you going to be on Excom?"

"Our distinguished leader," Smitty said, nodding toward Wilson, deep in conversation with that new colored boy he had brought up to the house, "has asked me. You?"

"Yup. I believe he wants us to meet him for lunch in the Union day after tomorrow, doesn't he?"

"So I hear it," Smitty said. "Routine, I suppose."

"So far," Ari said, looking speculatively at Willie chatting away like old folks at home with Bayard Johnson. "So far."

Smitty, who kept his ear to the ground at all times, wondered about Bayard Johnson and Willie as he stepped off the Quad and cut briskly across in front of the library and so on down to the athletic facilities. It was "up," actually, since he was going northeast according to the map, but somehow everything in that direction seemed "down" from the Quad, just as the Row seemed "up," men's halls were "over," and women's halls "up there." He supposed that was because the Quad actually was the center and everything either rose, or fell away from, there.

Willie, he reflected, might be getting himself into more than he anticipated with his well-meaning partisanship for the University's new addition.

It was all very dramatic to confer the accolade on him in front of everybody on Reg Day, and it was all very well to face down Jeff Barnett and the others by inviting him to dinner, but there Smitty suspected it had better end. There had been a lot of post-dinner mutterings. A lot of people were uneasy about it in addition to Jeff, whose opposition might be expected, and Rudy Krohl, who could be counted on to raise hell just because he was a prejudiced and obstructive jerk, and Gale Bryce, who wanted to run an experiment—Smitty agreed with Franky on that—and Renny Suratt, who was a general spoiler and liked to stir things up. Quite a few others were genuinely concerned. Willie could draw on a big reservoir of respect and goodwill, but this time it might be running dry. Smitty didn't know his own position yet. He didn't feel any particular prejudice, neither did he feel any particular urge to be a hero. He guessed he'd have to wait and see and size up the guy for himself.

Meantime he was already on four committees and about to undertake the fifth and that was crazy, even for him. He had sometimes thought of converting all this activity into political clout and trying to run for student-body president next spring to succeed Willie. But poor Bob Godwin had his heart so set on it that he'd be absolutely devastated if anybody, particularly a fraternity brother, tried to get in his way. Smitty had some time ago decided that he wouldn't. For him, it would just be a nice honor and a pleasant responsibility. For Bob, he knew, it was going to be absolutely the justification of his entire college career. He'd probably be marked for life if he didn't make it. If Smitty tried and failed—which he considered highly unlikely—it would be just a slight hitch in the steady onward progress of Smith Carriger toward . . . what?

He told himself rather bleakly that he didn't really know. To succeed his father as chairman of Carriger Corp.? Probably. Marry a wealthy, socially acceptable, frightfully suitable girl? Probably. Have two or three kids, all of whom would come here to the University and carry on the tradition? Probably. Do good works and live in justice and mercy all the days of his life? Probably. But what, really, did that all add up to, when you came to the end of it? Just another tombstone alongside all the rest in the family plot:

Smith Carriger, 1919–19—

Who would ever care whether he had been or gone?

Who would give a damn that he had passed this way?

Christ! he told himself abruptly. What a morbid son of a bitch! And on such a lovely day, too. What was the matter with him? He was generally a pretty even, good-tempered, steady sort of guy. With his money, he could have been a heller, a spendthrift, a tramp, a nothing. He wasn't any of these, he was a damned good citizen. So why all the gloom and doom all of a sudden? And again, why on such a sweet and gentle day?

What he probably needed to do, he told himself with an amusement that helped, was fall in love. Except, he wondered, rather wistfully, where was she? Unlike Marc Taylor, who was a decent enough guy but seemed to be laboring under some sort of continuing mental burden right now, Smitty was a little disturbed but not devastated by the fact that his particular girl wasn't on hand this very moment. He fully expected to find her one of these days, and if he didn't find her here by the time he graduated, he was sure the family would have her all lined up for him when he got home. He came of a social class whose rituals were as rigid as India's, particularly in the area of the selected bride. It was breaking down some, gradually. Nowadays girls were more and more making up their own minds, but few were so foolish or so careless of the goodies of life that they would willingly pass up a Carriger. He wasn't worried about *that*. He just rather wished that he knew who she was right now, and preferably here, not back home. He needed her company to help change his mood on this gently drifting, sleepy afternoon.

He sighed and thought: Oh, well. Right now he had three heavy business administration courses and all his committees to worry about, and he thought that was a good thing. It kept him occupied. It kept them all occupied.

Excom; Rally Committee; the Political Union; the Concert Series Committee; the freshman orientation committee; dance committees as numerous as there were dances, and that was plenty; picnic, barbecue and special-event committees; various Big Game committees; the Row's rushing committee; the committee on public exercises; Interfraternity Council; Interclub Council; the various religious clubs; women's and men's riding clubs; the rifle and pistol club; the drama club; the various Young Men's and Young Women's Christian Associations committees; the Women's Glee Club; the Men's Glee Club; the various honorary societies in the chemistry, engineering, business, journalism, French, German, English and other departments; the athletic letter societies; Young Democrats; Young Republicans; the American Student Union; the International Committee; the Japanese Students' Association; other nationality associations; the tennis club; the polo club; the badminton club; the debating club; men's and women's bridge clubs—

And on, he thought.

And on.

And on.

"If the sports don't get you," Franky summed it up, "the committees will."

And he was just about right, Smitty thought, as he reached the gym and prepared to add one more to his own list of activities. He hadn't paid too much attention to intramural sports before—it was hardly his area of interest, as he had told Hank—but he was a good citizen and a fast learner: he'd be an expert by the time he'd been on the committee a week. He had this compulsion to serve. It was just the way he was.

After the meeting he decided to use the pool as long as he was there. Jeff Barnett and Randy Carrero were practicing laps together and he joined in for a while. The subject of Bayard Johnson came up but they didn't reach any conclusions. Jeff sounded adamant, Randy undecided. Smitty said he was, too. He left them still faithfully splashing up and down and went forth again into the sleepy afternoon, heading back toward the Inner Quad, the bookstore and so home to the house. Looking into the Inner Quad through the arch that supported the huge old clock whose Westminster chimes bonged away the hours, he saw Billy Wilson and Janie Montgomery, arm in arm, strolling slowly along. He thought for a moment of hailing them and stopping to chat, then decided against it. Far be it from him to interrupt young love. Lucky Billy, he thought, with a touch of envy rare for busy, industrious, solid and secure Smith Carriger. Billy had *his* girl, all right.

And indeed he had, Billy told himself happily as they wandered slowly along. Everything about Janie suited him just fine and everything about him seemed to suit her just fine. Some people might make cracks about their almost overwhelming felicity but they didn't care. They were convinced it was jealousy, "and to hell with them," Billy sometimes remarked with rare profanity.

Now as they wandered across the center of the Quad in the lazy sun, the campus quiet around them, virtually the only sound the distant drone of some pedagogic voice exhorting sleepy students in some afternoon class in some distant, dusty corner, Billy found himself idly puzzling, as he often did, exactly what it was about Janie that so powerfully appealed to him.

She was small and petite, but lots of girls were that. She was amiable and friendly, but most here were. She had a good but not brilliant brain, which Billy told himself was just fine because that was the kind of brain he had, too. She wasn't any raving beauty but then he wasn't any Gil Gulbransen–Lor Davis type himself. He was a nice-looking kid, she was a nice-looking kid, they were just nice, average people. They both had open, honest, welcoming faces which told the world that they were disposed to like and trust most everybody.

"Maybe that's it," he said aloud. Janie gave his arm a squeeze and demanded, "What?"

When he told her what he was thinking she laughed, the gurgling little laugh he had forgotten to list among her qualifications. He did like that laugh.

"You sound pretty smug to me," she remarked. "Pre—tty satisfied, if I may say so."

"You may," he said. "It won't stop me, though. How about *that*?"

"You're shameless," she said, laughing again.

"Absolutely," he agreed, and stopped abruptly in front of Memorial Church. Mourning doves murmured their soft "Croo-*croo*! Croo-*croo*!" above the glowing mural.

"What is it?"she asked, a little alarmed by the suddenness of his action.

"Isn't it a *beautiful* afternoon!" he exclaimed. She gave her funny little laugh again.

"Want to go in for a minute?" he asked.

"I haven't been in Memorial Church for months," she said, looking a little embarrassed. He laughed.

"Me either." His expression sobered. "But you know, once in a while—it's good to stop in, don't you think? I mean, it's nice to have it there. I'm glad the founders built it for us. It's nice to have it when you want it."

"You mean it's good for the soul," she suggested with a twinkle.

"That's exactly what I mean," he agreed. "Come on."

The church was deserted, absolutely still. Sunlight slanted down through the stained-glass windows, dust particles danced. Although the muraled facade was large and impressive, centerpiece of the Quad and so of the University, the general effect inside was small, comforting, "almost cozy," in the words of Bill Lattimer, a regular attender. It had been created with care, and with love for the dead boy whose untimely passing in Italy had inspired the founding of a great university. It had been built to scale, as it were, not only for the regular services held there but for the occasional students who like Billy and Janie might decide to pause in their busy lives and just drop in for solace, meditation or just plain silence. Some attended every Sunday, some now and then, some rarely saw it from one year's end to the next. There was never anything compulsory about it, but it was there when needed, a comforting presence in everyone's mental geography of the campus.

They went halfway down the aisle, stepped into a pew and sat down, holding hands. A solemn silence. Finally he broke it softly.

"I do thank God for you," he whispered. "I really do. I don't deserve you, but He brought you to me and so—I do thank Him. Is that all right?"

"You silly!" she said, tears coming into her eyes. "You absolute silly! What do you mean, is that all right? Of course it's all right! I do the same. So there."

And, rather shakily, she uttered again her little chortling laugh.

She snuggled into his arm and he kissed her. Then he looked around guiltily: he had the sense that someone else was there. But he could see no one.

He relaxed and kissed her again. Gently the organ began to play: "Oh, you beautiful doll—you great big beautiful doll—"

They moved apart with a start and suddenly grinned.

"I'll bet I know who that is," he said, half rising, half turning. "Hack! Come out of there!"

With a grand thunder the organ crashed into the opening chords of the wedding march, then as abruptly ceased. Haggerty appeared and came forward with a grin.

"Hi, Billy," he said. "I must congratulate you on finding the ideal place to smooch. Fran and I used to do this sometimes, when we were young and foolish."

"You never do now, though," Billy suggested.

"Never." Haggerty laughed. "Too old and dignified, now. I dimly remember it as fun, though. How are you, Janie?"

"Fine, thanks, Hack," she said. "Do go on playing for us. We'll be quiet."

"Nah," Hack said. "I just come in to fool around a little—the chaplain told me I can whenever I want to, if the organ's free. I just have a little something in mind I want to work out this afternoon. This is a lot quieter than the house."

"Please," Billy said. "We really will be quiet."

"Of course you *can* applaud after the more brilliant passages," Hack said with a chuckle. "I wouldn't mind."

"What is it?" Janie called after him as he returned to the organ.

"Sort of a sequel to 'A Walk on the Quad,'" he called back. "I may title it 'Lollin' on the Lake,' or something equally frivolous. Anyway, it's going to be campus-oriented. I'll play you the first part and the scraps I've got so far for the second. It's very disorganized."

"I'll bet."

"You'll see," Hack said. He seated himself and sat quietly for a moment. Billy and Janie held hands again and were very still.

Very softly Hack began to play.

Seated thus in the soft amber light of the beautiful building, alone with his thoughts, Haggerty found his mind swirling with all those thousand and one ideas and intimations that ultimately coalesce in the creative process, if one is fortunate, into a coherent whole. He was here to compose and he was also here to clarify and define his own feelings and attitudes. This was often the case when he sat at piano or organ in a nonprofessional situation. On most occasions, his musings revolved around the same thing they had revolved around for the better part of two years: Fran. She was intermingled with all his music—she *was* his music. But they seemed to be no further along than they always had been on the difficult path to reconciliation of their differing ideas on marriage, family and career.

He let his fingers stray for a minute or two, scales, arpeggios, glissandos, chopsticks, anything to limber up. Then, almost automatically, since he knew it so well by now, but with the infinite delicacy and attention to detail that marked all his playing, he swung into the first movement of his newest opus. He wasn't going to call it "Lollin' on the Lake" or anything like that. He was simply going to call it "You."

It began very quietly with a lovely limpid line that rose slowly to a stronger, more powerful statement; hesitated for a while on a graceful, contemplative theme; slid gently down again to a sustained, driving yet almost moody combination of minors; and ended quietly on a reprise of the opening theme.

He paused. Down below Billy and Janie applauded quietly. They were joined by several others who apparently had come in, drawn by the music. He dismissed them all from his mind and began to ramble through what he called "the scraps." Each was melodic—everything he wrote was melodic—fluid, appealing, frequently almost hypnotic in its power. He was not a wildly experimental composer, his instinctive sense of form and beauty was too great; but he was a very good one indeed.

He thought that possibly he should take the four themes stated in the opening movement and develop each into a separate segment, rather than try to add further movements based on the "scraps." He thought perhaps he might do that; and, musing and rambling and letting his particular daemon take him where it would, he started again on the first, lovely melody and let it grow and expand, advance, turn back upon itself, find its path again and go forward to a sweet and lingering conclusion.

He paused to make notes and as he did so, Billy and Janie peeked around the edge of the organ, mouthed "Got to go—thanks—see you," and went on their way back out to the sleepy afternoon. He smiled, waved, turned back. He could stay there until dinnertime, just running over things, repeating, embellishing, adding, discarding—and probably would. The world was far away and he was quite content.

In a creative sense, that is.

On the other level, where tall and gracious Fran Magruder resided always in his mind, he was not so content. He was writing this piece for her—essentially, he had written everything in the past two years for her—and about her, and because of her. It was as though he were trying to find in his music some easy solution to what at times appeared to be their almost insoluble differences about their mutual future. That it would be mutual, neither had entertained the slightest doubt since they had met at a dance in sophomore year. But how they were going to reconcile its opposing but equally insistent demands, they didn't quite know; and although they did their best to conceal it from one another, they knew they were equally uncertain and equally apprehensive.

Their latest argument had occurred just last night on the way back from studying together at the Libe, and he supposed that was really what had impelled him to come in here and thump away. (His playing was the farthest thing from "thumping," but that was how he often casually referred to it.) He was walking her home to the Union where she lived. Along the way, as often happened, they got into what she referred to as "Topic A-1."

"It seems to me," he said finally after fifteen minutes of increasingly emphatic exchanges, "that for you to go to work for a law firm in San Francisco would be just as disruptive and destabilizing of family life as it would be for me to play an occasional gig on the side just to keep my hand in."

"It wouldn't be 'just a gig on the side,' " she said, "and you know it, Hack Haggerty. Before I knew it you'd be trying to establish your own band and go on the road somewhere. What would that do to family life?"

"Others do it," he said stubbornly. She snorted.

"Yes. And look at their family lives!"

"I don't know much about them, actually," he said in a superior tone which, instead of annoying her further, as he rather hoped, just made her laugh.

"You sound so knowledgeable," she said.

"So do you."

"Well," she said, "from what I *read* about them, it's pretty disruptive. Of course, maybe all the articles are false. But *my* research indicates—"

"*Now* who's sounding knowledgeable?" he inquired with a chuckle, tucking her hand more firmly under his arm. "You lawyers! '*My* research shows—!' How pompous can you get?"

"Not much more, probably," she said with an answering amusement, "but if anybody can do it, I imagine you can. Stop ducking the issue. You know perfectly well—"

"I don't know *anything* perfectly well!"

"All right, imperfectly, then—you know imperfectly well that a musical career is not conducive to a settled and stable family life. *I* can get somebody to stay with the children, but it's difficult when the father's away—"

"Oh, *ho*! Now we're discussing the children already. Who said we're going to have any?"

"*I* say so," she said, "and since I'm the one who's going to have to do all the work in that department, if *I* say we're going to have them then I assume *I* will, O.K.?"

He halted their slow progress and gave her a mock-intent look. They both laughed.

"Let's go once around the Quad for exercise before I take you to the Union," he suggested. "We can't settle this in the short time it takes to walk a direct line up there."

"Fine," she said, pulling him determinedly forward. "Let's go!"

"Slow down!" he protested after a minute or so along the dimly lit, deserted colonnades. "Slow *down!* We don't have to race."

"It's good for us," she said, but relenting and coming down to a more comfortable pace. "No, really, I'm not kidding, Hack. I can get help, once I get established with a good firm, but I'll be there at both ends of the day. You might not be there except at both ends of the season."

"Suppose I get a contract with some hotel or night club right in the City? I might be sleeping while they are in school, but I'll be up when they come home and I won't leave until after they've gone to bed. Wouldn't that be enough?"

"It doesn't work that way," she said. "Bands move around, they don't stay all the time in one place. Maybe that would be true for a month or two or even six months, but after that you'd be in some place like—*Cleveland*, maybe!"

"Who ever goes to *Cleveland?*" he demanded, mock-aghast, and they stopped again and broke into laughter. "Now listen," he said as they resumed stride, "you're making such a big deal about this and we're not even married yet. Don't fret. It will all work out. Believe me."

"Oh, I believe you," she said, again amused. "You just mean it will work out as Hack Haggerty wants it to. I believe you. I believe you're quite convinced of that."

"Well, the alternative," he said in a reasonable tone as they rounded Engineering Corner, "is for it to work out as Fran Magruder wants it to work out, isn't it? Where's the compromise in that? And isn't compromise what marriage is supposed to be all about?"

"If you really insist on starting a band," she said, "I suppose we'll compromise some way if we want to be together—"

"Which we do."

"Which we do. But I still think it would be very risky to have it all depend on something as shifting and uncertain as a musical career."

"Well," he said, "maybe law is a little more certain, I'll grant you that, particularly with the grades you're piling up. But I still maintain you'd be away almost as much and it would be just as disruptive and just as threatening to us."

"No," she said in a firm tone he had come to know pretty well, the only tone that made him wonder—but only fleetingly—whether it really would work out. "It wouldn't. There's no comparison. So I'd suggest we abandon that fruitless and obviously unprofitable line of argument."

He stopped dead again and regarded her with an amazed shake of the head.

"Lawyer talk!" he exclaimed. "Lawyer talk! Why don't you sound like a human being? Anyway," he said in sudden exasperation as she started an annoyed retort, "why the hell discuss it anyway? You know I'm taking economics. You know I'm going to be a broker. That's stable enough, isn't it?"

"Yes," she conceded. "But I know you'll be miserable. And I don't want that for you, either."

"What in hell *do* you want?" he demanded. "And don't say 'you' because I won't believe it."

At which they laughed ruefully, gave each other a quick kiss under the arches, linked arms again, rounded English Corner and strode briskly up the Quad and so to the Union for her and back to the house for him.

And that, he thought now as his themes grew and expanded and began to flow fully and easily under his inspired fingers, was about where their arguments always ended. He supposed they'd settle it someday, but he was beginning to wish he knew when. He never doubted that it would all work out somehow, though. He quite literally couldn't conceive of life without Fran.

He ran softly once more through the entire composition, ending on a lingering, yearning note that died out gently in the silent church. His audience had dwindled down to two, a couple of fellows he didn't know, who applauded quietly and gave him a cordial wave when he left the loft and started for home.

The afternoon was moving on when he got outside.

The sun was a little farther down in the west, first shadows were beginning to fall across the sandstone. All pedagogic voices were stilled now, nothing disturbed the Quad save the gentle crying of the doves that still mourned gently along the eaves. The nonstop life of the campus was proceeding elsewhere on this glowing afternoon when nobody, he thought, should have to do anything but just enjoy being alive.

One who was doing so, although his enjoyment was rudely interrupted from time to time by what he regarded as the raucous and totally unnecessary bellowing of the coach, was that swain of swains of Welcome Waggoner's, that athletic adornment and scholarship marvel of the house, Theodore Krasnik Musavich.

Moose and his sweating teammates were plowing the earth, as they put it, on the floor of the stadium. Shadows were already lengthening far across the field, although it was only three-thirty. It was beginning to be downright chilly in the bowels of the giant oval. Eighty-nine thousand spectators were going to scream there Saturday at the first game of the season, but right now their seats were empty, the swirling color and mounting excitement absent. The stadium's occupants consisted of the varsity team at one goal and the freshman team at the other. With them were the usual outriders, the second strings, the coaching and assistant coaches, the water boys and miscellaneous helpers plus a few students with nothing else to do at that moment. Perhaps a hundred had dropped by to watch practice. They were scattered widely around the stadium, most of them moving every few minutes to keep ahead of the shadows advancing rapidly across the bowl.

Moose could hear the wild animal roar of the crowd, the great happy pounding in his ears that was abruptly hushed as the play began. He blocked his man and then, finding himself miraculously free, danced sideways with amazing agility to receive the ball—faded back—reached for it—almost fumbled—teetered for a moment—regained his footing as the crowd's roar stopped for a breathless second and then resumed in a rising frenzy—turned and ran like an arrow, an absolute fucking arrow—eluded his pursuers, successfully brushed aside the only real challenge to his hurtling progress—ran—ran—ran—forty yards—fifty yards—*sixty-seven yards*—TOUCHDOWN!

"MOOSE!" the crowd roared in a great exultant chant. "MOOSE! MOOSE! MOOSE!"

"Musavich," the head coach bellowed, "are you dead or alive, God damn it! Get into that scrimmage, boy! Throw yourself into it, God damn it! You can do it. I think," he added, turning to shake his head at an assistant coach with a rather frustrated grin. "I *think*, God damn it."

"Yes, sir!" Moose shouted back. "I'll do better next time, sir!"

"God, man, I hope so!" Coach exclaimed. "Now, move!"

And this time, quite successfully, he did. In fact, he often did, quite successfully. It just took him a little time to really get warmed up, that's all. After all, hadn't his blocking been largely responsible last year for nine touchdowns, two of them in Big Game? And hadn't he actually, once, done exactly what he'd been dreaming of when Coach chose to intervene in his usual crude and overbearing fashion? The son of a bitch was damned ungrateful, Moose thought. He was always implying that he might boot Moose off the team, but he must think Moose had something or he wouldn't have kept him on the team for three solid years. And Moose *did* have something. It might not produce touchdowns every time, but by God it was a necessary, helpful and *worthwhile* contribution to the University's many victories. He deserved some thanks for it, God damn it!

They had about another half hour to go, and for the rest of the time he really did throw himself into it, thinking resentfully that he'd show the coach. Who did he think he was, anyway? He wasn't so special, his tenure was always being challenged by disgruntled alumni every time the team suffered defeat, even though it wasn't often. His status was just about as stable as might be expected from the administration's rather nervous attempts to balance its desire for academic reputation against the necessity for athletic glory. So far Coach had successfully withstood all challenges, but it was thanks to Moose and other good guys like himself, Moose thought. They saved his ass for him all the time by being the skilled and dedicated players they were. And certainly, he told himself with what he felt was thoroughly justified annoyance, some might be more skillful but none was more dedicated than Theodore Krasnik Musavich.

Moose had begun playing football, as nearly as he could remember now, about age four when his father, an avid fan, had begun tossing toy footballs to him in the backyard. This had presently developed into their own special scrimmage in which he received the ball and then attempted to evade his father's not too serious attempts to block him. By the time he was twelve the pretense ended and his father was really trying to block him. Moose by then was a very big boy for his age and his father was increasingly less successful in standing in his way. This suited both of them just fine, and when he entered high school it was with the understanding that everything was to be subordinated to the game; not too difficult an injunction for Moose to follow, since it was by then pretty obvious that Mr. Musavich's little boy was not going to be president of the scholastic honor society. He was not, however, quite as dumb as he liked to make out, either then or when he reached the University. His grades were a steady and modestly respectable C-plus, an occasional F now and then but also rising with fair frequency to the glittering heights of B-minus. And his football, both in high school and at the University, while seldom brilliant, was reliable.

Most coaches were usually content to field a good solid team, hoping for brilliance in a few individuals now and then but counting on overall strength for the hard, slogging advances that were necessary for a consistent string of victories. Moose fitted in fine. Coach might bellow at him impatiently from time to time, but he had recognized early that Moose was one of his key men. His sixty-seven-yard touchdown run last year had been, in everyone's opinion, sheer fluke; nonetheless, Moose had pulled it off, and you never knew what he might do again when things got tense and heated up—you just never knew. Meanwhile you could count on him to keep slogging away—a little slow to get started, maybe, but in there doing his damnedest when you needed him.

In those mysterious realms shielded from public view in which coaching staffs, the administration and certain influential alumni dickered and dealt in cozy, off-the-record, Byzantine agreement, it had early been decided that Moose Musavich was going to survive the stresses and strains of academia and thus be able to play on the team a normal four years. Once in a while some professor who hadn't been apprised of this might be prompted by memories of youthful dreams of academic morality to attempt to grade him rather more severely than necessary. If this threatened Moose's ability to stay in school, as it had on two occasions, the professor was called in for a little chat with Dr. Chalmers and Coach, Coach carrying the ball, so to speak, and Dr. Chalmers from time to time interjecting a typically vague but nonetheless pointed comment which clearly indicated that it would be to everyone's best interests if Moose were to be permitted to try again and, hopefully, stay in school. Thus it had come about. Everyone was happy, or at least reconciled, no one more than Moose himself, because, as he often said, "Jeez, I don't know what I'd do if I couldn't play football!"

Wilson had sometimes attempted to point out, rather severely, that one of these days Moose was going to have to decide, because he was going to graduate and certainly he recognized that he wasn't good enough to play professionally? Willie didn't put it quite that bluntly, but he didn't have to: Moose agreed promptly that he knew all that, but he was hopeful that his physical education major would qualify him for a coaching job in "some podunk high school or other."

"After all," he remarked, "I went to one, and I never knew a happier guy than my high school coach. He couldn't throw a turd, you know, let alone a football, but he sure was one happy guy doing what he liked, which was fooling around with us kids and having a good time. I think he was about our mental age, actually, although I guess now he was probably thirty-two or so. I'm mentally older than he was," he added quickly, sensing the gleam in Willie's eye, "but I know I'd enjoy it too. It's a good life, these small towns. You can be a big frog in a little puddle there. I won't mind it so much."

"You're a fair-sized frog here," Willie pointed out. "You're sure you wouldn't mind?"

"I'll be all right," Moose said. "Don't worry about me, Willie. I'll be O.K."

"Well," Willie said doubtfully, "I hope so."

"I will," Moose insisted, not noticing that Willie had neatly done one of his 180-degree turns and had wound up with Moose feeling good about being able to reassure *him* instead of the other way around as it had seemed to start out.

Next to football, Moose thought now as he and the team headed for the showers in the chill of the fast-falling twilight, he guessed he really did love the house best of anything. They had such a neat bunch of guys (except for that creep Suratt and snoopy-superior Gale Bryce and Rudy Krohl the Hitler-heiler and one or two others—but *mostly*, they were nice). They sure were great buddies to him, particularly his own classmates, though a lot of the younger ones like Rodge Leighton were really nice to him, too. He hoped they'd be able to maintain contact. So many guys drifted apart after school ended, he'd heard alums discuss this when they visited the house; but he wasn't going to. They meant too much to him.

And the next time he needed tutoring or something, or the next time he got mixed up with some girl they didn't consider suitable—although, so far, Suzy Waggoner was proving too much for them; he certainly wasn't going to let Suzy go any time soon—they'd rally around and help him out.

"Did you ever read *Winnie the Pooh?*" Willie had asked Unruh one time, after they had helped Moose cram for a midterm.

Unruh nodded. "Grew up on it. I still read it once in a while."

"Moose is the Eeyore of the house," Willie said. "Absolutely Eeyore."

"Absolutely," Guy agreed. "Sitting there with his tail in the water."

"And us to pull it out for him," Willie said with a chuckle. "What will he do when we're no longer around?"

"He'll manage," Guy predicted. "Somebody will always look after Moose. He's that kind of guy. Everybody likes Moose."

And this was mostly true, Moose felt now, feeling lucky as Coach snapped a towel at him as he went by and said cheerfully, as though he hadn't bawled him out at all, "Hang in there, Moose. You'll have a good year."

"Yes, sir," Moose said. "I'm going to try, sir."

"I'm sure of it," Coach said. "Just don't climb into Welcome Waggoner's pants too often, that's all."

At this all his teammates hooted (half of them had been the same route, Moose thought, what are they laughing for?). Moose blushed and studied his feet.

"Yes, sir," Moose said. "I'll tell her you warned me, sir."

"You *will* not!" Coach said in mock indignation. "I may want to try that myself one of these days."

"I'm sure she won't be offended, sir."

"Or surprised, either," Coach retorted and everybody hooted again.

He really wasn't such a bad guy, Moose thought. Most people were pretty nice when they weren't being official or something.

He guessed it *was* going to be a good year, at that. He felt really good about it, now. All he prayed for was one more touchdown like that one last year, and it would be absolutely perfect.

On the basketball court in the sports pavilion the thoughts of that brilliant student, solid citizen and reasonably active ladies' man, Clyde Gaius Unruh, were far at the moment from *Winnie the Pooh* or indeed anything of any substance. He was shooting baskets all by himself on the deserted floor. Practice for the varsity schedule hadn't started yet but he wanted to limber himself up. It wasn't going to be difficult, as he had gone to his high school alma mater in Waikiki at regular intervals during the summer to do just what he was doing now. He had also, as always, done a lot of surfing on the north side of Oahu where the really big waves rolled in.

Guy Unruh believed in keeping himself fit, and now, as he dribbled the ball and ran through a series of shots of deliberately varying difficulty, he was quietly enjoying that state of euphoria that comes with a sense of complete physical well-being. He moved around the court with the characteristic easy, loose-jointed lope that Bill Nagatani, at that time covering sports, had once described in the *Daily* as being "the closest thing to the flow of mercury one is likely to see in human form."

"Gosh," Guy had kidded him next time they met on the Quad "You're a poet."

"And don't know it," Bill had said, blushing a little, embarrassed that he'd let himself go in print that way. "But you *are* good, Guy, of course you know that. Damned good."

"I'm adequate," Guy admitted with a smile.

"You can say that again," Nagatani told him admiringly. "No wonder half the girls on campus think so too."

"*They* find me," Guy said with a grin, "*more* than adequate."

"I wish *I* had said that," Nagatani said. He grinned, too. "I wish I were *able* to say that. How do you do it?"

"Just like basketball," Guy told him as the bell rang and they parted to go to their classes. "Grab the ball—run with it—feint left—feint right—get the opposition thoroughly dizzy—*and into the basket!* Easy as pie."

Well, he thought more seriously now as he ran the length of the floor, ducking and weaving and dodging as though he were already facing some crack team like University of Santa Clara or Cal, those days were beginning to wind down a bit. It wasn't that he had become a chaste wallflower overnight—he didn't expect that ever to happen completely—but he was slowing down somewhat under the earnest attentions of Maggie Johnson. In her quietly careful, determined way, she was changing him quite a bit. He wasn't entirely sure he liked it all that much—he still was pretty carefree in ways she couldn't even imagine—but he was getting more "conservative," as he put it to himself. He wasn't quite as carefree and liberal as he had been up to six months ago when he had really begun to consider Maggie seriously. With her he had never made the final conquest that had been his so easily with a dozen others on campus. He wouldn't dream of even trying because he knew it would probably drive her away in hysterics. He considered it almost shocking that he should feel so inhibited in her presence. It both fascinated and rather frightened him. If she could paralyze him that much now, what could she do to him if they were married? He'd function physically, all right, there was never any doubt of that with Clyde Gaius Unruh; but what would she do to his *soul?*

He soared off the floor like some long, sleek, supple seal and sank a basket while he pondered this conundrum. "Soul" sounded awfully stagy, he thought, but it was some word like that which he was after: his being, his integrity, his essence—the thing that made Guy Unruh Guy Unruh—the thing that *was* Guy Unruh, unique to him, untouched and uncaged by anyone else.

That was what he didn't want to lose; and that was what worried him most about his increasingly concentrated view of Maggie Johnson. It could happen.

Disturbed and for the moment frustrated by this, he again raced down the court and raced back, extending his comfortable lope, so deceptively easy, so all-conqueringly fast, into a single long continuum of motion so smooth and so swift that he felt as though he were flying. He soared again from the floor in a high, triumphant leap and sank another basket.

Behind him he heard the thud of feet and turned to see a dark blur approach, twist, turn, leap almost as high and with equal grace drop in a ball.

He paused, momentarily out of breath, grinned and held out his hand.

"Damn, man," he said as they shook hands, "you're *good.*"

"I'm not as good as you," Bayard Johnson said with a shy, pleased smile, "but I'm *pretty* good."

"*Pretty* good," Guy echoed. "You're *great.* Come on!"

And he dribbled the ball down the court in another of his long, smooth-flowing rushes with Bayard fast behind him; evaded him successfully, turned and dribbled back as Bayard again tried to intercept him. He took aim, made his toss—and Bayard leaped high, knocked it down, grabbed it and was off down the court himself with Guy in fierce pursuit.

Fifteen minutes later, exhausted, tingling and happy, they sat side by side on the bench and toweled off the perspiration with the comfortable camaraderie of two who had taken each other's physical measure and found it an enjoyable and rewarding thing. When they had both stopped puffing and returned to a reasonably calm state of being, Guy said as a flat statement.

"You're going out for the team, of course."

Bayard frowned and looked, for the first time in their exuberant contest, a little uncertain.

"I don't know," he said finally. "Do you think they'd want me?"

"What do you mean, 'want you'?" Guy demanded. "We'd be utter fools not to take you. Of course we *want* you. One run down the floor and the coach will be on his knees begging you to play. Were you on the team back east?"

Bayard nodded.

"Well, it's a natural, then. Be here next week Tuesday at two P.M. when we have the tryouts. You'll have to go through the motions, but we need a guard and there won't be any problem. I'll talk to him."

"I wish people didn't have to—" Bayard began, and stopped.

"Have to what?"

"Talk to people for me," Bayard said in a low voice, staring at the floor. "I wish people could just—just take me as I am."

"I'm taking you as you are," Guy pointed out with some sharpness. "I'm taking you as a damned good basketball player." He turned on him with a challenging air. "All right?"

"I appreciate that," Bayard said. "But it still sounded so—so patronizing, somehow. So far—" He paused and then continued in the same low-voiced way. "So far, Willie and Bill Lattimer have taken me under their wing on Reg Day—and then Willie and Ari Katanian arranged to shift my room in the hall so I'd have roommates who didn't—didn't try to—to hassle me. And then Willie invited me up to dinner and—and crammed me down everybody's throat. And now you—"

"Listen!" Guy exclaimed indignantly. "Listen, you poor, pathetic little boy! Who's patronizing whom, here? You didn't ask for some of it but you did ask Willie to have your room changed—no, hear me out," he said as

Bayard started to make a movement of protest. "I know Willie volunteered to, but he told me it was clear you wanted help so he gave you help. And anyway!" he said, sounding even more indignant. "I know Willie does a lot of things just because he's a kindhearted sap who doesn't like to see people unhappy. So don't put him down on that, either! And the only reason I said I'd talk to the coach is that I'm not such an ungenerous soul myself! So, fuck it! I won't say a word to the coach. I won't have to, he'll see it for himself. Will that make you happy?"

For a moment Bayard did not reply. Then he gave his sidelong glance and sighed.

"I'm sorry," he said. "I'm sorry. I'm oversensitive, I guess. But you would be too if you were—if you were me."

"Well," Guy said, not relenting too much, "don't overwork it. You don't have to, out here. Most people are disposed to be friendly. Just give them the chance, O.K.? We only want to help you. And if that sounds patronizing, then fuck you, too, buddy. We don't have to be anything. We can just be silent. Would you like that better?"

"No," Bayard said with a half-smile. "I wouldn't like that better."

"O.K., you touchy son of a bitch," Guy said, returning the smile and jumping up. "Let's have another round."

And he was off down the court like lightning in his easy, gliding fashion. And after a second Bayard was after him. And after another fifteen minutes they were exhausted, pretty well reconciled, and off to the showers.

But afterwards, Guy shook his head in considerable bafflement as he walked slowly back to the library, where he was to meet Maggie for a little predinner studying.

And Bayard, moody and alone, walked slowly back to his hall. It wasn't, he told himself desperately as he moved along, head down, eyes averted, barely returning the several friendly hellos he received along the way, that he didn't appreciate what they were trying to do for him. But they just didn't understand. *They just didn't understand.* And no matter how hard they tried, or how hard any white tried, he didn't think they ever really would.

Or could.

They couldn't know, he told himself as he scuffed occasionally at a weed or clump of grass as he walked along the dusty path, what courage it had taken for him to decide to leave Howard University, where he was cosseted by his own, and come three thousand miles to an environment whose anticipated attitudes had often made him physically tremble. They couldn't know that he had been sick to his stomach all the way out on the train. They couldn't know that he had been forced to turn into the bushes behind Memorial Hill on Reg Day and be sick again, while the assistant dean of men stood patiently shielding him from view until he could proceed.

They couldn't know that he had literally been unable to eat until Willie and Ari Katanian had taken care of his problem with his roommates. They couldn't know how queasy he had felt all through dinner at the house, that he had several times during the meal felt as though he were going to vomit right there and had restrained himself with such agony that he thought he might literally pass out. They couldn't know how every minute of every hour of every day was a challenge and a strain. They couldn't know that it was only in this last half hour with Guy Unruh, racing up and down the court and losing himself in the sport he loved, that he had finally found a little peace, and finally begun to come to terms with the University and come back a little to what he thought of as "my real self."

He *knew* Guy and Willie and most of the others were "disposed to be friendly," as Guy put it. He *knew* he was being oversensitive and touchy. But some things you just couldn't help.

"I will do better," he muttered aloud to himself. "I *will* do better."

"That's good," some older guy he didn't know remarked as he overtook him and hurried past, but he looked back with a smile and the smile was friendly; and weakly but determinedly, Bayard smiled back and watched him for a moment before lowering his head again.

"Keep it up," his father had said, chucking him under the chin with a worried affectionate smile when his parents and brothers had said goodby to him in Union Station in D.C. "Don't let it hang down, boy. Keep it up!"

"I will," he said now—again aloud, although this time he looked around to make sure no one was in earshot. "I *will*."

And did, and felt better.

But it wasn't easy, he told himself as he thought again, with gratitude, of Guy's basically good-natured—and, Bayard knew, basically concerned—bullying afterwards.

It wasn't easy to pretend all the time that you were calm and secure and sure of things, even though now, after the last half hour, he was beginning to see a glimmer that it might really come true.

He realized that he really was beginning to feel a little more relaxed. He just had to keep up the momentum. If he could.

With the swift transitions of youth, not even stopping to shift gears, his mind leaped to a much pleasanter subject: the girl Willie had mentioned. Maryetta Bradford. He had looked her up in the Bawlout. She was a sophomore transfer like himself, from Berkeley, majoring in sociology. He wondered if Willie had called her yet. Maybe he could call Willie and—

He caught himself up short with a frustrated shake of the head. There he went again, inviting their help, running the risk of being patronized again.

Then he lifted his head and told himself flatly to cut it out.

It wouldn't be that at all. Willie had volunteered to help and he trusted Willie enough to believe that he really wanted to. Why shouldn't he accept the help in the spirit in which it was offered?

He kept his head up and his stride became more brisk. He would try to reach Willie right away.

A warning voice said: Watch out, she's white, you may just be inviting trouble. But this was the West now, not the South or East. He dismissed it.

He felt, abruptly, a great deal better. For the first time since reaching the University, he was taken out of himself. His strenuous workout with Guy seemed to have been a turning point. He had some really interesting things to think about, now.

And so, Bayard would have been much surprised to learn, did his new-found mentor. In the Associated Students main committee room in the Union, Wilson was presiding over the first full session of Executive Committee. But his heart and—a little more obviously than he realized—his attention weren't in it.

At the moment Donn Van Dyke was giving a report on the fall quarter's activities—as she saw them. He was not too sure all of her program would get by Excom unscathed, but it was being delivered with her usual sunny enthusiasm, which he had never found wearing before but now found a little tiring. This was possibly because he had once more, quite unexpectedly, run into his green-gold girl. (He was all too aware now that her name was Marian Emerson, but it was still too prosaic to think of her by name. It brought her down to earth too abruptly. He wasn't ready for that yet. "My green-gold girl" was much more romantic. To his considerable surprise, he *felt* romantic. It had sort of crept up on him when he wasn't looking.)

"And so with all *that*," Donna said with a chuckle, cheeks rosy, blond hair tossing, lovely smile on her lovely face, "I guess we'll *all* keep busy this quarter!"

"And every quarter," Willie murmured. "Unto the last generation. What do you think, Ari?"

"I'm overwhelmed," Ari Katanian said, amused. "But if you say so, Donn, I guess we can do it."

"Of course we can!" Donn said cheerfully. "If everybody pitches in, it's a cinch. Don't you think so, Willie?"

"I'm only here to preside," Wilson said, at which there were skeptical snorts and murmurs around the table. "What does everybody else think?"

And he looked around the lively circle: Ari and two other guys from the men's dorms; three women from the women's dorm; three from the sororities; himself, Smitty Carriger, Duke Offenberg and another guy from the Row; the Rally Committee representative; the faculty representative (Dr. Stafford, who obviously relished her role, as it gave her a prominent stage for her campus-riveting performances), and so on. Fifteen in all, a rather unwieldy body, he had always felt, but in reality it came down to himself,

Donna, Ari, Smitty, Duke, Dr. Stafford and maybe one or two others whose votes he could count on, who really decided things.

Now Duke spoke up in a reasonable tone of voice to ask if maybe it wouldn't be possible to cut back on a few things to save a little money.

"After all," he said, "it isn't as though we have all that much in the till. That's a hell of a heavy program, Donn."

"Oh, we'll be fine," she said airily. "A lot of this is charity events, you know. They generally take care of themselves. And the rest just need a few volunteers. They always turn up." She looked about with a smile. "We did."

"I just think we should try to run a balanced budget, that's all," Duke said, sounding not too impressed. "I'm sure the administration expects us to."

"The administration," Dr. Stafford said crisply, plunging a heavily jeweled hand through her severely pulled-back bun of gray hair, "expects you to act like a bunch of kids. But responsible kids. If that isn't an utterly delirious contradiction in terms."

"We try, Dr. Stafford," Willie said mildly. "We try. I think you have a good point, Duke. Any ideas for cutting back a little, anybody?"

"Not necessary," Donna said firmly. "Not necessary."

But several others seemed to think so, so the upshot was that he appointed Duke, Smitty and a guy and girl from the dorms to make a special report to the next meeting. Meanwhile they would proceed with the calendar Donna had outlined, if there were no objections. There were none.

That was what usually happened, he thought as his mind began to wander—in addition to his personal concerns it was after four and everybody was beginning to Think Dinner, as Franky Miller often put it. Things usually wound up in a special committee, a study and report. If the adult world was like this, he thought, it must waste an awful lot of time. But he didn't think it was like that. He couldn't believe their elders would be so dilatory and procrastinating. Only "kids," as Dr. Stafford called them, and nuts to her, could waste *that* much time.

They finished the closed-door portion of their meeting, threw it open, received five appeals for approval from various groups that wanted to organize "jolly-ups," the informal dances in the women's gym that some group or other put on about every other week; gave them swift approval on the promise, insisted upon by Duke, that they wouldn't ask for funds; heard one or two more cuties from Dr. Stafford, who obviously relished their sycophantic chuckles ("Have to keep the old girl happy," Willie confided later to Ari. "She can raise *more hell* with Chalmers when she gets mad"); and adjourned at five-fifteen, content with their meeting. Typical of Excom, felt Willie, who had been on it for two years. Routine stuff, no surprises. He called the next meeting for a week from then "subject to call of the chair if any emergencies arise," and they left in varying states of briskness and amiability.

Duke and Smitty started to hang around waiting for him to accompany them back to the house, but he murmured something vague about having to "check a few little things—see you guys back up there," and managed to shake them. Then he ducked quickly down to the Quad and over toward the church, which was where he had glimpsed her in the distance on his way to the meeting an hour and a quarter earlier. Which was absolutely absurd, he told himself, because why would she be there now? She was long gone, he knew that absolutely. Yet here he was, drawn back on the flimsiest hope, persuading himself there might be a thousand-to-one chance that she was still hanging around the Quad at this going-home hour.

For what, just to see him? How stupid could you be?

And yet—maybe it wasn't so stupid, at that. She might have had a late meeting with her faculty adviser—she might have wanted to stop by one of the departmental offices on some personal business—she might even have just been visiting the church. She might even, though he rejected this sternly, have had a date to meet someone else. There could have been a lot of reasons, couldn't there? Of course, she might even have *been* someone else, to be realistic about it—recalling his last pursuit in the Quad when he thought he had seen her and instead had overtaken some earnest, freckle-faced freshman. But still, he thought, it might be worth a look.

The Inner Quad, however, was completely deserted at this hour except for the occasional homegoing student who walked across it bound for somewhere else. Otherwise, nothing broke its placid tranquillity as autumn's quick-dying twilight began to turn the colonnades and arches into temporarily darkened caverns, before the lights came on. He wandered idly along them for a few minutes, finally told himself to knock it off. This was stupid. She wasn't there and there was no hope she would be.

He turned abruptly, stepped up speed and headed back across the center of the Inner Quad.

It was about time, he thought wryly, to stop acting like a typical lovesick college kid and get on home. He didn't like to think of himself as typical and he certainly wasn't love-struck. But he did have to admit, with his saving inward humor, he sure was acting funny if he wasn't.

He looked up at the growing moon accompanied by the first planets and stars, lying against the rapidly darkening lemon-green sky. Do you belong to me? he asked one of them, probably the planet Jupiter. Jupiter didn't answer.

He laughed aloud at himself, said hi to a couple of late-passing girls on their way to the women's dorms, and went on his way. Willie Wilson, he told himself, you are a nut.

It had been Kay Ellsworth, hadn't it, who had said at Reg Dance that Marian sat beside her in an English class? So that meant talking to Latt— who in turn would talk more casually to Kay—who in turn would very casually mention to Marian that she knew that dashing soul the student-body president—who, he hoped, would probably hear that it would be all right to make a direct approach. Tinkers to Evers to Chance. Wilson to Lattimer to Ellsworth to *her*.

That was how it was done, he thought wryly, if you had a devious mind like his—and didn't want to take any chances on being hurt if you went at it too directly.

He began to whistle as he left the Quad, a cheerful sound with which he kept himself company all the way back to the house.

9

On weekends the house, like the campus, was relatively quiet. If there was a home game, Saturday was a day of happily rising excitement until it was over, after which the more affluent and adventuresome took the train to San Francisco or, if among the few who had automobiles, drove down to Carmel and Monterey or sometimes as far afield as Lake Tahoe or Yosemite. The nonaffluent majority stayed close to home, studying, relaxing, bullsessioning on politics or world events or sex, taking a break to see a movie in the town if the spirit moved.

On this particular October weekend the game was away, in Southern California. Moose, his teammates and several hundred loyal fans had gone south on a special train, having a great time and imbibing things of which Dr. Chalmers, with his famous (and sometimes, it sounded, rather desperate) insistence that "alcohol and gasoline do not mix," would not have approved. The president did not really think that alcohol and anything mixed, and in this he was probably entirely correct. The coach and his assistants did their best to keep their charges dry, with frequent threats of expulsion from the team and the University if anyone strayed. This worked quite well with most of them until after the game, at which time the coaching staff closed its eyes to what went on.

At that point, down came decorum, coaches and all.

For this, Gulbransen and McAllister, among the seniors, Carriger, Davis and Godwin of the juniors, and Carrero and Bryce of the sophomores had made the trip south. For the younger members, there were all sorts of implicit promises of delightful sinfulness in being out on the town in L.A. on a Saturday night five hundred miles from school, but the chances were very good that none of them would have the nerve to do anything about it except walk along the streets and imagine, with a tense and rather wan envy, all sorts of thrillingly evil things going on behind closed doors. Or they might all wind up in a beer joint somewhere on Sunset Boulevard, where, if they managed to gain entry, they would probably be severely restricted to soft drinks and frustrated fantasies. They would then go back to the Y.M.C.A., which was all they could afford, and try to get some sleep, which they would find very difficult. They would then come back to the house and boast that they had really had one hell of a satisfying and thoroughly sinful time, which would fool nobody among their elders, most of whom had been through the same experience a number of times.

At the house, life in their absence was proceeding at half-pace on what everybody knew would be one of the last glorious days of autumn. The heavy fogs, cold nights and drenching rains of the Bay Area's short winter would come all too soon. This was a weekend to relax and enjoy life, even if one did have to study or tend to house business. At least it could be done outdoors.

In pursuit of this pleasant objective, Ray Baker, Buff Richardson, Lattimer and Franky Miller appropriated the chaise longues and the two sagging old sofas on the southwest sunporch. Johnny Herbert, Duke Offenberg, Rodge Leighton, Rudy Krohl, Marc Taylor and Jeff Barnett were occupying similar dilapidated artifacts on the north porch. Out front on the balcony overlooking the lawn Unruh and Suratt were sharing an arm's-length silence and the two old rockers that resided there. Like most of the furniture in the house, the outdoor equipment was old, battle-scarred, sagging and worn. It never seemed worthwhile to assess members for new furniture because, as Franky pointed out, it became old furniture in a month. Hand-me-downs were good enough until they finally collapsed. Then some alum could usually be prevailed upon to kick in a few dollars to buy a replacement, usually secondhand for that same reason.

It was after lunch. Everybody had either gone to the Cellar for a snack or, more likely, had gone to the kitchen to put together a sandwich or two and a glass of milk from the supplies Dewey the cook laid in every Friday for this purpose. Now everybody was feeling drowsy and relaxed. Muted sounds of activity formed a pleasant background, the occasional shout of laughter from nearby houses—voices raised in idle, desultory, halfhearted argument—tennis rackets pinging and tennis balls thunking on the nearby court—birdsong—Haggerty musing softly on the piano downstairs—the rare car or two driving by, starting up, parking—a mild, caressing wind now and again rustling the leaves of the big eucalyptus beside the garage—the world drifting . . .

Into this placid scene Rudy Krohl brought reality with a capital R. It was not a pleasant half hour that followed.

Trying to reconstruct it later for Willie's benefit, Rodge Leighton said it had begun when Duke Offenberg returned from a trip to the john and accidentally brushed against Rudy's foot as he passed.

"Duke apologized," Rodge said with a puzzled shake of the head, "but it sure seemed to annoy Rudy. Out of all proportion, it seemed to me."

"He *is* out of all proportion," Wilson said grimly. "We've got to take that boy down a peg or two or he's going to be raising hell every time we turn around. What did Duke do?"

"Tried to keep calm," Rodge said, looking disturbed. "But Rudy wouldn't let him."

And that was how it had begun.

"Damn it!" Rudy exclaimed sharply. "What the hell are you doing, Duke? You kicked my foot!"

"I didn't 'kick' it," Duke said, at first mildly. "I brushed against it. I'm sorry."

"You kicked it," Rudy said, sitting up on the old army cot on which he had been sunning himself. "You deliberately kicked it."

"I did not!" Duke said with equal sharpness. "I said I brushed against it and I said I'm sorry. What the hell's the big deal about it, anyway?" His tone became acrid. "Did I break your little piggy?"

"I don't like to be touched," Rudy retorted. "Especially by people like you."

"What do you mean?" Duke demanded, turning back and looming over him while the others became still. "People like me? Say what you mean, Krohl, or shut your damned mouth."

"Oh, now," Rodge Leighton said nervously. "Now, Duke—"

"This is between this—this *Nazi*," Duke said evenly, "and me. I like you, Rodge. Stay out of it."

"Who's a Nazi?" Rudy demanded, trying to stand up. Duke pushed his chest and he toppled back with a shout of anger.

"Now, listen you guys—" Hank Moore and Jeff Barnett said simultaneously, getting out of their chairs and moving toward them. Duke turned on them with a look that made them stop.

"Stay out of it, I said!" he snapped as Rudy tried to struggle to his feet, sputtering. Duke gave him another shove and he fell back again. There was a ripping sound and the ancient canvas on the ancient cot finally gave up its ancient ghost, depositing Rudy, now livid with rage, flat on his back on the floor. "Now," said Duke, standing over him, "tell me more about it, little man."

"But you can't do this, you guys!" Rodge protested in a voice nervous but determined. "This is the *house*. We're all *brothers! You can't do this!*"

"I didn't begin it," Duke said, breathing heavily, "but I intend to finish it. If Hitler Junior here wants to make something of it."

"You damned . . . damned . . ." Rudy hissed—literally, Rodge thought, with a wild surge of near-hysterical inner amusement, hissed. He couldn't believe it.

"Damned what?" Duke demanded, voice now ominously quiet.

"Damned Jew!" Rudy said with a half-whisper, his face contorted as he struggled to get up. "Damned Jew."

Duke's fist caught him squarely on the jaw and he went back down—for the count, Rodge saw. He had never seen it happen to anyone in real life before.

"Ah'm goin' to get he'p!" Jeff Barnett cried. "We cain't handle this alone!"

And he raced out the door and across to the other porch yelling, "He'p! He'p! you guys! Ova heah on the othuh po'ch!"

"What the *hell*—?" Franky Miller demanded, half asleep in the sun. But they all responded at once, leaping off the chaise longues, rocketing off the sofas, racing on Jeff's heels back to the other porch, as Unruh and Suratt hurried in from the front balcony.

Rudy came to groggily a moment later to find them all staring down at him.

For a second he obviously did not know where he was. Then a fearful scowl took over as he blinked and sat up amid the wreckage of the cot, rubbing his jaw and wincing with pain—damaged, they could see, but not permanently. Duke still stood over him like an avenging angel.

"Now," Buff said sternly, "I'm president of this madhouse. Suppose you tell me what happened."

"He—" Duke and Rudy began together. Buff cut them off.

"You, Rodge," he said. "Tell us."

After Rodge had—with several bitter interjections from the combatants, loudly squelched by everybody—Buff said nothing for a moment. Then he turned to his fellow seniors. "What do you guys think?"

"Expel them both," Franky said flatly.

"Too harsh," Unruh objected.

"Much too harsh," Lattimer agreed. "And unfair. Duke was obviously acting under great provocation. I will admit," he added dryly, "that Rudy's provocation remains something of a mystery to me. But I gather he thinks he had one. In fairness we should probably find out."

"How about a house meeting?" Renny Suratt inquired.

After a little negotiating to accommodate various study schedules, it was so agreed.

"O.K.," Buff said. "Tuesday night after dinner. Meanwhile, you guys," he added, turning to Duke, who had stepped back, still looking like a thundercloud, and Rudy, who was giving scowl for scowl, "just stay out of each other's way, all right? You're going to have a chance to thrash this all out—"

"If necessary," Franky interjected, more lightly, "we'll set up a ring and referee a return match," which made everybody smile a little, except the two adversaries, who were still too angry.

"Could be," Buff said. "Anyway, we'll do it. Now I'd suggest everybody get back to whatever they were doing. Rudy, clear up that mess and take it out back to the trash. Duke, come join us on the other porch."

For a moment Duke looked as though he would refuse. Then he shrugged, picked up the textbook he had been studying and obediently followed them. Behind him Rudy let fly with a string of expletives that were, however, carefully muted so that only those close by could hear. Rodge, Jeff and Hank paid no attention and turned back to their books. Presently, muttering, Rudy picked himself up, gathered together the remnants of the cot, threw his towel over his shoulder and, still scowling, left.

Silence descended on both porches and on the front balcony, where Guy and Renny had returned to their studies.

The pleasant day was no longer pleasant. And the outside world, with all its growing horrors, not quite so far away.

Ten minutes later Duke stood up abruptly and snapped shut his book. His face was pale.

"I'm feeling sick to my stomach," he said. "I think I'll go to my room and study."

"Watch out for lurking Nazis," Franky suggested and Latt said quietly, "That's not funny, Franky."

"No, it isn't," Buff agreed as Duke, expressionless, went out the door.

"Just trying to be helpful," Franky said, for once looking and sounding genuinely abashed. "I just thought maybe a little joke would—"

"Your timing is usually impeccable," Latt told him with a wry smile, "but not this time. I hope they don't run into each other somewhere else in the house."

"They will," Buff said. "But I get the feeling they'll avoid another round."

"For now," Ray Baker said. Tim looked from the writing pad on which he was scribbling notes for an editorial.

"It's a good thing Duke is bigger than Rudy," he remarked. "They like to kick around littler people, these Nazis."

Buff looked at him with his amiable, good-will-to-everyone smile.

"Now *you're* being prejudiced," he said. "Is that going to be the subject of the next editorial?"

"It might," Tim said. "It might. I think I'm going to take off on the Japanese in this one. They're really raising hell in their invasion of China. Where are they going to stop?"

"Nagatani won't *like* you!" Franky said in a half-singsong, only half kidding. Tim frowned.

"I don't know what to make of Bill. I like him—always have liked him— he's a hell of a good newspaperman and writer—he's going to make a good editor of the *Daily*—he'll probably wind up somewhere very successful in the profession, if he wants to stay in it—but—I just don't know. There's something there I can't get at."

"He hasn't signed a treaty with Krohl, has he?" Ray Baker asked with unexpected wryness. "The Campus Axis?"

They all laughed but it was laughter with uneasy overtones: the world really wasn't all that far away at any time these days.

"I don't think so," Bates said with equal dryness, "but you never know." He looked across at Richardson's lengthy bulk, stretched out on one of the chaise longues in the sun. "What are we going to do about Krohl, Buff?"

"I don't know," Buff said from under the towel he had drawn across his face. "What do you want to do?"

"I still think we ought to expel him," Franky said. "I wasn't kidding."

"And I still think that's too harsh," Lattimer said. "But he certainly ought to be disciplined somehow. He's getting to be a very divisive element."

"Like his countrymen," Tim said. Latt looked at him with a troubled frown.

"Well, we're his countrymen, they're not. We can't hold him responsible for what happens in the old country."

"We can hold him responsible for bringing it over here," Ray Baker said in his mild but determined way.

"Yes," Latt said, still troubled. "I suppose one can look at it that way. But I still don't think it's right to judge him by what goes on in Germany."

"I think we're getting to a point," Bates said gravely, "where *everybody* is going to have to be judged by what's going on in Germany. How we react to it—how we don't react to it—whether we do something about it—whether we turn our backs and pretend it isn't there—we'll all be judged."

"Oh, well," Franky said, rolling over on his back, a large and comfortable mound on the other chaise longue, "we all know you've come back from vacation an avid interventionist. A lot of us don't see why we can't just stay out of it and let Europe stew in its own juice."

"I've *been* there," Tim said grimly. "And so have you, Buff. How about giving me a hand here?"

"Well—" Buff said from under his towel, and paused. "Well . . . I don't know, Timmy. I'll grant you it was disturbing to see those little kids who don't even know where we are chanting about how much they hate us and the British and the French—"

"And the soldiers," Tim said grimly. "And the tanks. And the planes. And the hysteria in the streets and the rallies, just as frightening—just as evil—just as blind. . . how can we ignore it?"

"I don't ignore it," Buff said mildly, as on the nearby tennis courts somebody shouted a triumphant cry as he scored a happy point. Feminine voices were also heard. A game of mixed doubles was apparently underway. "I just question whether it's really as serious as you seem to think, that's all. Understand me—" he pulled away a corner of the towel and gave Bates a friendly glance—"I'm not disparaging your feelings or your worries about it. You're sensitive to these things, that's part of your job as a journalist. And also—" he smiled before pulling the towel back in place—"that's you. That's the way you are. You feel things more deeply than a lot of us do."

"Sure, Timmy," Franky said. "That's why we *love* you."

"Oh, sure," Tim said, smiling a little, drawn momentarily out of his earnestness. "That touches me deeply, Brother Miller, you've no idea . . . I *do* think it's serious and I *do* worry about it and I *don't* think it's funny."

"I don't think it's funny either," Franky said, rolling over on his stomach and lifting himself as much as possible on his elbows, "but I think there's got to be some proportion about it. A lot of people on campus think you're getting pretty rabid in the *Daily*, you know. A little too much Johnny One-Note. Maybe you should relax a bit."

"Well, the hell with you," Tim said angrily.

"Just telling you," Franky said mildly, plopping his head down on his arms. "What else is a brother for? If we don't, who will?"

"Plenty of people, if they disagree," Tim said, still ruffled.

"And you haven't been getting letters about it?" Franky inquired.

"Well—" Tim said, and paused.

"Lots?"

"A few."

"Come on, now. Be honest."

"I *am* honest," Tim said, but less certainly. "Quite a few. But there've also been quite a few supporting me. It's about even. And that *is* the truth. So I have to decide what I think is right and go ahead with it, don't I? It seems simple enough to me."

"What's simple these days?" Ray Baker asked, looking up from his book with a rueful smile. "Doesn't seem to me that much is."

"I'm sorry," said Tim. "You either see it or you don't. I do."

"Well!" Latt said with a laugh. "I guess that tells us. You wouldn't be getting a little arrogant about it, would you, Timmy?"

"No, I'm not getting arrogant!" Tim protested with a sudden desperation in his voice. "Somehow I've got to make them *see*. I've got to make them *see*."

"But maybe not so insistently," Latt suggested gently. "Maybe—a little more lightly?"

"How can you be 'light' about Adolf Hitler and Nazis?" Tim asked bleakly. "How can you be 'light' about an imperialistic machine that seems bent on conquering the world?" Then he relented and relaxed. "Look, you guys: I appreciate your concern—I hear what you're telling me—I know you want to protect me—and I appreciate it. I really do. I don't mean to sound 'arrogant,' and I don't mean to be 'rabid,' and I want you all to think well of me. I realize you're helping—as you see it—and I'm grateful for that. I'll try to be fair about it and not let my concern override my sense of balance. It's just that sometimes—" he looked out at the lovely day and sighed—"it's difficult, that's all . . . difficult. But I'll try."

"Can't ask for more than that," Buff observed from under his towel, and Franky extended his arms out far enough to clasp his hands awkwardly and cry, "Hurray! Hurray! Crusading Editor Sees Light, Vows to Wage a Balanced Fight! Thousands Cheer as Bates Abates!"

"Jackass," Tim observed, but smiling. "What's everybody doing tonight?"

"Katie and I are going to see *Dracula*," Franky said. "We're going to get a hamburger at Sticky Wilson's first. Want to come?"

"Or you can join me and Kay," Latt suggested, "and see *Frankenstein* instead."

"Doesn't anybody like Shirley Temple?" Buff inquired plaintively from under his towel. "I *like* Shirley Temple."

"You kids," Bates remarked.

"It would be good for you," Buff told him. "You need something frivolous."

"All right," Tim conceded with a smile. "I'll go."

"Good!" Franky said with exaggerated relief. "I am *so* glad to hear it." He too struggled to his feet. "Meanwhile, the game ought to be on pretty soon, shouldn't it?"

"Yes," Latt said, "but hold the radio down to a low roar, will you? Some of us still have to study."

"Me too," Franky said cheerfully, "but I never allow it to stand in the way of really important things."

Downstairs in the living room they found Taylor, Leighton and Barnett already sprawled on the floor in front of the radio. They joined them as U.C.L.A. got the toss and the game began with a surge of happy, excited sound.

An hour later, after he and Ray had taken time out to go over the house accounts in Ray's room and found that the first month's budget had been almost an exact balance between income and outgo—which was about the best they could hope for—Buff decided to go back to the room he shared with Duke and find out how things were proceeding in that quarter. His first intention had been to go down and listen to the rest of the game, but the thought of Duke and what he must be going through kept nagging at him. Buff was not among the greater brains in the house but he had almost the kindest heart. And since he was now, as Wilson had said upon turning over the gavel to him just before vacation last June, "the leader of our little flock," he thought perhaps he should lend a helping hand.

If one was needed: Duke was a touchy soul and this was a very touchy subject. It was with some inner trepidation, not visible on the always ami-able and good-natured exterior, that he knocked on his own door.

"Who is it?" Duke growled: no ecstatic welcome there, all right.

"It's me," he said. "May I come in?"

"It's your room," Duke retorted. "I can't stop you."

"Your tone can," Buff said, deciding to be blunt. "I'll see you later."

"No!" Duke said sharply. He opened the door and Buff could see that he wasn't feeling much better. "Damn it, *come in!*"

"O.K.," he said, trying to ease things a little with the friendly grin that almost never failed to elicit a favorable response. "I *will!*"

"*Good!*" Duke said, relenting a little with the start of a rather shamefaced smile. "I'm *glad!*"

"So am *I!*" Buff said, dropping into the depths of their sofa. "How are you?"

"Oh," Duke said, taking a seat at the other end of it. "All right, I guess."

"Stomach feel better?"

"Some," Duke said. He looked fierce. "My mind doesn't."

"No, I imagine not," Buff agreed. He gave him a long look. "Tell me about it."

"You just can't know," Duke said somberly, and stopped. "You just can't know—" he stopped again. Buff decided to wait patiently until he resolved the struggle, whatever it was.

"You just can't know—" Duke said finally in a half-whisper, "what it means to be a Jew."

"Nope," Buff agreed crisply, deciding the last thing he would do was humor self-pity. "I cannot. But I'm not entirely without some imagination." He turned on the charm. "Dumb, maybe, but not without some imagina-tion. I know it isn't easy."

"Sometimes it's hell," Duke said in a low voice. "It's hell. Absolute hell. Particularly with that monster in Berlin doing what he's doing to us. But," he added, "it's broader than that. It's what everybody sooner or later tries to do to us. Good people, decent people, well meaning—even when they refrain from being unkind to us, the refraining itself is an unkindness. So few of you," he said with a wry little smile, "can manage to conceal it. At some point, it comes through. And that's equally bad."

"You don't concede, then," Buff asked in a tone of genuine interest, feeling that he suddenly had to defend the whole gentile population of the world, "that *anybody* can be genuinely uncaring about it? I think I am. I think Willie is—and Latt—and—well, really, most of the house. I mean, I honestly *do not* have any feelings like that, myself. And I don't think they do either."

"You're very decent," Duke conceded. "And Willie and Latt and most of you. But the horrible thing that Hitler's doing—that anybody, anywhere, anytime, is doing, when they start to jump on us—is to bring it out in everybody. Maybe not strongly—maybe not consciously, even—but to the point where it results in, that—that damnable *refraining*, if nothing else. And it's just—" his voice became very low and for a moment, until he made an obvious effort to control himself, Buff thought he was going to cry—"It's just *hard*, that's all."

Buff sighed a couple of times. Heavily. And wished Willie and Latt were indeed there to help him. But they weren't, so he shouldered what he regarded as his responsibility, and did his best.

"I know it's—"

"How *can* you know?" Duke interrupted with a sad, sidelong glance.

"Oh, damn it," Buff said, "shut up, will you? You don't make things easy for anybody, you know—"

"Why should I?" Duke asked. "Has anybody made it easy for us?"

"Oh, Christ!" Buff said in a frustrated tone, for once not sounding quite so amiable. "Your family's prospered here, your folks are as well off as mine are, you're liked and respected in the house, you're on Excom and half a dozen other things, you're a big man on campus, you're practically a straight-A student, you're going to make Phi Bete, you're one of the stars of the ed school, you really *may* wind up as president here someday, or if not of this university, then of some other. What's your gripe, Duke? Why can't you relax?"

"Because none of us can ever really relax," Duke said in the same desolate voice. "There's always somebody around like that damned Krohl to—"

"Fuck Krohl," Buff said. "He's an asshole."

"Yes," Duke agreed, "but he's a dangerous one, because he's just like Hitler, who he thinks is so wonderful. He's a catalyst. He's a touchstone. *He brings things out in people.* He's too much of a fool to do it deliberately, like Hitler does, he just expresses it for himself because that's the way he is—but that's enough to get it moving in other people." He looked far away for a moment and added in a sudden, youthfully innocent tone of profound satisfaction, "I'm glad I knocked him on his ass."

"So am I," Buff said. "Just between you and me. That doesn't mean we may not have to pass some sort of judgment on you Tuesday night. You may have to pay a fine or something. We can't have guys going around here popping each other in the nose every time somebody says boo. We'd have complete chaos in twenty-four hours."

"He said a lot more than boo," Duke said stubbornly. "And he deserved to be popped in the nose. Anyway, it was the jaw."

"Whichever it was," Buff said, "it isn't going to happen again while *I'm* president. Do you understand that?"

"Yes, *I* understand it," Duke said. "Do you suppose he does?"

"He will after Tuesday night," Buff promised. "Now why don't you stop

brooding about being a Jew and call Shahna and go to a show tonight? I was
going with Tim and Ray but I might even go with you, except you know now
that I'll be watching you both and feeling superior all the time. You know I
do that. That's the way I am. Right?"

And he gave his roommate the amiable grin, which, as Franky said, could
charm Attila the Hun on one of his off-days. In spite of himself Duke responded with a smile. One couldn't help it with Buff.

"Yes," he said, "I know that's how you are. But I guess Shahna and I can
stand it."

"I should hope so," Buff said. "O.K., it's a date. Meantime, why don't you
sit in the rocker and let me take a nap on the sofa. And study quietly if you
will, please. I don't want to wake up until it's time to go to dinner."

"All right," Duke said. He looked suddenly bleak again. "I had thought I'd
go down and listen to the game but I guess I won't, now. I don't want to see
Krohl again."

"Listen," Buff said, rolling over to face the wall, "if you want to go down,
you go down. Sail past that son of a bitch as though he doesn't exist. I'm sure
he doesn't want to see you, either."

He felt drained by two hours in the sun and the emotional strain of their
conversation. Hardly anyone ever thought Buff felt much of anything, he
was always so good-natured, but he did, he thought with a mild defensiveness as he drifted off: he did. He felt sorry as hell for the Jews, but Duke
would probably regard that as patronizing too. You couldn't win—you just
couldn't win. They couldn't win—and you couldn't win. But he was damned
if he was going to let it affect the house if he could help it. He was snoring
in half a minute.

Duke sat in the rocker for a little longer not thinking much of anything.
Then he stood up abruptly, took a deep breath, straightened himself to his
full six feet three, stepped into the hall, closed the door quietly and went
downstairs. Jeff Barnett smiled and gestured him over and he lay down
beside him on the floor, turning on his back with his hands clasped under his
head, closing his eyes as the announcer's excited voice poured over them.
Krohl wasn't there, and anyway, Duke had decided to take Buff's advice and
ignore him. This worked fine—as long as he wasn't there.

"I don't see," said Hank Moore, one of the gentlest and most reasonable
of youths, "why you feel you had to make such a damned row out there.
What are you trying to prove, Rudy?"

"I'm not trying to prove anything!" Rudy said in a loud and angry voice,
but his roommate, as he was beginning to realize to his annoyance, was not
an easily intimidated type.

"Don't yell," Hank said calmly. "I'm right here. I was just asking."

"I just can't stand them!" Rudy said.

"Why?" Hank asked in his usual pleasantly courteous tone.

"Damned—" Rudy began but Hank wasn't having any.

"Oh, knock it off!" he said with a sudden vigor that quite startled Rudy. "Just can it, will you? I don't want to hear a lot of ranting and raving. I'm asking a question because I want to know the answer. If all you can give me is loudmouthed crap, then forget it and we won't mention the subject again."

"You won't, maybe—"

"We both won't," Hank said firmly, and he turned back decisively to the history text he was studying. There was silence for several minutes. Then he observed, without looking up, "If that's all you can say for yourself Tuesday night, you're going to have one hell of a time of it, I'm afraid. I won't be the only one wanting answers."

Rudy snorted scornfully.

"I may not even go Tuesday night."

"Good," Hank said indifferently. "Then I'll have the room all to myself this quarter. I'll enjoy that."

"They wouldn't dare!" Rudy exclaimed. "They wouldn't fucking dare! My father told them when they pledged me he's going to give the house five thousand bucks to build a special library and study room. They won't sacrifice *that* no matter how they hate my guts! You wait and see what pious old Willie and Richardson and Saint Lattimer and the rest do when *that's* the option!"

"I think Saints Willie, Richardson and Lattimer have a little more guts than you think they do, Rudy," Hank remarked, finally putting aside the book and turning full toward him. "Tell me something—do you *want* them to hate your guts? Is this some sort of involved psychological thing Galen Bryce would like to analyze? Maybe you should talk to him."

Rudy snorted again.

"Bryce? That pansy? Don't talk to me about Bryce, that creep. *No*, I don't want them to hate my guts! I just want to make them see how the Jews are running the world, that's all, and how that superior bastard Offenberg is—"

"Is *what*?" Hank demanded, sounding completely disgusted now. "What has he ever done to you except be decent to you—as much as possible?"

"I heard he opposed taking me into the house," Rudy said, "He said I would be disruptive and a troublemaker."

Hank looked skeptical.

"Who told you that? I don't believe it."

"Gale told me that, that's who!"

Hank shook his head.

"I thought you just said you despise Gale. You *are* weird, Rudy."

"He has his uses," Rudy said with a disparaging smile. "You ought to cultivate him. He knows most everything that's going on around here. Very useful."

"Well, I don't know whether Duke opposed you or not," Hank said, "but considering what's happened since, if he did I'd say his instinct was correct. Anyway," he added as Rudy looked as though he might lunge at him but thought better of it in the face of his calmly impervious manner, "he didn't succeed, did he? You're here, aren't you? And so am I. You didn't know there was some opposition to me, did you? A few of them thought I was too 'quiet.' I guess they finally decided"—he smiled, a little wryly—"that I have the potential to be louder if I have to. What do you think?"

Rudy studied him for a minute. Then he said carefully, "I think you say what you think."

"That's right," Hank said. "And I don't make a nuisance of myself doing it, either. I still don't know what your gripe is with Offenberg except that he's Jewish. So what? I'm half Irish and half French—a hundred years back somewhere, that is. Right now I happen to be an American. How about you?"

"So am I American," Rudy said with a scowl. "But," he muttered, staring angrily at the floor, "I'm not a mongrel like some people. I'm pure-blooded."

"Oh, Lord," Hank said. "Oh, *Lord.* Pure-blooded what, if I may ask? Wienerschnitzel?"

"And don't make fun of the Germans!" Rudy said, suddenly sounding genuinely threatening. "They're *my people!*"

"*Your* people!" Hank echoed, not at all intimidated. "Well, forgive me. I thought you were American too."

"I'm *German*-American," Rudy said, and if he hadn't sounded so genuinely proud of himself Hank would probably have laughed out loud. But he could see his roommate was quite sincere, and that ridicule had been carried just about as far as it could profitably go.

"Look," he said quietly. "I really don't want to talk about it anymore, except to say I think you're making a big mistake if you approach Tuesday night in the mood you seem to be in now. More fundamentally, I think you're making an even bigger mistake to carry on a feud with Duke Offenberg—and Jews in general. It's a tough world out there and it's getting tougher, and that sort of thing doesn't help us here in America. We've got to stand together for whatever's coming—"

"Nothing is coming, if the world is just sensible and gives the Germans what they want," said Rudy, "which is to correct the Versailles Treaty and take their rightful place in the world."

"Well, Versailles," Hank said. "I'm not going to get into an argument about Versailles today. I just want to keep it down to what we have in front of us, which is you and Duke Offenberg and getting along in this house, which is a microcosm of a lot of things."

"You were the one who brought up 'whatever's coming,' " Rudy pointed out in a tone between scorn and sulk. "I didn't. As for Offenberg, he can stay out of my way and I'll stay out of his."

"And we'll all have to walk on eggs," Hank said. "That's great. That—

is—just—great." He closed his book and stood up. "I'm going to go down and listen to the game."

After Hank left, outwardly calm but inwardly annoyed, frustrated and troubled, Rudy sat doing nothing much, a scowl on his face, anger in his mind, unforgiveness in his heart.

He was, as Willie said, "out of proportion."

Not really out of control.

Yet.

But certainly out of proportion.

No one could have looked more in proportion, more calm and relaxed, than the house member who was now sauntering slowly back from the library.

He had made a casual detour through the Inner Quad, which on this lazy afternoon was almost deserted.

Almost, but not quite.

On the off-chance that someone might be there, he had gone to the usual place, found the usual company, received, and given, the usual response.

Now, feeling that curious dichotomy of singing satisfaction and savage remorse which he had long since found to be characteristic of such occasions, he was in a state of mental suspension in which he was hardly thinking at all as he walked along.

He did realize, though, with the recognition that somehow never failed to surprise him, that the Quad, the campus, the University, the golden world, all looked exactly the same.

And so, he knew as he responded with his usual cheerful grin to the greetings of half a dozen never-suspecting friends along the way, did he.

He would never quite get over the wonderment of that fact.

Never.

Long ago when it had all begun he had thought that he must carry some sign of it that the world could see.

But then he had realized that he was one of the lucky ones.

There was no sign.

On a distant field in the slanting rays of the afternoon sun each loyal comrade brave and true shoved back and forth in sweaty pursuit of the elusive pigskin while thousands cheered. Sometimes Moose and his teammates had the advantage, sometimes U.C.L.A. The announcer was equally excited by them both. His hysterical voice echoed up and down the Row and indeed all over campus from a thousand radios in house, hall and dormitory. It was enough to drive a man to drink, Guy Unruh thought as he sat with

Suratt on the front balcony, making one last attempt to study as the excitement mounted to them from the living room.

Shouts of *"Get him!"*—"Block that kick!"—"Yeaay!"—and "Oh, *SHIT!*" heralded the shifting fortunes of battle in familiar voices from below.

"I'm going to give up in a minute and go down and join the mob, I guess," Guy announced—the first comment he had volunteered to Renny all afternoon. "Want to come along?"

At the other end of the balcony Renny looked up from his Advanced Economics book with a deliberately exaggerated surprise.

"Are you talking to me?"

"Now, who the hell else," Unruh demanded, "would I be talking to? Myself?"

"You might," Renny said. "Some people around here do."

"Well, I wouldn't know," Guy said. "I don't go around listening."

"You should," Suratt suggested with a dry smile. "It can be very interesting. Did you know, for instance, that—"

"I don't care!" Guy interrupted sharply. "I don't give a damn, understand? Knock it off!"

"I just wanted to make life more interesting for you, that's all," Renny said serenely. "You seem to lead a rather narrow existence."

"I do?" Guy demanded, and then stopped himself abruptly: Why the hell was he falling for this obvious game, anyway? He laughed, though it sounded a trifle forced, as he knew they both realized. Why did the guy possess such a talent for throwing people off balance? And why did it give him such obvious satisfaction? He decided that this was the time to beat him at his own game, and ask.

"Suratt," he inquired in a pleasantly conversational tone, "why are you such a son of a bitch to everybody all the time?"

He was gratified to note that this seemed to have hit home. Renny's superior self-confidence seemed to be shaken. He actually flushed with anger for a moment.

"I'm not a son of a bitch to everybody all the time!" he exclaimed. "I don't mean to be a son of a bitch to anybody!"

"Oh, yes you do," Guy said calmly. "You couldn't be so consistent if it weren't deliberate. Why is it, I wonder?"

"I don't have to talk to you," Suratt said, half rising from his chair. Guy waved him back down.

"Oh, come on," he said, enjoying himself. "Don't be so thin-skinned. We're just talking. I'm curious. It might help you to talk about it with somebody."

"Well," Renny snapped, but settling back down for the moment at least. "Not with you!"

"And why not?" Guy asked blandly. "I lead a narrow existence, true enough, but I've been here a year longer than you have. Maybe I can really help."

"I don't need anybody," Suratt retorted, "to 'really help.' I'm doing all right, thank you! What the hell is this, some kind of game?"

"Quite similar to the one you play, as a matter of fact," Unruh said with the same pleasantly reasonable, deliberately infuriating air. "Only in your case I think it's a serious problem. It puts your whole life here on such an uncomfortable basis. A lot of us wonder what you get out of it."

"Who's 'a lot of us'?" Renny demanded scornfully. "Nobody else has ever talked to me like this."

Which wasn't true, as Moose had. But Guy didn't need to know that.

"Maybe nobody else thinks you're worth the time," Guy suggested.

Renny flushed again and Guy decided he had probably gone far enough. His own motivation in this had just sort of developed as the conversation went along: he just wanted to give Renny a jolt and make him think about himself—it really might do him some good. But he didn't want to be mean. They did have to live with each other in the house, after all.

"Look," he said reasonably, "I don't mean to be harsh, Renny, but you do have a way of getting under people's skins and making them feel that you're taking advantage of them—psychological advantage, I mean. You like to throw us all off balance. Apparently you get a kick out of it. Most people don't. We'd like to understand. It wouldn't only help you, it would help all of us to know how to get along with you better."

"Just leave me alone," Renny said flatly. "That would be the best way."

Unruh leaned forward and stared at him across the length of the balcony. "And you'll leave us alone?"

"For Christ's sake!" Renny said, exploding at last. "What the hell are we talking about, anyway? If you guys can't take a little kidding now and then—"

"It isn't kidding," Guy said, echoing Moose though he didn't know it, "it's hurting. And"— his voice grew firm—"there's no excuse for it. And we want it to stop."

"Well, if you've managed to live with me for a whole year already," Suratt said, "and nobody's ever complained before, then I guess—"

"Plenty of people have complained," Unruh told him, "but I'm apparently the first to lay it on the line."

"I can't be responsible for what people say behind my back when they don't have the guts to face me," Renny said. "That's too damned bad. I haven't heard about it."

"Oh," Guy said. "I thought maybe you'd picked it up in the course of your eavesdropping."

"I don't—" Renny flared up, and then turned crimson and stopped.

There was a silence while Guy watched him with the same clinical interest he might have shown toward a dissection specimen in pre-med. Then he decided to end the discussion: he was pretty sure Renny wouldn't change, no matter who said what. And he was probably only making it worse.

"Look," he said reasonably, "I'm not riding you just for the hell of it. It really would help you, and it would help all of us, if you'd make a real effort not to be so sharp with us. I guess there's a reason, everybody has a reason for everything, but whatever it is, I guess we'll never know and don't need to know. It would just make it easier all around if you'd change some, that's all I'm saying. If I've hurt you, and I guess I have, I'm sorry. But think it over. Some people can be a lot rougher than I am."

"Then why haven't they jumped me long since if I'm such a bastard?" Suratt demanded with a revival of scorn and combativeness. "Why should I believe what you say?"

"It's a tolerant house," Unruh observed.

Suratt gave him a scornful look.

"Oh, shit," he said.

"O.K.," Guy said, closing his book and standing up. "Play it your way, friend. Just stay out of my way and a lot of other people's way, that's all. We'll all be better off."

Suratt started to make an angry retort but a hail from the lawn below forestalled him. Billy Wilson, Marc Taylor, Tony Andrade, Johnny Herbert and Smitty Carriger, all carrying books, had apparently come back together from studying at the Libe.

"Hey, you studious bastards!" Smitty shouted. "Why aren't you listening to the game? Who's winning?"

"We're just coming down," Guy responded. "I think they are, at the moment, from all the groans we've been hearing. But there's the last half to go."

"That's what we figured," Tony said, "so we came on back. Coming down, Renny?"

"No," Renny said, "I've still got a lot of studying to do. I'm not as bright as the rest of you."

"You're bright as hell," Smitty said. "Come on down, why don't you? You'll make us all feel bad unless you do."

"I'll bet," Renny said with a sudden naked bitterness that momentarily shadowed the afternoon and surprised them all except Guy, who had paused at the door. "I'll see you later."

"You know what you remind me of?" Unruh said slowly as the others climbed the front steps and disappeared from view. "A mean old tomcat spitting at the people who want to pet him."

"I don't want people to pet me!" Suratt snapped. "So keep your damned patronizing analogies to yourself!"

"As you wish," Guy said. He turned on his heel and left him, an angry, lonely figure brooding on the balcony.

There Latt and Franky found him a couple of minutes later when they decided to take a break at halftime and get, as Franky said, a breath of fresh air and a new perspective on life.

When they came out on the balcony and saw it wasn't deserted, they hesitated.

"You can come on out," Suratt said with a bitterness they couldn't understand. "I'm leaving!"

"Well, all right," Lattimer said mildly, stepping aside startled as Renny pushed roughly past them. "Now what was that all about?"

Franky made a disgusted sound.

"Who knows? I'm not going to spend my time worrying. He isn't worth it."

"Everybody's worth *some* worrying," said Latt, the ever-tolerant. "But," he admitted thoughtfully, "sometimes I do wonder a little bit about *him.*"

"He makes me tired," Franky said, pulling the two rockers closer together. "Guy was out here with him. Maybe they had a fight."

"Oh, I hope not," Latt said, sitting down and stretching out. "One fight a day is enough around here."

"We haven't heard the last of that one," Franky said, settling down. "I hope the local branch of Hitler Youth gets his comeuppance."

"Something's got to happen," Latt agreed.

"Well," Franky said, "we'll just have to hope the madness passes before it goes too far. Anyway"—his tone brightened—"enough of that now. Did you say you and Kay are going to see *Frankenstein?* Why don't you join us at *Dracula?*"

"Speaking of madness and horrors," Latt said with a laugh. "It doesn't much matter, does it? They're both supposed to be entertaining. Sure. Anything to lighten up the studying a bit."

"Yes," Franky said gloomily. "It won't be long till midterms. I'm in my usual state of ravaged preparation."

"You'll probably pull at least a B in most of them," Latt said. "I know you, I'm not worried. You always moan and you always get there. Much to our surprise, I'll admit," he added with a chuckle, "but you *do* get there."

"Bastard," Franky told him. "You great brains have absolutely no pity. B's are not like A-pluses or whatever the hell grades you pull down."

"I have been known to get A-pluses," Latt said with an amusement that robbed it of smugness, "but most of my professors restrain themselves to A's. Anyway, I think B.J.'s probably going to beat me this quarter. It's her turn."

"Is that how you two divide it up?" Franky inquired. "By 'turns'? Jeez! It must be nice to share that kind of monopoly."

Latt laughed.

"I can't *help* it, you know. It just comes out that way. You wouldn't want me to deliberately flunk, would you?"

"It would do wonders," Franky said solemnly, "for the morale of us all. Where have you been, anyway?" he demanded as he saw Haggerty cross the lawn. "I thought you were up in your room studying all this time."

"No," Hack said casually. "I've been down on the Quad. Actually I've been in the church playing the organ. There was something I wanted to work out and I knew as soon as the game began the piano would be out of the question here. What's the score at halftime?" When they told him he grunted. "We can do better than that. I'd better go in and join the crowd, I guess,"

"How was the Quad?" Latt asked. "Many people around?"

Hack yawned.

"Practically deserted." He smiled easily. "I like it that way. You guys coming down?"

"Oh, sure," Franky said. "We're just taking a breather."

"Willie in there?"

"I haven't seen him all afternoon," Latt said.

"I think he's still up in his room. He's been damned quiet all day."

"Well, that's O.K.," Hack said. "I'll see him sooner or later. See you guys."

"We'll be right down," Franky said. "After a few more private words with Latt."

"Few more private nothing," Latt said, getting up. "Hey!" he called down to Hack. "You and Fran want to go see *Frankenstein* with us tonight?"

"Sure," Hack said. "We've been talking about it." He grinned. "It's my night for girls."

"If Fran could hear you say that," Franky said, "she'd kick you around the block. Every night is girl night with you. And she's the girl, right?"

"Right," Hack said comfortably. "You know me well, Brother Miller. Come on down, let's bet on the game."

"Be right there," Franky said as the radio rumbled up again below and the announcer's voice boomed out across the Row to announce the start of the second half. "Willie!" he shouted up the stairs as he and Latt reached the landing and started down. "Hey, you, *Wilson*! Get your ass down here! You're missing the game!"

But there was no response and after a moment they looked at each other and shrugged.

"Guess he's just not feeling sociable today," Franky said and Latt said, "Oh, Franky, for heaven's sake. Maybe he just wants to *think*. People do, you know."

"Not me," Franky said cheerfully as they entered the living room and prepared to find their places again. "It's just too damned much trouble, any way you slice it."

My tale's soon told:
Born old.
Lived old
Died old.

In his aerie on the third floor under the eaves, the only member remaining unaccounted for on this football afternoon was suffering one of the occasional bouts of melancholy that now and again assailed him for no apparent reason he could analyze or understand. This bothered him: he liked to analyze and understand. His usual antidote was to read, reread, and sometimes polish and add to, the occasional scraps of poetry whose origins he found equally inexplicable.

As furtively as Bates with his box of character sketches, Wilson too had what he referred to wryly in his own mind as "the most secret of my secret vices."

That terse farewell to a barren life, for instance, conceived and put on paper a couple of years ago at the great age of nineteen: where had it come from? He was damned if he knew. It wasn't about *his* life—at least, he hoped it wouldn't prove to be. Yet from somewhere, piercing his heart with the potential of a pointless life, had come this inner bleakness he hadn't even known existed. He didn't *think* it had any place in the successful, well-ordered career of Richard Emmett Wilson, but there it was—fit for some shriveled old monk, maybe, but certainly not for Perfect Boy Politician, Superman on Campus.

Very curious.

And the opening verse of an elegy, origin a little more obvious, result of a family trip a year ago to Washington, D.C., come to him full-blown at Arlington National Cemetery. It was filled with an ominous foreboding he had not known he felt. A reflection on the past or a forecast? Lately he was beginning to feel, in an increasingly unhappy way, that it was the latter. But how could it be, when, so far as he consciously knew, it had been inspired by what had gone before, not by what might be yet to come?

Here among the pleasant grasses
Where the wind of springtime passes
I see in bitter veneration
The wreckage of a generation . . .

And the love poems, derivatives no doubt of Shakespeare, Housman, Millay, but with a lot of himself in there too—the rhymes and free verses, speaking in tongues of the heart he had barely sensed so far and had never actually experienced in such depth. Where did *they* come from? One might think he had suffered the grand passion of the age, but he hadn't: just a couple of unhappy adolescent love affairs that he had survived, he thought, with reasonable success.

Nonetheless, here was written word: it had come to him, it was his. How, he did not know:

> *When first mine eyes met thine I knew thee.*
> *Heart unto heart, strength unto strength. You smiled.*
> *I saw that in that same swift way you knew me*
> *And took my heart forever, as simply as a child.*

Who was she, this *belle dame inconnue* (if he remembered his high school French correctly) who had apparently raised echoes of things even before they happened? No one he could recall, he was positive of that. From what secret caverns of the heart did things like that originate? What inspired the adolescent mind to make these leaps into sensibility based on the flimsiest of intimations, yet, he felt, intuitively sound?

Whence came this voice:

> *All, all have I done with thee*
> *All asked, all given, all received from thee:*
> *Nothing denied, or been denied by, thee.*
> *Thus I, in you imprisoned, am forever free.*

And what about the affair seen in retrospect, looked back upon as some yearning perfection that shut out the world, so that it became a jealous temple no one else could enter.

> *With you I never laughed when there was no need for laughing.*
> *With you I never spoke when there was no need for speaking.*
> *With you I never sought, for there was no need for seeking.*
> *You were. I was. We two together*
> *Were all the need in any weather.*

And from somewhere equally mysterious, the darker and more somber note, the other side of Willie Wilson—the other side, in truth, of anyone:

> *Love me not. My name is pain.*
> *My heart will kill your heart. Refrain*
> *From all commitment too intent*
> *Of love foredoomed ere it is meant.*

And in the same vein:

I, within the castle keep,
Live and breathe, eat and sleep.
Pass by the door.
Beeseech no more.
I within the castle keep.

And the dissolution, the ending, the wryness, the ache that time could assuage but did not heal:

They say:
"After it is over, you will wonder how it happened."
They say:
"After it is over, you will laugh."
I saw you yesterday.
I still knew how it happened.
And I did not laugh.

And the final bitterness, desolate and unleavened:

I too have lain in darkened rooms and heard myself called wonderful.
How little it takes to make some happy.
How much—too much—to comfort such as I.

And the afterthought, which he recognized wryly as probably the quintessential Willie, to which he had given the only title in the lot:

THE HUMAN RACE CONSIDERS SEX
What we dreamed, it wasn't.
What we hoped, it doesn't.
But we will not betray its glories.
We will sing you ballads.
We will tell you stories.

On the last of the pages, torn from classroom notebooks, examination blue books, the occasional piece of typing paper, he came once again upon the epitaph: gentler—not so savage—but still not what you might call ho-ho hysterical. He could imagine dramatically how, years from now, on some distant tombstone so far ahead in time he could barely envision it, the impressed passerby would stop and ponder the enigmatic, touching soul who lay beneath:

You I have hurt, forgive me.
You I have comforted, remember me.
Stranger, think well of a stranger.

Where in the *hell*, he asked himself again while distant echoes of the game rumbled up through the house, did things like that come from? Maybe just from being about to leave adolescence—from being on the verge of adulthood—maybe just from being twenty-one and possessed of a vivid internal life and imagination that he had so far disclosed to no one except Latt, who had once asked him out of the blue, when they were studying history together one night in Latt's room, "Do you ever write poetry?"

His first instinct was to utter a surprised laugh and say, "No. Why?" But Latt had the quality of bringing out the truth in people because he was so dead-center honest himself. He had simply stared at Willie with a gravely thoughtful expression until Willie had laughed again, not embarrassed but conceding, and said, "Oh, yes. Once in a while. Do you?"

"Sometimes," Latt said. "It isn't very good. Is yours?"

"Some of it," he said. "Not all, by any means."

"I'd like to read some of it sometime."

"Maybe," he said. "Sometime." He grinned. "I'll show you mine if you'll show me yours."

Latt smiled and shook his head.

"Nope. Mine isn't worth anything. But yours might be. You're an interesting character, Brother Wilson. You intrigue me."

They were then juniors and had known each other for almost three years.

"I didn't know you were making a study of me," he said. "I should either be flattered or terrified."

Latt looked puzzled.

"Why?"

"Oh," he said. "You see through people, Latt. It makes us all nervous."

"Oh, I hope not," Latt said, sounding genuinely distressed. "I wouldn't want to think I had that effect on people."

"It's all right," he said quickly—the last thing anyone wanted to do was wound Latt. "It's good for us. It keeps us on our toes. We need someone to maintain a standard. We need a measuring stick."

"I'm thin enough for that, all right," Latt said with a smile, though he wasn't thin, really, only slim. "But I'm not really—you know, I'm not critical. People just interest me. And you more than most. You always have. I hope you don't really mind."

"Well," he said, looking quizzical, "it's a little unsettling to know you're being observed."

Again Latt was honest. He smiled.

"Nonsense! You know you love it. You'd be devastated if you thought people weren't paying attention to Richard Emmett Wilson."

That made Willie smile too. He was pretty honest himself. Most of the time.

"I suppose you're right. So: what have you concluded about me?"

"I'll tell you someday," Latt said. "I wouldn't want to increase an already enormous ego by—"

"Bastard," Wilson said amicably. "Where were we? Somewhere in the Reformation, wasn't it?"

And they had gone back to their books and the subject of poetry had never arisen again. He would like to see what Latt's was like, though: generous, compassionate, religious and full of good thoughts, he'd bet, because that's what Latt was. Not a Thing of Hidden Depths, dark and dour and akin to something dragged in off the moors via Shakespeare and Emily Brontë, like himself.

And yet it was a funny thing: he wasn't like that, really. It was just the way things hit him sometimes—a passing mood. Most of the time he was calm, cool, steady and in command of his world. Or so he liked to believe. Maybe *that* was the pose. Maybe that was just the veneer he maintained to get himself through the day. Maybe the demon lover dank and dour was the true Willie, after all.

He snorted and pulled himself up short. Demon lover! That was a crock! Awkward schoolkid was more like it, given the pace of his so-called romance with his green-gold girl.

He did not feel so proud of that right now, though really there was no need to be ashamed of it. It was going along all right, even if he was beginning to think restlessly that it was too damned slow.

First of all, he had talked to Latt about it, more frankly than he had so far to anyone else, including Unruh. You could count on Latt's discretion absolutely; his acceptance of things was as compassionate and nonjudgmental as anyone's his age could be. And Latt had talked to Kay, as requested. And Kay had evidently mentioned Willie casually to Marian Emerson, because a couple of weeks ago, during one of the snap quizzes their German history professor loved to spring on them, he had seen her look around casually—carefully-casually, he had told himself with inner delight—from her seat in the second row, and had let her eyes wander briefly past him as he sat in the back row. No way to move up from W to E, he thought with amusement, but at least eye contact had been established; and the inevitable process began.

It was a standardized procedure, immemorial in structure and design. You saw a girl. You looked at one another a few times. Then you didn't look at one another a few times. Then you exchanged a direct, appraising glance or two. And then you decided whether it was going to be worth it.

If it wasn't, you soon found somebody else to look at. If it was, you presently found yourself investing all sorts of time, effort, energy and sometimes considerable money in the project.

If you were a child of nature like Gulbransen, things moved on swiftly and naturally to a pleasant conclusion in a car parked in the hills behind campus, or in a hotel room in San Francisco. No agonizing, no regrets, and that was that.

If you were one of the thinkers, that part of it might or might not occur but even if it did, it really wasn't the most important part. You had to own each other, and ownership only meant pain, and sooner or later the whole thing fizzled out in a rash of jealousies, hurts, misunderstandings, disputes and disappointments.

This side of it the Gulbransens of this world never even saw, lucky them. If you happened to belong to the non-Gulbransens, you went slowly and took your time, knowing that nine times out of ten what had begun so pleasantly would end sure as shooting in your getting involved, with the lively potential for unpleasantness all around.

Anyway, there was Donn Van Dyke. She had him signed, sealed and delivered, so everybody was concluding. So, really, why bother with anyone else, if everybody was correct?

With a sudden impatience, which he hoped Marian didn't sense, he turned back to his blue book and began writing with a stern attention to duty. But when the exam ended they passed one another going out.

They didn't look.

But they knew.

A week later they saw each other again. He had done a lot of thinking and so, obviously, had she. It wasn't an impulsive mistake, he concluded: it was meant to be. *I Saw You—You Saw Me—We Both Said, "Whee!"—It Was Meant to Be.* Number 2 on next week's *Hit Parade*. Wilson, you jerk, he told himself, can't you be serious about anything? Nonetheless, he found himself haunting the Cellar, more or less casually. Donn couldn't understand why he was there so much. He wasn't entirely sure himself, every other minute. On the minute in between he knew damned well why. On Monday of the current week it had all begun to fall into place.

After class ended that day, she walked slowly ahead of him up the Quad. He followed at a casual distance. Suddenly she turned around, so abruptly he didn't have time for dissembling. He made a quick and awkward pretense at it—suddenly thought, How silly!—stopped and smiled. She smiled back.

"Hi," he said. "I'm Willie Wilson."

"I know," she said. "I'm Marian Emerson."

"I know," he said, and started to repeat automatically, "I'm—"

They laughed and the world instantly became an easier place. But not entirely. It still had a way to go, he thought now, as shouts and exultations came up from the game below.

"You always wear green when I see you," he said.

She smiled.

"I always wear green hoping you will see me. Besides, it becomes me."

"That it does. I'm on my way to the Union to do a little politicking and incidentally get something to eat at the Cellar. Will you join me?"

"Well—"

"Of course, if you have something better to do—" He smiled. "But of course you don't."

She laughed.

"Of course I don't."

But they kept a decorous distance all the way, not saying much. And in the Cellar, where they saw many people and caused some comment, none of the tentative intimacy remained. Their conversation was awkward and there was a watching and a distance between them which he could not break down, though he tried—rather too hesitantly, he thought now.

Afterward they walked together to the post office.

She turned off to the women's dorms and he went on up to the Row.

Aside from class, where they knew their paths would cross, he did not know at that moment whether they would ever see one another again.

So much, he thought now with recurring gloom, for the old Wilson charm. She had reacted with about as much enthusiasm as a frog in freshman biology. Everything seemed to have subsided after her initial opening gambit. But she *had* initiated it, he told himself, seeking straws. She *had* turned around first and spoken to him, not vice versa. It was her idea to respond to his idea. He must have failed her in some way he couldn't imagine. His apparel? It was the usual college scruff. His hair? It was combed pretty well, though it tended to curl loose sometimes: he had always thought that was cute. His breath? She hadn't been close enough to tell. His attitude? He had tried to be his usual witty, casual, easygoing self, the one most people seemed to like. His language? Aside from the occasional "damn" or "hell," which shouldn't shock anyone but the most puritan maiden, it had been as innocuous as a hymnal. His assumptions? They had been those of any normal, red-blooded American boy in such a circumstance. He had carefully tried not to let them show, in any event.

So what was wrong with Richard Emmett Wilson that he had failed this opening test, as he so obviously had? Was she shy? Was she coy? *Was there already somebody else?*

Horrors. Or *Zounds!* as McAllister might say. Heaven forbid.

Anyway, he couldn't believe it. She *had* given him the come-on in class, hadn't she? She had turned around and said hello, hadn't she? She was obviously as interested as he was, wasn't she? *Wasn't* she?

Very well, then.

At that point the team made a touchdown and a universal bellow of joy roared up the stairwell. He supposed he really probably should go down and join the fun. He had long ago established the right to retreat when he wanted to, but perhaps this wasn't quite the time: he was president of the student body, after all, even if he hadn't had the money to go down south to the game.

He was about to put away both his moody poems and his moody thoughts when Jeff Barnett yelled, "Willie! Somebody wants y'all on the phone!"

"Male or female?" he yelled as he came out into the hall and started to clatter down the stairs to the second-floor phone booth.

"Male," Jeff responded. "I think I recognize the voice. Have fun."

Something in his tone, faintly mocking, subtly patronizing, gave Willie a pretty good idea.

"Hi," he said, closing the phone-booth door to shut out the still-raucous sounds of jubilation from the living room. "This is Willie."

He was not surprised when a voice half hesitant, half muffled, replied, "This is Bayard."

"Oh, *hi*," he said, putting a lot of cordiality into it because Bayard seemed to need it. "Where have *you* been?"

"Oh," Bayard said with a deprecatory little laugh. "Around. I haven't seen you, though."

"I've spotted you a couple of times across the Quad, but you were obviously hurrying to a class and so was I. You know how it is—we all get wrapped up in our own little circles. Guy tells me you're getting along great with basketball. That's fine. He's proud of you. So'm I."

"Well, thanks," Bayard said, sounding shyly pleased. "He's certainly been awfully nice about encouraging me."

"He says that's about all you need, a little encouragement," Wilson said. "He says you're a natural and Coach thinks so too."

"Coach seems to like me," Bayard agreed with the same shy satisfaction. "Maybe I'll be out there on the varsity someday, after all."

"No 'after all' about it," Willie said firmly. "It's inevitable. When are you coming up to the house again?"

"When do you want me to?" Bayard asked. He uttered his shy little half-laugh. "I can't just—just bust in, you know."

"It's my fault," Willie said. "I should have gotten back to you a lot sooner. But one gets so damned busy on campus." An idea, tentatively considered earlier, took root. "How's it going in the hall? Everything O.K. now? Ari Katanian keeping an eye on you?"

"Ari's great," By said gratefully. "He's a kind person."

"He is. The best. And the roommates?"

"The roommates are fine. One's pre-med and the other's studying archaeology. We have some interesting talks."

"I'll bet you do. And the hall in general?"

"I'm accepted. For the most part. I guess that's about the best I can expect."

"As long as life's livable. Let me know if it isn't."

"I'm kind of ashamed of myself now for complaining," Bayard admitted somewhat sheepishly. "I guess it would have worked out all right."

"Maybe," Willie said, "but there's no reason why you should have been subjected to uncertainties about it." He reached the decision he had been considering. "How about coming up next week—say, Thursday?"

"Thursday would be good," Bayard said promptly, sounding pleased.

"Good," Wilson said, and added casually, "That's our first formal rushing date, you know."

Instantly Bayard's tone changed. Wilson thought, Now, God damn it, don't back out on me. That's what Jeff and some of the others want.

"Oh," Bayard said cautiously. "No, I didn't. In that case, maybe I'd better make it some other time. Don't you think?"

"No, I don't, or I would have suggested some other time. What's wrong with Thursday?"

"Well, I mean—that makes it too—too definite, doesn't it? I mean, that's a special night for people you might want to pledge, isn't it?"

"So?"

"Well, I mean, I'm not—not in that category."

"Aren't you?" Wilson asked calmly. "I thought we discussed that."

"Yes, but—"

"All right, then. This is it. I'll expect you Thursday at seven-thirty, bright and shiny, O.K.?"

"Well . . . I'll . . . have to think about that."

"Not too long," Willie suggested, "or the invitation might be withdrawn."

"Oh," Bayard said hastily, "I hope not."

"Well, then. Do or die. Yes or no. What's the answer?"

The response was a heavy sigh at the other end of the line.

"Stop agonizing," Wilson told him, not unkindly but firmly. "I won't let anybody bite you. O.K.?"

"Well—"

"O.K., I said?"

"Well . . . O.K."

"That's more like it. Have you talked to Maryetta Bradford yet?"

Bayard uttered a startled little laugh.

"How did you happen to think of her?"

"I thought that might be why you called. Aside from just wanting to talk, that is."

"You're too smart, Willie," Bayard said, sounding more relaxed, and amused. "That is why I called, really."

"I suppose you've been shy about that, too."

Boy! he thought. Listen to me! And I've been circling around Marian Emerson like some two-bit quaking little high school kid! What a fraud, Willie Wilson, what a fraud! But his tone was perfectly matter-of-fact when he added:

"That's no way to win a fair lady, you know. You've got to get in there and fight! Give 'em hell!"

"I know," Bayard said, genuinely laughing now. "But," he added, tone abruptly sobering, "it isn't that simple."

"Nonsense!" Wilson said grandly. "Simple as A, B, C. Want me to call her for you?"

"Oh, *no!*" Bayard said. Then he paused and reconsidered. "Well," he said cautiously, "maybe. But you'd better start right off by telling her."

"Telling her what?" Wilson demanded. "That you're a handsome, dashing, intelligent, charming, absolutely ravishing—"

"That I'm a Negro," Bayard interrupted. "As you know very well."

"It'll come out," Wilson promised glibly, though at the moment he wasn't quite sure how he was going to handle it. "Anyway, I think that'll be an asset with Maryetta, if my impression of her background is correct. I told you her mother and mine went to the University of California at Berkeley together, and from what Mom says, Mrs. Bradford was always in the lead when it came to social causes. Not that there were very many in those days, but she was always in there pitching when there were any. In fact, she still is. I saw her name in one of the San Francisco papers just the other day as one of the sponsors of a committee to aid the longshoremen's strike. Maryetta's been brought up in that kind of atmosphere."

"Then," Bayard said with unexpected dryness, "she certainly won't mind anything as liberal as dating a Negro. It certainly *ought* to be as simple as A, B, C. Nothing to it, right?"

Wilson uttered an exasperated sound.

"Now, I didn't mean it that way—"

"That's the way it came out," Bayard said flatly.

There was silence during which Willie thought: Oh, the hell with the prickly bastard. But he decided to wait. After a moment Bayard apparently reconsidered.

"All right, so she probably won't be shocked. It probably will make things easier for her, as you say."

"Will it for you?" Wilson demanded. "Because if it won't, Bayard, I'm not going to be a party to getting you into anything you aren't comfortable with."

"Like rushing at the house?"

"Oh, Christ! To hell with both. Goodbye."

"No, wait!" Bayard said with a sudden youthful desperation. "I'm sorry, Willie. You're trying your best for me, I know that, and I guess I'm not being very appreciative."

"Not very," Wilson agreed bluntly. "Are you coming Thursday?"

"Yes"—voice low.

"And am I to call Maryetta?"

There was a hesitation, but—still very low—"I'd appreciate it if you would."

"All right. I'll get back to you. And I'll see you Thursday at seven-thirty. Right?"

"All right . . . and thank you."

"You're welcome!"

And he hung up the receiver rather more emphatically than he had intended.

And being Willie, had instant second thoughts.

May he *was* forcing the pace. Maybe it was wrong to push Bayard into situations he perhaps wasn't psychologically ready for, however much he might seem to be ready for them in other respects. Maybe he was using the boy to push his own ideas, using him as a means of advancing his own beliefs—which seemed to be formulating themselves with surprising rapidity, almost as though they possessed a life of their own—instead of exercising a fair regard for Bayard's very real, and obviously in his mind entirely justified, hesitations and uncertainties.

Maybe it was just an ego trip for Willie Wilson, when all was said and done. Maybe he just wanted to surprise people who considered him conservative, and take satisfaction from their astonishment.

Maybe he was an egotistical son of a bitch, within the castle keep.

All of this did nothing to lighten his moodiness, even though he made a conscious effort to sound cheerful and assured a moment later when he called the women's rooms in the Union and asked for Maryetta. He was told that she had gone home to Berkeley for the weekend and would be back Sunday night.

He left his name and went, rather disconsolately, back upstairs to his room. There he closed the door, put his poems safely away, and sat down on his sofa. There he did absolutely nothing for a while.

Downstairs the tumult of the game rose to a climax and at last concluded.

"Hey, Willie!" Franky shouted. "We won! Seventeen to fourteen!"

"That's *nice!*" he shouted back. "*Real* nice!"

"Well, don't take my head off," Franky retorted. "It *is* nice."

He offered no answer. The noise died away below. The house became relatively silent as afternoon lengthened into evening.

He was still sitting on the sofa, staring out the window, when he heard the door open behind him. Six feet four of happily healthy masculinity coiled itself into a seat beside him and a protective arm went around his shoulder.

"Willie, my boy," Guy Unruh said, "don't worry, don't fret. Uncle Guy is with you all the time. Have you problems? Have you worries? Have you—*ow!*" he cried indignantly as Wilson dug him suddenly in the ribs. "Is that any way to treat your old pal, your old buddy?"

"Unruh," Willie said, mood successfully broken as Guy had intended, "stop necking me and make sense. How the hell are you?"

Guy gave him an appraising sidelong glance.

"*I* am fine. How are *you*, Mr. President? That is what matters to *me*, and indeed to the whole damned universe. On you so much depends. On you—"

"Oh, stop that stuff. I'm all right. Why? Don't I look it?"

"I haven't lived with you, man and boy, for three years without knowing the signs. Something's on your mind. What is it?"

"I don't know," Wilson said soberly.

"Menstruating?" Unruh asked kindly.

"Unruh," Willie said severely. "For Christ's *sake*. I'm just thinking."

"You never stop," Guy said, removing his arm to tie a vagrant shoestring. "You never stop ticking away, my old Willie Think-Machine. Why don't we get ourselves organized and find a little relaxation for the night?"

"What do you want to try for?" Willie inquired dryly. "A Theta? A Tri Delt?"

"Not tonight. I want mine captive. I want to be sure of it. O.K.?"

"What about Maggie? I thought you and she—"

"Not Maggie!" Guy said, looking exaggeratedly shocked. "Heaven forbid! Anyway she's gone to some hen party with some friend down in San Jose. And what she doesn't know won't hurt her. I thought I'd go up to the City. Want to go along? I've arranged to borrow Buff's car."

Wilson gave him a thoughtful stare.

"You know I don't make a habit of that."

"You know I don't either," Unruh said, "but I feel a little restless. Maybe it's the war situation."

"Is it a 'war situation'?" Willie asked. "I thought it had all sort of died down, since Munich." He looked wry. "Except for Rudy Krohl, maybe."

"Screw Krohl," Guy said. His expression sobered. "I don't know. Has it?"

"I don't know either," Wilson said. He paused, far away. Then he nodded. "All right, I'll go. Where will it be, Sally's?"

"They're the best," Guy said, "but damned expensive. I know a couple of other places."

"All right."

"There! Tell *me* I'm not going to be a good doctor! I made the right diagnosis and prescribed the right cure, didn't I?"

"Well," Wilson said, "*a* cure. Now if you will remove your carcass from mine, I think I'll go take a shower and get ready."

Later that night, around eleven, Haggerty returned from his regular date with Fran. The house was relatively quiet. He saw light under Ray Baker's door—Ray was always studying or working on house books, one of the two. There were similar signs of life in several other rooms, the muffled sound of a bullsession somewhere as several great minds went at it hot and heavy about Socrates, Plato and their relevance to modern life.

Hack decided he wouldn't get into that; went quietly up the stairs to Willie's room, knocked, got no answer; went back down to the second floor; hesitated for a moment, then walked along the hall until he came to the door he was looking for. Light was showing beneath it. He knocked, softly. It opened and he stepped inside, shutting it behind him.

Friendly eyes and the usual open smile greeted him. "We sure do have a smiley bunch in this house," Franky had remarked the other day. And, with some notable exceptions, they did.

"Hi, Hack," the room's occupant said. "Want to talk? Have a seat."

"No, thanks," he said, smiling back. "I've got a lot to do tomorrow. I'm going to play the organ for the service in the morning, go to the beach with Fran for a picnic lunch and then come back and study. But I just wanted to stop by for a minute."

"Yes?" his fraternity brother asked, eyes innocent, face untroubled.

"I just wanted to give you a little advice," Hack said. "I was down on the Quad this afternoon around quarter to two—"

"Yes?"—eyes still candid, expression still untroubled; but now, Hack thought, with just the faintest air of wariness.

"Yeah," he said slowly, "I know it's because you probably don't know about it, but just as a word of friendly advice—I think I'd stay away from the corner of the Inner Quad, if I were you. It has a reputation."

"Oh, really?"—shocked now, and earnestly troubled. "For what?"

"Well, you know," Hack said, a little awkwardly because he wasn't sure of his ground here—yet. "For guys that—that want to go there."

"Oh." Really troubled, now, genuinely concerned. And in a rush: "Gee, Hack, thanks for warning me! I really *didn't know*, you know—*really*—nobody ever told me anything like that and I just—just wandered in there because I had to go, you know." A sudden thoughtful look. "There *were* a couple of guys in there that looked at me—well, a little *funny*, you know, but I just dismissed it, did what I had to do, and got out of there. I didn't hang around, believe me!"

"No, I know," Hack said soothingly. "I saw you come out." Thinking: I wasn't there when you went in, however, so I don't know how long you'd been there. "Anyway, I just thought I'd mention it. I was sure you didn't know."

"Oh, *no*"—the earnest expression more earnest than ever, the eyes wide and candid as could be. "I'll never go there again, you can be sure of that! Golly, Hack, I don't know how I can thank you enough! It's real kind of you." And then, perfectly naturally, "You won't tell anybody, will you? They might think—and it was just because I didn't know. *Really*. Boy! Am I relieved you told me!"

"I knew it was a mistake," Hack said, smiling and turning to the door. "I know you won't go back."

"Never." Solemnly. *"Never.* And gee, Hack, thanks *again."*

"Don't mention it," Hack said, giving him a last smile as he stepped out, closed the door and headed for bed, thinking: Well, I wonder. I really do wonder.

And leaving behind a frightened mind telling itself desperately: Oh, God. Oh, God, Oh, God. I never will go there again. Never, Never, EVER.

It took three days before the helpless fascination drew him back. It took about that long before Hack was in a position to have a private talk with Willie and by then he had decided not to. It would probably never come to the point of needing action of any kind, anyway.

He thought he would keep an eye on it, though. If true, it was a dangerous game, whose inducements he was sensitive enough, as a creative mind, to understand, though he had decided long ago that it was not for him. He didn't judge it: if that was the way it was for some, that was the way it was. But at least he might be able to help with a little preventive damage control for a young friend of whom he, like everyone, thought highly.

10

The special meeting to discuss what Buff had described, in the note he pinned to the bulletin board by the dining-room door, as "The problem of brother striking brother and other unfraternal conduct," began shortly after seven P.M. Tuesday.

Everyone was present with the single exception of Rudy Krohl, whose absence from dinner had caused considerable comment—the intention, as Wilson remarked dryly to Gulbransen, who nodded. A certain amount of tension inevitably filled the living room as Buff took his seat on the piano bench and told Andrade to call the roll. The tension, mingled now with the anticipation of the uproar that might occur if Rudy didn't show, began to mount.

Tony went down the list to "Herbert." Johnny dutifully replied.

Tony paused and the tension grew further. But Rudy had apparently been eavesdropping, because when Tony called his name he appeared and, looking neither right nor left, walked across and sat down on a sofa beside Galen Bryce, who gave him a small welcoming smile. Tony finished and everyone looked expectantly at Buff.

"We are gathered together—" he began, and Suratt murmured, "In the presence of these witnesses," which caused considerable muffled amusement.

"Now, see here, you guys," Buff said sharply, "cut the crap. This is serious business. We are gathered together to find out why Brother Offenberg saw fit last Saturday to deck Brother Krohl just before the game. And what we should do about it."

"Mr. President," Galen Bryce said with his usual unctuous smile, "I'm wondering why it is necessary to do *anything* about it. Is there some reason the president could give us why we should intervene as a house in what was apparently a purely private quarrel?"

212

"Mr. President," Smitty Carriger said, ignoring him, "some of us were down studying and didn't get back from the Quad until after it occurred. Could somebody tell us what it's all about?"

"You mean you haven't heard?" Franky demanded and Smitty replied crisply, "About seventeen versions. Is there an official one?"

"Latt," Buff said, "you're the most objective man in the house. You tell them."

"I'll try," Latt said, "although I will say I've heard as many reports as Smitty has, if not more. Anyway. It was a beautiful day, as you recall, and many of us were out studying or lying in the sun on the porches and the balcony. Brothers Offenberg, Krohl, Moore and Barnett were occupying the north porch. The rest of us were draped around."

"You should have seen Franky," Tim suggested. "Nobody drapes like Franky."

"A thing of beauty," Franky remarked placidly, "is a joy forever."

"Now, God damn it," Buff said. "Proceed, Brother Lattimer."

"I will," Latt said with some severity, "if all the amateur comedians will shut up. There came a time when Brother Offenberg decided he had to go to the bathroom, so he left and did so. When he returned he accidentally—" Rudy stirred and Ray Baker said amicably but firmly, "We lawyers don't want adjectives or adverbs, please"—"when he returned, he brushed against Brother Krohl's foot. This provoked a response from Brother Krohl. Maybe I'd better call on Brother Leighton, who along with Brothers Moore and Barnett, was a principal witness."

"O.K.," Rodge said from his seat beside Moose. "Rudy—Brother Krohl—responded, all right. He muttered something we couldn't understand"—he looked across the room at Hank Moore, who nodded—"and Brother Offenberg apologized."

"How?" Gale Bryce inquired.

"How does anybody apologize?" Duke demanded. "I said, 'I'm sorry.' "

"Not, 'I'm sorry, buddy,' " Gale murmured. "Or, 'Gee, I didn't mean it.' Or anything like that."

"No," Duke said, "because it was obvious to me, and I thought to any sensible person, that I didn't mean it."

"And you *weren't* sorry," Gale murmured in the same deliberate inciting-to-riot tone.

"Another of his damned psychological experiments," Gulbransen snorted, not too quietly, and North, seated beside him, amended, "Psycho experiments."

"Now, see *here!*" Buff said with a real anger, very rare for him. "You guys *be quiet!* All of you! And I mean it! Go ahead, Rodge."

"His apology," Rodge said, "didn't seem to satisfy Rudy. He started to swear and demand what Duke was doing, anyway. He told Duke—Brother Offenberg—that he had 'kicked' his foot, 'deliberately kicked it.' Brother Offenberg again denied it. He got a little sarcastic, I'm afraid, and Brother Krohl responded by saying he didn't like to be touched 'by people like you.' I tried to intervene and calm things down, but Duke—Brother Offenberg—said this was between him and this—"

He hesitated and Duke said coldly, "Go ahead. Say it."

"This 'damned Nazi,' " Rodge said, looking unhappy. There was a sharp intake of breath around the room. Rudy glowered and stirred restlessly again. Gale Bryce put a soothing hand on his arm, looking very professional.

"So then Jeff and Hank tried to intervene too, but Brother Offenberg warned us off—"

"How?"

"Just *looked*. And then told us to stay out of it. And then he gave Brother Krohl a shove. He was sitting on that old army cot we had, you know, and the cot collapsed and deposited Brother Krohl on his—on the floor. Duke then called Brother Krohl 'Hitler Junior,' I believe it was—" Jeff and Hank nodded—"and Rudy," Rodge concluded simply, "called him 'a damned Jew.' "

Again there was a sharp reaction. Buff glared and there was silence.

"And then Duke socked him in the jaw," Rodge said, "and he passed out for a minute and then came to and we ran for the other guys and then you came in, Mr. President, and broke it up and decided to have this meeting, at Renny's suggestion. And told them to stay out of each other's way in the meantime. And that's about it."

"Bad enough, I'd say," Randy Carrero commented thoughtfully.

"Absolutely disgraceful," Galen Bryce agreed gently.

There was another silence while everybody thought, carefully not looking at the two combatants, both of whom were flushed and angry again.

"Do you agree with that, Jeff?" Buff asked. Jeff nodded. "And Hank?" Hank nodded. "And Duke?"

"Yes," Duke snapped. "Essentially."

"And Rudy?"

"Oh, sure," Rudy said with a studied indifference. "As far as it goes."

"What was left out?"

"The way he did it."

Duke sat up straight.

"Now, listen—" he began angrily but Buff interrupted.

"*You* listen. We'll get to you. What was 'the way he did it,' Rudy?"

For a moment Rudy looked at his antagonist, the first time their eyes had met since the incident. Then he looked away and the frozen, stubborn expression they were coming to know took over his face.

"Just like I said. Deliberately."

"I did *not!*" Duke said, and beside him Unruh and Lor Davis grabbed his arms as he half started to rise. "That is a dirty lie, typical of—"

"God DAMN it!" Buff exclaimed, vehemence so unusual that it momentarily silenced them all. "I'm going to fine both of you a couple of hundred bucks if you don't settle down!"

"Oh, now, Mr. President," Galen Bryce began in a soothing tone as several others made sounds of protest.

"And you, too, doctor!" Buff snapped. "And I'll put it to a vote, too, and we'll see what happens! Now," he said, breathing hard. "How many think Duke did it deliberately? Raise your hands!"

But the direct challenge was too much. Nobody moved.

"Then I take it," Buff said, still breathing hard, "that everybody agrees that there wasn't anything deliberate about it, so therefore Rudy *is* telling a lie when he says—"

But that too was too much. Wilson leaned forward.

"Mr. President," he suggested, "I think maybe the problem is that nobody really wants to be forced to take sides on this or do anything too drastic about it—"

"That's the trouble with the world right now," Tim Bates interrupted bleakly. "Nobody wants to take sides. Nobody wants to do anything drastic. And so—"

" 'So' what?" Renny Suratt asked in an aloof and scientific tone.

"And so people get away with things," Tim said moodily. "Like Hitler."

"And Rudy?" Renny inquired blandly.

"Yes," Gulbransen said with a distaste he made no attempt to conceal. "Like Rudy."

"Mr. President!" Rudy cried. "Mr. President, God damn it, is this some kind of one-sided lynching party or am I going to get a fair hearing?"

"The question we have to decide, I think," Wilson said, "is whether you were fair to Duke and Duke was fair to you. In my opinion I think you both went too far. But I think you started it."

"*He* started it!" Rudy cried. "*He* started it when he deliberately—"

"Oh, stop using that word!" Duke interrupted loudly. "I didn't 'deliberately' do anything!"

"Except call him a damn Nazi," Suratt remarked dryly.

"And 'Hitler Junior,' " Smitty Carriger noted.

"And knock him out," Gale Bryce said with a cozy little laugh. "Other than that, nothing."

"But I didn't start it by doing anything deliberate," Duke said stubbornly.

"And all he did to you, really, that I can see," Renny said in a clear, judicious voice, "is say that you hit his foot deliberately, and call you a damned Jew."

Again there was a silence that lengthened—and lengthened—and lengthened—until into it Tim said, "Exactly. . . . I really think," he added quietly, "that we're finally in real danger of tearing the house apart, here. I

think the sickness of our times is right here. And I hate it," he said simply.
"*I hate it.* I don't condone everything Duke did, I think he reacted too
quickly to Rudy's first remark, which I think *he* thought *was* deliberate. And
so do I. I think he flew off the handle too fast and said and did some things
that weren't necessary, and they in turn provoked Rudy into saying what he
did. But I think Duke is under a lot of pressure about events in Europe and
I don't blame him. Rudy's made no secret that he sympathizes with what's
going on, and supports it, and I don't like that and I don't blame Duke for
reacting to it—overreacting, sure, but maybe if we'd put ourselves in his
shoes for a minute, we'd see why. Nobody else in this house has ever been
hostile to him the way Rudy is. We like him. We value his membership. We
value his friendship. Whatever he did, Mr. President—and I believe there
was deliberate provocation, all right, but not from him—it doesn't warrant
being called a vicious name. It doesn't warrant bringing that Nazi death's-
head into this campus and into this house. That," he concluded quietly, "is
my belief."

"And that, I suppose," Suratt said with a wry little smile, "is the editorial
for tomorrow. And tomorrow. And tomorrow. And—"

"Yes, smart-ass," Tim said evenly. "And as often thereafter as necessary."

"Mr. President," Willie said before Suratt, flushing, could reply; and Buff,
who had been listening quietly to Tim, making no attempt to interrupt, said,
"Brother Wilson," in a resigned tone.

"Mr. President, I can sympathize with Brother Bates and his statement of
the case against Brother Krohl. I agree with a lot of it, and I think he's right
that Brother Krohl, in his ineffable fashion which we are all coming to know
and love, did deliberately provoke what happened and then found himself
dealing with an explosion bigger than he had counted on—an explosion
grown out of anger and frustration . . . and fear. I don't condone the explosion, but I think it was provoked. Deliberately. And Brother Krohl, in one
sense, got exactly what he deserved.

"But, Mr. President," he said, and they were all very quiet and intent,
"we can't have members trying to settle their arguments with physical responses. That's just not the way things are done—in this country—on this
campus. We've always been able to discuss anything here and come out of
it without that kind of thing. We'll be losing something very precious, I
think, if we get away from that. And that's where Brother Krohl, finally, in
the last analysis, is way out of line and had better, in my estimation, shape
up—or get out."

Rudy actually turned pale. Willie ignored him and went calmly on.

"If he can't conduct himself decently here, then we don't want him. But
that's a separate issue and one we don't need to decide right now. Maybe a
warning's enough, on that score. That's up to him. The issue of intolerance
. . . and anti-Semitism . . . and all that ugliness we see going on in Europe,

and which—Tim is right—can so easily raise its head here, as witness this very incident that's brought this meeting—is something else. But that, too, I don't think we can settle here, either, except to say that we're against it. As far as we're concerned, it may come under the general umbrella of how Brother Krohl behaves—it may come down to a focus as narrow as that. As far as we're concerned in this house and on this campus, if he restrains himself, that may be enough. If he doesn't"— he looked thoughtfully at Rudy, who did not meet his eyes—"then we can face that later.

"Right now, it seems to me, we just have to decide, in my opinion, Mr. President, the narrow issue of physical violence. Somebody hit somebody. Somebody hit back with ugly words we don't want to hear again in this house. In my opinion, Mr. President, Brother Krohl and Brother Offenberg should each be fined the sum of fifty dollars and be suspended from all house activities except room and board for the rest of the quarter. And I so move."

"But that's just a slap on the wrist—" Tim began.

"Second," Unruh interrupted firmly.

"Vote!" Franky cried.

"All those in favor!" Buff said.

"Aye!" roared nearly everybody. "No," said a handful.

"So carried," Buff said.

"Mr. President!" Galen Bryce shouted as everyone started to get up. "Mr. President, I demand a show of hands!"

"Mr. President," Gil Gulbransen shouted him down, "I move to lay that motion on the table!"

"Second!" North McAllister said.

"All those in favor—"

"Aye!" roared an obvious majority again. "So ordered!" cried Buff, already halfway out the door. "Sorry, Gale," he shouted back over his shoulder. "I think we all have to go study now!"

"Well," Hank Moore asked his roommate, "are you happy?"

"Fucking sons of bitches," Rudy said. "I'll get even one of these days, see if I don't."

"I wouldn't try, if I were you," Hank said. "I think they're bigger than you are."

"Huh!" Rudy said scornfully. "Nobody's bigger than what's going on in the world right now. It's *justice*. Nobody can stand against that! *Nobody!*"

"Some may want to try," Hank suggested. "I wouldn't push it here, if I were you."

"Well, you're not me," Rudy retorted, "so keep your fucking sermons to yourself!"

"Yes, sir," Hank said. "Excuse me."

And he went down the hall to Ray Baker to ask him if he couldn't move to some other room. Ray looked thoughtful and went to see Latt while Hank waited. Latt didn't hesitate a moment to say, sure, of course, he wouldn't mind sharing. When Willie told him later that he was being awfully generous because he had certainly earned his privacy for senior year, Latt just smiled and said, "I don't mind. He's quiet and steady, and so am I. It won't be any problem." That was Latt.

When Hank came back ten minutes later to gather his books and clothing, Rudy demanded, "Where are you going?" but Hank didn't reply.

"See if I care!" Rudy shouted after him as he went away down the hall. "See if I God damned care!"

And he slammed the door as hard as he could, which made him feel a little better and brought several of his brethren into the hall to ask each other what was going on. He didn't care, he told himself stoutly, though in a very odd way he felt as though he might cry, *he just didn't care.*

They could isolate him all they liked but they weren't going to change him, because he was *right.*

And he was going to stick to it, too.

"I'm sorry," Buff said, back in his room. "But we had to do it. And we had to make it equal."

Duke looked up from the big jagged red stain on the floor, origin unknown, that he had apparently been studying with great concentration when his roommate came in. It was known as "The Mortal Sign of Brother X" and many were the legends of mayhem and murder that had been woven around it by successive generations.

"That's all right," he said, eyes haggard and unhappy: for once, Buff thought, the Offenberg assurance had been badly shaken. "I understand. Nobody needs to apologize."

"We knew you and Rudy wouldn't," Buff said with a half-smile, a feeble attempt to lighten things up a little. It wasn't enough.

"That's right," Duke said, and returned to his contemplation of The Mortal Sign.

"Well," Buff said as the silence threatened to lengthen uncomfortably, "at least I think we've given him a lesson he won't forget. He'd better not, or next time he'll be out."

"That would be nice," Duke remarked, without inflection.

"And of course," Buff added, turning to his desk and preparing to open his books, "so might you be. If it came to that."

"I understand," Duke said in the same toneless voice. "It won't. I've made my little protest. I'm through. We Jews aren't supposed to hit back, you know: it makes everyone uncomfortable. We're just supposed to sit and take it. I believe it's known as 'being civilized.'"

"Oh, now," Buff said, genuinely disturbed by the depth of bitterness. "That isn't right. Don't say that."

"Why isn't it right?" Duke inquired, meeting his eyes again. "Why shouldn't I say it? Do we have Nürnberg Laws here too?"

"Oh, Duke," Buff said, and "Yes, 'Oh, Duke!' " his roommate responded.

"I mean," Buff said, "you just can't condemn us all. *We* don't feel the way Rudy does. *We* don't say and do the things he does. *We* aren't your enemies. We're your fraternity brothers and friends."

"Why didn't you condemn what he said, then?" Duke inquired, eyes on the floor again.

"We *did* condemn it," Buff said, almost desperately. "Willie condemned it. Timmy condemned it. Everybody condemned it."

"Then why didn't you put it in a resolution and have it voted? I'll tell you why: because you're not sure it would have carried, that's why. Not 'everybody' condemns anti-Semitism. Willie and Timmy and Latt and you and Unruh and Gulbransen and North and a lot of others, maybe. But not all."

"But, Duke," Buff protested, easygoing heart deeply troubled, easygoing face showing signs of a rare unhappiness, "you weren't entirely innocent, you know. You did respond pretty violently. And Willie thought it was best to present a resolution that would go right down the middle and clear the decks and get it out of the way."

"Sure," Duke said. " 'Get it out of the way.' That's what the whole world wants to do right now, 'get it out of the way.' So you rushed through your equal-punishment resolution and now we can all forget about it. Hooray."

"We did our best," Buff said, sighing but deciding the hell with it. He seated himself at his desk and opened a book. "I said I'm sorry and I am. If we didn't hit all the fine points, it's because things could have gotten out of hand if we'd had too much discussion. Willie didn't tell me beforehand what he had in mind, but when he spoke up, I thought, Here's a way to get it over with as fast as possible. Obviously a big majority agreed. So it's done. There's no point in rehashing it. Just stay out of his way and he'll stay out of yours and we'll get through the year. That's about all I can suggest."

"It's deeper than that," Duke said, returning to his contemplation of The Mortal Sign. "It's a lot deeper than that."

Buff started to reply, thought better of it, tried to force himself to concentrate on his text. This was never easy, particularly when it was *The Social Theories of the New Deal,* with which he and his parents violently disagreed. But he tried.

Neither spoke further. Finally Duke got up abruptly and went out to telephone Shahna. When he told her what had happened she started to cry and he almost did too. But he told her grimly that they weren't going to break him, no matter how they tried. She told him that she loved him, and he was entirely right. The situation wasn't quite that dramatic, perhaps, but

in the context of the times no one, understandably, could have convinced
them otherwise.

Later that night in the room Renny Suratt shared with Johnny Herbert
(a mismatching if there ever was one, Latt remarked to Ray, but Ray said
they were crowded and he didn't have much choice in assignments), the
postmortem of the house's decision had already gone from Rudy, Duke,
Nazism and anti-Semitism all the way back to the shortcomings and results
of the Versailles Treaty. Tim could hear the voices raised in heated argument on this perennial subject as he came along the hall on his way to call
the night editor of the *Daily* to check on the progress of tomorrow's paper.
For a moment he decided to ignore it. Then the combativeness aroused by
the tensions of the evening came to the fore and he decided no, by God,
he wasn't going to let anybody get away with the kind of stuff he heard
Suratt spouting as he approached the door. He owed him one anyway
for that "tomorrow and tomorrow and tomorrow" crack, snotty son of a
bitch.

"The only reason President Wilson dragged us in," Renny was saying with
absolute assurance, "was to increase American markets and help the big
munitions makers rake in the money. The usual conspiracy of big business,
big profits, big politicians. That's the way it always works. Always has, always
will. And the poor damned Germans took a screwing and have had to pay for
it ever since. Which is why," he said as Tim walked in and dropped into
a seat beside Smitty Carriger, "I can't get so crazy-mad upset about Hitler
as Tim does. He's only righting the wrongs of the Versailles Treaty, which
was a dictated peace and a lousy one." He gave Bates a challenging look.
"Right, Tim?"

"Oh, sure," Tim said. "And the damned Germans didn't have a damned
thing to do with it."

"A little," Renny said airily. "A little."

"Sure they did," Lor Davis said, blond hair tousled as always, classic
forehead creased by an earnest frown as he leaned forward, "but only after
being denied all their just claims by the Allies . . . at least," he added
somewhat doubtfully, "that's what my history prof says."

"And do you always have to believe everything your history prof says?"
Bates demanded. "Can't you think for yourself?"

"Think?" Gale Bryce echoed with a fatherly chuckle that was supposed to
foster the illusion that he didn't mean it. "Loren wants to know: what's that?"

"I *do* think," Lor said in an aggrieved tone, smiling uncertainly, "so don't
be a bastard. I agree with my professor. The Germans started it but they were
deliberately lured into it by England and France. And they're just as bad as
the Germans ever were. Look at what they've done in their empires, look

how they've treated their colonial peoples. Look at their unemployment problems and what a mess they're in domestically. I mean, why blame the Germans? It's an equal blame, isn't it?"

"Boy!" Smitty said, pleasing Tim with an unexpected ally. "Put on that phonograph record and let it roll! That's the sort of stuff I get from my profs too. That's the fashionable way to teach nowadays: Who's to blame?—we're *all* to blame—therefore *nobody's* to blame. There aren't any standards of right and wrong to judge by anymore, it's all equal. Well: that isn't how I was brought up."

"Me either," Johnny said. "My dad fought in the World War—"

"They all did," Suratt said dryly. "More fools they. That old professor from Princeton led 'em down the garden path and they *went*. Just because they were fools enough to do it doesn't mean we have to, twenty-two years later."

"My dad isn't a fool!" Johnny said angrily. "So don't be such a smart-ass. He's a good, patriotic—"

" 'Patriotic!' " Renny echoed. "*That* tired old word!"

"Yes," Johnny said heatedly, " 'patriotic!' Which is more than you'll ever be!"

"If it means swallowing every lie from the dirty politicians and the lousy warmongers," Suratt snapped, "then you're right, I never will be. If it means having the sense to see what's right and do it, then I'll accept the label."

"Oh, there *are* standards of right and wrong, then?" Smitty inquired. Renny snorted.

"No you don't. You can't trap me, Carriger. Yes, there are standards. If you have 'em, you don't swallow the warmongers' arguments. You don't set out to kill millions of people—"

"But the Germans killed millions of people! They killed millions and millions and millions in the war. And they're killing more right now, in Austria and Czechoslovakia. And what about the Jews?"

"Oh," Suratt said in a tired voice, "forget the Jews. They're always belly-aching. So a few of them got their shops closed and have had to flee the country. So what? They're probably happier somewhere else. I'd rather leave than stay where I'm not wanted."

"It's their country too," Tony Andrade spoke up unexpectedly from his seat beside Lor Davis. "What about that?"

"They don't have countries," Renny said coldly. "They have groupings. They're international. That's why they run things everywhere, because they're so powerful. Hitler has a point there, too."

"Jesus!" Andrade said. "Haven't we got enough of a problem in the house already without you mouthing that junk?"

"Ah think the vote tonight was pretty damned high-handed, myse'f," Jeff said, drawn by the noise of the argument and entering to squeeze in beside Tony. "I think ol' Rudy got railroaded a bit, don't you?"

Tim started to retort, then decided to hold his tongue and listen to the younger generation. A split existed, he was pleased to note.

"He didn't deserve anything better," Tony said flatly. "He's been laying for Duke since we pledged him last year."

"And of course Duke tried to keep him out of the house, you remember," Gale Bryce recalled dryly. "Not exactly a reason for Rudy to want to be buddy-buddies."

"Duke was right," Smitty said. "He could see him coming."

"I wonder why the rest of us didn't?" Tony inquired. "He's certainly been open since about what he thinks."

"He wasn't then, though," Johnny said. "He was very diplomatic and discreet."

"And his dad has a lot of money," Renny said. "That overcomes a lot of objections, doesn't it, Tim?"

"It apparently did in your case," Tim couldn't resist, and went on smoothly before Renny could make the angry retort he obviously wanted to. "Rudy seemed personable, his grades were good, he seemed to have a good deal on the ball and be bright and pleasant—the usual criteria. It just seemed like a good idea at the time. We all thought Duke's fears were exaggerated." He looked grim. "Not now."

"So what's going to happen the rest of the year?" Galen inquired. "Do we all have to go around walking on eggs?" He looked quite pleased by the explosive potentials.

Tim shrugged.

"If we do, we do. But let's hope they have sense enough to drop it. They ought to be able to stand each other until June. If not, we may have to discipline them again."

"As long as things keep on the way they're going in Europe," Tony said, "nothing's going to settle down, really. Everybody's going to be on edge."

"Hitler says he's going to get back everything they took away from Germany at Versailles," Smitty remarked. "He still has quite a way to go."

"What's wrong with that?" Renny inquired.

"Oh," Smitty said, "only a war, maybe. Nothing at all, Renny. Nothing at all, really."

"In the first place," Renny said, "he's entirely justified, and in the second place, we wouldn't be in it anyway. So what's the problem?"

"F.D.R. wants us to be in it," Lor said.

"Oh, Christ!" Renny said. "F.D.R.!"

And they were off into fifteen minutes of overheated, overreactive, overly repetitive discussion of the President which as usual resulted in a draw. His big, bouncy presence was everywhere. There was no escaping it. His supporters were as vehement as his detractors. He was always good for a wrangle, anytime. Arguments about him always ended in a noisy, name-calling stalemate.

"Anyway," Jeff said finally, "I know that tricky old bastard. He'll have us in it the minute he thinks he can get away with it. You mark my word, Miss Suzy!"

"Who's Miss Suzy?" Tim inquired. Jeff grinned.

"I don't know. It's just somethin' we always say in my family—'You mark my word, Miss Suzy!' Probably some old mammy years ago. But she comes in handy, doesn't she? She's got that old bugger's number, just like I do."

"Well," Smitty said, getting up to leave, "we can't settle Roosevelt—or Hitler—tonight. And I've got to study."

"Me, too," Tony said, and Johnny Herbert also stood up and went over to his desk.

"Not to run you guys out," he said with a smile, "but here's your hat, what's your hurry. Eight-o'clock classes come mighty early."

"I don't have anything until ten tomorrow," Renny said complacently. "I could go on all night." His expression became the usual, mocking and perverse. "Just remember, Smitty: the blame is equal—everybody shares it— nobody can take a high moral ground because there isn't any—nobody's to blame for anything because everybody's to blame for everything— everybody's morally equal because everybody's immorally equal—nobody can judge anybody else because we're all bad. Isn't that great?"

Smitty made a face as he paused at the door.

"Like I said, that's the popular way to teach and argue nowadays. But I— don't—believe it."

"Me, either," Tim said shortly. "How do you arrive at any kind of judgment on anything, if that's your theory?"

"You don't," Renny said blandly. "And the world stalls at dead center. That's the beauty of it."

"You're nuts, Suratt," Tim said, turning away. "Good night."

"Not only nuts," Smitty agreed, following suit. "But dangerous. *I* think."

"*Me?*" Renny demanded cheerfully, pleased because he realized that in the process of wanting to provoke he had apparently hit on something that could be used often to bait his more earnest brethren. "*Me,* dangerous? Come on, now! How do you arrive at that?"

He looked exaggeratedly innocent and the rest bade him farewell with dutiful laughter as they left.

But down the hall Tim and Smitty paused for a moment before saying good night.

"That's the trouble," Smitty said, genuinely worried. "It's what a lot of people, including several of my profs, seem to be trying to do—destroy the basis for judgments of any kind. If you succeed in that, then nobody can take a firm stand on anything because, as Renny says, we're all alike. How do you get a hold on things? How can you attack or defend anything? It puts us all on quicksand."

"One keeps trying, I guess," Tim said moodily. "But you're right, Smitty. It's getting tougher."

He went on to call the night editor and make sure all was calm on the *Daily*.

Smitty went to his room to hit the books for a while before turning in.

Neither could foresee how tough, in time, the making of judgments would become, nor, until they looked back years later, how explicitly, in a casual fraternity argument prompted by an unhappy racial incident, they had accidentally touched upon the near-fatal weakness that would underlie their generation's passage through the twentieth century and eat away, patiently and implacably, at the very foundations of organized society itself.

Half in jest, half in perversity, Renny Suratt had stumbled upon the great fulcrum with which not only Adolf Hitler would seek to move the world. Many of his heirs both spiritual and political, in many and many a land, would also see it and try to use it, all too many with success.

11

On Thursday night, as planned, "Willie's Little Black Sambo" (Suratt, egged on by Galen Bryce), or "Willie's Latest Cause" (Franky, encouraged by an amused but not unfriendly McAllister and Richardson), or "The Kid Everybody Wants and We're Going To Be Lucky If We Get Him" (Unruh, firmly supported by Lattimer, Gulbransen and Musavich), came up to the house after dinner with some twenty other nervous rushees.

They were served drinks (nonalcoholic) and cookies (Dewey the cook's attempt at chocolate-chip, only mildly disastrous as compared with some of his productions, which were masterpieces of malnutrition).

They were examined, which they were vividly aware of and which did not make them any less nervous, awkward and self-conscious.

For an hour or so they stood about uneasily while members made determined attempts to draw them out on any conceivable topic that could be prolonged into a sustained conversation.

That was the night Bayard got his nickname. The minute they left and went mumbling self-consciously off into the night "like a flock of scared little sheep," as Franky put it, Jeff plopped himself down on one of the sofas and demanded, "Willie! What y'all have planned for that boy By'rd?"

" 'By'rd?' " Willie echoed, playing for time. "I haven't got anything planned for 'By'rd.' "

"I'd plan By-*Bye*, if I were you," Jeff suggested, smiling to soften it but not really kidding, as Wilson could see.

"Now, I don't see why you say that—" he began, but Jeff shook his head.

"Willie," he said patiently, "we've all just been through a big battle over Duke and Puke"—neither was there, and there was a startled burst of laughter—"and I don't think any of us really wants to get into another one soon over a nice nigrah boy like By. Now, I like By—I'm not sayin' I don't—he seems to be a good-lookin', well-mannered, pleasant, intelligent colored boy. He knows his place and I respect him for it. But I don't want him in my house. It's *my* house and I want to associate with who I want to. I don't want a nigrah boy, however nice he may be, forced down my throat. I told you that before and you didn't listen. I mean it, Willie! I mean it!"

"I know you mean it," Wilson said soberly, sitting down beside him as the rest began to draw into a tighter, interested circle around the sofa. "And nobody wants to force you into anything. It's my hope that when you get to know Bayard—By—better, you'll—"

"I know him," Jeff said reasonably. "I've known him all my life. I told you, I grew up with him. I played with him as a kid, he was in and out of my family home every day in a way you Yankees never know—and would never permit. I *know* him, or leastways I've known maybe—" he paused, mentally counting—"six or seven of him in my growin'-up days. Some of 'em, two or three in particular, will be my friends till the day we die. I see 'em every time I go around my hometown, I ask how they're doin', they ask how I'm doin', we wish each other well and it's genuine. Later on when we all marry and have families, I don't doubt a bit but what one or two of 'em will name a son for me, and I fully expect, Willie, in a way you Yankees will *never* undersand, I fully expect that they'll be comin' to me for help of one kind or another as long as we live. And I'll give it to 'em gladly, without even thinkin' about it twice, *because that's my obligation.* And not only that, I *want* to. But I don't want to be *forced* to do it. That's the difference, you see. That's where I understand certain things and y'all don't. Believe me, Willie. Y'all just *don't.* So I hope y'all won't push it, because I'd hate to have to beat y'all on it. How many votes does it take to blackball somebody?"

"More than you can line up," Willie retorted. Jeff was unimpressed.

"I wouldn't be so certain of that. Come on: how many?"

Wilson hesitated. Latt intervened.

"Because we had such a battle over Bill Nagatani a couple of years ago, it now takes five. It used to take two, but that got out of hand."

"Five," Jeff said thoughtfully. "O.K., call in your chips, Willie. I'll see you and raise you."

"It's not a poker game," Wilson said in an annoyed tone.

"Damned right it isn't," Jeff agreed. "It's serious business. But I guess it still comes down to votes."

Wilson gave him an appraising look.

"I predict the great majority will be perfectly willing to try it and give him a chance. Anyway, he may not even want to join if we ask him, so it all may be academic, anyway."

Jeff looked blank.

"Then why force it? What are you tryin' to prove?"

"Oh," Wilson said slowly; and sighed. "I don't know . . . some concept of human decency and tolerance and—and elemental goodness, I guess. I suppose 'decency' is the operative word."

"Listen," Jeff said. "I'm decent. I can talk to that boy anytime on any subject and we'll get along just fine. I can sit beside him in class, we can see each other at a dance or a party or whatever and talk just like you and me. As long as I'm a gentleman and he's a gentleman, which I'll concede he is. But I don't have to live with him to do that—"

"As long as he 'knows his place,' right?" Unruh interrupted, finally breaking the virtual spell that had seemed to hold them all while Jeff and Willie argued. "As long as he *knows* and you *know*—"

"But we *do* know, you see," Jeff said simply. "That's the point. We *do* know. He understands just as much as I do why we can't be in the same house and *have* to live together. It wouldn't be fittin'. It just wouldn't be fittin'."

"You mark my word, Miss Suzy," Tim said wryly. It broke the tension a little. Something of Jeff's usual cheerful grin came back.

"That's right! That is absolutely right. And his feelin's won't be hurt. We understand each other. I'll bet you'll find, Willie, that when it comes right down to it, he'll back off. 'Cause he knows what's right and so do I."

"It's got to change sometime," Wilson said bleakly.

"Well, try it," Jeff said. "But don't say I didn't warn you. It'll be more than five, too." The grin deepened. "You mark my word, Miss Suzy."

And on that note they all laughed, kept their own counsel, and parted for the evening. Later Wilson tried to reach By at the hall but he hadn't come in yet. He told himself firmly that he wasn't going to give up, even though he suspected uneasily that Jeff might be right: even if he called in all the chips, it still might not be enough.

He wasn't prepared to concede that yet, however. His main worry was that Jeff might be right on another score: By might not have the guts to go through with it even if the necessary votes did fall his way.

Willie reflected somewhat grimly that he might be going into battle for someone who didn't really want to be saved. And what became of fine principles then?

In this gloomy foreboding, however, he would prove to be mistaken. A very determined little lady was about to take the matter firmly in hand.

He had finally reached Maryetta Bradford around nine P.M. Sunday when she had returned from Berkeley. Theirs had been quite a cozy conversation, the girlhood friendship of their mothers making for instant ease. She had transferred from Mills College to the University, she said, "because, frankly, I just got bored. It's a nice little school but things here are so—so much—"

"Bigger?" he suggested and she laughed.

"Bigger and a *lot* more stimulating. People here really like to *think* about things. I mean, they do at Mills, too, but not on the broad scale they do here. I like that. My mother, you know, was *very* active in social causes and still is. I like to think I'm following in her footsteps."

"I'm sure you are," he said, "and I'm sure you will be here. . . . I'm calling because I have a young friend who's also a sophomore transfer, who may be calling you. I just wanted to let you know about him so that you won't be surprised."

"Oh, nice," she said. "Tell me about him."

"His name is Bayard Johnson—"

"I *like* it! It sounds romantic!"

"Well, he isn't exactly Rhett Butler. But he does come from the South."

"Oh, *good!* Southerners are such interesting people. They need to be *converted* so!"

Lord! he thought. What am I getting poor By into?

"I don't think you need to convert this one," he said carefully. "He's already, you might say, er—converted."

"Then I know I'll like him even more," she said firmly—her soft little voice, he was already beginning to suspect, could be *very* firm. "He must be a very tolerant person, then. Most Southerners are so *rigid*."

"He is tolerant," he agreed. "In fact, he was—uh—born tolerant, you might say."

"Oh?" she said, puzzled. "How was that?"

"Because of his parents."

"Oh, they were like my mother! Then we *will* start off with a lot in common."

"Well—not—*exactly*. They were born tolerant, too, because *their* parents were born tolerant, because their parents—it runs in the family. It's By's heritage, you might say. His difficulty is that other people—other Southerners and—and—*others*—are not always tolerant toward him."

There was a silence.

"Oh," she said finally, in a tone he couldn't quite analyze but at least she was still talking. "I know who you're talking about now. By Johnson. So that's his name. I never really heard, but I did so admire what you did for him on Reg Day. I've been looking forward to meeting you because I've been wanting to tell you that, ever since. It was *splendid!*"

"Thank you," he said, beginning to feel relieved, although he shouldn't have worried, obviously: she was her mother's daughter, all right.

"Yes, I was *so* proud of you. I was proud of him, too. I felt that he conducted himself with great dignity in a *most* difficult situation."

"Indeed he did. So. Will you talk to him if he calls?"

"I would be *thrilled*," she said. "In fact, where is he living? I'll call him."

He hesitated, then thought: What the hell. He needs to be shaken out of himself. He told her.

"He's a little shy. A very nice guy, you know, very good-looking, but he is a little shy."

"We'll fix that," she said with serene assurance, and again he thought, with some amusement, Oh, Lord. Watch out, By. Watch out, everybody.

"You do that," he said. "Let me know how it goes. Maybe I can get Donna Van Dyke some night and the four of us can go out together."

"Let's do it soon," she said. "That would be absolutely *great!*"

Tonight during the rushing period he had managed to ask By quietly if she had called. By said, oh, yes, and they were going to see each other soon. He had sounded quite overawed and Willie had been tempted to say, Look, kid, don't let it throw you. She's just a girl.

But because he was sensitive and intuitive he realized that to By she was already something far, far more. He didn't quite understand fully yet what it meant to By to have a white girl call him out of the blue, take the initiative and suggest very directly that they have a date. But he was already beginning to get a glimpse of it. His uneasiness turned serious, and grew.

Yet, as they walked slowly along beside the dimly lighted Quad on their way to the Cellar from the Libe, where they had arranged to meet and study—thereby causing a considerable stir of which he was acutely aware and which she seemed to ignore with a serene relish—By could not have been happier. In fact, he thought that he had never been so happy in his life—or, as he realized with recurring flashes of terror, quite so frightened.

Where he came from, if he had dared to walk along in public in the obvious companionship of a white girl, he might have wound up bruised and bloodied if not far worse. He kept telling himself that he was far away now, sheltered by the embracing arms of the University, away from intolerance, away from fear. But fear had been a lifelong companion and he could not shake it. Nor, thinking back to his reception at Willie's house, was he all that certain that he might not meet there punishments more subtle, if not as physically devastating, as those that could have faced him back home.

And they might not be so very subtle, either. There had been something in the eyes and manner of Mr. Barnett—*Jeff* Barnett, he kept telling himself—that had instantly put him right back where he came from, mentally almost hat in hand saying Yowzza. Jeff had been polite enough—more polite and actually more cordial this time than during that first visit when Willie had virtually stood over him with a blacksnake whip and demanded it. But his eyes said: We know each other, you and I. We know where we fit. You're a nice boy and we're both a long way from home, but don't try to take advantage of it. You keep to your side of the street and I'll keep to mine and we'll get along just fine. All right?

And hating himself for it, By knew that his eyes had said: Yes, sir. I appreciate your kindness, sir, and I won't take advantage of it. Oh, no, sir. You can be sure of that, you surely can. Oh, yes, sir.

And so the hour had passed with great tension for him; and it was not made easier by his instinctive knowledge that Jeff was just as young and inwardly just as tense and unsure of himself as he was. But buoyed up by the rules and rituals of the ancient pattern from which they sprang, Jeff, By knew, would be able to maintain his outward assurance far longer than By could. And so it had been a miserable hour, not made easier by his conviction that there were others, not bound by heritage but equally hostile to any further advances across a line invisible but in their minds unbreakable.

And now, suddenly, this cute girl beside him—again, Willie's doing and, again, throwing him into turmoil. He thought with a sudden wryness that in some ways Willie was a hard friend to have: a great one but a hard one. He gave so much but he demanded so much and expected so much, too. By wasn't entirely sure he could stand it, though he was sure he couldn't stand it if he didn't have him as a friend, either.

A sudden sad little sigh, totally unconscious, escaped him. So quickly that it seemed to his startled mind that she actually, physically, pounced, Maryetta responded.

"What's the matter?" she demanded sharply. "Are you worried about those stupid gossiping twerps in the Libe?"

"No," he said. "I really wasn't thinking about them at all."

"Don't," she said. "They aren't worth it. What's worrying you, then?"

"Nothing," he said. But as he expected, she would have none of it.

"Yes there is," she said. "People don't sigh"—and she went *Whooosh!* in a way that he at first thought was meant to be funny but realized was meant to be emphatic—"just like that without some reason. What is it?"

"I don't know whether—" he began.

"Tell me," she said firmly. "It doesn't do any good to keep things bottled up inside. What?"

"Well, I told you Willie invited me up to the house for rushing—"

"Yes," she said impatiently, "and they gave you some funny-tasting punch and some soggy chocolate-chip cookies. I don't see why that should make you sigh, though."

He started to smile but realized that she was totally humorless. He wondered if she was that way about everything. He hoped not.

"That wasn't it," he said obediently. "There's another Southern boy—gentleman—there—"

"Southern boy," she said. "Just like you. Who is he? What about him?"

"His name is Jeff Barnett and he's a nice guy. But all he can see is my color and he—he doesn't like it."

" 'Doesn't like it'?" she repeated sharply. "What did he do? Spit?"

"No," he said, marveling again that the exaggeration wasn't humorous but realizing that wasn't her way. "I don't mean he doesn't *like* it, I mean that when he sees it he automatically puts me in—in a certain place in his thinking and it changes the way he regards me. . . . I'll bet," he added wistfully, "that if we'd grown up in the same town together, we could have been real good friends."

"But he still wouldn't want you in the house."

"No," he said in the same wistful way, but honestly. "I guess he wouldn't."

"What about the others? How do they feel?"

"I don't know."

"You must sense something," she said, and just then they passed one of the lights along the Quad and he could see her clearly. Small, blond, pretty. Intelligent. Purse-lipped. Dead serious.

And determined.

Was she ever!

"I think there's some," he said, "who agree with Jeff. Not for the same reasons, but they—they feel uneasy about me. And I don't blame 'em. I'm unusual out here. I'm something new. I'm not your ordinary student. I'm a change. Change challenges. I can understand it."

"Well," she said shortly, "I can't. Change makes people grow. It makes them strong. You can't stop change. What are you going to do if they ask you to join?"

"They won't."

"If Willie wants them to," she said flatly, "they will. What will you do? Run away?"

"Now, listen—" he began, stirred to protest.

"Well," she said, "what *will* you do?"

"I think," he said slowly and carefully, because this was the first time he had been forced to think it through and state it out loud, "that I'll probably say no."

"You will *not!*" she exclaimed, so vehemently that another couple, over-taking their slow walk that had come to a virtual halt at the corner of the Quad, looked back at them, startled—and, he thought uncomfortably, dis-approving. "I won't let you!"

"My," he said, but mildly and with a little laugh. "You're taking on an awful lot of responsibility for my life on pretty short notice, aren't you?"

"You need someone to help you," she said. "You're just a kid, really. What do you know about things out here? You'd let yourself be scared off if I weren't here to help. That's why we met. Of course you're going to join that house. You're going to stay in there and fight! And I'm going to help you!"

He shook his head with a bemused little smile.

"You are something," he said. "You're sure something, Maryetta."

"I'm your friend," she said, tucking his hand firmly under her arm and pulling him forward. "Now, come along. The Cellar's going to close in fifteen minutes, we just have time to go in there and have a cup of coffee. We're going to march in there as though we owned the place and that's how you're going to act from now on, on this campus, everywhere you go. Right?"

"If you say so," he said, again shaking his head in amused wonderment.

And that was what they did, eliciting further looks, murmurs, half-hidden laughter, bafflement. He walked her to her dorm. No one was around downstairs, which he thought was just as well. He didn't know what she expected by way of good night, didn't dare offer to kiss her. It wasn't necessary. She held out her hand, gave him a firm, commanding shake, said, "Thank you for the coffee. Call me tomorrow. Good night!"—turned on her heel and marched up the stairs without a backward glance.

He walked slowly back down to his dorm through the now deserted campus; found both his roommates in bed; undressed, went down the hall to the toilet, used it, brushed his teeth, came slowly back to bed. There he lay wide awake, staring at the ceiling, for quite a long time before he finally dropped off into uneasy sleep.

You are one confused boy, Mr. Johnson, he told himself, one confused boy.

But at least he had a girl now, apparently—and she apparently intended to take control of his life—and she was very determined—and she was white.

And he couldn't figure out why she had decided to zero in on him as her project.

And that confused him even more.

12

Overnight, autumn retreated. Fog rolled in over the Coast Range. Lovely Indian summer seemed to have come at last to an end. Regularly every morning the campus lay shrouded in mist. Dim forms loomed up and vanished. Breath left trails. Disembodied voices and the sound of hurrying feet echoed along the Quad. Heavy sweaters appeared, woolen skirts, clodhoppers, suitably dirty heavy-duty pants lovingly preserved in their grime against this turn in the weather. Overcoats went on sale downtown for $29.50.

It wasn't really time for winter yet; maybe this was just a preview. Or maybe the dreary months had really begun and life must narrow in for a while. The best time to study, said Latt who didn't need a season to assist him, was winter.

Thanksgiving loomed a few days away. Quickly after would come final exams, end of quarter, Christmas, the new year—1939, and a third of the academic year gone already.

For some, the first three months seemed to pass in a sort of ponderous dream, heavy with the apparently endless eternities of youth, so quickly gone but, for some, so slow of passage:

Marc Taylor, lonelier, unhappier, more and more the waif despite the efforts of such as Gulbransen and Richardson to give him a boost, befriend him, introduce him to girls, "get him *moving*," as Gil put it with a frustration half annoyed, half amused . . .

Randy Carrero, sinking deeper into his agonized relationship with Fluff Stevens, who was seemingly unaware that one of the University's brightest minds and normally steadiest personalities was floundering because of her—or maybe, as he darkly brooded, perfectly well aware, relishing it, enjoying his unhappiness, regarding it in some perverse way as a tribute to herself . . .

Rudy Krohl, increasingly ostracized and increasingly, though he would never admit it, unhappy and beleaguered, a state of mind that produced more and more bluster and an embittered belligerence whose potential for trouble increasingly worried his elders . . .

Renny Suratt, sharper, more sarcastic, more annoying, cutting himself off with apparently reckless determination from all who tried to be friendly, until most gradually gave up . . .

Galen Bryce, more and more all-knowing, more and more supercilious, he too more and more isolated . . .

Johnny Herbert, never free from worry about his health, dreading the approach of winter and the almost certain recurrence of his debilitating respiratory infections, knowing that when they returned he would go through another bitter struggle with himself just to keep going and keep smiling . . .

And the uneasy wanderer of the Quad and other secret places, outwardly relaxed and cheerful, inwardly tense and unhappy, caught between two worlds as he understood all too well, knowing that ultimately society would probably force him to choose the one, even though perennially hopeful of the dream-friendship in the other that would provide him with the answer to everything; haunted increasingly by the feeling that he would never find it, that all, forever, would be empty . . .

But for most, fall quarter was a relatively happy and rewarding time, of continuing, if sometimes rocky, progress toward whatever goals they had consciously or unconsciously set themselves. There were some failures, some successes: a normal human baggage of each, it seemed to them. Life went on in the accustomed campus routine, not particularly unusual, not particularly sensational. At least, so far.

Over all brooded events in Europe and Asia and the ominous, oncoming drift toward war. No matter what individual problems they might or might not have, they all hoped, anxiously if not always articulately, that it would pass them by.

Sitting at his desk in the *Daily* Shack, Bates thought about this. Barricaded as always behind piles of exchange papers from other campuses, copies of nearby metropolitan dailies, the occasional magazine, endless sheets of gray copy paper on which he had jotted down ideas for news stories, features, editorials, headlines and front-page makeup, recent letters to the editor, pens, pencils, paper clips, erasers and all the other junk that normally covered the editor's desk, he was in his usual state of worry that his seemingly carefree fellow students might not care enough about the things he thought they ought to care about.

On the surface of it, he didn't think they did. His pages, which he congratulated himself were shaping up into one of the best volumes of the *Daily* in years, faithfully recorded all the major events of the campus as well as the ongoing events abroad. He wondered how much the student body was affected by the latter, really. He suspected that campus news was much more important. To them anyway.

Through the *Daily's* pages strode Willie, that larger-than-life figure (or so he often seemed to his fellow students and even, sometimes, to his fraternity brothers), holding Excom meetings, fighting for student rights (brighter lights for the long, communal study desks in the Libe, for instance; and other major issues); meeting with Dr. Chalmers to discuss drinking on campus; with Dean Maggie to discuss lengthened weekend passes for women students; with "Happy" Harmon, the campus cop, to discuss the possibility of raising the speed limit to twenty miles an hour for automobiles on campus, now approaching a congested and bothersome total of three hundred; taunting the University's athletic opponents with suitably sarcastic and witty statements; being announced as a finalist candidate for a Rhodes scholarship; being Perfect Boy Politician, Superman on Campus, and, as far as Tim could see, a good and extremely popular student-body president.

Almost as dazzling was Guy Unruh, subject of recurring headlines as he loped to basketball glory against outmatched opponents, assisted by Bayard Johnson, "the brightest young star on the team," according to the coach.

Moose had not been able so far to duplicate what Franky called his F.A.T.—"Fucking Asshole Touchdown"—but had performed capably and well all season and had been the subject of a recent interview by Randy Carrero, who had found to his surprise that he didn't have to doctor Moose's responses much to make them sound intelligent. "When you get old Mooser onto football he can be quite coherent," he had told Tim admiringly, for the moment taken out of his own unhappy concerns.

Latt and B. J. Letterman had received their usual admiring little feature squib—BIG BRAINS SHAME US AGAIN—when midterm results were posted. Once again they had received the highest grades on campus, B.J. leading by one A-plus—"her turn," as Latt had predicted to Franky, though he would probably overtake her at finals.

Billy Wilson had been the featured second lead in a Little Theater production of *Our Town*, and Bill Nagatani had given him a very favorable review.

Jeff Barnett had led the swimming team to a string of victories, his engagingly mischievous face, flashing grin and sleek little body gracing several sports-page photos. He had also begun to move up the tennis ladder as Randy's game noticeably fell off.

Bob Godwin had chaired four committees, two charity drives and four jolly-ups, these last featuring Haggerty and his aggregation. Hack's latest composition, "You," had been given a preliminary and very successful introduction at a jolly-up a week ago. It would be featured at the Big Game Ball on the eve of the uproarious annual football contest with Cal, the University of California at Berkeley, across the Bay.

These were the house members who most often hit the paper. In and around their various activities swirled the lives and public doings of many other prominent students as the *Daily* recorded the games, dances, meetings, concerts, lectures, forums, parties, charity drives, good works, academic interests, achievements and failures, fun times and serious accomplishments, of the University family.

Things were moving forward at a good clip, generally in line with the student-body president's latest poetic effusion. He knew Tim would never have agreed with it, had he seen it: he would have considered it too frivolous. But, Willie thought, it wasn't all *that* frivolous:

> *Dream your dreams and laugh your laughter.*
> *Enough of the other will come after.*

Timmy was more serious than that. He wanted them to worry, right *now*.

Or maybe, he thought wistfully as he heard the sounds of another edition cranking up outside his door and various incoming staffers stuck their heads in to say hello, maybe he just needed to fall in love, or something. He still didn't have any particular girl, although there were a couple on the staff whom he dated off and on, and a pretty classmate whom he liked in Armpits McGee's course The Romantic Mode from Chaucer to Coleridge ("Just a chance to talk about sex and indulge her own fantasies," hooted Suratt). But, so far, nobody to really inspire him. He supposed it would happen someday but it hadn't yet. It didn't occur to him that possibly his preoccupied aspect and general air of carrying the world on his shoulders might be a little intimidating to the average coed.

Even if he had realized it, he probably wouldn't have changed.

It was just the way he was.

Particularly when confronted by the steadily more dangerous activities of Herr Hitler and what Tim thought of as "the slant-eyed little bastards in the Orient." He had never called them that in Nagatani's presence and they had never discussed the subject directly again, but he sensed—or thought he sensed; maybe he was overreacting—a certain satisfaction in Bill's attitude as the Japanese army struck ever deeper and more bloodily into China.

Between Bill's subtle satisfactions (as Tim saw them) and Rudy's defiant cheerleading for Hitler, he reflected, the Axis was pretty well represented in his vicinity. Personally, he had had quite enough of the Axis.

Still, he really had tried to present things fairly and fully and not be too adamant or hysterical about them. He was doing his best to heed the advice of his closest friends in the house. He riffled through the growing file of "his" *Dailies.* It was an ominous ongoing story the headlines told:

"EUROPE NOT PREPARED FOR WAR"—RETURNING PROF DISCOUNTS GERMAN READINESS . . . HITLER TO ENTER SUDETENLAND TODAY. PEACEFUL INVASION BEGINS . . . HISTORY PROF WARNS HITLER MAY FOLLOW CZECH TRIUMPHS WITH FURTHER DEMANDS . . . CHAMBERLAIN DEFENDS MUNICH PACT, WINS CONFIDENCE VOTE . . . CZECH PRESIDENT QUITS, PRO-NAZI GOVERNMENT FORMED . . . CHURCHILL LASHES MUNICH AS "UNMITIGATED DISASTER," SAYS AIR BUILDUP ONLY WAY TO SAVE EMPIRE . . . U.S. NAVY OPENS LOCAL RADIO CLASS, EMPHASIZES "NO OBLIGATION TO SERVE" . . . CZECHS ASK MUSSOLINI HELP SAVE FREE PLEBISCITE PLAN. IL DUCE IGNORES PLEA . . . GERMANS FIGHT WAY INTO DEEPEST AREA OF SUDETENLAND . . . JAPAN CUTS HONG KONG–CANTON RAILWAY IN MASSIVE AIRGROUND DRIVE . . . U.S. AIR GAMES SAID SUCCESS. N. CAROLINA TO HOLD PRACTICE BLACKOUT . . . CHURCHILL URGES U.S. JOIN BRITAIN AGAINST HITLER "BEFORE IT IS TOO LATE" . . . FRANCO FORCES DRIVE LOYALISTS STEADILY TOWARD DEFEAT . . . AMERICANS FLEE CANTON . . . CHAMBERLAIN URGES PARLIAMENT APPROVE ANGLO-ITALIAN FRIENDSHIP PACT . . . HANKOW FALLS . . . HITLER DEMANDS RETURN OF FORMER GERMAN AFRICAN COLONIES . . . GERMAN EXCHANGE STUDENT DEFENDS HITLER COLONIAL DEMAND (*"Germany must get her colonies back. And I am sure they will be returned to her without a war. All Germany wants is a place in the sun, and that is what our beloved leader is struggling for. Eighty million Germans are living in a territory too small for comfortable existence, without a sufficient supply of raw material. Germany has to expand and regain the colonies taken away from her by the Versailles Treaty."* Tim assigned Randy to it, hoping to weaken his pro-Rudy sentiments. Randy had come away disgusted, written one of his best stories in weeks and a harsh editorial.) . . . F.D.R. SAYS U.S. WANTS PEACE BUT SEES NO ALTERNATIVE TO ARMS BUILDUP . . . FRENCH PRESIDENT DALADIER HINTS CLOSER TIES WITH DICTATORSHIPS . . . BRITISH CABINET BACKS NEW CHAMBERLAIN-HITLER MEETING TO STRENGTHEN EUROPEAN PEACE TIES . . . HITLER OFFERS FRANCE "GENTLEMEN'S AGREEMENT" TO FORGO WAR FOR 25 YEARS . . . U.S. NAVY TO BUILD FIVE BATTLESHIPS AT COST OF 70 MILLION . . .

And the other, parallel headlines, now in November building toward a crescendo that seemed equally dark, though neither Tim nor most in the outside world had sufficient information to know with any certainty what they might portend:

GESTAPO ROUNDS UP POLISH JEWS, DUMPS THEM ACROSS BORDER . . . "NON-ARYAN" CHILDREN BARRED FROM GERMAN SCHOOLS . . . GOEBBELS SAYS GERMAN OFFICIAL'S DEATH IN PARIS "JEWISH PLOT" TO START FRENCH-GERMAN RIFT . . . HITLER NEGOTIATING WITH LATIN AMERICA TO TAKE UNWANTED JEWS . . . NAZIS REVIVE MEDIEVAL YELLOW STAR OF

DAVID . . . NAZI LABOR PARTY SEIZES JEWISH HOMES, STORES, ARRESTS
THOUSANDS . . . JEWISH DOCTORS RESTRICTED TO "JEWS ONLY" . . . NAZI
RALLY CALLS FOR "EXTERMINATION" OF NON-ARYANS . . . GOEBBELS CALLS
PARTY LEADERS TO PLAN STRONGER ANTI-JEWISH PROGRAM . . .

Where would it end? Tim asked himself with a shudder. They were going
crazy, absolutely God damned crazy. An idea he had been kicking around
tentatively in his mind for weeks suddenly coalesced. He picked up the
phone and called the house. His man wasn't there at the moment but he
found him in his room with Buff after dinner.

"I think you should do it," Buff said, when Tim described his idea. "I think
it's a perfect opportunity. I think Tim's giving you a wonderful chance and
I think you ought to take it."

And since it wasn't characteristic of Buff to take such a strong stand, his
words, Tim could see, carried considerable weight with his roommate. But
Duke still was not convinced.

"I appreciate what you're trying to do, Timmy," he said slowly, "and I
think it's—it's—" he hesitated, and for a moment emotion shone through—
"very kind. But I'm afraid it would just—just make matters worse. It would
call attention—and maybe calling attention isn't what we ought to be doing
right now." His eyes widened; he looked somewhere far away. Self-assured
and sometimes arrogant Duke seemed to have vanished, at least for
now. The thought flashed through their minds that maybe Rudy had succeeded more than he knew. "I don't know," Duke said. "I just don't
know. . . ."

"You can have my column for the day," Tim repeated, "or you can write
a front-page editorial, whichever you want."

"I just don't know. . . ."

Buff got up with a swiftness they hadn't seen him display in months, went
to the door, pulled it open, bellowed up the stairwell:

"Willie! Hey, you, *Willie!* Come on down here! WILSON!"

The retort was muffled but emphatic.

"I *hear* you, God damn it! WHY?"

"I'm not going to tell you until you get down here!" Buff shouted as doors
opened, heads popped out, and muffled cries of "We're *studying*, God
damn it! What the hell is the matter with you, Richardson?" and similar
brotherly comments increased the din. There was the shattering slam of a
door, a distinctive thump—jump—bang—thump! on the stairs.

"Now," Wilson said, somewhat out of breath but amicably combative,
"what the hell *is* the matter?"

When they told him he said slowly, "I think I can see your point, Duke.
You don't want to aggravate things. You don't want to draw attention."

"That's exactly the phrase I used," Duke said, " 'draw attention.' But they won't listen. They think I should do it anyway."

"Of course you didn't hesitate to pop Rudy Krohl in the mouth," Willie observed. "Then why—"

"That was different," Duke said. "That was private to the house. Anyway, it was just an impulse. I've regretted it ever since."

"Why?" Willie asked simply. "The jerk deserved it. It made you feel good to strike back. It said something. So would an editorial. Or a column."

"I know," Duke said, "but I think it would just inflame things over here that maybe—maybe won't be inflamed if we don't make a fuss about it." He gave them an unhappy look. "I know you probably think I'm a coward—"

"No, we don't!" Willie said sharply. "Not at all!"

"—but I'm not. It's just a matter of—of strategy, you know? Of what's best—and how to handle it. And it—it really isn't our tradition, either." He looked bleak. "We aren't taught to—to strike back. I know a lot of us are aggressive, sometimes, and maybe I am too, but that's just compensation. Inside is a little fellow saying, 'If I'm nice to you, maybe you'll be nice to me. How about it?' But sometimes"—he looked even bleaker—"sometimes they're just—just *not*."

"Not in Germany right now," Wilson agreed somberly, "that's for sure. Why don't you ask Shahna?"

"That *is* a good thought," Duke said, suddenly looking brighter. "I will."

"Right now," Willie suggested. "She may be in."

"She is," Duke said. "Wait for me."

"Isn't it nice to know where your girlfriend is every minute?" Buff inquired with a smile as Duke went down the hall to the phone booth. "I wish I could be that certain of mine."

"You don't have a girlfriend," Willie said. "Just casuals."

"*And* look who's talking!" Buff retorted. "Here we thought we had you all fixed up with Donn Van Dyke and lately I hear you've been chasing after some little gal who lives in the Union—"

And they were off into a lively discussion in which Wilson protested that there wasn't anything at all between him and that little gal in the Union, and they commiserated heavily with poor Donna, left and bereft.

"Well," Willie demanded, amused but relieved when Duke returned, "what did she say?"

"She agrees with me," Duke said, closing the door and leaning against it with an unhappy expression. "She doesn't think I should write anything. She thinks it would be too much special pleading and too easy to discount and too personal and too—" he sighed heavily—"too dangerous. So—"

"Well, by God, then," Tim said flatly, "I will."

"She doesn't think anybody should," Duke said. He sighed again. "And I think I agree."

"But we can't just sit here and say nothing!" Tim exclaimed. "My God, who knows what's going on over there, really?"

"Maybe that's why we shouldn't jump to conclusions. Maybe it isn't as bad as—as it sounds."

"Back to the Middle Ages?" Wilson demanded. "Back to the ghetto? Come on, Duke. It doesn't look good and you know it."

"There was a confidential note on the news wire today," Tim said, "that as a result of this meeting of top Nazi leaders they're going to establish camps and make all the Jews live in them. That sounds bad enough to me."

"Shahna's folks have heard worse rumors than that," Duke admitted in a low voice, "but that's all they are—rumors. We have to be fair."

"Fair?" Wilson exploded. "What the hell's fair about the Nazis?"

But Duke, fortified now by Shahna in his worried hesitations, refused to budge.

Tim's editorial appeared the next morning, reviewing the Nazi anti-Jewish campaign from Kristallnacht to the latest rumors of "so-called concentration camps," as the wire services designated them. Like many of his editorials and columns this was alarmed, concerned and hortatory: it had a Purpose. And like many, it was read with respect but generally dismissed with the sort of tired O.K.-we-know-all-that-but-really-what-can-we-do-about-it? attitude that unhappily, he felt, reflected the attitude of the country as a whole.

"Wilson's latest God damned project," as Suratt referred to it, was launched the same day. It drew considerably more attention and, among other unexpected results, brought him abruptly closer to his elusive green-gold girl and made it quite likely that from that point on they would be seeing more of each other.

Tony Andrade and Lor Davis, hurrying together, as was usually the case, toward their respective eight-o'clocks in engineering and geology, were the first house members to realize that something was going on. Willie hadn't been at breakfast in the dilapidated old kitchen known to all as "Cockroach Heaven"—somebody said he'd left 'way early, around seven, which was unusual. Subsequently Tim's absence was also noted. Tony and Lor rounded the corner of the tiny little old post office building and started down toward the mist-filled Quad where Angie D'Allessandro and Lou Gianfalco were waiting for them. The mystery was solved.

Directly in front of the post office a card table had been set up. Three hand-lettered placards had been nailed to the large live-oak tree that shaded the building.

DOWN WITH NAZI TYRANNY! exclaimed one. FIGHT HITLER BRUTALITY! urged the second. STOP ANTI-SEMITISM! DON'T LET IT HAPPEN HERE! admonished the third.

Behind the table in three canvas camp chairs sat three students. In the center was the student-body president looking, Tony and Lor thought, pretty pleased with himself although trying not to show it. On his right sat the editor of the *Daily*. On his left was the lean, lanky figure of the president of Interclub Council, Ari Katanian.

"There's a powerhouse!" Tony murmured with a chuckle. "Do you think we dare just walk right on by?"

"Do you want to?" Lor inquired. Tony shook his head.

"No, of course not. It's a good cause." He walked purposefully over to the table. "Hi, Willie—Tim—Aram. Where do we sign?"

"That's the spirit," Wilson said, flashing him a smile. "Right under us, why don't you? Abou Ben Adhem, you can lead all the rest."

"Honored," Tony said, and complied. "Lor?"

"Sure," Lor said, also signing. "What's this all about, Willie?"

"Just what it says," Willie said with a grin. "We're starting a campus revolution."

"Jeez!" Lor said, looking startled. "Tony, maybe we shouldn't put our names on—"

"Oh, for God's sake, Lor, come on!" Andrade ordered, grabbing him by the arm to pull him away to join the cousins, who were now walking toward the table. "Hi," he said, concentrating his usual cheery smile upon them. "Want to join a good cause?"

"Hi, Willie," Angie said. "*And* Tim. *And* Aram. My goodness, what a powerhouse."

"That's what I said," Tony told her. "But a powerhouse is only as strong as its foundations, right, guys? They need a list of signatures to hold them up. So sign here, ladies! You may win the door prize!"

"It isn't exactly a funny thing, you know," Tim remarked somewhat stiffly. Tony's grin diminished but his cheery pragmatism held firm.

"Of course not, and I admire you for going to bat for it. I'll spread the word to everybody I see. What about classes? Do you need somebody to spell you later?"

"Thanks," Tim said, mollified. "I'm going to cut all mine this morning. We might need some help later when I have to go to the *Daily*."

"Don't you need a little feminine help?" Louise asked in her practical, businesslike way. "You don't want to make this an all-male project do you? Where's Donna?"

"I haven't talked to her," Willie said. "She'll be by soon, I'm sure. Yeah, thanks, why don't you come join us when you get a break? That's very nice of you."

"We'll be back at eleven," Angie said. They left, Lor still looking doubtful.

"Hey!" Willie exclaimed in a pleased tone. "*Look* at *everybody* coming to see *us!*"

And for a few quick minutes thereafter it seemed as though everybody was, as student after student paused to scrawl a hasty signature before hurrying on to class. Of the six or seven hundred who passed the post office before the eight-o'clock bell rang and brought its sudden hush to the Quad, perhaps a third signed immediately; perhaps a third muttered embarrassed promises to return later, which they probably wouldn't keep; and a third looked disapproving and passed by without comment.

Not bad for the first hour, Wilson thought. They spelled one another to go to the Cellar, use the men's room, get some coffee. At nine they picked up another sixty signatures.

Duke and Shahna came by at nine forty-five when things were most deserted to scribble their names and then slip hurriedly away.

"Thanks, guys," Duke said tersely. Shahna gave them a quick, shy smile and said, "We don't know how to thank you enough."

"And your editorial, too, Timmy," Duke added. "It said it all. Much better than I ever could. You know we were doubtful, but maybe this is right. . . . What do you plan to do with the signatures?"

"Send them to Dr. Chalmers and the trustees, first of all," Wilson said. "And probably duplicates to the governor."

"And the top people in the legislature," Ari suggested. "And California's two United States Senators—"

"And some influential Congressmen—" Willie added.

"And the big-city dailies," Tim said, "and maybe New York—"

"How about Adolf Hitler," Ari suggested, not entirely in jest. "Might as well do it up right while we're at it."

But at the mention of this name, even though so far away and unable to touch them directly, both Shahna and Duke looked quite genuinely alarmed.

"Oh, I don't know," Shahna said hurriedly in a nervous little voice. "Do you really think you should?"

"And why not?" Willie demanded. "We ought to let the bastard know what we think of him."

"But I have relatives over there," Shahna protested, looking really very upset. "Suppose he sees our names and they trace my relatives and—and—"

"Where are your relatives?" Tim asked. She looked stricken.

"We don't know," she said forlornly. "They were in Austria."

"And *you* can't trace them," Willie said gravely.

"No," she admitted in a half-whisper.

"All the more reason to let him know what we think," Ari said. "But we can eliminate your names if we ever do send it to him."

"Oh, I fully intend to," Willie said. "Nothing would please me more."

"Maybe you had better eliminate them," Duke said, feeling slightly ridiculous but also very uneasy. "We don't mind them being used here but Shahna's probably right about over there. It might cause trouble."

"They're very efficient," Tim observed. "Buff and I saw that last summer.

I don't blame you. We'll take care of it. . . . How absurd it is," he added in a bleak, unbelieving tone, "that we here, on a campus six thousand miles away, should actually be talking seriously about eliminating names to appease a raving madman in Berlin."

"Well, thanks, guys," Duke said with a nervousness increased by Tim's tone, which made distant horrors all too real. "We appreciate it."

He took Shahna's arm and they started to turn away. Suddenly they froze. Coming toward the table from the Quad were three tall, blond figures side by side, marching with a defensive unity and an unconscious rhythm prompted by a combination of anger, determination, self-consciousness and a defiant apprehension that could of course not be known to their immediately hostile viewers.

"Are they in a parade?" Wilson inquired loudly, but Duke and Shahna didn't wait to find out. They turned hastily away and hurried off toward the bookstore.

Breathing heavily, Rudy Krohl, Helga Berger and the German exchange student, whose name was Wolfgang Hubner, arrived in front of the table and, as Willie described it later during the meeting with Dr. Chalmers, plunked themselves into place.

"What are you doing?" Rudy demanded, voice shaking a little with nerves, though to them it sounded like anger and inevitably provoked an angry retort.

"Getting signatures for an honorable cause," Wilson replied in an icy voice. "Want to sign up?"

"You are insulting my country!" Wolfgang Hubner said, voice also shaking but, in his case, with complete self-righteousness and genuine anger. "You are insulting my leader! I do not like that!"

"Well, get you," Wilson said scornfully. "What do you think you're going to do about it, call in the Gestapo?"

"Now—" Ari began in a conciliatory tone, but Tim was in no mood for patience either and Ari's tentative start toward rational discussion was overruled.

"Yes," Tim agreed with rising anger, "why don't you? That's the kind of justice you get in *your* country under *your* great leader. Maybe you'd like to kill a few Jews here while you're at it, how about that? Have a little bloodbath in the center of the Quad, maybe! Have storm troopers throw stones at Memorial Church! There's lots of things you could do here if you only had your bullies with you. But you don't, Hubner, so shove off, O.K.?"

"This is absolutely illegal!" Helga Berger exclaimed, so indignant her usually rosy cheeks were positively crimson. "Absolutely *wrong*! We should complain to the president! We should write letters to the *Daily*—" She paused, suddenly remembering whom she was addressing. "*Oh!*" she cried furiously at Tim. "*You!*"

"Go ahead and write it," he snapped. "I'll print it. But right now, get the hell out of the way, all of you, so decent people can get to the table and sign this petition. Go on! *Get!*"

And indeed, as they now realized, a quickly growing crowd was beginning to gather as the bell rang and classes poured out on the Quad.

"We're 'decent people.' " Rudy exclaimed, voice now no longer nervous but filled with an angry resentment. "And we have as much right to be here as you do! *And we don't like what you're doing!*"

"You don't have any right to block this table," Willie said, standing up and raising his voice, shaking off Ari's restraining hand on his arm. He was conscious of Tim standing too; and, after a moment, Ari doing the same with a wry shrug and a grim face. "Now," he said. "Will you get away from here or do we have to force you to get away from here?"

"Don't let him talk to you like that!" Wolfgang Hubner shouted. "Don't let him do it, Rudy! Who does he think he is, big student-body president!" Without any irony at all but with genuine rage he reached for the most awesome analogy he could think of. "Who does he think he is, *Adolf Hitler*?"

"No, by God!" Wilson said loudly as hoots and shouts and a scattering of applause came from the fascinated audience—the academic morning was seldom as much fun as this—"I wouldn't be that scum of the earth if you paid me! I wouldn't be that vicious, worthless, two-bit murderer—"

"My *leader!*" Wolfgang bellowed. "*Mein Fuehrer!* Rudy, *help me!*"

And he grabbed the table and overturned it in their faces as Rudy obediently scurried to catch the fluttering sheets of signatures and begin tearing them in two, and Helga rushed for the placards and started to rip them down.

The next couple of minutes, until Happy Harmon the campus cop arrived, puffing and out of breath, from the Cellar, where he had been having his customary midmorning cup of coffee and sweet roll, were rather lively. Books and binders were gleefully tossed aside, pro- and antiwar cries filled the air, lovely women screamed and strong men rushed into battle with delighted howls. There hadn't been so much fun on campus since the night the halls invaded the Row a year ago.

Fortunately—very fortunately, probably, since for a few wild moments all restraints seemed to have disappeared in a glorious burst of excitement and sheer animal spirits—nobody was injured.

Wilson and Wolfgang engaged in a brief shoving match across the overturned table but, with it flapping between their legs, were unable to get close enough to each other to do any damage.

Tim, who had never struck anyone in anger in his life no matter how violent his pen might be at times, managed to grasp Rudy firmly by the shoulders, send him sprawling off-balance much as Duke had, and rescue most of the signatures intact.

And Ari, equally peaceable physically but possessed of a considerable authority when he wanted to use it, advanced upon Helga Berger with such an ominous expression that she turned pale, uttered a frightened squeal, dropped the placard she was trying to destroy, and fled.

At that point Happy, who had thoughtfully grabbed his bullhorn from his car en route, made full use of it:

"GOD DAMN IT, STOP THIS GOD DAMNED NONSENSE OR I'LL HAVE YOU ALL IN JAIL! GOD DAMN IT, *STOP IT*!!!"

Half an hour later, together with Donna, who had apparently been summoned from class, they were cooling their heels in Dr. Chalmers' outer office. He let them glare at each other and sweat it out for a while under the stern disapproval of his secretary, who gave them one disdainful glance and returned to her typing.

At last the big oaken door swung open and he stood there surveying them with the coldest expression any of them had ever seen on his face. When it suited him, he spoke.

"I won't make the mistake of addressing you as ladies and gentlemen, except for Miss Van Dyke. Come in."

When they were seated in the overstuffed leather chairs and sofas that faced his big oaken desk, on whose gleaming surface only a yellow legal notepad and two needle-sharp pencils were visible, he told his secretary to hold all calls until further notice "and cancel my luncheon date with Dean Magg—with the dean of women."

And ignoring the nervous, hastily muffled snort of laughter at this near-gaffe which came from somewhere in the room—could it have been from the student-body president?—he closed the door, walked slowly and grandly to his desk, sat down in his antique high-backed rocker and stared at them, with absolute impassivity, one by one.

"Now," he said finally, "Officer Harmon, will you please describe what you saw and know of this disgraceful incident."

"Well, sir," Happy said, not very happily because sooner or later he got to know most of the outstanding kids on campus and, being childless himself, was fond of all of them, "I didn't see how it began but it ended with the temporary apprehension of the individuals in this room. I was peacefully having my usual midmorning coffee break in the Cellar when two students— Mr. Andrade and Mr. Loren Davis, I believe, from your house, Mr. Wilson and Mr. Bates—dashed in shouting for me. They told me that there was a riot at the post office and that my presence was urgently needed. Dropping everything—I did go back and pay my bill later at the Cellar—I rushed, with Mr. Andrade and Mr. Davis, to the scene of action." He chuckled suddenly. "There was plenty of action."

"Yes," Dr. Chalmers agreed gravely. "Don't embellish, Happy. Just tell me the story."

"Yes, sir," Happy said hastily. "My apologies, sir, but some of it was rather funny. Mr. Wilson and Mr. Hubner seemed to be doing some sort of dance with a card table. Mr. Bates, whom I have always considered quite peaceful in spite of some of his columns and editorials"—he winked at Tim, who was too tense to respond in kind—"was busy tipping Mr. Krohl over. Mr. Krohl was shouting his protests. Miss Berger was attempting to rip down a placard which had been nailed to the oak tree next to the post office, but uttered a sort of *eek!* sound when Mr. Katanian advanced upon her—"

"With what?"

"Just a look," Happy said, "but it seemed to be sufficient." He chuckled again. "It was a pretty fierce one. And all around, maybe two hundred students were milling and shouting. So I took my bullhorn and told them to stop this minute. I had to shout a few times but pretty soon everything calmed down. I told the principal participants that I thought we had all better come along and talk to you."

"Nobody defied you," the president said, in a tone that indicated that to do so would be absolutely unthinkable at the University.

"Oh, no, sir," Happy said. "We have a good bunch of kids here. They respect authority."

"But not, apparently, each other," the president observed. "So much for your part of it. Now, Mr. Wilson, you are supposed to guide and direct and generally set the standards for this student body. Suppose you tell us how you happened to recede so far from that worthy position."

"I must apologize, sir," Willie said with a humility that appeared to be genuine—he really did look shaken—"for my part in all this. In fact, I suspect I am really the most guilty of all. Probably I am the only one who should really be punished. I am prepared to accept my responsibility."

"That is most noble of you," Dr. Chalmers said with the very faintest trace of amusement in his eyes, "but for the moment I think we can put aside the question of punishment. I still don't know what this was all about. What was it?"

"Well, sir," Willie said, "it's a rather delicate matter—"

"It was an insult to my country and my leader!" Wolfgang Hubner interrupted loudly. The president was on it like a flash.

"*You* will speak when spoken to, Mr. Hubner. You are not in your country now, nor are you under the protection of your leader. You are in the United States and you are under the protection of our laws—and their obligations, which I am empowered to enforce by virtue of the authority vested in me by the board of trustees of the University. Is that clear?"

For a second it seemed that Wolfgang might give him an angry retort. But the president possessed a monumental dignity when necessary, and was giving it full scope now. Wolfgang subsided. Momentarily.

"It was something to do with Germany, then," Dr. Chalmers said.

Willie nodded.

"Yes, sir. And the Jews."

"Oh?" Dr. Chalmers said with surprise either real or feigned, no one could be sure. "Are they a problem here?"

"They are a problem everywhere!" Wolfgang snapped. This time the president looked at him directly and his expression, which had begun to soften a little, became again as cold, Willie thought in the standard campus lingo, as a witch's tit.

"Mr. Hubner," he said, "you are here as a guest of this university. You will either be courteous enough to be silent until I ask you to speak or you will leave this room and I will arrange for you to leave this university. Do you understand that?"

Again it seemed for a second that Wolfgang might defy him. But, characteristically when confronted by real opposition, he backed down.

"All right," he said sullenly. "All right. But you will ask me to speak later!"

"Certainly," Dr. Chalmers agreed, "when I am ready for you. So, Mr. Wilson, proceed, please. How did the Jews get into this? And Germany, for that matter? And how did it all wind up in front of the post office?"

"I am afraid that was my fault, as I said, sir," Willie replied. He considered quickly, and rejected, the idea of giving the Krohl-Offenberg background. That would only complicate matters. "Mr. Bates had decided to write the editorial on the Nazis and the Jews that you may have read this morning"—the president nodded—"and he, Mr. Katanian and I—at my instigation—decided that it would be a constructive thing if members of the student body as a whole were enabled to take some direct action that would indicate to—to anyone who might be interested that we here at the University do not approve of what Herr Hitler is doing in Europe, and specifically, what he is doing to the Jews."

"Did you consult the administration about the wisdom of doing this?" the president inquired, fixing him suddenly with the piercing look that could, Franky said, make strong men faint and weak ones drink cyanide. Willie met it straight on.

"No, sir," he said quietly. "I did not."

"And did you consult any of your fellow students—Miss Van Dyke, for instance—Excom—anybody—about the wisdom of doing so?"

"No, sir."

"Ah," the president said gently. "Executive privilege."

"Well, sir," Wilson said, trying not to protest too much but anxious to make his point, "it just seemed to us that we should do *something*, that's all. And the petition idea seemed like a good one. And we were doing well with it, as a matter of fact, peacefully and constructively, we thought—"

"But without any permission."

"No, sir. No permission but the permission of conscience, sir."

"*Aha,*" the president said with the second slight trace of amusement they had been able to discern. "You always have been a phrasemaker, Willie. So *you* thought you were proceeding in order on all fronts, right?"

"Yes, sir," Wilson said, encouraged. "Not exactly in *order,* maybe, but at least in an orderly way. Lots of people were signing up, and then suddenly along came Rudy and Helga and Hubner, encouraging them to disrupt things—"

"I *didn't*—" Wolfgang began but stopped at the president's casual, almost absentminded glance in his direction.

"We *wanted* to break it up," Rudy said defiantly and Helga agreed loudly, "*Yes!*"

"In due course, if you please, Miss Burger and Mr. Krohl. Mr. Wilson, continue."

"That's about it, sir. We were signing 'em up and Rudy and Helga and Hubner were trying to knock 'em down. And they did succeed in disrupting and probably stopping for good, I don't know, that's up to you, what we conceived of as a peaceful but necessary protest against the *brutality*—" his voice took on a certain relish as he hammered out the words—"and the *ruthlessness*—and the *vicious violence*—of the present German government. And"—he could not resist a sudden swing around to give Wolfgang a nasty look—"its great leader."

"Mr. Hubner," the president said, "do you want to comment on that?"

"Yes, I do!" Wolfgang said, returning the look with interest. "I come here as a friend. I come here as an ambassador, maybe you might say, between our two countries. I come here to discuss very grave world problems with friends I may make in America, because I think it is necessary to talk. Or we may fight. I do not want that to happen. I am not like Wilson, who doesn't care if he insults my government. Or Bates, who slanders Germany in his paper every time I turn around. Or others here who may use any pretext to try to stop the great work my leader—*my leader*—is doing.

"Germany has a right to her place in the sun, I say that every time I talk to anyone here, and most of your history and political science teachers in America agree with me. Most of them say, 'Yes, Germany was greatly wronged in the Versailles Treaty. Germany was robbed in the Versailles Treaty. Germany was almost destroyed by the Allies after the World War. Germany has a right to live and be strong. Germany has a right to regain her colonies, as much right to have colonies as the British Empire, as the French Empire. Germany has a right to live again!'

"That is what the professors say, almost all. It is what they are teaching right this minute, right here on the Quad. That is why I already hear this morning that lots of students do not agree with Bates and his editorial. That is why Wilson gets not so many signatures—he will say there were a lot, but not so very many in a student body of forty-five hundred—on his silly petition. That is why not so many pay attention to his silly posters. Because your professors tell the truth, that is why! Because thanks to them your students know the truth!

"Germany has a right to live! You cannot deny it to us! And Germany has a right to do as she pleases with difficult citizens of an alien race who refuse to cooperate with Der Fuehrer's plans for Great Germany. That is why the Jews must be put in their place! That is why there are laws to make them behave! That is why they will soon live separate from the rest of us, so that we can proceed *as we must* to make Germany pure and strong again!

"Let them write their editorials!" he concluded into the rapt silence that his fluent (and, Tim thought, very well rehearsed) vehemence had created. "Let them try their silly petitions! It will not matter to us! We cannot be stopped! We will win!"

And with a sudden grim, satisfied shake of his head he sat back in his chair. Rudy and Helga, looking slightly dazed, regarded him with approving, almost adoring, looks.

"Is that all, Mr. Hubner?" Dr. Chalmers inquired with a calmness so absolute it was far more deflating than any opposing rhetoric would have been.

"Yes! For now!"

"For as long as you stay here, I think," Dr. Chalmers said. Wolfgang looked startled, half-alarmed and puzzled. The president ignored him and turned to his other concerns.

"Mr. Wilson, I am not saying that you can't work on your petition. Nor, Mr. Bates, that you can't write editorials that are about as free and uncontrolled, I think you will agree, as any you will find in any American college newspaper. But I do say that there are rules that have to be followed here, that you must obey them or risk serious disciplinary action which could result in consequences very unhappy for your campus careers.

"As for you, Mr. Krohl, and you, Miss Burger, I want you to refrain from any further attempts to interfere with the free expression of opinion on this campus. If you wish to try to circulate a petition saying Jews are a bad thing and should be isolated from society in Germany, or even here, that is your privilege. I doubt that you will get very far with it here, or on any American campus, but go ahead and try it, if you like. I suspect that may be the only way to convince you. Just don't try again to interfere with the expression of contrary opinion or you too may find yourselves the object of severe disciplinary action. Very severe . . .

"As for you, Mr. Hubner, as long as you are a guest on this campus, you are to refrain from any further public statements attacking the Jews, defending the Nazi regime, or in any way attempting to influence students here to your way of thinking. The role of an exchange student, as I see it, is to learn about the country where he is temporarily resident. It is not to be a propaganda agent for his own country, particularly when his convictions are such that they lead him to participate in, and encourage others to participate in, violence. We don't want that here. If you violate these conditions—" he paused before continuing with quiet emphasis—"under which I am permitting you to remain—you will either be on your way to some other campus the day after, or on your way home to Germany, whichever you prefer.

"Now you may go. Miss Van Dyke, Mr. Wilson, Mr. Bates, Mr. Katanian, please remain."

Those he had dismissed filed out. Wolfgang looked defiant and ostentatiously scornful. Rudy looked defiant and sullen. Helga looked upset but determined. Happy Harmon followed with the quizzically personal shake of the head to the president to which his thirty years as campus cop entitled him.

As soon as the door closed behind them Dr. Chalmers completely surprised the others by picking up the telephone to his secretary and ordering "five hamburgers with everything, and—" he glanced from face to startled face and took their orders as given—"two coffees, two iced teas and a Coca-Cola."

Then he put down the receiver and turned, with an expression as quizzical as Happy's, to Willie, Tim and Ari.

"Well, children," he said, "what am I going to do with you? What would you suggest, Donna?"

She giggled.

"I don't know, sir. Make them run around the Quad barefoot seventeen times? A public whipping at high noon in front of Memorial Church? Or maybe revive stocks and make them sit in front of the post office every day for a year?"

Dr. Chalmers smiled.

"I think you're with them in spirit even if you weren't in the flesh. Obviously some disciplinary thing has to be done—or be perceived to have been done. I've already heard from one trustee—his daughter's here and she apparently called him immediately. He doesn't approve. No doubt I'll be hearing from others. And not all of them will approve, either. In fact, I suspect a majority will want something rather severe to happen. . . . The problem for me, you see, is that, essentially, I agree with you. I think I made clear in my little talk at Reg Dance where I stand in the matter. But we have to keep a balance here. A lot of people in this country aren't convinced yet that there's any great threat from Mr. Hitler. I'd like to think there's still a chance he can be contained. But I am not," he admitted with an unhappy expression, "very sanguine about it.

"However, whatever I may think or you may think or many others on campus and through the country may think, it is still pretty apparent that a majority does not agree with us. Therefore, I can't preside over a campus that's suddenly going all-out for intervention. The country is still isolationist—always has been—at heart probably always will be. Until that changes, I have to keep a balance in my small part of the world. At the same time, I have to try to remain loyal to the motto we have here, taken from the very nation that now appears to be threatening everything we believe in—the motto I first admired as an undergraduate here myself, and still admire: *Die Luft der Freiheit weht*—'The winds of freedom blow.'

"They will continue to do," he said firmly, "as long as I am president or until such time as we are actually at war and views such as those of Herr Hubner, Mr. Krohl and Miss Berger come under the heading of aid to the enemy."

"Do you think we will be, sir?" Ari inquired soberly. "At war?"

The president sighed.

"I think it gets likelier all the time. I hope and pray we can stay out of it, but I don't rule it out. Events have a way of overtaking nations as they do individuals. It happened before, and I went. It may happen again, and you may have to go. I survived. Pray God you may too. In the meantime, we are confronted with a campus and a country that may soon become deeply divided. The argument may result in bitter clashes and violent expressions. My point is that, if at all possible, it must not come to that kind of irrationality.

"Violent or even excessively unfair advocacy from any side of any issue can only result in the diminution"—his voice actually became a little husky, and they were moved—"of this beloved place. This is not a place for violence, it is a place for free minds—arguing vehemently, perhaps, that's been the case as long as I can remember, but not with violence or in fear of violence. Reasonable, decent, constructive debate, lively, honest, frank debate—but not violent and unfair debate, destructive of all rational decision.

"So," he said as there was a knock on the door, his secretary delivered the food and they distributed it quietly among themselves, "that's where we stand. I think, Tim, that you should try to be not quite as positive and declamatory—exclamatory, too—in your editorials and columns and the way you play the news in the *Daily*. I'm not censoring you and I shall certainly argue most vehemently against any attempt by the trustees to censor you. But you have to help me by showing a little restraint. All right?"

"But I have to express my honest convictions!" Tim protested. "Why shouldn't I warn people? Why shouldn't I try to educate them? It's my job as a journalist!" He looked very earnest. "I feel it's what the Lord put me here for."

"But with calmness and restraint, Tim," the president repeated. "With calmness and restraint. All right?"

Tim was silent for a long moment. Finally he spoke, quietly and obviously moved.

"Yes, sir . . . I'll try."

"That's all one can ask," Dr. Chalmers said. "And you, Willie—and Donna—and Ari. Don't try to get too far out in front of the parade, all right? Petitions may be offered, challenges may be made—but I'd feel very much obliged if you wouldn't give them too much official sanction by being the ones who spearhead them. You can support and endorse and go along with— but try to help me keep a balance. Is that unreasonable?"

They looked at one another and Willie spoke.

"No, sir, that's not unreasonable. But on the other hand—" he paused— "on the other hand, what is leadership for? What does it consist of? What is expected of us, if it is not to lead the parade and get out ahead and take stands that should be taken?"

"I lead," the president noted, "but I'm not on a soap box every day or waving placards every day. Still, you don't doubt that I'm in control here, do you?"

"No, sir," Wilson said, meeting his eyes squarely. "But subject to the board, right?"

"Surely," Dr. Chalmers agreed with a smile. "That's *my* balance. As I am trying to be yours." The smile broadened. "Since you've just made the analogy.

"Now I think what we'd best do is just say nothing publicly about this matter. That means that you, Tim, will refrain from an editorial and will also see that there's a very brief and very straightforward account in tomorrow's paper. No indication that I have given you all a lecture on responsibility. No reference to any conditions I have imposed on Herr Hubner." He smiled. "I may be exercising a little censorship right there, but for the moment I think it would be best. Do you agree or don't you?" Tim hesitated and the president went comfortably and unchallengeably on. "I'll give you a statement to print—very short—something to the effect that 'The president's office announced that Dr. Chalmers had discussed the incident with all of the interested parties and all are agreed that a repetition of violence is unbecoming to members of the University family and will not be encouraged or tolerated.' " He smiled again. "Wishy-washy, no doubt you'll say, but that's one of the things you learn while growing up: sometimes wishy-washy is best. And the student body will read between the lines and think I really gave you hell." The smile deepened as he noted their obvious surprise at this uncharacteristic use of what was, for him, really quite strong language. And added another surprising colloquialism: "O.K.?"

"We'll do our best, sir," Wilson said, and they all nodded vigorously. For the moment, the president knew with a wryness he refrained from expressing, they absolutely genuinely meant it.

"Fine," he said comfortably as they prepared to finish their lunch in companionable silence. "Then we'll all survive in good shape."

Afterward they walked away from his office along the busy colonnade under the sandstone arches in thoughtful silence until Ari said softly,

"Well. Now I understand why he's president of the University. I don't think I ever really appreciated it before."

"He's quite a guy," Willie agreed. "I guess you got *your* marching orders, Timmy."

"I think you all have too!" Tim rejoined with some vigor. "We're none of us supposed to do anything, I gather."

"He didn't say that," Donna objected. "He said we could support and endorse and do anything we wanted to as long as we don't initiate it and don't let it get into violence. At least that's how I understood him. He just doesn't want us 'leading the parade.' "

Ari smiled.

"But Willie *wants* to lead the parade. Otherwise it won't get led properly, right, Willie?"

Wilson had the grace to grin.

"Something like that."

"Anyway," Tim pointed out, "you only told him we'd do our best. It was a pretty qualified promise."

"Now, don't be tricky, you guys," Donna said, half joking but half in earnest too. "You know how he took that."

"With a grain of salt, probably," Ari suggested. "But I suspect it would be a good idea to lie low for a bit. I'm off to the gym. See you around."

"Excom Thursday afternoon," Willie reminded.

"I'll be there," Ari said, gave them a cheerful wave and left.

"I'm off to the *Daily*," Tim said. He smiled rather dryly. "To refrain from writing an editorial. And to make sure that our account of what happened is as dull as possible."

"Don't forget Dr. Chalmers' statement," Donna suggested.

"It'll be on my desk when I get there," Tim predicted. And so it was.

For a moment, as Willie and Donna watched his earnest figure depart, a sudden surprising awkwardness seemed to come between them. Wilson felt guilty because he hadn't even taken her for coffee in the Cellar for almost a week, though they had met and chatted amicably a couple of times in the student government offices in the Union.

"What have you been up to?" he asked, rather inanely, he thought; but her response, as usual, was bright and cheerful.

"Oh, nothing much. We had a rushing tea the other day—some good prospects. And I've been doing a lot of studying getting ready for finals. And making plans for Thanksgiving."

"Going home?" he asked, and realized instantly that was the wrong thing to ask, because she turned toward him eagerly.

"No, I'm not. New York state's much too far away for even a long weekend. Are you?"

"No," he said cautiously. "My folks are going to be away visiting my dad's brother in Denver, whom they haven't seen in three years, so Guy and Buff and Hank and Billy and I have rented a big house down in Carmel."

"Are the girls going with you?"

"I suppose so," he said in an offhand way, though he knew perfectly well they were.

"My!" she said, determinedly cheerful as always. "What a houseful! That should be fun!"

"Are you going to be with someone from your house?"

"Nobody's asked me," she replied with a bright smile that said: Isn't that a silly situation to be in? But I am. She looked suddenly sad. "People think I'm so *self-sufficient*."

"Me, too," he said. "And I'm not at all, really."

For a moment they were united in a glance of mutual commiseration.

Then he thought: Oh, what the hell. It's habit—it's expected of me, and not only by Donna—I'd be an ungenerous son of a bitch if I didn't—

"Look, why don't you come with us. I mean, it would be fun to have you. There's lots of room, it's a big place. I know everyone would be delighted—"

"Would you be?" she asked, and fortunately some friends went by just then and in the midst of greetings his stout "I certainly *would!*" apparently didn't sound as defensive as he had feared. She sounded genuinely pleased and excited.

"I will, then! It will be *such fun!* Thank you!"

"Good, it's a date. Let's cut our eleven-o'clocks on Wednesday, grab a bite at the Cellar and take off. O.K.?"

"Fine with me," she said with a happy laugh. "You're so masterful, Mr. Wilson. Are you going to class now?"

"It *is* almost one, isn't it?" he said, surprised. "Yes, Modern German History, ironically enough. Hubner's in the class, trying to be a sort of resident reproach, I think. No doubt he'll already have told the prof all about it. We may be the subject of today's lecture."

She looked thoughtful.

"I'm really sorry you didn't let me know in advance. I would have loved to be a part of it."

"Probably just as well you weren't. Somebody has to maintain the dignity of our administration."

"But it meant something," she said with a surprising wistfulness. "Sometimes it's nice to *mean* something."

He gave her a reassuring look.

"There'll be other chances, no doubt. Take care. I'll see you soon."

"Before Thanksgiving, I hope," she said, for once sounding not like a completely assured, cheerful Donna but a rather uncertain, tentative Donna.

"Of course," he said firmly. "Of course."

After class, during which Wolfgang shot him several triumphant glances which he finally squelched with a savage glare, he walked slowly back to the house in the pale sunshine and moderate warmth that had succeeded the morning's chill. When he got there life and his relations with Donna changed abruptly and, he felt at last, probably permanently.

A message was pinned to his door in Latt's familiar tiny, neat script: "Call Marian as soon as possible."

He had talked to her on the phone a couple of times since their first unsatisfactory luncheon at the Cellar, she had agreed to meet him there one other time for a visit equally uneasy and awkward. After that, aside from an occasional exchange of fleeting and formal hellos in the class they had together, there had been no further contact. He had hesitated and she apparently wasn't interested.

With a sudden quickening of heart which he told himself was silly, but there it was, he called the women's residence switchboard in the Union and after a moment was put through to her room.

"Oh, yes," she said, sounding flustered. "I wanted to apologize. I am so sorry."

"For what?" he asked blankly.

"My father."

"What about your father?" he inquired, mystified. "Do I know him?"

"You must. He's a trustee."

"No, I don't. I really haven't paid much attention to the trustees."

Which was true: one didn't unless there was some emergency of some kind. They met in mysterious places, usually in San Francisco, at mysterious and unannounced times, and their impact on the student body was remote under ordinary circumstances. One knew the name of the chairman, vaguely, and perhaps two or three other members who were former athletic greats, but in general the board lived in a world of its own, Dr. Chalmers its only direct and visible conduit to the students.

"Walter Emerson," she said. "He graduated in 1920, after the war. He was elected four years ago. He's a contractor in Piedmont in the East Bay. I thought maybe you'd run into him."

"I knew there was an Emerson on there, but I didn't make the connection. I'll have to try to meet him."

"It may be possible," she said with a wry and rather forlorn little laugh. "He's quite upset about what happened at the post office this morning."

"Oh!" he said, light dawning. "Dr. Chalmers told us that the daughter of one of the trustees—you must be the one."

"I'm afraid I am," she said, sounding more forlorn.

"But why? I don't get it."

"I didn't *intend* to tell him, but I did want to call him about something else this morning, and then I went by the post office just as that German exchange student and those two other students started making a fuss—"

"That was not," he said wryly, "my finest hour."

She laughed, much more naturally.

"I thought you were *splendid*. Anyway, then I went and called my father and naturally I told him what I'd just seen. I was excited about it, because I agree with what you were trying to do. But I'm afraid he doesn't. He got quite upset, in fact, and said he was going to call the other board members. I expect he has, by now. He can be very determined. So in case there's any trouble, I wanted to apologize. It's all my fault."

"Oh, no, it isn't," he said firmly. "It would have gotten out sooner or later anyway."

"Yes, but he said he was going to call the City newspapers and give them a statement."

"Oh," he said, less confidently. "He *is* an active one, isn't he?"

"Yes," she said, sounding forlorn again. "I'm afraid so."

"Well, we'll just have to meet it when it comes. Dr. Chalmers is on our side—"

"But he has to listen to the board. At least, that's what my father thinks." His tone became a little tart.

"Dr. Chalmers told us we should do it more quietly but he didn't put any ban on it. I would hope the board would be equally mature."

"Daddy *is* mature," she said, not sounding as offended as in retrospect he thought she might well have been. "He just has his ideas, is all."

"So do we," he said, more respectfully. "I sure hope there won't be any conflict with the board. Surely they don't approve of hounding the Jews, do they? Or of German expansionism? Or of Germany starting another war?"

"Oh, *no*," she said in some alarm. "Daddy's not anti-Jewish at all. And he was in the war, so he's really quite anti-German. It's more that he doesn't want *us* to get involved again. He thinks we have everything we want right here and shouldn't let ourselves be dragged into another European war."

"What they're beginning to call 'isolationist,'" he said. "I can see that, too. But I think people have to take a stand against what they think is evil."

"I agree," she said. "I told you I do. Anyway, I just wanted you to know that I do apologize for getting my father upset. Maybe he wouldn't have heard about it if I hadn't told him. I just hope it doesn't mean any trouble for you."

"If the father is upset," he said—thinking suddenly: Come on, Wilson, what the hell!—"then maybe the daughter should make amends by going out to dinner with me some night soon. Like Friday, maybe. How about it?"

"Oh," she said, and there was a silence. He was just on the verge of thinking, Oh, the hell with it, when she spoke in a tone he couldn't analyze. But there was no need to, since it was affirmative. "All right," she said slowly. "If you want to."

"I asked," he pointed out, and she gave a sudden little laugh.

"And usually, I suppose, *they* ask *you*. Is that right?"

"I didn't say that—" he began indignantly and then relaxed. He was halfway home, no point in making issues. "But of course," he amended with a chuckle. "It's one of the privileges of office."

"I thought so," she said, sounding relaxed also, which he hoped she would be from now on. "I guess I'll just have to remember to follow the pattern."

"I won't tell anybody if you don't," he said lightly. "Why don't I pick you up at six and we'll go up to the City? I think Ted Weems and his orchestra are at the St. Francis. We can also go on up to the Mark Hopkins later, if you like."

"We'll see," she said, suddenly sounding formal. He thought: Now what?

But his tone was completely self-assured as he said, "Fine! That'll be great! I'll see you at six Friday, then. And thanks for tipping me off about your dad. I'm sure if he carries it further we can work it out all right. And I certainly don't blame you for it. It was just one of those things. And here *we* are, going to the City. So I guess *everything's* going to work out all right, hmm?"

"We'll see," she said again in a noncommittal voice—but not an unfriendly one, he told himself, half pleased, half apprehensive, which he thought might be how he was supposed to feel.

He decided as they hung up that she would take some study, that girl. But at least he had his foot in the door at last; and suddenly he knew that he was committed—to what, he did not know exactly at this moment. But that he was, he had no doubt.

Seconds later, having played the grand seigneur, he looked in his wallet and discovered that there was, as McAllister had remarked the other day about his own, a great wasteland inside. There was only one thing to do about that. He walked along the hall and knocked on the door of the house banker.

"Yes?" Latt inquired. "Come in, come in, whoever you are . . . oh, hi, Willie. I was wondering what had happened to you after the big excitement. You guys disappeared rather suddenly with Happy." He smiled. "I thought maybe he'd thrown you all in the clink downtown."

"No," Willie said, sinking into a chair in his usual break-back recline. "He just took us down to see Chalmers, who was amazingly mellow. He even ordered hamburgers from the Union and gave us lunch, believe it or not. Thank you for the note about Marian. I did call her. It seems her father is a trustee, which I didn't know, and she told him about what happened, having just come by the post office and being full of it although she'd originally planned to call about something else. And he's very upset and she thinks he's probably called the other trustees and the City papers, which means that hamburgers with the president may not be the last we'll hear of it. She was very apologetic."

Latt smiled.

"At least you've made contact again."

Wilson looked satisfied.

"I did indeed. Not only made contact but invited her to go to the City Friday night for dinner and dancing."

Latt looked genuinely interested.

"And she accepted?"

"You bet," Willie said, satisfaction growing. "Like a shot. I've never known a girl to be so enthusiastic—"

"Wilson."

"Well, at least she *did* accept," Willie said with a grin. "There may not have been any loud screams of joy you could hear all over the Quad, but at least she *did* accept. And that, old friend, leads directly to you."

"Are Kay and I being invited to go with you?"

"Indeed," Wilson replied crisply. "After you loan me thirty bucks."

Latt sighed in mock despair.

"Why is it that nobody loves me just for myself? Why does money always get involved?"

"Because while you don't have as much as some people, like Buff and Smitty for instance, you're even more generous than they are about lending it. You never make anybody feel even the slightest bit bad about borrowing from you. It's a *pleasure*."

"Do I ever know it!" Latt said with a groan, but humorously. "Do I ever know! So you want thirty bucks. What do I get in return?"

"Depends on how soon you want it back," Wilson said with a grin. "And what the interest is."

"The usual. *Nada.* And I would like it back by next weekend if you can possibly manage it. With Big Game weekend coming up, I'll have a few obligations of my own. I can't bankroll *everybody*."

"If past history is any guide, this house is going to be such a turmoil of high finance on Big Game weekend that Ray Baker is going to have to add keeping everybody's personal books to keeping the house books. Wall Street won't be in it. So: can I have the thirty? It's my turn to write the folks this week and I'll explain everything. My dad will make an honest man of me."

"He will? That's not the story you usually give me about your father."

"He will this time," Willie assured him, "when I explain about this perfectly wonderful girl I've been trying to make time with for most of the quarter, and how she's finally tumbled, and all. He won't be able to resist. He was young once himself."

"Always an uncertain assumption with fathers," Latt remarked with a smile. "Well, I hope so, Brother Wilson. I'd hate to have to wash dishes somewhere to get Kay and me dinner Big Game Night."

"Oh, pish, tush!" Wilson said grandly. "Somehow it'll all get scraped together. One for all and all for one." He grinned. "It's just that right now, it's one for all. O.K.?"

"You're incorrigible," Latt said, going to his closet and reaching into some recess known only to himself. "All right," he said with a severity not entirely joking as he handed it over. "Don't spend one cent until Friday and return it to me the moment you hear from home. All right?"

"You're being so *rigid*. This isn't like you."

"Also, I want a full account of everything that happened. If I'm going to invest in this, I want to know what the money went for."

Willie looked abruptly not so cheerful: a little apprehensive, Latt thought.

"Probably not much," he said gloomily. "You know how she is."

"No, I don't, really. Kay seems to like her."

"Oh, I'm sure she's very pleasant on a girl-to-girl level. She's certainly played hard to get with me."

"I wasn't aware that you were besieging her very hard," Latt observed. "It hasn't really been much of a campaign, has it?"

Wilson looked thoughtful.

"To tell you the truth, Latt," he said slowly—"and you and Unruh are probably the only two I would tell the truth to—I'm a little afraid of her, actually. She's got me a little baffled."

"By design? Or just because you let yourself feel that way?"

Wilson frowned.

"I don't think by design, really—I don't *think* she's that calculating. I don't know her that well yet, of course, but from my impressions so far, she isn't. Maybe it *is* just me. It makes me feel like I'm in the sixth grade or something. Funny feeling. I don't know that I've ever had a feeling quite like it, in fact."

"And Donn?" Latt inquired, giving him a shrewd look.

"Oh, Donn," Willie said. He sighed. "I went overboard this afternoon and invited her to come down to Carmel with us. And as it turned out, that was just before I found your note about Marian. Now I'm really confused. I'll have to pretend I'm having a big old time with Donn and the guys and all the time I'll be thinking maybe I could have worked out something with Marian."

"Wow!" Latt exclaimed. "I think you've got it, Willie. I've never heard you talk like this about anyone before. Aren't you going awfully fast, all of a sudden? Are you sure about this?"

"Hell, no. I'm not sure about it at all. It may all collapse Friday night. But I hope—" His voice and expression changed. "I hope it won't."

"If that's how you feel," Latt said loyally, "I hope it won't, either. And if you really do feel that way, then I don't think it's going to."

He was glad, Marc Taylor thought gloomily in the pin-neat room he shared with Rodge Leighton, that somebody was happy on this chilly afternoon. Actually, he supposed, quite a few were. Out on the lawn he could hear exuberant yells and barks as Richardson, McAllister, Gulbransen, Lor Davis, Andrade, Smitty Carriger and Napoleon raced about in an impromptu touch-football game. At the piano downstairs Haggerty was rambling again, a phrase here, a few chords there, bits and scraps of special favorites as the mood struck: "Stormy Weather" . . . "Smoke Gets in Your Eyes" . . . "Summertime" . . . "Night and Day" . . . "Sweet Leilani" . . . "Sophisticated Lady" . . . "Begin the Beguine" . . . "Autumn in New York" . . .

Marc had walked back from an afternoon business administration course with Billy Wilson and Franky Miller, both in good spirits, Billy happy because he had just been selected for Puck in the upcoming winter quarter production of *A Midsummer Night's Dream,* Franky happy because he had been able to make last-minute arrangements for Katie and himself and Latt and Kay to spend Big Game weekend at the Lodge at Pebble Beach.

Lots of people, Marc reflected, seemed to be happy.

Except himself.

And somehow that never quite seemed to come off.

As always, lately, he just couldn't think why. He knew he wasn't the handsomest guy in school, or the greatest brain, or the most active, but surely he had *something* to offer people. His folks told him so: the nervous, worried letters from his mother, the occasional gruff telephoned admonition from his father to buck up, boy, get in there and *pitch*—he knew they meant well, he knew they were worried about him, he knew he was failing them.

Just as he was failing himself.

And everybody else.

He heard Gulbransen give an extra loud and joyous shout and thought: There's an example. For quite a while there, Gil had sort of taken him under his wing, starting with Reg Dance and running on until only about a week or so ago, when he had suddenly seemed to have given up. It was nothing definite, no crude rejection, no big scene, no specific termination: just a loss of interest that Marc could sense even though Gil had not said a word or been any less pleasant. He just *didn't care* anymore whether Marc succeeded or failed in the campus world. Marc could tell and it hurt him more than he could possibly have said. Certainly he could never have said it to Gil himself. The only response, he knew, would have been a polite, "Are you crazy, kid? What's the matter with you? Sure I give a damn. Just get in there and *pitch*, that's all." Which would have been so like his father that Marc literally, he told himself, could not have stood it.

He wondered how many others there were like him on campus—some, he was sure, found the world a monstrous and unending challenge which, in adolescence, seemed impossible to master. There was a dark underside to student life everywhere which surfaced now and then, he supposed, on all campuses. Within the past two weeks there had been two suicides. SOPH SHOOTS SELF NEAR PARENTS' HOME—a kid from Burlingame, who, as near as family, friends and teachers could tell, was doing pretty well but in his own mind evidently wasn't. And JUNIOR FOUND DEAD IN CAR NEAR BEACH— "a loner . . . modest grades . . . studied terribly hard . . . not many friends . . . seemed depressed . . ."

Those descriptions fitted him too, Marc thought; and yet not for any reason he could analyze, try as he might. His grades were only adequate but not disastrous. He had the love of his parents, however awkwardly expressed. He had the support of the house just by virtue of being a member, even if he had no really close friends there—they tried to keep him from being a loner and he tried, halfheartedly, himself. But he was depressed, there was no doubt about that. The world was gray, inimical, beginning to be somehow off-balance, out of focus, as though seen dimly through a haze that deranged and distorted. And the focus, though Gulbransen had done his best, and several of his classmates such as Randy and Rodge had gone out of their way to do their best, was becoming increasingly strange and increasingly far from reality.

He was beginning to walk through his days, he felt, as through a fog more profound than any that drifted in over the Coast Range. The imminence of winter wasn't helping, but it was deeper than that, and more confusing. Something was seriously and alarmingly wrong. He flailed about in his mind, not knowing how to fight it, not knowing where to turn to get help—not yet ready, in fact, to admit to himself that he needed help or to throw himself on the mercy of those around him and ask for it.

Events like those in the headlines were no encouragement either. *Others have had the courage to do it: why not I?* It was a dreadful and seductive thought which kept recurring with a growing insistence: a small drum throbbing away in the back of his head somewhere that he couldn't silence. *Go away!* he kept silently crying to it: *Oh, go away and leave me alone!* But it wouldn't go away and it wouldn't leave him alone. And just a few moments ago, scaring him terribly, it had begun to transform itself into a tiny, insistent, awful voice saying: *Well, now, suppose you did? Not saying you will, now, but if you did—what do you think would be the best way to go about it?*

He had actually cried out in protest when that voice hit him:
"Oh, *no!*"

But having thought it once he could not keep himself from thinking it again. It was with him now forever, maybe. Or until he did—what?

And all *for no real reason he could understand.*

It just didn't make sense.

Which was why it was so terrible, because there seemed to be no way he could take hold of it and fight it.

It just *was,* that's all—in him, and all around him.

The contrast with the predinner conviviality that was beginning to fill the house was suddenly too much.

Quietly and with no volition of his own he began to cry, silently and uncontrollably, no sound, just desperate, inexorable tears flowing down his cheeks. Thank goodness, he thought, Rodge was off at football practice in the autumn dusk encouraging Moose. But he would soon be here and Marc would have to have himself in order by then.

He gulped and one sob did escape him, so deep and profound that Buff, passing in the hall, stopped abruptly, listened, shook his head and frowned. But he didn't knock or try to come in: he didn't want to presume on anyone's privacy even though that might have been the only thing to do right then that would have been really helpful. But Buff wasn't like that, nor, indeed, were very many. Latt might have, out of instinctive sympathy and compassion. Suratt might have, out of curiosity and a chance to mock, and even that might have been helpful just then to break the mood. But nobody did.

And presently, somewhere through the fog, came the realization that the happy skirmishes on the lawn had ended and that the hour of dinner must be drawing near. Gil did go past the door, gave it a quick rap and called out, "Hey, Marc! How's my guy?" And even though he showed no sign of pausing before going on to his room, that did help a little: maybe he still cared a bit, after all. But it didn't help much, and the tears continued to flow awhile longer, desperately though Marc tried to stop them.

It was thus that Rodge found him a few moments later when he came cheerfully in after trudging back from the stadium with Moose, both of them pleased because Moose had really done well that day and Coach had clapped him on the back and predicted, "Moose is going to give us another great touchdown in Big Game or I'll eat my hat!"

So they were both feeling pretty good, and came happily into the house to find the living room already beginning to fill up, the radio blaring out Benny Goodman, a lively game going in the pool room, a fire roaring, a nice end-of-the-day feeling, everything cozy and warm in contrast to the outside chill that was deepening toward frost as night came on.

Rodge was innocent of worries and totally unsuspecting when he flung open the door. His instinctive reaction when he saw his roommate huddled by the window was to step inside and slam the door hastily shut again.

"Hey!" he said in a hushed voice. "What's the matter with you, Marc? Are you all right? Is there anything I can do to help?"

"I'm sorry," Marc said miserably. "I'm *sorry*. I was h-hoping this would be all over when you got home. I'm *sorry*."

"Well, that's all right, guy," Rodge said, voice still hushed as he turned to the door, engaged the bolt and then seated himself earnestly on the floor at Marc's feet. "Seriously, pal, what's it all about? I mean, I do want to help if there's anything I can do. Is it a girl?"

"*Girl,*" Marc said in a sarcastic voice through the tears that were finally beginning to subside. "That's all anybody ever thinks about, is it a *girl*. No, it isn't a *girl*—or maybe it is—or *I don't know*. I just *don't know*. I just feel miserable, is all."

"Yeah," Rodge agreed with a tentative smile, trying to lighten things a little. "I can see that, all right. That's pretty obvious, I'd say. Is it grades, then? I mean, mine aren't so hot, either—"

"No, it isn't grades," Marc said in the same miserable tone. "It's just—just—*everything*." And in spite of his best efforts the tears resumed.

"Well, gosh," Rodge said, upset now himself and not knowing, really, how to handle the situation. "I mean, it can't be *that* bad—"

"It is. It's *awful*."

"Well, then, I think you ought to talk to somebody about it. A doctor, maybe, or—or something."

"I don't want to talk to a doctor! He'd just say it was school-kid nerves and he'd tell my folks and then they'd get upset—they're already upset, they suspect something anyway—and everybody else in the house would know about it, and—and—"

"Oh no they wouldn't!" Rodge said stoutly. "*I* won't tell anybody. Who else would know?"

"You'd probably tell Moose."

"Not if you don't want me to. Anyway, Moose wouldn't be such bad support to have, you know. He's a sympathetic guy. But I won't tell him, I promise on my word of honor."

"Oh, you can tell anybody you want to," Marc said with a sudden despairing tiredness in his voice. "It doesn't really matter."

"Of course it matters," Rodge said firmly, "if it's got you in this state of mind. You sure you don't want to tell me about it? I'm your roomie. I really won't tell anybody."

"Why should *you* have to be burdened with it?" Marc asked, turning to look at him squarely for the first time through tear-red eyes. "It isn't your problem."

"Well, damn it," Rodge said with a first show of impatience, "I am your roommate, damn it, and I am your fraternity brother, and we do have some obligation to each other, though maybe you think that's all nonsense—"

"No, I don't think it's nonsense, but why hasn't anybody been able to help me, then?"

"Have you given anybody a chance?" Rodge retorted, deciding that maybe impatience might provide a necessary jolt where gentler concern seemingly could not.

"Gulbransen's tried," Marc said, "but all he can do—" and for a moment a wry little half-laugh broke through the gloom—"is give me a series of sex lectures on how to go about it with freshmen women."

"I'll have to talk to him," Rodge said, joining the laugh in the hope he could encourage it. "I could use a few of those myself."

"And you've been kind," Marc conceded. "And Randy. And Latt. And—well, 'most everybody. But—" his expression changed, desolation returned—"I don't know what it is. It's just *there*. It's just—just *eating* at me, that's all. *And I just can't seem to get out from under it*." And he repeated in a tone of utter abandonment: "It's *awful*."

For a moment they stared at one another with a bleakness that Rodge suddenly felt was beginning to suck him in too. He shook his head sharply as if to break its spell and put a hand earnestly on Marc's knee.

"Well, look," he said. "I really do think you should talk to someone else about it, really frankly, because nobody really knows how you feel. I know a lot of us have been a little worried that you seemed to be feeling kind of depressed, and as you say, everybody's tried to help on that level. But I don't think anybody has had any idea that you were—" he looked strained and earnest and very young as he sought to give encouragement where he now realized it was desperately needed—"that you were fighting this kind of battle. You should talk to some of the older guys, I mean, the ones who really think about things. We all like Gil, he's great, but he is pretty much of a lightweight, essentially. I mean Willie and Latt—and Tim, maybe—and Unruh, he's going to be a doctor. And maybe Franky. And Buff. And even Moose, he's kind. They'd all want to help."

Marc gave him a scornful little glance and the tears, unbidden, began again, worrying Roger intensely.

"I don't want a damned 'C-Committee on Marc Taylor'!" Marc said with something between a sob and a hiccup. "It's b-bad enough for me to get y-you all worried and upset. Now you'll probably want to move out, and—"

"I will the hell not! We get along fine in this room! I'm not going to move out just because—because—"

Again Marc gave him a bleak and desolate look.

"Because I'm a weakling and can't take it?"

"God *damn* it!" Rodge said, a rare—and real—anger breaking through. "Will you for Christ's sake stop that? That's Step One—stop putting yourself down. You're not a weakling, you're just in a bad corner at the moment, but you'll get out of it. Do you think you're the first college student who ever felt this way?"

"No. Two of them killed themselves this week."

An actual physical sensation like a stream of ice water raced down Roger's back, so sharp and strong that he almost cried out. For a moment he was too paralyzed—and now too frightened—to move. But he had to rally, and he did.

"If you talk like that," he said carefully, "I *am* going to talk to Willie and

Latt and maybe Unruh about it, right away. Right this minute, I mean. I won't even wait till after dinner."

And using Marc's unresisting knee as a prop he pulled himself upright and stood over him with determination in every line of his wiry little body.

"Now," he said in the same careful, deliberate way, "you tell me what you want me to do, roomie. Are you going to straighten up or do you want me to go and tell everybody?"

"You'd better not leave," Marc said with a wry, forlorn, scary little laugh. "I may have a gun in the room."

"You don't have any gun in the room!" Rodge said flatly, although for a terrible instant that left him actually shivering inside he wasn't at all sure.

Harsh, familiar, jangling and imperative, the sound of the first bell for dinner filled the house.

"What's it going to be?" he demanded. "What do you want me to do?"

There was a long pause during which he held Marc's eyes with his as though afraid that if he glanced away he might lose him forever. Finally Marc laughed again, a little more naturally this time.

"Well, I sure can't go down to dinner looking like this. Will you tell Buff I'm sick and bring me back something to eat?"

"All right," Rodge said, still in the same careful way. "I'll do that. You sit tight, O.K.? I'll go get it right now and bring it right back. O.K.?"

"Yes," Marc said. "I won't go away."

"And don't do anything crazy, either," Rodge said, voice beginning to tremble a little at last from sheer nervous exhaustion and release of tension. And without looking back he went to the door, unlocked it, and hurried down to the kitchen, where he had Dewey prepare a plate.

"Hurry up, Dewey!" he ordered as the enormous black bulk moved with a floating, unhurried grace about cluttered Cockroach Heaven and the amiable black face displayed its usual unhurried smile ("Get used to 'most anythin'," he often told his friends, "workin' 'round them boys.")

"Mr. Taylor," Rodge added with an urgent emphasis, "isn't feeling very well."

"This'll fix him up," Dewey said confidently, slapping a grayish slab of liver on the plate, smothering it with onions, dumping on a ladleful of mashed potatoes, plastering the whole with greasy brown gravy and adding two slices of bread and an enormous blob of butter for good measure. "This'll fix him up in no time a-tall."

"I sure hope so," Rodge said, grabbing it and hurrying back upstairs, fending off interested inquiries along the way with a terse "Marc's a little under the weather. Nothing serious."

"You think *that* will cure him?" Franky demanded, pausing in mid-descent on the stairs. "My *God.*"

"Kill or cure," cheerfully offered McAllister, coming along behind; and could not understand the strange, almost wild look Roger gave him as he climbed past with plate tightly clutched in both hands.

"Tell Buff he isn't well, will you, please," he requested breathlessly. "I'll be down as soon as he's started to eat."

Marc's attitude, he found, was quite similar to Franky's; but at least he did eat the bread and butter and some of the mashed potatoes and gravy and a tiny bit of the liver before he looked up with a rather wan but apparently reviving equilibrium and said, "Don't hover. Go on down. I'm feeling better."

"I hope so," Rodge said, sounding not at all convinced. "I'll be back as soon as I've had dinner. I'm going to study in, tonight. Will you be here?"

"Nowhere else to go," Marc said, suddenly sounding bleak again.

"All right," Rodge said sternly, "knock it off. Stop feeling sorry for yourself. I'll be back in fifteen minutes."

"You mean well," Marc said. "You're a nice guy. I do appreciate it. I only wish things looked—" his face threatened to crumple again—"looked *brighter*, that's all."

"They will," Roger said emphatically as he went out. "They *will*."

But God, he thought, will they? And in the few brief moments he lingered after dinner before returning upstairs he managed to tell Willie, Latt and Buff that they had a problem on their hands. He didn't have time to murmur much more than "Seems terribly depressed—talking about suicide—" but that was enough to make them thoroughly alarmed. He saw Willie and Latt go over to Unruh and take him aside, and went back upstairs hoping they could manage to work something out damned fast.

He had great faith in their ability to do so, and reached the room feeling much better about things. Until he heard the smooth professional chatter— or what its originator obviously conceived smooth professional chatter to be—going on inside.

Oh, God, no, he groaned to himself. That's all we need.

"What in the hell are you doing here?" he demanded, flinging open the door.

"Hi," Galen Bryce said with his bland Cheshire-cat smile. "Marc and I are having a little chat. I overheard you telling Willie and Latt that there was a problem and thought I'd offer my professional services."

Rodge snorted, ignoring Marc's reproachful look.

" 'Professional services'! What a crock! Just a chance to butt in and get some material for a term paper, is what I'd say!"

"Now, now," Gale said, not at all ruffled. "I'm sure I can be of assistance, otherwise I wouldn't be here. Now, Marc," he said, voice dropping to a low, intimate, conversational level, "when did you first notice this depression coming on?"

"I don't know," Marc said, actually, to Roger's disgust, treating the creep

with some respect. That proved how sick he must be, Rodge told himself
with a shiver.

"Look," he said harshly, "I *have* talked to Willie and Latt about it, Gale,
and they're going to work something out. So why don't you run along?"

"I'll leave that up to Marc," Gale said smoothly. "What would *you* like me
to do, Marc?"

"Well," Marc said uncertainly, looking from one to the other and back
again, "I guess—I guess if you really think you can help, Gale—"

"I do," Gale said in his most soothing tone, the one he often practiced
when alone. "Incidentally, Rodge," he said comfortably, "perhaps you might
take your studying and go somewhere else for a little while, so that we can
talk privately? Nothing personal, you know—doctor-patient confidentiality,
and all that. Would you mind?"

"Well, of all the damned nerve!" Rodge exploded. "This is *my room*, I'll
have you know! Yes, I'd mind! And I'm not going!"

"Well," Galen said, with what appeared to be real regret, although you
never knew with the creep, Roger thought, it was probably all part of some
elaborate psychological ploy, "then I'm afraid we'll have to defer our little
talk, Marc, to a later time. Perhaps tomorrow. Because you know I *would*
like to help. You do know that, don't you, Marc?"

"Oh, yes," Marc said, in a voice that seemed, to his roommate, a little
dazed. "Yes, I appreciate it, Gale. We'll talk."

Over my dead body, Roger told himself, and was pleased to see that Galen
looked decidedly taken aback for a moment when the door opened just as he
reached for it and the tall figure and self-confident face of Guy Unruh appeared.

"Hel—*lo!*" Guy exclaimed. "What are *you* doing here?"

"I just came to talk to my friend Marc a little bit," Gale said, holding on
to his dignity with some difficulty. "It seemed to be interfering with Roger's
studying. So I'll say good night."

"Good night," Guy said in a tone mild but implacable. "What did *he*
want?" he inquired, settling in a chair. "Was he planning to psych you
out, Marc?"

"I think he was trying to help," Marc said, giving him a look half hesitant,
half resentful.

"Maybe," Unruh said calmly. "Maybe." He could not have appeared more
relaxed as he added casually, "I hear you're having a tough time of it at the
moment. Care to tell me about it?"

"Oh, why not!" Marc said. "Everybody knows now, anyway!"

He shot a glance at his roommate, who promptly stood up and started to
gather his books together.

"Stick around, Rodge," Guy ordered in the same calm tone. "You're in on
this too. You obviously do want to help."

"I felt I had an obligation," Rodge said, obediently sitting down again.

"And quite right," Guy agreed. "Now, Marc, can you put your finger on anything?"

"No," Marc said in a voice beleaguered and tired. "I can't 'put my finger on anything.' "

And although Guy continued to probe, much less self-consciously and with considerably more genuine concern than Galen had, foreshadowing the very good doctor he hoped someday to be, he did not have any real success. He only realized that there was a very genuine and very deep-seated melancholy that did not seem to have its roots in anything social, sexual, academic or familial—a profound sense of inferiority, failure and un-worth that neither gentle joshing nor impatient challenge could seem to shake. It left him deeply worried, and when it ended in a return of tears he stood up, put his hand on Marc's shoulder and said gently,

"Well, look, Marc. You just go ahead and get all of that out of your system and then we'll start to rebuild, O.K.? You have lots of support here and you're going to have more. It's going to be *all right—you're* going to be all right. The day's coming, and very soon, when you'll look back on this and wonder what all the trouble was about. And nobody—*nobody*—will think any the worse of you for having gone through it." He smiled across at Rodge. "Why, hell. We've all had our moments. You know, I may be the big basketball hero now, but I can tell you when I first got off the *Lurline* from Hawaii and arrived on this campus, I may have put up a good front, and I guess I did. But inside for a couple of months I was almost as miserable as you are. And *I* didn't know why, either. It was just *there*—I know what you mean when you say that. But I worked my way out of it and so will you. And we're *all* here to help. Right, Rodge?"

"That's for *damned* sure," Rodge said fervently.

"Now," Guy said as Marc's convulsive tears continued to shake his frail little frame, "I brought you a couple of sleeping pills. I want you to take them and turn in. Rodge, you see that he gets to bed—"

"I'm not a b-*baby*," Marc protested, and Guy laughed but didn't moderate his firm tone.

"Nobody thinks you're a *baby*, but Rodge is going to see that you take those pills and get to bed right this minute or I'll have your ass in a sling. All right?"

Marc stared up at him and did manage the smallest of smiles, though his body continued to tremble with gradually diminishing tears.

"All r-right," he said finally. "All r-*right*. And th-thank you. I know you m-mean well."

"I do," Guy said dryly. "Roger: I'm counting on you, buddy. See that he minds, O.K.?"

He winked, Rodge nodded, he left. Ten minutes later Marc had taken the pills, undressed and was in his bed on the sleeping porch, to which Rodge had escorted him, stonily ignoring Suratt, who met them in the hall and started to make some smart-ass comment but stopped at Rodge's expression. Gale also stuck his head out his door but also saw Rodge's expression and quickly pulled it in again.

Roger stood outside the sleeping-porch door until he heard Marc breathing evenly and starting gently to snore. Then, much troubled, he went along to Guy's room. There, as he expected, he found Guy, Willie, Latt and Buff in council of war.

"What are we going to do?" he demanded, not even asking if he could be included in this august group. Nobody seemed to mind.

"I'm going to call his parents," Buff said, "and tell them there's a problem and he may conceivably have to leave school for a while."

"They'll be terribly shocked," Latt demurred. "Maybe you should just tell them he's not feeling too well and we think it might be a good idea for him to go to the Men's Rest Home for a few days."

"That's my idea," Guy said. "I'm going to call Dr. James at the Student Health Service first thing in the morning and give him my impressions and ask if we can't get Marc over there right away."

"That'll mean he'll have to go through another conference with James and get all upset again," Rodge objected. "Can't we just—get him in there, somehow?"

"I'm afraid not," Unruh said regretfully. "Regs are regs. But I'll go with him and you can too, if you like. And maybe you, too, Buff, and Willie—"

"I haven't anything better to do," Latt observed with a smile and Guy smiled too and nodded. "Of course, and you. And Gil deserves to, too. Hell, we'll have a committee."

"He told me earlier he didn't want a 'Committee on Marc Taylor,'" Rodge said with a rueful smile, "but it looks like he's got one."

"It looks like he needs one," Wilson said. "And that's the main point."

Their mood was not easy as they went to their respective rooms to study. Their thoughts returned often to Marc, so lonely and unhappy, asleep out there on the porch—hopefully, as Willie remarked to Buff when they happened to meet in the kitchen around eleven for a go-to-bed snack, without dreams.

Ten beds over toward the other end of the porch, Gulbransen hadn't been having any dreams, at least none that he could remember. But he awoke suddenly with Marc insistently on his mind.

Willie had come by his room and told him about the situation just before he had gone to bed.

Now Gil, too, wondered what the hell could be done.

God knew he had given it *his* best shot. Starting with Reg Dance and for quite a while thereafter, he had diligently tried to instruct young Marc in what he seemed to be most lacking, social grace, ease, self-confidence and the proper techniques with which to go after girls. It just hadn't done any good. Maybe the kid was queer but he certainly hadn't acted that way. He seemed to show a very anxious interest and had obediently accompanied Gil, Karen Ann Waterhouse and a blind date (handpicked by Gil) to several campus dances and one evening in the City. The adventures had been only moderately successful. A couple had been downright disastrous.

Karen Ann, who in her coolly superior, girls'-finishing-school way was not tolerant of the socially inept and not very impressed with what she referred to as "your charitable causes," had urged Gil several times to let it go.

"Marc's a nice boy," her most recent comment had summarized it, "but you have to admit he *is* dull. I wouldn't want him mooning around *me* looking scared, self-conscious and unhappy. What makes you think any other sensible girl would?"

Gil looked stubborn.

"I just feel I ought to help him, that's all."

"Why? What's he to you?"

"Just a fraternity brother," he said patiently. "And a kid who just can't seem to pull himself together. What's wrong with that?"

"Nothing's *wrong* with it," she said, "except it's a waste of time. Some people are destined never to grow up. I'm afraid Marc is one. You've got better ways to spend your time."

"Do you mind him being with us occasionally? It hasn't really been very often. And I didn't know you valued my time so. You often find other guys to be with."

"And you find other girls," she said crisply. "Do you drag Marc along on your dates with them? He really *must* be learning a lot, if you do."

"You're the only one who's kind enough to accept him."

She tossed her long blond hair impatiently and shot him a level glance.

"And don't be sarcastic. I don't like it."

He returned her look for look.

"You never are? Not the way I heard it, McGee."

"If you don't like it, go somewhere else."

At this he rolled over on his stomach—they were on the lawn in front of the Libe absorbing some of the last of the cool autumn sunshine—plucked a blade of grass and began nibbling on it with a faraway expression in his eye.

"Why do I hang around you, Karen Ann?" he asked presently. "All I get is insults."

"Not always," she said with a wry little smile. "Maybe that's why."

"If you think you're the only one—"

"I know I'm not the only one," she said calmly. "That's what I was just saying. Am I supposed to be impressed by it? Or cry about it? Neither one would do me the slightest bit of good. Even if I cared, which I don't."

"Then why—?" he asked. She gave him an amused glance. "We understand each other. As they say. Maybe that's why. There are worse foundations for marriage."

"Who was mentioning marriage?"

"We often do," she said dryly. "Indirectly."

"Well," he said, "if I ever start to directly, make me stop. It isn't really what I have in mind."

"Me, either," she remarked. Her tone became brisk. "And now, with that settled—"

"*God.* Will you stop it?"

"What?" she asked innocently.

"*That,*" he said loudly.

Again she gave her hair a disdainful toss. It caught the thin sun and gleamed and glinted as it fell in perfect waves around her stark, high-cheekboned, aristocratic face. They did indeed make a handsome couple, tall, blond, beautiful: "You and your carbon copy," Latt had told him one time in a rare moment of amused personal comment. Perhaps that wasn't such a bad basis for marriage, either—as long as they understood one another. The kids should be spectacular.

"Well," she said, "I think I'll go inside and study for a while. It's getting cool. Want to come along?"

"Why should I?"

"O.K.," she said cheerfully, rose gracefully to her feet and started to move away. He caught the hem of her skirt. She uttered a startled squeal, not at all Karen Ann–like, which made several nearby students laugh, and cried, "*Stop it!*"

"You stop," he said, hanging on. "Or you're going to start unraveling right here in front of God and everybody. We wouldn't pay attention but God might. Or Dean Maggie. Or somebody."

"Very funny," she said, perforce complying.

"Are you going to wait for me?"

"Let go and get up!"

"Not without a promise."

"I *promise,*" she said. "Lord!" she added as he let go, stood up, brushed himself off and picked up his books. "You don't care if you make a fool of yourself, do you?"

"Not where you're concerned, madam," he said, bowing low and gesturing her forward with knightly gallantry. "It happens all the time. I'll never know why."

"Neither will I," she said, and with a sudden sunny smile tucked her arm in his. They headed off to the entrance to the Libe chatting away with complete amicability, leaving behind several baffled onlookers, including Franky and Ray Baker, who happened to be passing by.

"I'll never understand that," Franky remarked. "Never."

"I think they're in love," Ray suggested with a smile.

"Must be," Franky agreed. "No rational explanation would suffice."

And it was true, Gil thought now as he began to feel drowsy again. He often did wonder why he and Karen Ann stayed together. But together they were, and they both knew it; and despite his many other adventures, which she suspected though he tried to be careful that she never knew for sure, and her own occasional dates with other fellows, which he also was kept informed of by kind friends, it was gradually becoming apparent to them in senior year that they were probably going to remain together for a long time to come. They had never discussed marriage except as she said—indirectly—but it was increasingly on both their minds as the year moved on.

He would be the perfect Handsome Doctor, she would be the perfect Doctor's Beautiful Wife. They would probably settle in La Jolla, where she came from, or nearby San Diego—he had already decided to make that concession, since four years of mild California weather had gradually spoiled him for Minnesota winters. Also, Southern California was steadily and rapidly expanding in population, opportunities and need. He would have a very smart, very popular and very lucrative practice, they would have a beautiful home and possibly two or three beautiful children. Before, during and after which, he would continue his amiable ways and perhaps she would too.

But as long as they understood one another—

In another minute he had forgotten all about Marc Taylor, except to determine that he would make some renewed attempts to get him lined up with some nice girl—any nice girl, for God's sake—and ask Willie in the morning what else he could do to help them handle the kid. He didn't discount the seriousness of the problem but there was a limit to what you could accomplish brooding about things in the middle of the night.

He rolled over on his side, closed his eyes and was out in five seconds.

Above on the third floor, having given Hank Moore some pointers on how to organize a term paper for one of his education classes and then waved him off to bed, Latt was still up and thinking.

Latt, according to an admiring Moose, "just never stops thinking. He just never does."

And, he supposed now as he finally closed his books, yawned deeply and began to contemplate going to bed himself, he probably never did except when he was dead-asleep. And even then he found that if he had some academic problem on his mind, it had usually worked itself out by morning when he woke up.

Academic problems had, up to now, been the principle problems of Bill Lattimer's life; and because he had always solved them so easily, it did not seem to him, looking back, that he had been much burdened in twenty-one generally serene and happy years.

It had not taken very long for his parents—his father a successful hardware-store owner in agricultural Fargo on the vast plains of North Dakota, his mother a longtime teacher, and finally principal, at the local high school—to realize that in their only child they had produced a very bright son indeed. They had immediately begun a calculated campaign to push him to his limits. He had responded first with placid compliance and then, as he grew older and the realms of literature and history began to open up for him, with an active hunger for knowledge that soon took him to the top of every class he was ever in. Somehow through it all he had managed to escape the jibes and jealousies of his contemporaries; he couldn't remember a single cry of "Teacher's pet!" although there must have been a few in grammar and high school. The great majority of his classmates might have begun by feeling envious—farm kids in North Dakota, like farm kids everywhere, were not notorious for their tolerance of academic success—but it really had taken very little time for them to feel a genuine and respectful admiration for his achievements.

Along the way, he had also acquired a deeply devout religious feeling. He was one of the few house members—Ray Baker, Johnny Herbert, Smith Carriger, Billy Wilson and, surprising some, Jeff Barnett, were the others—who seldom failed to attend services in Memorial Church if they possibly could.

"It makes me feel good," Smitty had responded to some crack by Franky about "There goes Latt and his Hallelujah Chorus." He said it made him "feel more complete, somehow. I know you think it's old-fashioned but that's the way it is. Sorry."

"Oh, don't apologize," Franky said, more soberly. "I admire you for it. I wish I could believe that deeply in something that isn't there."

"Tell Latt it isn't," Smitty suggested, "and see how far you get."

But not even Franky was flip enough to do that; nor, indeed, did he or anyone else care to challenge Latt on anything, let alone his faith. Latt, as Franky subsequently remarked to Wilson, was just about as impregnable a human being as could be found. There was an inner certainty, strength and serenity that was unshakeable. And the record of his many kindnesses, as Willie observed, went back to where the mind of man runneth not.

"He's too good to be true," Suratt had remarked when he first joined the house; but even he admitted honestly after a few weeks' acquaintance, that it was all real.

"He *is* too good," Renny conceded. "And it *is* true."

It was also, in a way which few were perceptive enough to realize, a burden for Latt at times; and having just concluded a conversation with Randy Carrero which followed within minutes the upsetting news about Marc Taylor, he was, he realized now, physically tired and emotionally drained.

He had just returned to the room after the discussion precipitated by Rodge Leighton's report on his unhappy roommate when there was a small but determined knock on the door. Unlike some who never bothered to lock their doors, Latt always did and it was always respected. He had established the practice when he first moved into the house as a sophomore. ("Latt a sophomore?" Tony Andrade had once inquired quizically. "I can't imagine Latt as ever having been less than ten years older than everybody else. At least mentally.") He felt he needed the privacy for study; and also, in some subtle but determined way, he felt he needed it simply to define himself as a gentleman who respected the privacy of others and expected the same respect to be accorded to him.

So the knock; and, as always prompt and courteous, he called out, "Yes?"

"It's Randy—" not sounding very happy. "Can I come in and talk for a minute?"

"Sure," Latt said, pushing aside his books and swinging his chair around. "What's up?"

"The usual, I guess," Randy said, dropping into a chair and looking glum. "I thought maybe you wouldn't mind if I talked to you about it. I realize it's an imposition, but—"

Latt studied him for a moment.

"Why would you think that?"

"Oh, I don't know," Randy said. "I just did. After all, it's my problem."

"Not getting any better, I take it."

"No," Randy said, stocky figure seeming to shrink with worry, once-cheerful, always-smiling face drawn, dark eyes dull and even bigger than usual under the tousled black hair he kept pushing off his forehead with a repetitive, almost compulsive gesture. "Latt, why are women like that?"

Latt smiled.

"I don't think all of them are, although I'm certainly not an expert. But if you think it would help for me to listen to you cuss them out—"

"You're so nice to everybody," Randy said, "I feel you'll understand and won't judge me." He drove a fist suddenly into his palm. "I'm in such a rut. I'm so confused."

"No, you're not. You're upset—you've been upset all quarter, I guess. But people get upset and get over it, and so will you."

" 'People,' " Randy said darkly, "don't always feel things as deeply as I do."

"That's what we all think," Latt said, but not unkindly. "Maybe it's the age group we're in. It's a time for taking things terribly seriously. Some of us more than others. You're one who does, that's all."

"*You* don't," Randy said, giving him an unhappy look.

"My name's Lattimer, not Carrero," Latt said with a smile, "and while I don't believe much in racial stereotypes, there's something to be said for them or they wouldn't be stereotypes. You do react a lot more than a lot of people do; your feelings are rubbed a lot rawer. At the same time, you probably bounce back faster than most of us. Why don't you just try to forget her and find somebody else? I know that's easier said than done—"

"You said it," Randy agreed tersely. "And you're lucky, you have Kay Ellsworth. She's a very nice girl." He looked suddenly very young. "Why can't I find a nice girl? Why did I have to get involved with a no-good, two-timing, two-bit little bitch on wheels?"

"Oh, I wouldn't call her that—"

"I sure as hell would!"

"Well," Latt agreed, "you do know her better than I do, of course. As for Kay, she *is* a very nice girl, but I assure you our romance is very low-key. We're not burning up the Quad with it."

"I'll bet she might like to," Randy said shrewdly, "but you're too reserved to cooperate."

"I prefer to call it 'steady,' " Latt remarked with a twinkle, "but maybe you're right, I don't know. Anyway, I don't even know if she'll have me. I haven't asked her."

"You know she'd say yes in a minute. Why are you afraid?"

"I'm not afraid," Latt said mildly. "It just hasn't—come right, that's all."

"It never will unless you make it."

For a second Latt looked more wistful than he knew. Then he laughed.

"I thought *you* were in here for *my* advice, not the other way around! Fluff probably *is* a blind alley for you and you just can't afford to let yourself get sidetracked on it. You're too fine a guy and you have too much to give. Isn't that right?"

Randy stared down at the floor as though he could bore a hole in it. Then he sighed heavily.

"Maybe. But what can I do? I seem to really, genuinely, love her, in spite of everything." He looked up, a candid agony in his eyes. "It's awful."

Lord, Latt thought, somewhere between exclamation and prayer, save us from unhappy sophomores! We've got too many on our hands. Outwardly his expression was grave and sympathetic, which accurately reflected his basic feelings.

"You've got to pull out of it some way," he said. "You've just got to. Timmy tells me your work on the *Daily* is suffering and I imagine your grades are going downhill to some degree—"

"Slipping," Randy admitted unhappily. "Slipping."

"Well, you see? You've got to get it turned around, somehow, as soon as possible. And you're the only one who can do it. I can't do it for you. I'm sympathetic and I'm always here to listen, but—" He paused. "You don't want me to talk to her, do you?"

Randy looked startled and appalled.

"Christ, no! That would be the worst thing that could happen. There isn't anything you could say that wouldn't make me look like a fool, and she'd just—just—" his face contorted—"come out of it despising me more."

"I agree. But you seemed to be expecting me to do something, so I thought I'd make the offer."

"Just be here," Randy said. "Just be here, so I can have somebody to talk to—" his face contorted again—"and keep myself sane."

"I'm always here," Latt said simply. "Anytime."

"For everybody," Randy said. "That's why you're so great." He sighed heavily and stood up. "Thanks, Latt. I appreciate it."

Latt shook his head.

"I'm afraid I haven't been much help."

"Oh yes you have. Maybe I'll just—maybe I'll see her, or write a note, or something, and say, 'Go to hell, it's over, get out of my life.'" He looked wistful. "Do you think that would do it?"

Latt smiled.

"It will if you mean it. But I don't think you're ready yet. I wouldn't try it until you are. If I were you."

"No," Randy agreed forlornly. "I've come pretty close several times but I've never quite—quite felt that I could really go through with it. And she knew it, of course. She just laughed and told me I'd be back. Which I have. But then there've been times when *she* told *me* to shove off and refused to see me until I—" his voice sank so low Latt could hardly hear it—"until I came crawling back. Like a faucet!" he exclaimed, voice suddenly louder. "Like a God damned fucking faucet, the way she turns it on and off! I ought to kill her!"

Latt gave him a long, grave look until he blushed and looked away.

"No, that's crazy talk," he admitted. He looked bleak. "But she's got to leave me alone. She's just got to!"

"Well," Latt said, suddenly brisk, "we're repeating, now. If you won't leave her alone she won't leave you alone. I think this is where I came in—or you came in, rather." He smiled and stood up. "Go to bed, Randy. It will look better in the morning. You're too strong to let it get you down permanently. It will begin to improve soon. It's got to."

"I wish I had your confidence," Randy said. "But then," he added with an abruptly recurring bitterness as he went out, "it isn't your problem."

Which was true, of course, Latt reflected as there came to him, as on many occasions, the same unsettling thought that he knew often came to Willie: Who am I, to set myself up as the be-all and end-all of superior wisdom? They had often discussed this and had finally come to the conclusion Willie had stated bluntly: "We don't 'set ourselves up.' They come to us. It isn't as though we seek them out to give them advice. Why should we feel qualms about it? It doesn't seem to bother them any."

But, they agreed, it did impose a burden that often made them feel humbled and inadequate. Quite inadequate, really, considering their own problems, which they often discussed candidly with one another.

Willie and Marian Emerson, for instance. Thank heaven, Latt thought as he went methodically, as he did everything, about the business of undressing, hanging his clothes neatly in the closet and putting on his pajamas. Thank heaven events seemed finally to be precipitating that relationship into something potentially more solid than Willie's slow-motion approach so far. Latt could understand why he'd hesitated, Donn being such a habit and universally accepted expectation—but on the other hand, it wasn't as though they were engaged or anything. So why shouldn't Willie seek Marian's company if he wanted to? Kay considered her a thoroughly nice, decent, intelligent and attractive girl.

And so, he told himself with the glumness that hit him now and again on this particular subject, was Kay. Randy was perfectly right: she had made it quite clear that she would prefer a closer relationship and a formal commitment that they would marry when school ended. He was the one responsible for hanging back. Why? He often wondered, and now he wondered again. Years ago, for a while, he had been afraid it might be some failure in himself, some sinister thing such as he had overheard other boys kidding about furtively in the gym. He had done a lot of earnest prayer during that period and a lot of soul-searching which had carried over into his early days at the University. Suddenly one day in his first spring, walking alone along the Quad in the soft sweet air of the Santa Clara Valley, he had said to himself: "*Nonsense!*" And so, he had realized once and for all, it was.

He had emerged from all his soul-searching serene and sure of himself: it wasn't that.

Then what was it?

Some innate delicacy, he had concluded—some essential reluctance to force issues—some excess of consideration—a native caution compounded by a deep and genuine respect for the dignity and feelings of others—the combination of all these seemed to hold him paralyzed in this important area. He knew Kay probably loved him, he knew she would probably, as Randy said, "say yes in a minute"—but still he hesitated. He hadn't finished his studies, he didn't have a teaching job lined up although the University was hinting, he was in no position to support Kay—it wouldn't be fair to her. He just wasn't ready yet. But maybe Randy, seeking advice but also not hesitating, in his direct, emotion-impelled way, to give it, was right. Maybe he should stop hesitating and plunge right into it. All of his closest friends seemed to agree with Randy.

He shook his head in some puzzlement as he walked thoughtfully down the hall to the sleeping porch: a tall, thin, straight-backed figure with a plain,

pleasantly attractive face and level, honest, kindly eyes that looked with
unblinking integrity at most things in life, including himself. He didn't have
Randy's problem, of a tangible, tantalizing, hurtful and apparently unattain-
able dream, nor Marc's, of an intangible, mysterious, terrifyingly pointless
pursuer who could not, at least for the moment, be successfully defined or
grappled with.

He just had himself.

He was his problem.

Amazing, he thought as he climbed into his lower bunk next to McAllister's and automatically blocked out the mild cacophony of snores with the
little prayer for comfort and guidance he had offered up every night of his life
since he could first remember.

Quite amazing, what a figure of steadiness and serenity Latt was to everyone.

And how uncertain and inadequate Latt sometimes felt himself to be
inside.

In one of the upper bunks down the porch a bit, the wanderer of the
Quad, still awake and watching Latt's discreet and silent passage to bed,
thought again, as he had many times, that if he were ever to consult anyone
about what he too thought of as *that*, it would be Latt to whom he would
turn. Latt was always so solid, always so steady, always so understanding and
always so kind. He could trust Latt, he felt, not to scorn, not to judge, not
to turn away in horror and contempt. Latt, he thought—perhaps along with
Willie, and perhaps even Hack, who was on the verge of suspecting
anyway—would be the refuge.

He, too, said a little prayer for guidance and for help; and presently his
snores, like Latt's, were joined gently with the rest.

"But I've told you!" Marc protested next morning in the Student Health
Services office. "I've told you and told you! *I don't know why I feel this way!*
I just *do!*"

And once again, as he had dreaded he might, he began to cry.

A long, silent look passed around the circle: Dr. James, that fussy, graying, impatient but kindly man who had seen students in their thousands
come and go with their homesicknesses, their love-agonies, their fractures
and frustrations of body and heart, on rare occasions their "social diseases,"
on even rarer their drug problems or their generalized, inexplicable malaise
. . . and Willie, Buff, Guy, Gil, Rodge and Latt, who had cut classes to come
and hover over their hapless young fraternity brother like a pride of protective lions.

Usually, Dr. James had found, he and his staff could prescribe successfully for most things—except for the malaise, which seemed to inflict some young-sters much more than others. Apparently he had a classic case on his hands now. This kind of excessive melancholia required much more patient and specialized treatment, which usually worked but sometimes didn't: he still felt a deep weariness and unhappiness concerning the two recent suicides, both of whom had come in his door and gone out again without ever, ap-parently, finding anything at all to make them feel better about themselves. With some kids, fortunately very few, one never knew; one just never knew. This one was so open and on the surface that he felt considerable hope; but one never knew.

He addressed himself to Guy Unruh with a deliberately flattering air of doctor to doctor.

"What do you think, Mr. Unruh? Is it your opinion that a preliminary stay in the Men's Rest Home would be the best course of treatment for the time being?"

"That is my conclusion, sir," Guy said, looking judicious, "and I believe my fraternity brothers agree." They all nodded gravely. "And you, too, Marc?" he added, giving him an encouraging glance. "Isn't that right?"

"I g-guess so," Marc said. "If the doctor thinks it will—will do any good."

"Obviously he does," Guy said, but not unkindly, "otherwise he wouldn't suggest it. My only additional advice would be that Mrs. Steadman give him extra helpings of everything and try to build up his weight. If you agree, sir. He's lost quite a bit lately and he doesn't have very much to lose."

"Quite right," Dr. James said. "You must try to cooperate, Mr. Taylor, even if you don't feel very hungry. Just pile it in, as much as you can, all right?"

"I g-guess so," Marc said again in the same woebegone way. "I don't think it matters, really, but—"

"Of course it matters," Guy said firmly, "so no more crap. You *eat*, O.K.? Have you ever been to the Men's Rest Home?" Marc shook his head. "You'll like it. It actually used to be Mrs. Steadman's home, when Dean Steadman was alive, and it's a very comfortable, easy, old-fashioned place. There are a couple of gals from town who do the cooking and they're damned good. All you do is eat and rest and read and sleep, and it's great. In fact, we all envy you, getting away from Dewey."

Marc smiled, a little feebly, but he did smile as the others laughed and Willie explained, "Our cook, sir. A character."

"Aren't they all," Dr. James remarked. "Why don't we try it for a few days, Marc, and then we can review things and see how you feel. Jot down your professors' names for me and I'll give them a call and tell them you're going to be absent for a few days—"

"But finals will be coming up pretty soon," Marc interrupted, looking as though he might cry again. "It's awful to—to chicken out just when—"

"You let me and the administration worry about that," Dr. James said.

"You may have to take formal leave for a while, but if you do, well, you do. You can always make it up, they'll understand. The University isn't inhuman. Thank God. Right now all that matters is that everybody wants you to get well. That's the main thing. We can worry about classes when you're back on top of things again."

"I don't think I'll ever be back on top of things again," Marc said in a slow, desolate voice, sounding completely down again. The reaction was strong among his housemates.

"For God's *sake*," Wilson said in a deliberately disgusted tone, hoping it might break through the disturbing lethargy, "we're all trying to help you, and the doctor's right, all that matters is getting you well again, so *knock it off*. All right?"

Marc looked at him as though perhaps he had never seen him before, which alarmed them further.

"If you say so," he responded finally in the same lifeless, disinterested way.

"*You* say so," Unruh directed. "You're the only one who matters. *You* say so, or it won't work. And you *will* have to drop out permanently."

"I wouldn't care," Marc said and again began to cry. Now thoroughly dismayed, they turned to Dr. James.

"We're not going to argue this anymore," he said, closing Marc's file with a decisive snap. He picked up the telephone, dialed, said, "Hi, Grace. I'm sending you a nice boy right away. Marc Taylor. Give him lots of food and take care of him. I'll talk to you later. Many thanks. Now," he said, standing up briskly. "Can one or two of you fellows walk him up there? Not everybody, that would make his arrival too much of an event."

"I will," Wilson volunteered. "And I," Unruh said. "And I," Gulbransen said. "After all, he's sort of been my case, up to now. I have an interest."

"Three's enough," Dr. James said. "Mr. Lattimer, Mr. Richardson, Mr. Leighton and all of you, thanks for your support. I know Marc will truly appreciate your concern for him after he gets a little rest and begins to feel better. It's very good of you, I think. And truly a help."

"It's what we're here for," Buff said matter-of-factly. "Pretty poor friends, if you can't stand by one another. Take it easy, Marc, and don't worry. We'll all be dropping in from time to time to see you. You'll be back in the house before you know it."

But Marc did not reply, except for a wan, disbelieving little smile that again made them glance at Dr. James. But this time he ignored it and moved them out quickly: probably, they agreed later, best for everybody.

For Willie, Guy and Gil it was a difficult walk over to the Quad and up the Row to the house, because Marc either could not or would not respond to their determined attempts at conversation. At the house, fortunately deserted in the midst of morning classes, they waited patiently while he slowly—very slowly—got his toilet articles, pajamas and books together.

Then they walked him over to the nearby faculty residential area where Mrs. Steadman, plump, gray-haired, warm and smiling, awaited them at the door of her rambling, dark-shingled, ivy-covered old house.

For Marc, who said almost nothing as he went automatically about what seemed to him suddenly, in some overwhelming way, to be actions almost final in their crushing impact, it was a gray passage through a gray world whose outlines were rapidly becoming stranger and more unfamiliar by the minute—when he could discern them through the terrifying haze of disassociation that seemed to be gathering all around him. The Quad, the Row, the house—suddenly nothing seemed recognizable. He didn't really know where he was. His fraternity brothers were only dim figures who now and then uttered awkward sounds of encouragement he seemed barely able to hear, and couldn't understand.

Mrs. Steadman was a blur, the Men's Rest Home nothing. He knew he was handed an enormous eggnog, which he drank obediently although he couldn't taste it. Obediently he undressed and put on his pajamas when he was told to. The sedative Dr. James had ordered put in the eggnog quickly took effect and he dropped off to sleep. But never once, now, did he know exactly where he was or understand, really, what was happening to him.

Much troubled, his brethren walked slowly back to the house.

"Damned if I know," Willie said morosely.

"You and me both," Guy agreed.

"You can say that again," Gil concurred.

"I'm scared," Willie said.

"Poor kid," Guy said with a sigh. "So am I."

"Me, too," Gil agreed. He shivered. "God knows I've tried—"

"We've all tried," Willie said. "But maybe not enough."

"And maybe," Guy said bleakly, "too late."

13

But life, as always, moved on because it has to, and by the next morning Marc was already being relegated to a compartment labeled "Must Visit," which many of them made plans to do but not many, in their busy lives, found time for during the next few days. Buff wrote Marc's parents a soothing letter and took on the task of keeping in touch with Mrs. Steadman. And for a couple of days running Willie and Latt dropped by to see their patient, who received them with a vaguely polite disinterest which they did not find encouraging. Dr. James assured them all that it would take time, so be patient and don't worry.

Wilson in particular did not have much time to, because events growing out of what he thought of as "the post office protest" began to overtake him with some rapidity.

The Excom meeting he had called for Thursday afternoon turned out to be much livelier than he had anticipated. And inevitably, this time, it made a much bigger splurge in the pages of the *Daily* than the initial incident. This was due to the presence of Walter Emerson, who provided most of the fireworks.

Wilson knew when he came into the meeting room in the student government offices in the Union that trouble was on the way, because he was immediately challenged by Dr. Stafford. He had arrived a few minutes early and so, unhappily, had she. They were alone in the room temporarily and, as he told Latt later, "She really let me have it. I hardly had time to say hello."

"Hello, yourself," she snapped. "What is this nonsense you've been stirring up, Willie Wilson? Haven't you more sense than to act like an irresponsible juvenile delinquent?" Her jewels sparkled, the heavy bracelets on her wrists jangled, her bun of severely drawn-back gray hair emphasizing her sharp-nosed features and the Elizabeth I–Dame Edith Sitwell resemblance she deliberately cultivated. Her famed acid sarcasm was in top form.

"One would think," she said—"No, don't interrupt!—one would think you had no sense of responsibility whatsoever. Student-body president! Spoiled brat, I'd say! You've always had everything your way. Everybody is supposed to kneel down and worship Willie Wilson, no matter what he does—"

"Dr. Stafford!" he interrupted, at first overwhelmed at the vigor of her attack but then beginning to get angry himself. "Dr. Stafford, I have discussed this thoroughly with Dr. Chalmers and he isn't all that upset about it—"

"Have you discussed it with him lately?" she demanded scornfully. "He isn't so pleased with you today!"

"But," he began, dismay in spite of himself beginning to come into his voice, "he assured me—"

"He told *me* not an hour ago," she said triumphantly, "*not* to let you and Tim Bates and Ari Katanian defy the board of trustees. He said—"

"But he *told* me—"

"*Don't interrupt!*" she ordered, eyes snapping, "obviously enjoying herself," as he remarked bitterly to Latt. "I hope we teach you people at least minimal manners at the University."

"I'm sorry," he said more strongly, "I don't mean to be rude, but I can't believe Dr. Chalmers would—"

"Are you telling me I'm lying?" she demanded, voice rising sharply.

"No, ma'am," he said, shaken but sticking to his guns, "I'm telling you my understanding of Dr. Chalmers' position. I'm also saying that until he transmits a change to me in person, I intend to proceed on what that understanding is. I'm sorry."

"You *are* accusing me of lying," she said with one of her dramatic changes to icy calm. "I can tell you you are treading on extremely dangerous ground, Mr. Wilson. Extremely dangerous."

"Yes, ma'am," he said, his voice to his annoyance trembling a little, but not yielding. "I will have to take that risk, I guess." He hesitated, then added what he knew would make her an enemy for life, but what the hell, she couldn't do him any damage in his senior year. "If you wish to retire as faculty adviser to Excom, that would be your privilege."

"I won't give you that satisfaction," she said. "I'll stay around and watch how the great Mr. Wilson gets out of this one."

He shook his head in genuine bafflement; and went on to make the breach irreversible, but so upset by the very personal nature of her vehemence that he couldn't seem to help himself.

"Why are you so violent?" he asked in a wondering tone. "I'm only a student. Why do you hate me so? Why are you so jealous of me?"

"I don't hate you and I'm not jealous!" she said furiously. "You're so—so—*superior!* You think that because the student body thinks you're so great you can get away with anything! You think that just because you're Willie Wilson—"

She stopped abruptly as Donn Van Dyke, all joy and liveliness as usual, he thought tiredly, swung in the door. But he was glad to see her, Miss Boundless Cheer though she was.

He immediately felt ashamed of the thought, because she was always, and even more obviously now, on his side. She had apparently heard just enough of their raised voices as she came down the hall so that her expression actually was quite shocked and uncertain. But her voice was quite calm as she asked politely, "What is it, Dr. Stafford? Can I be of any help?"

"No!" Dr. Stafford said flatly, and turned away to take her usual seat at one side of the conference table at which the Executive Committee usually met. There she sat in monumental, disapproving silence, a large, heavy, implacable-looking woman, breathing heavily and staring straight ahead as her fingers drummed on the table. How unhappy she looks, Willie thought; and with a sudden flash of intuition: I don't believe she ever has been happy, in all her lonely life.

Normally this would have moved him to pity, sensitive as he was. But not now.

"Hi, Donn," he said, voice still trembling a little with anger, pain and baffled resentment. "I'm glad you came in. We were just—just talking."

"Yes," Donna said with only a little extra brightness to indicate her nervousness. "I heard. . . . Did you know we're going to have a member of the board of trustees with us today?"

"No, I didn't," he said, and was aware from the sudden change in the rat-a-tat-tat of her long polished nails on the table that Dr. Stafford hadn't known either.

"Yes," Donna said. "The president's secretary just called me. Apparently he just came by. It's a Mr. Walter Emerson and he wants to discuss your—your little episode at the post office."

"Good!" Dr. Stafford said, not looking up. "So do I!"

"And so do I," Wilson said evenly. "Did you call Timmy? He'd better be here, too."

"Yes, I did," Donna said as Ari Katanian and other members of Excom began to drift in. On their heels came Tim Bates and Bill Nagatani, a little out of breath after hurrying over from the *Daily.* And right after them came a short, solid, compact individual in mid to late forties whom Wilson took to be his next problem: Mr. Walter Emerson, trustee.

Mr. Emerson did not look unpleasant but he did look very determined and very firm. He also looked a little self-conscious as he took a seat in the row of public chairs. He did not look like the type who would be easily deflected once he set his mind on something. Nagatani took a seat a few chairs away.

Everyone looked expectantly at Willie when he called the meeting to order. After a moment's hesitation he did the only thing he could do, which was to sail right into it.

"Are you here for some purpose, sir?" he inquired politely. "If so, Excom will be glad to hear you."

"Well, yes I am," Mr. Emerson said. "I appreciate your courtesy, Mr. President. My name is Walter Emerson and my daughter Marian is a student here. May I?"

"Yes, by all means," Wilson said. "Draw up a chair to the end of the table. Perhaps we should introduce ourselves," and did so. Fifteen earnest young faces stared somewhat blankly at Walter Emerson as he took his seat and leaned forward, arms on table, hands folded upon them.

"You won't believe it," he said in a pleasant voice—but, again determined—"but I was on Excom a couple of years myself, when I was here. I was also on the football team. You may have heard of the Wow Boys"—he smiled—"succeeded some years later by the Vow Boys. They took a vow to go to the Rose Bowl. We took a vow to have a lot of fun." He chuckled in a way they had to admit was disarming. "We did, too. . . . Anyway, we're all members of the family, as you can see, and I know your problems in running the student body. That's why I find it hard to understand, Mr. Wilson, Mr. Bates and Mr. Katanian, why you wanted to compound them by staging a most unusual demonstration that can only give the University a bad name with the general public. And, I might add, with a number of my fellow trustees, whom I have consulted on the matter."

"Can I answer that, Mr. President?" Tim asked, and with a quick glance that told him *Keep it polite,* Willie nodded.

"Well, sir," Tim said, "we staged a 'most unusual demonstration,' as you put it, because we sincerely believe that Adolf Hitler is an evil human being who is doing monstrously evil things to the Jews in Germany and will, unless stopped, very possibly do terribly evil things to the world as a whole."

"Well," Walter Emerson said, "that's frank enough. Does it occur to you, though, that there may be millions of your fellow citizens who might concede all that and still prefer that this country not get directly involved?"

"Yes, sir," Tim said. "I think we're aware of that."

"Then why—?"

"Because we felt we should take a stand," Tim said sharply. "We feel all decent people should."

"But lots of decent people don't agree," Walter Emerson said reasonably. "Why should you impose—"

"We didn't 'impose,' " Tim objected. "We just offered a petition."

"In a pretty prominent place," Walter Emerson said with a smile, "which caused a small riot. I've also seen some of your editorials in the *Daily*. They're sort of 'imposing,' aren't they?"

"They're my prerogative as editor," Tim said with a certain note in his voice that prompted Ari Katanian to intervene.

"You have to allow Tim freedom of the press, you know, Mr. Emerson," he said.*"Die Luft der Freiheit weht,* and all that."

"I was also on the *Daily* a couple of years, believe it or not," Mr. Emerson said with another chuckle—everything very jolly so far, Willie reflected. "Before I got really serious about football. I got around, boy! You've no idea. Of course I know about freedom of the press," he said, more seriously. "I also know that there are—or should be—certain restraints of good taste and decorum that should guide a publication such as the *Daily*. I don't mean official censorship, of course—don't look at me like that, Mr. Bates, I really don't—unless it becomes absolutely necessary."

"Exactly," Tim said in a tight voice.

"I should tell you frankly," Walter Emerson said, his own tone not yielding anything either, "that there are a number of my fellow trustees who seem to be coming perilously close to that. We wouldn't want that to happen, would we? So perhaps the restraint should be self-imposed before it becomes necessary for the administration to impose it."

"Dr. Chalmers told us—" Willie began.

"Dr. Chalmers told us what he told you," Walter Emerson said with sudden bluntness.

"It was a form of censorship," Wilson said. "Gentle, but there."

"Not at all," Walter Emerson said reasonably. "It was self-control—restraint—the hope that you wouldn't overdo it, is what he told me. He emphasized that it was up to your good sense, but he didn't rule out the possibility he might have to step in later if you refused to—if you couldn't see your way clear to complying with his suggestion. From what I gathered from the board," he added firmly, "the board is ready to support him in whatever action may be necessary . . . if you don't agree."

"I seem to detect a threat there, Mr. Emerson," Tim said sharply, "and I don't like it."

"I'm just laying the cards on the table for you," Walter Emerson said, continuing to sound reasonable but obviously not giving an inch. "We can have a pitched battle over the *Daily*—and over whether anyone should be allowed to have anti-Hitler demonstrations—which essentially would be pro-war demonstrations, if it comes to that, and let's pray to God it doesn't—or we can all agree to calm it down and proceed in a decent and respectable way."

"We're already in a pitched battle, aren't we?" Ari Katanian remarked. "Since you've already told the City papers. They'll be wanting to know what happens next, I suspect."

"And I intend to tell them," Walter Emerson said calmly. "So"—he opened his arms and turned his hands palms up on the table—"what's it to be?"

Wilson could see from Tim's expression that he was about to tell him in no uncertain terms, but just as he was getting ready to intervene and try to calm things down, the door opened and Marian came in, looking flustered, out of breath, and, he thought, quite lovely. She gave him a quick, shy smile that did not pass unnoticed and sank into a seat. Her father swung around, beamed, said, "Hi, baby," and turned back.

"This is my daughter Marian," he explained with obvious pride.

"I hope you aren't being too fierce," she said with the immemorial self-conscious little laugh of children when they suspect their parents are going to do something that will be monumentally embarrassing to them.

"Not at all," he said comfortably. "Excom and I are just having a quiet discussion of that inexcusable little riot the other day. I think we understand each other. Right, Mr. Wilson?"

"We're trying to understand, sir," Willie said, being careful not to look at Marian over her father's shoulder. "I'm not sure we're exactly clear what you want us to do. Not express any opinions at all? Express them but don't make a fuss about it? I think most of us are a little puzzled."

"And resentful, I'll bet," Walter Emerson said with another easy chuckle. "I remember how touchy we used to get when anybody tried to tell *us* what to do. Nobody wants to interfere with your right of expression, of course, but maybe it would simplify matters if you just didn't express any opinions at all about what's going on in Europe—at least for the time being, that is. Until we see how things develop."

"I don't think there's much doubt how they're developing," Tim said in a flat, resentful voice. "That seems clear enough. If one isn't blind."

"I'm not blind," Walter Emerson said, for the first time sounding a little sharp himself. "It doesn't look good over there, anybody can see that. But Hitler may stop one of these days, things may change; nothing's inevitable. But no matter what happens, I for one am completely opposed to sending our boys and money over there again to pull other people's chestnuts out of the fire. Once is enough. And 'our boys' means you, don't forget. It's not just a philosophical exercise. We're talking about your hides here, not mine. I want to save you from what I went through."

"I'm sure that's very kind of you, sir," Wilson said before Tim could make some other retort that might inflame things further, "but I do think each of us has to face up to that for himself. You made your decision in your time—"

"We thought it was the war to end wars," Walter Emerson said wryly. "What a crock. But we hoped, fellows—we hoped. I don't want you to get all fired up with hope and idealism and then get disillusioned as we did, after all we went through over there. And now it seems to be starting all over again. . . ." His voice trailed away and for a moment he was looking far away into regions of hell they hadn't even begun to imagine yet. In the silence that fell as they all watched him intently, a surprising voice intruded.

"I lost someone over there, Mr. Emerson," Dr. Stafford said with a crisp lack of emotion, back in character again. "I couldn't agree with you more."

"Thank you, ma'am," he said with a little bow. "I appreciate your support. We're dealing with people who just don't know, here."

"But they think they know," she said with a bleak glance around the table. "That's what makes it difficult."

"Yes, ma'am," he agreed. "We have to guide them a little. If we can."

"You don't have to 'guide' us," Tim protested with sudden bitterness. "Do you know how patronizing that sounds? Sir?"

"I don't mean to be patronizing," Walter Emerson said calmly. "At the same time"—his tone became more emphatic—"I think I can speak for the board when I say that we don't want pro- and anti-war riots on campus, either. Nobody knows yet what the best policy will be to keep us out of whatever may be coming over there, but I think it's safe to say we *do* intend to keep out. We want you to take that into account."

"Your minds are made up then," Ari Katanian said. "Everybody toes the line. Or else."

"No, now, not quite that," Walter Emerson said. "Be reasonable, you guys: that's all we're asking. Don't inflame a situation that's becoming almost daily more difficult."

"President Roosevelt seems to think we ought to oppose Hitler," Donna observed. Walter Emerson snorted.

"Roosevelt!" he said. "When did we run the University by what *Roosevelt* thinks?"

"Yes, sir," Wilson remarked as there were various sounds of amusement and/or protest around the table, and Marian looked terribly embarrassed, "that *does* represent a certain point of view around here, there's no doubt about that."

"And in the country as well," Walter Emerson said, "not just old fogies at the University. You've got to keep a balance. You've got to exercise restraint. The board would really appreciate it if you'd just ease up for a little while."

"I can't suppress my opinions," Tim said doggedly. "I'd rather resign from the *Daily* first. Too many bad things are going on. I have to speak out. I just can't sit still."

"But you can keep calm!" Walter Emerson said. "Try it. It might show that you're growing up. Well!" he said, before Tim, flushing, could make the angry retort that was obviously building. "I guess that does it as far as I'm concerned. I just wanted to bring you that message from the board, for your guidance. It's really about the same as Dr. Chalmers told you, except we're in a position to have him put a few teeth in it if we have to. We don't really want to, though. After all—" and once more his comfortable chuckle as he stood up—"we were young once, too, you know, believe it or not. Thanks for your patience, Excom. I appreciate the opportunity. It's been like old times, yammering away about things in here. Coming, baby? You can walk me to my car."

"No, Daddy," she said, looking flustered and, Willie thought, even more appealing. "I think I'll stay for the rest of the meeting, if you don't mind."

"Oh?" he said. "Well, O.K. We'll see you on the weekend, then." He bent down, gave her a kiss, tossed them all a farewell wave. "So long, Excom. You've restored my youth."

"Thanks, sir," Willie said with a smile as he went out the door. "I think you may have reaffirmed ours."

After that, there didn't seem much more to say. Dr. Stafford retreated again into her disapproving silence, and nobody wanted to discuss Walter Emerson's intervention in her presence; that would have to come in private talks around campus later on. Routine business was quickly disposed of and Willie adjourned the meeting. Nagatani, who had said not a word but scribbled busily throughout, left with Tim to go back to the *Daily*. Ari yawned and stretched, smiled amiably and went back to the halls. The rest dispersed with routine jokes and inconsequential banter. Dr. Stafford rose without farewells or even a glance at Wilson and stalked out, invariable red velvet jacket swirling. Donna and Willie were the last members to leave. Marian was still sitting nervously in her chair.

"Did you want to see us about something?" Donn asked politely.

Marian hesitated, then said quickly, "Oh, no. At least—that is—I did want to talk to Mr. Wilson—Willie—about something. If I could, that is."

For a minute Donn looked quite upset. But she covered it instantly with her usual smiles.

"Why, sure," she said and then laughed, quite naturally. "I mean, I guess you can. I can't speak for Willie."

"O.K. with me," Wilson said, feeling foolish. "What's it about?"

"Can I just walk along with you and—and tell you about it?" Marian asked, and without a moment's hesitation Donna said, "Of *course* you can. Excuse me and I'll just run along. Don't forget we have that date later, Willie."

"We do?" he asked stupidly. "O.K., I'll see you later."

"Good," she said, tossing him her biggest, cheeriest smile. "I'm counting on it."

And with a quick little smile and wave to Marian, she swept out of the room, head held high.

"Want to go to the Cellar?" he asked, that being the only thing he could think of to say at the moment. But she shook her head.

"No, let's just walk down to the Quad," she said, still looking nervous but determined. "I want to apologize for my father." She smiled rather forlornly. "Again."

"Oh, he wasn't so bad," he said as they emerged from the Union. "He was a *lot* better than I expected."

At this she laughed aloud, quite spontaneously, and it was his turn to look embarrassed.

"I mean—I thought he'd be—well, a real—"

"A real monster?" She laughed again. "He's too smart for that. Plus, he's really quite a nice guy. When you get to know him."

"Oh, I'm sure," he said hastily. "I didn't mean that he wasn't."

"He didn't come here until after the war. He was already married then and they had me. He only graduated sixteen years ago. He isn't so far away from us. Probably we should be thankful the board didn't send down somebody else. He says there are 'a lot of old dinosaurs' on the board."

"Yes," he agreed. "I suppose if we have to have any contact with the board, he's the best. He has a knack for slipping in little zingers, though. I thought Timmy might climb over the table after him, at a couple of points."

They laughed heartily together at the mental picture this evoked, and he reflected with some relief that they were really becoming quite easy with one another at last.

"I hope," he said as they started down the Quad, lying peaceful and deserted in the thin autumnal sun, "that we *can* strike a balance on things. I think people have to express what they feel in a situation as serious as this could be, but I can also see where the administration doesn't want it to get out of hand. Even, though," he admitted wryly, "I suppose I did a lot to help it get out of hand the other day."

"I liked what you did," she said simply. "I'm going to tell my father that this weekend." She smiled. "I'm not afraid of him."

"I don't imagine you're afraid of much," he remarked and she looked shy again.

"Well, I don't know," she said, and quite suddenly, baffling him considerably, she seemed once more far away. He decided he couldn't let that get started again.

"Surely not of me," he said quietly. "I wouldn't want to think I have that effect."

"You're quite formidable," she said, her smile easier again. "I don't think you quite realize the impact Willie Wilson has on people."

"I got a little taste earlier," he said in a rueful tone, still genuinely disturbed by Dr. Stafford but thinking also that enlisting sympathy and understanding wasn't such a bad way to proceed. Willie Wilson, his inner voice told him, you are an incorrigible cynic. No, he replied, I really want her support. It could mean a lot to me.

"I thought you were a little upset about something," she said. "You concealed it well but I thought I sensed something."

He nodded. A sharp girl, his little voice said, and full of surprises. Be on your toes.

"I was. Dr. Stafford really lit into me just before the meeting began, and I don't quite know why. We got into a real row for a couple of minutes before the others came. I'm afraid I wasn't very polite, finally. I told her she was jealous of me, which seems ridiculous, the head of the English department jealous of a student. But I think she is. And I don't understand it. It's very puzzling."

"I can understand it," she said thoughtfully as they turned into the Inner Quad and began to walk slowly toward Memorial Church. "You're young. You're handsome—oh, yes, you are, don't be modest. You're successful. Everything's going your way. You give off a sort of glow—"

"Lots of people our age 'give off a sort of glow,'" he remarked wryly. "It's called youth, I suspect."

"Yes, but it makes a lot of older people jealous. And sad. I can see why Dr. Stafford couldn't help striking out at you. She's a real sad lady. And youth was a long time ago, and even when she had it I suspect she was always the ugly duckling. I can understand."

"You're very sympathetic to other people," he said, not to flatter, quite sincere. "I like that."

"I try to be," she said with her sudden shy little smile.

"And fair," he added. He frowned. "I doubt if you can realize what an odd feeling it is to know that somebody dislikes you just because you're you—that no matter what you do, it doesn't matter, it won't make any difference, it won't change them because their dislike is something almost instinctual . . . and terribly unfair."

She gave him a sidewise glance.

"Isn't that what your demonstration at the post office was all about? Doesn't that sum up what you were protesting against in Germany? A state of mind? Jealousy? Instinctual? Terribly unfair? I thought it was."

"Of course it was," he said. "But that was an intellectual conclusion on my part. I'd never had it presented to *me* in quite that personal fashion until Dr. S. let fly." He looked puzzled. "I don't know why I've never run into it from my contemporaries, though. Odd that it should come from someone so much older."

"Who knows what makes other people unhappy? Something just struck her all of a sudden. As for your contemporaries—" a quick smile which, he realized with pleasure, was, or at least appeared to be, genuinely admiring— "I repeat, you don't realize the impact of Willie Wilson. I'm sure there are jealous ones. It wouldn't be human if there weren't. But they've never quite dared to express it openly because you're so—so secure, somehow."

"I am?" he asked with a sudden bitterness that he told himself he certainly mustn't show to her. "Is that how everybody thinks of me? 'Secure'?"

"Yes," she said, giving him a curious look. "Aren't you?"

He laughed his noncommittal laugh. "Oh, sure," he said elaborately. "Isn't everybody?" And was thankful he didn't have to expound further. From a corner of the Quad, a trim, familiar little figure trotted toward them with its usual happy, puppy-dog grin.

"Hey, Jeff!" he called, "What's doing, pal?"

"Faculty adviser wanted to see me," Jeff explained casually as he came up to them and paused, running slowly in place and, Willie noted enviously, not puffing at all. "Just on my way to swim practice. Who's your pretty girl, Willie?"

"My fraternity brother Jeff Barnett," he said, "Marian Emerson. Marian, Jeff. Jeff, Marian."

"*Real* pretty," Jeff said admiringly, deciding to stand still. "Y'all got good taste in *some* things, Willie."

"I know who you are," she said with a smile. "You're our swimming star."

"And resident rebel," he said cheerfully. "Don't let Willie here give you a lot of Yankee nonsense, Miss Marian. He's a good guy but he's full of it."

"I'll be on guard," she said.

"You do that," he said with his most charming grin. "Got to be runnin' along or I'll be late. Nice to have met you. See you at the house, Willie."

And he trotted off, turning just before he left the Quad for a farewell wave.

"He's very nice," she said. "And very fond of you, obviously. *He's* not jealous."

"And not afraid of me, either," he said with mock ruefulness. "I may be 'formidable' to some people, as you say, but not to Jeff Barnett. He has no respect for me *what*-so-*ever*."

"Yes, he does," she said, with a smile, "and you know it. I think I'd better be getting back to my studies," she added abruptly, sounding, suddenly, oddly formal. "I just wanted to reassure you about my father. It's been an interesting talk. I appreciate your taking the time—"

"Come *on*," he said. "Don't be so formal. I'll walk you back to the Union."

"I have to go to the Libe first."

"All right, the Libe, then."

"Well—" She hesitated, abruptly shy. He thought: Now what? "I think maybe, if you don't mind, I mean—you really needn't. I appreciate it, but—I can walk over by myself. I wouldn't want to trouble you."

For a moment he stood there in the center of the Quad and stared at her, puzzled and, he realized though he fought against it, hurt. Then he said quietly, "O.K., if that's what you want. It really wouldn't be any trouble, of course; that's ridiculous. But suit yourself."

"I'd really rather," she said. "I'm sorry."

"Oh, no," he said. "I do think it's ridiculous, but there we are. Do we still have a date for tomorrow night, then?"

"Oh, yes," she said hastily. "Six, didn't you say? I'll be ready."

"Good," he said shortly. "I'm glad something I do pleases you."

"Oh," she said, in a dismayed voice. "I didn't mean it that way. You just don't understand."

"Afraid not," he said. "See you tomorrow night." And turned on his heel and strode off, not looking back.

All the way back to the house his thoughts were angry, baffled, resentful and hurt. Was she meeting somebody else? He couldn't figure out what in the hell—his thoughts went 'round and 'round.

When he reached the house a note in Buff's generous scrawl was pinned to his door: "Call Donn."

That, he thought, was the last thing he wanted to do at the moment. But then he thought: At least *she* likes me—what a great gal *she* is.

Really.

"Hi," he said. "Just got in."

"Yes," she said, sounding nervous and defensive. "I was just wondering if—if you still want me to come to Carmel with you Thanksgiving. I can always make other plans if—if it would be inconvenient. In some way."

"Why, sure," he said, more impatiently than he intended. "Of course," he reaffirmed quickly. "We're all looking forward to it very much. It's a deal."

"Are you looking forward to it?" she asked in the same defensive way.

"I certainly am," he said stoutly. "We're going to have a lot of fun."

"Well, good," she said, sounding relieved. "I just didn't want to—to get in the way of anything. If you had other plans."

"No other plans," he said firmly. "Believe me. No other plans."

"O.K.," she said. "Take care now."

Christ, he thought as she hung up. *Women.*

Once he got over that instinctive male reaction he was able to concede honestly to himself that perhaps he might have had something to do with it, too.

He had scarcely returned to his room when the phone rang again and on the second floor Lor Davis shouted, "WIL—SON!"

Calm and unhurried but obviously concerned about something, the voice of the president came over the line. Abruptly Willie tightened up.

"Good afternoon, Willie," Dr. Chalmers said. "I heard you had an interesting Excom meeting."

"Yes, sir," he said, trying to match the president's even tone, "we did. Mr. Emerson livened it up. And so," he added pointedly, "did Dr. Stafford."

"Yes, they both told me. Dr. Stafford sounded genuinely upset. Were you impertinent to her?"

"No, sir, I was not! She jumped me the minute I entered the room, for no reason at all that I could understand. I actually thought she was jealous of me, which seems ridiculous. But she was certainly more violent than usual."

There was the slightest trace of amusement on the other end.

" 'Violent'? Is that how the students think of Dr. Stafford?"

"Well, sir," Willie said, "She *is* very positive. You have to admit that. She also said—" He paused. "She said that you told her that she was not to let us defy the board." In spite of himself dismay and some resentment crept into his voice. "I thought our understanding with you was that we could continue what we were doing but just not be quite so—so strong about it. When I told her that was our understanding she got all upset and said I was accusing her of lying. What *was* our understanding, sir?"

"I think you both understood me," the president said. "I did agree that you and Tim and Hank, and whoever else wants to, could proceed as you were doing but in a somewhat milder and more decorous way. I did tell Dr. Stafford that she should make sure that you did not openly defy the board. I don't see any discrepancy. Do you?"

"Well—no, sir. Except that she implied that you wanted a complete clamp-down on us and I didn't think we had agreed on that."

"Just between you and me," Dr. Chalmers said comfortably, "Dr. Stafford sometimes interprets things a little more emphatically than they're intended. . . . Are you still in doubt?"

"No, sir," he said slowly, "I . . . guess not."

"But you're not sure."

"No, sir, not—not exactly."

"Express yourself, Willie, but be discreet enough about it so that you don't stir up a major controversy with the board. Which is the purport of this call, because apparently you already have."

"Oh?" he said, dismayed. "How's that, sir? Mr. Emerson disagreed with us but he seemed reasonable. There wasn't any clash. He stated his point of view and we stated ours. We thought he was quite a nice guy, actually."

"Walter Emerson," Dr. Chalmers said, "*is* a nice guy. A little pompous, as he grows older, and a little abrupt, but one of our nicer board members. Left to himself, all would be well. Unfortunately he also has a tendency to be a bit excitable, so that he did, at first, contact a number of other members with a somewhat skewed version of what occurred. And then Mr. Nagatani, who happens to be campus correspondent for the *Chronicle* along with his other duties, got in touch with him and sent them a long dispatch this afternoon after your meeting. The emphasis, I think, was more on controversy than conciliation—a characteristic of journalism, I'm afraid—and now the fat is, at least temporarily, in the fire. Has he called you for further comment yet?"

"Not yet."

"He has me, and no doubt is trying to reach you even as we talk. He is a persistent young man, Mr. Nagatani, though a very able one, I think."

"He's good. What did you tell him, sir?"

"Basically, the gist of the conversation in my office—without reference to Wolfgang, though he's heard his name somewhere and intends to call him too." There was a slight chuckle. "This may turn into an international incident yet. Are you prepared to repulse storm troopers?"

"I'm prepared to repulse Wolfgang," Willie said dryly. "Then what am I to tell Bill when he calls me?"

"Just stick to the basics, leave out personalities, leave out Hitler and the Jews, just say we agreed that reasonable, orderly and courteous disagreement is a hallmark of the civilized mind and of this university, and that we all intend to proceed in that spirit whenever there's a genuine difference of opinion. Period. 'Thirty' and the end, as I believe the journalists say. All right?"

"If that satisfies you, sir, it seems reasonable to me."

"Good. We must prepare ourselves, however, for the possibility of some rather sensational headlines. If they occur, we must not dignify them with comment, disputation or reply. We must ignore them. They will pass."

"If you say so, sir."

"Trust me," Dr. Chalmers said. "It happens all the time."

When Bill called some five minutes later—"Where've you been, Willie? Somebody in your house must have a really heavy date tonight, the phones have been tied up for the last fifteen minutes"—he did as instructed, kept to basics, did not elaborate, mention Hitler, Wolfgang or the Jews, wave any flags, raise any issues, make any points. Nagatani sounded quite disappointed when he hung up.

"I'm going to talk with Wolfgang. He'll liven things up."

"No doubt. Give him my love."

"Are you kidding?" Bill asked, startled and apparently quite sincere.

"Yes," Willie said, "I'm kidding."

Next morning, sure enough, the headlines said: ANTI-NAZI STUDENTS DEFY TRUSTEES. BOARD MAY CRACK DOWN ON PROTESTS. MEMBERS FEAR "WAR HYSTERIA" GRIPPING CAMPUS. Journalists, he agreed wryly with Dr. Chalmers, did not always seek the Golden Mean.

He decided to go downstairs and see if Latt was around. He wasn't but Franky was. They decided to shoot some pool to kill time until dinner, "not being athletic like our famous fraternity brothers," as Franky said. Jeff was swimming, Randy was doggedly working on his tennis game, Moose was at the stadium practicing for this week's easy contest with Oregon and next week's tough Big Game with Cal, and Unruh was on the basketball court with By Johnson, whom, Wilson remarked, he must look up again soon.

"Why?" Franky inquired. "He's a nice kid, but—"

"No 'buts,' " Willie said crisply. "Because I want to get him in this house, that's why."

"I thought you'd forgotten all about that," Franky said. "I was rather hoping you had, as a matter of fact. Aren't you satisfied with defending the Jews and taking on Adolf Hitler? Seems to me that's enough controversy for a while. It would be for me, anyway."

"You don't know my capacity," Wilson said serenely, sinking one in the corner pocket and caroming two more into the side pockets. "Top that, Fatso."

"I am *not* fat," Franky said with dignity. "Just hefty." And with bland accuracy he sank two of his own and the eight ball, to win the first game. "Tell me," he said as he racked them up for the next round, "are you convinced you can get him approved? Jeff seems pretty sure he's got enough votes to beat him, and I agree. There are quite a few of us who have doubts, you know, Willie. It's a nice gesture on your part but I don't know that we're ready for it."

"It's going to happen someday," Willie said as Franky hit the triangle of balls and sent them rolling in all directions across the table. "Why not now and why not here?"

"That's what Katie says," Franky acknowledged. "And Kay Ellsworth and Maggie Johnson. The women are all for it, apparently—even though none of the sororities will touch Shahna Epstein, nice girl that she is. Nor would they touch a colored girl if they had the opportunity. Very consistent, the ladies."

"That's why we've got to show 'em it can be done," Wilson said, accidentally sinking the eight ball and therefore having to rerack the balls for another game. "I'm going to invite him up here for one more dinner before the holidays. At the first house meeting in January we'll have a discussion and put it to a vote and we'll see who wins."

"You sound pretty confident," Franky observed. "How do you know he wants to join? From what I heard the last time he was here—"

"He had doubts for a while," Wilson admitted, "as who wouldn't, in his position. But Guy told me the other day that he's been sounding him out during practice and he seems more agreeable now. Also, I got a call from Maryetta Bradford and she said—"

"Who's Maryetta Bradford?"

"Maryetta Bradford," Wilson said, "is hell on wheels. She is also a real little dynamo. She's a sophomore transfer from Mills who has decided to make By her Cause with a capital K. Last time I talked to him I got the feeling he's fallen in love with her. I don't know whether she has the capacity to fall in love with a human being but she sure has the capacity to fall in love with an idea. And By's her idea right now."

"And she's white, of course," Franky said, pausing in midshot to give him a thoughtful look. "That's a pretty tricky area, Willie. That's even trickier than getting him into a fraternity. Are you sure you know what you're doing?"

"I did introduce them," Willie admitted, "but after that it was out of my hands. Our mothers—mine and Maryetta's—were friends at Cal, and I had an obligation to look her up, and when I mentioned her to him he got interested, and so I called her and *she* got interested, and—"

"And the poor guy didn't know what hit him," Franky finished soberly. "Just imagine if you were a Negro brought up in the south and some flashy little white babe suddenly moved in on you. I'm not so sure you did him any kindness that time."

"Well, now, listen, damn it," Wilson said. "I just introduced them. I didn't know then what I know now."

"Is she one of those barricade-stormers?" Franky asked dryly.

"I'm afraid so. She told me she's joined that noisy little bunch that's raising money for the Loyalists in Spain. And she went up to the City last weekend for a demonstration in support of the longshoremen's strike."

"I'm surprised she wasn't out there with you at the post office," Franky observed, sinking a perfect shot in a side pocket.

"Probably would have been if she'd known about it," Willie said. He grinned. "It didn't last long enough for her to get involved."

"How are things going on that?" Franky inquired as Wilson took careful aim and missed. "Everything settled down?"

"Reasonably," Wilson said, deciding not to tell him all the details. "Things seem relatively quiet here, too. I notice Krohl and Duke don't speak, which is probably just as well."

"Duke's very grateful to you, you know. He and Shahna are really worried about things. They think you walk on water, now."

"They told me they appreciated it," Willie said, looking embarrassed as he remembered the quite emotional scene when they had seen him in the Union that same afternoon. Shahna's influence always had a tendency to make Duke more emotional, but he was emotional enough on his own. They had reiterated their admiration and thanks several times while he tried to shrug it off, aware of all the watching faces. Finally he had managed to move off, rather awkwardly. "I didn't think I did all *that* much," he said. But they seemed to think so.

Maybe he had. He wondered now, as he and Franky prepared for a final game before knocking off to shower and get ready for dinner, what it had really added up to. He wondered also whether it really did make sense to pursue the issue of By Johnson further. Maybe, as Franky said, "defending the Jews and defying Hitler" was enough for a while. But he had the feeling By's matter wouldn't rest, now that Maryetta was involved. She had sounded very determined when they had talked on the phone last night. He wondered if By knew the lobbying she was doing for him. If so, he reflected as he sent a quite sensational shot down the table and back again to drop neatly into an end pocket, it was probably making By even shyer than before.

Down at the gym, By and Unruh had finished practice and were showering. By now they were much more at ease with one another, and in
addition to what the coach called "a beautiful working relationship" on the
court, had become comfortable friends as well. Guy suspected that he and
Willie and Latt were by now By's closest friends on campus. So he did not
hesitate to raise the subject while By lathered and splashed beside him,
spluttering with enjoyment in the needle-sharp hot water.

"When are you coming up to the house again?" he inquired casually.
"Willie and I would like to wrap up the rushing and get your name before
the group as soon as possible."

"Oh," By said, pausing and turning to give him a serious look before
ducking back under the shower. "That's nice. I haven't heard from Willie for
several weeks. I didn't know if he was still interested."

"You've heard from me," Guy said with a smile. "I wouldn't mention it if
Willie and I weren't in agreement. We coordinate."

"Yes, I know you do," By said with an answering smile. "I'm aware of that.
When do you want me to come up?"

"Final rushing is next Wednesday," Guy said. "How's that?"

By thought for a moment as the water cascaded down on the shining
blue-black body that could move with such swift and sinuous rapidity when
going for a goal. Then to Guy's surprise, because he had seemed so hesitant
before, he nodded his head with a decisive vigor.

"Yes," he said firmly. "I think I'd like that. Then I can move in at the
beginning of winter quarter."

"That's right," Guy agreed, surprised both at the acquiescence and the
apparently serene confidence. Where had that come from? He decided it
might be best to slow it down, just a little bit. "Of course," he added
cautiously, "you realize that it does have to go to a vote, so we can't guarantee it absolutely. But things look good."

"Do they?" By asked, giving himself a final soaping and starting to rinse off
as Guy did the same. "I'm glad to hear it. I thought Jeff Barnett and one or
two others might try to make some trouble."

"Jeff doesn't exactly 'make trouble,'" Guy said, "he isn't that type. But he
does—"

"He does 'take against you,' as my grandmother used to say," By commented with a wry little smile. "I haven't done anything to him but—but be
what I am. But I know that in his mind that's quite enough."

"He's not prejudiced, exactly," Guy said awkwardly as he turned off his
shower and began to towel vigorously. "He's just—the way he was brought
up, that's all."

"And so am I," By said simply. "We understand each other. I was telling a friend of mine that if we'd been reared up in some small town down South we'd probably be good friends. It wouldn't have helped him welcome me into his fraternity, of course, but I probably could have worked around the yard all right."

"Oh, now," Unruh said, startled by the sudden bitterness: By sometimes had capabilities one wasn't prepared for. "That isn't right."

"No," By said, "it isn't right. But that's the way it is. Who else will vote against me?"

"There may be one or two," Guy said carefully. "It's a—" he paused almost apologetically, although he rather resented the feeling that he had to be apologetic—"it's a fairly big step for us out here, even though much less than it would be in the South, of course. Or probably in the East, also. But you mustn't let that bother you. After it's over it'll be over, and if you get in everybody will close ranks and—"

" 'If!' " By interrupted, pausing with one leg of his trousers on. "Then you really think there's some doubt?"

"There could be," Guy said, almost impatient though he tried not to sound it. "Nobody can guarantee anything like that. It can happen to anybody. Somebody doesn't like the way a guy looks or the way he eats or talks or the way he dresses, or—you name it. There's more damned nonsense goes on in that kind of voting. You just have to be prepared for it. It isn't going to happen to you, I'm sure. But—it could. Of course," he added, as By slowly finished dressing, a thoughtful expression on his face, "we don't think it will, you understand. We think it's safe."

"I don't care if it's 'safe,' " By said finally, going to a mirror and running a perfunctory comb through his tight-curled hair. "I just feel it's something that ought to be done."

"So do I," Unruh said, looking over By's shoulder and combing his blond mane in companionable proximity. He looked him in the eye in the mirror. "You've changed your tune. You weren't so enthused about it earlier."

"I'm not 'enthused,' exactly," By said gravely, returning look for look. "I just said I thought it should be done."

"Even that's a change," Guy remarked, turning away to his locker and getting out the heavy sweater he had worn down to practice. "You weren't so anxious to be a test case a few weeks ago. What happened?"

"Oh," By said. A bemused but pleased expression came into his eyes. "I met someone."

Guy nodded.

"Willie told me. She must be something."

"She is," By said softly. "She's great."

"And she's the one who put you up to—persuaded you—to go through with this. Full speed ahead, I mean. Damn the torpedoes."

"Isn't that what you and Willie and Latt wanted me to do?"

"Yes," Guy said emphatically. "We're delighted. We were afraid you were going to back out."

"I thought about it," By admitted. "But *she* told me that I'd really be letting my—my people down if I chickened out. She told me I owed it to myself and—'to Negroes everywhere,' she said. So I've decided to do it." For a moment he looked worried again. "I hope you're not going to be disappointed."

"Not if we can help it," Unruh said firmly. "We're going to do our damnedest."

"All right, then," By said with a pleased little smile. "Then I'll do mine."

They left the gym and walked along together until their paths diverted. Damn it, Guy thought, as he watched By's tall, lithe figure go pantherlike across the meadow to his hall, the house had better *not* disappoint you. It would be a real sad day if that happened.

When he reached the house he found Willie taking a shower, told him the gist of it, and suggested he call By as soon as possible. This he did and was gratified to hear the tone of anticipation and confidence that came over the wire.

Willie, too, was pleased by By's change of heart. He too felt that something very important was at stake. He too felt it would be a great mistake if the house rejected him. And like Guy, he knew unhappily that it was a real possibility.

In his room on the third floor across the hall from Unruh's, North McAllister was not thinking about By Johnson or other such sociopolitical issues, although he had given some thought on the first night Willie had brought By to the house. North had made up his mind then: he was going to vote against him. Not because he found him personally objectionable, far from it, but just because it would be, as he had agreed when Jeff Barnett sounded him out, "too disruptive." North was basically a pretty conservative guy, he often told himself, aside from the one area of his life where he was far from it, and his general attitude was to keep the peace, divert attention with a wisecrack and stay out of the way as much as possible. There were various advantages in this, the major one being the privacy of his personal life, to which he was dedicated in a way and for a motivation which hardly anyone at school, and certainly not B. J. Letterman, had ever suspected.

Contemplating that now, he experienced that curious combination of seductive satisfaction and knifelike regret that one or two others of his housemates would have recognized. He did not know who they were but he suspected. Nothing overt had ever passed between them except what he had heard described as "the look." That was quite enough to establish an instant understanding, unexpressed, silently supportive but never articulated. Nor, he suspected, would it ever be articulated, although he had a vision of them all meeting years later and exchanging surprised and amused confidences about various housemates and campus figures concerning whom there might then be certainty where now there was only speculation.

He knew from rueful experience that it was hard, in this area, to separate fact from wishful thinking, and so he had always been absolutely circumspect on campus and around the house. Unlike his younger fraternity brother who wandered the Quad, whose affinity North suspected but had no intention of ever confirming, he himself never engaged in such dangerous practices. He had a handful of reliable friends, one on the Row, two in the halls, one young professor in the chemistry department, whom he had acquired over his years at the University, but all of them he had first met in the City, and it was to the City that they repaired on the relatively few occasions when they felt they could safely meet. Not for him the taking of chances and the flaunting of the gods of conventional society: he had too much at stake. This did not mean that there had not been, on a few occasions, wild and insanely chance-taking moments: everybody had those once in a while, under the influence of liquor or on the occasion of unexpectedly proffered, irresistible opportunity. But fundamentally, North McAllister was a steady and responsible young man who tried to manage, with more skill than many, what he had long regarded bitterly as a most unfair problem handed him by a mocking and inexplicable fate.

He sometimes thought that there might eventually come a time when he would, in the clichéd phrase, "adjust," either by accepting altogether or returning to the safe havens of societal convention. But the time had not come yet. He was still in the period of protest; as, he suspected, was his younger housemate. And the protest was even more unhappy and bitter now because recently, quite inadvertently, quite against his better judgment and his firm intentions, he had fallen in love.

He could pinpoint exactly when it had occurred. The autumn afternoon had been golden, the lazy peace of weekend had lain upon the campus, the air was soft and gentle, the world in perfect harmony amongst all things, as it could be, then, in the Santa Clara Valley. He had been studying on the front balcony and had looked up to see someone coming back from studying at the Libe. North had seen him a hundred times, talked and joked with him at the house, run into him on the Quad for friendly greetings on the way to or from classes, sat beside him at dinner. It had all been so orderly. But suddenly now in the golden light he seemed to glow with youth and happiness—an extra aura surrounded him—North had never seen him before. The wonder hit him with devastating force, his heart was lost and gone, totally out of his control. The world in an instant narrowed down to one laughing face and one pair of friendly eyes.

"Hi," the other called cheerfully, as he always did. "Haven't you anything else to do than study all day?"

"Nothing like it," North had called back, managing to sound natural, though his heart was pounding and he realized he was physically trembling. God, I will have to get over that, he told himself, and managed to control it sufficiently to get successfully through their brief exchange.

"Well, don't overdo it"—with a completely innocent and happy laugh. "We wouldn't want to lose you that way."

"No fear," North had responded as the other disappeared into the front door below. He wanted him to come to the balcony—and he wanted him never to come to the balcony. He did not, and that was the full extent of the moment. The initial crisis passed. But the wonder and the agony of it were with North now night and day. He did not know, in real despair, how he was going to handle it until he reached the end of the school year and the blessed release of graduation, which would take him, as he planned, to med school and thus out of the direct way of this new, fearful and almost irresistible temptation.

The thought that kept occurring to him was: Why not? He's a wonderful guy (everybody agreed on that), he wouldn't hate me, he wouldn't despise me, he'd accept me as I am, and maybe—just maybe—if I put it to him frankly—then just maybe—

The thought had become an obsession. He told himself it was insanity. It could very well destroy him if he gave in to it. Far from being the understanding forgiver of his wishful dreams, the other might well turn upon him publicly, expose him for what he was, devastate him utterly, the house, the campus, his future career—

North did not think he would succumb to an impulse so dangerous: but he was increasingly unsure. It would be a terrible, terrible chance to take. And yet he knew, with a sick certainty that if some intervention of God or fate or whatever you wanted to call it did not occur soon, he was almost certainly going to make the approach that could so easily end the world of acceptance he had so carefully crafted for himself.

He thought for a while now—as he heard the sounds of his brethren gathering for dinner, the house beginning to come alive, Haggerty on the piano as usual, the radio droning the latest from Europe, the sharp crack of the balls on the pool table—of B. J. Letterman and their curiously uneasy, unstable, half-serious, half-joking relationship.

His heart was swept by a sudden wave of pity for her, so appealing, so vulnerable, so overwhelmingly bright—and so baffled and upset by an adversary whose presence she was simply not equipped to suspect, or successfully do battle with if she did. He was not sure any woman could do battle with it, but he knew already of married situations where the wife did and either went away defeated or managed to convince herself that she had won a tenuous and ever-threatened victory. He could not conceive of B.J. in such a situation, affronted in the very heart of her femininity: it would destroy her. Certainly it would drive her from him forever. And if they were married—and if they had children—

It was why he had resisted, so far, her attempts and those of their friends to place them in the category of sure-to-be-marrieds into which so many of his classmates were beginning to fall as senior year progressed. He couldn't—it wouldn't be fair to her—it would be a betrayal of them both. It would, or so he thought now in his twenty-first year, destroy not only the loving and innocent heart of B. J. Letterman but the very essence and integrity of North McAllister.

And yet—and yet. Women did not repel him. He was not a virgin in either area. He could do it if he had to. And there were several excellent reasons why he should.

One was the paramount fact that she loved him: of that he was quite sure.

The second was that he had developed for her an affection that, while not right up there with Romeo and Juliet, was at least deep, compassionate, considerate, caring and quite capable, he believed, of making her happy and of lasting a lifetime. It could be "a good marriage," as good as, and in many ways a lot better than, a great many in the world. Millions settled for less. Why should he hesitate?

And there was his career. Bachelor doctors existed but most were married. In medicine perhaps more than most professions it conferred an aura of stability and solidity that patients valued and felt comfortable with. Like Guy Unruh, North intended to be a very good doctor; a settled family life was certainly a major part of it—and having reached that point, which he always reached in the merry-go-round that was his mind on this particular subject, he was confronted again in his mind's eye with the smiling face and engaging personality of his laughing love; and all else vanished.

He fought himself to a standstill for the better part of ten minutes. Then he went downstairs to the phone booth on the second floor and called his special friend on the Row, a football player in the Zete house. In matter-of-fact tones, with hearty references to girls in case they might be overheard, they arranged to meet in the City Friday night. Then he went back to his room, locked the door, flung himself into a chair and cried for a few agonized moments as though his heart would break.

Then he stood up, blew his nose, combed his hair and went down to the washroom, which fortunately was empty at the moment. There he mopped his face with cold water until the redness and swelling began to subside.

Got to be strong, he repeated in the dogged litany with which he encouraged himself when life threatened to become too much.

Mustn't give in.

Mustn't let it break me no matter what hell it puts me through.

Got to be strong . . . got to be strong . . . got to be *strong*.

And then he thought: Even as I'm being strong I'm being weak. So how do you figure that one, O God of Justice?

Or do You even bother to try?

For Moose, who had never had the problem, or if he had had long since forgotten it in the headlong chase for girls, it came as quite a surprise to find McAllister apparently getting over a crying jag in the washroom. At least, that's what Moose was pretty sure had been going on: there was an awful lot of splashing and extra water running if all North needed to do was wash his face and hands for dinner.

"Hey!" Moose said, never one for tact but always one for sometimes heavy-handed but unfailingly good-hearted sympathy. "Hey, Mac, what's up? I mean, are you O.K.?"

"Sure I'm O.K.," North said, looking him straight in the eye though his own were still inflamed. "How'd practice go today? Going to give 'em hell in Big Game?"

"Oregon first," Moose pointed out, "then Big Game. No, seriously, North, if there's anything I can do—"

"Nothing to do anything about," North said, rather shortly, Moose felt. He paused at the door. "I appreciate it, though, Moose. It's good of you to ask."

"Well," Moose said doubtfully. "Like I say, if there's anything—"

"No, no," North said quickly. "Forget it, O.K.? I'll see you at dinner."

"Sure," Moose said, still doubtful but deciding it would be best to drop it. "Let's hope Dewey has something besides that damned beef stew he always serves on Thursdays."

"I think he put one of Josephine's kittens in it last week," North said, sounding more like himself, and on their mutual laughter took himself away. But it was still a little odd, Moose thought. Kind of a funny guy, McAllister: pretty much a loner, not quite in the Main Group, as he thought of them proudly—himself and Willie and Latt and Unruh and Buff, with Haggerty sort of an independent, as Haggerty was, but still part of them. Everybody liked North and he apparently liked them, but there was a difference there, a separation. Moose had always felt it and so had the others. They had all mentioned it from time to time in rather baffled tones.

There was an inner core to North that was very reserved—not like Willie, who had it too but could open it up and let you in if he considered you worth it. Moose was grateful every day that Willie considered him that way. He would have been absolutely devastated if he had been kept out. He wasn't like North, who apparently didn't need any particular support from anybody.

Moose, he reflected humbly now, was not very self-sufficient and he did need support. He felt himself to be the luckiest guy in the world because he certainly had it from the guys in the house as well as from Welcome Waggoner, whom he hadn't seen in a couple of weeks and was beginning to get pretty hot for.

He knew the symptoms: he wouldn't rest now until he called her and they had another of their rough-and-tumbles. He had confided to Unruh not long ago that it was rather like tackling the entire U.C.L.A. backfield. Guy, who had been there himself on two or three occasions, grinned and said he found it more like riding the big wave at Waimea Bay. In either case, they agreed, it was an experience not to be scorned and perhaps not to be duplicated in a lifetime. If the lifetime was as domesticated as theirs would probably be.

Lately, though—which is why he had sort of cooled it with her in the past two weeks—Moose had found that Suzy was beginning to talk like the rest of them. Domesticity, he confided to Willie, seemed to be breaking out. There were little hints of a desire for something more long-term, a conspicuous cooing over babies when they had been at Fisherman's Wharf in the City recently, a sudden interest in attractive houses they happened to see; dreamy speculating on what it would cost a married couple to occupy one of them "after we graduate."

The whole thing had made Moose damned uncomfortable. He was beginning to think maybe he should get out of it before it was too late. When he had run into Willie in the hall a few minutes ago he had said as much.

"Just tell her, then," Willie suggested. "Don't be bashful. You know Welcome. You'll probably have to beat her head in with an ax to get her to let go. Which," he added severely, "is because you're probably the most easygoing sucker she knows. It would be like you to ignore all the other guys she's had and let her glom on to you as her ticket to a respectable married life." His tone softened into the amused affection so many of Moose's close friends used with him. "You're dumb, Moose. You'd better run like hell or Welcome will have you trapped before you know it."

"She can't 'trap' me," Moose said firmly. "I'm not going to get her pregnant, for Christ's sake. I always use a rubber."

"She doesn't have to trap you that way. You're so easygoing it isn't necessary. All she has to do is play on your good nature. You'll start feeling sorry for her pretty soon, and that'll be your doom."

"I *am* sorry for her," Moose admitted. "She's had a kind of a rough time of it, really, everybody always thinking they can sleep with her all the time—"

"Well?"

"Well, I *know*. But still, she's a nice gal, she always thinks the best of everybody—well, damn it, she *does*. She—she just *likes* it, that's all. And so," he added stoutly, "do I."

"Most people do," Willie remarked dryly, "but that doesn't mean you should get all gooey sentimental about a calculating character like Suzy Waggoner. I repeat, she's going to have you signed, sealed and delivered before you know what's hit you. You're halfway there already. For your own sake, pal, knock it off."

"But she's got to have *some*body! The poor kid is—"

"Anybody who refers to Welcome Waggoner as a 'poor kid,'" Wilson observed, "is lost already. I'm going to wash my hands of you, Moose. You're on your own with this one. God help you!"

"I'll do all right, thank you," Moose said with dignity. "Say, what's the matter with McAllister?"

Wilson looked surprised.

"I don't know. Is something?"

"I caught him in the washroom a while ago throwing water on his eyes. I think he'd been crying."

"Son of a gun. I wonder why."

"That's what I wonder too."

"Well, one thing's for sure," Willie said. "He isn't going to tell us. North's a pretty elusive character." He frowned and made a mental note which he filed away for future consideration. "I wonder what it is. It isn't like him to let his guard down."

"I don't think he meant to," Moose said. "I just stumbled in."

"You, Mooser?" Wilson inquired, giving him an affectionate poke. "You *never* stumble. The fleetest, the fastest, the most surefooted—"

"Sure, sure," Moose said. "I only hope I can be that way in Big Game."

"You will," Wilson assured him as they heard the first bell for dinner. "You'll be the star of the game."

"God," Moose said fervently. "Wouldn't that be *wonderful?*"

And all during dinner he dreamed of Big Game, absentmindedly feeding Napoleon, that malodorous beast, who had managed to crawl under the table when nobody was looking and then half-crouch just high enough to rest his drooling head beseechingly on Moose's knee. Completed passes in glorious succession, daring feints, sensational end runs, spectacular touchdowns chased themselves across Moose's mind until Napoleon, overcome by his own enthusiasm, tried to include his hand with a piece of meat.

"*Ouch*, God damn it!" Moose yelled. "Get out of here, you fucking monster!"

"Serves you right," Buff said as everybody laughed and Napoleon crawled rapidly away and out from under the table on the other side. "You know the rules about feeding that dog at dinner. Did he make a clean cut at the wrist?"

"Very funny," Moose said, nursing his hand, fortunately undamaged. "Very funny, Buff. He could have hurt me seriously."

"How could he do that?" Suratt inquired. "He doesn't have any teeth."

"*Oh*, yes he does, smart-ass," Moose retorted. "He could have ruined my game."

"Easy to do," Renny observed. "And no great loss."

At this some laughed but more hissed. Buff banged the table sternly with his spoon.

"Knock it off, you guys," he ordered. "Cut that crap, Renny, or I'll fine you. And Moose, *stop feeding that dog.*"

Down the table, Willie had made a point of sitting next to North, and observed him joining in the general hilarity just as always. His dark eyes sparkled, his rather florid good looks seemed the same. But still, Willie thought, he'd keep it on file.

Relieved of Napoleon's slavering attentions, Moose returned to his day-dreams. The great day was approaching. Ten days later it came. Various things advanced in the interim.

In the Men's Rest Home, Marc Taylor seemed to be eating and resting well. But he was, Mrs. Steadman reported, still very withdrawn, reading some, sleeping a great deal, not showing much interest in the copies of the *Daily* and the City newspapers she brought him, or the increasingly ominous news from Europe that came in crackling voices over the small Philco by his bedside. Dr. James stopped by every other day or so; Willie, Latt and Unruh visited at fairly frequent intervals. Galen Bryce tried a fatherly visit, unsuccessfully. Rodge Leighton, Hank Moore and Randy Carrero also came by. They filled him in on the latest doings at the house, where everybody was beginning to get swept up by the growing excitement of the coming game. Marc expressed a wanly polite interest but could not seem to rouse himself sufficiently to respond with any enthusiasm. His fraternity brothers worried. Dr. James shook his head and decided to call his parents. The possibility that he might have to leave school became stronger in all their minds, except Marc's—who, disturbingly, didn't seem to care one way or the other. Mrs. Steadman made plans for a big Thanksgiving for him and the two other boys who would be staying with her over the long weekend. Marc expressed only the vaguest interest. Mrs. Steadman, too, shook her head and pursed her lips. His parents offered to fly out from Pennsylvania for the holiday, but Dr. James advised that they wait a few days in case it might be necessary for them to come and take him home a little later on. He said he thought this would become clearer in another couple of weeks. Marc expressed no interest.

Moose did have another date with Welcome, Randy did make still another attempt to rid himself of the incubus that Fluff Stevens had become for him. Moose found Suzy as stimulating and satisfying a workout as ever, even if there were some more references to marriage, babies, houses and "after graduation." He attempted to ignore these and for once was not his usual amiable, responsive self when she made some pointed remark. Suzy sensed this and was smart enough to drop it and concentrate at the business at hand, which, as always, went very well. She was not at all nonplussed by his seeming disinterest in the future. She was quite confident that she had a good solid base to build on: certainly his gasps and groans and cooperative frenzies reassured her that her hold on him was as strong as ever. She told herself with comfortable complacence that there would be plenty of time for serious matters before the school year ended.

Randy, who had been carefully prevented from enjoying such transports with his tantalizing lady love, tried again to banish her forever from his life, and again failed. He was able to get a date with her—after several teasing changes of mind—for the same Friday night on which Willie and Marian, and North and his friend from the Zete house, went to their respective destinations in the City. Randy took Fluff there, too, after borrowing another thirty bucks from Latt, who, obliging as always, curtailed his own plans to go to the City and decided instead to take Kay to dinner at L'Omelette, that popular peninsula restaurant. Unruh and Maggie Johnson and Gulbransen and Karen Ann Waterhouse decided to join them. Other members of the house took various dates to various places. Some, less fortunate, joined company to go to a movie (*The Thirty-nine Steps* with Madeleine Carroll and Robert Donat and *Marie Antoinette* with Norma Shearer were the most popular at the moment) or stayed home and studied.

Everyone who dated had a pleasant evening except Randy and Willie. Marian seemed to have retreated, curiously, into the shy and elusive distance where she had kept herself prior to her father's appearance on campus. Fluff played her usual games with Randy. Try as he would, he could not get her to take him seriously when he said he didn't want to see her again.

"Oh, come on!" she said, laughing the carefree laugh with which she customarily greeted what she called his grumpiness. "You don't mean that! Why, it wouldn't be any *fun* if we didn't see each other!"

"Fun for you," he said, staring unhappily into the darkness of the eucalyptus grove near the stadium where he had parked his car after their return from dinner and dancing at the Mark Hopkins. "No fun for me."

"You're such an old *spoil*sport," she told him lightly. "All I get is grump, grump, *grump. Honestly!*"

"Why don't *you* be honest?" he asked bitterly, falling helplessly into the personal tone he always told himself he must not use but could not help. "You know we aren't getting anywhere and you know it's driving me bats. Why don't you just shove off?"

"And leave you all by your little self on this great big campus?" she inquired with the chuckling mockery he had come to hate. "I wouldn't do a thing like that to little old you! Besides," she said with a pretty pout, "I *like* having you around."

"Why? All you do is try to hurt me."

"I *do not!*" she exclaimed with great indignation which greatly became her, as it flushed her perfect face with highly attractive color. She looked the picture of complete sincerity and boundless health. He could hardly stand it.

"I'm not going to be calling you anymore," he said, "so don't expect it. And I'd appreciate it if you don't call me."

"You *know* I will," she said with a little gurgle of amusement. "I can't help it. You're so dashing!"

"Even your words are stupid," he said, hoping maybe that would do it. But as he had learned repeatedly, insults only made the game more fun.

"I love it when you get mad," she said solemnly. "I just *love* it. It makes you sound so *masterful.*"

"Oh, Christ," he said again in a muffled voice. "Of all the God damned crap."

"It is *not*," she protested indignantly. "It's the absolute truth. When I hear you use talk like that I think, oooh, what a man I've got. *I like it!*"

"You haven't got me," he said. "That's where you're in for a big surprise."

"Oh, *good!*" she said with mock excitement. "What will it be? Tell me!"

For a split second he considered grabbing her by the throat and saying something insane like "It could be *this!*" But he knew that really was insane, even to think it. With great difficulty he controlled himself. But he had broken out into a cold sweat and his hands and whole body were shaking.

"What's the matter?" she asked lightly. "Are you cold or something?"

"Yes," he said through clenched teeth. "You're walking on my grave."

"Oh!" she said, and for just a second the banter stopped and she did look genuinely upset. "What an *awful* thing to say! How can you *say* such a thing, Randy Carrero! Do you want to scare me half to *death?*"

"I want to make you listen to me," he said desperately. "You're de-stroying me—"

"Oh, don't be so dramatic!" she ordered, cheerful giggle returning. "People don't destroy people. You're so *serious* all the time. Can't I *ever* make you *laugh?*"

"Listen," he said, and was shouting though he didn't realize it. "*Listen.* I *do not want* to see you again. I *will not* call you. I *do not want* you to call me. I'm going to take you back to your house now and that's the last of it, do you hear me? The last of it! If I'm ever fool enough to try to see you again, may God strike me dead!"

"You see?" she said in a tired voice. "That's what I mean. You're always so dramatic."

The world suddenly seemed to whirl away and a furious anger seized him, a great roaring, raging tumult that seemed to be accompanied by a blinding white light. And so it was.

"It sounded pretty dramatic to me, too, miss," Happy Harmon said calmly, holding his flashlight about two inches from Randy's eyes. "What's the mat-ter, young fellow? Had too much to drink?"

"No, I haven't!" Randy said loudly.

For another second or two the world continued to spin out of control. Then it stopped abruptly and he slumped back exhausted in his seat for a moment. Then he cried in a strangled voice, "I'm going to throw up!" He wrenched open the door as Happy jumped back, staggered a few feet to the nearest eucalyptus tree and proceeded to do so.

"What is going on here, miss?" Happy inquired mildly. "Just a lovers' quarrel?"

"He thinks he's my lover," she said scornfully as Randy came woozily back to the car. "I guess. I don't know *what* he thinks he is."

"I was just telling her," Randy said between gulps of air, holding on to the hood to steady himself. "I was just telling her—that I didn't want—to see her—ever again. *That's* what it's all about."

"And were you agreeing to that, miss?"

"No, I wasn't," Fluff said. "He's said that so many times, and then come back, that I'm sick of hearing it. Just plain *sick*. He'll be calling me tomorrow morning and falling all over himself again. You just wait and see!"

"I really don't want to," Happy said with a smile which he tried to suppress out of respect to the dignity of the law. "I'd better have your names in case I decide to report this. You aren't supposed to be in this area at all, you know. Certainly not parking. I would highly recommend, Mr. Carrero, that you *do not* call Miss Stevens again."

Randy gave her a long bitter look. "I won't call her," he ground out, "and you tell *her* not to call me, either!"

"You heard him, Miss Stevens," Happy said. "Is that a deal?"

For a moment Fluff hesitated. Then she smiled a beatific smile.

"I'll try not to," she said sweetly. "Of course, there might be some reason that would come up . . . I mean, one never really knows, does one?"

"Mr. Carrero," Happy said solemnly, "good luck. Follow me."

The evening for Willie and Marian was in a much different key but, for him, equally frustrating. Not that he had in mind any great passionate culmination at this stage, he told Unruh next morning, but he did think things might advance a reasonable distance now that he thought they had an understanding. That seemed to be his mistake.

Not that she was unfriendly or uncommunicative or excessively withdrawn, or anything. She was just so *polite*, to the point where he finally said, "Look. Are you enjoying this at all? Would you like to go home? I don't want to impose myself on you if—"

She gave him a startled look. Her eyes widened and she shook her head. All around them the diners at the St. Francis were busily eating, talking, gossiping, clattering silverware, clinking glasses. Quite a few were already dancing. It seemed to him this table had been an island of conspicuous silence ever since they arrived. The ride up had been that way, too, in spite of his increasingly desperate attempts to keep the chatter going.

"Oh, no," she said. "I'm enjoying myself. Really I am. I'm just quiet, that's all. You'll have to understand that if—if we're going to be seeing each other."

He gave her the long slow candid look which he had found effective in similar situations.

"Are we?"

"Oh, yes, I hope so," she said quickly. "Also—" She paused and a little smile came into her eyes. "You don't understand what it is to be dating the student-body president. It's rather awesome, to tell you the truth."

"Now you're pulling my leg," he said with mock severity, "and I'm not sure I like it. You should have more respect for your elders."

"How much older?" she inquired, and when he said, "Probably about two years," she laughed again and said, "My, how ancient. I had no idea."

"I hope you won't mind pushing my wheelchair. Or would you rather dance?"

She looked suddenly shy again but stood up and moved gracefully into his arms as they took the floor. Her back, however, was rigid and when he touched it he realized she was trembling.

"Hey," he said, "I'm not going to bite you. Relax."

"You're not supposed to know I'm not relaxed!" she said, so strongly that he stopped in midstep, astonished. "You're not supposed to know all about me!"

"O.K.," he said hastily. "O.K., I don't know anything about you. I'm sorry I made the date, I'm sorry we're here, I'm sorry I ever thought it might be possible that we could be friends—let's go sit down."

"No, *I'm* sorry," she said with an uneven little laugh, resuming the dance. "I don't mean to be difficult. I just thought it was pretty personal, what you said."

"I apologize," he said, for a moment finding it difficult to pick up the rhythm again. "I just wanted to reassure you, that's all. I don't feel so easy either, if you want to know. I feel that I'm definitely on trial."

"I'm sorry—"

"No, I'm sorry—" he began, and laughed. "I think we'd better stop apologizing to each other or we won't finish a dance, let alone the evening."

He gave her a comical look that seemed to do the trick, at least for the time being. She laughed again, quite naturally, and did seem to relax finally. He realized that she was a very good dancer when she let herself go. He had learned his lesson, though: he mustn't tell her so.

"Did you like my father?"

"I liked him. Firm, I'd say. Somewhat set in his ways. In fact, I'd say likeable but quite inflexible. Has he ever struck you that way?"

She frowned thoughtfully.

"No, not really. He's a very indulgent father where my sister and I are concerned."

"Well, who wouldn't be? I think you'd be pretty easy to indulge, if you want my frank opinion."

"As long as it's as flattering as that," she said with a laugh, "I'll take it. You don't know how difficult I can be."

I'm beginning to get a faint inkling, he thought, but maybe that will prove to be just a passing thing. I hope.

"Not at all," he said firmly. "You're delightful. And I do appreciate your taking my side. I hope you will tell your father so. It would be a help."

"Oh, yes," she said as the dance concluded and they returned to the table, his hand on her back, which he was disturbed to find was still trembling despite the outward calm. "I'll tell him, all right. We have quite a few arguments at home about world affairs. We don't agree on very much."

"What about your mother and sister?"

"They agree with him, usually," she said. Again a smile. "I'm the difficult one. As I told you. I don't think you believe me, but it's true."

"I refuse to accept it," he said lightly. "Nobody as pretty as you are could be difficult about anything."

"I'm not pretty," she said. "Lots of girls at school are a lot more attractive than I am. Take Donna Van Dyke, for instance."

"Donn—" he said carefully, thinking: Oh-oh. Here we go. "Donn is a very beautiful girl, and a very bright one. And very, very capable. But that isn't everything."

"Oh, you mean there's something else?" she inquired with a skeptical little laugh. "I'd say that pretty well covers it."

"Look," he said, with a slight exasperation he thought was justified, "are we going to argue about Donna? I like her, she's a great gal, we met quite a while ago and have been friends ever since, she's vice-president of the student body, we work well together and always have—"

She gave him a wide-eyed look, apparently in all innocence though he wasn't so sure.

"They why are you here with me?"

"I repeat," he said, with real annoyance now, "if you want me to take you home, we'll go. Is that what you want?"

"No," she said, looking startled and stricken, which he considered somewhat exaggerated in view of the way she had appeared to deliberately twist the conversation, "that isn't what I want. *I* want to be here with *you.*"

"And I want to be here with you," he echoed dryly, "so can we stop this inane discussion and concentrate on enjoying ourselves? You aren't the first girl who's been jealous of Donna Van Dyke and no doubt you won't be the last. But you don't have to be jealous of her where I'm concerned. She's just a good friend, in my eyes."

"Does she know that? That isn't the way they talk about you two on campus. You're really an item, so I hear. I understand she's going to Carmel with you and your fraternity brothers for Thanksgiving—"

"Where in the world," he demanded in a wondering tone, "did you hear that?"

"Things get around."

"O.K.," he retorted in a tone deliberately indifferent. "Want to come along? There's plenty of room. It's a big place."

"What a gracious invitation!" she exclaimed, half angry, half laughing.

"Well!" he said shortly, digging into his food with some savagery. "I don't think this subject deserves much more."

"*Oh!*" she said in a stricken little voice, and he looked to see—*what else,* he thought disgustedly—the trembling lip, the crumpled jaw, the tender tear, beginning to roll down her cheek and drop, if she didn't stop it, squarely in the salad.

"*Oh,* come *on,*" he said. "Can't we stop this discussion? I felt sorry for Donn, that's all. She isn't going home for the long weekend, her folks live in New York state, she's going to be alone—"

"You mean nobody else invited that *popular girl?*" she demanded, removing the tear with a surreptitious swipe of her napkin. "She didn't have *anywhere else* to go? I don't believe it!"

He almost said, "Neither do I," but reflected in time that he did, after all, owe some loyalty to Donna. "It was just—just something I felt I should do, that's all. I just felt it was expected of me."

"Exactly," she said. "And so you did it."

"That's right," he said. "Sometimes you have to do what people expect of you. You can't be too unreliable. It's unsettling. Plus a betrayal to some degree . . . at least," he said, looking at her with half-closed contemplative eyes, "that's how I see it."

"What am *I* supposed to expect from you?"

"I don't know," he said, more lightly. "What do you want to expect?"

"I don't know," she said in what appeared to be a genuinely puzzled tone. "I really don't know."

"I think we'd better dance again," he said, standing up. "Service seems to be a little slow tonight and that will speed it up."

He held out his hand, she hesitated, then took it; they moved onto the floor. The back, he noticed, was still rigid and still trembling. What *was* this all about? For all the bravado, she must be terrified of him. A sudden wave of pity swept over him. He felt, not for the first time nor, he suspected with some considerable foreboding, the last, that he was stepping into quicksand. But he couldn't seem to stop, evidently. Nor, he knew, did he want to.

From then on, as he told Unruh next morning when he drove him into town rather than face the forbidding collection of odds and ends Dewey had left behind for their delectation on his weekend off, things reverted to meticulous politeness and seemed to go steadily downhill.

They danced a few more dances, finished the meal, did not linger. Neither seemed to want to. Their conversation on the way home was sparse and stilted. They were both relieved when he took her to the door, did not offer to kiss her, said good night with polite formality and drove off.

"How about you and Maggie?" he inquired next morning. Guy frowned.

"Oh, the usual. She comes on pretty strong, does old Maggie. Not climbing into my pants yet, though I know she'd probably love to if she could get over her upbringing. But very possessive in all other respects. We might as well be married already."

"You know you want to," Wilson said as they drove up Palm Drive, peaceful in the cool haze of oncoming winter. Guy sighed.

"Yes, I suppose so . . . yes," he said more strongly, "I do. But I had thought when I got to that stage there might be more—more romance to it, you know? Instead I find myself heading toward it pretty much because I'm expected to—and she expects me to—and *I* expect to."

He shifted his long legs, stretched a long arm along the back of the seat and gave his old roommate and permanent pal an unabashed affectionate hug. "Let's go up to the City and get laid. Want to?"

He removed his arm and leaned forward with half-mocking seriousness to study Wilson's face. Willie gave him a quizzical glance and shrugged.

"Nyaah. I haven't got any money. I still owe Latt thirty bucks for last night."

"I've got some money. I'll take care of it. You know you want to. There'll be no problems there. No sweat, no strain, no love, no pain. Everybody has a job to do, everybody does it, and that's that. I prescribe it as your doctor."

"You medical men," Willie said. "Always so *practical*."

Unruh chuckled. "Somebody has to be, otherwise what would growing boys do?"

"Listen!" Willie said, pulling abruptly into a parking space in front of Sticky Wilson's. "I only go up there with you about twice a quarter, if that often, and you know it."

"Do you enjoy it?" Guy inquired, studying him again. Wilson shrugged.

"I manage. Come on, let's go get something to eat."

"Right, I'm famished."

Shortly after five as they started out of the house to go to the City they ran into Latt, who was just returning from the Quad where he had been correcting freshman history papers in his capacity as assistant to the head of the department. Unruh looked expectant, Wilson philosophical. They were not feeling particularly proud of themselves but not particularly ashamed, either. It was just the way life was sometimes when you were twenty-one and the juices were flowing. Latt, who had seen those expressions and sensed that mood before, gave them a look they knew.

"Now, don't look so disapproving," Willie said. "We can't help it."

"You can and I am," Latt retorted, looking, for him, quite severe. "But it's none of my business. You do as you please."

"We'd rather have your understanding," Guy said, striking an elaborately beseeching pose. "Or at least your sympathy."

"Never," Latt said, smiling in spite of himself. "I've no patience with you."

"Oh, come on," Wilson urged. "Be human."

"Never," Latt said. "I just don't countenance it."

"O.K.," Guy said lightheartedly. "Some people are honest enough to go get it and some people jack off in the shower. Go ahead and do what you like."

"And I don't—" Latt began indignantly.

"Never?" Guy interrupted. "Now, come *on*, Latt."

"Never," Latt said firmly.

"Yeah, I know," Willie said. "Never in the shower. O.K. for you, Latt. We know what a hypocrite you are. We'll think of you."

"If you really did," Latt said with dignity, managing to suppress all traces of smile, "you'd be ashamed of yourselves and wouldn't go. I wash my hands of you. And don't forget you owe me thirty bucks, Wilson."

And he turned grandly away and stalked up the stairs, not looking back.

"You suppose he really is that disapproving?" Guy asked, more or less seriously, as they hopped in the car to begin the hour-long drive to San Francisco.

"Probably," Willie said. "But he'll get over it."

"And do you suppose he really does—?"

Willie looked wry.

"Doesn't everybody? And who gives a damn, anyway?"

"Well, that's right," Guy said. "I was just wondering." He grinned with sudden affection. "Good old Latt. What would we do without him?"

"I don't want to think," Willie said. "I just don't want to think."

14

Now Big Game was upon them and in the rising excitement all else became temporarily subordinate. Even Bates, whose editorials in the last few days had seemed unnaturally muffled though still concerned, stopped arguing with Hitler for a while and devoted himself to extolling the traditional rituals of interschool rivalry. He even permitted Nagatani to run an editorial that concluded exultantly, "Overriding the worries of our hectic age, this is the *real* reality. This is fun. This is what college is all about!"— even though everybody knew perfectly well that it was only a portion, though perhaps the happiest portion, of what college was all about.

Some members of the house confined themselves to the social side of it and participated only as spectators at major events. Others were more actively involved. Billy Wilson, who was developing a surprisingly good tenor, was one of the stars of the Big Game Gaieties the night before the game. Haggerty had contributed two songs, "simple little jingly melodies," as he called them, and several throwaway rhymes. He was always one of the mainstays of the production, which capped the pre-game festivities and set the final mood.

Thursday night always featured the Big Game bonfire at the lake, that seasonal body of water which, after winter's normally heavy rains, swelled in spring to a size adequate to accommodate sailboats, swimmers, divers, sunbathers, and the Water Carnival, featuring various competitions which this year seemed sure to be dominated by Jeff Barnett. The rest of the year the lake sank to an expansive reed-filled mudhole, abandoned by its vernal devotees to frogs, salamanders, turtles and mosquitoes.

Freshmen and sophomores had built the thirty-foot pile of wood and trash under the supervision of a committee of upperclassmen chaired by Bob

Godwin, "seeking his votes," as Suratt remarked, "wherever he can." It made a gorgeous blaze, flames and sparks shooting high into the chill November sky, the trash-stuffed effigy of Cal's Golden Bear expiring satisfactorily on the top to the accompaniment of recorded screams and bellows.

Willie, Latt and several others were involved in planning the reception for the alumni which would be held at the house immediately after the game. Hack of course would play the piano for it, Billy and Unruh had agreed to sing. A committee headed by Ray Baker was in charge of arranging food and drinks, officially nonalcoholic, although a few surreptitious injections would probably be added to the punch from time to time from some unidentified source. Dewey was given stern instructions on what to prepare and how to present it, to the point where he finally protested, "Now, y'all jes' leave me alone, hear? I know what to do and I'm goin' to do it. Ain't nobody complained about my cookin' yet!"—a statement he made, staring them blandly in the eyes, which provoked a burst of raucous laughter to which he responded by turning his back upon them and proceeding to do, as always, exactly what he pleased. "I only hope to God the result is edible," Ray remarked, a sentiment echoed fervently by his brethren. Going on past performance, they decided it probably would be—just. They knew it wouldn't matter, though. In the happy euphoria of Big Game, and after a few slugs of the mysteriously fortified punch, nobody would mind. Particularly if the University won.

For this outcome, one house member felt he had to assume responsibility for the whole team, and to his care, feeding and general morale Rodge Leighton found himself devoting considerable time in the final hours before the game. A few weeks ago Rodge had asked Coach if he needed an extra hand, and Coach, remembering how loyally Rodge had attended practices and the bond that had grown between himself and his big, lumbering friend, had said he sure could. Rodge was happy, Moose was content and, Coach hoped, would duplicate his Fucking Asshole Touchdown, or at least perform at the peak of his abilities.

To do this, however, he would have to be convinced that he could, and this, Rodge found, demanded all his talents of friendship and persuasion. Along about Friday noon, as was his habit before a game, Moose went into a blue funk. This time it seemed excessive: Rodge had never seen his friend so apparently buffeted by the harsh winds of fate. One would have thought the whole world was collapsing around him.

"Look, Moose," Rodge said patiently, massaging his neck and shoulders in the comforting way he had learned in the fieldhouse, while Moose sat dejectedly in his room staring at the big toe that was popping out of one of his woolen socks, "you're going to do a great job Saturday. What's the problem?"

"I don't think I am," Moose said mournfully. Rodge stopped massaging.

"Then of course you aren't," he agreed matter-of-factly. "Why don't you call in sick and tell Coach you can't play? Or I'll call him, if you like."

Moose swung half around and glared at him over his shoulder, so fiercely that Rodge thought for a moment he might have gone too far.

"Are you *crazy?*" Moose demanded. "What the fuck do you mean, I can't play?"

"I didn't say you couldn't play," Rodge said calmly, pushing him back into position and renewing the massage. "I just said if you were going to chicken out I'd call Coach and make your excuses for you."

There was a surge under his hands but he kept them firmly in place. "What more can you ask of a friend?"

"If you weren't my friend," Moose growled, "I'd pop you one." But the tension eased. "I'm not chicken."

"No, I don't think you are," Rodge ageed. "I was afraid maybe *you* thought you were. You were beginning to talk that way."

"I was *not!*" Moose said indignantly. "I just said I—"

"You just said you weren't going to do a great job Saturday. Lean back a little."

Moose obliged.

"Work on my right shoulder a little more," he directed. "There's a little muscle strain there . . . that's it. Good. I didn't say I wasn't going to do a great job on Saturday—"

"You said you didn't *think* you were. That's what counts, what you *think*. You've got to think positively about it, Moose. If you have to think at all. *I* think it would be a lot better if you stopped thinking and just went out there and played. You've had all the training—all your instincts are right. Let 'em go!"

"But it's Big Game," Moose said with an abrupt return of gloom. "I can't afford to let everybody down in Big Game."

"Who the hell," Rodge demanded, "said you were going to let anybody down? It's Big Game. Anything can happen in Big Game, you know that. It doesn't matter what team it is or what its record is, when it comes to its own special Big Game, anything can happen."

"But I'm afraid I might not—"

"Stop it!" Rodge ordered. He gave Moose's shoulders one more deep squeeze and a concluding slap and stepped back. "There. That ought to make you feel better."

"It does," Moose said gratefully. He swung around and looked up. His tone became earnest. "And *you* make me feel better. You're a real friend and I appreciate it. Everybody thinks a guy like me is big and tough—(No, they don't, Rodge thought affectionately. Not if they know you.)—but I'm not, really. I just fool 'em. I need people to build me up. And you really support me, you really do. You're really a nice guy, Rodge, you put up with me right down the line. I don't deserve you, really. I'm sure damned glad you're my friend. It means a lot."

"Well, thank you, Moose," Rodge said, surprised and touched by this unexpected and uncharacteristic effusion but not embarrassed by it because it was so obviously spontaneous and genuine. "It means a lot to me, too, and I appreciate your telling me. You know how you can prove it? You can get in there Saturday and play like hell and—"

"—and help us win the Game," Moose concluded with him, nodding his head vigorously and looking suddenly less burdened by life. "I'll sure as hell try! By God, I sure will!"

"That's more like it," Rodge said, picking up his books to go along to the room he now occupied alone in Marc Taylor's absence. "That's all anybody can ask."

And maybe, he thought, it would be enough. One would sure hate to see old Mooser trip on his own shoelaces on his last day as a football hero.

From all over Row and dorms and rapidly filling parking lots, eighty-nine thousand lucky ticket holders streamed toward the stadium. Along Highway 101 and down Palm Drive the traffic crept bumper-to-bumper. In the groves that surrounded the stadium, thousands of tailgate parties were under way. Picnic hampers were open, wine and heavier drinks were flowing freely despite University regulations which on this particular day simply could not be enforced. Good-natured jeers and catcalls greeted the arrival of each new car bedecked with Cal's blue and gold, each grinning party of Cal students and alumni sporting the enemy colors. With happy exuberance the jeers and catcalls were returned at every glimpse of the University's cardinal red. The world was a happy place. Hitler and the threat of war were almost forgotten. For one of the last brief happy times in quite a while, the world was carefree, innocent and fun.

In through the gates they went, surrendered tickets, climbed patiently in their thousands up the outside stairs and then worked their way slowly down the crowded stairs inside. Over all the vast bowl there rose a rustling hum of excited talk, laughter, shouts, anticipation. Eveyone's prayer had been answered: the weather, beginning to turn more frequently bad, was blessedly perfect for this one day—clear, crisp, bright, the sky an unbelievable blue, the grass truly an emerald green, the whole vast restless crowd a constantly moving spangle of blue and gold and cardinal red.

Most of the house had managed to sit together in the student section on the fifty-yard line and as the team in its brilliant crimson and white came trotting into view a loyal shout of "MOOSE! YEAH, MOOSER!" went up, echoed and relayed around the stands until it was presently lost in other shouts for other heroes. Down on the field a familiar figure clasped hands above its head and did a little dance.

There was constant movement and swirl of color down there for a few moments as members of the teams jumped up and down, swung arms, felt arm and leg muscles, slapped each other encouragingly on the back, went through their usual pre-game rituals of firing themselves with the requisite enthusiasm. Somebody spotted Rodge's wiry little figure bustling about on the sidelines, and another brief shout of "YAY, ROGER!" went up. He stopped dead and turned to look up with a grin so broad and pleased they could see it from where they sat. The teams took their positions, a great hush fell on the stadium. Cal won the toss, kicked the ball high and far into the sparkling air. A great shout succeeded the great hush and the game was on.

For the first quarter, Moose hardly knew where he was. Twice he dropped the ball when it was passed to him, several times he failed to do the blocking he was supposed to do. Waves of sound rolled over him as the teams moved back and forth and their respective supporters gave voice in the stands. He felt as though he were operating underwater or on some mountaintop where he was, curiously, all alone. He was vaguely aware at one point of Rodge yelling at him, "Get in there and fight, Moose! Get in there and fight!" But when he turned his head to acknowledge it, which of course he shouldn't have done, he tripped, fell down and was momentarily lost beneath a wave of pounding thighs and trampling boots, from which he emerged luckily unharmed but badly winded.

"What *is* the matter with that friend of yours?" Coach demanded. Rodge, looking white, said, "I don't know, sir, but I'm sure he'll be better."

"He'd God damned well better be," Coach snapped, "or he's going to sit on a bench for the rest of the game!"

"Oh, that would kill him, sir!" Rodge cried in dismay.

"Better him than the whole fucking team!" Coach retorted and turned his back.

Rodge slumped down on a bench, thinking: Oh, God, Mooser, come *on*.

The first quarter dragged by, the second followed at an equally uninspired pace. It was not, all agreed, one of the more brilliant Big Games of all time. Cal, though the favorite going in, was not playing well either. Moose continued to function as though in slow motion, although just before halftime he seemed to snap out of it somewhat and began to move at a livelier and more competent pace. It was not enough to save him from a locker-room blast at halftime from Coach, who told him he was going to be benched in the third quarter, "and after that we'll see what happens."

Moose looked absolutely stricken and all Rodge could do was give him a surreptitious grip on the shoulder. Moose looked up with such a lost and desolate expression that Rodge was quite sure he didn't even know who Rodge was. Oh, *God*, Rodge thought, not exclamation but appeal. Help him, help him, *help him*!

Out on the field during halftime the bands marched, played school fight songs, Sousa, popular show tunes. Cheerleaders bobbed up and down before the opposing stands, led their fellow students in card displays of varying degrees of taunt and insult, concluded finally with renditions of the famous yell that paid tribute to the trophy that always went to the winner for temporary custody:

"Give 'em—the Axe—the Axe—the Axe! Give 'em the Axe, give 'em the Axe, give 'em the Axe, WHERE? Rightintheneck the necktheneck, right-intheneck the necktheneck, rightintheneck, rightintheneck, rightintheneck, THERE!!!"

Hoots, shouts, yells, applause—excitement building up again: maybe the second half would be better. The hush fell, the gun sounded, the ball was kicked again into the clear blue sky, becoming golden now as the air turned chill and the dying sun slanted low across the deep green field and the spangled stadium. The welcoming roar went up again. Two minutes into the quarter Cal intercepted the ball and scored a touchdown. The blue-and-gold segments of the stadium went into ecstasies. The cardinal reds sank into glum and anxious silence, not much relieved when Cal failed to convert and was stopped at six points instead of seven.

"That's what happens when he takes Moose out," Hank Moore said loyally, and his elders smiled tolerantly.

"I wish Moose made all that much difference today," North McAllister said, "but I'm afraid he doesn't."

This made them all even glummer as the third quarter slogged to its end after a lot of pushing, shoving, feints, pile-ups, passes and attempted field goals that did not succeed. It began to appear that the game was settling down to a grim determination by Cal to protect its lone touchdown and an increasingly weary attempt by the University to break through and score at least one of its own. The conviction was growing in the stands that this was not to be. At the end of the third quarter some cynics began to leave, although most settled in grimly to see it through, telling each other frequently that you never knew, with Big Game. You just never knew.

All through the fourth quarter, however, the pattern continued . . . until three minutes from the end. At that moment things changed, history was made, the stuff of collegiate legend sprang full-blown from the brow of Zeus or somebody, brave men bellowed, frail women wept and screamed, and the world became an insane, unbelievable, marvelous, magical, wonderful place.

Back in the game, chastened, desperately determined and also muttering his own little prayer to the Almighty, Moose did it again.

He wasn't where he was supposed to be, nobody including himself knew exactly how he got where he was, but by some miracle of man or nature it put him directly in the path of a desperate Cal defensive pass. He did intercept it—he did find the ball precariously dancing on the tips of his fingers—he did sway, turn, writhe, contort, almost tumble full-length trying to capture it as the stadium went wild—he did rescue it, just barely but enough—he did clutch it desperately to his chest, turn and begin to run as fast as he could toward the Cal goal—he did duck, dodge, weave, evade, plunge headlong foward as throats whose owners thought themselves incapable of further sound managed more—he did begin, it seemed to him as he loped down the field and the opposition melted finally away, almost to fly—for a magical few seconds he became the daring young man on the flying trapeze, he sailed through the air with the greatest of ease, he was flying—flying—flying—floating serenely through the heroic skies of November toward his triumphant moment—twenty yards—thirty—forty—forty-seven total, this time—carrying them all with him into a universe filled with glory in which he and they were forever young—forever masterful—forever free from care and worry and the ultimate burdens of growing old—forever frozen in their shared moment of wonder and exultation—MOOSE! . . . MOOOOSE! . . . MOOOOOOOSE!

"HE'S MAKING ANOTHER GOD DAMNED FUCKING ASSHOLE TOUCHDOWN!" Franky bellowed, pounding Willie so hard that he yelled, "O.K., O.K., I see him, you don't have to break my God damned shoulder!" "THEN BE EXCITED!" Franky roared, grinning. "I AM EXCITED!" Willie roared back, turning to pound him with equal vigor while everywhere among the dots of cardinal red others were doing the same as the sky split open and the universe became for them one great roar of happy, hilarous sound.

North's friend from the Zete house kicked the ball between the goalposts. Above in the stands, with a curious mixture of pride and poignancy, he thought: That belongs to me. And then he thought: For a little while.

The University had triumphed 7–6.

The closing gun sounded and the game was over.

In the wild flurry that followed as students and alumni swarmed down on the field for the transfer of the Axe and team members thwacked each other over the heads and whatever other parts of the anatomy were reachable, Moose looked through the phalanx of congratulatory arms and bodies that surrounded him to see a familiar figure racing toward him. He broke away to race toward it. "I did it!" he shouted. "I did it, I did it, I DID IT!" "*You sure did!*" Rodge shouted back as they met with a thud and began hugging each other ecstatically, happy tears and exultant laughter mingling. They quickly broke apart, self-conscious, but they needn't have been because many others were doing the same. A lot of people cried from sheer excitement and glee over that one.

Back at the house an hour later it was congratulation-time all over again as upwards of fifty alumni and their wives drifted in to drink what Buff called "Wowee Punch" and consume (somewhat tentatively, after the first bite) some of the rather peculiar-looking hors d'oeuvres Dewey had prepared for display on the dining-room table. Smitty Carriger, Tony Andrade, Lor Davis and Hank Moore stood behind the table dispensing the refreshments, Haggerty played the piano while Billy and Guy led school songs, and the room was filled with camaraderie, reminiscences, graying heads and round little paunches. God, Wilson thought, there we are twenty years from now. The thought made him shiver, and when he caught Buff's eye and saw his expression he knew it was making him shiver, too. But they all were on their best behavior, perfect hosts, friendly and gracious and chatting away like magpies, as Gulbransen expressed it when the last alum and his beginning-to-get-scrawny wife finally wandered somewhat wobbily out the door two hours later. The scene was replicated everywhere up and down the Row and in many of the hall eating clubs. The campus was awash with sentiment.

Moose did not appear until about half an hour into the party, having been delayed in the field house by a constant stream of students and alumni wanting to shake his hand, pound his back, hug him, kiss him and otherwise "maul me over," as he murmured to Rodge when, dignity restored, they stood side by side in an impromptu receiving line.

Finally they were able to break away and walk back to the house, Moose acknowledging cheers and applause everywhere along the way from the crowd now streaming back to cars or campus domiciles. Even Cal rooters cheered him good-naturedly, which he rather expected but still thought was pretty nice of them.

"Feel pretty good, don't you?" Rodge inquired as they finally left the last of the celebrants and started up the Quad.

"I sure do," Moose said with a big grin. Then he suddenly looked forlorn. "Except now, you know, Rodge—it's all over. That's all there is. I won't ever play a game for the University again. I'm going to graduate in a few more months. *It's over.*"

And he looked for a moment as though he might cry again, until Rodge, much touched, hit him on the shoulder and said briskly, "Oh, come on now, Mooser! You've just got the senior blues. There's plenty of things left to enjoy between now and June. Snap out of it. You're the biggest hero in the whole university right now, so be happy. *Be happy!*"

"Yes," Moose said, brightening again. "I did play a pretty damned good game, didn't I?"

"You sure did," Rodge said loyally. "You couldn't have been better—at least," he added, "the ending couldn't have been better."

"That's right," Moose acknowledged with a sheepish grin. "That ending made up for a lot, didn't it?"

Haggerty was the first to spot him when he came in—Rodge entered, deliberately a little ahead, and the minute Hack saw him he swung into a foot-stomping rendition of the fight song. The alumni cheered, his fraternity brothers cheered, everything was happy and excited again as the man of the hour shambled in, suddenly feeling quite awkward and shy. Two quick belts of Wowee Punch soon relaxed him, however, and he even wolfed down a half-dozen of Dewey's hors d'oeuvres in rapid succession, which mightily pleased Dewey, peering through the peephole in the kitchen door.

There was a lot more contratulatory talk, a lot more "mauling over."

Then the last alum departed and Wilson shouted, "Hot damn! All aboard for the City!"

And Big Game Night began.

High and happy on the sheer excitement of it, Moose drifted through the evening in a euphoric daze. He told Suzy at the end of it (when they were safely ensconced in a small, complaisant hotel near Union Square) that he figured he had shaken the hands of at least a thousand woozy alumni, been kissed by at least as many amicably groggy alumnae as the party from the house moved through the hours from the Fairmont to the Mark Hopkins on Nob Hill and then down Powell Street to the Sir Francis Drake, to end up at the St. Francis. The streets were filled with happy University and Cal students shouting, cheering, singing, blowing horns, cranking noise-makers, dancing in impromptu conga lines and weaving snakes in and out of hotel lobbies and through and around Union Square. Big Game Night in those days engulfed the City in a way it was not to do in more sophisticated, and therefore drabber and less carefree postwar days. Life could be fun, then, and the young were still young enough to enjoy it. The town turned itself over to them and they and the town reveled in it.

With the exceptions of Franky and Katie Sullivan and Latt and Kay Ellsworth, who were driving down for a weekend together at the Del Monte Lodge at Pebble Beach, all the other seniors were in the party from the house. Baker, Bates and Richardson were with not-so-serious dates they had arranged for the evening, the rest were with their regulars: Haggerty and Fran Magruder, North and B.J., Moose and Welcome, Unruh and Maggie, Wilson and—Donna, Willie having considered and rejected the idea of trying to set something up with Marian.

Got to make the break with Donna sometime, he told himself, but somehow he couldn't quite bring himself to do it Big Game Night. Not only had he committed himself for Thanksgiving, but it was so—*expected* that he and Donna be together on this occasion, as they had been for the past three years. He knew it would devastate her if he were to abandon her on this particular night of all nights; he knew he just couldn't do it. He was impatient with himself for what he felt was cowardice and reluctance to come to grips with it, but he just couldn't. Perhaps he would see Marian somewhere along the way and at least get a chance to dance with her. That would be something.

But when he did see her and catch her eye across the dance floor of the Mark, he knew it was a futile hope. She looked startled, he saw her eyes sweep over Donna, a closed expression came over her face, that was it. She didn't even acknowledge his tentative attempt at a greeting but looked vaguely past his ear as she was swept away by her date, some immature and scrawny little kid who looked too young to be even a freshman, though he was probably at least a sophomore or maybe even older. Willie didn't know him and wondered what she was doing with such an obviously callow jerk. Probably something that had been set up weeks ago and she couldn't get out of it. Forgetting that he hadn't even asked her to get out of it, he figured that must be the only explanation.

"See somebody you know?" Donna asked brightly and attempted to swing him around so that she could see too; but for once he refused to cooperate with her invariable tendency to lead. She didn't get away with it this time. He held her firmly in check and said cheerfully, "Oh, just some guy from the halls. I wonder if Ari Katanian is here tonight?"

"Probably here somewhere," she said, conceding to superior force and snuggling her head against his chest as the most effective alternate strategy, which he hoped Marian didn't see. "We'll probably run into him sooner or later. . . . It's a great night, isn't it?"

"It's always a great night," he said. "Our last Big Game Night as undergrads."

"We'll be back," she said confidently. "Won't we?"

"Oh, I suppose so," he agreed, thinking: Here we go again. "It depends on where I'm living, I suppose, whether I'll be back."

"It depends on where we'll all be living," she said with her little gurgle of laughter. "I expect it'll be somewhere around the Bay, won't it? That's what I hope happens to *me*, anyway. It's in my blood, now."

"Mine too," he conceded. She gave his arm a little squeeze.

"Then it *will* be here, right?"

"I'm more or less expecting it will be, for me," he said carefully.

"Oh, good!" she said. "Then I don't have to worry."

He started to challenge this, then thought better of it and decided to say nothing. But he did sigh, quite heavily, then coughed and pretended he hadn't as the band swung into another number and they moved out across the floor, Donn humming happily in his arms.

Damn it, he thought, why do I get into these situations? Across the room he saw Marian and her date leaving. She looked back for an instant and her eyes swept over them again without a sign of recognition. Then they were gone. Ah, well. If they were going on to the other hotels, he'd catch up with them again before the night was over. And if they weren't, but were going somewhere else? And to do—what?

He didn't want to think.

Her date was such a *jerk*.

"Hey!" Unruh said, bumping his elbow as he and Maggie sailed by. "A penny for your thoughts."

"Aren't worth it," he called after them. "How about yours?"

"Ha, HA!" Guy said in a tone that was designed to make Maggie giggle, and did.

Actually, he thought as he saw Willie and Donn stop dancing and work their way off the crowded floor to the two tables where their party was established, their thoughts were probably quite similar. Here was Maggie, short, a bit plump and obviously going to get plumper, loving, cheerful, considerate, concerned—just begging to be a doctor's wife—why in the hell was he restless, vaguely uneasy, vaguely dissatisfied? It was stupid. She was everything he needed, she obviously felt she needed him, it was probably inevitable—why not relax and enjoy it? They hadn't, as the saying went, "gone all the way," but that would come when they were married and its absence had nothing to do, he believed, with his current mood. Whatever he wanted in that line he could get elsewhere on campus or he could persuade Willie to come up to the City with him and they'd find it in the commercial area. He and Willie weren't the only ones and Guy honestly didn't think it made the slightest difference to either of them or to their respective characters, which he thought were pretty damned good when all was said and done.

He didn't feel guilty about it at all, he told himself firmly now as Maggie clung gently to him while he swung her masterfully about the solidly packed floor in what he referred to later as "a real butt-bumper." It was that clinging softness that was going to win out in the end, he knew. He too sighed and when she rested her head gently on his chest, responded by lowering his cheek to rest against her soft brown hair.

What could you do? You couldn't fight it. Mrs. Doctor Unruh, here I come.

For Haggerty and Fran, still squabbling intermittently over their respective desires for a career, no such thoughts on either side disturbed the evening. For them, the basic question had been decided a couple of years ago, and it wouldn't have occurred to either of them to worry about it now.

"Hey, lady," he said, squeezing the hand she was resting comfortably on his arm as they sat close together watching the crowd. "Having a good time?"

"Oh, yes," she said. She chuckled. "I get such a kick out of watching Moose. He's so pleased with life right now."

Hack smiled.

"And so he should be. It's a great way to wind up his football career. Particularly when we were all convinced nothing like it was ever going to happen again. He showed us."

"He sure did," she said. "And yet, you know? I don't really think Moose looks at it that way. I think to him it's just something that happened and he was very lucky it did, and he's deeply grateful, and—and sweet."

He smiled again.

"Yeah, he's like that. A gentle soul, our Mooser, underneath it all." He chuckled suddenly. "He's getting scared of Welcome's matrimonial intentions, though. He's been telling some of us that he thinks she's really after him now. He's getting worried."

"I would be, too," she said becoming serious. "I like Suzy—as who doesn't, in spite of her reputation—but, really! Moose can do better than that."

"I have," Hack said complacently. "But then, not everybody's so lucky."

"You!" she said. "You certainly sound smug about it. How do you know you can be so sure of me?"

"If I'm not by this time," he said, squeezing her hand again, "I must be in pretty bad shape. Do you make cow eyes at anybody else? Do you—"

"I don't make cow eyes at you!" she interrupted with mock indignation. "Where did you get that—that *twenties* expression?"

"I'm a twenties kind of a guy," he said, suddenly jumping to his feet and pulling her after him as familiar music began. "Let's Charleston!"

"How old-fashioned can you get?" she demanded. But she matched him twirl for twirl and hop for hop and in a minute or so the crowd had parted to make room for them and they were really putting on an exhibition that brought cheers and whoops at the end.

"There!" she said, dark beauty flushed with laughter and excitement as they walked, hand in hand and out of breath, back to the table. "I hope you're satisfied!"

"With you," he said with an exaggeratedly low bow as they sank down beside North and B.J., who had just come in from the Fairmont, "*always.*"

"I heard that!" B.J. said, clever little face alight with its usual warmly welcoming expression. "What a compliment!"

They both sensed the slight wistfulness she couldn't keep out of her voice and assumed North did, too. But he only continued to scan the crowd with a vague little smile. So Hack decided to plunge in.

"I'm sure old North here pays you compliments all the time," he said. "I try to parcel mine out at intervals so Fran won't get too spoiled."

"*I'm* not spoiled!" B.J. said, with what in a girl more sure of herself and her companion would have been irony. But it came across as ruefulness and made them both considerably annoyed with North; which, as Fran remarked later when they were driving back to campus, "you expect to be on other occasions. But *Big Game Night?* Honestly!"

"Have you two been dancing, North?" she asked now, a little more sharply than she had intended. He pulled his eyes, apparently searching for someone or something on the dance floor, away and gave her a slow, contemplative look.

"We've managed a few. B.J.'s damned good but I'm not so hot. So we decided to sit it out for a while."

"You are too!" B.J. protested. "You're very good." She laughed and tried to keep it light, but again, her next comment didn't sound that way: "I think you just don't want to dance with me."

"Well, *I* do," Hack said, rising to his feet abruptly, taking her hand and pulling her after him as he had Fran. "Let's go! . . . To hell with him," he said cheerfully as they swung out into the sardinelike crush of butt-bumpers. "Isn't that right?"

"That's *right!*" B.J. agreed, a little shakily but sounding more like herself. "*We'll* have fun, anyway!"

"That's the only way to handle him," Haggerty said. "Let him stew in his own juice if he wants to."

"He gets so moody sometimes," she said, sounding worried again. "I don't know what it is, Hack. Do you suppose it's me? Am I failing him in some way?"

"No, you're not," Hack said very firmly, because he had suspected from time to time that he might know what North's problem was and found himself in the delicate position of wanting to protect them both from hurt. The sooner they got married, *he* thought, the better for them both. His tone became even more positive. "He *is* a moody guy sometimes, we notice that in the house, but that doesn't mean he isn't a good guy or that he doesn't like you, because we all know he does. He *really does* enjoy being with you, B.J. Believe me."

"That isn't the same as saying he might—might—" she hesitated and then decided to trust Hack, always so kind, considerate and understanding of everybody—"want to get married when school ends."

"Do you want to marry him?" he asked, keeping time for a moment to let them be carried a few steps by the human tide around them as he stared down into her troubled eyes.

"I think I would like to, yes," she said finally. "But—" she looked suddenly desolate—"if he doesn't really want to—"

"He does," he said emphatically. "He *does*. Now, you just hold on to that thought and don't let the temporary moods throw you off."

"But what's the matter?" she asked in a bewildered tone. "Why does he have these moods if it—if it isn't me?"

Hack, he told himself, hang in there. You can't afford a slip now. They're both depending on you.

"Who knows what another person is really thinking?" he asked, more lightly. "One just has to have trust. It makes every sense in the world for him to want to marry you, attractive and clever and bright—*God!*" he interrupted himself to say dramatically, and it evoked a smile—"*how bright you are!* It's a crime! I mean, you have everything, B.J. If I weren't hopelessly involved with that—that *lawyer* over there, I'd snap you up in a minute, myself. You'd be a great catch for anybody. And North knows it, and one of these days he's going to tell you so. You'll see. Take my word for it."

"Well," she said, with a wistful little smile, "I'd like to, Hack. I would like to—"

"Believe me," he said firmly, thinking: Don't let me down, pal, don't let me down. It's for your own good. "Everything will be *all right*. You'll see."

She smiled the wistful little smile again and made no comment. He swung her back firmly into the lively rhythms of the dance and they said no more on that subject.

For several moments after they left the table Fran had remained silent while North continued his slow survey of the floor. A waiter came by, they showed driver's licenses proving they were over twenty-one, ordered two light gin and tonics, her second for the evening, his third. They clinked glasses and he said, "To Moose."

"I'll drink to that," she said with a smile. Then she added evenly, "And to B.J., who is a wonderful girl who doesn't look happy tonight."

He looked startled but she didn't stop.

"Why isn't she happy, North? Why do you make her unhappy?"

He shot her a sudden look, dark eyes and handsome face shadowed for a second by emotions she couldn't analyze, sensitive though she was and good at the legal profession she had chosen for herself. Then whatever it was vanished and he smiled, a perfectly natural smile.

"I'm sorry," he said. "I wasn't aware I was making her unhappy. I *am* sorry for that."

"Come on, North," she said. "You're a very bright guy. And a perceptive one. You know she's unhappy. She tries to hide it but it's pretty obvious. To Hack and me, anyway."

"I bow to your astuteness," he said, and did so with a gesture tinged with mockery. Then he looked more serious. "I said I'm sorry if I'm the cause of it. I don't mean to be. I'll just have to try harder, I guess."

"It isn't a matter of 'trying,'" she said. "No girl wants to feel a fellow is 'trying' to enjoy her company. She wants to feel he really does want to be with her. I don't think B.J. feels that with you. And we don't sense it either."

"Well," he said sharply, "if I'm made to feel that I'm under observation and judgment all the time, I might as well be by myself—"

"No," she said with equal sharpness, putting her hand on his arm. "That's silly. That isn't what I'm saying at all. I'm just saying you shouldn't hold back. I think you are. I think you really would enjoy being with her if you'd just—just—if you weren't so—so—reserved, I guess is the word. You *are* reserved, North, very much so. You do a lot of laughing and joking with everybody, but you *yourself* are hidden away inside somewhere where nobody seems to be able to reach you."

Again the quick play of emotion, indecipherable, impregnable, swiftly gone.

"Isn't everybody?" he asked quietly. "Isn't everybody 'hidden away inside'? Isn't that the human condition? Isn't that why it's so hard for *anybody* to really know *anybody*? What's so strange and unique about that? And if I may ask, *counselor*, what's so wrong with it?"

"Nothing," she said, rather helplessly. "I'm not saying it's unique and I'm not saying it's wrong—except as it hurts other people. Then I think it gets into an area where it's debatable whether it's wrong or not. If what we do hurts others, *I* think it's wrong."

"Perhaps others expect too much," he said, staring moodily out at the dance floor. "Perhaps it's their problem, not mine."

"No," she said. "No, that's not it. If you allow them to believe they should expect a certain response from you, and you don't give it, then that's your problem too. At least I think so."

"Then perhaps," he said, turning to face her squarely, "perhaps I should retreat permanently into a cave and not impose that kind of burden on anybody. Would that be better, Fran?"

"You're trying to confuse me," she said, half laughing.

"You're the lawyer," he said, half amused too but giving no ground. "You're supposed to do the confusing. You're not supposed to be confusable."

"Well, I am," she said, "and I admit it. So why do you put yourself in a position where B.J. expects things of you, if you have no intention of giving them to her?"

"Who said I won't?" he asked quickly. "Just because my timetable may be different from yours or—" he added with some sarcasm—"the other people who judge me—doesn't mean that I'm not working on one. You see—" and for a second the strange unhappiness came and went again across his face—"maybe I put myself in a 'position,' as you put it, because that's the way to make myself live up to what people expect of me—perhaps it's so I won't have any choice but to get out of my cave. If I don't move as fast once I'm out as people want me to, then maybe it's because—" his voice sank so she had to lean forward to hear it—"because it's *hard.* Does that make sense to you?"

"I guess so," she said hurriedly, not knowing exactly what he was trying to tell her, if anything, but feeling finally that she *had* pried too deeply into someone else's privacy and had best back off before he said, and she heard, things neither of them wanted exposed.

Big Game Night! she thought. And senior year! The things they sometimes got you into!

"Well," she said with a bright thankfulness as Hack and B.J. came toward them out of the crowd. "Here they are back again!"

"And in good time, too," he said with some irony as he rose to pull out B.J.'s chair for her. "Not a *second* too soon."

And resumed perusal of the dance floor as B.J. chatted on brightly and nervously at his side.

Half an hour later they were all walking down Powell Street calling out greetings to the occupants of overloaded cable cars as they clanged laboriously up and down the hill. Autos still clogged the streets, horns still hooted, revelers still shouted. Below in Union Square they could see happy crowds singing and dancing their way along. It was almost eleven but the festivities were still going full pitch.

"About another hour," Wilson predicted, "and we're all going to collapse like the One-Hoss Shay." He raised his voice as they neared the Drake and he spotted his brother arm in arm with Janie in the midst of the crowd that still surged along the sidewalks. "Hey! Come join us!"

Billy grinned up at them as they came happily down the hill and almost started toward them. Then he hesitated and called out cheerfully, "No, thanks. We're supposed to meet Tony and Lor and Johnny and the cousins at the St. Francis. And Smitty and Hank and Rodge and Randy and who knows who else. Maybe we'll see you there later."

"O.K.," Willie called back. "Don't count on it."

"We won't," Billy responded. "Have fun."

"You, too," Wilson said as they moved off, smiling happily. "Our younger group is getting pretty exclusive, aren't they?"

"As our older group gets older," Ray remarked.

"I feel as though I'm being swept out the door already," Unruh complained humorously. "What's the hurry? It's a *long* way to June."

"Hah!" Gulbransen said. "You wait and see, boy. It'll be here so fast we won't know it."

"Meanwhile," North said before they could all get too sentimental about it, "here's the Drake. Want to go in?"

They paused on the sidewalk surveying the lobby packed to the doors, the waiting line stretched halfway down the block toward the Square.

"It'll be just as crowded at the St. Francis," Guy said.

"Maybe not," North said. "It's bigger."

"O.K.," Willie said decisively. "Let's go."

They had to wait there too, but after about fifteen minutes Smitty and Randy came out to go to the men's room, saw them in line and hailed them effusively. Smitty slipped the maître d' ten bucks and five minutes later extra chairs were being squeezed around a table that normally seated twelve but presently held twenty with the spillover obligingly accommodated at an adjoining table occupied by Cal rooters. Billy seemed to make sure that he and Janie were on the opposite side of the table surrounded by the younger group, but that seemed natural enough. Everybody was prepared to settle in amicably for the rest of the evening when Bates suddenly called out, "*Achtung!*" in a disgusted Oh, Christ! voice.

Across the room a quartet dazzling in health, blondness and general air of superiority was being seated at a table of noisy celebrants who obviously didn't know them but were making room for them with typical Big Game hospitality. And just at that moment, in one of those coincidences that could have happened anywhere during the evening but somehow hadn't until everyone reached the St. Francis, Buff returned from his own visit to the men's room with Duke and Shahna, whom he had found waiting in line.

A rather excessive, and secretly somewhat defiant, fuss was made over greeting them, and since the group from the house was one of the two or three largest in the room, it was an obvious and highly noticeable display. On the other side of the room it produced a response that no one had quite anticipated.

"Oh, oh," Willie said, raising his voice in a tone that cut through the merry chatter and commanded instant attention. " 'Achtung!' was right, Timmy. Here they come."

And sure enough here they did, looking self-conscious but very determined: Rudy and Helga, Wolfgang and some other junior Valkyrie, unknown to them but obviously a true believer. With a sort of grim concentration they worked their way—plowed, Willie described it to himself—across the crowded floor until they were standing on the outer perimeter of the group. Everyone turned to stare up at them with a variety of expressions that did not include welcome. A silence fell.

Into it Rudy blurted, "Hi! How about making room for us?"

"Well, I don't know," Buff began. "The table's awfully full, Rudy, and—"

"You're making room for *them*," Rudy said in a belligerent tone. Helga and the junior Valkyrie nodded vigorously and Wolfgang said, "*Ja,* that's right, Rudy. They sure are!"

"Perhaps this is a table for people we like," Randy suggested in a clear, carrying voice whose coldness was aided by several drinks and his general frustration at being alone for the evening.

Rudy flushed but before he could reply Willie said calmly, "I don't know whether I'd put it quite like that, Randy. But we are awfully full, Rudy, as you can see. I thought you and your friends had found a place over there—?"

"We thought we'd prefer being with you," Rudy said, gaining confidence from their obvious uncertainty. "You know Helga—Wolfgang—and this is Annalise Gunther, one of the other German exchange students. So, can we sit down?"

"There aren't any chairs," Willie said simply, just as a waiter approached with two for Duke and Shahna, who took them, looking tense while trying to ignore the intruders.

"They have more," Rudy said flatly, and Wolfgang said, "*Ja,* sure they do."

"Well, perhaps they do," Buff said firmly, "but there isn't room to put them anywhere. So why don't you go back to your table before someone gets your seats?"

"*This* is my table," Rudy said, standing his ground. "Waiter! Bring us four more chairs, will you?"

"Don't do it, waiter," Willie said.

"Well, sir—" said the poor waiter, stranded between.

"Here!" Rudy said, pulling out a ten-dollar bill and tossing it to him with a grand gesture.

"Yes, sir!" the waiter said, seizing it just above the floor and scurrying away.

"If you can make room for *him*," Rudy said with complete contempt in his voice, "and *her*, then I guess you can make room for me and my friends. So move over!"

"We make room for *our* friends," Moose said. Rudy swung around with a glare.

"Listen, big hero!" he said. "If you want to make friends with that—that—"

But he was unable to finish because Gulbransen, who was seated nearest, reached up, grabbed him by the tie and pulled his face down to a level with his own.

"Listen, boy," he said in a level voice, "if we wanted you at this table we would have invited you. We didn't. Take your Nazi friends and shove off."

"God damn it—" Rudy began, and even in the midst of the convivial din in the room his voice rang out loudly enough to quiet conversation at neighboring tables.

"Move!" Gil said, letting go of the tie and rising to his full height of six feet two. "Now!"

For just a second Rudy visibly contemplated striking him; so visibly that the maître d' and several nervous waiters began to move toward them.

Then Wolfgang said scornfully, "Come on, Rudy! If these *Dummköpfe* want to associate *mit den Juden*, let them! We have too much self-respect. Come!"

And grabbing the two girls by the arms he turned on his heel and marched them back to the other table, which by now, as several house members noted with glee, was indeed occupied by someone else.

"Well—" Rudy began. But no one responded. Gil's face was expressionless, the others took their cue from him: a circle of stony faces looked blankly up. Finally, muttering something furious but unintelligible, Rudy too turned blindly and walked away. Seconds later they saw with satisfaction that he and Wolfgang were engaged in another verbal battle, this time with the newcomers at the other table. With some laughter and considerable satisfaction, they turned away and left them to make the best of it.

"We're so sorry—" Shahna began nervously, and Duke agreed, "If we'd had any idea we were going to cause such a rumpus—"

"Listen," Buff interrupted calmly. "If we didn't want you with us we'd have made the same excuse of a full table and you wouldn't be here. It's no problem, it's nothing to apologize for, it isn't even a rumpus."

Randy said, "Is there some way we can get rid of the guy permanently? I was sort of on his side before but I'm really getting teed off. You guys are going to graduate, you'll be rid of him in June, but the rest of us are going to have to suffer with him for another two years."

"I agree," Jeff said with his amiable grin. "I may have my problems, Willie, but they sure aren't like his."

"The pledge class is still on probation until the first house meeting in January," Willie said. "It's possible something can be done then. Right, Buff?"

"Right, Willie," Buff agreed dryly. "Doesn't anybody want a drink?"

"Get that waiter over here," Unruh agreed. "He's ten bucks richer and didn't have to do a thing. He ought to be willing to cooperate."

And so he was, and so the evening got back on track and went along merrily until one A.M. when they heard the familiar strains of "Good Night, Ladies," followed by the slow, swaying last dance of romantic couples, so butt-bumped, as Guy remarked, that they couldn't move, only pulsate.

From there they all went their separate ways, Tony, Lor, Johnny and "the cousins" up to Napa Valley, where Louise Gianfalco's father had invited them for the rest of the weekend; Moose and Welcome, Gil and Karen Ann, and Buff and his date off to their small compliant hostelry in the Tenderloin, on the shadier side of Union Square; the rest, by car, late bus or train, back to campus.

A hundred miles south in Del Monte Lodge, Franky and Katie and Latt and Kay ate a sumptuous meal and had some drinks, three each for Franky and Katie, one daiquiri for Kay and a ginger ale for Latt, who smiled and refused to succumb to Franky's desperate pleadings that he "have a real drink just once—just *once!*" Then they danced for a quite a while and finally went to bed, the girls in their room and Franky and Latt in theirs.

"I'm frustrated as hell!" Franky exclaimed as soon as they had bade the girls good night, heard the firm click of the deadbolt on their door and returned to their own room. He made an exaggerated face, not entirely in jest.

Latt chuckled.

"That's too bad. Read the Gideon Bible and go to sleep."

"You're heartless! There's the cutest little girl in the world and here I am with—what? *The biggest brain in school,* for God's sake! *That's* Big Game Night?"

"I can't help you. Try Corinthians."

"Oh, shut up!" Franky said, throwing a shoe after him as he disappeared into the bathroom.

However, Latt noted when they had finished and he turned off the light ten minutes later, Franky did begin snoring the moment his head hit the pillow. Latt concluded, as he often had before, that while Franky talked a good game, when it came right down to it the courage and the expertise weren't there. Nor, of course, the necessary cooperation of the cutest little girl in the world.

All in all, everybody agreed, it had been a great Big Game, thanks to Moose, and aside from Rudy's little nastiness, a wonderful Big Game Night: the last for the seniors as undergrads, as they commented to one another with increasing frequency—and increasing sentimentality—as the night progressed. It made them all a little wistful and hurried them just a little faster toward whatever it was they were headed for.

They didn't know, and on that night of nights did not really want to imagine. They shut it out and, for the most part, had fun. Which, as Nagatani had said in his editorial, was what college was all about . . . at least on that particular traditional occasion.

Years later those who survived the war and were able to come back would still feel that happy surge of excitement, that happy innocence, when Big Game came around again and once more all of living narrowed down to autumn light slanting low across a stadium, the roar of a good-natured crowd and two teams running on a bright green field.

15

Thanksgiving was cold. The weather, so cooperative for Big Game, turned abruptly cooler the day after. First rains fell, drenching the campus, slashing palms and eucalyptus, drumming on tiles, standing in puddles in the Inner Quad, imparting an air of desolation to the concluding days of the quarter. A massive storm, first of the season, hung off the coast for almost a week, dumping a total of three inches from Mendocino in the north to Big Sur in the south. Then the rain stopped but not the depressing weather, which turned consistently overcast, gray and sullen.

"It makes it cozy, anyway," Buff remarked when they built up the roaring fire in the living room of the big old barn of a house they had rented just off Carmel's Ocean Avenue.

"It could be cozy and sunny and I'd like it better," Guy responded.

But they were young and there were sufficient semibright times of scudding clouds and fleeting blue so that they could do a lot of wandering around town, hiking and playing impromptu volleyball on the beach, driving 17-Mile Drive up to Pacific Grove and back to see the seals and sea-lions and watch the otters drifting placidly in the tossing kelp or cavorting happily in the cold and restless sea.

They had stocked up Wednesday on the way down with three turkeys and all the necessary supplies, and on Thanksgiving morning the three girls, Donna, Maggie and Janie—neither Buff nor Ari Katanian having brought a date—were up early and puttering happily about in the kitchen. Maggie was an excellent cook, Donna not far behind. Under their direction things moved smoothly toward an excellent and enormous meal. The fellows were in and out, commenting, tasting, teasing, interfering, their interventions greeted with squeals, giggles, protests and stern commands to get out which they happily ignored.

Buff and Guy had been put in charge of liquid refreshments and had managed to acquire a goodly supply of liquor from a dealer Buff knew in Menlo Park. The general hilarity was increased by the standard drinks and by an oddly colored but powerfully emphatic concoction Buff put together and named, with a flourish, "The You-Better-Believe-It." After one taste, everybody believed it. Only the fact that they were essentially responsible youths kept things on an even, if pleasantly glowing, keel—that and the fact that Ari Katanian did not drink at all, and the others were sensible enough not to overdo it . . . and, possibly, the presence, off there on some distant but effective astral plane, of a ghostly Dr. Chalmers, saying firmly, "You know I don't approve of That Sort of Thing."

So they drank moderately, ate until they could eat no more, and, after charades and other innocent games around the fire, went to an early bed. The old house had five bedrooms, which was just right. The Wilson brothers bunked together, the rest drew straws: Guy with Hank, Donna with Maggie and Janie and Buff with a room each. This was not a holiday for romance, save of a casual and public nature, and in truth no one missed it. They were there for fun and a good time and they had it, quite innocently and without regrets for anything else.

Willie in particular was happy to have it that way. It made it easy to sidestep any confidential heart-to-hearts with Donn, which he could sense disappointed her but suited him just fine.

On Friday they rose late, whiled away the day, ate enormously again of what was left, and it was substantial, of Thursday's meal. On Saturday they were down to turkey soup and turkey sandwiches. On Sunday, after a big brunch at one of Carmel's cheaper and more relaxed places where you could get away very amply for about two dollars apiece, they prepared to drive back to campus.

The phone rang shortly before they left. Its message, and the one heart-to-heart conversation Willie did have with anyone, were all that marred for any of them an otherwise perfect weekend. But those were enough to set it quite permanently in memory.

On Friday night Billy, who had spent most of the afternoon lying on the beach with Janie, blissfully enwrapped in an old army blanket while sharp winds attacked but could not invade their cozy cocoon, tossed and turned for almost an hour. Finally his brother rolled over to face him from his own bed and inquired in a testy half-whisper, "What in the hell's the matter? Having a wet dream or something? Why don't you settle down?"

"No, I'm not having a wet dream!" Billy whispered back with an asperity quite unusual for him, particularly when addressing his big brother.

"Well, then, what is it? It must be something—and something you want to talk with me about, otherwise you wouldn't be making all that noise. So let's have it. Is Janie mad at you?"

"Did it look like she was mad at me this afternoon?" Billy retorted scornfully.

"No. As near as I could tell you were quietly fornicating on the beach under that blanket. Everything looked very cozy to me."

Billy gave a snort of laughter.

"Not that it didn't occur to me," he said dreamily. "Not that it didn't seem like a *damned* good idea. But no, Dickie. Nothing like that."

At this use of the old childhood nickname—the "Willie" had only been acquired through his own deliberate encouragement when he reached the University—Richard Emmett Wilson began to pay closer attention. He opened his eyes and tried to penetrate the darkness, but without much success. His brother was a small lump in the other bed. But there was something about the lump's outline that indicated a certain rigidity and tenseness. Inevitably this produced a tenseness in him. As a result he sounded sharp.

"All right, then: what is it?"

Billy sighed, a deep and uncharacteristic sound that tightened his brother up further.

"Dickie," he said with a reluctant slowness, "somebody. . . somebody's. . . after me."

"What do you mean, 'after you'?" Willie inquired sharply.

Billy sighed again and twisted uncomfortably in his bed.

"Like that—that man at the lake."

The old dark incident, buried among the memories of a summer long ago and never related to their parents, came back suddenly in its terrifying surprise. They were much older now and more knowledgeable about many things, but the episode still retained its ability to shatter security. Willie shivered. Once again he was ten years old, protecting his baby brother from the world's endless onslaughts.

"Here?" he asked in a shocked whisper. "Here at school?"

"Here in the fraternity house."

They stared across the darkness at one another, Billy's eyes enormous and dark with trouble, Willie's wide and full of chaotic thoughts.

"Do you want him?"

Billie managed to smile a little, though his brother could not see it.

"I think you'd stand by me even if I did."

"You belong to me. I stand by my own. Well, do you?"

"No," his brother said quietly, "I do not."

"Well, then," Willie said impatiently, "tell me who he is."

"No."

"Why not?"

"Because in the mood you're in right now you'd hurt him, and I don't want him hurt. I don't like him like—like that, but there's no point in being cruel to him. He's going through hell about it, he told me so and I believe him. I do like him. Not like—that, but enough so that I don't want you to hurt him."

"Then why tell me at all, if you don't want me to do anything about it?"

"Because you're my brother," Billy said simply, "and you asked my why I was bothered and so I told you. I can handle it all right . . . I think. If I can't, I may ask for your help."

"You do that," Willie said. "And Billy—I don't hurt people. I'm not like that."

"I know you're not," his baby brother said humbly. "I guess I'm really kind of confused about it all."

"Well, so am I," Willie confessed. "But we can't afford to let it get you down."

"No," Billie said, and again there was the deep, uncharacteristic sigh, "we can't do that. . . . Well, goodnight, Dickie. And thanks."

"I haven't done anything."

"Maybe just thanks for being you," his brother said with a sudden little laugh that sounded more, for the moment, like himself again. "Isn't that enough?"

"I hope so in this case," Willie said soberly. "I sure do hope so."

"Yes," Billy said gravely as he took another deep breath, "I sure do, too."

And for a few minutes they both lay tense, staring at each other across the small, intervening space, unable to penetrate the darkness but comforted by each other's presence. Down the hill at the bottom of Ocean Avenue they could hear the distant heavy rollers crashing in on the enormous, sandy crescent. Keep them away, Willie thought with an almost superstitious transference of image: keep them away from my brother and from me.

Presently Billy turned on his other side and, tensions for the time being relaxed, began gently to snore. Presently Willie followed suit. The big old house was silent save for a few steady rhythms here and there.

Down the hill the rollers came heavily, insistently, implacably, crashing in.

They were packed and about to leave when the phone jangled insistently and it seemed to Willie that there was something implacable about that, too.

"Does anyone want to get that?" Buff called, turning from packing the big Buick sedan his folks had given him at the start of senior year. "No, wait a minute. I'll get it. I left the number with Carriger, although I can't imagine what . . . Yeah?" he said, puffing a little from his sprint up the steps. "Hi, Smitty. What's up?" His expression changed, his face turned pale, a shocked disbelief transmitted itself to the others, looking up anxiously from the driveway to where he stood framed in the kitchen window. "Oh, what a God damned shame! Where is he now? . . . O.K., you do that. Yes, we're just about to leave. We'll be there by four, I should think. . . . O.K., boy, thanks. It's good to know you're in charge. See you in a little while."

He put down the phone, came out on the porch to meet their upturned faces.

"Now, isn't that a God damned shame! Marc Taylor tried to commit suicide"—there were horrified exclamations of protest and disbelief—"and almost succeeded. Mrs. Steadman just happened to come into his room to see if he was taking a nap and managed to cut him down"—Janie and Maggie started to cry—"and now he's in the hospital and Dr. James is with him. Doc has called his parents and Smitty suggested he do the same on behalf of the house, which was damned thoughtful of him—Smitty's a hell of an organized guy, you know it?—and when we get back I'll do the same. I guess we'd better get on back now as fast as we can. Although I guess everything's under control and there isn't much for us to do, really."

"Just be there," Guy suggested quietly. "That will probably be more help to him than anything."

"Yep," Buff agreed. "Off we go."

And much sobered, they locked the house, piled into his car and Willie's and Ari's, and drove back through the Sunday traffic, on many occasions quite a lot faster than the law allowed. None of them had ever confronted anything like this before. The initial horror of it was presently compounded by the bafflement and mystery of it. It was an uncharted sea. The waves, Willie thought grimly as he pushed the rattletrap old Chevy convertible along as fast as it would go, were suddenly coming in from all directions.

When they reached school, Buff called Marc's parents but found they had already left home to catch a plane. Dr. James said he was pleased to see Marc's fraternity brothers but they would have to wait until tomorrow to visit their patient. He said Marc was in shock and "will need a lot of help."

"I know you boys can give it to him," he said and they promised fervently that they would. Everybody felt somehow disconnected, pointless and useless for the rest of the evening. It was a hell of a way to wind up Thanksgiving vacation, Unruh remarked. They started to agree until Buff replied quietly, "Worse for him," which made them all feel ashamed of themselves and even worse than they felt already.

Next day Marc's parents arrived and thanked them profusely for "what you've done for our boy." They all said it wasn't much, not anywhere near as much as they should have done and would have liked to have done—"but somehow he just—didn't want us to." Marc's parents nodded sadly. They said they were going to take him home as soon as Dr. James said he could travel, which Dr. James said he thought would be Tuesday. Everybody fell to and got Marc's things ready for shipment.

On Monday evening they all went in a body to the hospital, almost the entire house, even Rudy Krohl, who snapped, "I'm not inhuman!" when Suratt made some dry comment about his presence.

Marc knew them but made virtually no response except to blurt out, "I'm *sorry!*" and start to cry, clinging like a child to the hand Buff with instinctive compassion placed against his cheek.

Life, they all agreed as they walked somberly back to the house, could be a fucking son of a bitch.

"And what about our responsibility?" Latt asked later that evening when a lot of people, having been unable to concentrate much on studying for the finals that now loomed ahead, gathered restlessly in the room he now shared with Rodge Leighton on the second floor.

"God damn it," Unruh said, "don't go making us feel guilty, Latt. We tried."

"We sure did," Gulbransen agreed. "I took that kid everywhere for a while." He grinned. "I think Karen Ann thought we had something going."

"That would be the day," Willie said dryly. "That—would—be—the—day. I agree with both of you. I don't see that it's our fault, Latt. I think he's basically unstable for some reason we may never know, and school just touched it off, somehow."

"I just think he was damned lonely and unable to relax with us, or himself, and finally it got to him," Rodge said. "I'm the first one he confided in, and I tried, too. I couldn't seem to get through to him any more than the rest of you could. I think he got himself into a box where all the doors seemed to be closed and so he tried to get out the only way he could think of. Thank God he didn't succeed," he added fervently. "I'd hate to have *that* on our consciences."

"We did what we could," Gulbransen reiterated. "I set up dates for him, I tried to get him started with girls—"

"Your universal solution," Latt remarked with a smile, "but it doesn't work for everybody. And I tried to help him with his studies, and that doesn't work for everybody, either. I'm just wondering if we were sympathetic enough, that's all. Life gets awfully busy on campus and everybody has his own concerns and his own problems and the days go hurrying by and we don't stop to think enough about our fellows, maybe."

"You can't," Franky said. "There's just too much, Latt. It's all you can do to keep abreast of your own problems without taking on everybody else's. At least that's the way I find it. I'm not unsympathetic—at least I don't think I am—but you get so involved with your own headaches . . . I think we're a reasonably sympathetic house. Maybe more than most." He grinned suddenly. "In general, I think we're an absolutely smashing, utterly superior, really stupendous group of fellows. Does anyone dare to disagree? If so, speak up and be dismembered."

There was raucous cries of "Hear! Hear!" and he added, "So take *that*, you Dekes and Zetes and Chi Psis and Phi Delts!" Which produced more hear, hears, considerable amusement, and some reduction of the tensions.

But they thought about it often, as the hours and days went by and Marc gradually began to fade from the forefront of their concerns. His parents had taken him home to Pennsylvania, but not before Dr. Chalmers had visited him in the hospital—an event which got around campus very fast and increased respect for the president to an even higher level—and had assured his parents that he would be given temporary leave and would be welcomed back at any time their doctors felt he was physically and mentally able. Marc did seem to respond to that with the first faint little smile anyone had seen, which made his parents cry and brought Buff, Unruh, Willie and Latt, who were with them, perilously close to doing the same. The four of them went to the airport to see the family off on the long, laborious flight to Philadelphia and added their assurances to the president's that he would soon be back, they were sure of it. He said, "I hope so," in a wan little voice and everybody got misty again. At the top of the boarding ladder he turned and gave them a little wave and all waved back, much moved.

"God!" Buff exclaimed as the door closed and they turned away, "I'm glad that's over!"

But it wasn't. The memory would continue to turn uneasily in their minds for a long time to come, even when Marc did recover and did come back. It was all so strange: one could never really grasp it or come to terms with it. It would always have an afterlife of its own. Many a bullsession would revolve around it, until Guy finally cried, "Enough, enough, God damn it! We'll never understand it, so let's get on with it!" Willie, privately carrying the double burden of Marc's act and Billy's revelation, mused that while understanding things was part of growing up, maybe finally realizing there were things you couldn't understand was part of it, too.

And then came finals, Christmas and the holidays, and a general scattering to their respective homes and destinations across the country.

Willie, after small presents and farewells to Donna and Marian, the first pleased and grateful, the other shy and unfathomable, told himself to hell with it, hopped in the Chevy and drove straight home to the ranch. His journey was almost the exact reverse mirror image of the journey to school, except that it carried with it, as for all of them, even heavier and more insistent overlays of origin, childhood, family, truly old, accustomed things— the ineffable essence of a place where you know everybody and everybody knows you and there are hardly any secrets about anything. . . .

It would begin as soon as he left the campus and turned south, the familiar, inevitable stripping away of college, the gradual resurgence of home. The process was almost like a change of clothes: as you progressed deeper into the Valley one set of garments came off and you began, almost against your will, to put on the other. Except in summer, when you were home for more than just a visit, this left you curiously suspended between two worlds, not altogether at ease in your appreciation of the one or your memories of the other.

Ordinarily this vague unrest did not go very deep, but this time you knew it would, for this time you were going home for a vacation that would probably be your last of any extended duration, and the day whose coming you had long foreseen would be soon upon you: the day when the conflict between your two worlds had to be resolved.

You had put off the thought of that for four years which had passed in golden procession as in a dream, but it could not be avoided now. You felt a little guiltily that you should be prepared for it. And yet, what time had there been for preparation? Mentally and physically, yes, in the courses you had taken and the plans you had made; but for emotional preparation, what time had there been? Four years, gone in a day and full to overflowing with things that left no room for the future, save as something so far ahead that it hardly seemed to exist at all. It was hard not to feel resentment at the way it had crept upon you, even though you knew you were in part to blame; you often tried to push it aside, even now, as though it could still be denied. Underneath you were saying no to the sea. For all your determination to keep it far away, off on the other side of the brief paradise in which you lived, it had come at last. Here it was, and there was no denying it now.

The realization gave him an uneasy driven feeling as he packed. Accompanying it was a heightened perception such as he had not experienced since he first set foot on campus. Everything seemed suddenly unrelated and alien. Haggerty, not yet on his way, was playing the piano downstairs. A pool game was going on at the other end of the house. Voices were calling on the lawn. Someone was singing in the shower. The phone was ringing.

For several minutes these sounds, so much a part of his life, seemed strangely sharp and separate, as though he had lost the thread which held them together.

When he had finished packing he went soberly downstairs and out to his car, not even remembering, perhaps subconsciously not even wanting, to look in the living room and the pool room and say goodbye.

Once he got over Pacheco Pass and into the Valley, it was as he had known it would be. He was going home through the folded hills of California, lying like great lazy elephants along the road, and his mood could not stand long against them. They were brown and cold now, but already, in the way of California's hurrying seasons, they were starting to turn green again with the first faint flush of new grain. Before long their shallow freshets would be in flood, red-winged blackbirds would flash among the sedges and cool yet gentle over all the great valley would move the searching, changing, sundrenched winds of spring.

Under the Valley's compulsion his thoughts began to turn away from what lay behind and look toward what lay ahead. School began to recede from his memory in an almost physical sense. Names and faces yielded to others, long remembered: old scenes obscured the new. When he thought of the house it was to remember consciously where it was on the Row, how it lay in relation to the campus and Quad. There was temporarily lost to him the unthinking physical reality of relationship which is so much a part of living in a given place over a period of time. At school he never thought of the road running along the Quad, turning by the bookstore, going by the Union, and so on to the Row; rarely did he stop to consider the University in relation to the town, the town in relation to the City.

Thinking back to it on the way home it was necessary to do that, it was necessary to give your progress close attention in mind's eye; and because it became more and more a conscious progress, and because you were getting deeper and deeper into the Valley, you presently began to stop thinking of school and began instead to think of home. And because home was a warm and all-absorbing thought, your unrest became temporarily submerged, temporarily obscured, until there came stretches of time when you could almost forget that it existed at all.

When you stopped to consider it, this ability of home to engulf your mind struck you as strange and almost frightening. Home was no single definite plan and scheme of things, possessed of component parts which lay together like those of a complete puzzle. Home was no unity of Quad and campus and house and Row and town and city. Home was a thousand things, funny, disconnected, unrelated, that hardly fitted together at all, much less in a pattern you could grasp and hold firmly. You noted that a new filling station had been built outside Fresno; it hadn't been there when you drove up three months ago. That was home: knowing it hadn't been there then, knowing it was there now. You took pains to look at the vine-yards around Madera and remembered that everyone always wondered whether they'd be hit by frost; that was home, that interest in the grapes around Madera. You saw the great Valley stretching west and south, seeming to reach the limitless horizons; and home was the knowledge that way over west beyond Lost Hills was the sea, and beyond that Guy's Hawaii and the Orient.

Home was orange trees and orange prices, smudging in the winter and dusting in the summer. Home was fruit stands along the highway at Kings-burg and the cotton crop in Corcoran, and fruit tramps and dilapidated cars and disease-ridden camps and Okie-grower hatred swirling like a bitter stream along the Valley. Home was small, hot, dusty towns and long, hot, dusty days, and the long, cool twilights that came after with the soft winds rising from the sun-exhausted fields. Home was high school memories and high school friends, shows at the Monache Theater in nearby Porter-ville and sodas at the drive-in, baseball games under the arc lights with everybody shouting, horse shows at the county fair, the Armistice Day parade and the Legion carnival, Main Street on Saturday night when the ranchers came in to shop and the sidewalks were so crowded you could hardly walk.

Home was a series of names and places as worn and familiar as an old shoe: Fresno, Merced, Madera, Visalia, Tulare, Hanford, Lindsay, Exeter, Strathmore, Porterville, Terra Bella, Bakersfield, Corcoran, Taft.

Home was the ranch, waiting patiently to claim your youth and your dreams. Home was a changing, shifting stream of memories and im-pressions, of ideas, of people and places, of things half remembered, of things half forgotten, harmless in themselves but conspiring together to build an all-consuming, all-devouring force whose possessive domina-tion you sometimes felt hopelessly you could never fight, could never break away from.

Home finally—and he saw as he turned off the two-lane macadam flanked by oleanders that one of the palm trees had been pruned too closely and was dying—home was the long drive climbing through the orange grove, the three dogs running by the car, the comfortable old brown house waiting among the acacia trees.

He had been back just a day before he stopped fighting against the tide which engulfed him and turned to drift with it. As always his subjugation was accomplished, not by his parents, but by the town.

"Well, Dickie!"—childhood again—the town had said when he came in from the ranch on his first morning home and stopped for gas. "How's the big college man?"

"Hello, Jimmy," he said. "I'm fine. How're you?"

"Top-notch," Jimmy said heartily. "Put her there, boy. Wouldn't be wanting some gas, would you?"

"That's the idea."

"What's the matter, run dry out at the ranch? Thought you people never stooped to trade with us common folks."

Why do they always have to be envious of the ranch, he asked himself; I have to defend it, and that only makes it harder for me. He grinned uncomfortably.

"Nope. We're doing all right. As a matter of fact, I thought I *would* trade with you common folks this time; help me feel at home, see?"

"I get it," said Jimmy. "Guess you're pretty glad to be back, aren't you?"

"You bet I am," he said, hoping he sounded sincere.

"Nothing quite like it," Jimmy assured him. "No, sir, nothing quite like it."

"You bet there isn't," he said, as heartily as he could. "By the way, how about giving me five?"

"Sure thing," said Jimmy, running around the back of the car, "sure thing. . . . Say! Did you hear about Mort Evans?"

Evans? Evans?

"Oh, sure," he said hastily, then corrected himself. "No, I didn't, Jimmy. What about him?"

"He and Dorothy Merritt had to get married."

"No!" he said, hoping he sounded suitably impressed. "When did that happen?"

" 'Bout a month ago. Didn't your folks write you?"

"No, they didn't."

"I thought maybe they had; quite a scandal for a little while. Kid's coming sometime in August, what they tell me."

"I thought she'd hook him sooner or later."

"I'm surprised she didn't get him a lot sooner," said Jimmy, finished with the gas and busy on the windshield. "After the way they raised hell that last year in high school."

"Yeah," he said, "I'm surprised, too. How's high school getting along these days, anyway?"

"Took the league in basketball, you know."

"Is that right? That's damn good."

"Sure is," said Jimmy proudly. "Sunk us in football, but we showed 'em who knows how to play basketball, all right, all right. . . . There, I guess that'll do for a while."

"Thanks, Jimmy," he said. "Our credit's still good, is it?"

"You bet it is," said Jimmy. "Don't the Wilsons own the town?"

"Hey, come off that."

"O.K.," said Jimmy, laughing. "Just kidding. What're you going to do next, anyway? Finishing up at college pretty soon, aren't you?"

"Yeah," he said soberly. "Christ, Jimmy, I don't know. I may go to law school."

"Aren't you coming back to the ranch?"

"I haven't decided yet." Jimmy looked disturbed.

"You're coming back sometime, aren't you?"

"Oh, sure," he said hastily. "I'll be back sometime, even if I do go to law school."

"I hope so!" said Jimmy. "Isn't everybody has a place like that to take over."

"I suppose I have got a pretty good deal there."

"*Suppose* you have!" said Jimmy. "My God, Dickie. Best ranch in this part of the Valley, and you *suppose* you've got a pretty good deal! Who says you can be a lawyer, anyway?"

"Well, by God!" he said. "I do!"

"O.K.," said Jimmy, beginning to laugh. "O.K. Just kidding again."

"Always the card," he said shortly.

"Yeah, that's me, all right. I didn't mean it the way it sounded. I'm just like everybody else, that's all. The whole town expects you to come back and settle down."

"I know it does," he said glumly. "That's just it."

"Well, anyway," said Jimmy, "we'll see you at the community supper at the church Wednesday night, won't we? I guess you can do that much for the old home town!"

"I didn't know there was one. We'll probably be there."

"I'll pass the word along," said Jimmy. "The town'll get a kick out of seeing the local boy who made good in the big college. Might even have the band out to welcome you."

"You do that," he said, starting the car.

"Sorry if I said something I shouldn't have."

"That's O.K., Jimmy. Only it isn't as simple as you think. Take it easy."

"Sure thing," said Jimmy. "Sure thing."

And this, he reflected as the morning wore on, was what you met every time you came home: this admiring envy of the ranch, this unquestioning picture of your own future, this unhesitating assumption that you wanted to plunge back at once into the gossip and life of the town. You got it on every hand as you went about your business on Main Street, and however good your defenses might be, they were never good enough. The town was glad to see you back. It wanted to know about school, and guessed maybe you were glad to be home on the ranch for a little while. It asked your plans and expressed so much surprise at your doubt concerning them that you presently stopped admitting it. It introduced you to its friends as "the oldest Wilson boy . . . you know the Wilson ranch east of town." It asked you about orange prices and how you hoped to come out this year, and said it had heard you were thinking of buying up the Ellison ranch next to yours and was it true. It asked after your family with a protective interest. That was annoying, but you had to concede finally, friendly. It called the ranch "A fine place . . . yes, sir, a fine place." And slowly, subtly, surely, it raised around you the iron wall of Duty, Responsibility, Family, Position.

And when you came right down to it, why should you object? Where, after all, did you get the right to be so God damned supercilious about it? This was your town, these were your friends and your people, this was where they expected you to live your life. What made you so perfect that you could patronize? It was a damned good ranch and a nice little town, and what call did you have to be so Johnny-From-College about it? Who did you think you were, anyway, J. P. Morgan? Maybe they did laugh at you a little bit for going to college, and maybe they did think a career anywhere else was a little silly when you had the best place in the county to come back to, but that was just because they weren't used to looking much beyond the business of making a living, which wasn't easy these days and only a very short time ago had been damned hard for almost everybody. Take it all in all, they were pretty damned nice to you, and you ought to be shot for not being grateful for it. A fellow ought to be proud to be fixed as well as you were. There certainly wasn't anyone at school you'd like to change places with.

By the time he returned to the ranch for lunch he was more than half convinced that he should give up the idea of law school, or any other career away from this place, entirely.

The surrender was sufficiently complete the following evening so that he could accept with a calm approaching acquiescence the inevitable talk with his parents. Aided by a growing distrust of his own desires, he found it at first less of a burden than he had foreseen. Not till it neared its close did the rebellion return and the dream become once more demanding; and later he could not have said why, or what marked the turning point.

Reasonably—so reasonably that for a time he was at a loss how to meet it—his father began to discuss the ranch. As quietly as though they had formed the basis for a comment on the weather, arguments old and familiar were presented again: the slow growth from forty acres to six hundred, the lavished care and pride, the name, the place, the position: the gradual approach of old age, the inevitable retirement, the tragedy of wasted years if the ranch should pass to other hands or fall to other masters. To his quick protests that there was Billy—who he knew didn't want to stay either—or that a manager could be appointed and the property maintained no matter what happened—this last point was yielded. But he was given to understand that little faith was put in his ability to withstand the slow but treacherous disaffections of a career elsewhere when his right and natural place was here. After all, he was the elder son.

Impressed by the impartial way in which these considerations were offered, he reflected presently that here in a California valley he was face to face with a concept as old as feudalism. Given his position, argument was superfluous. Certain things were so: if you were born a Wilson you had a Wilson's place to fulfill, and if you were heir to a property like the ranch you succeeded to it without question. Vehemence was unnecessary in the light of this self-evident logic. While you were free to make your own decision—and you knew you were, for your parents, whatever their disappointment, would not stand in your way when the final decision came—still it was assumed that the obvious pressure of facts would convince you. No attempt was made to condemn or belittle your plans for a life elsewhere; your sincerity was accorded you, your intelligence and ability conceded. Only a quiet repetition of points already made, a gently increasing pressure and the faint beginnings of emotion served to indicate an inflexibility as iron as your own.

He felt suddenly that he could stand it no longer. This patient insistence, this elusive but rigid opposition, seemed to be hemming him in on every side, crushing his resistance and obscuring his plans and his dreams. If they would only come out in the open—if they would only fight him and give him something to fight. But they would not. They were reasonable and infuriatingly tolerant, because they knew this was the way to wear down. This was the way to worry and make uncertain. This was the way, in the end, to bring about acceptance.

He stood up abruptly.

"I'm sorry," he said, trying to keep his voice from becoming sharp. "I don't want to talk about it anymore. I'll tell you what I've decided to do when the time comes; but right now I want to be left alone. I'm sorry."

A little silence fell, widened. Now if you will only argue with me, he thought, if you will only—

"Why, all right, son," his father said calmly. "You work it out your own way. Your mother and I want you to do what is best for you. It's your life, after all."

"I think I'll go outside for a while," he said. And was surprised to note that he had managed to say it quietly.

He walked out to the edge of the lawn, out where the orange trees began, and stood there for some moments listening to the night. Only country sounds broke its stillness: somewhere, far, a dog barked once; in reply a lone cock woke and welcomed midnight, two hours early. A few late frogs still chorused from the standpipes in the orchard, a little whisper of wind stirred the leaves of the umbrella trees, and from the pump house in North Hill pasture came the steady, rhythmical grinding of the pump, muted by distance. But other than that, no sound; no sound.

Presently the lights went off in the wing of the house from which he had come, and he was left alone in the darkness with only the massive bulk of the hills and the slow swinging of the stars to keep him company.

Watching their orderly progress, reflecting for a second on that even course so infinitely far and inviolate, an angry bitterness stirred his mind. What did it matter that you had plans and dreams and ideals? What good were youth and brains and ability? What though the world did need decency and integrity and a clear vision toward the light now more than ever? Nobody cared. Nobody even had time to find out whether or not you had them. Life went on too fast for things like that: life was real, life was earnest, and to hell with you, Dickie-Willie Wilson, you and your silly little ideas about "helping people" and "contributing something" and "doing what one can to help keep things going" in a world made awful by Adolf Hitler.

That was some other world you were thinking of, some world free of the thousand nagging hands of care and duty and responsibility. You'd travel a long way to find that world; and you certainly wouldn't find it in this heartbreakingly beautiful night, with its winds so gentle, its hills and valleys so still and dark, its stars so unutterably remote in their timeless serenity. Maybe it didn't even exist. You thought it did because you were young, and because you knew only the young, who were your friends and had not learned the necessity for accepting less. You could dream with them because they dreamed too and had not yet been asked to forget how. But they would be. They would be. Even as they passed in quick review across your mind you could see the eager smile vanish from this face, the quick laughter pass from that, the frank and open friendliness go from some other.

Where will we be, my friends, when the years have had their way with us? What will be left of our dreams and our courage then? Will we know one another still, when we are old?

As though it had come upon him from the night, he felt a melancholy so profound that it cut into his heart like a knife.

He realized that the wind, at first unusually warm for this time of year, was becoming steadily sharper. He must go in. The night of youth, the night of the world, was coming on.

16

So soon they could barely believe it, vacation ended, school began. Another quarter.

Another Reg Day.

Another Reg Dance.

The swift resumption of old friendships.

The tentative beginnings of new.

The unexpected occurrence of new problems.

Continuing struggles with old.

The start of new classes.

The adjustments to new professors.

The immediate start of the frantic whirl of campus activities, academic, social, eleemosynary.

The holidays swiftly receding.

Winter quarter swiftly begun.

Oddly, though in some cases they had spent part of the holidays together, it seemed to many of them almost as though they had been apart for quite some time. Youth's clock, ticking more slowly then than it ever would again, seemed momentarily to have stretched things out, to have created a substantial psychological gap in which weeks, not days, seemed to have passed. Back on the other side of Christmas everything somehow seemed long ago and far away; on this side, all seemed fresh and new with endless miles to go: except for the seniors, for whom the clock was different.

No sooner were the holidays over than time, for them, seemed to accelerate in almost frightening fashion. It did not matter that it was raining heavily on Reg Day: spring seemed suddenly just around the corner. Graduation, hitherto an uncomfortable but rather remote concept, suddenly became real and more than a little threatening. Decisions that before had seemed far away were now all too imminent.

"Memorial Church," Unruh remarked dryly, "here we come."

So it was that Franky, not even pausing to unpack, hurried to the phone to call Katie, only to find Gulbransen in the booth talking to Karen Ann; and when Guy and Moose came along ten minutes later to call, respectively, Maggie Johnson and Welcome Waggoner, they found Franky in happily voluble possession, chattering on as though it had been months since he had seen Katie; and after Guy and Moose concluded, North was waiting patiently in line to call B.J.; and after him Latt, somewhat self-conscious but determined, talked to Kay; and after him Haggerty, much more comfortably, with Fran; and finally Willie, waiting until last because he characteristically did not want everyone knowing his business, talked first to Donna—bright, cheerful and honestly pleased to hear from him—and to Marian, a little shy and remote but also pleased—he thought.

So it was, also, that Billy spent fifteen minutes cooing back and forth with Janie, to the finally exasperated impatience of Randy, who wanted desperately to talk to Fluff Stevens but instead got the usual knowingly amused runaround from her sorority sisters, which started him off on winter quarter in the same foul mood in which he had concluded autumn quarter. Tony Andrade, Lor Davis and Johnny Herbert shared the phone to call Angie and Louise; it was obvious that their essentially sexless companionship would continue as before. Duke Offenberg, who had called Shahna every day during vacation when he wasn't actually with her, arranged to take her to dinner at Beltramo's that very first evening. His clash with Rudy Krohl, though it had resulted in what others considered a triumph, had left him with a peculiar and apparently insatiable need for reassurance. This Shahna, as always, quietly and loyally offered.

Other associations also resumed. North came down from his third-floor room later that evening and put in a call to the Zete house. And on the afternoon of the next day, when the weather had turned milder with scudding clouds and steadily decreasing showers, Haggerty went down to the church to try out his latest composition on the organ and was surprised and troubled to see, far across the Inner Quad, the figure of the wanderer disappearing under the arches in the direction Hack had warned him against. It might not have meant anything—the guy had seemed genuinely abashed when Hack had talked to him, and Hack hadn't happened to see him there since—there were any of a dozen innocent reasons why he might be there now—but there had been a certain indefinable furtiveness about his movements . . . and the conviction was growing in Hack's mind . . .

God damn it to hell, he thought as he settled himself at the keyboard and let his fingers play idly over the minor keys. God damn it, he's a *nice* guy—and everybody likes him—and *I* like him—and I don't want to have to blow the whistle . . . but somebody may have to, if he doesn't stop. Because if he doesn't, then sooner or later he may get caught and then there'll be a big scandal for the house . . . and devastation for him . . . and I don't want that to happen . . .

And finally, on a plane both innocent and inescapable, there came the mutual disclosure and discussion—pleased, disappointed, proud or profane—of last quarter's grades. Most had survived the finals in reasonably good shape, although Buff, Moose, Lor and Franky had each received an F in at least one subject. From there things rose to a plateau of C-plus to B-plus in which were to be found such as Baker, Gulbransen, Haggerty and Bates, along with most of the juniors and sophomores. Hank Moore, Rodge Leighton, Tony Andrade and Bob Godwin managed to pull down two straight A's and two B's apiece. Unruh and Wilson both bettered that with three straight A's and two B-pluses apiece. North had racked up three straight A's and a B in spite of his problems. Rising serene and, fortunately, ever-modest above them all was, as usual, the one Franky called "the Inevitable Latt" with two straight A's and three A-pluses, "whatever the hell that means," as Franky also remarked. Close behind came B.J. with four straight A's and one A-plus in spite of her own North-generated problems.

All in all, they agreed with satisfaction, not bad for a house that sometimes took a ribbing for being "just a bunch of grinds."

"That's my fault," Latt remarked with a wry smile. Whatever its origin, it tagged after them in spite of Wilson's student-body presidency, Godwin's potential succession to same, Tim's editorship of the *Daily*, Moose's F.A.T.s, Guy's basketball, Jeff's swimming, Randy's still formidable tennis and the fact that their intramural touch-football team was right up there with the best of them. They congratulated themselves that they were a damned well-rounded group, as Buff remarked whenever some other house president greeted him at an Interfraternity Council meeting with "How are you and all your Phi Betes?"

"You fuckers are just jealous," Buff always responded with a comfortable smile. "We've got brains *and* quality."

They were also a pretty damned congenial bunch, in spite of a few rough spots. One of them, he reflected as he prepared to call the first house meeting of the quarter to order on January 4, lay dead ahead. Fortunately it wouldn't be his direct responsibility: with a little luck he would be out of office in fifteen minutes.

"If you bastards will settle down," he said severely as Franky and Jeff rolled on the floor tussling for a pillow from one of the sofas, and the others wandered in by twos and threes to collapse on the floor, sink into chairs or perch on the arms and seats of sofas, "the sectretary will call the roll and we'll have the election of new officers for winter quarter."

Whereupon, despite his vigorous protests, he was reelected president by acclamation; Ray Baker house manager and Tony Andrade secretary, by the same method; and Smitty Carriger, after Franky announced that he absolutely would not accept the job again, vice-president. All of this to the accompaniment of choruses of "AYE!" so loud and exuberant that Napoleon, aroused, began racing around the room in wild excitement until his tail caught Franky squarely across the chops, prompting a howl of "Jesus *Christ*, you antediluvian canine!" from that temporarily stunned individual and prompt action by Jeff and Billy, who threw themselves upon Napoleon, tripped him up and lay upon him so he couldn't escape despite flailing limbs, more excited barking and happy thumping of tail on floor.

Josephine, surveying all this serenely from atop the piano, uttered a small, dignified "Prrrt!" which said, as clearly as anything, "What a hopeless bunch of rowdies!"

"Does anybody have any business to bring before the house?" Buff inquired, thinking: Christ, I hope it doesn't get too bloody.

From the sudden tension and the stern expressions on several faces, however, it was obvious that it well might. For several seconds no one spoke.

"Go on, Duke," Willie said finally. "Tell us about it."

On the sofa where he was flanked by Johnny Herbert and Rodge Leighton—not by their choice, their expressions made clear—Rudy Krohl began to look both belligerent and a little frightened.

From across the room where he was sitting on the arm of a worn leather chair occupied by Gulbransen, Duke gave him an odd look, half antagonistic, half something that Wilson thought might be, but hoped was not, apprehension. Then he sighed.

"Mr. President," he said, "I think I'll pass."

"*Pass?*" Willie exclaimed. "After what he's been doing to you? You're going to *pass?* What the hell's the matter?"

"Well—" Duke paused and sighed again. "I think maybe I've contributed too much to this situation already. I think it's best to just let it go. After all, maybe it isn't that important—"

"It's exactly as important as you think it is," Unruh remarked, and Latt nodded.

"I think so, too," he said gravely. "Better put it on the table, Duke. You aren't alone."

"Oh, no," Duke said quickly. "I don't think that. But I just wonder what good it will do, that's all."

"It will stop this harassing and help us clear the air," Wilson said crisply. "A consummation devoutly to be desired."

"Only if you have the votes!" Rudy said, voice rising to a sudden surprising shrillness oddly incongruous with his blond bulk. "Only if you have the votes!"

"I think we have them," Willie said with a calm assurance he did not altogether feel.

"Jeepers!" Jeff said. "What *is* this all about? *I* don't know. Has something new happened? Does everybody know but me?"

"No," Smitty Carriger said, speaking for the majority, who looked equally puzzled. "Lots of us don't. What is it, Duke? Come on, now. You owe it to us. What is it?"

Duke sighed again; stared at the floor; rubbed his chin; started to speak; stopped; started again; stopped.

"For Christ's sake," Willie said impatiently. "This"—he jerked a thumb in Rudy's direction—"guy over here has apparently been engaged in a deliberate campaign of harassment ever since Big Game Night. A lot of you were there and you know what happened Big Game Night. Since then there's been some sneaky stuff that—well, go ahead now, Duke, and stop this coy act. That's no way for—for people like you—to fight people like him. *Come on!*"

Finally persuaded, Duke took a deep breath and proceeded in a straightforward voice, clearly and without hesitation. A shabby little picture emerged—kid stuff but, as Gulbransen remarked later, sinister kid stuff.

"It began on the Monday after Big Game," Duke said. "Ever since then, almost every day, somebody's slipped the latest clipping on Hitler's anti-Jewish campaign under my door—usually late at night after I've gone to bed, I guess, because either Buff or I have found it next morning. I must have left my binder lying about someplace, too, because one day I found that somebody had scrawled—well, I won't tell you what he had scrawled, but it wasn't pleasant—across the front page of it. I've found similar notes tucked into the pockets of my lumber jacket too, made of cut-out newspaper letters, no handwriting. And when I got back from vacation there was a cheap sheath knife stuck through a piece of paper on my desk." His tone became momentarily wry. "I didn't mind disfiguring the desk, it looks as though it's been around since the founders, but I didn't like the words on the piece of paper."

"What were they?" Smitty asked into the intently listening silence.

"*Blut und Ehre*," Duke said, "which I think means 'Blood and Honor' and is one of the chief Nazi slogans, I believe. Also, 'Watch it, Jew!' which is something original from my secret admirer. Who I don't think," he added with a sudden vigor that sounded more like himself than had been the case in quite some time, "is really such a secret, after all."

Everybody looked at Rudy, who looked at nobody in return but whose face had a closed, stubborn, resentful expression, both defiant and uneasy. Finally Wilson spoke quietly.

"Is this all your doing, Rudy?"

"No!" Rudy said flatly. Skeptical sounds responded. "O.K., if you don't believe me, prove it!"

"Do you still have the knife, Duke?" Willie inquired.

"Oh, yes."

"Then we can always get the fingerprints—"

At which point Rudy, who was not a clever unpleasant boy but just a rather stupid one, minor except for the major evil with which he had chosen to align himself, blurted out, "There weren't any fingerprints!" and was overtaken by a quick gust of laughter. But it was uneasy laughter, quickly stilled as Buff held up his hand for order and looked thoughtfully around the room.

"So there we have it," he remarked, and paused. Silence lengthened. "What do you think," he asked finally, "we ought to do about it?"

"I think," Willie said calmly, "that it's time to pass the usual resolution approving the pledge class for full membership."

"Isn't that a little ahead of time?" Renny Suratt asked quickly. Willie gave him a bland look and said, "Maybe."

"We haven't had Hell Week yet," Gale Bryce pointed out, manner earnest, eyes bright with anticipation of fascinating psychological clashes to come. "We don't approve pledges until they've been through that."

"There's been a form of it," Wilson said, "as Duke's just told us—only in this case it's been a pledge putting a member through a private little Hell Week. We'll get to Hell Week, you guys, don't worry about it; next week, in fact. Prior to that, since we know we aren't going to reject anyone on the list anyway, I think we ought to vote. Here's the list, Tony," he added casually, getting up from his seat beside North and taking it over to him. "Why don't you read it to us and we can make it formal?"

Tony took the paper, obviously surprised at what appeared to be, and was, an unusual intervention; scanned it quickly; kept his usually smiling face impassive but glanced at Buff. Buff nodded.

"Go ahead. Read it and we'll vote."

"Well . . ." Tony said in a doubtful tone that increased the tension greatly. "O.K. . . . Jefferson Davis Barnett . . . Randolph Carrero . . . Roger Leighton . . . Henry Moore . . . Marcus Taylor . . . William Wilson . . . and that's it."

"Where am I?" Rudy cried in a strangled voice, lunging to his feet, face pale and contorted as he turned desperately to Buff. *"Where am I?"*

"I think that's a fair question, Mr. President," Latt remarked quietly. "Where is he?"

"He doesn't seem to be here," Tony said, rather lamely. Gulbransen hit Duke on the knee and said explosively, *"Good!"*

"No, Mr. President," Latt said in the same quiet tone, "I don't think it is good. It isn't fair and it isn't right."

"It is certainly fair under all the circumstances to separate him from the list and take a separate vote on whether or not we went him as a member,"

Wilson said with a calm equally adamant. "Surely you can't object to that, Brother Lattimer."

"Not if that was the house's intention, Brother Wilson," Latt said. "I wasn't aware that it was. We certainly weren't given any advance notice before it was sprung on us."

"All right," Buff said with a sudden decisiveness. "Make a motion, somebody. If enough agree, we'll do it that way. You can sit down, Rudy," he added, not unkindly. "You're going to get a fair shake, one way or the other."

"All *right*," Rudy said, and turned almost blindly to take his seat. There was a subtle but definite drawing-away by Rodge and Johnny.

"I so move, Mr. President," North said. Moose said, "I second!" in a loud voice.

"All those in favor," Buff said.

"AYE!" responded a large segment.

"Mr. President," Gale Bryce said, "I ask for a roll-call vote on that."

"I move to lay that motion on the table," Wilson said promptly.

"All those in favor of the motion to lay on the table—" Buff said quickly.

"AYE!" said an even larger segment.

"The motion to separate the lists stands as approved by voice vote," Buff said. "All those in favor of Jeff Barnett and the guys on his list—"

"AYE!"

"All those in favor of Rudy Krohl—"

"Mr. President!" Renny Suratt said firmly. "Mr. President! I hate to interrupt this steam roller but there is such a thing as elemental fairness—"

"What would *you* know about *that*?" Moose growled but Renny chose to ignore him.

"—so before we cast a vote on Rudolph Krohl which looks very likely to go against him, he ought to have a chance to state his side of it. Or am I being completely out of line with this great, objective lynching party?"

"It isn't any lynching party," Franky spoke up from the floor where he was resting his head on a pillow which in turn rested against the flank of a once more serenely sleeping Napoleon. "It's a carefully thought-out plan to remove an impediment to the future peace and happiness of this house. And I for one," he said with a sudden vigor that made Napoleon raise his head sleepily and then drop it again with a thud, "am all for it! Vote! *Vote!* VOTE!"

"Mr. President," Latt said, "Brother Suratt has a point. We've heard Duke. Surely we ought in all fairness to hear Rudy before we vote. Do I have to make a motion to that effect, or," he added with a most uncharacteristic sarcasm of his own, "will the basic nobility of this perfect house reassert itself and permit him to speak?"

"Oh, hell," Gulbransen said in a disgusted voice, "let him speak. Tell us why you've been bothering Duke, Rudy. Tell us all about it."

"Go ahead, Rudy," Buff said. "Why don't you stand up here by the piano?"

"I'll stay here!" Rudy said defiantly. "I'm not on trial!"

"I'm afraid you are," Buff said, "but suit yourself."

And so for the next ten minutes, from his seat between Johnny and Rodge, who drew even further away as he proceeded, he gave them what Franky referred to later as "your basic German-American Bund."

All the slanders ever perpetrated against the Jews spilled out in Rudy's rambling but doggedly determined account. His final charge was that they were trying to drag England, France and maybe even America into a war against an innocent, noble, beleaguered Germany that had no choice but to arm and fight back. If Hitler was doing things to them, they had brought it on themselves by trying to thwart his glorious plans to revive Germany and restore her place in the sun. They deserved whatever they got. Personally, he didn't believe any of these crazy rumors that were beginning to spread about tortures and maybe even mass murders—they were all just part of the whole big Jewish lie that was being spread across the whole world in an attempt to discredit Germany. Hitler wouldn't do anything like that. He was too great a man.

Finally the spew of hatred stopped. An increasingly appalled silence had fallen. Into it Bates inquired at last, "You really believe all that crap?"

"It's true!" Rudy cried. "It's true!"

"Suppose it were true," Smitty asked carefully, "which I don't for a single minute believe—what has that got to do with Duke? Why are you harassing him?"

"He's Jewish, isn't he?" Rudy asked simply. "He's been my enemy since I pledged this house. Why should I worry about *his* feelings?"

Tim and several others started to reply, then stopped, frustrated. As Gulbransen remarked later, "It's hard to believe these horrors exist when you find them on your own doorstep."

They couldn't believe that they had fellow countrymen who actually, blindly, accepted all this. But they did: some silent, some swept away by emotion like Rudy. What did one say in a situation like that, here on a campus known always for its tolerance, its fairness and its decency? It was an alien thing.

For several seconds more the silence held.

Into it Willie said finally, "Mr. President, I move the question on the admission of Rudolph Krohl." He glanced briefly at Latt. "If we're all satisfied, now, that he's had his say."

"Second," Latt said impassively.

"All those in favor of the motion," Buff said.

"I suggest a roll call," Latt added, and Buff hesitated.

"Go ahead," Rudy said bitterly. "Let them have their fun."

"It isn't fun," Buff said sharply, "and you aren't doing yourself any good with that tone. Tony, call the roll."

Calmly and steadily, Tony did; and at the end announced what they all knew, because everybody had been counting:

"On this vote the yeas are six, the nays are nineteen and the motion to admit Rudolph Krohl to membership in this house is defeated."

"What am I going to do?" Rudy cried in sudden incongruous anguish. *"What am I going to do?"*

"You should have thought of that," Gulbransen told him bluntly. "Go live in one of the halls, I guess. Unless the dean's office will give you permission to live off-campus. Which might be best for you and everybody."

"But you can't—" Rudy began, face suddenly crumpling. "You can't just—you can't just—"

"We just have," Buff said. "I'm sorry, Rudy, but that's it, I guess."

"I'm not sorry," Franky said from his recumbent position beside Napoleon. "I say good riddance to—"

"We don't need that, Franky!" Buff said sharply. "This is no joke, it's a serious and unhappy business. It's no light matter to bounce somebody out of a house. I'm sorry it had to come to this, Rudy, but I'm afraid you've made it inevitable. We'll give you a few days to make other plans but I'd suggest you try to be out of here within a week."

"You'll be sorry!" Rudy cried. "My father won't give you any library now!"

"We can stand that," Buff called after as Rudy rushed from the room. "We can stand it. . . ."

He looked suddenly tired, rubbed his eyes, asked in a tired voice, "Is everybody satisfied with what we've done?" Nobody spoke and presently he said, "O.K., I'm going to adjourn the meeting. I think that's enough drama for one night. Without objection, it's so ordered."

And they left the meeting soberly and went off to their rooms or to the Libe to study; and later regrouped soberly here and there throughout the house to rehash and reargue what they had done. It was, as Buff had said, no light matter under any circumstances to expel a member duly chosen and pledged; but, as Willie demanded defensively of Latt when he climbed the stairs to the attic around ten-thirty, "What else would you have had us do? You can't let the guy get away with that sort of thing. It's childish, and in the context of Hitler it's sinister. It isn't any kid game he's playing, and for his own good, the sooner he realizes it the better. Maybe this will turn him around and save him and others a lot of trouble."

"Maybe," Latt said gravely. "I hope so. . . . I don't disagree with our decision, because he has made it impossible for himself and Duke to get along in the house and we'd be constantly on edge about them. I do still question a little bit the way you sprang it on us, though. I don't like it when you get tricky, Willie. It isn't like you."

Wilson gave him a wry, unhappy look.

"Maybe it is," he said moodily. "I did it, didn't I?"

"Don't be smart," Latt said. "I'm concerned."

Wilson sighed.

"Damn it, so am I. But if it had been announced beforehand with all sorts of fanfare—or if we'd taken up the entire list and then had to have a big fight to get him off of it—those approaches would have been worse, it seems to me. Somebody had to force the issue in a way that would decide it: I did. I'm not entirely proud of it but I'm not entirely ashamed of it, either. It worked, he's out, we can go on about our business."

"That seems to be Hitler's attitude toward the Jews," Latt observed softly.

For a moment Willie looked genuinely angry.

"God damn it, stop being holier-than-thou! You don't have a monopoly on concern about moral positions, I'll have you know!" Then he softened it with a smile because nobody wanted to, or could, stay mad at Latt for any length of time. "*Almost* a monopoly, maybe, but not complete. . . . I'm concerned about it, too, Latt, but God *damn* it! We're coming up on something internationally, I think, that's going to be damned serious for our generation and for everybody on earth, maybe. It's a small blow we strike here, but it seems to me it's an important one."

Latt nodded.

"I agree. But I think it's important to do it in a fair and orderly fashion that will maintain our way of doing things, that's all."

"Is Hitler doing things 'in a fair and orderly fashion'?"

Latt sighed.

"No, he's not, and I don't defend him. But I think we have to be careful that in opposing him we don't lose something precious in ourselves—that we don't allow him to force us into changing ourselves into something we're not. Or shouldn't be, anyway."

"The classic argument," Willie said moodily. "How far do you go in opposing evil before you become evil yourself? And yet, damn it, we can't let him get away with what he apparently wants to do in the world. We just can't. Can we?"

"I don't know," Latt said with equal moodiness. "I just don't know. I happen to believe in the Christian ethic, myself. I think we have to be true to ourselves first, and that if we are, the forces of evil will ultimately be defeated."

"By what, our noble example? Tell that to the Czechs. And the Austrians. And the Jews on Kristallnacht. Or to any threatened people, at any time through history, now, in the past or in the future. I don't think it works, Latt. I think sometimes you have to be as tough as the forces of attack. And if that means as ruthless and as dirty and as—as evil, then maybe that's what it means. Maybe that's the only way to win—be as harsh and cruel and cold-blooded as they are."

"I don't want to think that!"

"I don't *want* to think it either. But logic and realism and the facts of life tell me that it is probably true."

"No!" Latt said sharply. "I refuse to believe that!"

"Then go down with the good-hearted," Willie said bitterly, "and the evil will sing over your graves. . . . I'm sorry, Latt, but I think there comes a time when there's just no other way, if you want to survive. You have to operate on the same plane as your enemies or they have all the advantage. And we just can't afford to let them have all the advantage. Otherwise there'll be nothing left of us. Or Europe. Or the Jews. Or anybody. I think that applies to any situation in international affairs where a drive for world domination exists. You can turn the other cheek if you want to, and see what good it does you. You'll be the next to dance to the slavemasters' tune, if you do."

"Well," Latt said with a gravity that indicated that he was speaking now from the very heart of his convictions, "I'm sorry, Willie, but I don't—I can't—agree with you. It violates everything I believe, everything I hope for, everything I am. I think we have to remain true to ourselves, no matter what. Whatever *they* do, I think *we* must adhere to the Christian ethic and to our own belief in what is true and good and right. Otherwise, we're lost even if we win."

"And so we won't win and we *will* be lost. At least if we follow your way."

"Better that," Latt said quietly, "than become the evil we oppose."

"I'm sorry. I don't agree with you."

"Then we'd better leave it there, hadn't we," Latt said, and stood up to leave.

Willie held out his hand.

"But as friends, I hope."

"Oh, for heaven's sake," Latt said, taking it. "Of course." He smiled and repeated what they often said to one another in moments of self-mockery: "It's only college."

"But like a lot of things in college, it reaches far beyond."

Latt sighed.

"Let's hope in this case it doesn't have to."

"We can hope," Willie said bleakly. "But it will."

And there you have it, he thought as he closed the door and turned back to do a little more studying before knocking off to get ready for bed. He had overstated his case, as one usually did when attempting to assail Latt's impregnable moral core, but essentially he thought he was right. He wasn't "ruthless" or "cold-blooded"—at least he hoped he wasn't—but damn it, there *were* times when the end justified the means, and Hitler was making it a major issue for everybody. Which was why the case of little Mr. Rudy was more than "just college," and why, he felt, it had been necessary to meet it on terms laid down by its inspirer in Berlin.

In terms of the immediate future, he could tell that Latt was probably going to be what was already being referred to as "isolationist" while he and Timmy and others were already well on the way to being "interventionist." Latt's motives would be the purest, most Christian, most selfless and most idealistic. His own and Timmy's would be much more realistic, Willie believed, but equally selfless and idealistic—they might, after all, be called upon to offer their lives to support their convictions. In the long run the basic motivation would be the same: how best to do it? There lay the argument. One could only go forward. And pray.

He sighed as there came renewed into his mind the knowledge that the battle between differing versions of right never ended; and the reminder that in another few days it would have to be fought out in still another area.

First, however, came Hell Week, that essentially infantile rite of passage that, in houses like theirs, was a relatively mild form of hazing that hurt no one. In others it sometimes became something much grimmer and uglier.

The farthest they ever went in their house was to order the pledges to strip and perform some awkward and humiliating act, varying from year to year according to the richness of senior imaginations. This was supposed to be a test of character, and essentially it was: those like Tony, Smitty and Johnny Herbert who said flatly, "Hell, no!" or "Fuck you!" or (in Johnny's case) a more dignified variant, were excused amid loud applause. Those like Godwin, Lor Davis and Bryce, who didn't quite dare defy what seemed to be the will of the house and so took a quick dab at it, were hooted out of the room and their knuckling under was never quite forgotten. But aside from this one juvenile rite, which perhaps did account for something in the way they were regarded and treated subsequently, most of Hell Week for this house consisted of cleaning up the yard, applying fresh paint where needed, reseeding the lawn and generally sprucing up the place—all this accompanied by an exaggerated deference toward their elders which was usually enforced with paddles and no great degree of severity.

From two or three of the most aggressively macho houses, however, there came more sinister and less innocent rumors. And every two or three years, on this as on many another campus in this and many another land, there would be a tragic episode in which, at a drunken party carefully held off-campus away from administration surveillance, some pledge would be drowned, or forced to drink a death-dealing amount, or suffocated, or killed in a fall, in some prank gone horribly wrong. This would always be followed by a clamor to abolish the fraternities and for good measure the sororities as well. Alumni would get up in arms—potential loss of future contributions would be quickly calculated in the comptroller's office—the furor would presently die down. A house might be temporarily suspended for a year or two as proof that discipline, too late, was being imposed. Then things would proceed as before.

In the long run the fraternity system survived because it was one of the best crucibles in which to forge friendships, camaraderie, mutual tolerance and character. "If you can learn to put up with your fraternal sons of bitches," as Franky put it, "you can learn to put up with anybody." The lessons of adaptability learned then would stand them in good stead when it came time to enter the greatest crucible of all and go to war.

After Hell Week came initiation. Again, some houses made a great to-do about this, full of abracadabra, secret code words, special handgrips, darkened rooms, candlelight, solemn processions, semireligious promises of eternal brotherhood. They prided themselves that their ceremony was much simpler. It too featured the darkened room, the candlelight, the procession, the promises of eternally binding brotherhood; but, as they liked to tell each other, "without a lot of that pompous crap." They pledged their friendship to one another in ritualized words handed on to them by national headquarters, and their attitude, both toward friendship and toward one another, was suitably respectful—but their whole proceeding was relatively simple and consumed only about twenty minutes. As Latt said, "If we don't like and trust each other at the end of our years together, ceremonial words aren't going to do it." The ceremony made it all a little special and they were all glad afterwards that they had been through it. But in essence, Latt was right.

So Hell Week and initiation came and went. Rudy Krohl, sinking ever deeper into a dazed and bitterly resentful silence, packed his belongings and left, nobody (including even Latt, his almost endless patience finally exhausted) knowing or caring where; the routine of classes and the rising drumbeat of campus activities began to sweep them along in earnest; and the time for final rushing and the assembling of next year's pledge class was upon them.

With it came the time for the immediate acceptance and induction of any transfer students they might wish to take in. And with that, as Jeff Barnett went around reminding them, came the time "when y'all's got to decide what to do about Willie's li'l ole starry-eyed crusade for that boy By."

Prior to his last visit before final decision, intensive discussions began in the house. They were equally intense, if not more so, elsewhere. They made him, as he told himself during several restless and increasingly sleepless nights, one unhappy, upset and confused little nigger.

The first to approach him was Guy Unruh. Their basketball collaboration had deepened into a genuine friendship as the practice months ended and the varsity winter season began. "He's a really nice kid," Guy told Willie on several occasions. "He means well, he thinks well, he acts well. I like him." "Work on him," Willie directed, and Guy replied with a grin, "Every day."

It wasn't quite that often, but it was enough to establish a considerable, and growing, influence: strong enough so that Guy was almost able to convince himself that there really weren't any problems, and that it would all turn out exactly as he and Willie and a lot of others wanted it to.

This, he knew, was a deceptive frame of mind he shouldn't let blind him to the difficulties. But inevitably it did, and this produced a confident tone that almost—almost—persuaded By that it was all clear sailing. Only inherent inbred caution kept him from, as he put it to himself, "really getting stupid."

"I've got to be realistic," he told Guy a couple of days before he was scheduled to come up for dinner. "I can't just assume that Mr. Bar—Jeff— and the others who don't like me are going to greet me with a brass band. More likely it'll be tar and—"

"Stop that!" Guy said sharply. "Cut it out! And don't say they don't like you. I haven't heard anybody, and that includes Jeff, say he doesn't like you. Jeff likes you."

"Oh, I know," By said, a sudden bitter little twist to his mouth. " 'Ah lahk that boy By. Ah jes' don' want him in mah house, 'cept to mop the floah, mebbe.' "

"God damn it!" Guy exploded. "When are you going to get over that crap, anyway?"

"Not in our lifetimes," By predicted bleakly. "That's my guess. Oh, I expect eventually there'll be some organized national attempts to gloss it over some, but it'll still be there, sometimes open, sometimes underneath, but always there. . . . I think," he said, suddenly gripped by a conviction he hadn't articulated before because it had never hit him with quite the force it did now, "that I may devote my life to that."

"To what?" Guy inquired, although he expected he knew.

"To making things better," he said, face alight; and for the first time used to a white man a phrase he had always been too self-conscious to use before: "For my people."

"Is that you talking," Guy asked bluntly, "or Maryetta?"

"Who cares?" By said, "if it comes out the right thing in the end?"

But it was, he knew, really Maryetta; and he realized in that moment that it had probably been her aim from the beginning. That first half-bullying, half-affectionate talk on the way home from studying together at the Libe had been followed by a number of dates and talks, each more solemn and insistent than the last. Maryetta was a type that would become increasingly prevalent as the years went on: the grimly earnest, ruthlessly good-hearted, savagely well-intentioned, terrifyingly intolerant lovers of mankind who mowed down all before them in their monstrously idealistic pursuit of the overwhelming Truth to which they, and they alone, had been given the key . . . they believed.

All her life she would be in pursuit of Causes. By the time she was sixty she would have participated in every drive, every protest, every campaign, every Cause of A Worthy Nature that the wildest fringes of idealism could conceive. Increasingly tense, increasingly grim, increasingly intolerant of any viewpoint save her own, starting from a point of little humor and progressing inexorably to one of no humor at all, she would be found all her life on the barricades. Enemies might shift and change, causes fade and be replaced. Maryetta would go on forever, living in a constant flurry of plans, programs, petitions, proposals. She would find that her native California, the state of ballot initiatives, was made for her and she for it. All her life she would be opposing this, supporting that, helping to generate, when things appeared too quiet, something else.

As such she would be the willing servant of many even more ruthless, and certainly infinitely more cynical, than she.

She would never know this.

Poor By, Unruh told Willie after the house had worked its will, never had a chance.

Nor, By found as his date for dinner came ever faster upon him, did he really want to. Jeff Barnett was the reality he had grown up with all his life, Maryetta the radical departure. Presently he had found that the radicalism was not all that hard to accommodate. "Stand up to them!" she was always urging, pert little face pursed and determined. "Don't let them push you around! Stand up to them!"

Any chance of "working from within," as Guy and Willie both urged him in last-minute phone calls the night before he came up to the house, was lost in the newfound, exciting feeling of independence. With Maryetta's help he seemed to have discovered his vocation. At her urging he painted himself into a corner from which it was impossible, for all practical purposes, to do anything else.

Yet it had taken him all of autumn quarter to come to that conclusion. The habits and thought processes of a lifetime in the South were not swiftly overcome. The transition had been made no easier by the reaction at home over the holidays, where his family, old-fashioned and alarmed, vehemently protested his attempt to enter the white man's citadel.

His parents and siblings simply couldn't understand. If the house didn't want him, why did he try to force himself upon the house? "Haven't you got any dignity, boy? Haven't you got any pride?" He tried without success to explain that it *was* a matter of pride and of dignity—his own. When he said it wasn't "the house" that opposed him, only a small handful, maybe, led by Jeff Barnett from Charleston, South Carolina, his father said By was getting mighty uppity to challenge a Barnett from Charleston. If Mr. Barnett didn't like him— Oh, Mr. Barnett *did* like him. Then what was the purpose in— Oh, Mr. Barnett just wanted him to stay in his place? Well, what was wrong with that? He *should* stay in his place, shouldn't he?

They battled through most of the holidays, only pausing, at his mother's finally exasperated demand, for Christmas, New Year's Eve, and New Year's Day. All the rest of the time, it seemed to By looking back, they argued and argued and argued and *argued.* He returned to the University emotionally exhausted, only to find Maryetta waiting and primed to overwhelm him all over again in a grim attempt to shore up what she had convinced herself was a wavering intention and an uncertain will.

Finally, when they had paused in the chill winter sunshine to sit on one of the benches in the Inner Quad for a few moments between classes, he had rebelled against this. But mildly. He was not equipped by nature or temperament to be too harsh with anyone, let alone the small, determined, insistent figure at his side. He didn't know whether he loved her or not—never would know, no matter how closely their lives might become entwined—but whatever the emotion, it was enough to tie him to her in a way that inhibited any real break. Or even any very harsh words, though on this occasion he surprised them both with the vigor of his response.

"Why do you keep after me so?" he demanded. "That's all I got, all vacation, was nag, nag, nag about it. Except they want me to do the one thing and you want me to do the other. I'm exhausted, Maryetta. I am *really* exhausted."

"Well!" she said shortly. "If everybody in this world who backed a good cause got *exhausted* then humanity would never get anywhere, would it? Do you suppose Jeff Barnett gets *exhausted* when he goes about trying to keep you out of the house? Do you suppose President Roosevelt gets *exhausted* when he tries to fight the evils in our rotten social system? Did Booker T. Washington get *exhausted* when—"

"Maryetta!" he protested, overwhelmed by this rather hodgepodge invocation of the pantheon. "Maryetta, stop it! I can't keep up with you when you get like this. You seem to think it's all so easy, and it isn't easy at all. It's hard, that's what it is, and I'm doing my best to see my way through it and you just keep yelling and *yelling—*"

"Very well!" she snapped, and he realized that her face had literally turned white. "Very *well!* If that's how you feel, By Johnson, *you can just go on without me!* I'm leaving!"

And she stood up as if to do so; and, as always when someone he had come to rely upon seemed about to abandon him, he grabbed her hand and besought her not to.

"Now, wait," he said breathlessly, aware that across the Quad not too far away Johnny Herbert and Louise Gianfalco, on their way to an English class, had paused momentarily, caught by their raised voices. "*Wait!* Sit down again. Everybody's looking."

"Not everybody," she said scornfully, glancing about so angrily that Louise and Johnny hastily turned and went on their way. "Who's that?"

"Only Johnny Herbert from the house," he said. "Only somebody who will probably vote for me. But you don't care, as long as you can make your point. You don't care as long as you can work out some fantasy on me."

"Yes!" she cried—the grim, determined expression—the little old-fashioned bun of hair—the face growing old and strained already, at eighteen. "And why not? The only way mankind ever advances is if people work out their 'fantasies' and try to make things better! What's wrong with that?"

"You don't care if you ruin the whole thing for me!"

"*Ruin* it for you?" she cried, voice again rising so that he put his finger to his lips and begged desperately, "Maryetta, *shhhh! Please!* I'm not *ruining* it for you! I'm trying to save it for you! And you want to run away! You don't want to fight!"

"Maryetta," he said, "I do want to fight. Honest I do. I've made up my mind to go through with it. What more do you want of me?"

"I want you to *put your heart in it*," she said in what he was coming to recognize as one of her characteristic shifts of mood, this time a soft, fervent, almost evangelical tone. "I want you to be *convinced* of it. I want you to *enjoy* it. I want you to *believe* in it and *believe in yourself.* As," she concluded solemnly, "*I* do."

"Well, I do," he protested, baffled. "I mean, I *do.* I mean, I've made up my mind to it. I'm going through with it. I'm letting my name go in. I'm not running away. Why are you so fierce about what I've already decided to do?"

"Because I'm afraid you'll back down at the last minute," she said calmly. "I'm afraid you'll get afraid again. I'm trying to prevent that."

"What you're trying to do," he said with a sudden bitter insight, "is knock me off balance so that I really will hesitate—and then you can push me back up again—and then you can take credit for what I do. You're just building up your own ego. You're just trying to obligate me, that's what you're trying to do. I don't like to be obligated like that." His handsome face set into stubborn, resentful lines she had never seen before. It gave her momentary pause but did not deflect her in the slightest from her purpose.

"I'm not trying to obligate you," she said with a quick change to a lighter, almost jocular tone. "You're so *serious,* By! I'm just trying to encourage you and make sure you won't lose heart, that's all."

"I'm not losing heart," he said, reverting to his characteristic mildness, looking a little shamefaced that he had abandoned it for even a moment. "I've decided to go through with it. You can stop fussing at me. After all," he said with a wry little smile, "it isn't all that important, it's only a college fraternity house."

"It is *too* that important!" she cried with a shocked indignation that, again, drew some notice from passing students. "It's *terribly* important! It's a symbol of—of *everything*." Her voice sank to a normal level, became earnest and intent. "You've got to learn to think of yourself as a symbol, By. You were a symbol when you entered on Reg Day last fall and you've been a symbol ever since. You're a symbol now. You can't escape it. I think you can be a symbol all your life, if you want to be." Her voice took on its intimate, evangelical challenge again. "You can do *great things*, By. I want you to. I want to help. Don't you understand?"

He gave her a look half quizzical, half accepting; he realized that she was setting them on a course for life, if he would acquiesce. He still wasn't sure he wanted to, entirely, but he knew he was coming closer, through the sheer force of her righteous, insistent, demanding little personality, if nothing else.

"Anyway," he said, not responding directly, "I'm going to do what you want about the house because it's what I want, too. So you can stop riding me about it. I'm going to do it." The ten-past bell jangled through the Quad. He jumped to his feet and pulled her up too. "There's the bell! We'll have to run for it!"

And so they did, and in the flurry of racing across the Quad and arriving late, flustered and highly visible, at the sociology class she had persuaded him to take this quarter, doubts, hesitations, uncertainties were finally wiped out . . . until much later that afternoon when he walked slowly back to the hall from the gym and heard behind him the tread of someone apparently trying to overtake him.

He was so engrossed in his thoughts that he did not really pay attention or look up until a small, compact figure swung into step alongside and a voice he recognized all too well said, with a fair attempt at jauntiness, "Hello, there, By, what's y'hurry? Y'all's goin' like a house afire!"

But he wasn't, really, and the awkwardness of the remark showed him at once that Jeff might be as nervous as he himself instantly became. But that didn't make it any easier.

"Oh, hi, Jeff," he said with an instant resolve: he wasn't going to dance like a good little nigger just because it was "Mr. Barnett from Charleston, South Carolina."

But again, that didn't make it any easier.

"Mind if I walk along with you a little ways?" Jeff asked, and By thought wildly: Suppose I say yes I do mind? But of course he didn't.

"No. That's O.K."

"Good," Jeff said, and for a minute or two neither said anything; until By finally asked, because somebody had to say something, "Have a good swim?"

"Oh, sure," Jeff said. "Always do. I love it, just like you do basketball. But we're tightenin' up a bit now, as we get ready for varsity competition this quarter. Imagine y'all are too."

"Yes," By said, as they walked along through the open meadow, brown with the dead grass of winter. "I'm sure Guy's told you all about that."

"Yes," Jeff said. "Guy's a good buddy of mine."

"Mine, too," By said, and for a second Jeff said nothing. Then he laughed.

"Guy likes everybody," he said. Then he added firmly: "And so do I."

"So do I," By said; and somewhere around them, hanging in the air, there seemed to be another voice, a great universal voice, demanding in wonderment, "Then why can't—" But it was only imagination. Jeff's response was another little laugh and, "Well, that's good."

For a couple of minutes they watched, with serious concentration, their feet moving side by side along the well-worn path. Then By took a deep breath and said, "But you don't like *me*."

Jeff stopped dead and By perforce did too. Jeff actually put a hand on his arm. He actually sounded, and By believed him because they were both natives of the same unhappy landscape, genuinely upset.

"I do!" he exclaimed. "I do like you, By! I just don't think you ought to—ought to—"

"What?" By demanded with a sudden bitterness that broke through his self-imposed restraints of courtesy and, yes, deference. "Try to join your house? Why not, Jeff? Why not?"

"Now—" Jeff began. Then he took his hand from By's arm and spoke in a quiet voice. "Y'all know why, By. We're not kiddin' each other. You know why."

By sighed heavily; and then gave words to what he now truly believed, at last. Suddenly it *was* all settled in his mind, in a way it still hadn't been even with Maryetta. "No," he said, equally quiet. "No, I really do not."

He didn't know for a moment what Jeff might do: curse him, turn and walk away, wither him with some contemptuous remark, maybe even offer some violent physical rejection, though he was much shorter than By and By wasn't really worried about that.

But Jeff, surprising and yet not surprising him, because Jeff really was a gentleman and not some redneck from the piney woods, again responded quietly.

"First of all," he said, "because I think I've got the votes to beat you, and I wouldn't think you'd want to deliberately put yourself in that position, of bein' humiliated. Secondly, it's an all-white house and you'd just simply be like a fish out of water, By, you know that. And thirdly—"

"Thirdly," By interrupted, "*you* think it would make *you* uncomfortable to have me around, and so *you* don't want me in *your* house because it *is* your house. Isn't that right?"

"Well," Jeff conceded, "maybe. But I think the first two reasons are just as valid. I wouldn't have the votes if others didn't agree with me, By. Some of them must think you'd be out of place—they must think they'd be uncomfortable too—otherwise they wouldn't vote with me. Would they?"

"Maybe they won't," By said, but he knew with a sudden sickening feeling that Jeff wouldn't let himself sound so confident if he didn't have reason to be.

"They will," Jeff said. "They will. It takes five to do it, and I've got 'em.

I've got 'em. So why don't you think about it and tell Willie you don't want to do it? Nobody'll think badly of you if you just withdraw. It'd save us havin' to vote, and you havin' to be beat, and it would be the best way out of an embarrassin' situation for all of us. Why don't you just do that, By? Everybody'd be much happier."

"*You'd* be much happier," By said bitterly.

"So would you," Jeff said, "once you get over this feelin' that you have to prove somethin'."

By gave him a long look as the last rays of the cold winter sun died over the meadow, crisscrossed now by many returning to their dorms.

"But I *am* proving something," he said bleakly. "Can't you understand that, Jeff? I *am* proving something."

Jeff looked sincerely baffled.

"Why do you have to?"

"Because I do," By said miserably—but miserable or not, he wasn't yielding, he told himself. Not ever again. "Just because I do."

"Then I'm sorry, By," Jeff said, and he did sound sorry, "but I'm just goin' to have to beat you, that's all. I'm just goin' to have to plumb right-out beat you."

"I don't care. You'll be beating yourself too."

Jeff looked startled for a second. Then he nodded.

"I think I understand how you mean that. But I don't think it's true."

"We'll see who's right in the long run," By said as the evening chill began to come up out of the ground; and they both knew he was talking far beyond the house.

"That's right," Jeff agreed quietly. "We'll just have to see."

They stared wide-eyed and motionless at one another for a moment more. Then they turned and walked away in the deepening twilight, Jeff back to the Quad and on up the Row, By through the meadow to his hall. And next night he came up for dinner and the night after that stayed in his room tensely and futilely trying to study until he got the call from Willie telling him what the house had done.

They were draped as usual in various stages of relaxation around the living room, some on sofas, some in chairs, Franky and a few others lying on the rug, Napoleon serving as support for Moose's feet, Josephine curled in Gulbransen's lap.

Buff called them to order, Tony called the roll: everybody was there. Relaxation tightened swiftly to close attention as Buff announced that, as everybody knew, they were there to vote on the nomination of potential transfer members, if any. Once again Willie took the lead.

"Mr. President," he said, "we all know there's only one, and that's By

Johnson, whom we all know pretty well by now, I think, as he's been here a few times for dinner."

"How many?" Suratt inquired. Wilson shrugged.

"Three or four, isn't it? Opportunity enough for everybody to get acquainted with him, I would think. Plus we all know he's developing into one of the rising stars of the basketball team, as Guy can testify. He's a hell of a nice, bright, decent, likeable kid, and a lot of us think he would be a damned good member and a real credit to the house. So I move that we pledge Bayard Johnson and invite him to join the house immediately."

Buff, knowing he would be interrupted, made the gesture: "All those in favor—"

"Mr. President," Jeff said quietly, "I don't want to prolong this and I know we all want to get it decided once and *for all.* But I do think we're goin' to have to talk about it a little bit. I think we all agree on what a nice boy By is. He really is a nice guy for a—for what he is—and I don't have anythin' against him on that ground—"

"Then why—?" Latt inquired and Jeff retorted with a rare flash of annoyance, "Because it isn't *right,* that's why!"

"Oh, come on, now," Unruh protested. Jeff shot him an angry look across the room.

"It isn't right in my book," he said flatly, "and that's what I have to go on. I'm not goin' into all the reasons I said when the question of him joinin' originally came up, but they haven't changed any. It's against the way I was raised, and furthermore—*furthermore*—it's against the way *he* was raised. I don't think in his heart of hearts he'd want to come in here knowin' that some of us *just don't want him.* I wouldn't want to do that, would you? I'd be damned uncomfortable if I came in like that, knowin' there were people not wantin' me here. And so would he, *I* think."

"He didn't sound that way last night," Gulbransen observed. "Some of us talked to him after dinner and he seemed quite ready to do it. He didn't sound reluctant at all."

"I know," Jeff admitted. "I know. I talked to him myself after gym night before last—yes, I did, y'all don't look so surprised, us Southerners can talk to one another—and he sounded pretty determined then. But I just don't believe him. I think he may have *convinced* himself that he wants to join—or maybe somebody had done the convincin' for him—but I can't believe that in his heart of hearts, comin' from the South as he does and knowin' how I feel, he'd really want to bust right in. I mean—" He looked earnestly around the room. "I mean, who'd want to do it? I can't conceive that—"

"Why don't we vote," Wilson suggested, "and if the vote goes his way, then let him decide. Why should you take it on yourself to decide for him, Jeff? Why don't you let us vote him in and then see what happens when we ask him to join?"

"Yeah, Willie," Jeff said with a grim little smile. "You'd like me to back down, wouldn't you? You'd like me to give up my votes, because you know that unless I do, he's licked. I've been checkin' and you've been checkin' and we both know what the score is. Isn't that right?"

"As of this morning—" Willie began, but Jeff interrupted triumphantly.

"And as of this afternoon—and as of before dinner—and as of after dinner—and—why don't you admit it, Willie? Y'all just *haven't got the votes*. It's as simple as that."

"Well," Wilson said, "if you're right—"

"You know it."

"If you're right," Willie repeated with dignity, "then I think those who are planning to vote with you owe it to the house to tell us why. You don't have the excuse Jeff does, that it's bred in you so you don't even have to think twice about it because it's just there. I think I can understand that. Somewhat. But the rest of you weren't born in the South and you don't have that excuse. If it is an excuse. So what's with you?"

"Mr. President," Franky said, propping himself up on his elbows from his recumbent position, giving Willie a thoughtful look, "I'm going to vote with Jeff because I think we just aren't ready for it. I think it may be coming someday—sometime—somewhere—maybe. But I don't see why we here in this house and at this university have to stick our necks out and take the heat. I think we'd get a lot of b.s. from the alumni and a lot of b.s. from the national and a lot of b.s. from the administration and a lot of b.s. from the press. I don't see why we need to borrow trouble. He's making a good place for himself on campus with basketball and all that and I think he ought to be content with that. He shouldn't try to put us on the spot. And neither, dear old chum Willie," he concluded as he lay back down, stretched and yawned, "should you."

"I agree," Renny Suratt said. "I don't see that there's any obligation on us to take the lead. There are more than a dozen other fraternities on this campus, and I don't see any of them stepping out in front in this noble crusade. Why have you selected us, Willie? What have we done to deserve your distinguished and flattering attention?"

Wilson started to snap out a retort but before he could Guy intercepted him with an admonitory gesture.

"Mr. President," he said, "let's don't get too personal here, O.K.? Willie isn't the only one who favors this. I do. Latt does. Gil does. Moose does. Timmy does. You haven't told me, Hack, but I think you do—" Hack nodded from the piano bench—"and Ray?" Ray nodded. "Pretty much all the seniors, and I think most everybody else—"

"Except me," Galen Bryce said cheerfully, eyes bright with the prospect of controversy that might bring really exciting psychological revelations.

"And me," Smitty Carriger said.

"And that makes five," Jeff said triumphantly, "and that's that."

"But why?" Guy inquired quietly. "Why? I can accept your point of view, Franky, and yours, Renny—it's a valid concern, that we're maybe going too fast and it might bring public embarrassment in some way. And I think," he added dryly, "that I can understand your motivation, Gale. But what's your problem, Smitty?"

"I guess I'm six of one and half a dozen of the other," Smitty said. "To some extent I agree with Jeff. I wasn't brought up in the South but I was brought up to believe that there's a difference, and that while we're morally obligated to do all we can to help improve financial and living conditions, which my family does all the time in our companies, we're under no obligation to endorse or support social crusades. And like Franky and Renny, I don't really think we ought to be taking the lead, because I don't really think it's time, yet."

"Well, when does it become time?" Willie inquired with some exasperation. "1940? 1950? 1960? '70, '80, '90, 2000? I mean, after all, damn it, there's got to be a start. There's nothing wrong with this guy except the color of his skin, right? Everything else about him is O.K. except that, right?"

"He's *different*," Jeff said desperately. "They *are* different, Willie, God damn it, you just don't know. They're reared up different, they think different, they act different—"

"And why is that?" Willie demanded. "Because you and your people have kept them down for three hundred years, that's why! They've never had a chance to—"

"We haven't either kept 'em down!" Jeff cried bitterly. "My family's always—"

"All right!" Willie overrode him as the tension rose sharply in the room. "All *right!* Your family's different, you say they've been good to them, I accept that. But that's not the case with the majority, and you know it!"

"Maybe," Jeff said. "Maybe." He turned to Buff with a look of appeal and said almost forlornly, almost like a bothered and hard-pressed child, "I want to vote, Mr. President. I don't want to argue anymore. Can we just vote? Please?"

Buff nodded.

"Right. We aren't getting anywhere like this and it's obvious we aren't going to get anywhere. All those in favor of the motion to invite Bayard Johnson to become a member—"

"Roll call, Mr. President," Galen Bryce suggested brightly. "Roll call."

"Call the roll, Tony," Buff directed, and when Tony had and the five had stood their ground, he said, "On this vote the yeas are nineteen, the nays are five, and under the rules of the house the motion is rejected. Will you so inform By, Willie? Tell him it's nothing personal—well," he concluded lamely when Willie shot him a look, "well, I mean—well, *you* know what to say."

"I don't know what to say," Willie retorted bitterly. "I can't think of any words for it that will do it justice."

After procrastinating for half an hour he knew he could not procrastinate any longer. With Unruh leaning against the wall on one side and Latt on the other, he picked up the phone in the second-floor booth and put in the call.

By answered on the first ring.

"Yes?" he said eagerly, and though Willie only hesitated a split second, when By said, "Willie?" it was in a much different, preparing-to-be-hurt tone that came clearly to his three intent listeners.

"By—" Willie began and By said instantly, "They rejected me."

Willie sighed heavily.

"Yes, I'm afraid they did. Jeff had his votes, all right. But I want you to know that there were nineteen of us for you, and of the five against only Jeff was really—really blind about it. The others had mixed motives but their main feeling was that we might be going too fast and would get a lot of criticism."

"Why would you get criticism," By asked in a tone half pain, half bewilderment, "for doing the right thing?"

"I agree with you," Willie said. "That wasn't my argument, I'm just telling you what motivated the opponents. I fought hard for you and so did a number of others."

"I appreciate it," By said. "Thank you, Willie, you've been a real friend. And thank Guy for me too, I know he helped. And Latt. And all the others." His voice remained clear but he sounded, suddenly, very remote. "I guess I won't be seeing you much any more. I'll have to see Guy because he's on the team, but I'll try to stay out of his way as much as possible—"

"Give me that!" Guy said, and Willie obediently slid out of the booth.

"Listen!" Guy said. "Stop that crap, O.K.? What kind of friends do you think we are? We'll be seeing you a lot—"

"Not at the house," By interrupted in a muffled voice. "You won't have me up to the house any more."

"Well—" Guy hesitated. Both Willie and Latt urged him with violent gestures to go ahead. "Of course we will! We'll have you up here for dinner whenever you can make it. And when we have a dance—"

By uttered a wry little laugh.

"Even if I'd come, which I won't, you know Maryetta wouldn't, now. From now on we only go places together. She's the only real friend I have on this campus. We all know that now."

"She is *not!*" Guy protested. "Nothing's changed up here, for Christ's sake! You've got your friends, we're just the same—"

"No, you're not. You're there and I'm here. And that's the way it is. So, thank you again, and—"

"Wait!" Guy demanded. "Wait!"

"For what?" By asked as he hung up, in a voice so low they could hardly hear him. "It's all over now."

"Oh no it isn't!" Maryetta exclaimed when he called ten minutes later after fighting a first bitter burst of tears to a standstill. "*Oh* no it isn't! I've been considering what you should do if this happened, and here's what I think. . . ."

Next morning in the *Daily*—published only after a tense closed-door argument between editor and associate editor that was clearly audible to fascinated staffers clustered outside—there appeared:

FRATERNITY REJECTS SOLE NEGRO STUDENT
Johnson Gets Boot in
Race-Dominated Decision
By Bill Nagatani

The University's only Negro student, Bayard Johnson from Richmond, Va., was rejected for membership in the Alpha Zeta house last night. Strong opposition led by swimming star Jefferson Barnett of Charleston, S.C., resulted in Johnson's blackballing by the five votes necessary under house rules.

Questioned by the *Daily*, Barnett freely admitted that his opposition to Johnson was motivated by traditional Southern racial attitudes.

"I don't believe," Barnett said, "that Negroes are capable of association with white men on an equal social footing. I don't believe By Johnson, whom I like as an individual and admire as a great basketball player, would be happy in the all-white environment of fraternities on this campus. Certainly I do not feel that my house would be comfortable with him in it."

The other four anti-Johnson members, who did not wish to be quoted by name, emphasized that they did not wholly share Barnett's racial views but had principally opposed Johnson because "it isn't time."

One summed up their views by saying they were "basically agreed that, while the Negro must advance in America, neither the University nor the country is ready to move too fast in this area."

Their view, and particularly Barnett's, was vigorously opposed by Willie Wilson, president of the student body and former president of the Alpha Zetes, who led the fight for Johnson's approval. He pointed out that nineteen members of the house had approved Johnson's try for membership and only the blackballing five opposed it. He said he "sincerely hoped" the house might reconsider Johnson's application "at some future time."

Johnson, however, told the *Daily* that he would "never again" seek membership in a fraternity "or association with any other group that does not admit Negroes to its membership." He said that the Alpha Zete decision had "confirmed me in the belief that in America the Negro can only advance through his own actions in an active campaign to secure his constitutional rights."

He said that as a result of the fraternity's action "I intend to devote my whole life to achieving equality for Negroes everywhere in America."

Queried by the *Daily* concerning his opinion of the Alpha Zete action, President Chalmers said he "deplores any action that needlessly wounds fellow beings," but would have no further comment at this time.

Off the record in his customary fashion, however, he did not hesitate to make his views known where he thought they would do the most good.

"Willie," he said when he finally connected by phone around three that afternoon, "what do you make of Bayard Johnson's statement in the *Daily*?"

"I think he means it."

"So do I. I think your house's action may very well turn out to be one of those events which, coming at or about college age, really does determine the course of a life. I am much disturbed about it. I worry that it has turned a potential constructive citizen vengeful."

"Oh, I don't think so, sir," Willie said earnestly. "At least I hope not. I don't know him awfully well, but I have cultivated him some because I really did want him in the house. I thought it might help us all in some way—that it *would* encourage him to be constructive. From what I've seen, he strikes me as an essentially gentle character, very shy and yet quite trusting and disposed to be friendly toward everyone. I don't *think* he'd be vengeful, but I just don't know. . . . I do know he's bitterly disappointed but I'm going to talk to him some more during the rest of the year and see if I can't head off any vengeful feelings."

"You did your best for him," the president said, "and I give you much credit for that."

"Thank you, sir. My feeling, as I guess yours, sir, was that perhaps we could make him a collaborator and coworker in trying to better conditions, and not an opponent. I think that's the only way to get anywhere." He uttered a wry little laugh. "I'm afraid little buddy Jeff put the kibosh on that. But you can't blame him, really. I've been around and around with him, but it's just instinct. Wrong instinct, *I* think, but he can't help it."

"I think perhaps," Dr. Chalmers said thoughtfully, "that we're coming to a time, or we're going to come to a time before long, when that instinct is just going to have to be overridden. What's right is just going to have to be done, that's all. The pressure will rise eventually, and it will occur. I'm pleased that you wish to keep talking to By. I think you probably have a lot of influence."

"And Guy Unruh, too," Willie suggested. "They're pretty close, on the basketball team. And Bill Lattimer."

"Who's everybody's good influence on everything," Dr. Chalmers said with a chuckle that was positively affectionate. "A rare bird, Latt. I think," he added thoughtfully, "that I will talk to Jeff, too. A fine young man, I think, and certainly an adornment to our athletic prowess. But he needs toning down on his native beliefs."

"Good luck, sir."

"You don't sound as though you have much faith in my persuasive powers." Willie laughed.

"The kid's a charmer but he's about as malleable as a piece of sandstone on the Quad."

"Which can be sculpted quite nicely," the president said comfortably, "when one uses the right tools."

"All I can say again, sir, is: good luck."

"Thank you," Dr. Chalmers said with another chuckle. "I'm not under the illusion that I won't need it. . . . Willie tells me," he remarked an hour later after his secretary had located Jeff in class and requested him to report to the hushed, oak-paneled office, "that I am going to have a great deal of difficulty persuading you that what you did last night was wrong."

"I'm sorry, sir," Jeff said evenly, only a slight tremor in his tightly linked fingers indicating the tension he was under in thus being summoned to the presence, "but I don't think it was wrong at all. I think it was for the best for everybody, the house, the University and that boy By himself, though I expect he can't see it that way right now."

"Apparently not. I suppose you saw his statement to the *Daily.*"

"Yes, sir."

The president gave him an appraising glance.

"It doesn't trouble you, a little bit?"

"No, sir. We got a few of 'em once in a while down South that don't seem to know their place, too. But it always quiets down. He'll forget it."

"How can he forget it, Jeff? Would you forget if somebody slapped you in the face?"

"Well, sir," Jeff said, "if I tried to bust in where I wasn't wanted, I'd *expect* to get slapped in the face. If he was so ignorant he didn't expect that, then I do feel sorry for him."

"But you wouldn't reconsider changing your stand so he could apply again."

Jeff's expression set in lines the president could see were just as stubborn as Willie had indicated they would be.

"He says he won't. He says that flatly. Why should I change my position when he's accepted that it's right?"

"I don't think you can quite draw that inference."

"Well, at least he's accepted that he can't break down the walls here, anyway. And I don't see you encouragin' him too much, either, sir—I mean with all respect, he's the only one you've admitted, right? If it's such a good cause, sir, why haven't you admitted more? Why aren't we just swarmin' with 'em, like—like little black beetles, or somethin'?"

"That's not a very nice comparison, Jeff," the president said, but still mildly: long experience told him that anger was no way to deal with a boy in this mood. "I think you could manage something a little more respectful."

"Yes, sir," Jeff said, looking abashed. "You're right, sir. As long as they stay in their place."

"Yes," the president said, a little more tartly. "Well: the reason the place isn't 'swarming with them,' as you put it so graciously, is that Bayard is, I'll admit confidentially to you, an experiment. The trustees have been thinking, and so have I, that we should begin to admit a small, carefully selected group, see how that works, and then go on from there until in a reasonably short time, there's a reasonable representation—"

"Why, sir?" Jeff interrupted, and Dr. Chalmers could see he was really asking, he wasn't being fresh. "Why do we have to have a 'representation'? They've got their own places, there's Howard University in Washington where By went before comin' here, and Tuskegee and some others in the South, and they can go there. Why do they have to come out here, where there aren't so very many of them?"

"Because in due course, I suspect, more and more will be coming to the West Coast. I think the University, which prides itself, I think rightly, on being in the vanguard of constructive change, should be helping to prepare the way."

"Well, sir," Jeff said, "all I can say is, I'm glad I won't be here. I'm glad I only have two and a half more years to go and then I'll graduate and I'll go back South and I won't worry about it. They're *never* goin' to achieve equality down there, I can tell you that!—sir. *Never.*"

"Well, Jeff," the president said mildly, "if you'll take it from an old man, 'never' is not an advisable word to use. About anything. But since you're looking into the future, I want you to carry this with you when you go: I want you to ask yourself how you will feel if you return to the South knowing that the principal legacy you have left your alma mater from your years here is a fellow American who, because of you, hates his country. Do you really want to live with the knowledge that that is the most long-lasting thing you have achieved here?"

At this Jeff looked, as the president had intended him to look, as though he had indeed been slapped in the face. His engaging young visage almost— almost, but not quite—crumpled into uncertainty, dismay, possibly even tears. But there was a fierce pride at work here, as the president realized, and after a moment of almost physical flinching from his words, it rallied.

"Well, sir," Jeff said in a voice that trembled with emotion but did not break, "I would hope that I'd be judged on something else besides that." His head came forward into his hands, he rubbed them across his eyes in a beleaguered gesture. But he did not give in. He looked up, terribly upset but unyielding. "I'd like to think I'd be remembered as a good student and a good athlete and a good friend to—to a lot of people, includin' By. I don't hate *him*, Dr. Chalmers, why should he *hate* me? Why should he *hate* America just because of me? I'm only doin' what I was reared to do, what I truly believe in. He's the one who's out of step, not me. He's the one who's tryin' to get out of his place, I'm not. I can't he'p it if what he's tryin' to do is *wrong* in my eyes. I just can't he'p it!"

The president gave him a long, thoughtful look. Then he nodded.

"I can understand. Perhaps I was too harsh—"

"You can't take back the words!" Jeff cried. "I'll remember them as long as I live! I surely will!"

"As perhaps you should," Dr. Chalmers said gravely. "Perhaps you should. Because there *is* another point of view, Jeff, and in your lifetime, and perhaps not too much further along into it, you may *have* to adapt to it: you may have no choice. So shouldn't you, perhaps, begin to think of it in terms of accommodation rather than confrontation? Shouldn't you begin to apply that lively brain of yours to the question of how we go about it, instead of how we try to stop it? You could contribute a great deal to your country, it seems to me, if you would do that. You have the brains, you have the position in your community, you have the very likeable personality that would permit you to act as a good mediator between the races.

"Why not think about that as a possibility? I'm afraid there's nothing you can do now to change the situation where By is concerned, but perhaps with that memory, and perhaps my own words, in mind, you can accomplish a great deal in a constructive way. I'd like to think the University had helped you to leave here with that purpose. Dare I hope just a little that this might be the case?"

It was Jeff's turn to give the president a long, thoughtful look. For several moments, neither flinching, they stared at one another. Finally Jeff's eyes dropped and he shifted uncomfortably in his chair.

"Well?" Dr. Chalmers asked. "What do you think?"

"I'll—think about it," Jeff said, voice low and not yielding very much. But it did yield a little, the president thought with a feeling of quiet triumph. That's something. With this boy, that's really quite a great deal.

"Good," he said comfortably. He stood up and held out his hand. "That's all anyone can ask. Thank you for coming by, Jeff. I appreciate it."

Jeff shook his hand gravely. Then his engaging smile began to return.

"Did I have any choice, sir?"

"Of course," Dr. Chalmers said. "I'm not a dictator."

"I can't think of a better one," Jeff said, smile broadening.

"Good luck with your swimming," Dr. Chalmers said. "Mrs. Chalmers and I will try to make it to one of the meets before the quarter's over."

"I'll win that one just for you."

"You'll win them all," the president predicted as he placed a fatherly hand on Jeff's back and moved him along to the door. "The University is counting on you."

"I hope you'll be proud of me," Jeff said, suddenly sober.

"Up to you," the president said as he stood in the doorway and smiled goodbye. "Up to you."

And Jeff went away thinking, just as the president had intended he should.

Dr. Chalmers could not imagine any sudden conversion, any dramatic reform. The patterns of a life, even an eighteen-year-old life, did not often change that quickly. But he had planted a seed—which was about all he could do, from time to time. He could only hope that the ones that took root were as worthwhile as this one potentially could be.

He told himself, as he went back to the big desk and resumed work on the unending problems of the University, that if he could look back on a hundred successfully planted out of all the thousands he had cast out during his presidency, he would be quite content.

Without thinking consciously about where he was going, Jeff found himself walking along in the mid-classes hush of the Inner Quad. He looked up with a start to see the muraled front of Memorial Church looming over him. After a rather self-conscious moment he opened the door and went in. It was cold in there—the University saved on heating bills except during the Sunday services—and deserted. The thin winter sunshine did not make the stained-glass windows glow as they would a little later, in the spring. But the room was, as always, beautiful, peaceful and restorative.

He sat in one of the pews for a long time, thinking. He could not admit to himself that he had been wrong—he wasn't ready for that yet, if he ever would be. But he did think about it, very seriously and very carefully. He was beginning to feel that maybe, just possibly, he might not have been entirely fair to that boy By. It was goin' to be pretty awkward tellin' him that, and maybe he never would—after all, it was By's fault, wasn't it, he shouldn't have tried to push in where white folks didn't want him. But *if* he *did* say somethin' to him, it wouldn't come easy. He'd have to think about it some more before he made any decision.

It wasn't easy to change your whole way of thinkin', and there wasn't any need to, really: just a feelin' that Dr. Chalmers—and Willie—and maybe some others—would think better of him if he did. It was just a question of which was more important, the folks at the University or all the folks back home who'd tell him he was absolutely right. He'd have thought it was an easy choice, before he talked to Dr. Chalmers; but to have the whole university and what it meant thrown in your face, to be made to think that you were betrayin' somethin' very *special* and *precious* if you didn't live up to its standards—well, he didn't quite know how to handle that one, at the moment. He'd have to think about it some more. And he would, too. He wasn't any coward, he faced up to things he did and accepted their consequences. It was just that he'd have to think some more, that's all.

The bell rang at eleven o'clock for the start of the ten-minute recess. He remembered with a start that he had a class coming up, hastily scrambled out of the pew and out into the noisy throng swarming through the chilly morning air. In a moment he bumped into Lor Davis, Tony Andrade and Rodge Leighton and walked along with them to the English class they all shared next. As they passed under the arches he saw in the distance a dark, familiar figure and that smarty little white gal who always seemed to be hangin' on him. Jeff felt a quick revulsion and looked away. Dr. Chalmers—Willie—the University—were askin' an awful lot of him, when you came right down to it. He'd do some more thinkin' for their sakes, but they *were* askin' an *awful* lot.

Seeing him across the Quad with his three housemates—had any of them, he wondered, been among the fateful five?—By felt a moment of blind panic, followed by an almost equally blinding relief as Jeff disappeared from sight. Sooner or later they would probably come face to face again but for the moment the thought of such a meeting was enough to turn him almost physically ill. He did, in fact, step back behind a nearby pillar so abruptly that Maryetta first exclaimed, "What—?" then turned, saw Jeff and immediately added in a scornful tone, "For heaven's sake, By, you aren't afraid of *him!*"

"I don't want to see him," By said almost inaudibly. "I just don't want to see him."

"He saw you," she said, having intercepted Jeff's look of distaste and returned it, with interest. "He's probably bragging all over campus about what he did to you. Well, I hope he's satisfied. I guess your statement showed *him.*"

"*Your* statement," By said. "I guess," he added wistfully, "that it showed everybody. I guess I'm through on this campus now."

"You're *not* through!" she said fiercely. "You're only beginning! You keep your head up and act as though you own this place and they'll come around. I'll bet you some other house will step in and—"

"Are you crazy?" he interrupted. "Are you absolutely crazy? No house is going to do anything at all. I'm through here and you know it."

"Well," she said shortly. "You're not through in the whole United States. You're not through—" she made a wide (and, he thought, rather wild) gesture in some general direction off-campus—"out *there*. And you're not through here unless you let Jeff Barnett really win. What do you want to do, leave the campus? Drop out of school? Wear a sign saying, 'I'm licked'? No, sir! You're not going to do that! I won't let you!"

He gave her a half-smile.

"You've taken on quite a responsibility for my life, Maryetta," he said with a certain wryness that he knew went right past her. "You're really totin' a load, with me."

"Listen!" she said fiercely. "Maybe that *was* my statement you read to the *Daily*, but you agreed with it, didn't you? You *asked* me to prepare something, didn't you? It's what you *wanted* to say, isn't it? You said you *liked* it, didn't you? It's a little late to get scared about it now!"

He sighed. The warning bell rang. He was thankful, for the moment, that she was going one way, he another: the intensity always got to him, sooner or later.

"They didn't have any *right* to do that to you," she said. "They just didn't have any *right*."

Under her prodding he forgot that "they" were only five of twenty-four and not the whole wide world. He found himself overwhelmed anew with a flood of pain and humiliation. And with it, deeper than he had realized, a dark and growing anger.

"No," he said somberly. "They surely did not."

And that afternoon when he, too, found himself sitting opposite Dr. Chalmers, he responded with only the minimum of courtesy to the president's attempts to assure him that the great majority of the student body was for him, that he need not take it personally, that there might well be other opportunities.

He said he didn't think there would be, and that even if there were, he intended to stand by his statement to the *Daily*. He reiterated this several times, so strongly that Dr. Chalmers soon abandoned the point.

For the most part in their brief talk By was so subdued and so stubborn as to seem almost sullen. The president was much disturbed but could not seem to break through and make real contact. He wished him well and let him go, telling him that he could stop by anytime he wanted to talk. By said politely that he didn't think he'd be wanting to talk about anything, thanks. From now on he intended to just concentrate on his studies and basketball and do his best to get through the rest of his college career "without troubling anybody else about anything."

"I hate to see you go away in that mood," the president said. By shrugged.

"What other mood is there for me, sir?"

The president, frustrated, said, "I know, but—"

And there it ended.

Or, as Dr. Chalmers told himself as he watched By go ramrod-stiff down the hall, there, perhaps, unless something powerful happened to prevent it, it began.

17

For the next few days repercussions continued. Furious arguments raged in the house. Smitty and Franky, disturbed by By's statement to the *Daily*, were having second thoughts. Jeff, far from being triumphant, was moody. Willie, hero to many, found himself the recipient of a call from Walter Emerson which he found unsettling even if it did impel him into his first date of the quarter with Marian.

In the *Daily* Shack, Bates and Nagatani were still in sharp disagreement over Bill's insistence on breaking the story after he received a phone tip from some anonymous female caller. Going through the pile of letters that by afternoon of the first day had reached 103 with no letup in sight, Tim was not in a very cordial mood when his presumptive successor knocked on the door and asked, with that politeness that always seemed to conceal a certain mocking amusement, if he might come in.

"Why not?" Tim inquired dryly. "This is going to be your office in another couple of weeks." He gestured toward the letters. "I hope you're satisfied."

"How are they running?" Nagatani inquired; and smiled when Tim told him, "Close."

"Pros ahead?"

"Cons at the moment, but only by about five. It seems the campus is fairly evenly divided, if these are any example. A lot of them seem to think my house is the shits."

"W-e-ll," Nagatani said in a politely regretful tone.

"Well, we're not," Tim said flatly. "Nineteen of us wanted him and only five voted no."

"Three more necessary than when you blackballed me," Bill commented blandly. "I guess I contributed something, after all."

"Don't say I did it," Bates said sharply. "I wanted you in, as you damned well know. I'm not going to discuss that with you again. I know that's why you're out to embarrass us now, but—"

"Not embarrass," Bill said, not at all flustered. "It's a good story. You wouldn't want me to pass up a good story, would you? What kind of journalism is that? It's a *good story*: University's only Negro gets it in the teeth from all-white frat—"

"Fraternity," Tim corrected automatically. "We don't use 'frat' here."

"Anyway," Bill said, concealing a smile with difficulty, "we had a duty to run it, right? Particularly when it got around campus. You didn't really want to censor it, did you?"

"No," Tim said in an exasperated tone, "I didn't want to censor it. I just wanted it kept in proportion, that's all."

"What's 'proportion'?" Bill inquired in a reasonable tone. "It's a big deal. Look what the City papers have made of it."

And he held them up: CAMPUS RACE PREJUDICE BLOCKS NEGRO; and FRAT NIXES NEGRO.

"Again, thanks to you," Tim noted. " 'By Bill Nagatani, Campus Correspondent.' Big deal, indeed. I'm sorry you were able to provoke Johnson into that statement. Did you write it for him?"

"I didn't write it for him," Nagatani said indignantly. "He volunteered it. And good for him! I like it, myself."

"Yes," Tim agreed, "you would."

"And why not?" Nagatani demanded, suddenly no longer so bland and smiley. "Why not something that says exactly the truth? He's got some pride. What's he supposed to do, crawl to you white guys? I say more power to him."

And for a moment he stared at Tim with an unusual open hostility in his eyes. Then the mask came down again, he smiled and relaxed. "Anyway, it's stirred things up a little. Want me to do an editorial on it? No, I'm just kidding. Probably best to let it pass without comment. I guess."

"I didn't say anything," Tim pointed out. Bill laughed comfortably.

"Didn't have to. I know how your mind works, Timmy. Are we going to take after Hitler again today?"

"Why don't you write about F.D.R.?" Tim suggested, deciding with relief that they were back on familiar ground.

"The budget message?" Bill inquired.

"Yeah. Nine billion bucks, biggest budget in history. One point nine billion for defense, biggest ever. Thirteen thousand warplanes, most ever."

"He's taking us right on in, isn't he?"

"He's doing what he thinks is necessary," Tim said.

"Is it?" Bill asked dryly.

And that, Tim thought, was exactly why he was waking up in the middle of the night worrying, now that his days on the *Daily* were numbered and he was coming up fast on the moment when its editorship would pass into the hands of this blandly smiling little figure in front of him.

"What do you plan to do with this paper, Bill?" he inquired. "Turn it into an isolationist sheet?"

" 'Isolationist,' " Bill echoed thoughtfully. " 'Interventionist.' That's getting to be the jargon, isn't it? I notice you're using them both a lot more in your editorials. And other papers are too. And radio. I'm not sure I like that. It just pushes people around more and more into two camps."

"There are two camps," Tim said flatly. "So what do you plan to do?"

"What do you care?" Bill asked. "You'll be out of here." Then his expression sobered. "I agree with you a lot of the time, Timmy. I'm just going to be a little quieter about it, that's all. I don't think even if Hitler took Europe and the Japs took Asia that we'd be in such terrible shape. We'd manage. So the *Daily* will be a little less outraged, for the rest of the year."

"While the situation gets worse," Tim said. "That's a hell of a note."

"That's your judgment. It isn't mine."

"You'll be the boss," Tim conceded, more amicably than he felt. He really felt like Moose after his last touchdown, that his college days, unhappily, were over. So much of his life for the past four years had been spent in this dirty, dilapidated, lovable, tumbledown old shanty; and suddenly he wouldn't be part of it anymore.

Bill grinned.

"You'll have lots of chances to express your concern. Let us hear from you. Don't go too far away. Write me a Letter to the Editor."

And on that comfortably patronizing note, which made him feel like an old horse being put out to pasture, Tim turned to the makeup of tomorrow morning's front page and Bill went out to write his editorial on F.D.R.

More and more, Tim thought as staffers began to drift in and the newsroom became alive with gossip, laughter and the sound of ancient Underwoods being belabored, he was beginning to feel that even the *Daily* was not enough to satisfy his growing concerns about the world. Even if by some impossible rearrangement of tradition he could stay on as editor, it might satisfy him sentimentally but it wouldn't be enough. Vaguely but with an increasingly insistent unease, he felt that there must be something else, some other gesture or affirmation to be made. He didn't know what, exactly. But there must be something.

He decided he would have to raise the question next time a senior bull session developed in the house. Some of his classmates were like Nagatani: they didn't suffer from his own ominous sense of urgency and oncoming crisis. But some, like Willie, had certainly given proof that they felt it too. Something inchoate, half-glimpsed and growing, was in Tim's mind. He'd have to kick it around with the others and see if it would take a shape that would make sense to any of them.

For the moment, although he too was having increasing periods of profound worry about it, the world situation was not in the forefront of Willie's concerns. He had already made one attempt to talk to By. Their conversation had consisted of two sentences:

"Hi, I just thought I'd call and—"

"Thanks for your interest, I appreciate it, I really do, but I don't have anything to talk to you about."

Click.

For a moment he had felt as though he were back in high school being rejected for the junior prom. Then he thought, Well, hell with you, buster boy. If you think you can slough me off that easily, you don't know Willie. I'll get back to you in due course. I'll *make* you talk to me. We'll see who wins this little contest of wills.

He didn't have time to think about it long, however, for he had no sooner gone back upstairs to his haven under the eaves than the phone rang and Hank Moore, passing the booth, picked it up and yelled, "WILSON! Mr. Emerson wants to talk to you!"

"Oh, oh!" Renny Suratt called out from somewhere below. "Watch out, Willie! Going to get little bottom spanked by big bad trustee!"

"I heard that," Walter Emerson said with what was evidently a characteristic chuckle. "Your fraternity brothers sound as disrespectful as mine used to be."

"Yes, sir," Wilson said, a little more brusquely than he had intended. "What can I do for you?"

"Take the chip off," Walter Emerson said comfortably. "Take the God damned chip off. I just thought we should have a little chat about this colored boy of yours down there."

"Mine and Edward H. Chalmers'," Wilson remarked and then decided to play it in a more comfortable key. "Yes, sir," he said amicably. "What about him? It's all over, of course. The house has made its decision, there's nothing more, as far as I know."

"And he's made his statement to the *Daily*," Walter Emerson said, "which has been picked up by all the papers in the City, and no doubt in the East as well. It puts the University in a bad light, you know, Mr. Wilson—Willie. Particularly coming after your little war demonstration. We can't have too much of that sort of thing. It's getting to seem like part of a pattern."

"Oh?" Wilson said. "A bad pattern?"

"Well," Walter Emerson said, "not really, I suppose. But bad from the standpoint of the University's reputation. We can't always be getting ourselves in the newspapers, you know. It makes us look like a bunch of crazies."

"Oh, now, sir!" Wilson said. " 'A bunch of crazies'! That's a little strong, isn't it? One anti-Hitler demonstration and one attempt to do the decent thing for a very deserving Negro student. That hardly makes us 'a bunch of crazies.' Or me, as their leader, which I guess is what you're getting at."

"Not at all," Walter Emerson said comfortably. "Not at all. You are a little out front for your time and place, maybe, but it's good to have somebody stirring things up."

"It is?" Willie said blankly. "You just said—"

"Within reason," Walter Emerson said with the chuckle Willie found he was coming to mistrust quite a bit. "Within reason. You referred to Johnson as Chalmers' boy too, and so he is. I suspect Chalmers told you that the board agreed to experiment with him for a year and see if it worked out, the idea being that if it did, we could then admit some more. But there's sort of an implicit bargain there, that nobody would tip the applecart and stir up too much notoriety while the initial experiment was going on."

"Too bad," Wilson said dryly, "that nobody thought to inform me."

"Dr. Chalmers told me he warned you to go slow, right after your gesture on Reg Day last fall."

"He did, but it was so circumspect that I probably didn't get it."

"Don't be disingenuous," Walter Emerson said, suddenly blunt. "You're a damned bright kid. You got it."

"Maybe so," Willie said, deciding to be blunt in return. "Too bad I ignored it in favor of doing the right thing."

"Which only resulted, when all was said and done," Walter Emerson pointed out quickly, "in defeating Johnson and apparently turning him into an embittered enemy of all that you and I stand for."

"I don't think it's that bad," Willie said, somewhat lamely. Walter Emerson snorted.

"His statement didn't sound very conciliatory to me. Maybe you can find some comfort in it. I can't. Too bad you just didn't leave well enough alone, Willie. You really don't have the answer to everything."

"No, sir," Wilson said, feeling suddenly tired. "I do not. I'm going to talk to By and see if I can't . . ."

"What?"

"Get him to calm down and be more reasonable about it. It isn't the end of the world, for God's sake."

"He sounds as though it is for him," Walter Emerson remarked, "and maybe it is. Good luck if you do talk to him. And Willie: I want you to promise me one thing."

"Yes?" Willie asked, guarded and suspicious.

"No more dramatic public gestures on this, O.K.? Just play it close to the vest—keep it quiet—discourage him from any more defiant statements or any big dramatic gestures—*hold it down*. O.K.? That's the only way to come out of this with anything constructive. Believe me. All right?"

"So far," Wilson said wryly, "he's refusing to speak to me, so all this advice is probably useless, anyway."

"I have great faith in your determination," Walter Emerson said with equal wryness. "You'll get to him. When you do, remember what I said. We may be entering a highly sensitive area on this subject. It behooves all of us to tread easy. Help him do so, if you can—and do so yourself from now on. O.K.?"

"I'll try."

"Give that daughter of mine a hug and a kiss for me," Walter Emerson directed. He chuckled again, sounding much more genuine this time. "Three or four, if you like. She spent most of Christmas vacation talking about you."

"She did?" Wilson inquired, sounding, he thought, pretty stupid. He *was* somewhat astounded, actually. "I'm surprised."

"You sound surprised," Walter Emerson agreed. "Oh, yes, you're quite the boy, in her mind. Mine too, I have to admit. Why don't you bring her over to Piedmont for dinner a week from Saturday, and plan to stay over? We have plenty of room and we'd love to have you."

"Well—I mean—"

"Don't you want to?"

"Oh, hell, yes," he said hurriedly. "I mean yes. Yes, of course. But I haven't talked to her in the last few days"—actually, he thought, not at all since a brief and awkward hello on Reg Day—"and—well, maybe she's already got a date with someone else—"

"She hasn't," Walter Emerson assured him with another chuckle. "She's counting on this one. So are you coming over?"

"Thank you," Willie said, venturing a laugh. "I guess I don't have much choice, do I?"

"Not a damned bit," Walter Emerson said happily. "We'll expect you a week from Saturday at six."

"Well, thank you, sir," Wilson said, sounding more bemused than he knew. "Thank you. Thank you."

"Three thank-yous and you're out," Walter Emerson said. "Saturday at six."

"Yes, sir," Willie said; and hung up, shaking his head.

And all the time, he'd been going through contortions trying to think of the best way to approach her. And she and Walter—he would have to call him that right off, to show he wasn't intimidated—had gone right ahead and planned this—this kidnapping.

"Hi," he said half an hour later when he got the phone again. "I hear I'm being kidnapped for dinner a week from Saturday."

She laughed, sounding quite at ease.

"Do you mind?"

"No. I think it's great. Six o'clock, your dad said. That means leaving here what, about five?"

"Probably, to be on the safe side. It's usually pretty heavy traffic Saturday getting across the Bay. Have you ever been to Piedmont?"

"Years ago when my mom went back to a reunion at Cal and we stopped to visit a friend of hers. That was in the days when we thought I might go to Cal."

"What changed your mind?"

"Well," he said, ignoring Franky, who had loomed up alongside the booth and was making faces in an attempt to break him up, "I was in the honor society at Porterville Union High School, where Billy and I went, and we had a state convention at Cal in June. And afterward one of the gals in our car who was already set to go to the University said, 'Let's take Dickie'—that's what they called me then—'over there and see if he likes it.' And we drove down Palm Drive and saw Memorial Church and came to the Quad and everything was bare and brown and deserted"—his voice began to get a little husky in spite of himself—"and you know, at that instant I fell in love with it and a week later I was taking the entrance exam and in September I entered. And I've been in love with it ever since and always will be, and that's how it happened."

"That's sweet," she said. "And touching. My dad will like that. He's a sentimentalist, like you."

"I'm not a sentimentalist!"

She laughed again.

"If you say so. O.K., I'll see you here at five on Saturday. Don't bother to bring a jacket and tie. We're very informal"—she laughed again—"except when we're formal. This time we won't be."

"En famille," he suggested and she laughed again. He really was going over as Mr. Hilarity today, all right, there was no doubt about it.

"There goes that high school French again," she said. "Not bad. See you a week from Saturday."

"I'll be there," he said, thinking: Not before?—and hung up, feeling quite absurdly on top of the world as he turned the phone over to Franky.

"You and Donn starting right in again?" Franky inquired. "That's nice."

"That wasn't Donn," he said. Franky gave him a look of elaborate surprise.

"Oh, Miss Trustee's Daughter! Well, well!"

"Just call Katie," Wilson ordered, "and slop all over, please, and forget me. All right?"

"Donn will be up—s—e——e——t!" Frank caroled.

"Screw you, buddy," Willie said, turning away with dignity.

"I have to study tonight," Franky called after him. "Can we make it Thursday?"

"Oh, go to hell."

But back in his room he reviewed the two conversations in a less carefree mood. He wasn't entirely sure that he liked to have Marian's father moving in on it: it destroyed spontaneity, made him feel much more rushed and obligated than he wanted to be. And the way she fell right in with it indicated that they must have talked it over and planned it very carefully. After all her pretense of being shy and withdrawing! What a fake!

He felt pretty annoyed about that, really. Maybe he should call back and say he'd forgotten a previous engagement—but the mere thought stopped him cold. And give up the opportunity that was being handed him on a silver platter? She would never speak to him again if he did that. And Walter Emerson would really get on his back.

Maybe Walter was the catalyst who would solve their problems for them. The hesitation waltz of autumn quarter—he felt it was kind of ridiculous, looking back. Gulbransen would have had her bedded or dismissed in a week. So would Unruh, although being a gentler person he might at least be kindly about it. Why had *he* been pussyfooting around?

Because, he told himself stoutly, this was Different. This could Really Mean Something. She was Special. She wasn't Just Any Girl Who Could Be Had for the Asking. She had Standards and so did he. She was Too Good to be Demeaned by Thoughts Like That.

Actually, he reflected wryly, for all he knew she might be sleeping with half the junior class. She might be another Welcome Waggoner. She might be on the prowl all the time, round-heeled, easy mark, best lay on campus. She might really be An Absolutely Worthless Tramp.

Oh, for Christ's sake, he admonished himself impatiently, stop trying to shock your own mind. You know damned well she isn't any of those things.

Everything indicated that she was exactly what he thought she was: Special, Completely Worthy of Respect, and, in all probability, Just What He Was Looking For.

Which left poor old Donn Van Dyke—like that "poor old," his mind told him wryly—well, where *did* it leave her? He knew for certain that *she* was Sincere, Honest, Trustworthy, positively bubbling over with Brains, Beauty, Integrity, Character and all those other good things. She was an exemplary girl in every way; her only problem being, as Unruh had once remarked, that she was almost too good to be true.

"Such endless perfection wears me out," Guy had said. "I don't see how you stand it. If just once she'd break down and yell or shout or cry or cuss or something! She's always so *cheerful*."

Which was entirely true, Wilson thought, beginning to defend her now just as he had when Guy said that. She was cheerful because she was good and because she genuinely liked everybody and wanted everybody to be happy.

He couldn't just dismiss her. No one in the world had given him less cause to. She had always been a true friend, and now that they were in tandem in student-body office it was perfectly natural that she should convince herself that it would lead in due course to a more permanent relationship. "I'll bet she's already secretly reserved the chapel for June," Latt had said recently, not entirely in jest; and while Willie didn't think she had, he really wouldn't have been all that surprised to find it true. But now came Marian, supported surprisingly by Walter, who had obviously made up his mind that Willie was just the man he had always hoped to find for his older daughter. And suddenly closer by a quantum leap had come the day when Willie must decide.

He sighed. All the knowns were on Donna's side, all the unknowns on Marian's. But Marian was new and interesting and even, he was beginning to feel, exciting, for all her inner hesitations and possibly difficult character, of which he had already caught some small glimpse. He knew himself to be strongly attracted and now he was being swept along by Walter, whom he was beginning to appreciate as a formidably determined man.

He decided presently that the best decision was, as before, no decision: ride with it, let the tide carry him, keep his own counsel, don't commit, see what happened—let events decide, as much as possible.

Which, he told himself, was not a very brave example of Perfect Boy Politician—or was it? Maybe that was the best thing a politician could do, at times—coast. Except, he thought ruefully, with Donn on one side and Walter on the other, there might not be time to coast.

Time, in fact, was growing shorter everywhere, in everything. The days were whirling faster. Senior year was moving on. Time which had always been so leisurely, time which had always been youth's luxury, time which had always been youth's friend, was winding down, and friend no more.

In their respective rooms on the second floor, several of his fellow seniors were feeling the same. A general unease seemed suddenly to have hit them all. Here they were in winter quarter—and in no time at all they'd be into spring—and then there they'd be at graduation—and where in the hell had it all gone, and what the hell did it all add up to, anyway?

Unruh, thinking back over these opening weeks of winter quarter, was more than a little appalled to realize that he had taken to Reg Dance, met on the Quad, shared classes with, had lunch at the Cellar with, telephoned, talked to, been really *absorbed by*, God damn it, Maggie Johnson *every single day* since returning to campus. *Jesus.* And yet how could he have avoided it? She was always *there*, plump and soft and adoring and clinging and *helpful* and *thoughtful* and *considerate* and *concerned* to the point where he thought he was about ready to yell from the sheer *smothering*. He knew he wouldn't, though, that was the frightening thing: he knew he wouldn't because he really rather liked it.

He had tried to have a little talk with her at Reg Dance, suggest that maybe it might be a good idea if they tried a little experiment for a while and didn't see each other quite so *much.*

"But why?" she had asked blankly, snuggling deeper into his arms as they danced.

"Oh," he said lamely, "just to try being with other people now and then— see how we feel—make us appreciate each other more—variety—" He felt he wasn't making much sense. Obviously she agreed.

"But *why?*" she repeated, raising her head long enough to give him a worshipful look. "Why? I don't *want* to be with other people. I just want to be with you. I'm *perfectly happy.* I don't *need* other people. Do you?"

"Well, no," he said hastily, thinking: Damn it, I've already talked to Willie about going up to the City next week, what will he think if I—?

"Really," Maggie said with a comfortable little laugh, dropping her head on his chest again, "you are so silly sometimes. I don't want to hear *another word* about it!"

"But," he protested, "I didn't mean—all I want—I just meant—"

"Silly!" she said affectionately. "You don't really know *what* you mean!"

Oh, yes, I do, he thought bleakly. But the time is fast afleeting when I'm going to be able to do anything about it, little girl, I can see that all right, all right.

And so *every* day, *every* night, *every* minute almost—*Jesus!*

If she weren't such a nice girl, and so strongly devoted to me, and if she weren't so perfectly cut out to be a doctor's wife, I'd—I'd—

But she was.

So there he was.

Pinned to the mast.

He stood up, locked the door, unzipped his pants, pulled down his shorts and began furiously masturbating. This was supposed to be some sort of innately masculine gesture of defiance, but after a few seconds it struck him as being not only quite boring but really rather ridiculous at this particular moment. So he stopped, put himself in order and returned to his books.

But *Jesus!*

Down the hall in the room he shared with Ray Baker, Gulbransen was in something of the same mood about Karen Ann, although Lord knew there was nothing cloying about *that* relationship. On the contrary. After Reg Dance he had hardly seen her, and she had only gone to that because, in some inexplicable burst of what strangely enough seemed to be anxiety, he had dated her up for it way back in December before the holidays.

"My, my," she said coolly. "You *are* being premature. What's the rush? Aren't you afraid I might say yes?"

"I want you to," he said, keeping it light, "believe it or not."

"O.K.," she said, distributing her blond mane across her shoulders with her characteristic toss of the head. "Then I will."

And they had kidded about it lightly during his brief holiday stay at her home, which only served to increase her parents' conviction that things were getting serious. And since Reg Dance they had hardly seen one another. They hadn't even telephoned, for Christ's sake. It was true he had dated one of his old senior flames once, and a new, cute little sophomore three times in the past three weeks, but even so, he did feel, with a certain uneasiness that quite surprised him, that Karen Ann could have maintained *some* contact.

That was why he had been on the phone tonight. She had professed great surprise at not hearing from him sooner. He had, against his better judgment, allowed a little annoyance to show because *she* had not been in touch with *him*.

"Ah, well," she said airily. "I'm not your slave, you know. I've had things to do."

"I'll bet."

"Perfectly respectable," she assured him calmly. "Meanwhile I hear you've been dating up a storm. What *is* this, anyway? I'm just supposed to be part of your harem?"

"Oh, hell! I haven't got a harem. I've just been wondering where you were, that's all."

"Right here at the other end of the line," she said, cheerfully. "Also on the Quad and in the Libe at frequent intervals. How come I haven't seen you? I know! You've been giving some cute transfer geography lessons on how to find her way around the Peninsula, including Sand Hill Road after dark."

"Nonsense!" he said indignantly, because that was exactly what he had been doing. "Sheer, unmitigated nonsense! I swear by Dr. Chalmers' beard—"

"He doesn't have a beard," she said with her sudden sharp little bark of laughter. "Might be becoming, though. Very Lincolnesque. So, what do you want now?"

"I want to take you dancing Saturday night. In the City. Want to go or don't you?"

"You put it so graciously. Of course I want to go."

"All right then. Pick you up at the house at six?"

"All right then. Pick me up at the house at six."

"All right!"

"All right!"

And suddenly laughing, as they usually wound up doing, they had hung up, both feeling a good deal better about things.

And that was probably why, he thought now as he tried to concentrate on studying, they really were going to get married, eventually: they didn't take each other too seriously and they made each other laugh. He did find her frustrating at times, though, because now and then, after all, she *was* supposed to take him seriously—and she just didn't. There were lots of times when she didn't seem to want him around at all, other times, like now, when she suddenly seemed to be his in some way much more personal even than their occasional (very occasional, although that wasn't the impression he liked to give the house) episodes of a more intimate nature.

Like Guy, he didn't want to be tied down—knew he probably would be—accepted it even as he rebelled against it—felt pleased about it—felt restless about it—didn't really know *how* he felt about it—and was getting himself into such a frustrated state of mind about it that he was almost on the point of doing what Guy had just done—when the door opened and Ray came in.

The world returned to the solid and steady basis on which Ray lived. And Gil became the fatherly adviser he liked to fancy himself with those who obviously didn't Know About Women the way he did.

"Hi," he said cordially, for he was fond of his roommate, as everyone was—good old Ray, the cornerstone of the house, they all said. "Had a wild date?"

"Oh, shucks," Ray said with a comfortable grin, peeling off his streaming raincoat and hat and throwing them in a corner. "It's too cold to have a date tonight. Raining like hell, too. I practically drowned getting back from the Libe. You been in all evening?"

"Yeah. Got to hit the books hard this quarter. Five subjects this time."

"Ouch," Ray said. "Is that going to give you time for all your women?" Gil grinned.

"Oh, sure." His tone became warmly confidential. "How about you? Are we finally going to get that big Baker romance everybody's been waiting for, for the past three years?"

Ray grinned too, an innocent and healthy grin that Gil secretly found a little frustrating: how could Ray be so happy when he apparently didn't have any of the romantic entanglements a lot of them did?

"I don't see any signs of it so far this year," he said cheerfully. "But I tell you, Gil, you'll be the first to know."

"Well, if you need any advice—" Gil said, quite seriously. But Ray just looked amused.

"I'll remember," he promised, putting his books on his desk and sinking into a chair. "I guess you're really the expert around here, all right. It must be great to have so much sex all the time."

But again, frustratingly, he didn't seem at all upset that he didn't. He just seemed calm and steady and unperturbed, as always: good old Ray, cornerstone of the house, salt of the earth, Mr. Average, calm as a summer's day.

"How do you manage?" Gil asked, deciding for once to force the issue: nobody ever quite got up the nerve to challenge Ray on this subject; there was something reserved and dignified there that was effective as a wall. "I mean, really, what do you do? Jerk off? That can't always be so much fun."

Ray gave him a calm look and a comfortable laugh.

"Oh, now, Gil. Don't try so hard. I'm getting along all right."

"No, but seriously. I mean—"

"I know what you mean. I repeat, I'm getting along all right. What's your worry?"

"Well, it just—just isn't normal, that's all. I mean, if you don't have a girlfriend and you don't beat your meat—and I know you aren't queer—then what—I mean, what—?"

"Look," Ray said, not at all bothered, perfectly at peace with himself. Damn it, Gil thought, honestly baffled, how does he do it? "Look, Gil. I'm doing all right, really I am. I'm twenty-one years old, right? And I've never been to bed with a woman, right?"

"Well, I didn't know," Gil said, finding that it sounded, oddly, quite apologetic.

"It's true," Ray said calmly. "I haven't. And I guess I have my normal share of wet dreams, and now and again, you're absolutely right, I expect I do—er—induce them a bit, as who doesn't—but basically, that's it. And you know something? I don't mind it at all. I feel perfectly good about it. I'm looking, you know; I'm not standing still. But I'm not fretting about it. I'm hoping that one of these days the right one will come along. She hasn't yet, but that's O.K., she will. And when she does, I'll be able to offer her something that—well, I know *you* can't understand this, but to me it's a little special and I like to think that she'll regard it that way too. If she's the kind I have in mind, she will. That's the way I was brought up and that's the way it is with me. So don't worry about it, O.K.? I'm managing very well, thank you."

"Well—sure," Gil said, feeling again, for some odd reason he couldn't define, almost ashamed of himself for asking. "Sure, Ray, that's O.K. I mean to each his own, right? Whatever's best for you, is the way I look at it."

"Do you?" Ray inquired, and for just a second Gil thought he might be poking fun at him, behind his pleasantly good-natured expression. But of course nobody would do that, in this area where Gil was such an expert. "Do you? I wasn't quite sure."

"Oh, yes," Gil said earnestly. "I hope," he added awkwardly, for suddenly, and again inexplicably, the answer seemed quite important, "I hope you don't—don't think the worse of me because I—because—"

"Oh, no," Ray said comfortably. "Of course not. To each his own, remember? Whatever's right for you. I'm rather proud of you, in fact—" and again Gil wasn't quite sure but what he was being made the butt of gentle humor— "I'm rather proud that my roommate is the biggest cocksman on campus. It gives me something to write home about. Makes college sound very dashing, when I tell my folks."

"Oh, I'll bet you do!" Gil said, grinning and beginning to relax. "I'll just bet you do."

"Once a week," Ray said solemnly, "regular as clockwork. Hey! Want to go down to the kitchen with me? I'll make us some hot chocolate before we turn in, O.K.?"

"O.K.," Gil said gratefully—and again, he didn't quite know why, he did feel genuinely grateful. "You know something?" he said as he shut his books and stood up. "You're a hell of a nice guy, Ray, you know that?"

"So are you," Ray said with a grin as they went out the door. "That's why we get along so well in this room. . . . North!" he called, banging on the adjacent door. "Come on down and have some chocolate with us before we go to bed."

"Thanks," North responded in a muffled voice. "Be down in a minute, guys. Thanks for the thought."

And rubbed his tired, uneasy eyes and carefully tore to tiny pieces the fifth version of the note he had begun to write. No point, he told himself over and over again. No point, no point, no point. But he knew he would come back to it and do it anyway.

He closed his door firmly and, in his turn, rapped on Moose's as he went down the hall.

"Hey, Mooser!" he called in a voice that sounded perfectly natural and at ease. "Baker's making chocolate for everybody."

"Big deal," Moose responded, but he sounded pleased to be interrupted.

And he was pleased, because for the better part of two hours he had been sitting over an opened but unread book, brooding about Welcome Waggoner and what he should do about her now that he had been formally introduced to her parents in a brief visit during the holidays.

Ever since school resumed they had been going at it hot and heavy. His visit home had been an unhappy one—his sister embittered by divorce, his younger brother beginning to drink too much, his mother, as always, "not feeling very well" as the result of some never-diagnosed ailment. Only his father had greeted him as the hero he was. He couldn't wait to get back to school. Most everybody *really* liked him there—not the least of them being Suzy, who had zeroed in on him from way across Memorial Hall on Reg Day. The way she had plowed through the crowd to his side had been noted and joked about by all. It had gone on from there as though it had never stopped, as it hadn't, really, except for ten days or so while he visited his unhappy family in Chicago.

Actually he had been as eager to see her as she seemed to be to see him—although you never knew with Suzy, she had so many irons in the fire. "*I* prefer to say 'rods in the fire,' " remarked Suratt, that little snot. But when she clutched his arm and breathed fervently, "Hey *Moose!*" it was apparent that she really was pleased to see him again. As soon as they finished registering they had taken off in Carriger's Cord, most sensational car on campus, kindly loaned without hesitation ("Just watch the leather, though. It costs like hell to have it cleaned"), and had hightailed it out to Sand Hill Road to the hidden and highly popular nooks familiar to successive college generations. There everything had been every bit as satisfactory as always.

"Well!" she had said when they finished, leather, if nothing else, intact. "Now what about us?"

"What do you mean, what about us?" he had inquired, genuinely puzzled. "Wasn't that about us?"

"I mean long-range. *You* know."

"Well, I—I don't, really," he said cautiously. "It was nice to meet your parents, though," he added helpfully. "They're very nice people."

"They were pleased to meet you, too," she said, thinking: Pleased to meet you so they'd know what they were up against. They had really given her fits about it, after he left. "Why don't we run away and get married? Wouldn't that be fun to do?"

This, however, was apparently going too fast for Moose. His expression for a moment was as shocked as her mother's had been in the glare she threw at Suzy behind his back when they met.

"Oh, I don't know," he said. "We couldn't just—just run away. What would your folks think?"

"Who cares what they think?" she inquired scornfully. "They're a couple of typical Piedmont snobs. All they think about is money and social position."

"Well," Moose said with a rather sad little laugh, "I don't have either one, so I guess that leaves me out."

"It does not," she said firmly. "It most certainly does not. You have so many more good qualities than they do that it's just—just ridiculous!"

"They're your folks," he protested. "You shouldn't talk about them like that."

"You ought to hear how they talk about—" she began; then started over. "If you heard them talk about even their closest friends, you wouldn't pay much attention to their opinions on anything. I don't."

"But they still have a lot to say about who—who you'll marry. They may not like me at all."

"They do," she lied firmly. "They most certainly do. Anyway, they'll go along with what I want." She laughed complacently. "I'm an only child. They always have."

"They *seemed* to like me," he said wistfully. "I hope they did."

"Don't worry about it. It will all work out all right." She looked thoughtful. "It might be simpler, though, if we just did it. That would avoid a lot of complications."

"Such as what?"

"Oh, just—fussing around. My mother would do that. She loves to fuss. I just don't want to waste my time on it, that's all. I tell you what!" She cuddled against him suddenly, which he didn't quite understand. "Why don't we just take off this weekend, like I said, drive up to Reno and *do* it? What could be simpler?"

"I don't know," he said with a worried frown. "I mean—"

"Don't you want to marry me? Is there somebody else?"

"N—no," he said; and, being Moose, came out with it honestly. "But— why me? That's what I can't figure. What am I to you, that I'm so special?"

"Well, if you don't know! After *that*! If you don't *know*!"

"That isn't everything," he said, because he had begun to realize in the last few months that it wasn't, really. "I mean, there's a lot more to marriage than just—just jumping into bed."

"Really," she said with her wicked little chuckle. "How would you know?"

"Oh," he said, "I just—I just think so, that's all. And why you pick on me when you've got so many other richer and handsomer and smarter guys on campus, I really don't know. I honestly don't. I mean," he added, putting it in the context that still conditioned much of his thinking, "I won't be making any more touchdowns. That's all over."

She laughed, but with a surprising affection.

"Oh, Moose! As if I cared about you making any more touchdowns!"

"Well, I do," he said forlornly. "I miss it like hell. I just hate to see it all end, I really do. It was *such fun* and I was *so happy*."

"I know you were," she said seriously, and he realized with an inner wonderment that it was the first time he remembered when she had really sounded serious about anything. "But life goes on, Moose. You have to grow up eventually and leave football behind. That's why," she added, reverting to target, "I think we should get married just as soon as possible."

"But I'm not going to leave football behind," he said stubbornly. "I mean, I know it's all over for me, but if I get a coaching job someplace then I can still be part of it and contribute something to the kids—"

"You aren't going to get a coaching job someplace," she said firmly. "My family's got so much money you can't even imagine it, at least I can't. It began with a store my great-grandfather opened in Jackson up in the Mother Lode country in Gold Rush days and it's gone on from there into mines and investments and stocks and bonds and oil and God knows what all, I don't. Anyway, my father can find a place for you in there somewhere. That will take care of everything."

He snorted.

"Hell, I can't add two and two and get anything but five. What do I know about high finance?"

She dismissed it with an airy wave.

"There are people on the staff to take care of that stuff. The people who own big businesses don't have to *know* anything. That's one of the privileges of being an owner. You can be as dumb as—"

"As me?"

"As dumb as my father," she went on serenely, "and still get along just fine. He's really a stupid jerk, when you come right down to it. But that doesn't stop him from getting richer all the time. As long as he has the right people under him."

"Well," Moose said shortly, "I'm not one of them. I'm as dumb as he is. And I must say," he added, "you kind of shock me the way you talk about your folks, Suzy. I may have problems with mine but at least I was brought up to respect them. I guess you weren't."

"Oh, I was," she agreed, again with her wicked little chuckle, "but I outgrew it. So: how about this weekend?"

"To get married? I don't think so."

"Why not?" she demanded, pulling back and giving him a sharply challenging look. "Is there something wrong with me?"

"No, no," he said hastily, though he could think of quite a lot. But to say so would only end something he really did enjoy immensely.

"Then what's the problem?"

"I really just don't see," he said patiently, "why you want *me*. I mean, I'm really not any genius, and I'm not sure I could help with any business even if I had the smartest guys in the world working for me, and I'm not all that good-looking, and—"

She interrupted with a genuinely hearty laugh.

"Oh, Moose! You really are a sad case, all right. Let's just say you have a good heart and you're steady and decent and kind and honest and reliable— and I'm sick to death of the other kind. Will that do it?"

He had to laugh too, in spite of all his reservations, which he knew she wasn't going to eradicate just in one complimentary statement.

"It sounds pretty good," he said. "I wish I could live up to it."

"Well," she said, voice suddenly incisive and cold, "if you're that uncertain about it, you can start this fancy gadget of Carriger's and take me back to campus and forget all about it. And don't call me again!"

"Oh, Suzy."

"Yes, 'Oh, Suzy'! Start the car!"

"O.K.," he said, his own tone suddenly becoming matter-of-fact: he had learned from long experience that it was the only way when she got into what he thought of as "one of her moods." He thought suddenly that it would be rather nice, probably, if she really meant it this time. It would relieve him of what had actually become quite a burden, when he stopped to think about it.

"This," he said with satisfaction as the Cord roared into life at the gentlest touch, "is quite some buggy, I must say."

"You could own one just like it if we got married," she said in the same cold voice. "You could have a Rolls-Royce or anything, if you weren't so dumb."

"You see, that's why you're absolutely right," he said agreeably as he hit the gas and they shot down the country lane that would presently take them back to Sand Hill Road. "I *am* dumb and there's no getting around it. You're much better off without me. And so's the business."

"Fuck the business," she said, which quite shocked him. He had heard that word from her before, but not in what you might call a social context.

Their return to campus was entirely silent until he drove her up the Row to the accompaniment of envious catcalls from several fraternities and applause from several sororities.

"It isn't mine!" he called cheerfully—and unnecessarily, because the car was famous on campus and everyone knew it was Smitty's.

"Just get me there," she ordered evenly, "and stop being a clown."

"Sorry," he said. "Just being friendly."

"Yes. Well. Do it some other time."

"O.K.," he said amicably. "*Here* you go!"

And stopped so abruptly in front of her house that it threw her forward a little, not enough to hurt, just enough to upset her dignity, which was what he intended. She shot him a venomous look, yanked open the door, jumped out, slammed it and stalked up the walk.

"See you!" he called happily.

"Not if I see you first!" she snapped over her shoulder.

He tooted the horn ironically—toot, toot, too-toot, toot—toot, *toot!*—and drove off grandly to cheers, applause and ironic laughter all around.

Now, however, as he wriggled his feet into new Christmas slippers and cinched up the rope on his ragged old bathrobe preparatory to joining the others in the kitchen, he rather wished he hadn't been quite so definite about it. Not that he thought for one minute that they wouldn't see each other again, but still. It was the closest they'd come to a real fight in a long time and he didn't really want it to rest, even temporarily, on that level. He really was becoming increasingly uncertain about the wisdom of even contemplating marriage with Suzy, but she certainly was a hell of a lay and he didn't want to antagonize her to the point where she'd really put a stop to their favorite pastime. He didn't see why they couldn't just continue as they were, particularly since he really couldn't understand why she had decided to pick on him to marry when there were so many more suitable guys around.

Furthermore, he was decidedly leery about tying himself up with a gal who really was a campus character and was not called "Welcome" Waggoner for nothing. She might consider *him* steady and decent and honest and reliable, but what was he to consider her? How could *he* ever trust *her* to be steady, decent, honest and reliable? He'd be stuck behind some boring desk helping her father with stocks and bonds and what would she be doing, meanwhile? He'd never thought he'd be a puritan but suddenly, faced with the prospect of a married Suzy (married to *him*) he found his masculine pride definitely uneasy. Not for nothing had Hack brought down the house at Big Game Gaieties with a parody on "If you knew Suzy like *we* know Suzy—"

I mean, Moose told himself, she's *active*. And if he wasn't enough to satisfy her now, what made him think he could do it when she had him trapped in the family business and was running around loose all the time?

"If you're really that crazy," Willie had advised recently, "then better keep her fat and pregnant all the time. And even then, I'll bet your kids wouldn't know who to call Daddy."

This brotherly comment, even if inspired by affection and a really genuine interest in his welfare, still stung pretty hard, because of course he knew it was probably basically true.

He decided as he went down the hall, banging on Latt's door, Buff's and Franky's, that he'd allow a decent interval—say overnight—and then give her a call. He was pretty sure she'd be agreeable, after she got her little snit out of her system: they just had too much fun together for her to be able to stay away. But he was increasingly determined that it would be limited to that. He didn't know of anybody else at the moment whom he wanted to marry but he was becoming quite sure he didn't want to marry her.

Latt was rarely thankful to be interrupted in the midst of studying, but tonight he was glad of it. He had started the evening diligently taking notes, in his tiny, neat, rather spidery hand, on the collapse of the slave economy in the South in the decade immediately following the Civil War, a subject he intended to pursue for a term paper and later expand into his Ph.D. thesis. His master's thesis, already half completed, was titled "The Influence of the Small Entrepreneur on the Opening of the West." A couple of years of graduate study, he figured, and he would have both degrees completed. He had already been assured by the history department that there was a place waiting for him right here if he wanted it. "You are undoubtedly," the stately head of the department had told him recently, "the most brilliant historical scholar who has ever attended the University. It will be a great pleasure to have you with us."

Such brilliance! he had told himself ironically shortly before Moose's welcome invitation to come down to the kitchen. Such brilliance, and what a timid soul he was when it came to the business of ordinary living! Tonight was a prime example.

He had begun by studying but had rapidly and most uncharacteristically drifted off into another subject. Like North, he too was writing a note: different object but essentially, perhaps, same objective.

"Dear Kay," it began. And there, though he had written the same salutation half a dozen times in the last hour, it had stopped.

What should the next sentence be?

"I've been doing a lot of thinking over Christmas, and since winter quarter began, about us; and I think—"

Or should he plunge right into it and say, "I guess I'm pretty much of a coward or I'd tell you this face to face, but ever since Christmas vacation I've been thinking that you and I—"

Or really go all out and say, "Marriage to me is probably the farthest thing from your mind, but—"

He had consulted Willie and Guy about this a couple of days ago and Guy had said, "Hell, Latt, just lay it on the line. The worst she can do is say no. Which," he added hastily at Latt's crestfallen expression, "she isn't going to do. Now, you know that! You know that perfectly well!"

Willie, approach innately more cautious, had also urged candor. "Every time I see her she tells me how much she likes you and—and—well, she wonders, Latt. She wonders why you haven't mentioned it already. She thinks maybe it's her fault."

"Oh, *no!*" Latt exclaimed, genuinely upset. "I hope she doesn't think *that.*"

"Well, she does," Willie said bluntly, figuring: *Somebody's* got to get him off the dime or he never will get around to it. "So you'd better tell her something before it's too late. Make a clean breast of it and tell her you know it's your fault for dilly-dallying but you aren't going to dilly-dally any more. And then tell her it's her decision and see what she says."

"But suppose she says no?"

Willie snorted.

"Listen! Not only won't she say no, she'll jump at the chance. Don't put yourself down, Latt. You're a pretty damned remarkable guy in lots of ways, and you have a great character to boot. A girl should be so lucky."

"W-e-ll," Latt said doubtfully.

" 'W-e-ll,' nothing," Willie retorted crisply. "I want you to do it!"

So he was trying, Latt told himself wryly, but, as witness six "Dear Kays" on the otherwise blank sheet on his desk, it wasn't easy. He had to keep trying, though, Willie had him convinced of that. He hadn't had the slightest idea that Kay was blaming herself for his silence—that seemed really appalling to him. Every instinct of a kind and generous nature told him he must at least relieve her of that anxiety. Whether he could quite go all the way at this time and mention marriage, he didn't really know. But he knew he had to keep trying.

He had just completed the seventh "Dear Kay" when Moose pounded on the door.

"O.K.," he called back with a feeling of great relief as he tore up the paper, pulled on the favorite old green cardigan he wore around the house all the time, and opened the door. "Count me in."

Franky, who had been dreamily and with great satisfaction contemplating the fact that in another five months he and Katie would be most securely and happily tied for life, was just coming out of his room as Latt came by; and next door Buff, who had been lazily going through his list of phone numbers, deleting a few and adding a few in preparation for winter quarter, stepped out to join them as they followed Moose downstairs to the kitchen. There they found the other seniors, rounded out a couple of minutes later by Willie, for whom Moose had bellowed up the stairwell. He came bounding down with his usual leaps and crashes, arousing protests from younger members still studying upstairs. A moment after that Bates and Haggerty, shaking off hats and raincoats, entered half drenched from the heavy wind-whipped rain that was still pounding down so hard it seemed to make the old house shake.

The class was complete in Cockroach Heaven, some sitting at the kitchen table, some leaning against the sink, some sitting on the floor as Ray, standing at the huge old-fashioned stove, prepared to ladle out the steaming contents of a huge pot of hot chocolate.

"Do you realize," Willie inquired when all cups were filled, "that this is the first time we've all been together by ourselves without a lot of juniors and sophomores underfoot since—well, since pledge night in '36, I guess." He raised his cup. "Here's to the Class of '39!"

Feeling suddenly very solemn and sentimental, everybody echoed, "Here's to the Class of '39!" and drank.

It was not, however, a mood that could last very long, in that house.

"Jesus Christ, Ray!" Franky exclaimed. "What did you put in this, Drano?"

"More like Clorox, to me," Buff observed thoughtfully.

"Or possibly Mercurochrome," North suggested.

"Well, I'll be damned!" Ray said with mock indignation. "If that's the thanks I get for coming down here and standing over a hot stove for you lousy ingrates, then you can just—just—"

"Don't say it, Ray!" Gil advised. "It would spoil the image. You don't raise your voice to anybody."

"I try not to," Ray said with a grin, "but sometimes the provocation gets pretty great around here. Are we going to have some sort of formal senior party before graduation?"

"You see, Willie?" Latt said. "You've started something."

"Always," Guy said. "Always. He can't help himself. Ideas sparkle off Perfect Boy Politician like horse piss off a dung heap."

"What a lovely thought," Tim remarked. "You sure do have a way with words, Mr. Unruh."

"I try," Guy said modestly. "I try. I think that's a damned good idea, Ray. Why don't we? Start on it now and get everything in shape—maybe arrange for one of those small banquet rooms at the Mark or the Frantic—"

"Too expensive," Ray said. "Let's stay closer to home."

"O.K. L'Omelette? Dinah's Shack?"

"L'Omelette," said several and everybody nodded.

"Not a minute too soon to get it lined up," Buff observed. "Lots of parties going to go on that week."

"Appoint yourself chairman of a committee," Franky said, "and get going."

"I'll appoint somebody chairman of the committee—" Buff began, but they hooted him down. "All right, damn it. Willie and Ray, we're it. We've decided on the place already, now we need the date." He took down the big calendar on the wall, hen-scratched all over with Dewey's undecipherable notes for menus, flipped the pages. "My God, that's only four and a half months away. Getting close, guys, getting close. . . . How about Thursday, June fifteenth? Finals end Wednesday the fourteenth—Senior Class Day is Friday the sixteenth—let's squeeze it in the middle, O.K.? . . . Shall we bring dates? . . . No dates. . . .formal or informal? . . . Formal. O.K. Franky, you're in charge of food—well, we want to be sure and get enough to eat, don't we? Hack, you take care of entertainment—namely, arrange for a piano and play it for us. Franky, you explain to Dewey that he just *can't* cook for us, the restaurant won't allow it, which I believe is true, but anyway we've got to convince him. We can't risk ptomaine our last three days in school. And I guess that does it. Everybody happy?"

"Gad, Buff," Unruh said in a tone of genuine admiration. "What a whirlwind of efficiency! I haven't seen you move that fast in four years."

"He's glad to be leaving school," Franky suggested with a grin.

"*Nobody's* glad to be leaving school," Moose said morosely, and suddenly they were all solemn again.

"That's right," Willie agreed softly. "Nobody is. . . ."

"What are we all going to do?" Tim inquired into the silence.

"What do you mean?" Gil asked, puzzled. "Guy and North and I are going to med school and Ray is going to law school and Mooser's going to coach football somewhere and—"

"No, that isn't what I meant," Tim said, stepping to the stove and getting himself another cup of chocolate. "I mean, what are we going to do about the war?"

"What war?" Franky demanded from his seat on the floor, back against a cabinet. "You're always talking war, Timmy, but there isn't any war. So calm down. Stop brooding about it. It's going to do you good to get off that *Daily.* You're obsessed."

"I am?" Tim inquired. He reached into the folds of his soaking-wet raincoat draped over a chair against the wall and pulled out his advance copy of tomorrow morning's paper. "Look," he said, and pointed to headlines: HITLER DEMANDS RETURN OF COLONIES TO GERMANY, ITALY, JAPS. WARNS U.S.: DON'T MEDDLE. . . . NAZIS THREATEN EUROPE AS HITLER NEARS SIXTH ANNIVERSARY . . . and, accompanied by a picture of U.S. Ambassador to

Great Britain Joseph P. Kennedy after testifying before a secret joint meeting of Senate and House armed services committees—PREDICTS WAR BY SPRING.

"If I'm obsessed, Franky," Tim said tartly, "a lot of people are obsessed with me. And with good reason."

"Well," Franky said in a dismissive tone, "I know that's how the warmongers and the interventionists want us to feel, but I don't see why we have to get frantic about it just because they are. Whatever Hitler's doing, or the Japs or Wops or whatever, they're doing it *over there*. They aren't doing it *over here*. So why should we get *our* balls in an uproar? I don't see it."

"Well, I do," Willie said.

"And so do I," Guy agreed.

Haggerty sighed.

"And I too. I guess."

"And I," North said. "I'm planning on med school but I won't be surprised if I wind up pushing bedpans in an army medical unit somewhere before I get to it."

"I don't want to think about that!" Franky said with an uncharacteristic, almost desperate vehemence. "I just don't want to think about that!"

"Well, you may *have* to think about that," Willie said coldly, "so better get ready."

"There's got to be a way out without that!" Franky insisted. "There's got to be!"

"I think," Latt said quietly, "that with tolerance and patience and goodwill on both sides—"

Tim turned on him.

"But there *isn't* goodwill on both sides! Can't you see that?"

"I believe there may be," Latt said gravely, "as long as men are decent and kind to one another and reason together like rational human beings. After all, when given half a chance mankind *is* rational—"

"Huh!" Willie snorted. "You a historian, and you believe that?"

"I do," Latt said, with the sort of unassailable, implacable goodness that had frustrated Willie and other opponents in ethical arguments before, "because I believe in an order in the universe, and in a Being who controls that order, and I do not believe He put us here simply to destroy one another."

"You and I have been around this track before," Willie observed. "A lot of people in history haven't received your message, I'm afraid. It's nice that you're kind and decent and God-fearing, but I don't think Adolf Hitler is. Or a good many others in this world. And they're the ones we have to deal with."

"But that's *my* point," Franky said. "Why do *we* have to deal with them? Why the United States? Why do we have to be policemen to the world? Why can't we just *let* them stew in their own juice? What's our call to go around messing in everybody else's business?"

"Your friend Hitler calls it 'meddling,'" Tim remarked. "Why don't you use his word?"

"He *isn't* my friend," Franky retorted. "He's a son of a bitch. But he's *there*. He's not *here*."

"He was here in this house with Rudy Krohl last quarter," Unruh said, "until we got rid of him. You voted for that. Nobody was more determined to bounce Krohl than you were."

"Right," Franky agreed, "and I don't regret it for one minute. And I admit all those subsidiary aspects of Hitler and I despise them and I don't want them here. What I'm saying is that we don't have to volunteer to get in his way—as long as he stays out of ours. I don't want to go to war to save the Czechs or the English or the French or the Chinese or anybody else. I want us to tend to our business and *stay put*. That's all."

"You don't want to do anything," Tim said, "because you're afraid you may have to go and fight, right?"

"That's one reason," Franky said bluntly. "Hell, yes. And if you try to tell me *you* want to go and fight, I'll say you're a liar."

"Hey, hey, hey," Buff said sternly. "Stop that personal crap, both of you. That's no way to argue."

"It's the way everybody else does," Franky said, but a little more amicably. "Why not us?"

"Of course I don't want to go and fight," Tim said, "any more than you do. But I happen to believe that there are some things in this world, and some issues, that sometimes have to be fought for. I think freedom and democracy do. I think America does, when she's really threatened—"

"But I don't think she is, don't you see?" Franky replied. "That's the difference between us, Timmy. Look: I know what you're doing. You're looking way ahead and you're saying, Now, suppose Hitler really gets on the move, and England and France can't hold him, and he takes the Continent and suppose meanwhile that the Japs really mop up on China and maybe move south into the rest of Asia, and then they decide to gang up on us together, and we don't have any allies left, and there we are all alone, and—well, I'll admit that's a frightening picture. But it's assuming an awful lot, I think. It's assuming all those catastrophes are going to happen. You say: Let's jump in now because someday they *might* happen. I say: Let's wait and see and maybe they won't happen. And then we won't have to jump in."

"At which point," Haggerty remarked, "it may be too late for us to save even ourselves. So then what?"

"I still think," Latt said quietly, "that there's a way out through goodwill and patience and negotiation among reasonable men that will avoid either extreme. I think it's the only way."

"Oh, I agree," Willie said. "I just don't happen to think it's an option that's open to us. I think Munich and the destruction of Czechoslovakia have already proved that there are only two ways open, Timmy's or Franky's, and I've about decided that as far as I'm concerned, Timmy's is the more likely. So I for one have also been doing a lot of thinking about it lately, and I've about come to the conclusion that I'd like to find some way to start doing something about it right now. It would be a small personal way at the moment, I'll admit, but—well—as proof of good faith, let's say. Does anybody agree? I know you do, Timmy."

Tim nodded. "I do. And there is one little thing that's come along. It's in the paper for tomorrow." He opened the *Daily* to an inside page and began to read. " 'The University Flying Club—' "

"I didn't know we had one," Buff interjected, sounding interested.

"About six guys, I think," Tim said. "All wealthy as hell, so they can afford planes of their own—" He laughed and everybody joined in, glad to relieve the tension a little—"I mean, *do* be our guest, Buff, we *know* you can afford one—anyway, the club is announcing that they've established a relationship with the Army Air Corps reserve flying unit in the Bay Area and they're hoping to play a part in training air reserve officers. So—"

"So?" Gulbransen said.

"So, I've been thinking—maybe that's something to do. Would anyone join me if I decided to give it a try?"

"I haven't mentioned it to anybody," Willie said, "but I did sign up for Reserve Officers' Training Corps this quarter. I guess I could easily combine regular R.O.T.C. and Air Corps training."

"You'll be a baby Hitler yourself," Franky observed, but sounding more like his usual joking self. "We're going to be afraid to have you around."

"You'll join me, then?" Tim asked. Willie thought for a moment, then nodded.

"Yeah. Why not?"

"O.K.," Guy said. "Count me in."

North and Haggerty hesitated. Then Hack said firmly, "Me, too."

"Not with your hands!" Franky protested, genuinely alarmed. "Suppose something happened to your hands!"

"Oh," Hack said moodily, "things may happen to a lot of guys' hands, if this goes on. Who am I to be special?"

"Or I," North remarked quietly. "I'll join you, Timmy."

"Me, too," Buff said.

"Wonderful," Tim said, obviously moved. "Latt?"

"I'm sorry," Latt said, quietly and firmly as ever. "I'm afraid I can't. I know a lot of you probably make fun of me—"

"Never," Buff said, equally quiet. "Nobody ever makes fun of you, Latt."

"—but I just believe in certain things, that's all, and I can't violate them or I'll destroy something vital in myself. I'd just absolutely destroy it. . . . 'Pacifist' was a harsh term in the World War and I guess it will probably soon be a harsh term again, but I guess that's what I am. I believe in a just and forgiving God who protects all creatures and regards them all as His children; and if I believe in that God, which I do, then I have to feel the same way as He does about all things. I think war is always morally wrong, I think it's never justified. I think it only brings unspeakable horror on the world, and that if another great war comes it will be infinitely more horrible than the last." He paused and smiled at North. "You may find me pushing bedpans alongside you, North, but I'm afraid that's the extent of what my conscience will permit me to do. I'm sorry, everybody. I know you're disappointed in me, but that's—" he sighed, a sound that seemed to come from some infinite depth inside him— "that's the way I am."

They were silent for a few moments after that until Tim said quietly, "I can respect that," and everybody chimed in to assure Latt that they could too, and he was a wonderful guy, and they could understand his point of view, and they would always admire and respect him, and—

He said nothing, only sat with a half-smile on his face, staring somewhere far away until Tim spoke again.

"Think it over, the rest of you guys. There'll be time."

"Gosh," Moose said, "I'd be scared shitless to fly. Isn't there something else I could do? Maybe I could work on the ground crew or something."

"Mooser," Willie said, reaching down to where Moose was seated on the floor leaning against his leg, mussing his hair in the old familiar way, "if Adolf Hitler hears that you're on the ground crew, *he's* the one who'll be scared shitless."

"Well," Moose said, with a self-conscious little smile, "I want to do *something* helpful."

"So do we all, I expect," Ray Baker said. "But let us think about it a little, Timmy, O.K.?"

"Sure," Tim said with a lighten-up grin. "I'm not on a quota for recruits."

There was a general laugh and everybody started getting up, stretching, getting ready to leave. Willie held up his hand, feeling a tensing inside.

"Just one other thing, which Timmy knows and it's in the *Daily* but he's just helping to build the suspense—I got a call from the Rhodes scholarship committee this afternoon—"

"*No!*" Gulbransen exclaimed, jumping up and starting to pound him on the back. "YI—PEEEE!"

"Is it true?" Franky demanded, looking absolutely delighted.

Willie nodded.

"It's true. And not only that—*not only that,*" he shouted over their wild sounds of jubilation, "but Mr. Clyde Gaius Unruh and Mr. Aram Katanian have also been chosen. So I guess," he said, feeling as though he might cry in the midst of laughing, "I guess we've—I guess we've done all right by the old house."

"YOU SURE HAVE!" Franky bellowed, as upstairs doors began to open and feet began to pound and younger generations swarmed downstairs to find out what all the uproar was about.

"If anybody wants any more hot chocolate," Ray yelled above the din, "there's plenty more in the pot!"

"I'd say quite a lot came out of that one," Latt told him with a smile, and turned to Willie.

"Willie—" he said, and shook his hand, hard.

"I wish," Willie said awkwardly, "I wish you could have been with us, Latt, but—"

"Oh, no," Latt said cheerfully. "I'm much too sedentary. Mr. Rhodes was a doer as well as a thinker, and that's what he wanted. And that's what he got, with you three. Heartiest congratulations. Really."

"I know," Willie said. "I know you mean it."

"Never more so," Latt said with a smile that lighted up his face. "I couldn't be happier."

"I know," was all Willie could manage then. "I know."

A few minutes later on the way upstairs after the whole house had jammed the kitchen to offer congratulations and finish the by-now-not-so-hot chocolate, Guy put a hand on his arm and stopped him for a moment.

"I have to tell you," he said in an apologetic half-whisper, "that I won't be able to go up to the City with you next Saturday night. I promised Maggie—"

"And I promised Marian."

They began to laugh, rather helplessly.

"What a mundane topic!" Willie said. "And just after being named Rhodes scholars, too! What *lèse-majesté!*"

"First things first," Guy said with a grin. "I'm sure Mr. Rhodes would understand. Or would he?"

And laughing they went on upstairs and so, eventually, to bed. But it was a long time before the house quieted down that night. As Latt had said, a lot had developed out of that pot of hot chocolate; and it would take a long time indeed before, in time and tide, it all got itself worked out.

18

I t rained that night, it rained the next night and the next and the next.
It rained right on into the weekend, mostly light, misty, cold and
penetrating, but now and then, for several hours at a time, a thundering,
torrential downpour that gushed off the roofs, flooded the Inner Quad an
inch deep and drowned the world in a blinding curtain of silver-gray. They
sloshed off to classes bundled up in hats, scarves, raincoats, umbrellas,
sloshed off to the Libe, sloshed to the gym, sloshed to the bookstore and the
post office, sloshed to the minimum of places they felt they absolutely had to
go and then sloshed home again. The fire in the big fireplace in the living
room was kept constantly stoked during the day, allowed to die down to coals
only late at night. Napoleon barked at the door to be left out, dashed shivering onto the lawn, defecated like lightning—"Ten seconds, I make it,"
Unruh said after they started keeping book; "Eight, I've got," said Carriger—
and then dashed in again. Sometimes he forgot—or, as Franky grumbled,
"Damned beast knows perfectly well what he's doing, he just doesn't want
to get wet"—and an impromptu clean-up detail had to be organized. Josephine graciously accepted the basket Ray fixed for her on the raised brick
hearth and seemingly never stirred from in front of the fire. North went
around quoting, "If winter comes, can spring be far behind?" until there was
a near-unanimous roar of, "Oh, for Christ's sake, *can it!*" The weatherman on
the radio described another massive storm just off the coast and predicted
that it and still another he said was forming in mid-Pacific would be delivering more of the same off and on for probably the next two weeks.

Everyone felt moody, restless, snappish, down; the only saving grace was
that spring really wasn't far behind. In that thought they all managed to
survive without taking each other's heads off too frequently.

Actually, as Duke Offenberg remarked one night when most of them were lingering in the living room after dinner, it was really rather cozy, everybody relaxed, the pets around, the fire blazing, everything snug, comfortable and reasonably warm inside, whatever the weather outside. Ray agreed that was fine but reminded them that there were two spots in the roof that had leaked a little last year and were now potential threats to the two eave-dwellers, Wilson and Haggerty.

"If this keeps up," he warned, "it may mean we'll have to have a new roof this spring, and that means an assessment and that means—"

There were universal groans and he had no trouble at all organizing the work crew he wanted. For two nights running everybody pitched in with a real sense of accomplishment and did a really good caulking job on all the potential weak spots. Ray, who secretly had thought the roof in pretty good shape but, as the careful house manager he was, wanted to make absolutely sure, was well pleased.

Rain or no, life went on. Tony and Lor Davis continued to escort Angie and Louise to classes, snacks at the Cellar and a midweek movie. It was a toss-up between *Boys Town* with Spencer Tracy and *The Cowboy and the Lady* with Gary Cooper and Merle Oberon. The guys liked both Tracy and Cooper but the girls just adored Merle Oberon, so that was the choice. Johnny Herbert, afraid of the weather and its effect on his susceptible lungs, had to beg off and stay close to home: it was all he dared to do, he said unhappily, to go to classes, without taking any extra chances. Everybody commiserated and the girls entertained them all at tea in his honor one afternoon in the DG house. He appreciated their kindness greatly but knew it was no real compensation for his perennially fragile health.

Bob Godwin, undaunted by the weather, was deep into planning for such spring activities as the Water Carnival and the Convalescent Home Drive, and also putting the final touches on his campaign for student-body president. The latter impelled him out around campus no matter what the weather: he was always showing up in unexpected places, having by junior year acquired enough friends that he was constantly being invited over for dinner at other houses and also to quite a few of the eating clubs, thanks to Ari Katanian's quiet interventions.

"Here comes the Orphan of the Storm," Franky remarked when Bob, bundled from head to foot, came puffing and blowing through the front door, scattering water all over the already muddied front hall.

"I remember him from the Blizzard of '91, by cracky," Willie responded. "Couldn't believe a living soul could make it over that pass. Don't believe it now, but *here he is!* How goes it, kid? Making headway?"

"Oh, *yes,*" Bob said, sounding increasingly confident now that his constant campaigning seemed at last to be paying off. "I really think everything's going fine. Are you going to endorse me?"

"Is it really important?" Willie inquired, still teasing.

"It would be nice," Bob said, "but I think maybe I can make it on my own now even if you don't."

Whereupon, of course, Willie said cheerfully, "Why, sure I will, Bob. I'd be happy to."

And Bob, having finally, inadvertently, found the key, was ecstatic.

Randy, his work on the *Daily* suffering and his tennis game shot pretty much to hell, went into what seemed to be a really deep funk as the rain continued. He told Jeff and Smitty morosely that he doubted if he would even try to stay on the team this spring. They told him he was crazy and did their best to buck him up.

"It's all right for you guys to talk," he said gloomily. "You aren't in love."

"I'm not sure you are, either," Smitty remarked in his pragmatic way. "I think you're obsessed, maybe, but that isn't what I think of as love."

"I know it'd be hard to do," Jeff agreed, "but y'all ought to tell that li'l gal to take a runnin' jump. She's no more worthy of you than—than—" he sputtered into his engaging gurgle of laughter—"than I am! No kiddin', Randy, get rid of her, man! It's the only way!"

But that only led Randy into another lengthy embittered diatribe about what a bitch she was and how he couldn't break loose no matter how he tried. And that made them sad, because, like everyone, they were very fond of Randy and anxious to have him get back on the ball again. Nagatani, debating whether to let Randy take over Tim's column in the *Daily*, called him in for a heart-to-heart that also quickly turned into a morose description of Fluff and her infuriating but hypnotic ways; and while Bill concluded by saying, "The column's yours if you want it—let's try it for a while and see how it goes," he did so with a lot of reservations, and also real regret.

"A guy with that much promise—!" he said to Tim, and Tim looked sad too. "I know it," he said, "but how do you break up something like that?"

It *was* an obsession, and something that went that deep was so rare in the swiftly shifting affections of the young that they really had no idea how to help.

Duke and Shahna, facing the new year and the gloomy weather, were also in the grip of an obsession of a different kind, being as worried as Tim about the course of events in Europe and with an even more personal interest. The removal of Rudy Krohl from the house had eased the immediate problem for Duke, though he did have one class with him and Werner in which the two of them went out of their way to give him nasty looks and mumble vague and unspecific threats. He had taken this for about two weeks and then braced them one day after class.

"Look," he said, "I don't like you guys and you don't like me, but suppose you knock it off, O.K.? I'm tired of this kid stuff. I'm staying out of your way, now you stay out of mine."

"And what will you do if we don't?" Rudy inquired unpleasantly. "Tell Dr. Chalmers?"

"*Ja, Jude,*" Werner added gratuitously. "What will you do?"

"Maybe I will tell him," Duke said.

"That's right!" Rudy jeered. "Run to somebody! Be a cry-baby! Get other people to fight your battles for you! That's what your kind always does!"

"Do you want me to knock you down again?" Duke demanded, suddenly in the grip of a rage so icy that he might very well have done so right then and there if Rudy hadn't backed down. But of course, as always when challenged, he did.

"Oh, take it easy," he said scornfully, but moving back a step. "You don't have to be such a big hero. Just stay out of our way, that's all."

"And you stay out of mine, God damn it!" Duke said. "Just *stay away.*"

This had apparently made an impression, because there were fewer portentous looks, fewer mumbled, ostentatiously ominous incoherencies in his ear as he passed by. But it left him as deeply troubled as ever, because the disease might be six thousand miles away in Europe but the symptom was still present in America—and growing, both he and Shahna felt uneasily as they read of German-American Bund activities in New York, anti-Semitic outbreaks inspired by the Ku Klux Klan in the South, swastikas painted on Jewish stores in the Pacific Northwest, Los Angeles, San Francisco.

Shahna's family still hadn't heard from their relatives. Rumors in the press were still vague but persistent. Instinct told them to be afraid. They still studied together at the Libe every afternoon but every time Duke bundled up and started out in the rain to meet her he felt as though nature itself were conspiring with everything else to challenge him. When he heard that some of the seniors were thinking about joining the army air reserves program he told Timmy to count him in.

Rodge Leighton, finding that he had to mother-hen Moose almost as much about not playing football as he had about playing football, still found time to be fascinated by developments in his field of physics.

"Did you see this?" he asked Tony, and proceeded to read from one of the City papers:

" 'SPLIT ATOMS RELEASE TWO HUNDRED MILLION VOLTS.

" 'Washington—Dr. Enrico Fermi of the University of Rome told a meeting of theoretical physicists today that atoms have been split to release two hundred million volts of energy. He said the awesome power was released in an experiment by a German physicist, Dr. Otto Hahn, who used neutrons to bombard a synthetic element known as ekauranium. Physicists at the meeting said the experiment was as important as the original discovery of radioactivity, but said it would take "at least twenty years" to put it to practical use. Efforts to duplicate Hahn's work are already under way at Columbia University and the Carnegie Institute . . .' "

Rodge had shaken his head in awestruck wonder.

"God, imagine that! Just think what could be done with that power! You could light cities, run trains, power all the appliances in the world—there's no end to what you could do with it! It could be a marvelous thing for humanity, it really could! Such a force for *good!*"

Tony had agreed and said he was equally impressed with something in his field of engineering.

"Did you see where that guy at Tuesday Night Lecture Series said television is ready to go? He says it isn't correct that it can only be transmitted on a line-of-sight trajectory—he says it can be transmitted beyond the horizon for at least fifty miles. He thinks that means that it will basically be useful only in rural areas, and then probably only black-and-white because color would cost so much that it would be 'economically outrageous.' But he does say it'll be here before long. He says it would be 'the most perfect instrument of propaganda yet devised by man,' and that's why Hitler is really encouraging its development in Germany. But Jesus, think of it! It could be a wonderful thing too. All the education it could bring to people—all the culture—so many good things—we could really be standing on the edge of a new Age of Enlightenment, Rodge. Wonderful things could lie ahead for the world in our lifetime. Isn't that *exciting?*"

They agreed that maybe no generation in history had been blessed with such great potentials as theirs. They congratulated each other on their choices of profession, because so much of this wonderful future they could glimpse for humanity was going to come directly from physics and engineering and their children the split atom and television.

When they were overheard by Renny and Gale, the two professional cynics, they got the kind of reaction they expected.

"Sure," Renny said. "Absolutely. The minute atomic power is perfected it will be in the hands of big business and there goes the little guy. So much for humanity."

And Gale said that in the first place, he didn't believe television was going to be developed any further—"Radio and Hollywood will kill it off, it's too much competition"—but even if it were, it would be an instrument for mind control rather than culture.

"Why does that bother you?" Tony inquired. "You want to control minds."

"If I can be one of the controllers," Gale said with a cozy little laugh. "But if *they're* going to control *me*, then no thank you."

The others went quietly about their usual business, Hank Moore faithfully going from house to class to Libe to house through the downpour day after day, reading, studying, beginning to think already about midterm papers and exams; Billy, looking a little strained at times, practicing for upcoming productions at the theater and spending the rest of his time, as always, with Janie.

On the rainswept Quad, where most hurried and few lingered, the restless wanderer still managed to find his like and break free from the conventional social patterns in which his easy charm guaranteed him such warm acceptance. Twice in the first week of winter quarter Haggerty, inspired to start work on a shimmering piece entitled "Rain on the Quad" saw him near the notorious corner; and sighed and went on into the freezing organ loft to strike some moody chords and wonder gloomily what to do about it. Unbeknownst to him and to the wanderer, someone else had become conscious of the visits and was quietly beginning to keep an eye out.

Midway in the second week of rain Buff offered something at dinner one night that made them all feel relieved. They quieted down with some difficulty when he rapped spoon on glass but swiftly paid attention when he spoke.

"I thought you guys would be pleased to know that I got a letter today from Marc Taylor—"

"His folks?"

"Nope, Marc himself. He says, 'Dear Buff and Guys: I thought I'd write and let you know that I'm feeling a lot better.' "

There were sounds of approbation and relief.

" 'I've been out of bed now for almost a month and I'm doing a lot of eating and exercising and am beginning to look like Unruh or Gulbransen.' "

Guy grinned, Franky remarked, "No finer models," and Gil said, "*I'm* happy"—and found that he really was, for his erstwhile forlorn little protégé.

" 'I guess I really went through a kind of crazy period out there, and I think of all of you more than I can say for your understanding and kindness. It really made me appreciate what a great group of fraternity brothers I have.' "

"I'm going to sob," Renny murmured and Moose glared at him and said, "For *Christ's* sake!"

" 'I really don't know now,' " Buff went on, ignoring the exchange, " 'what made me try to do what I did. But whatever it was, I can honestly tell you that it seems to be all gone now. I only want to get fully well and get back out there. The administration has been wonderful about letting me take leave, but I owe it to Dr. Chalmers and my teachers—and particularly to you guys—to prove that I'm ready to get back to work and really make a go of it.

" 'I promise all of you that I won't ever again let myself feel that you don't like me, or don't want me around, or don't support me. You've proved that just isn't true.' "

Buff paused and cleared his throat. He wasn't the only one.

" 'I also feel that I owe God thanks—and Mrs. Steadman, who I really believe was His instrument—for saving me from what I crazily thought I wanted to do. I repeat, I really don't know what got into me. But I can tell you it's really gone, and I believe forever.

" 'My doctors here are wonderful and so are my folks. The doctors tell me that if I continue to improve the way I am now, I will be able to come back spring quarter. So here's to you and here's to the University and here's to the new Marc Taylor! I'll see you in three months.

" 'My best to everybody, including Napoleon and Josephine.

" 'Marc.' "

There was a silence that even Renny didn't dare break. Buff did, by saying as matter-of-factly as possible, "Well, there's the good news. Timmy, you help me write him a note and we'll all sign it. O.K.?"

"O.K., Renny?" Moose demanded in an ominous voice and Renny said, "Oh, for Christ's sake, yes! I'm not inhuman, Moose!"

"You could have fooled me," Moose said, and found with satisfaction that for once he had the last word as Renny turned away and didn't reply when they scraped back chairs and began to leave the table.

So the rain went on . . . and on . . . and on . . . and on the second Saturday afternoon, as per previous arrangement, the president of the student body, Richard Emmett Wilson, Perfect Boy Politician, drove up to the Union in his battered old '34 Chevy convertible and picked up Miss Marian Emerson en route to her home in Piedmont across the Bay.

19

He didn't relish driving in the increasingly heavy downpour that had begun just as he left the house, particularly on a winter's night already starting to get dark by five; but that was the chance of the game. Marian was waiting just inside the door, swathed in raingear, rosy and flushed with what appeared to be excitement. He hoped it was. He felt somewhat excited himself.

This could be a portentous weekend—or, as he reminded himself with customary caution and logic, not so portentous.

The best thing to do, he decided as he hopped out into the deluge, ran around the car, opened the door, grabbed her bag, tossed it into the backseat, hurried her into the front, slammed the door, dashed around and hopped in again, breathless—the best thing was just to assume that it would be great, just absolutely great, and proceed firmly in that conviction.

For the first few minutes, as they drove up Palm Drive and joined the heavy traffic north on the Bayshore Highway toward the Dumbarton Bridge, their conversation was pleasant and more or less what he had expected. She congratulated him on the Rhodes scholarship, told him how much she loved England, agreed that it would be a wonderful experience for him "unless there's a war," which they agreed was possible, Hitler being the monster he was. She wondered what Willie would do if war came before he left for Oxford and he said he assumed that if that happened he would still be able to accept the scholarship after the war was successfully concluded.

At that time they had no doubt of the outcome, for in those days the British Empire was a political and psychological colossus that loomed over the world in a way that had never happened before and could never be imagined later. It was the greatest aggregation of subject nations and peoples ever assembled in all of history by one conquering power. The map was colored red with imperial ownership that literally encircled the globe. The sun literally never did set on the British Empire in those days. Fifty years on it would still be hard for them to realize how swiftly, utterly, completely and unbelievably it had vanished into history.

"Suppose you go over there and then it starts while you're there?" she asked. "What would you do?"

He was silent for a moment, negotiating the rain-slick traffic. And thinking.

"I might . . ." he said slowly. "I just might . . . enlist."

She looked startled and said she thought he was very brave to even contemplate it. He said, hoping to gain points thereby, that he didn't confide his plans to everyone like that. She inquired: "Not even Donna?" He refused to be drawn on that subject, and, when she began to be critical of Donna, suggested that she ought to get to know her, and offered to introduce them.

"Oh, no," she said hastily. "I wouldn't want you to go out of your way to do that. I'll probably meet her one of these days, just in the normal course of things. Why don't I do that?"

"O.K.," he said, making it sound completely indifferent. "And in the meantime, don't make up your mind about her too quickly. She's a great gal."

"Obviously," she said in a suddenly remote voice. "Obviously you think so."

The remaining half hour of their journey was scrupulously silent. He thought a couple of times of trying to lighten it up but then thought: Hell with it. She may have thought the same, for all he knew. Anyway, the result was silence, which continued until they reached Piedmont in the East Bay, drove up an obviously expensive street lined with obviously expensive houses and came finally to one even more obviously expensive. It had two stone gateposts and a short winding drive. Chandeliers illuminated a pillared portico. A massive oaken door was opened by a beaming Walter as they stopped before it.

He ushered them in with great good cheer and immediately offered drinks. Marian accepted his suggestion that she have a "very light" gin and tonic.

"And Willie?"

He thought for a split second and decided: What the hell.

"A martini, please, sir."

"Man after my own heart." Walter beamed. "Olive? Lemon? Onion? One, both, all three?"

"Whatever you're having, sir."

"Stop the 'sir' stuff, this is family! I take both an olive and an onion." And he bustled toward a bar at the far end of the room just as a golden retriever bounded into the room and they turned to see a pleasant-faced woman, perfectly coiffed, perfectly tailored, apparently perfectly cordial. She kissed Marian, held out a perfectly manicured hand.

"This is the famous Mr. Wilson," she said in a perfectly modulated voice. "A fellow alumnus. Marian has told us a great deal about you. Flip, get down."

"Thank you, ma'am," he said, fending off the wildly loving Flip with his left hand and shaking with his right rather more firmly that she did, but feeling at ease nonetheless. "He isn't bothering me, I love dogs. I didn't know you'd gone to the University, too."

"We're very inbred," Walter said, returning with the drinks. "Wanted Marian to go there as a freshman but she decided she had to experiment with Mills first. Now I think she's much happier. Right, baby?"

"I'm finding it enjoyable," Marian said politely. "Where's Cee?"

"That's her sister Cecilia," her father said. "She's up there just dilly-dallying around, as usual. She'll be down. Well, everybody sit down! When will dinner be ready, Mother?"

"I thought seven," Mrs. Emerson said. "Give these children a chance to get settled. And finish the drink you've made for them."

"I thought they deserved it after that drive in the rain," Walter said, a trifle defensively, Willie thought. "Lord, what a night!"

"Not a fit night out for man or beast," Willie agreed, reprising the old W. C. Fields line. Walter guffawed.

"Right on the nose with that one! First of all, house rules. You can call me 'Mr. Emerson' if I show up at Excom again, but here it's Walter. And this is Mary, right, Mary?"

"That's right," Mary said without the slightest hesitation. But Willie made a mental note to wait a bit, all the same.

"You're at the top of the stairs to the left, right across the hall from Mary and me," Walter said with an emphasis that brought the slightest glint of amusement into Willie's eyes. "The girls are on down at the end. Mary prefers breakfast exactly at nine, right, Mary?"

"That seems to me a civilized hour," Mary said.

"If that's O.K. with you, Willie?" Walter asked. Mary looked a little surprised and Willie hastened to oblige.

"Fine," he said. "I expect to sleep like a log tonight. Rain always does it for me anyway, and getting away from twenty of the world's master snorers will make it even better."

"Oh, do you belong to a house?" Mary asked, though he was sure Marian must have told them.

"Yes, the Alpha Zetes."

"Oh," she said politely. "I'm Kappa Kappa Gamma."

"A *wonderful* house," he said, hoping his tone was as reverential as was obviously expected. Apparently so, for Mary said, "It is," in a tone of complete and complacent satisfaction.

"Well!" Walter said as a sulky but beautiful teenager appeared in the doorway. "Here's Cee. Cecilia, this is Willie Wilson, president of the student body. Cee is going to the University as a freshman next year."

"Will you pledge Kappa also?" he asked as they shook hands; but Mary preempted her answer.

"We certainly hope so," she said. A faint unhappiness crossed her perfectly composed features. "We've been a little disappointed in Marian. She's preferred to be a little more independent, I'm afraid."

"Well, g—" Willie began, and stopped himself just in time from saying, "Good for her!"—"girls nowaways have to make up their own minds, I guess."

"Yes, I suppose so," Mary said. She uttered a slightly wistful little smile. "Not like my day, 'when Mother knew best!' "

"Well!" Walter said heartily. "Why don't you kids finish your drinks and take your things up and get settled—you're to the left at the top of the stairs, right opposite us, Willie—and then we'll eat. I'm starved!"

"I'm sure there will be ample," Mary said comfortably. "Dora's outdoing herself. We'll see you downstairs in fifteen minutes, Mr. Wilson."

"Yes, ma'am," he said, thinking: *Jesus.*

Dinner was served and he established immediate empathy with the cook. She was of Dewey's color and about the same vintage, somewhere between forty-five and one hundred, her face wrinkled and kindly, her hair graying fast, her manner one of calmly unruffled acceptance of the family to which she had, they told him, been attached for fifteen years. Mary made some remark about "When I was at the University we Kappas always felt that—" which was about the tenth time, he thought, that she had mentioned the Kappas. Dora, serving a wonderfully tender roast to Walter, glanced up with a smile and caught his eye. They understood each other and he could tell she liked him. He had now won the approval of the dog and the cook, he thought with amusement. He thoroughly enjoyed every mouthful, as he told her at the end of it. He left the table surrounded by the warmth of her approval and in the living room was overwhelmed once more by that of Flip, who like Napoleon loved everybody and was convinced he was a miniature and just the right size for laps.

"Flip, damn it, *get down*," Walter ordered when they all took seats in what seemed to Willie a rather awkward half-circle facing the fire and the enormous oil painting of a much younger Mary that hung above it. "Damned dog," he said, dragging him gently but firmly out of the room by the collar and closing the door. Flip collapsed with an enormous sigh just outside. Walter turned back with a smile.

"Well, Willie, how are things going on campus these days? Any more dramas? How about a nightcap, by the way?"

"Well, sir—Walter—" the familiarity still a little difficult in spite of a lengthy dinner-table discussion of Walter's golf problems.

"Why not?" Walter demanded, going to the bar. "How about a brandy?"

"You must keep Walter company, Mr. Wilson," Mary remarked. She smiled pleasantly. "It gives him an excuse."

"He doesn't really need it," Cecilia, absolutely silent during dinner, volunteered with a sudden nervous little giggle.

"It eases his conscience," Marian agreed with her own little laugh, which Willie had now realized was much like her mother's. "Doesn't it, Daddy?"

"You see my problem, Willie," Walter remarked with a determinedly hearty amusement as he returned with two well-filled brandy snifters. "As the only man in a houseful of women, I really take it in the neck. So how's it going? Anything new on the Jews and the colored boy?"

Willie hesitated a second, then decided to give as good as he got.

"No, sir," he said crisply. "Niggers—kikes—everybody—we seem to be getting along just fine."

There was a moment's silence but Walter was not so easily daunted.

"Ho, ho!" he exclaimed, giving Willie a shrewdly amused look. "He bites! The boy has spirit! He doesn't like old grads and trustees interfering with what he wants to do!"

"Not at all, Walter," Willie said, taken aback for a moment but again deciding to give as good as he got. "They're fine, too"—he gave Walter what he hoped was a charming smile—"in their place."

Walter laughed, quite genuinely.

"You know, there are some ten or twelve of my fellow trustees who, if you said anything like that to *them*, would go straight to Ed Chalmers and try to get your scalp, my boy. You're probably lucky I'm me . . . I really am curious to know about our friend By Johnson. What's he up to these days?"

"To tell you the truth," Willie said more seriously, "I haven't seen or talked to By in the past three weeks since the house made its decision. I've tried a couple of times but he's hung up on me before I could get started. I have Guy Unruh and Ari Katanian working on him. If they can get him loosened up a little I'm planning to go down and see him some night. Guy tells me he's still pretty bitter, but he thinks he'll come around in time."

"Is that the Negro boy your house tried to pledge?" Mary inquired. Willie nodded. She gave him a disbelieving little smile. "What a quixotic idea! We Kappas would never try a thing like that."

"No, ma'am," he agreed. "Nor would any other house on campus, probably. At least no one has. It was just my own crazy idea."

"It was a thoroughly decent and wonderful idea!" Marian said with a sudden vehemence that obviously startled her mother.

"Well!" she responded. "I'm not saying it wasn't a worthy idea *as an idea* but there are limitations, of course. To be practical, one does have to work within the framework of one's society as it exists. Otherwise progress is defeated by—well, by the sort of reaction within your house, and by the general reaction on the campus."

"Most of the campus approved, Mother," Marian said. Mary smiled.

"Yes, dear, and so did you, I know. But there was still such a large group opposed that—well, that it just wouldn't have *done*, that's all. I think in time Mr. Johnson will realize that everything probably worked out for the best. And I'm sure you will, too, Mr. Wilson."

"No, ma'am," Willie said. "I'm afraid not."

For the first time since he had arrived, he thought, she really looked a little upset and disorganized.

"Well!" she said—her favorite exclamation, he was beginning to think. "Then I must say, Mr. Wilson—" She paused and with the closest she permitted herself to come to sarcasm, said, "*Willie*—I must say that I think you are a most ill-advised and unwise young man. I certainly don't blame Dr. Chalmers and the board if they feel they must oppose what appears to be an attempt at really radical change on campus. Why, it virtually amounts to revolution, in terms of what the University has always been."

"Oh, Mo—*ther!*" Marian exclaimed, and Cecilia again uttered her rather hysterical little giggle and chanted, "Watch out for the Reds, watch out for the Reds!"

"I don't care," Mary said, maintaining her untroubled air with difficulty but maintaining it, he had to hand her that. "I think, had it been successful, that it could very well have led to a disruptive situation on campus that the Communists most certainly could have profited from even if they did not inspire it. Which, Mr. Wilson, I assume they *did not.*"

"No, ma'am," he said, annoyed but realizing he must keep his temper or risk losing any chance of anything with Marian. (Was that really what he had come here for? He seemed to have almost forgotten.) "No, ma'am," he repeated, "the Communists had nothing to do with it, I assure you." (Very briefly the stubborn little face of Maryetta Bradford shot across his mind, but he rejected it out of hand. That was ridiculous.) "It was all my own idea. I was given to understand by Dr. Chalmers—and indeed by Mr. Emerson—Walter—however, that the board itself was willing to make some modest experiment in that direction."

"Walter!" Mary exclaimed, and they could see she was struggling with some difficulty to maintain her air of judicious calm now. "You never told me that!"

"No, I didn't," Walter agreed. "Thought it would be more peaceable not to. Which was correct. Willie, how about some more brandy?"

"And don't turn it aside," his wife snapped with a sudden ferocity that startled Willie far more than it seemed to startle her family, who were apparently used to it, "by appealing to Mr. Wilson to have more brandy! That is typical of you, Walter Emerson, both the evasion and the brandy. What do we have to do to get the truth told in this house?"

"Now, Mary," Walter began, but she would have none of it. She stood up and turned to Willie with a reasonable semblance of dignity restored.

"I'm sorry that you have to be subjected to a family squabble, Mr. Wilson, but perhaps it is best that you see us as we are. And that we see you the same way. It will permit us all to judge the future better."

"Yes, ma'am," he said, standing up awkwardly and automatically holding out his hand. "I'm sorry if I—"

"Nothing to worry about," she said, ignoring it. "You haven't done a thing but be yourself, which has been quite enlightening to Marian's parents, I think. Or at least to me. I hope you sleep well and I will see you at breakfast."

"Yes, ma'am," he said. "Nine o'clock."

"Good night." She turned gracefully and went out, saying, "Here, Flip, boy," in a calm voice, taking him with her up the stairs.

"Good night," he said, and after a moment sat down, aware of the stillness in the room. Walter was staring into his brandy snifter. Cecilia was humming softly to herself and leafing through the pages of a movie magazine she had picked up from a side table when the going began to get rough. Marian finally spoke.

"I'm sorry," she said. "I apologize for Mother. She gets quite—upset about things, sometimes."

"Not at all," he said. "I expect I was pretty positive myself—"

"You were entirely within bounds," Walter said. "But perhaps it would be best for us not to discuss By Johnson again during your visit. Keep me advised, though. Give me a call after you've talked to him. I'd like to know how he's getting along."

"Yes, sir. It may be a few weeks, though."

"Whenever. *Would* you like some more brandy, incidentally?"

"No, thanks," he said, beginning to feel relaxed enough again to smile. "It's excellent, though."

"I think I'll go along up," Walter said, going to the bar and pouring himself another hefty slug in preparation.

Cecilia yawned, closed her magazine and stood up, a gangly but striking string bean.

"Good night, then," Walter said. "See you in the morning. Come along, kiddums."

" 'Kiddums'!" Cecilia exclaimed. "*Daddy!*"

"Gosh," Walter said with a wink at Willie. "I can't do anything right around here. There are books and magazines in your room, Willie, if you want to turn in early too."

"Thanks," he said. "I expect I will. I brought some reading for class that I'm supposed to have done by Monday, though. I expect I should do it."

After they left, Walter closing the door carefully behind them, a silence fell during which he and Marian did not look at one another for a few minutes. The fire sputtered and crackled, sinking rapidly. Finally he glanced at her and was startled to find her eyes filled with tears.

"I am *so* sorry," she said. "Mother can be so—so *beastly* at times, and

Daddy's so—so heavy-handed. I don't see how they ever got married. Do you ever wonder that about your parents?"

"Sometimes," he admitted. "I suppose everybody does, once in a while. But they did—" he smiled— "and so here you and I are—and so maybe it was just as well."

But she didn't smile in return, just looked more forlorn and dashed the tears away with a hasty hand.

"You won't ever want to see me again, after this!"

"Oh, now!" he said, surprised by her vehemence. "Don't take it so seriously. Every family has its little arguments. It isn't the end of the world. Your mother's entitled to her opinions."

"But she'll hold yours against you, that's the problem. You don't know her."

"No, but she seems like a nice lady—er—essentially."

Marian smiled then, still rather forlornly.

"Yes, I guess 'essentially' she is. But I'm glad I'm away at school now. And I am sorry I subjected you to this. Daddy and I thought it would be a nice break for you to get away from campus for a few hours. It was basically his idea, but she seemed to be for it too."

"Oh," he said, feeling a surprising little sting. "I thought maybe it was your idea."

"Oh, it was," she said hastily. "I didn't mean that *I* didn't want you to come over, I did. I meant that Daddy really thinks you're great and he was *really* enthused. Mother was very interested, too."

"I'll admit I was," he said with a smile. "I thought maybe getting to know them would help me to know you better." As I think it has, he told himself with some wryness. "Anyway, don't worry about it. I'm sure we'll all get along fine in the morning."

"I hope so," she said in the same forlorn voice. "Can I get you a glass of water or a Coke or something to take up to bed with you? Or more liquor?"

"Certainly not more liquor," he said, startled and again a little stung by what appeared to be abrupt dismissal. "Are you going up so soon? I thought maybe we could just—just talk for a bit? I mean, we really haven't talked about much, up to now."

She frowned.

"We've already talked about the Rhodes scholarship," she said earnestly. "And Hitler—and war—and—well, I suppose we could talk about your house but—" She paused, rather helplessly.

"O.K.," he said, standing up. "Let's get a Coke and then I will turn in. I really do want to do some reading. Is there Coke in the bar or do we have to go to the kitchen for it?"

"There's some in the bar," she said, looking distraught but leading the way obediently across the huge white room. They went silently and solemnly up the stairs side by side, each with a glass of ice in one hand, a Coke in the other.

At the top of the stairs he noticed that the door to her parents' room was open a substantial crack. Through it he could see Walter, glasses on nose, sitting up in bed and pretending to read. Apparently he and his wife had resolved their differences for the time being: all was silent and serene. Marriage! he thought, and marveled at its wonders. He couldn't see Mary— probably they had twin beds, her choice, Walter's concurrence.

Walter grinned and waved with elaborate fellowship, other hand to lips indicating that Mary was asleep, which Willie didn't believe for one minute. He waved back cordially.

"Well, good night," he said loudly to Marian as he reached his own open door directly across the hall.

"Good night," she said, and added in a whisper, "I hope you're not too— too upset with us."

"Not at all," he whispered back emphatically and gave her what he hoped would be a reassuring smile.

She went on along the hall. He stepped in, closed his door with a re-sounding click he hoped would satisfy her parents, and slowly got ready for bed. Marian remained an enigma. She could be so apparently at ease and relaxed at some moments, so instantly tense at others. Was there any con-sistent thread underlying? If so, he hadn't found it yet.

The house and neighborhood were silent as a tomb. For a few minutes he really did try to read. Then he snapped off the light with a sigh and finally, after some long and uncharacteristic tossings and turnings, drifted off to sleep. But not before he thought again: *Jesus.*

In the morning he woke promptly at six-thirty, campus hours, but man-aged to drift back to sleep again after a quick trip to the bathroom. The house was silent as before. Outside the rain continued, steady, heavy, monoto-nous. It would probably go on for days; the weatherman hadn't offered much hope of an early break. He looked out at a cold green world before climbing back under the covers and pulling a pillow over his head: a beautiful neigh-borhood, chaste, orderly, painfully well kept. He liked the ranch better. It was almost always casual, sometimes sloppy, undeniably lived-in. He won-dered for a moment how Marian would fit into such an environment and then dismissed it as he got back into bed. He'd worry about that later— maybe.

He was beginning to think he might have exaggerated things a bit, which wasn't like him. He felt that maybe balance was returning, after three months. Sleep reclaimed him before he could pursue the idea further.

Shortly after eight someone apparently opened his door with great delicacy and discretion, for suddenly a wet nose was stuck in his face, a slurpy kiss bestowed on his forehead and two heavy paws rested on his chest. Flip was obviously his alarm clock.

Fifteen minutes later he was dressed in gray slacks, red University pullover and his best Roos Brothers loafers. He gave himself a last look in the mirror, decided he was presentable and stepped out into the hall just as Walter, who had no doubt been waiting, emerged beaming from across the way.

"Hi!" he said. "Like a Bloody Mary to start the day right?"

"No, thanks," Willie said. "I'm afraid I'm a pretty conservative drinker. You don't suppose Dora would have an advance cup of coffee, would she?"

"For you, Willie," Walter said with a grin, "anything. You've made a great hit." After Dora had delivered the coffee and paper and kindling were crackling in the fireplace he said, "What do you think of my girls?"

"I like them," he said, tone becoming cautious, which he knew Walter noted. "Cecilia's a little character but she's a beautiful girl and obviously very bright. Marian—" he paused and Walter said, "Yes?" giving him a seriously interested look—"Marian's a very nice girl, also obviously very bright. I like her," he added simply. "Otherwise I wouldn't be here."

"Do you like her mother?" Walter asked and Willie almost demanded, "What is this, an inquisition?" But Walter was so obviously genuinely interested that he decided to keep talking and make it an honest one.

"Also very beautiful and very bright—and very determined."

"Domineering, you might say," Walter suggested. Willie decided to give him a grin and see it through.

"I'm not in a position to say that, but you might."

"She means well," Walter remarked seriously, not at all offended. "And she does do a great deal of good. She's involved in half the charitable projects in the Bay Area, I do believe. She's quite a remarkable person, in many ways. And she's a good mother to the girls—even though," he added somewhat wistfully, "they don't always appreciate it as they should."

"That's sometimes the way with strong mothers," Willie said politely.

"Which," Walter said with a candid grin, "may be why weak fathers are sometimes necessary. Someone has to indulge the kids once in a while. . . . Have you and Marian seen much of each other?"

Willie hesitated, then decided to be honest.

"Not too much. A few dates, a few snacks at the Cellar, a movie or two—not exactly heavy dating."

"Not too serious," her father suggested. Willie frowned and gave him a contemplative look.

"I've thought it could be."

"Past tense. It isn't now?"

Willie shook his head in some bafflement.

"It could be. It could be. But—"

"What?" Walter asked quietly; and again, encouraged by his direct and companionable manner, Willie decided to be honest.

"She can be, " he said carefully, "a—rather difficult girl. Great qualities, you understand, but . . . changeable, sometimes. That's intriguing at times, but other times—you wish you knew where you stood, if you know what I mean."

"Oh, I do," Walter said with a smile. "I'm married to her mother." He paused and gave Willie another of his shrewdly analytical looks. "Perhaps you should consider someone else."

For several seconds Willie was so taken aback that he literally did not know what to say. It was one thing to be coming up on that kind of thinking yourself and quite another to be told politely, "Here's your hat, what's your hurry?" That was the sort of decision a man should make for himself, not have it made for him by the girl's father. It startled, shocked, offended, dismayed. It was damned unsettling, in fact, particularly when you had basked in the complacent glow of the thought that the father couldn't wait to get you committed. It was quite a blow to the ego, actually.

It took him several seconds to recover enough to respond.

"Shocked you, didn't I?" Walter chuckled, nailing him exactly. "Hurt your manly pride. Offended your masculine dignity. Indicated you might not be quite the God's gift to women that you thought you were. Went at it bass-ackwards, like I do most things. *You* ought to be telling me, with a fine show of reluctance, that yes, Marian's a great girl, but maybe she isn't quite the one for you. *I* ought to be startled, shocked, offended. "Right?" He grinned. "Sure you don't want that Bloody Mary?"

Willie gave him a long, slow, solemn look; and then, in spite of himself, responded to Walter's cheerful brashness with the beginnings of a smile.

"Yes, I think maybe I will, Walter."

"Good!" Walter said, going to the bar, mixing it quickly and bringing it back. "Let's be honest. You have been rather a reluctant Romeo, haven't you? You have been pretty slow to—"

"Only because I respected Marian," he said. "And, frankly, I've been trying to understand her. And, frankly," he added, deciding to be completely candid, "she's made me a little afraid of her. She can be so easy and natural at times—and so puzzling at others. I *have* been wondering whether I wanted to put up with that kind of constant uncertainty for a lifetime. Tell me," he said, with an abrupt directness he would not have ventured some other time, with someone less honest. "Has it been worth it for you?"

For a moment Walter looked offended himself. Then he relaxed.

"Fair enough. Fair enough." He too looked for a moment deep into his glass, as though for a second he really did think it might hold the answer to life's more elusive mysteries. "Let's put it this way. I have a nice construction business. I have a nice house. I have two beautiful and intelligent daughters. I have a beautiful and intelligent wife who has contributed greatly to, and supported me in, all these, and who is an adornment to me, my business, my kids and my life. What I've put up with in return for that, what I have had to compromise with and endure, is another matter: what I'm telling you is, that's where I am now. Is that a fair answer to your question?"

"Fair enough," Willie acknowledged in his turn. "Fair enough. So that leaves me about where I was before, right? Should I or shouldn't I 'consider someone else,' as you put it? You're not helping me make up my mind, you know, Walter."

"All I'm doing," Walter said, "is letting you understand that if you want to get out while the getting's good, I'll understand and there'll be no hard feelings. What other father you know can make that claim?"

Willie laughed.

"Not many, I guess. I don't have all that much experience to draw on, but I'd guess not many. I do appreciate it. I really do."

"Good!" Walter said and held out his hand. They were shaking on it solemnly when the door swung open, Flip galloped in and Mary appeared.

"Well!" she said. "What are you two shaking hands on? Some big business deal?"

"Some big deal," Walter said with a cheerful wink at Willie. "I don't know about the 'business' part, but it's some big deal, right, Willie?"

"I'll never tell," Willie said.

"So, Mr. Wilson," Mary said. "You like our Marian."

"Yes, ma'am," he said; and finally added, after so many "Mr. Wilsons," "Most people do call me Willie. If you'd like."

The two of them were seated in what he supposed would be called the conservatory in some even more grandiose mansion, a partially glassed-in room filled with plants, off what was obviously Walter's home office, a small room filled with a desk, files, bookshelves and papers. How he had been thus neatly cut off from the herd and corralled by himself, he didn't exactly recall, except that it had been done with startling speed and dexterity when they broke from breakfast shortly after ten. Now they were seated opposite one another in white wicker chairs, fortified with extra cups of Dora's special blend of coffee.

Outside the rain had stopped, but obviously only temporarily.

"I would call you Willie," Mary said with apparent pleasantry, "except that for me such familiarity with first names can only come when I really know and like someone."

"Yes, ma'am," he agreed quickly, thinking: Better be on your toes, boy. "I feel exactly the same way."

The tiniest glint in her eyes noted this opening exchange of fire, but her tone remained perfectly self-possessed and equable.

"Good. Then we understand one another. How long have you known Marian?"

"Only autumn quarter. Three months, really. Reg Day, fall quarter, I believe it was, when we saw each other. A month after that before we had a date."

"Is it what we would have called in my day 'heavy'?"

"We'd call it that, too," he said with a smile. Then he frowned. "I'm not quite sure. Mr. Emerson—Walter—asked me about that, too, and I didn't know quite what to say. I've thought at times that it might have that potential, but every time I've thought so, Marian has—retreated, I guess you might say. I think she's basically very shy."

"And of course very well brought up," Mary observed; and suddenly he decided he had not come here to be patronized, whatever the consequences. He gave her a cheerful smile.

"She certainly meets *my* standards," he said heartily.

"How nice," Mary said. "I suppose, coming as you do from a ranch in a small farming community in the San Joaquin Valley, that they are very high."

O.K., he thought: two can play that game.

"In terms of money," he said thoughtfully, "in terms of money—I would say that, yes, we have ranchers there who could probably buy half of Piedmont tomorrow morning without having to take off their dirty overalls or go to the bank. Yes, ma'am. In terms of money, our standards can be quite astonishing, to those who don't know us. Culturally, we may not be quite as—as overbearing as some people up here—" he gave her a between-us smile—"sometimes seem to be, but we manage quite well in that area, too."

"It must really be an ideal society," Mary observed with a dry little smile. "But we are getting rather far away from Marian. What are your intentions, Mr. Wilson?"

At this phrase, so old-fashioned in his view, he almost laughed aloud. But despite his keyed-up sense of insolent combativeness, which he knew did not become him but which unhappily she had seemed to provoke in him almost from the moment they met, he knew laughter at this point would not be wise. And also, he thought, he *did* have *some* manners, even if he was from "a small farming community in the San Joaquin Valley."

"I honestly don't know at this point what my intentions are, Mrs. Emerson," he said in a genuinely baffled voice. "Let me ask: is Marian interested in me?"

"Yes," Mary said with the faintest tinge of regret. "I'm afr—I believe—she is."

"How do you tell?" he asked with a relaxed and, he hoped, charming smile, though her deliberate slip annoyed him considerably. Which he knew it was intended to.

"She talks a lot about you when she's home, that's one way. She speaks of you with considerable warmth. She appears to admire you tremendously."

He told himself he mustn't be pathological about it but he really did seem to sense *I don't see why* in her tone. He tried not to be too challenging but couldn't seem to help it.

"Essentially, Mrs. Emerson, I gather that you don't approve of *anything* serious between your daughter and me, right?"

For a second she looked a little startled. Then she nodded, quite businesslike.

"She's really very young. And not really very sophisticated. It's possible you've been reading into her things and qualities that aren't really there, yet—perhaps never will be. Men, particularly young men, do have that habit. And there's the war. It's coming. If it comes to this country along with Europe, you will have to go—unless there's some disability Walter and I aren't aware of?"

"No, ma'am," he said dryly. "Not that I know of."

"Then you will. And if you have a romance with Marian, if, perhaps, you might even be married, then it would be intensely hard on her and greatly unfair. I know: I was a war bride myself. It isn't easy."

"No, ma'am," he agreed gravely. "But it's happened to millions before, and if necessary will happen to millions more, and somehow most of them seem to survive it. You did."

"But why should I willingly let my daughters be subjected to it if I can protect them, even a little bit? You're older than Marian, more sophisticated—I dare say you know more about 'life,' as we used to euphemize it, than she does—?"

She paused and stared at him but he knew he wasn't going to respond to that one. He continued to watch her attentively until she resumed.

"—and because of that, are probably already much more armored against the world than she is. No, Mr. Wilson. Walter thinks you are a very fine young man and I am inclined to agree. But I don't believe it would be wise for you to pursue a romance with Marian which could, I am afraid, lead only to unhappiness for you both."

"Well, ma'am," he said, "assuming anything were to develop, then by rights it really should be between us, shouldn't it? I mean, parents can only protect kids so far and then it's their lives, isn't it? . . . I must say, though, Walter hasn't given me much guidance and you aren't, either, except to tell me politely that neither of you would be the least bit hurt if I just got the hell out. And that *I* shouldn't be hurt either."

At this she did laugh, quite openly and naturally.

"Oh, Mr. Wilson! Willie! You *are* a nice boy and I *do* like you and there's really nothing personal in all this, except that I just want to protect my daughter from getting hurt, that's all. Surely that's a mother's prerogative?"

"The road to Piedmont," he said wryly, "is paved with good intentions. Do you think I can find my way back from here to campus?"

She smiled.

"We're counting on you to get Marian there, too. Safely. All right?"

"O.K., Mary," he said. "All right."

"Is it a deal?" she asked with a gleam of humor he didn't know she had; and offered her hand.

"It's a deal," he said, accepting it just as Walter came in red-cheeked and puffing from a romp on the soggy lawn with Flip.

"More damned hand-shaking going on around here!" he exclaimed. "What the hell—?"

"He'll never tell," said Mary.

And, "That's right," said Willie.

When they left to return to school around two o'clock, after a hearty lunch for which Dora again outdid herself, the clouds were solidifying again and a cold, scudding wind was driving the shards of swiftly resuming rain before it. Mary, Walter, Cecilia, Dora and Flip stood together under the portico to wave goodbye with many admonitions to drive carefully, watch out for Sunday drivers and be careful in the storm. They shouted back that they would and chugged off down the drive somewhat fitfully, the Chevy's always uncertain temperament not improved by a night in the open due to the fact that the Rolls and the Lincoln, as Walter apologized, had taken up all the garage space.

"That was nice," he said as they began the winding drive down through the Piedmont hills to the main highway where they would turn south to Dumbarton Bridge. "I like your family—even if Daddy is a little heavy-handed and Mother has her opinions," he suggested, but with a smile that robbed it of sting. He wanted to see how she'd take it. She took it fine.

"They're such characters!" she said with a cheerful laugh. "But they do mean well. I know I've disappointed Mother about the Kappas, but I just decided I wanted to be my own woman. I expect I could still join, if I really wanted to. But I'd rather be independent."

"Yes," he said with another glance, this one rather wry. "I've noticed that."

"Does it bother you?" she asked with a directness that caught him a little unprepared; but, "No," he said, and decided to toss it back. "Does that bother you?"

"What, that my independence doesn't bother you?" She looked thoughtful. "No, I probably wouldn't respect you if it did."

"I'm glad to know I have your respect, anyway."

"Admiration and respect."

"How about liking?"

"Oh, of course," she said blushing slightly. "That too."

"Good," he said. "I've wondered from time to time."

"You're the first boy we've ever invited to stay overnight," she said in a voice that held a certain triumph; overshadowed, for him, by the pronoun.

"I'm glad I passed the committee," he remarked with a little more overt amusement than he actually felt: there were wheels within wheels, here. He didn't want to get run over by any of them. "And did I pass muster once I was in the door?"

She blushed again, looking very pretty, he thought when he took his eyes away from the heavy downpour and the increasingly heavy southbound traffic to give her a quick glance.

"Everybody enjoyed you," she said firmly. "You made a big hit with everyone." She smiled. "Even Dora and Flip."

"But what about your mother?"

"She really liked you, too," she said seriously. "She told me she had a nice talk with you after breakfast. She said you were 'a fine and perceptive young man.' "

"Whom she thoroughly approves of as a friend and escort for her daughter," he suggested, again with a quick sidelong glance, which was all he could chance as the rain drummed on the canvas and the old car rolled along through traffic. Again Marian blushed. The strength of her response startled him.

"I don't care! What does she know about it?"

"Oh," he said, curiously not feeling annoyance or regret or indeed much of anything: perhaps this just made things easier. "Then she really *doesn't* want me in the picture."

She turned to look at him.

"Did she tell you that?"

He nodded.

"Pretty much. I told her it was something we had to work out together, and that I couldn't promise not to see you. Was that the right answer?"

She hesitated and he thought: O.K., girl, this is it. Which is it going to be, me or your family? But as he might have expected, her response didn't lend itself to that kind of simplicity.

"I guess—maybe—it was," she said slowly, and again a quick glance revealed that she was thinking about it very carefully. No spontaneity here, no bubbling Donn Van Dyke with honest emotions on sleeve. Why did Donn pop into his head just at that moment? Life was complicated enough. One thing at a time.

" 'Maybe'?" he echoed. "Is that the best you can do?" He grinned, hoping to elicit a more relaxed and affirmative response. "How about a little wild enthusiasm here?" Then seriously he said, "There does come a time to begin"—he almost said "growing up" but again caught himself in time—

"considering your own life too, you know. We all have to start branching out and making our own decisions. That's one of the things college is supposed to give us—the chance to mature independently of our parents."

"I have to take their opinions into account," she said stubbornly. "I can't just ignore them."

"No," he said, suddenly deciding what the hell, why try to keep on being diplomatic? "But you can tell them, Look, I'm growing up and I'm going to have to start making some decisions of my own, and this is what I'm going to do about Willie Wilson. If," he added with a sudden unamused, almost hostile exaggeration, "I'm not a leper, that is. Am I?"

"Oh, no!" she exclaimed in what appeared to be genuine dismay. "Of course you're not! How awful! What an awful thing to say!"

"I was beginning to feel that way," he said, not yielding much.

"Why do you say things like that to me?" she demanded, sounding close to tears. "Why do you try to make me feel as though I were—were failing you in some way? You shouldn't talk to me like that! Why, we hardly know each other, really!"

"Whose fault is that?" he asked—not being entirely fair, perhaps, but irritated enough so that he let it sweep him along.

"Oh!" she said, and did begin to cry. "You're impossible!"

"I'm sorry for that," he said gravely. "I didn't start out to be."

"But you are! You *are!*"

His subsequent attempts at more casual conversation were repulsed with silence, and so they concluded their homeward journey as they had concluded the outbound, in silence, in the pounding, pelting rain, in the cold, wet world of winter weather. They crossed the bridge, reached the Bayshore Highway, turned south, came presently to the massive sandstone pillars and turned onto Palm Drive. The rain was so torrential and so mixed with fog that they could not see Memorial Church or the red-roofed arches until they were halfway down the drive.

She had stopped crying by then and his own attitude had stabilized. He wasn't all that sorry. At least he had provoked some show of genuine emotion for a change, some honest display of feelings, some knocking-down of barriers. Something might be made of that, or nothing. He was beginning to think he didn't really care; and to wonder at his own capacity for self-delusion in the last three months. He hadn't thought of himself as being that vulnerable.

At the Union he hopped out again in the downpour, repeated his dash around the car, unloaded her bag, escorted her to shelter. They stood for a moment staring at one another. The rain made a heavy rushing sound all around.

"Thank you for a very pleasant visit with your family," he said formally. "I'll write your mother a note."

"It doesn't matter," she said, not looking at him. "It doesn't matter."

"I don't know, at this moment," he said. "But I will, anyway. See you around."

"Yes," she said, still not looking at him. "I suppose so."

"Well—goodbye."

"Goodbye. Thank you for the ride."

"You're welcome."

The house seemed silent, rather empty, rather cold, when he parked the Chevy in his space in their ten-car garage out back and went in through the kitchen door. He went through the dining room to the front hall and was about to climb the stairs to his room when he heard the crack of a cue ball in the poolroom. He dumped his bag at the foot of the stairs and wandered in to see who was there.

Seeking company, he admitted to himself.

Seeking reassurance that he was still Willie Wilson, for whom the world went right.

"Hey, Willie!" Unruh hailed him cheerfully as Latt, startled, hit a wild one, knocked the eight ball into a pocket and said, "Oh, *shoot!*" in a mildly reproving voice. "Look what you made me do, Guy."

"You were beaten anyway," Guy assured him with a kindly tolerance. "Face it, Lattimer, you're a no-God-damned-good pool player."

"I try," Latt said with dignity. "I try. If I didn't have so many comical friends. Did you have a good visit, Willie?"

He decided he wouldn't attempt to put a good face on it with these two old pals. He shrugged.

"Oh. Moderately."

"What's the matter?" Guy inquired. "Didn't like Momma, Poppa and the kiddies? Or they didn't like you?"

"We all liked each other well enough, but—come on up to the room when you're through, I'll tell you about it."

"We're through," Guy said. "Latt can't hit the broad side of a barn."

"I perhaps *might*," Latt said, "if I didn't get so much chatter. Lead on, Macduff. We'll follow."

Up under the eaves, after he had turned on his small space heater and his cubbyhole had become warm and snug, he did tell them all about it. When he finished Guy said tersely:

"Dump her."

Latt looked a little perturbed and said, "Isn't that a little harsh, Guy? She's apparently a nice girl—"

"But difficult," Guy said. "Who needs difficult? You have Donn, after all. I'll admit she's a little smothering, but hell, Maggie's smothering and *I'll* probably marry *her*. Why should you be unsmothered? Particularly when the alternative is to be in a perpetual emotional turmoil."

"But maybe there's some reason for it," Latt objected. "Maybe she's got some problem with classes or something that gets her on edge. Or maybe—"

"Oh, Latt," Guy said. "You're always so damned fair! It's *sickening!* Why don't we just destroy the girl's character and relieve our dear old brother here of any qualms of conscience he may feel about it? Wouldn't that be in the true fraternal spirit? Knowing Willie, I expect he's got a few. Right, lover boy?"

"I—" Willie began, and paused. "I don't want to be unfair either. Maybe it's me. Maybe I *am* to blame. Maybe I haven't been aggressive enough—or have been aggressive at the wrong moments. Or something. Damned if I know."

"There, you see?" Unruh demanded. "If you're that confused, get the hell out of it. Now's the time to do it. I wouldn't say either one of you is exactly head-over-heels. I think this is all in your mind, Willie."

Willie gave him a quizzical look.

"Is it ever anywhere else, when you come right down to it?"

"Now *that*," Unruh said, "is a thoroughly cynical attitude." He grinned. "With which I absolutely agree. Except sometimes. And I get the feeling this isn't one of them."

"I'm not really in a position to give advice to you experts," Latt remarked, "but I'm not sure I'd burn all my bridges if I were you, Willie. Unless you really decide you want Donna."

Willie frowned.

"That's the thing, damn it. I don't know whether I do or not. She's habit—she couldn't be brighter—or nicer—or more—" he smiled and said it wryly— "worth*while*—"

"She'd be a great wife," Latt said. "*I* think."

"Speaking of which," Willie said, "how are *you* doing?"

Latt actually blushed.

"Oh. We're getting along."

"Asked her yet?" Guy demanded.

Latt's blush deepened.

"No."

"Well, God *damn* it, *get to it!*"

"I suppose *you* have," Latt retorted. "You're always so full of advice."

"Well—no," Guy admitted with a grin. "But it's on the agenda. It'll come up, one of these days. I'm about convinced it's inevitable."

"So am I," Latt said, and smiled rather uncomfortably. "I guess. . . . Anyway, this isn't helping Willie."

"Willie can't be helped," Guy remarked. "He just wants us to be audience for another of his Hamlet acts. Correct, old buddy?"

"Oh, go to hell," Willie said with a grin, feeling suddenly better about it all.

"Dump her," Guy advised again. "It's the only way."

After they had gone off downstairs, Willie fell into a brown study. When he met them in the living room a couple of hours later he was no nearer a conclusion. The only thing that seemed to be pushing him in one direction as opposed to the other was the fact that having seen Mary in the context of the home she had created for herself and her family—in that order, he suspected—he thought he understood Marian better. Whether this was good or bad, he didn't know; and anyway, maybe it didn't matter.

Maybe he no longer had the option. He might never hear from her again. She might refuse to see him altogether. He might decide never to call her.

When the phone rang at nine, however, and Jeff yelled "WILLIE!" he felt renewed excitement. It subsided when he heard Donn's cheerful voice. But after listening to her bubble on for a bit he found himself responding with thankful relaxation and easygoing camaraderie.

She *was* a nice girl.

And she *was* comfortable.

And predictable.

And that *was* something.

Quite a lot, he told himself.

In fact, a hell of a lot.

20

After another week of alternating heavy rains and coldly penetrating drizzle, the weather finally broke—temporarily, they knew, for there would probably be at least another month of winter. But in a sudden unexpected harbinger of spring, a couple of warm, wonderful, sparkling-diamond days descended on the campus. Moods changed, hearts lifted. With a few exceptions, heavy-heavy gave way to light and happy.

For Bates, one of the exceptions, yielding to Nagatani the editorship, for which Tim had worked so hard throughout his campus career and to which he had devoted so much care and emotion during the four months when he finally had it, was not an easy thing. He went around complaining about his successor's news priorities to anyone who would listen, pointing out in the City papers information that HITLER THREATENS NEW MOVE ON CZECHS; that Fritz Kuhn, head of the German-American Bund, had drawn twenty thousand to a rally in Madison Square Garden; that the Nationalists had started a bloodbath in Madrid following the collapse of the Loyalist cause; and that the Japanese were continuing their systematic and frightful slaughters in China. All these, in Tim's view, Bill had relegated to relatively minor positions in the *Daily*. He grew so vehement that Franky finally suggested to Dewey that he mix him "an Alka-Seltzer cocktail with bourbon."

"You sure are upset, Mr. Bates," Dewey agreed with a cautious chuckle, quickly suppressed when Tim glared at him.

It wasn't that there weren't plenty of constant, lengthy and heated arguments about the world situation, as Gil commented to Latt. They occurred in the house and all over campus, all the time. The possibilities of war, the chances of staying out or being dragged in, occupied probably a good half of all conversations. Nor was it only in bullsessions: classrooms, too, were becoming frequent battlegrounds of opinion and emotion. Professors who theoretically were supposed to be objective were no more objective than Timmy in seeking to influence everyone they could reach.

Poor, battered, beleaguered little Germany, threatened and encircled by the big bad colonial powers egged on by invidious America—that was one loudly vocal school of thought.

Aggressive, militaristic, bloodthirsty Germany, out to destroy democracy and conquer the world—that was the other, coming up fast on the outside.

In this increasingly contentious atmosphere there was a subtle but inescapable change in campus discussion. Slowly but surely being driven into second place were the standard topics so appealing to the collegiate mind: sex, in all its various forms, manifestations and mechanics . . . philosophy, from Plato to Bertrand Russell . . . religion, from Christ to Buddha to Mohammed to voodoo . . . politics, local, state, national, international . . . those wonderful, long, late-night, inconclusive bullsessions of college days!—summed up precisely one time by Franky when he told Smitty:

"Buff and I really had the world's problems all worked out last night. He has this illegal beer stashed away, you know, and I think we each killed about four bottles, after which we became positively brilliant. The only trouble is, this morning we can't remember a damned thing we said!"

The topic of Hitler unhappily loomed larger and larger. Life, often earnest and sometimes real, was becoming more and more so in college talk. In the house, as elsewhere, they didn't want to be forced into it, that's all: they didn't want anyone, even Timmy of whom they were very fond, beating them over the head with it all the time.

It surfaced often enough—too often, many felt—as winter resumed with rain and cold, bitter wind and frequent fog . . . and then began, finally, to turn with all its old, familiar magic, slowly, seductively and inexorably, toward spring. . . .

But before that happened, there were still a few gray days.

On one of the last rainy weekends, when midterm exams were over and people were beginning to think quite seriously about finals and deciding that maybe they had better put on that last burst of speed, if they could, which would tip a B-plus to an A, or a D to a C, the president of the student body decided to go down to the halls to see the University's only Negro student.

It was a trip he had been contemplating for several weeks, during which Unruh had reported back at frequent intervals on By's uncertain and fluctuating emotions, and Ari Katanian had also relayed his impressions. Neither was exactly optimistic.

Guy said his friendship with By had dwindled down, at By's instigation, to a polite formality on the court and no relaxed kidding off of it. He had even suspected, in two or three crucial series games with other schools, that By had deliberately failed to cooperate with him, though it had been done with such apparent naturalness that the coach and the team had taken it as simple error on By's part. But after the failed plays his eye had caught Guy's for just a second. Behind his innocent, contemplative stare Guy thought he could see very well the message he was apparently meant to get. He was becoming increasingly annoyed but had not yet challenged By openly. Willie urged him strongly not to and had managed to exact a promise that he wouldn't. But Guy thought he might mention it to the coach sometime when it came right. There were ways of instilling doubt. Guy felt he was beginning to have sufficient provocation.

Ari, who had arranged to sit beside By at their eating club on a couple of occasions recently, had reported to Willie that he had been "frozen with politeness."

On the first occasion By had been scrupulously complimentary about Ari's Rhodes scholarship and after that had subsided into a silence broken only by monosyllables when Ari attempted to carry on an ordinary conversation.

On the second occasion By had taken a different and more aggressive tack, inquiring, when Ari moved in beside him, "Why are you sitting with me? Is there something I can do for you?"

Ari, normally one of the most outgoing and easygoing of individuals, had reacted mildly but with a certain underlying impatience.

"I just wanted to visit with you. Is that against the law?"

"Not here," By said wryly. "Not yet. But it is where I come from. I'm used to it. It just seems odd to me, you getting so friendly with—with someone who's—who's sort of a pariah around here."

"Who says that?" Ari inquired, lowering his voice as a couple of guys across the table began listening with an ostentatious air of inattention.

"Oh," By said, "it just seems to be the accepted thing."

"Not by me," Ari said. "I'm not like that."

"I know," By said with a wry little smile. "Ari Katanian's image wouldn't allow it."

"Well, f—" Ari began and then stopped himself with a considerable effort. "You don't have to be snotty with me, By," he said, more mildly. "I'm your friend. You can stop being defensive."

"I can't ever stop being defensive," By said, pretending to eat but, Ari noticed, actually just pushing the food around on the plate and hardly touching it. Lord, he thought, the poor guy must really be tight as a spring inside. A sudden pity moved him.

"Look," he said. "I won't talk if you don't want to. If you do sometime, drop by and see me in the room. This is no good here, and anyway, it's too public." He stared at the guys across the table until they blushed and looked away. "I didn't mean to embarrass you. I'm sorry."

"No, I'm sorry," By said, abruptly looking flustered and unhappy.

"Come see me," Ari urged, but By shook his head.

"I can't," he said in a desperate voice, very low. "I just can't."

After that, by tacit agreement, they said no more to one another.

"I think you're going to have a tough time with him," Ari told Willie a little later on the phone. "Want company?"

"No, thanks. We don't want him to feel we're ganging up on him. Just be friendly when you see him."

"I always am," Ari said. "But I don't think it's going to be enough."

Guy also offered to accompany him but Willie said no to him, too.

"You're beginning to get impatient with him, I can tell. And that's no way to achieve anything."

"Yes, I suppose I am," Guy admitted. "But damn it, he's getting to be annoying."

"It's defensive," Willie said. "The poor kid thinks the whole world is against him, now. We've just got to show him that isn't so."

"Good luck," Guy said dryly. "Have fun."

And so, about eight-thirty on a Sunday night, alerted by Ari that By was apparently alone in his room, Wilson walked down through the rain and fog to the halls, passing the deserted windswept Quad, the Libe with lights glowing through the mist, along the familiar, deep-worn paths, across the soggy meadows to By's hall.

Inside, he closed his umbrella, took off his raincoat and hat, started along the battered, brightly lighted old corridors, quiet now with the hush of study, only a few voices raised in vigorous argument, a few radios and phonographs emitting popular music in varying degrees of volume: "Deep Purple" . . . "And the Angels Sing" . . . "Beer Barrel Polka" . . . "Over the Rainbow" . . . "A-tisket, A-tasket" . . . and those most lively and hypnotic of all that kept a generation company, Glenn Miller's "In the Mood" and Tommy Dorsey's "Boogie Woogie."

Several friends hailed him and he stopped briefly to chat. He hoped their cheerful greetings would not alert his objective. Apparently they did not, for when he knocked there was no hesitation in the sounds of a chair scraped back, feet moving quickly toward the door.

"Oh. It's you."

"That's right. May I come in?"

For just a second By hesitated. Then he stepped aside without response.

Willie threw his things on one of the casually made beds. By closed the door.

"May I sit down?"

"Oh, sure," By said, hastily tossing books from chair to bed. "Go ahead."

Seated, Willie stared at him for a long moment until By's eyes, which met his reluctantly, glanced elsewhere.

"Am I disturbing you? I'll leave, if I am."

"No," By said. "That's all right." He smiled—a little. And briefly. "I could stand a break from studying."

"Good. That was my idea, too. How's everything going?"

"Oh. All right."

"Good. Tough classes this time?"

"Fairly. You?"

"Pretty tough, this quarter." He smiled. "I have to live up to my reputation, now."

"That's really good," By said, "you're getting the Rhodes scholarship." He smiled too, with a sudden shyness. "It makes me proud I know you."

Willie gave him a quizzical look.

"Do you? I haven't been quite sure in the last few weeks."

By sighed.

"I don't blame *you*. You did your best. And I suppose I don't blame Mr. Bar—Jeff, either. It's just the way he was brought up. He can't help it."

"Apparently not. You sounded pretty fierce in your statement to the *Daily*, though. It sounded as though you're blaming the whole white race for it. Forever."

But this, he could see instantly, was a mistake. The sudden curtain he had seen once or twice before dropped over By's face. His expression stiffened, became impassive, closed-off, almost sullen. He looked at Willie as though at a stranger, and this time his glance did not wander.

"What would you have me do? Dance down the Quad shouting, 'Hurrah, hurrah'?"

Willie shook his head.

"No," he said quietly. "I expected you to be upset. I don't blame you for being upset. But I didn't expect you to go overboard in the other direction. What good does that blanket defiance do?"

By looked off into some outer distance where Willie knew he could not follow.

"Maybe not much here—now. Maybe not much back home—now. Maybe not much in the whole country—now." He paused and then spoke with an almost messianic conviction that told Willie he wasn't going to get through, this time. "But the day will come. And when it does," he concluded very quietly, "*I will be ready*."

There was a silence while they stared at one another, eyes wide, locked, wanting to communicate but seemingly unable to cross the line that lay between them.

Finally Willie asked, "Ready for what?"

"Ready," By replied quietly, "for whatever it takes."

Again there was silence between them. It lengthened. "Boogie Woogie" suddenly boomed out as somebody opened a door, sank quickly back to a driving, throbbing rumble as the door closed. A phone rang in the booth down the hall.

"BY JOHNSON!" somebody shouted with an overtone of irony clearly perceptible. "Your lady friend's on the line!"

An expression of triumph flared across By's face as he stood up quickly.

"Excuse me," he said politely. "I do have one friend on this campus. I'll be back in a few minutes."

"Don't hurry," Willie said, standing up too and picking up his things from the bed. "I'm on my way."

"Thank you for coming," By said in the same polite voice.

"Not at all," he said. "I'll give you a call sometime"—knowing he wouldn't, knowing By knew it too.

"Likewise," By said—knowing he wouldn't, knowing Willie knew it too. "COMING!" he shouted and loped off down the hall.

Willie closed the door quietly and left.

All the way through the rain he cursed himself, By, Maryetta, Jeff, Smitty, Franky, Gale Bryce, Renny Suratt. There must be some way to get through, some way to head off what he could now clearly see coming down the road. But he hadn't found it, and he was pretty sure now that in all probability no one would.

Maryetta had won. By's future, for whatever it might portend for the country they all of necessity had to share, rested with her.

As if that wasn't depressing enough, there was Billy, knocking on his door with their special rat-*tat*, rat-*tat*, rat-*tat* as soon as he got back.

"Hi," he said. "What's up?"

His brother stood in the doorway, eyes wide and darkened with worry. "Are you busy?"

"Come on in and sit down," he ordered, clearing away from one end of the sofa the dirty shirts and underwear he was getting ready for their shared weekly package home. "What is it?"

"Things are getting a little hot and heavy."

"With Janie?" Then he saw immediately that this wasn't the problem. "Oh, that." He shot the bolt on the door. "Well, sit down and tell me about it."

"He's writing me," Billy said unhappily. "And I'm not encouraging him, Dickie, I swear I'm not."

"I know you're not. I'm convinced you belong to Janie. He isn't, though?"

"He tells me I could—could have both," Billy said, sounding miserable. "He says he does and it's—it's no problem. It obviously is for him, though."

Willie gave him a half-serious, half-teasing look.

"Well, you could. Want to? I wouldn't think any less of you."

"*No*, I don't want to!" Billy said indignantly. "I'm not like—like that."

"You never know. You never know. The more I learn about sex, the more I think anything's possible."

His brother gave him a startled look.

"*You* wouldn't, would you?"

"I've never had a really good offer," he said airily, some perverse little devil prompting him to shock. "So in all honesty I probably can't say."

But Billy looked so genuinely upset by this that he felt he had better curb the levity. He smiled and shook his head. "Don't look so horrified. I haven't any plans."

"But how you could even think—"

"Everybody thinks everything, sooner or later," he said, feeling very ancient in his wisdom. "It doesn't mean they're going to do anything about it. So. *You're* not. So what's the problem?"

"Oh," Billy said, fumbling in his shirt pocket. "Things like this." He sighed. "At least once a week."

There was silence while Willie read it. In one of the rooms below, somebody here liked "Boogie Woogie" too. Smitty, he suspected, who had one of the new high-fidelity record players that were just beginning to come on the market. The tune, as mesmerizing in its way as Ravel's "Bolero," chugged along hypnotically in the Sunday-night study-silence.

"Hm," he said when he finished reading. "Quite poetic and really quite moving, I'd say. He really likes you. And, I would say, quite selflessly. He really does wish you well."

"I know," Billy said miserably. "That's what makes it so difficult."

"Typed and unsigned, I see. Still not going to tell me who it is?"

Billy shook his head.

"Have you had any more talks with him?"

Again Billy shook his head. But there was the slightest hesitation.

"Hm. You have."

"Yes," Billy admitted defiantly. "Several."

"But you must feel it's getting really pressing now, or you wouldn't be bringing me into it again, right? When was the last time?"

"This afternoon."

"Ah," Willie said, mentally ticking off everybody he could remember seeing around the house earlier in the day. Billy smiled, more relaxed.

"I see you figuring," he said. "Don't bother. You aren't *everywhere*, you know. You don't know *everything* that's going on."

"Pretty much," Willie said with cheerful complacency. "Pretty much. So. Is it—"

"Stop guessing, Dickie. If I want to tell you, I will."

"Well, supposing you do," Willie demanded, "what am I supposed to do about it? Say, 'Villain, unhand yon innocent youth! Take your filthy hands off my brother's—" He stopped with an abrupt burst of laughter. "He hasn't had them on there, has he?"

"Oh, for gosh *sakes,* Dickie! No, he hasn't! *Be serious!*"

"I am," he said, curbing the laughter, "but you must admit it could lend itself to a certain amount of ribaldry."

"Not for me," Billy said, dead serious again. "And not for him. And it wasn't for you, when I first mentioned it. You were all set to boil him in oil when I told you about it in Carmel. Why are you so carefree now?"

"Because after thinking it all over," he said seriously, "I decided that my little brother was perfectly capable now of taking care of himself. So I stopped worrying."

Billy looked at him for a long moment, eyes again troubled and uncertain.

"I think I can," he said slowly, "and so far I have. And God knows I don't *think* I want anything like—like that. But he's so *nice,* Dickie—and so sad—and so troubled—and I'm so sympathetic with people anyway, that—that—"

"Oh, come now," he said, suddenly a little alarmed, realizing suddenly that maybe this was more serious than he had thought. "You're *not* going to do anything like that. You're *not* interested and you *don't* want it and you're going to let him down gently, as you know how to do, because you *are* sympathetic—and you're going to come out of it"— he smiled—"with everything intact and still belonging to Janie. And the two of you are still going to be friends and get along just fine, because I gather he's a gentleman and really a nice guy too, right?"

"Oh, yes," Billy said fervently. "Oh, yes, he is."

"Well," Willie said dryly, "that eliminates Bryce and Suratt, anyway. Only twenty-two left to go."

At this Billy finally did laugh, quite heartily.

"Lord, yes! Anybody'd have to be pretty hard up to imagine anything with those two!"

"So, seriously, what can I do for you? What's the purpose of this talk? Why did I get this progress report?"

Billy shook his head, looking rather baffled himself.

"Well, I wanted you to read it so that you'd—you'd know what's going on—and the kind of guy he is—and why I *am* troubled about it—and—and—I just needed you to tell me I wasn't going to do anything I shouldn't do, I guess—and that you have faith in me. I guess maybe that was the fundamental thing—just to know you're here for me when I need you."

"Have I ever not been?" he inquired quietly. Billy looked a little shame-faced.

"No. I never should have doubted it."

"I should hope not," he said. He gave his brother a contemplative look that was returned without wavering. "Would it help if I—if I did talk to him? Am I close enough to him that it—that it would do any good? For him, I mean?"

Billy continued to stare at him. His face got the intent, furrowed-with-thought look that Willie could remember from age one, three, five, ten, right on up, when he was really concerned about something.

"You're close enough to everybody," he said finally. "Everybody trusts you. . . . If you promise you won't ever—*ever*—tell anybody else—"

"Oh, for Christ's sake!"

"All right," Billy said hastily. "All right, I know. Just the same, I want you to promise."

"All right," he said quietly, "I promise. O.K.?"

"O.K.," Billy said, and told him.

"I can't claim," he said finally, "that I'm all that surprised. There's always seemed to be something there that wasn't quite—quite—right, somehow. I don't mean that in a bad sense," he added hastily at Billy's expression. "Just something that wasn't quite—I don't know quite how to express it, but it was there. . . . O.K., I'll talk to him."

"When it comes right," Billy said. "Don't go rushing down this minute. And gently."

"Oh, yes," he said. He smiled, a little ruefully. "It's going to take me a while to work out my strategy. And I hope I'm as sympathetic as you are, kid. I hope it runs in the family."

"It does," Billy said with a smile they had exchanged, over the years, when they really saw eye to eye on something. "I'm sorry to burden you with it, but in a way, you know—" the smile grew openly affectionate— "I really do feel relieved that you're involved." The smile faded, his tone became sober. "Maybe I was getting . . . closer . . . than I want to think."

"Maybe you were. I wouldn't have thought any less of you for it."

"I know," Billy said, smile returning. "That's why you're a hell of a guy, in my estimation."

"*And* that of thousands!" Willie said with a grin.

"*Millions*," Billy said with an answering grin, more prescient then than he could ever have dreamed.

A week later Willie still hadn't figured out exactly how he was going to go about it, nor had the opportunity come naturally to initiate any kind of intimate talk. He was sitting in his room about nine on the following Sunday evening studying after a quick trip into town with Buff and Moose to get a bite when the phone rang and Duke Offenberg shouted his name from below.

Haggerty was on the line and suddenly he was confronted with almost the same issue. Only this time, as he and Hack both instantly recognized, it was something much more serious for everyone, in its ultimate ramifications.

Happy Harmon didn't usually patrol the Quad at night much, though he suspected there were more goings-on there than there should be, of one kind and another. He was a domestic man, didn't have kids but did love his wife of thirty years and liked to be at home with her as often as possible. The University's kids, he often said proudly, were his kids. Not all were perfect, by any means, and they were young and full of p. and v., as he sometimes put it to President Chalmers. It kept him hopping just to check on the eucalyptus groves, Governor's Lane and a few other tucked-away trysting places constantly rediscovered by each succeeding college generation.

The Quad and the Inner Quad at night, with their long, shadowy colonnades, dimly lighted and generally deserted, were probably used more than he wanted to think by youngsters seeking outlet. On the occasions when he did patrol there, his familiar roly-poly, uniformed figure and his darting flashlight—whose beam he made sure to cast far ahead of him to give ample warning—were usually enough to scatter any activity that might be going on, sufficiently in advance of his approach so that he wasn't often called upon to do anything drastic. On this he and the president saw eye to eye.

To be too tough, they were afraid, would be to bring embarrassment for everyone. Neither really wanted to do that. Both had seen plenty of human nature, in the World War and later, and both were inclined to let it take its course as long as it didn't really hurt anyone.

"If they don't do things around here," the president told him, "they're going to go out in the hills someplace. They do anyway, but I'd like to keep as many as possible in the vicinity. It's safer than some of those deserted back roads out there at night."

This tolerantly practical attitude, which would have astounded most of the student body and appalled many of the trustees, was something the president did not disclose to anyone but Happy, with whom he had long ago developed a personal friendship and a very good working relationship.

Happy thought now, as he trudged down the colonnades through the cold and misty night, that the kids didn't give the administration much trouble of the kind he was principally supposed to guard against. Basically, considering that they were in charge of "forty-five hundred mostly healthy and heterosexual young animals," as Dr. James remarked to Dr. Chalmers, they could congratulate themselves that things rocked along on a reasonably even keel with few major problems and very few public scandals. An occasional pregnancy or case of V.D. was about as serious as matters became.

There was one thing, however, which was increasing and which worried everyone in authority who knew about it, and that was the graffiti—and, they suspected, the practices—that showed up from time to time in certain rest rooms around the campus. Some were female but the substantial majority were male; and to their elimination the administration was dedicated with all the determination imposed by the standards of a staid and relatively conservative generation. Not that very many of them were shocked—they had all been adolescent too and there were various notable examples in the English department, history, drama and indeed almost anywhere one looked closely enough among the faculty.

Professor A, for instance, did rather bounce when he walked. And Professor B at times became so exclamatory that it seemed he might flit right off into the stratosphere with his exaggerated diction and fluttery hands. And even Professor C, hale, hearty, masculine, married, full of wife, kids, honors and apparently unassailable rectitude, did not, at times, go entirely unsuspected by his colleagues when he cast an approving glance at some stalwart track star or football player. But, in the way of one of the most hypocritical subjects known to humankind, everybody pretended it wasn't so and society rolled forward, as it always does on any subject a bit too close to home, on wheels greased with determined pretense and mutually agreed-upon myopia . . .

Until somebody got caught . . . whereupon a devastating light was cast suddenly into dark corners and for a few days or weeks or months everyone went around on mental tiptoe and avoided the subject with great discretion and ruthless gentility until the next time it was thrust in their faces . . . which, of course, was not where they wanted it to be, and accounted for the diligence with which, in recurring spasms, they attempted, as some of the bothered (and perhaps threatened) trustees put it fiercely, to "stamp it out!" (Walter Emerson not among them—not condoning, just trying to be fair.)

At the back of his mind, Happy was always aware of their attitude—and aware also that at any time he might stumble upon some unavoidable situation in which he would be required to act. He hoped to hell that when he did it could be taken care of—as it had been on several occasions in the past—very quietly and in ways that would not do too much damage to those he felt were "basically kids just like everybody else."

"They are and they aren't," Dr. Chalmers said when they discussed it, as they did from time to time when Happy came across indications of occasional increases in activity: it seemed to rise and fall with the weather, like everything else. "They have a particular problem and unfortunately college administrators are supposed to take care of it. I've about concluded after all these years that there's very little we can do except make sure that it doesn't happen in the middle of the Quad at high noon where society can't pretend it isn't there. It's up to us, Happy," he added with a smile, "to keep the lid on."

"Yes, sir," Happy agreed. "I don't think there's a great deal of it, sir."

"Enough," the president said. "Enough. As well you know."

"Well—" Happy said slowly. "Some. I don't know how much. There are three or four places I try to check on a fairly regular basis. Usually all I have to do is stop in and—if you'll forgive the expression, sir—urinate—"

"I will," Dr. Chalmers said gravely, but with a twinkle.

"—and then hang around outside for a bit pretending to absorb the sunshine. That seems to slow down the traffic. But it's seldom very heavy," he added hastily. "Just now and then."

"A little more than that sometimes, I think," the president said. "I walk around this campus, too, you know, Happy. I don't conceive of us as being, in the broader sense, policemen. But we do have some obligation to guard against things that would offend the sensibilities and the moral principles of the majority. As I also think we have an obligation to help, if we can, rather than punish too drastically, when we come across them."

"Yes, sir," Happy said, sounding relieved because he really was a kind-hearted man. "That's exactly how I see it too."

Reviewing this conversation as he pulled his heavy scarf and the padded lamb's-wool collar of his windbreaker tighter around his neck, Happy felt a bit guilty about the errand he was on right now. He didn't often set out deliberately to get someone, no matter what the questionable activity might be: it went against his grain, as he had told the president, "to spy on anybody." The president said that was a good attitude to have, but now and then it had to be done, for the general good. Happy still didn't like it, but in this case he did feel that maybe it was necessary—the particular instance was becoming a bit flagrant. But he hoped earnestly that he wouldn't find anything when he got there. It was such a chilly night that he didn't see how anyone . . . but of course some students were out, even on a night like this.

Hack Haggerty, for instance. Happy decided to approach his objective by a slow and circuitous route—hoping for surprise, he told himself stoutly, but also, perhaps, hoping that by the time he got there, his quarry, if any, might have dispersed and gone safely home. So he had walked slowly around the perimeter of the Outer Quad, winding up behind Memorial Church, where he decided to cut through to the Inner Quad. Just as he emerged alongside the front of the church, he and Hack almost collided. Both had been walking slowly along, heads down, lost in thought. Both had jumped and exclaimed—"*Hey!*" from Happy, "*Jesus!*" from Hack—and burst into relieved laughter.

"Happy!" Hack exclaimed. "You scared the hell out of me! What are you doing out on a night like this?"

"I could ask the same question, Hack," Happy said—he had known him quite well over the years, admired his music, told him so on many occasions—no official "Mr. Haggerty" here.

"I came down to use the organ," Hack said, "as you know I do quite often. Got tired of studying, so I thought I'd play a little music for a change."

"I know," Happy said. "It's nice Dr. Morris lets you do that. I often hear you at night when I'm making my rounds."

"Be my guest," Hack said. "I'm working on a new piece I want to introduce at the senior ball."

"You've done some nice pieces about the University," Happy observed. "You ought to put them all together sometime."

Hack looked pleased.

"I'm going to. I've got five so far and this will be the sixth. I think I'll call them 'Suite for Sunny Days.' " He smiled. "Not that they have been, these past few weeks, but overall, I think that pretty well sums up how I'm going to remember the University."

"That's nice," Happy said. "I've been here thirty years and I must say that's how most of them seem to me, looking back. . . ." His tone became casual, so casual that Hack was instantly on guard—Happy, he later told Willie, was about as transparent as a pane of glass. "How's your young fraternity brother, by the way? What's his name—?" When he said it, trying so hard to be casual, Hack was ready for him.

"He was studying in his room when I left," he said calmly.

"Are you sure?"

"Yes," Hack said, and laughed, perhaps a shade too heartily: Happy wasn't quite as dense as he liked, for professional reasons, to let on. "I ought to recognize him by this time, shouldn't I?"

"That's right," Happy agreed with an easy laugh.

"Why, has he done something?"

"Not that I know of," Happy said. "I just wondered."

"Oh," Hack said evenly. "Well."

"Why?" Happy inquired, focusing in a bit more. "Do *you* think he's done something?"

"No!" Hack said, again perhaps a bit too strongly: it was made mental note of. "No, not at all. He was just studying, when I left."

Happy nodded.

"I know, you told me. We'll, I guess I'll be pushing along. Have a good rehearsal. Or recital. Or whatever it is."

"Composition," Hack said, at ease again. "Why don't you come in and listen for a few minutes?" He smiled. "Admission's free."

"I may just do that," Happy said. And added thoughtfully, "After I've made my rounds."

"Good," Hack said, trying—again, a bit too hard—to make it quite casual. "I'd like to know what you think."

"I'm no music critic," Happy said comfortably. Then he smiled. "But I know what I like."

"That's what they all say," Hack said, pulling open the heavy door and starting inside. He too smiled. "Good hunting."

"I'll let you know if I get any scalps."

"You do that," Hack told him with a laugh and disappeared inside, snapping on the lights as he closed the door behind him. Happy stood outside patiently and waited, mentally calculating how long it would take him to climb up to the loft. Within a suitable few seconds the first notes began to come from the organ—pure—lyrical—hesitating—pausing—sinking—rising again to heights that were indeed, as Hack had named them, sunny. It was going to be one of his very best. Happy could tell that already.

But why the protectiveness toward his young friend? Why was he covering for him? They weren't in it together, were they? Happy had heard that a lot of musicians—but, no, he couldn't believe it of Hack Haggerty. He was one of the most normal kids Happy knew on campus, aside from the special something that produced his music. And that Fran Magruder—who would ever want anything else, being so lucky as to have her?

He *had* known Hack a long time, and he finally concluded, after chewing the subject for a few more moments, that it was probably exactly what it appeared to be—Hack was genuinely worried about his fraternity brother and he genuinely wanted to keep him from being hurt, and so he had probably lied for him just because that's the kind of decent and compassionate guy Hack Haggerty was.

Happy sighed and resumed his slow, trudging walk, gradually narrowing his range and coming closer and closer to his objective in that particular corner of the Inner Quad.

At the organ, Hack continued playing for another five minutes. Then he stopped and went down to the door to take a look. If Happy was still out there, he would just have to say that he had decided that he wasn't feeling very inspired tonight and had decided to go back to the house.

If he wasn't there—

Far across in the corner, the flashlight beam moved slowly, casually, inexorably, under the arches.

Oh, Christ, Hack thought. I hope the poor bastard hasn't picked tonight of all nights to—

He remained, fascinated—hypnotized—paralyzed—until suddenly lights flashed on and voices youthful, turbulent, terrified, cried out in anguish and despair . . . and were as suddenly hushed.

An almost complete silence, in which he could hear only the occasional plop! of water dropping from palm frond to palm frond, descended on the Inner Quad.

The lights from the far corner shone dim but unwavering through the mist.

He began to run toward them, faster than he had ever thought he could go.

At Dinah's Shack "The Learned Owl," as Suratt had once called him, much to the annoyance of Buff and Gulbransen, who had overheard him, had just finished dinner with Kay Ellsworth and was preparing to leave. The meal had been excellent, the atmosphere as always congenial, lots of others and their dates from school all around—"a very pleasant place," as Kay said, giving it what for her amounted to a wildly enthusiastic endorsement.

"I'm glad you liked it," Latt said as they bundled up and started to make their way out through the happily chattering crowd still waiting to be seated. "I thought about L'Omelette or Auten's or Beltramo's but I still like Dinah's best."

"It was a good choice," she agreed, tucking her arm through his as they emerged into the misty night and started toward the parking lot. "Bill!" she said in a surprised voice. "Are you cold? Your arm's trembling."

"Oh, no, I'm fine," he said earnestly. "Really I am. This is a really warm coat, and the scarf you gave me for Christmas is just great. Thank you again for it. It was a *really* thoughtful present."

"I thought you could use it," she said with a smile. "I'm not sure you always take care of yourself enough, sometimes. I thought I'd like to help."

"You did," he said as they came to the Chevy convertible. "One good thing about this old buggy, anyway," he said brightly as he opened the door for her, "it does have a good heater. It's a good thing Willie decided to stay in tonight, so I could borrow it." He smiled as he took his place behind the wheel. "You know Smitty Carriger's Cord—"

She laughed.

"*Everybody* knows Smitty Carriger's Cord."

"Well, he offered it to me, because he said he was going down to the Quad to study. But fortunately Willie came by just then and offered me this." He uttered a self-deprecatory little laugh, sounding rather more wistful than he knew. "I haven't the slightest idea what I'd do with a Cord. It's about ten times my speed."

"You'd do perfectly well with it," she said firmly. "You mustn't put yourself down like that. You could handle it."

"Well—maybe." He laughed again. "But I'd rather not. It's too much responsibility."

"Now," she said, putting her hand lightly and momentarily on his knee, which made him start though he tried desperately to suppress it. She appeared not to notice. "Now—" calmly removing her hand and tucking it inside her coat—"I don't want you to say you're not capable of responsibility, Bill. You're capable of a great deal of responsibility. There isn't a person on campus who doesn't recognize that."

"Am I?" He looked doubtful and, for a moment, very young—even the famous Latt, she thought with an amused, almost poignant affection, could still look young sometimes. "I don't know. It's a funny thing, you know, the impressions people have of one—and how one really is. The guys in the house depend on me so. They're always seeking my advice—" he gave a sudden little smile—"to say nothing of my money, which I don't have much of but which they're always borrowing—and yet, really, who am I? I don't know much. I don't have all the answers. I'm just me. Why do people have this exaggerated idea of me?"

He shook his head in genuine bafflement as he eased the Chevy, coughing and bucking a bit but gradually catching hold, out of the parking lot and onto the road back to school.

"Because you're *good*," she said.

"Oh," he said, and gave her a sudden shy, sidewise little grin. "I thought maybe it's just because I'm bright."

"You are that," she agreed with a smile. "My goodness, yes!"

"Oh, well," he said. "Lots of people are bright. I just said that because it seems to be the one thing everybody always emphasizes when they talk about me. It doesn't impress *me* all that much."

"It certainly impresses all the rest of us! But seriously—that isn't all they say about you in the house. I know because I've talked to a lot of them. They do think you're good—a very fine, decent, honest, understanding, compassionate human being."

"My goodness," he said with gentle self-mockery. "All that?"

"All that," she said firmly. "Furthermore—" she laughed—"you go to church a lot, and that *really* impresses some of them."

"Yes," he agreed, amused too. "Some of my brothers aren't exactly noted for churchgoing. It does make me something of a puzzle for some of them."

"But they respect you for it. . . . Surely they must have told you all these things."

"Well, yes," he said, driving along carefully in the light fog that was swirling over the road—not enough to be dangerous, at least not yet, but warranting the care he and most others tonight were giving it. "They're really very flattering."

"It isn't flattery, it's truth. Why be bashful about it?"

"Well . . . I don't like to give myself airs."

"You aren't giving yourself airs! You're just acknowledging the honest truth of it. You are a rare human being, Bill Lattimer. You might as well accept it."

"I'm stuck with it?" he inquired quizzically. She nodded, amused but emphatically.

At which they both laughed and he felt suddenly much more relaxed with her tall, reserved beauty and dignified presence than he had all evening. So relaxed, in fact, that he really wondered for a moment or two if maybe tonight might not be the night to—

"Don't you think it's about time," she inquired quietly, voice tremulous but determined, "for us to discuss getting married?"

"*What?*" he cried, so startled that the Chevy swerved violently and almost left the road. He had to fight it desperately for a moment to bring it back in the lane.

"You don't have to kill us," she said with a shaky little laugh. "I was just asking."

"But—" he said. "But—"

"Is it such an awful idea?" she demanded, half laughing, but also, he perceived, on the verge of half crying too. "Am I that—that—repulsive?"

"Oh, *no!*" he cried. "Oh, no, no, no, not at all! But you—you just startled me so that I—I—"

"Haven't you even thought about it?" she asked, sounding so forlorn that it touched him terribly. "Hasn't it even occurred to you just a—just a—a *little* bit? I thought we were such good friends—"

"Oh, we *are!*" he cried, and in spite of the weather and in spite of the traffic and in spite of his own timidities and hesitations—and *just plain cowardice*, that's all it had been, he wasn't going to pretend to himself any longer—he took his right hand off the wheel, reached over and took hers. "We are, we are, we are! I'll say yes. I'll say yes, Katie! Oh, *yes!*"

"That's what *I'm* supposed to say!" she retorted, openly laughing and crying now, squeezing his hand with the strength of a desperate relief.

"I beat you to it," he told her with shaky triumph, laughing and crying himself. "I beat you to it, Katie! How about *that!*"

All the way back to campus they didn't say anything more, just held hands, blissfully silent. His grip was as desperate as hers. The only time he released her hand was when it was absolutely necessary to hold the car on course.

The fog had increased somewhat when he dropped her off but they didn't notice. They sat for about five minutes in the car, holding each other tight and kissing as they had never kissed before. Then she floated in and he floated off, neither aware of any ground beneath them.

He parked the car in the garage and sat there for several more minutes feeling that the world had changed for him in some great, fundamental and irreversible way.

When he got inside he found that it had for others too, though not so happily. One glance at Willie's face when he came upon him standing in worried conversation with Hack and Buff in the living room told him that, for others, the change was not so nice. He found himself brought abruptly down from his happy high plateau to a level sad and disturbing. But through it all he was buoyed up by the certainty, which would remain about him like a golden protective coat as long as he lived, that never, for anyone in all history, had the world changed so wonderfully and so marvelously as it had for him.

"Latt!" Willie exclaimed. "Thank God you're here! Come on up to my room. We have to talk."

"Sure," he said. "But what—?"

"Come along, we'll tell you," Hack said; and even disturbed as he was, he was perceptive enough to sense the glow surrounding the Learned Owl. "You look happy. What have you been up to?"

"She said yes!" he cried, still unable to believe it. "Or I said yes! Or somebody said yes! Anyway, it was *yes* all the way!"

"You asked her to marry you," Willie said, a pleased grin breaking through his obvious worry.

"Well," Latt admitted with a laugh that wasn't too steady, "somebody asked somebody. As a matter of fact, I seem to recall that she asked me. But what the hell! We both said yes!"

" 'What the hell'?" Hack echoed. "From our most gently spoken member? Boy, you really must be out there on a star somewhere!"

"I am," Latt said with a totally unself-conscious, totally happy laugh. "I am! Oh, yes, I *am!*"

"That's good," Willie said, solemn again. "Because I'm afraid we're going to have to bring you down with a bump. Come on up. We'll tell you about it."

The tableau Hack saw when he reached the men's room in the corner of the Inner Quad was one he would not forget for a long, long time, if ever. The merciless light—Happy's sad but stern expression—his young fraternity brother looking at him with haunted, tear-filled eyes as though Hack were the one thing that could save him—the other kid, whom he didn't know, in a frozen, apparently almost catatonic state, leaning against one of the wash-basins, the clothing still in some disarray—the sense of desperation—the general air of furtive assignation discovered—

"Happy!" he said in a voice that trembled in spite of his best efforts to hold it steady. "What's going on here?"

"That's—pretty obvious, isn't it?" Happy inquired in a voice that wasn't too steady either. "I tried to give them fair warning but they were too—too—they didn't hear me. I really didn't have much choice, Hack. I'm sorry."

"So am I," Hack said bitterly. "So am I."

"Hack," his young friend said, half crying. "Hack. Help me."

"If I can," Hack said, committing himself without a second's hesitation:

after all, what were friends and brothers for, if you didn't stand by them when they needed you? "Happy! Can I?"

Happy thought for a long moment.

"It's got to stop, you know, Hack," he said finally. "We can't just declare open season, you know. There's got to be some rules—and some decency—around here. We can't have the Quad turned into the—the Roman Forum, you know. This is *wrong*."

"Look," Hack said desperately. "Do you have to report it this very minute? Or have you?"

Happy again gave him a long look and Hack knew he had won—a little time, at least. He didn't know at that moment if it would, or could, be anything else.

"No," Happy said, "I haven't." A small smile crossed his face for a moment. "I rather figured you'd be along. Kind of thought you might be keeping an eye on things too."

"I have been," Hack said. He looked at his young friend, whose eyes were beginning to show faint signs of hope. The other kid just stood there. Pimpled and scrawny, Hack realized, not even—well, Jesus, mustn't get sidetracked on thoughts like that. "I have been," he repeated. His voice rose in challenge. "Haven't I?"

"Yes," the wanderer said humbly. "You—you warned me."

"So I did," Hack said with a disgusted bitterness. "And this is the thanks I get."

"I'm sorry," his friend said, beginning to cry again in a desolate fashion, a long, long way from his usual cheery, easygoing public disposition. "I'm sorry."

"Yes," Hack said. "Well. It's a little late to think about that. Happy, would you let me go call Willie before you do anything more?"

Again Happy gave him a long, considering look.

"You mean release these guys to you and Willie?"

"No, no, you keep them until I get Willie down here. Then we can talk and see what we should do."

"I know what *I* should do," Happy said. "I should take them right downtown to jail."

"*No!*" both cried sharply: apparently the other kid wasn't quite so catatonic, after all.

"Well, I should," Happy said. "How long will it take to get Willie down here?"

"He's at the house studying. Ten minutes. Five minutes."

"There's a phone just outside," Happy said. "Go to it. You fellows, get yourselves in order and try to look presentable. Hack!" he called as Hack started to hurry out. "You know my little office over in English Corner—to the left just as you come in from the Outer Quad. The lights will be on. Tell Willie to meet us there."

"So I got my tail down there just as fast as I could," Willie related as they climbed the stairs toward his room, "and Happy was very reasonable, wasn't he, Hack?"

"Happy," Hack said thoughtfully, "is one of God's noblemen. The sinners on this campus over the years have owed more to Happy that they've ever realized or acknowledged. There ought to be a statue of him as big as the Campanile at Cal. He couldn't have been nicer or more reasonable. Tough but fair."

"Right," Willie agreed.

"So he didn't report it," Latt said.

"No," Willie said. "He turned it over to us."

"At least, our boy," Hack said. "I don't think he's going to report the other kid, either. Just gave them both one hell of a lecture and let them go—called the other kid's house and turned him over to them, just as he did with us. He told me there's going to be a sign in all the men's rooms tomorrow, though—something to the effect that on such-and-such a date 'Two students were discovered engaging in an illicit act and have been severely disciplined. Close surveillance is now in effect and will be maintained in this and all other men's rooms on campus.' He said that ought to scare the hell out of 'em. And quiet things down for quite a while."

"I expect it will," Latt said. "How could anybody be so stupid? How could any guy as bright as—"

"I know," Willie said gloomily. "I know. But why do we expect rational answers to an insoluble conundrum? There aren't any. Anyway," he said as they approached his door, "here he is. He's scared shitless, poor bastard."

"And so he should be," Hack said grimly. "So he damned well should be."

And so he damned well was, Latt thought with a surge of pity when he got up awkwardly from the sofa and greeted them in a low, shy voice that, again, was very far indeed from his usual pleasant conversation.

"Oh, hello, Latt," he said, automatically starting to hold out his hand, then remembering and pulling it quickly back. "I'm sorry you have to be dragged into this."

Latt did not reply until he had held out his own hand and waited patiently for it to be accepted. In a moment it was, with a sad, tentative smile.

"I have a lot of charity to give the world tonight," Latt said. "Because guess what! I'm engaged!"

"To Kay Ellsworth?" the other asked, and a spontaneous, happy smile came momentarily to his face. "Oh, Latt! Congratulations! I *am* glad!" Then his expression changed, tears appeared to threaten. "I'm glad somebody had a—a nice normal evening tonight, anyway."

"Sit down," Willie ordered, but not unkindly. The wanderer returned to the sofa. Latt sat beside him, Willie and Hack took the two chairs facing them, Buff sat on the desk. Willie studied their problem child for a few seconds that seemed to the others to lengthen almost unbearably.

"What are we going to do about you?" he asked finally. "Do you think you deserve to stay in this house?"

The wanderer was silent for a moment. When he spoke it was in a lifeless, crushed voice.

"Probably not. . . ." The ghost of a wry little smile touched his lips. "Not if you tell everybody about it, that's for sure."

"Nobody's told anybody," Buff said sharply. "The only people who know aside from Happy and your—your pal—are right here in this room. Happy says he won't tell, right, guys?" Hack and Willie nodded. "And God knows we won't—*if*—"

" '*If*'—what?" —almost inaudibly.

"If you promise us that you won't ever do a thing like that again as long as you're on this campus," Buff said flatly.

"That's right," Hack said grimly. "Not *ever.*"

Willie shifted slightly in his chair, and they turned on him with such coordinated unison that he threw up his arm in mock defense.

"Maybe," he said, "we should allow a little bit for human nature, don't you think?"

Buff and Hack looked startled and inclined to be combative, but Latt without a moment's hesitation concurred.

"I agree," he said firmly. "I don't know much about the subject, but from the little I've seen and read there's sometimes a—a compulsion, you might say. There's no point in promises that can't be kept."

"Huh!" Hack said. "He can keep it if he wants to. Lots of people do. And don't ask me how I know," he added with a side glance and brief smile at Willie, "because I'm not going to tell you, and you can make of that what you like. Anyway, it can be done. *And we want you to do it.* O.K.?"

"I hate to argue," Latt persisted, voice gentle as always but firm underneath, as he could make it when he felt the need, "but I still agree with Willie that we've got to be practical. Maybe it's better just to say that if you're ever again found in a situation that will bring discredit on the University or the house, you're out. Does that make sense to you?"

Their young friend stared at them with unhappy eyes.

"Thank you, Latt," he said finally, again hardly audible. "I don't know if it does to you other guys, but it does to me . . . *yes*," he repeated desperately. "It does to me."

"And it does to me," Willie said. "I for one don't give a damn what you do privately but I sure as hell don't want you disgracing either the University or the house, as Latt says. I'll settle for a promise on that, bearing in mind that it's virtually self-enforcing because you can be damned sure nobody will go to bat for you next time, buster—"

"I know that."

"—and therefore you'd be smart to keep it damned well under control until you get out of here. After that, you're your own responsibility."

"He was his own responsibility," Hack said with recurring bitterness, "and he flunked the course."

Willie turned on him sharply.

"I know you're pissed off because you warned him and he didn't behave, but he doesn't look exactly happy about it, does he? He's being punished, isn't he? He won't forget it, will he?" He practically glared at their unhappy charge. *"Right?"*

"Right"—again, almost inaudibly.

"All *right*," Willie said. "That's good enough for me."

Latt nodded.

"And me."

"Buff?" Willie demanded.

"Hell," Buff said, "you know me. I don't believe in being hard on people as a general rule. I think he's learned his lesson."

"I hope so," Hack said, not sounding very convinced.

"I have," the wanderer said. "I *have*." And began to cry again, from sheer relief that the world, which had seemed about to end an hour ago, apparently was still there for him, after all.

"Here," Latt said, handing him a clean handkerchief. "Blow your nose and get yourself together. We want to see you tomorrow morning just as bright and cheery and natural as always so that nobody else will suspect a thing. O.K.?"

A rueful little smile managed to break through.

"I may have to tell them I have a cold for a few days, but I think I can manage."

"You damned well better," Hack said, not sounding quite so fierce.

"Thank you all for everything"—again, very low.

"You should," Hack remarked bluntly, "because we've been extraordinarily patient and protective of you—amazingly so, in fact. We ought to have kicked your butt right out the door. Most houses would."

"Yes," the wanderer said, very low and very humbly. "I know."

"We're counting on you," Latt said, more gently. "We know you won't let us down."

"Oh, *no!*"—with a desperate fervor. "Oh, no, I *won't*."

"That remains to be seen," Hack remarked after the wanderer had left, muttering a muffled goodbye and going off quickly down the stairs, by some lucky chance not running into anyone and so being able to get to his room, to the washroom, and then safely out to bed with no one the wiser.

"I think it'll work," Latt said as they bade Willie good night and started down the stairs. "Anyway," he said with a resurgence of happiness and a quick return of his awestruck, still-not-quite-believing-it smile, "I'm going to stop thinking about it for now. I'm engaged! I'm happy!"

"You use Pond's!" Buff completed the advertising slogan for him, poking him affectionately in the ribs. "Whoever thought *you* would be the first to take the plunge! Old Latt! Our Brain!"

"Even Brains are human," Hack noted.

"I guess there's always been some doubt," Latt admitted with a smile that was suddenly shy but still very pleased. "Maybe people will think differently now."

"They sure will," Buff agreed. "It's going to be the sensation of the campus tomorrow morning."

"Maybe Timmy can get Nagatani to put a special notice in the *Daily,*" Hack suggested. "Maybe we can get Dr. Chalmers to declare a special observance or something—"

"Maybe," Latt said with a happy laugh, "I can take you guys and knock your heads together and—"

But they were never to know what he would have contemplated next, because downstairs they heard the front door slam open and slam shut with a terrific bang. Randy Carrero passed them on the stairs like a bolt of lightning, looking neither right nor left, taking the steps two at a time, not returning their startled greetings, perhaps not even seeing or hearing them in his blind rush— "a regular baby tornado," Hack murmured when they turned in amazement to watch his stocky little figure swarm up the stairs and disappear on the second floor.

"My, *my,*" Buff agreed. "Dat boy is shuah mad 'bout sump'in. Lawsamercy."

"I think he needs help," Latt said, looking worried. "I think maybe I'd better go see—"

"Now, come *on,*" Hack objected. "Stop being the universal mother hen for once in your life, will you, Latt? It's none of your business. He's obviously had another fight with that little bitch Stevens and there isn't anything you can do about it but just let him get over it. He will."

"I know," Latt said. He still looked worried. "But it isn't good for him to—"

"He'll live," Buff remarked. "I agree with Hack. Let him stew in his own juice for a change."

"I know, but—"

"Look," Hack said patiently. "You're engaged—you've got enough to think about—you're happy—you're excited—it should be a wonderful night for you—you've already had to go through one emotional round with one problem child. There's such a thing as being *too* good, you know. Let it alone, Latt. You deserve better than that."

"Well—" Latt said; and hesitated; and smiled.

"You have your problem child, I have mine. He likes to confide in me. I think I can help him with my sympathy, it's what he wants from me. It won't interfere with my happiness, nothing can interfere with that. I'll just go in for a minute and chat. It might help. It can't do any harm."

"O.K.," Hack said. "O.K. You're an incorrigible nice guy, Lattimer. Absolutely incorrigible."

"Genuine, too," Buff observed with an affectionate smile.

"I know, damn it," Hack said. "That's what makes him so impossible. All right, I wash my hands of you" —and added, and would wish later with a terrible bitterness that he had not—"Your blood be on your own head!"

"Oh, come," Latt said, smiling up at them where they stood a couple of steps above him—they had never seen him so completely confident, so completely relaxed and happy—"Don't be so ominous."

"It's my nature," Hack said with a grin as Latt brushed past them and went on up to the second floor and the room Randy shared with Billy.

Billy, Latt was just as happy to see, was still out. (Was it only ten o'clock? What a night!)

Sometimes Billy had been a help in Latt's recurring sympathy sessions with Randy but sometimes the sheer weight of his overwhelming satisfaction with Janie had only made things worse for Randy. Randy had flared up not long ago, called Billy "smug" and then had to apologize when Billy looked surprised and hurt. Latt was too kind to use the word, but even he felt at times that the Billy-Janie combine was too icky-poo to bear, as Suratt had remarked to Randy.

Billy never seemed to have any problems: life was so uncomplicated, for him. That was among Randy's minor, but constant, irritations.

God knows *he* had problems, Randy often told Latt, and tonight Latt could tell that they had apparently reached some sort of grand, crashing climax.

Randy's face looked like a thundercloud, his hair was disheveled, his clothing looked flung-together, his eyes were red, possibly from sorrow but more likely rage, and in general he looked crutty, unkempt and really rather down-at-heel—a long way from the trim, neat, slicked-up, smart-as-a-whip youngster Latt and Willie had been responsible for bringing into the house a year ago. He was still smart as a whip, there could be no doubt of that even though his grades and achievements had all taken a nosedive since last September; but it was a high intelligence resting on the shaky foundation of a not very stable personality, Latt was afraid. He could not help but be emotionally involved in this deterioration of a young friend he had been deeply fond of from the first.

Randy was sitting at his desk with his back to the door when Latt entered. He made no attempt to turn around or greet him.

Instead, when Latt asked, "Are you O.K.?" he answered in a surly tone, "I might have known it would be you."

"Yes, it's me," Latt said mildly. "May I sit down?"

"Be my guest."

"Good. I will. Do you want to hear some good news about me or shall I keep it to myself?"

"I don't care," Randy said, still not turning around. "Everybody has good news but me, anyway."

"We-ll," Latt said, thinking back a half hour, "I wouldn't say *every-body*. I just thought you might like to know that Kay and I got engaged tonight."

At this Randy did turn around and was still gracious enough to look genuinely pleased and exclaim, "Why, Latt! I think that's great, I really do. Just *great*. When are you going to get married?"

"Graduation, I suppose. Probably join the mob in Memorial Church."

"Do they do it all at once?" Randy asked, sounding genuinely interested.

"No, just kidding. Two by two, like the Ark. You'll find out someday."

"I will *never* find out," Randy said, remembering to glower. "It is *all over*. There *isn't any more*. This time *we are really through*."

"You've said that before," Latt pointed out gently, being careful not to sound as though he were poking fun, "and it's started over again. It will this time, I'm sure."

"No," Randy said, and there came into his voice a certain bleakly final note that made Latt think that just maybe, at last, a conclusion really had been reached. "No. This time it won't."

And suddenly, making Latt jump, he slammed a fist on the desk and cried out, "God DAMN it!" in a hopelessly angry voice. "God damn it, God damn it, God DAMN it! . . . OH!" And he pounded on the desk again, both fists this time, a sound that prompted Moose, in the room above, to thump on the floor. "Oh, fuck you, too!" Randy cried up at him. "What the hell do *you* know!" Moose replied with a muffled shout they couldn't understand and thumped again. Then there was silence for a while until Randy said in a bitter and desolate voice, "I *really am* through, this time. *I really am*. I can't stand it anymore. I just *can't*."

"If that's really the way you feel," Latt said cautiously—he had been party to so many of these renunciation scenes since September that he didn't really trust this one, just yet—"then—then maybe it's for the best. Maybe it is time to just cut it off once and for all and then move on to something else. Is that agreeable to her?"

"Who gives a fuck what's agreeable to her?" Randy demanded bitterly, fingers moving restlessly over the desk, body twitching nervously. "I've spent too long trying to figure out what's agreeable to her. It doesn't matter to me anymore, Latt. It just *does not* matter."

He sat there for a second more, twitching and turning—"jumping in place" as Franky had put it, observing him in one of these emotional spasms. Then he suddenly sprang up, so quickly that he knocked over his chair. "I want to get out of here!"

Latt looked startled.

"What do you mean? Go downstairs or something? Get a bite in the kitchen? I'll go with you."

"No, I mean get out of here and get out of this house!" Randy said, beginning to pace up and down the room, which wasn't much pacing as it was only about twelve by twelve. "I mean just get out and—and *go!* I feel like I'm being smothered! I've got to *move!*"

"But at this time of night? I don't understand what you mean, Randy."

"I mean I just want to—just want to *go someplace!* Just *move!* Just *do something!* I'm going crazy sitting here!"

"But you just came in—"

"I know it, but I want to go out again!"

"That doesn't make sense," Latt said, determined to keep calm and quiet him down. "Why don't you sit here and relax for a while? I'll stick around and talk to you if you want me to—"

"I just want to go someplace!" Randy said, sounding a little wilder, alarming Latt, who was beginning to think he might have to call for reinforcements. He'd never seen Randy quite this wound up, though Lord knew he'd seen him plenty wound up. "I want to go downtown! I want to get something to eat!"

"But there isn't much open at this hour," Latt objected, trying to be reasonable. "Maybe a hamburger joint or two—"

"I'll find something," Randy said, yanking his windbreaker off the couch where he'd thrown it scarcely ten minutes before. "I'm going!"

"Well, I can't let you go like this," Latt said, standing up also and putting on his coat, which he realized he'd been lugging around absentmindedly ever since Willie had hailed him when he came in from his date with Kay. (How long ago was that? It seemed like a week. Again he thought: what a night!) "I'll go with you."

"Oh, no, you don't have to," Randy said; but he sounded relieved all the same, and Latt was glad he'd offered.

"Oh, yes, I will. You're in no shape to go by yourself, in this mood. Anyway, it's a miserable night—"

"I know that," Randy said, as he ran quickly ahead down the stairs. "I'm glad of it! I'm miserable too!" He paused abruptly. "Whose car can we take? You don't have one—I don't have one—"

A little warning voice told Latt: Pretend you don't either, then you'll both have to stay home. But honest as always, and considerate as always, he banished the thought promptly and said, "I still have the keys to Willie's. He loaned it to me earlier to take Kay out but I forgot to return them. He won't mind."

"Good!" Randy said, yanking open the kitchen door. "I'll drive."

And again the warning voice. This time Latt obeyed it.

"No, that's fine," he said quickly. "I don't mind."

"I'd rather," Randy said flatly. "I need to do something. It will take my mind off it."

"Well—"

"Come on!" Randy said impatiently. "Willie won't mind. And you deserve a ride." He laughed, a short, harsh sound in which admiration, envy, and perhaps irony were oddly mixed. "You're happy. You're engaged."

"Yes, I know," Latt said, feeling an uneasiness he couldn't have explained. "But really—"

"Damn it!" Randy said loudly. *"Give me those keys!"*

"Well . . ." Latt said, still doubtfully. Randy reached over and grabbed them out of his hand. "Come on! . . . Christ!" he said when they emerged into the night, rain almost gone but fog now heavy and hugging the ground. "What a son-of-a-bitching night!"

"We'll have to be very careful."

"Don't worry," Randy assured him, hopping in and slamming his door as Latt perforce did the same. "I'm a good driver."

And he gunned the car, shooting it out of the garage in reverse so fast he almost hit the back fence of the Beta house across the alley. He yanked the car around, stepped on the gas and shot down the street, narrowly missing a couple of cars parked along the curb.

"Are you drunk?" Latt inquired, half joking but feeling suddenly more than a little apprehensive because it *was* a fearsome night. "Randy," he said seriously, "you really must slow down. This fog is *very* dangerous. You don't want to have an accident with Willie's car, do you? At least, I don't."

"Don't worry," Randy said, beginning to sound impatient again. "I'm quite all right."

And slowed his pace a little. But as they swung onto Palm Drive he began to speed up again, even though the fog, swirling and winding in long ropes across the road, was so thick they could hardly see ten feet ahead.

Well, Latt decided after a moment, with a wry little smile as they drove rapidly along—maybe not too rapidly, but certainly more rapidly than he would have—Randy's obviously lost in thought. Maybe the best thing for me to do is stop worrying and get lost in mine.

So he called Kay back into mind and all his thoughts were happy and loving as they rolled on up Palm Drive in the misty, shifting, sinuously winding cotton-wool blanket that hid the world.

"They only had to go a mile," Gulbransen remarked in disbelieving wonderment next morning. *"They only had to go a mile!"*

Only a mile and, at most, perhaps ten minutes.

But it wasn't a mile that night.
And it took them only five.

The house was on its way to bed when the phone rang.
"WILSON!" Franky bellowed; and Wilson went down.
"Yes?" he said. And the world up-ended.
"What's the matter?" Franky demanded a minute later when he saw him
on the stairs, holding on to the railing and literally seeming to drag himself
up step by step. *"Hey! What's the matter?"* Franky repeated in great alarm
when all Willie could do was shake his head and stare at him as though he
had never seen him before. "Buff! Guy! Everybody! Come on out here!
Something's the matter with Willie! Hey, EVERYBODY!"
Doors opened, feet pounded, voices cried out. Willie heard them dimly
somewhere in the distance—couldn't distinguish between them—couldn't,
for a moment, remember where he was, who he was, what he was doing
there—
Then he remembered.
"Oh, God!" he cried in a voice they could hardly recognize. "Oh, *God!*"
By that time half a dozen were standing around him on the second-floor
landing, more hurrying toward them in various stages of undress.
"Happy—just—called," he managed to say, barely able to articulate; and
repeated in a dazed voice, "Happy . . . just . . . called . . ."
"Yes?" Buff cried in a terrible voice. "What *is* it?"
"Apparently . . . they . . . took . . . my car," Willie said in the same dazed
way. Then he began to speak very slowly, very carefully, enunciating each
word very clearly. "Happy said . . . Happy said Randy was . . . was apparently driving and they . . . they skidded off Palm Drive . . . into the euca-
lyptus grove and . . . and hit a tree. Randy's in the . . . the hospital with . . .
with a broken back . . . and Latt's . . . Latt's—"
"Oh, Willie," Guy said in a strange, harsh whisper. *"Don't say it."*
"Latt's dead."
"But he was here just half an hour ago!" Hack cried in anguished disbelief,
as though that could make any difference.
Staring at them blankly, Willie began to cry, with a hopeless sorrow as he
had not cried since he was a little boy.
They had never seen Willie cry before.
The stability of their world had been destroyed.
It was terrifying.

Five minutes later they had grabbed sweaters and coats and were on their
way to the hospital.
Buff, as always able to lift himself out of his amicable lethargy and take

command when he had to, said flatly, "Willie, Guy, Franky, Moose, you come with me. The rest of you stay here, we can't have a mob scene at the hospital. We'll tell you all we know when we get home. Smitty, can we all squeeze in the Cord? I don't trust myself to drive my car."

"Sure," Smitty said, starting to run back to his room. "I'll get the keys."

"You can drive us," Buff called after.

"Sure thing," Smitty said and was back in a flash.

Nobody said anything on the way up Palm Drive. Smitty slowed when they came to the car, upside down, one wheel ripped off, squashed almost flat between tree and ground. The lights were still on, reflecting off the swirling fog as though they still had some purpose.

Two patrol cars from town were there, spotlights revolving, along with Happy's red University car. Five or six other cars were parked across the drive. Little groups of late-homing students, white-faced and shaken, stood about talking aimlessly in hushed, frightened voices.

Happy turned, grim-faced, saw them, waved briefly, turned back to watch a wrecking truck trying to dislodge Willie's car from the tree; not an easy task, so deeply was its front end embedded in the trunk.

They shuddered and looked, trying not to look too closely, for a moment that would remain etched on their minds as long as they lived.

Horror utterly unbelievable, utterly implacable, hung in the air like a palpable thing.

"Go on," Buff said in a choked voice. "Don't stop."

"No," Smitty said.

At the hospital Dr. James was there, accompanied by several local doctors. The corridor lights were bright and garish. Nurses hurried up and down.

"Come in here," Dr. James said, leading them to a small visitors' room, closing the door when they were all in. "Sit down. . . . I am terribly sorry. There isn't much more to say on that score except—I am. It is a great loss to you in the house and certainly a very great loss to the University. He was a fine, fine boy and a marvelous intellect. One wonders why the Lord permits such things." He smiled slightly, wry and grim. "I have concluded after thirty years of practice and fifty-five of living that there is no answer."

"What—what happened?" Buff asked. "Does anybody know?"

"I talked to Happy just a moment ago," Dr. James said. "I gather you saw—" he hesitated slightly—"the wreck." They nodded. "The details of the accident itself are fairly self-evident. Either Randy Carrero was driving too fast, or he wasn't concentrating on his driving, or both. Happy told me he had been having some emotional problems with his girlfriend—"

"He had come in a few minutes earlier in a foul mood," Willie said. "We all thought they had probably had another fight."

"I guess he wanted to go out again just to get away, or something," Buff said, "and Latt—Latt decided to go with him, just to be helpful." He smiled a small, unhappy smile. "You know how Latt is." He corrected himself, very carefully. "Was, I mean."

At this the sheer enormity of it struck them all afresh and for several moments no one, including Dr. James, could trust himself to speak.

"What," Franky asked finally, "was the—the actual cause of—of—"

"They apparently both went out through the canvas top," Dr. James said. "Bill evidently struck the tree head-on, Randy caromed off it to one side. Bill's injuries were massive—concussion, basically—many, many broken bones—broken neck—" they flinched as if struck but he went firmly on— "massive brain damage, certainly—"

"Oh, that brain, that brain!" Guy said in a stricken voice. "How will we ever tell Kay and his folks?"

"You leave that to me," Dr. James said. "You'll probably want to write some sort of house letter to his parents—" they nodded—"and you will all have a chance to talk to the young lady as the days go by. I'd suggest you not make that too formal, just buck her up as much as possible whenever you get a chance. Other than that—" He stood up. "Want to see Randy?"

They looked at one another, so many emotions contending inside that for several moments no one could speak.

Finally Moose said softly, "I'd rather see Latt."

"I'm afraid you can't do that," Dr. James said. "He was—very badly disfigured—and he's going to be sent home tomorrow morning early to his parents—and I'm afraid you just can't do that. You'll just have to remember him as he was. I'm sure there are many happy memories."

"Oh, yes," Willie said and almost started to cry again; and was not alone.

"So," Dr. James repeated. "Do you want to see Randy?"

"After he killed Latt?" Franky asked bitterly; and again there was silence.

"Oh," Buff said at last. "He didn't mean to."

"That's right," Moose said. "He didn't mean to, for God's sake."

"Come on, Franky," Willie said, standing up, taking his arm and pulling him up. "We can't afford to think like that. He really didn't mean to, and he probably feels like absolute hell."

"He doesn't at the moment," Dr. James said, "because he's barely conscious and he's under heavy sedation; he hasn't spoken yet and he hasn't been told. But he will. He will."

"Is he going to make it all right?" Buff inquired.

"Oh, yes, we think so," Dr. James said. "Mild concussion, broken back, fractured pelvis, internal injuries—but he's young and strong and he'll make it. He'll probably have to be out of school for the rest of the year but he'll be back in the fall good as new, or I miss my bet. But as soon as he finds out—that's when he's really going to need the help and support of all of you. I hope you'll be able to give it to him freely and unstintingly, because when this emotional burden is piled on top of the other one he's apparently carrying—well, he's going to need a *lot* of support. How about it, Franky?"

Again for several moments Franky's face was a study; but he finally uttered a deep sigh and nodded.

"I'll try. I'll try. It isn't going to be easy, but I'll try."

"It isn't going to be easy for any of us," Willie said, "but the kid needs help, more now than ever. Come on, let's go."

Down the hall in the dimly lit room they saw a figure swathed in white that looked very strange and like no one they knew. Only one eye and one side of his mouth were visible.

For a moment after their entrance there was no sign of life save the rhythmic rise and fall of his chest, which, as Dr. James had indicated, appeared to be very strong.

Then the eye opened, the body stirred. They stood very still. The eye began to focus. The voice when it came was very weak and muffled, but recognizable.

"Hi, guys," he whispered. "How's Latt?"

"Oh, *God*," Unruh whispered to Willie. "Oh, *Jesus*."

Nobody responded.

"Hey, guys," Randy said in the same slow, painful whisper. "I said, how's Latt?"

"Hello, Randy," Dr. James said, putting his hand on Randy's shoulder and smiling down at him. "How's the boy?"

"I said," Randy repeated, obviously gathering his strength to make the effort to say it more loudly, "how's Latt?" Again no one spoke; and a sudden, convulsive movement shook his body, his voice surged up so suddenly it frightened them. "Latt!" he cried. "*Latt!*" Tears began to well up in the visible eye: he knew. "Oh, *Latt . . . It should have been me! . . . It should have been me. . . .*" His voice trailed away in utter desolation and he turned his face to the wall.

"I think you boys had better run along now," Dr. James said. "Say goodbye and go. *Quickly.* I'll handle this."

"Hang in there, buddy," Buff said huskily, giving Randy's shoulder a quick squeeze; and one by one, hurriedly, they followed suit, Franky included.

There was no further response from Randy.

Outside in the corridor with the door closed, they turned to Dr. James.

"Will he be all right?" Buff asked.

"We'll manage," Dr. James said. "Don't worry about it. I'll talk to him at length as soon as he's a little stronger. Right now he's in shock—he already was, of course, but this has compounded it. He'll have more sedation, and in the morning after he's had a lot of sleep I'll get to work. So *don't worry.* It will be *all right.* And now *you* get on home. Probably a lot of you aren't going to get much sleep and you have some rough days ahead, so—*git!* All right?"

"Yes, sir," Buff said gratefully for them all. "Let us know if we can do anything at all—"

"Comfort your dead brother's parents and girl and help build up the morale of your live one. That ought to keep you busy for a while."

And with a smile fatherly and encouraging, he saw them out.

Nobody said a word all the way back to the house.

When they passed the scene of the accident it was deserted. Police and spectators were gone, the car had been removed. Only wounded earth and the great gash on the tree bore witness.

Ironically, the fog had lifted, the clouds had broken.

A two-thirds moon looked down, diamond-bright, and cold.

They looked up at it for a moment as they paused by the garage to gather themselves together before going in to face the others.

Moose spoke in an almost childlike voice, innocent, bereft and wistful: "I wonder if Latt is up there somewhere?"

Nobody answered.

Nobody could.

Three days later, heartbreakingly beautiful, inexorably blithe, spring arrived.

Suddenly, in the California fashion, one season was gone and another was in place. Gently over the Santa Clara Valley blew the soft warm winds, white and graceful bowed the endless orchards of peach and plum and apricot and apple. No industry then, no Silicon Valley. Farmlands stretched everywhere, flanked to the west by the soft rise of the Coast Range and the hint of the sea beyond. An all-enveloping rural peace lay upon the campus and the fields around. Over all the lovely valley a kindly benison brought its annual promise of rebirth and growing things. Birds were everywhere. The wild, hysterical cries of quail sounded in the meadows and a lone mocker sang all day and all night in the big eucalyptus by the garage.

In the house the horror of that night still came back in surprising, unexpected ways at unexpected times and places. They had been so absolutely unprepared for it. It was such a monstrous derangement of the pleasant pattern of their lives. And yet, as they—and not only they, for the tragedy hung heavy on the entire campus—came gradually to realize, this was probably the way life really was. It did not always announce its triumphs or its tragedies—it did not always give fair warning. More often than not, "things just happen," as Haggerty put it during one of the many, many postmortems that occurred.

If only Randy had been a little less troubled and upset—if only he hadn't wanted to leave the house—if only Latt hadn't decided to go with him—if only Latt hadn't had Willie's car—if only it hadn't been so foggy—if only Latt hadn't been so kind and helpful to everyone—if only—if only.

The terrible uncertainties of life, from which most of them had been sheltered until then, were brought home in a shattering revelation they would never forget. In some fundamental way, in those areas of mind and heart where innocence still remained, none of them after that night would ever be a child again.

For many days they were simply unable to grasp the enormity of it. They kept expecting Latt to show up for breakfast, or come to dinner, or return from studying at the Libe or along the Quad; they kept expecting to hear his gravely gentle voice in the hall. They would think: I'll have to see what Latt thinks about that—or, Maybe Latt can loan it to me—or, I wonder if Latt would help me with this term paper—and then stop in midthought, devastated by the realization: *But he isn't here. He won't ever be here again. He's gone, gone, gone. Absolutely gone.*

They knew it would be a long time before they could really, completely, beyond all question, accept the fact.

For Randy, lying in the hospital, the days passed in a haze of gradually lessening sedation and gradually lessening pain—very gradually, as they had put him in a cast from hips to shoulders on the third day after the accident and he was not yet able even to turn himself from side to side. His back hurt with a pain he would never forget. Years later when he heard people agree that pain was something whose memory mercifully faded with time, he would think to himself: Not that pain. That pain you remember. Always.

And the other pain. He did not have to wait years to realize that the burden of the other pain would stay with him also. Stark and implacable, it confronted him at every bend of thought, overwhelmed him in the midst of every reverie: I killed Latt. I did it. I killed him, as surely as though I did it with a gun. I can never escape. He will be with me always, decent and gentle, honest and kind. I killed him.

And rising then to overwhelm him, further evil spawn of those thoughts, still others:

I am worthless. I am no good. I have robbed the world of a brilliant mind it needed, a profoundly worthy human being it should not have had to do without. God should have taken me instead. I didn't deserve to live. It should have been me.

His parents had come up from New Mexico, arriving on the afternoon after the accident. His father spent three days with him, then had to return to the ranch. His mother remained, silent, grieving, enormous dark eyes beneath the bun of gray hair never leaving his face for an instant as he woke and slept, woke and slept. At mealtimes she took over from the nurse and fed him; read to him when he asked her to; napped fitfully when he napped, on the extra bed they had placed in the room for her, slept there beside him at night; never leaving, hardly ever moving unless he asked for something.

In the second week of his convalescence, which they told him would probably take about six weeks before he could safely be driven home, she was called to the telephone one morning and presently came back wiping away tears and trying to speak, unsuccessfully, in a normal voice.

"That was Mrs. Lattimer," she said, trembling with emotion.

He said, "*Oh,*" in an anguished voice.

"Oh, no," she said quickly. "Oh, no, Randy. She wasn't angry or hurtful in any way. She was very nice and—and very concerned about you. She said they had been worrying and grieving about you right along, and she just wanted—wanted to know if you were all right."

"That sounds like Latt's parents," he said in a muffled voice, starting to cry himself. "They would."

"She sounded awfully nice," his mother said. "We didn't say much, but we understood each other. She said they were so afraid you would feel that it was your fault—"

"It *was* my fault!" he cried bitterly. "It *was* my fault!"

"No, dear," she said, placing a quick hand on his arm. "No, darling, you mustn't feel that way—"

"But, *Mother*—"

"I know," she said. "I know what you mean, of course, and in that sense you're probably right—"

" '*Probably*'!"

"But in another sense," she went on, undaunted, "it wasn't your fault, you didn't mean to do it—"

"Of *course* not!"

"Of course not," she agreed hurriedly. "You were upset and not yourself—and it was a bad night—and it just—just happened. Mrs. Lattimer said to tell you that if there was anything to forgive—*if,* she said—then they have already forgiven you. She said that—that Bill had mentioned you to them often and that he was very fond of you, and so she knows that you must be 'a very fine boy,' she said. She said to tell you not to worry but just to remember him with loving thoughts as they were doing, and that they will hold you in loving thoughts too and pray for your swift recovery. I told her that I could understand why you and the other boys thought so highly of their son, seeing he obviously had such fine parents. Then we both started to cry and had to say goodbye. But the main thing is, she said *you are not to feel guilty.* And you mustn't, Randy. You really mustn't. It will destroy you if you do."

"I deserve to be destroyed," he said, face turned to the wall. And of course that only made her cry some more.

But he did, he told himself. He *did*.

He had not been worthy of Latt's friendship.

And he would never recover from his death.

But he was, as Dr. James had said that night, young and basically healthy, and day by day he grew stronger physically and, in spite of his self-flagellations, more stable mentally. Dr. Chalmers stopped by, his words calm, supportive, free of blame, immensely strengthening. Many on campus sent notes or called. The burden of all was: Be strong. Get well. We're for you. He only heard from Fluff once, a brief note—at least he supposed it was brief; it was in a small envelope. He tore it up without opening it. There was nothing she could possibly say to him now. He realized that his instinctive reaction, instantaneous and final, really did mark the end. There really was nothing left, absolutely nothing.

He uttered a small, triumphant cry as he ripped the note savagely to shreds and tossed it in the wastebasket beside the bed. The sound startled his mother, who asked, "What was that, dear?"

"Oh," he said casually—and he realized that he really did feel casual, not all tensed-up and agonized as he had before, for which he was profoundly grateful— "Just somebody I used to know."

As the weeks went by, a lot of guys from the house came to see him at frequent intervals, sometimes alone, sometimes in small groups. At first he had greeted them with an apprehensive shyness, afraid that the love for Latt would spill over into some devastating remark that would utterly destroy his still very shaky confidence. But as Buff had remarked in the postmortems, "He's been devastated enough." And when it became apparent to them in their visits how genuinely shattered he was, even Franky had relented and their attitude had become uniformly supportive.

Even that jerk Suratt, he reflected, had been very decent and uncharacteristically mild-tongued; and Galen Bryce, though doubtless much tempted, had refrained from trying to do a patch-up job on his psyche.

At the start of his fifth week in the hospital, windows open, the soft winds of spring flowing in upon him, the sun bright outside, birds singing, everything urging him to get up and go and enjoy it like all the rest although he knew he couldn't—there was a shy knock on the door and the last person he wanted to see stepped quietly in when his mother opened it.

"Oh, hello," he said, hardly able to speak; and she said, "Hello," and he could see it was very hard for her too.

"Mom," he said, "this is—this is Kay Ellsworth. She was engaged to—" he gulped but forced himself to go on—"engaged to Latt. That—that night."

Without a word his mother opened her arms and took Kay into them; and for several minutes, he guessed it was, they were all crying together.

But presently, as he was gradually coming to expect, the crying ceased and things began to calm down. They had to, he was learning: they just had to. It didn't diminish the grief; it was no disrespect to the one who was gone—but they just had to. Those who were left couldn't manage to go on if they didn't.

"I've wanted to come," Kay said, sitting down beside him on the bed, drying her eyes as much as she could, "for a long time. Really since the morning after—after it happened. But somehow I just—just couldn't." And the tears threatened to well up again.

"I know," he said, feeling his own start. "I don't blame you. I wouldn't blame you if you never wanted to see me again."

"Oh, Randy," she said, taking his right hand where it lay clenched atop the blankets, "you mustn't say that. Things happen. It could have happened to anybody, anywhere, at any time, if the circumstances were right."

"But it didn't have to happen to—" he started bitterly.

"But it did," she said quietly.

"And I didn't have to be the one who—"

"But you were. Are you going to let it ruin your whole life?"

"That's what I keep telling him," his mother said. She smiled wistfully. "Randy is really a very stubborn boy. I don't think he believes me."

"Sometimes," Kay said with an answering smile and the look between them that, as often happens, shuts out men altogether, "sons don't believe mothers so well. Sometimes it takes somebody else to get them to accept something. Maybe he will listen to me." She gave Randy a smile that trembled between wryness and further tears. "I think maybe I have the right."

He gave her hand a desperate squeeze and choked out, "Yes, I guess maybe you do."

"All right, then," she said with a sudden vigor. "I've talked to his parents— many times—and they aren't holding a grudge. It's too—too awful for that. What good would it do? And I don't hold a grudge. And the house doesn't, I know, because Willie and Guy and all the others have told me so. So you're the only one, I guess—a grudge against yourself. To what purpose, Randy? To placate him in some way? I'm sure he doesn't hold it against you. That wouldn't be his nature."

He shook his head in sad wonderment.

"No," he said, barely managing. "He was *so good.*"

"He was. And if *he* can forgive you, and *we* all can—then there shouldn't be any more to be said. Isn't that right? Dr. James tells me you're coming along very well—"

"I'll never play tennis again."

"Oh yes you will. He says by the end of the year. He says your main problem now is to regain your confidence and your self-respect—and not look back too much. You've got to go on, Randy. We've all got to go on." Her face threatened to crumple again but she held it firm. "It isn't easy, but it's what he would want us to do. We've got to. We can grieve—"

"I'll always grieve."

She gave him a wistful little smile.

"You think I won't?"

"But you'll find someone else," he said earnestly. "You're young—you're a great person—you'll be rewarded."

"And so will you. With peace of mind. Which is what you need most badly, right now."

She gave his hand a final squeeze and stood up; kissed his mother; turned back to lean down and kiss him.

"Now you think of him and what he would want you to do. I think he'd want you to learn from it and be a better person. It's the only way to make his death mean anything."

"Thank you, Kay," he said, tears threatening again. "Thank you for everything. I don't see how you do it, but—thank you."

"Take care of yourself," she said. "You're going to be all right."

After she left they were silent for a while. Then his mother took his hand, which she noted was now lying relaxed and open at his side.

"What a wonderful girl," she said softly. "Do you feel better now?"

"Yes," he said with a drowsy smile, "I feel better now." And dropped off to sleep while she sat beside him, reading and still holding his hand.

When he awoke he lay for a long time with his eyes closed, thinking, as he was to do many times over many days and nights. Out of it all came the growing conviction that Kay was right: "He'd want you to learn from it and be a better person. *It's the only way to make his death mean anything.*"

He realized finally that it was the only way: that he must from now on be a good and constructive person, get back to what he had been before Fluff came along, not waste himself on people or causes that he knew to be worthless; not, as Latt had phrased it once in a rare moment of impatience, "throw himself away."

He didn't know what direction this would take, how he could really express it; but he knew the inspiration and the determination were there now, and he knew that in due time the way would be revealed to him. He had never been particularly religious, did not regard himself as being noticeably so now; but something had changed for him forever on the night he and Latt did not make it up Palm Drive.

His mother showed him a letter she was writing to Mrs. Lattimer:

"Something good in Randy will always be Bill's."

To the expression of that good, in whatever form it might take, he knew now that he would always be dedicated.

A week later Dr. James pronounced him fit to leave. When he got home he would be ambulatory but would remain in the cast for another six weeks, then be in a steel brace for another three months before he would finally be whole again. He would be able to return to school fall quarter, for a while would have to spend weekends in the Men's Rest Home, but could gradually resume his tennis and his activities on the *Daily* (where Nagatani said his place was waiting for him). By spring of 1940, Dr. James said confidently, he would be good as new.

His father drove up from New Mexico in one of the ranch vans, which he had fitted with a bed in the back. They would make it an easy journey, not trying to cover too many miles each day, stopping in the simple, inexpensive motor hotels that were springing up everywhere along the nation's roads.

The whole house came to see him off.

He would never forget as long as he lived the moment the warmth of the sun fell on his face when they rolled his bed out of the hospital to the van.

21

Time moved faster. For the seniors everything suddenly became the last.

The last spring vacation. The last Reg Day. The last Reg Dance. The last schedule of classes. The last house election (Smitty president by acclamation, Buff finally having convinced them he wouldn't serve again). The last house functions. The last chances to walk the Quad and the campus, green and lovely in the full flood of spring. The last chances to swim in the lake or drive out to the beach or go to the City or get a meal at Sticky's or a Coke at the Union or go to a movie in town or just lie in the sun and let the world drift by in a sleepy haze no more energetic than the soft white clouds, dimly seen through half-shut eyes, that slid slowly past against the endless blue above . . . the last chance to enjoy a world soon to change, never to be the same again.

For Ray Baker it was a time to concentrate on his concluding pre-legal course and begin to look a little more seriously for the nice girl who would be willing to come back with him to Arvin, or Bakersfield, in the southern San Joaquin and be a small-town lawyer's wife. He had told Gil, secretly amused by Gil's reaction, that the word "nice" held no pejorative connotations for him—that was exactly what he wanted. He was not sure at the moment whether he would return to law school at the University or go somewhere else, possibly Cal or one of the schools in Southern California. He knew that he would, as he put it to himself, "keep my antennae up" for Miss Right. Calm and steady, moving straight ahead on the course he had laid out for himself, he had no doubt whatsoever that he would find her in due course.

For those who considered themselves to be, and were considered by their

476

brothers to be, "the positives" (as Franky, one of them, described them), the
last quarter was a time to firm up everything that had gone before.

Francis Allen Miller and Mary Katherine Sullivan announced their engagement in April and their marriage in Memorial Church at eight P.M.,
June 18, 1939, Commencement Day. Edward Paul Haggerty and Francine
Helen Magruder announced in late May that they were engaged and would
follow suit in the same place at eleven A.M. the next day. Clyde Gaius Unruh
and Marguerite Johnson announced their engagement a week later and their
marriage in Trenton, New Jersey, on July 1. Guy, by no means feeling as
"positive" as Franky and Hack, had, as he told Willie, finally decided, "What
the hell!"

"That's a wildly passionate declaration if I ever heard one," Willie remarked. "Don't you love her even a *little* bit?"

"Oh, of course I do," Guy said, having the grace to look a little shamefaced. "She's a *wonderful* girl and she's going to be a wonderful wife."

"And what kind of a husband are you going to be?" Willie inquired dryly.

"People who live in glass houses," Guy retorted, "shouldn't sound superior. I'm going to be a good one."

"Faithful?"

"What's that got to do with it?" Guy inquired blandly. He grinned. "At
least I know the mechanics pretty well. She won't be disappointed. And," he
added more seriously, "I'll take good care of her. I'll be a good provider. She
won't have any complaints."

"I suppose that's as good a basis as any."

"You bet," Unruh said crisply. "Check us out in twenty, and see."

For those whom Franky characterized as "in-betweens," the final quarter
did not produce conclusions so definite.

Gil Gulbransen and Karen Ann Waterhouse continued their ironic dance-
of-detachment without ever quite getting to the point of pushing it to the
decision both felt was probably inevitable. Gil, as his housemates observed
wryly, seemed to take the sense of "the last" very seriously. "By June,"
Suratt remarked, "he won't have left a stone or a freshman girl unturned."
Certainly he did seem to be even more on the prowl than usual. They all felt
it was a wonder Karen Ann would still speak to him. But Karen Ann, as Hack
pointed out, was a cynic, and a very practical gal to boot.

"She knows exactly what she's letting herself in for," he said, "and after
all, there's a lot to be said for Gil. He's going to be a good doctor, he'll make
a very good living, he's handsome as hell and really, he's a nice guy underneath it all."

"If you're in a position where you don't have to be jealous every time he
sleeps with somebody," Buff remarked with a grin. "We are. But what about
Karen Ann?"

"I don't think she's jealous," Hack said. "She gets around a bit herself.

And I guess it depends on what a girl wants. If you're society like her family then I suppose you want a handsome guy who's a success in his profession and is as agreeable as you are to keeping up appearances. I don't expect it'll be the kind of marriages Franky and I will have—"

"Thank God," said Franky fervently.

"—Thank God. But I bet it'll work. I've seen a lot like that. As long as everybody obeys the rules, nobody gets hurt, everybody gets what they want out of it, and everybody's happy."

"Not for me," Buff said thoughtfully. "Not for me."

But what there was for him, he wasn't really sure as he approached the end of senior year. He supposed he could be called some kind of womanizer but he wasn't really a *serious* one, as he considered Gil, and to some degree Guy. He just sort of went along and women just—just kind of threw themselves at him, really. He supposed some of it was because he was rich, but there were quite a few girls who really seemed to like him just for himself—in fact, nearly all of them. He could say, and he was proud of it and felt he had a right to be, that almost every gal he'd ever dated was still a good friend. He liked that—he liked people to like him. He often thought, with a really nice feeling inside, of what Willie had said soon after they joined the house: "Anybody who doesn't like Buff Richardson needs to have his head examined. If a more likeable guy exists, I haven't met him yet and I don't expect to." That had been three years ago and just recently Buff, rather shyly but really wanting to know, had reminded Willie and asked if he *had* met anybody more likeable during their years together.

"Absolutely not," Willie had said without a second's hesitation. "You're tops, Buff. Everybody on campus knows it."

Why, then, wasn't he all set to march down the aisle in Memorial Church with the rest of them? Why hadn't he found the right girl? Why was his heart still uncommitted?

Why was he still alone?

He had discussed this really seriously with Duke not too long ago, one stormy night in winter quarter when they had been studying in the room and he had finally, along about eleven, opened his secret cache of beer and suggested they forget studying and just talk. The first thing he had done was raise the question.

"I think maybe," Duke said, "it's because you *are* so generous, Buff—you spread yourself so thin, in a sense, that you haven't had time to concentrate on any one to the exclusion of all the others."

"But I do like everybody," he protested. "It isn't my nature to shut anybody out."

"We know that," Duke said, "and of course from your friends' point of view, that's great. We all profit from it, you're such a generous friend to all of us. But where girls are concerned, maybe you should just deliberately narrow things down a little. I'm sure you know lots of gals who'd be absolutely delighted to be your principal date—maybe even fiancée someday, if you're ready to go that far."

"How did you happen to be so lucky?" Buff inquired wistfully. Duke's expression became a little guarded but he spoke frankly, the capacity to draw people out, quite innocently and without calculation, being one of Buff's qualities.

"First, of course," he said slowly, "there's—background. It's the same, obviously. That tends to draw—people like us—together."

"Because the Jews feel threatened?" Buff inquired with an innocent candor so direct that not even the most sensitive could feel offended.

Duke nodded. His expression darkened.

"That's what drew us together first, I think, that sense of—of kinship—and beleaguerment—and defensiveness—" his voice became low—"and fear. . . . But then, of course," and his voice rose, his expression became as relaxed and happy, Buff thought, as he would probably ever see it, "there's Shahna herself."

"She's a wonderful girl."

"She is," Duke agreed softly. "She is that. First we had a class together. And then we began talking between classes—and studying together—and dating—and pretty soon it just became an understood thing. And when we graduate next year we're going to get married. It's as simple as that."

"Well, hardly," Buff said with a smile. "But I do think it's wonderful. So the secret is background—and feeling the same way about things—and wanting to protect each other." He grinned suddenly. "You mean if I find some rich bitch from Montclair, New Jersey, who's just as mixed-up as I am, that will do it?"

Duke laughed.

"You aren't mixed-up, you're one of the most uncomplicated people I know. No, I don't mean that. Necessarily. But you might find somebody there."

"I'm sure my folks have half a dozen in mind for me," Buff said dryly. "But there are enough rich bitches here, and I haven't found one. So there must be more to it than that."

"Well, just don't worry. That's the main thing, don't worry. It'll happen someday when you least expect it. Boom! And there you'll be, Daddy Buff with ten kids, on his estate in Montclair, wifey off at the garden club, both of you happy as clams."

"Do you really think so?" Buff inquired, sounding wistful again.

"Positive," Duke said.

But *he* still didn't feel "positive," Buff thought. It wasn't like him to be introspective but he sure did wish she'd hurry up and come along if she was going to, particularly with things so uncertain and war maybe coming on. He didn't want to tackle that without somebody backing him up at home. But where was she?

Moose knew where she was for him, all right, but, managing to hold firm to what he described to himself as "my Sand Hill Road Resolution," successfully got through spring quarter without having to do anything about it.

Suzy recovered from her little pout after a brief return to being Welcome Waggoner to the whole male population, and they had some more damned good times—at least once a week and sometimes oftener, he told Gulbransen when, as frequently happened, they compared notes. But despite several more attempts on her part to entice him with tales of all-play-and-no-work, Rolls-Royces, country clubs, someday inheriting the business, and the like, he steadfastly refused to discuss matrimony any further.

Anyway, matrimony wasn't his principal concern as his college days grew inexorably toward their close. More than anyone besides Timmy, he sometimes thought, he suffered from what Rodge Leighton called "senior syndrome." He really missed football, he really did. Quite often he'd go out to the stadium on the long sweet afternoons to watch next year's varsity and backups run through spring practice. Everybody made a fuss over him and made him feel at home, Coach was always glad to see him and took him into his confidence on a lot of things, such as tips on the game and how to get along with the administration and the alumni, which he said with a cynical chuckle was 75 percent of any coaching job. He knew Moose wanted to land a coaching job in some high school somewhere, and promised to keep his ears open and see what he could do to help. But graduation was coming ever faster and there still wasn't anything and Moose was beginning to get worried. He didn't want to go back to Chicago and drive a truck for the city, like his dad, although he knew he could do it if he had to. He still wanted, if only vicariously through young kids, the thrill and the glory.

Sometimes as the shadows lengthened across the field, now even brighter and greener in the high noon of spring, he would wander off by himself for a few moments to stand alone in some deserted corner and just let it all flood over him again: the stands filled with brightly colored, screaming thousands, pennants flying, bands playing, two teams heroically clashing, the glorious passes, the daring runs, the ball soaring back—back—back—and there, hero of the hour, proud, confident, invincible, ever happy, ever triumphant, ever young—MOOSE! MOOOOOOSE! MOOOOOOOOOOOOOOSE!!!

Then he would come to with a start, shake his head, turn back self-conscious and shamefaced toward the benches. But Coach, if he noticed and of course he did, never kidded him, never said an unkind word, just clapped him on the shoulder with perhaps a little more warmth than usual and told him encouragingly, "Hang in there, Mooser! We'll make it!"

And he knew he would, somehow—somewhere—one of these days before too long. He simply had to. And he would.

So it was no wonder, perhaps, that he really wasn't as concerned about marriage right now as some of the guys were. He was still back there in glory days, as Rodge remarked when he urged him, as he often did, to let them go and think about tomorrow. He was doing that, too—hell, how could he not, when the choice was between coaching and driving a truck all his life—but it still wasn't all that easy to just cut off what in many ways had been the biggest and best and happiest time of your whole life.

He knew Timmy had the same problem because Timmy had told him so one time when they had fallen into step on the way back to the house from their one-o'clock classes. It had been a perfect spring afternoon, golden and wonderful as they can only be at twenty-one on a college campus (perhaps never more wonderful than they were everywhere in the doomed spring of 1939). Finally Tim had shaken his head and said, "God! All this beauty and over there in Europe—!" He hadn't finished but had let it trail away in the warm sun and gentle breezes that rustled through the palm fronds in the Inner Quad.

"Still worried about it?" Moose asked. Tim had given him an almost indignant glance.

"Hell, yes," he said with a sort of scornful impatience. "It's going right on in spite of the beautiful weather and kids who don't pay any attention to what's happening. Czechoslovakia's *all* gone now, Hitler wiped it out and took Prague at the end of March. And then he took the port of Memel on the Baltic from Lithuania. And in his speech to the Reichstag yesterday he really ran the gamut, told F.D.R. to take his peace plea and shove it, abrogated the Anglo-German naval treaty, abrogated the Munich consultative pact with Great Britain, abrogated his nonaggression treaty with Poland, demanded the return of Danzig from Poland and a Polish corridor right through Poland to the sea. Then the slimy fucker had the gall to offer nonaggression pacts to any nation that wants one, if they'll humble themselves to take the initiative and ask him. . . .Now that jackal Mussolini is threatening to cancel the Anglo-Italian pact he signed a year ago—and the French are beginning to say that maybe Danzig isn't the right place to take a stand, so they may try to break their pact with Poland—and the anti-Semites and the appeasers are getting more and more open in this country—and I tell you, Moose, it's one hell of a situation!"

And he looked gloomily down at the ground as he walked along, ignoring the glorious weather and barely acknowledging the many students who said hello.

"Gosh," Moose said, respectful of so much knowledge. "You're really full of it, aren't you?"

"Oh, Moose, for Christ's sake!" Tim exploded. "Don't you ever read the papers or listen to the radio?"

"Well—some," Moose said, a little taken aback by his vehemence. "I mean I read the *Daily*—"

"The *Daily*!" Tim snorted. "The *Daily*! What a namby-pamby sheet *that's* turned out to be since I left! *Jesus*!"

"Oh, I think Nagatani's doing a good job," Moose protested; and then added hastily at Tim's expression, "I mean, it's not *bad*. He gives us the news, right?"

"Not the way I did," Tim said flatly. "I ran a *good* paper. The University really knew what was going on when *I* was in charge."

"Well, sure," Moose agreed. "You were damned good, everybody knows that. But Bill still gives us a lot of news, plus—well, plus more of what's going on right here." His tone became tentative. "Don't you think?"

"Obviously not," Tim said with a snort, "or I wouldn't be complaining. I wish I were sitting in that editor's chair right now! Things would be different!"

"I know how you feel," Moose said sympathetically. "It's just like me and football. Those were the days, right?"

"Moose!" Tim exclaimed. "How can you make a comparison between me and the *Daily* and you and football—!"

"Well," Moose said, standing his ground, "just the same, Timmy, you miss it just like I do, isn't that true?"

For a moment Tim looked as though he was going to deny it with some vigor. Then innate honesty reasserted itself and he reflected that he was, after all, talking to a brother who had known him intimately for the past three years.

"Yes," he said quietly. "I miss it like hell."

"It really hurts sometimes, doesn't it?" Moose said wistfully. "There you are, one day the big hero or the big boss, and next day it's all over and somebody else is doing it. I don't think I've gotten over it yet."

"Me either," Tim admitted with a rather wan little smile. "But we've got to."

"That's what Rodge says," Moose agreed, "and he's right. But it sure isn't easy sometimes."

"Nope," Tim said as they reached the bookstore and he turned in to buy some typing paper, "it sure isn't. See you at the house."

He needed the paper not because he was doing anything about his "novel"—he'd been too busy to touch it since September, his notes and sketches were still just sitting there in that damned locked box in his closet. He needed the paper because he wanted to write another letter to the editor. He supposed part of it was nostalgia, as Moose said—he still couldn't keep his hands off the paper as long as Nagatani would let him get away with it—and part of it was because he was, as always, genuinely upset about the ongoing course of events. With Hitler's latest speech he now believed that they had taken a quantum leap toward the inevitable. He banged away at the rattly old Underwood portable he had up in his room so savagely he felt it might almost explode.

"Now, Timmy," Bill Nagatani said soothingly from the *Daily* Shack when he received the result, "do you really want me to print this thing?"

"Yes," Tim said shortly from the house. "Why the hell do you think I wrote it?"

"Oh," Nagatani said, "just to get it off your chest, I imagine. I'm really wondering if that won't be enough to suit you?"

"It will not! I want it printed!"

"Well," Bill said slowly, "I wonder if I can maintain my 'responsibility to my country and to the University family,' as you put it, if I print something that's pretty far out, in a way. You're genuinely concerned, Timmy, we all know that. But can't you tone it down a little? I mean, calling Hitler an evil maniacal genius—"

"He *is* evil. *And* a maniac. *And* a genius. I said so and I believe it. I don't think he deserves any courtesy or any tolerance or any pulling of punches, at all. I think we should call him exactly what he is."

"I know that's what you've been thinking since I took over," Bill said with a wry little chuckle, "and you've certainly been letting me know. Which letter is this I've received since I became editor, about number fifteen?"

"No. It's only the fourth one."

"Oh. Well, it seems like fifteen. I've printed 'em, too, haven't I? Without challenge."

"So why are you challenging this one?"

"Oh, Timmy. Because we all know what you think. You expressed it very well and at great length when you were here. You've expressed it very well in your other three letters. Can't we have a rest for a while?"

"No. Hitler isn't resting. If he were, I wouldn't have to write. So, are you going to print it?"

Nagatani sighed.

"Oh, sure. Of course. You're the ex-editor, aren't you? People respect your opinions—even if they are rather overstated," he couldn't resist adding. "I'll print it. I may have to cut it some, but I'll give you the gist of it. Then I can write a rebuttal. And so it will go, on and on."

"Until I get you to admit I'm right," Tim said with a laugh, relaxing now that he had won his point. "I'll have another for you next week."

"Oh, Christ. Surely you're kidding?"

"Maybe," Tim said airily. "Maybe not."

"Oh, incidentally," Bill said, "don't hang up for a minute. What's this I hear that some of you guys have joined the army air reserves program. Are you going to war or something?"

"We may," Tim said calmly. "If we do, some of us intend to be a little bit prepared for it. Any objections?"

"Oh, no. It just seems a little quixotic, to me. I didn't realize you thought we were *that* close."

"Close enough. Want to join us?"

"No, thanks. Flying makes me sick. Anyway, I think maybe you're getting a little hysterical."

"We'll see," Tim said grimly. "We'll see."

"That's right," Nagatani said amicably. "Can't argue with that."

It was no wonder Tim had no time to worry about marriage. He warn't agin it, he told himself with a wry humor, in fact it would be great if he had a steady and could be in a position to follow Franky and Hack and Guy down the aisle. But hell. There were so many more important things going on in the world right now.

For North McAllister, whose brothers with two or possibly three exceptions could not understand why he and B.J. weren't also altar-bound, the most important thing going on in the world was, as always, the internal struggle with himself, which seemed to be in one of its recurring periods of rising tension as he approached the end of his undergraduate days.

He had stopped writing to, and arguing with, Billy, who with his brother's support assured had managed to convince North gently but firmly that he really wasn't interested; but that, of course, didn't mean that North wasn't still interested. He hated himself for it sometimes; sometimes felt helplessly and hopelessly that it was impossible to fight; sometimes tried, without success.

His football friend in the Zete house stood by him loyally. They helped each other a lot even when they weren't together—just the knowledge of another understanding presence nearby meant a great deal. They managed to maintain their schedule of going to the City every couple of weeks; studied together occasionally; met now and then for lunch or a Coke at the Cellar. Their friendship occasioned no comment, melded smoothly into the busy fabric of campus life. It was a lifesaver for them both.

It did not, however, solve the basic problem, whose first stage, in North's mind, was: what do I do about It? And whose second was: what do I do about B.J.? He found that the approach of graduation was reversing the order. But they remained inextricably entwined; especially since he seemed to have succeeded to Latt's place in B.J.'s mind. She told him that "in a funny way, I feel that my life is sort of incomplete without Latt. We were almost like brother and sister."

"Everybody's life is incomplete without Latt," North said gravely. "He was unique."

And because B.J. really was devastated for a while, struggling with the same blue funk they felt in the house, he found himself drawn closer to her, not so much of his own volition as by what seemed to be her increased emotional dependence upon him as a result of Latt's death.

It made increasingly inescapable the question of what he was going to do about their situation.

The answer was something about which he fluctuated, it seemed to him,

on an almost daily basis as graduation neared. Some days he told himself
stoutly that he should commit himself, ask her to marry him, turn away as
much as possible from his more searing hungers and simply *do it*, as Franky,
quite innocently, urged him from time to time: "Don't hesitate, just *do it!*"
And quite frequently North could almost—almost—convince himself that he
was going to just *do it*. And then everything would, miraculously, be all
right.

Then he would have the same recurring nightmare and wake up sweating.
He *was* doing it, he *was* walking down the aisle, he *was* turning to face a
radiant B.J. on the arm of her father—and he would wake up crying out
(fortunately not aloud, or the whole sleeping porch would have been
aroused)—"NO!"—and sweating.

On one occasion he apparently had cried out aloud. He realized later that
Willie must have been waiting for just some such opportunity, for the next
night he heard a discreet knock on his door and opened it to find Willie
standing there in bathrobe and slippers.

"Mind if I come in?" he asked mildly, and North, after a split second's panic
which he could only hope did not show in his eyes, said easily, "Sure. I'm
honored. I don't recall you ever just dropping in on me, Willie. What's up?"

"Oh, nothing much," Willie said comfortably, easing himself into a chair,
lighting a cigarette, offering North one, which he took after a moment's
hesitation. He didn't enjoy smoking much but it was so much the current
symbol of collegiate sophistication that he felt almost obligated.

"Must be something," he remarked, "to bring you down from your eagle's
nest." And decided to sail right into it. "What have I done?"

Willie gave him a quick glance, apparently a little taken aback by this
directness.

"Nothing *I'm* upset about," he said in a reassuring tone that instantly
tightened North up inside. Why was he being reassuring? And why the
emphasis on the pronoun? "Do you realize that you yelled in your sleep last
night?"

"I did?" North asked blankly, thinking: Oh, God. What did I say?

"Yeah. You shouted. 'NO!' Real upset. Very strong. It woke almost everybody up."

"I'm sorry." He shook his head in apparently genuine puzzlement. "I
wonder what I could have been dreaming?"

"You don't remember?" Willie asked, studying him more closely than was
comfortable.

"No," he said; and then laughed, quite naturally, he thought. "Maybe I
was dreaming that Dr. Stafford had given us a surprise quiz in Shakespeare's
Contributions."

At this reference to the famous throwaway (as they regarded it) course
which she and the English department offered as a sort of universal catch-up

for seniors who needed a few extra units to complete necessary graduation totals, they both laughed. North was taking it because he needed three more units to complete a literature requirement, Willie, as he had explained wryly, "because I have to catch up with three units that got misplaced somehow when I flunked the requirement for freshman biology."

"You didn't!" North had protested with a laugh.

"Oh, yes I did. I had to take it over again sophomore year—and flunked it again. I told them I'd never in all my life have to know how to dissect a frog. They weren't amused and they were bigger than I was. I finally passed it last year, but somehow in the shuffle I misplaced three units. So now I'm taking good old S.C. from Stafford. She hates my guts but I'm depending on her elemental sense of fairness, which she prides herself on. Our relations are scrupulously polite but frigid, ever since she laced into me at Excom. I think I told everybody about that."

North nodded.

"But how could you get the Rhodes scholarship with that hanging over you?"

Willie shrugged and grinned.

"Sheer genius. The rest of my record is so dazzling they're gambling on my being able to correct the deficit by June. It's only three units."

North looked a little worried for him.

"I hope she doesn't get vindictive."

Willie dismissed it.

"Oh, she couldn't. It would be too obvious."

Now North's mention of her class provided some distraction, but, as he could instantly sense, not enough. Willie joined in the laugh but stuck to the subject.

"I can see where Stafford would give anybody nightmares," he agreed, "but somehow when you yelled it sounded a lot more—well, personal, if you know what I mean. You sounded really sort of—agonized, I thought. It worried me. So I thought," he said, a trifle too casually, "I'd see if I could help."

North gave him a look half puzzled, half amused, and shook his head.

"I appreciate that, Willie, but I really don't remember what I was dreaming."

"Really?"

"No!" he replied. Too strongly, because Willie got the expression that Renny referred to as "zeroing- in." "Watch out when Willie zeroes in—he's after something." Even if his nerves hadn't been one-sixteenth of an inch from the surface, North would have been uneasy. As it was, he overdid it.

"What on earth," he demanded, "would I have been 'agonized' about, anyway?"

He became conscious suddenly that the house was very quiet. Many were studying. The weeknight ban on loud radio and phonographs was being observed. He wished he had decided to go to the Libe to study. But it was too late now. He repeated his point, unfortunately.

"I am not 'agonized' about anything. What would I be 'agonized' about?"

"Oh, I don't know," Willie said, drawing thoughtfully on his cigarette. "B.J., maybe? Something else? Both?"

North looked blank though he was in turmoil inside.

" 'Both' what? If you know something I don't know, Willie, you're going to have to spell it out. I don't know what you're getting at."

Again Willie gave him a thoughtful look; but backed off a little.

"Well, first of all," he said quietly, "I don't want you to get the idea that I'm hostile about anything, because I'm not. I'm the farthest thing from it. So—relax."

"How can I relax," North inquired unhappily, "when you seem to be— pushing me on something—and I don't know what it is?"

"Don't you?" Willie responded, voice now very quiet—really gentle, North felt. It was almost enough to tip the balance. But a decade's defenses took a little longer to come down.

"No, I don't!"

"Oh," Willie said, in the same very quiet, very gentle voice, "I think you do, North . . . I think you do."

"Well, why—" North said, eyes haunted, voice really 'agonized,' he thought with a wildly crazy self-humor— "why are you after me? Why don't you leave me alone?"

Willie gave him a long look, stubbing out his cigarette, pushing the ash-tray aside.

"Well . . ." he said slowly at last. ". . . he is my brother, after all."

For a very long moment, then, they simply stared at one another while North first flushed, then became very pale. Moving it seemed almost with-out conscious volition, he got up, went to the door, locked it. Then he turned and he leaned against it, facing Willie. When he finally spoke it was in a voice choked and almost inaudible. It was a tribute to them both, Willie thought, that he made no attempt to dissemble.

"I haven't talked to him . . . or written to him . . . for a couple of weeks, now. . . . I've made up my mind, Willie. It's not—not there."

"But friendship is," Willie said quickly. And firmly. "From him and from me. Can you believe that?"

North's eyes never left his. Finally he nodded.

"Yes, I believe that. Just so long—" his voice sank almost to a whisper— "just so long as you don't offer to 'help.' I hate patronizing people who tell you they want to 'help.' There *isn't* any 'help' except what you can find inside yourself. So—don't patronize."

Willie shook his head.

"I'm not the patronizing kind. I do think there might be some help in the sense of—no, now wait a minute, let me finish—in the sense of, specifically, maybe you want to talk about B.J. in this context. It must be awfully difficult for you—"

"Terrible," North said with sadness so deep it moved Willie profoundly. "Just *terrible*."

"I know," Willie said. "Or I think I can sympathize enough to understand. Sit down, no point in standing. . . . Does she suspect anything?"

North obediently resumed his seat; shook his head.

"I—don't think so. I'm sure she finds it a little odd that I'm not more romantic sometimes." He managed a rueful little smile. "I do know how, you know, Willie. I *have* done it. It's just that I—I like—the other—better. And that's really why I've deliberately held back—why I haven't asked her to marry me—why I wake up crying 'No!' out of a bad dream that we're standing at the altar and suddenly I feel in my dream that *I shouldn't be in this situation—it's so sad and tragic—it's so terribly unfair.* Not so much to me, I can manage, there are ways and places and people, and it can be done with complete discretion and no one will ever know. That's what happens in many, many cases, far more than the conventional world ever realizes. But just at this particular time, when she's young and idealistic and hopeful and wants a good husband—I mean, I'd be that to her, Willie, I really would, and she would never, never know. But I still haven't quite managed to make the jump from what I know can be worked out fairly and well for both of us, to actually putting aside hesitations and scruples and accepting that it would give her what she wants, a loving husband—and I would be if I went into it, I would be, nobody has to worry about that—and a good home and the sort of life she dreams of for herself . . . does any of that make any sense?"

"It does to me," Willie said quietly. "And I'm sure it does to Billy, if you've talked to him about it—" North nodded—"and we're the only ones who are ever going to know, so . . . What does he say?"

North gave him a wry little smile.

"He wants me to get married. And I imagine you're going to tell me the same."

"I am," Willie said without a moment's hesitation. "And the sooner the better."

"Even if I—"

"Even if you do. Look at it this way: *you're making her happy.* Isn't that what you want to do?"

North nodded.

"You love her?"

"I'm—very fond of her. I *could* love her. I will, if we get married. You think that's good enough?"

"I think that's good enough," Willie said flatly. "Now go to it, damn it, and stop tying yourself in knots! O.K.?"

"Is that an order?" North asked with a shaky little laugh.

"That's an order! Don't *think* anymore! Just *do it!*"

"Yes, sir," North said with another shaky little laugh but sounding, suddenly, determined. "I *will!*"

For a couple of weeks, however, nothing happened; and the brothers Wilson, discussing the matter one night when Billy again climbed the stairs to Willie's aerie—across whose door somebody, probably Franky, had recently pinned a hand-printed sign, DON'T GO ON TO HEAVEN, WILLIE'S HERE—found themselves increasingly concerned. But midway in the third week, the day after all house members received invitations to the Magruder-Haggerty wedding, another set arrived for all of them from Salt Lake City.

Mr. and Mrs. Kenneth Letterman were pleased to invite them to the wedding of their daughter Betty June to Mr. North McAllister at two P.M. on Monday, June 19, the day after commencement, in Memorial Church.

Meeting Hack on the stairs, Willie remarked, "Great news about North and B.J."

Hack for just a second gave him a glance that said it all.

"Best for everybody," he agreed tersely and went on, leaving Willie to reflect that Hack, like one of the favorite songs he liked to play for them, knew a little bit—quite a lot, actually—about a lot of things.

He could not conceal from himself, however, that he was now afflicted quite severely with his own doubts and second thoughts. North was putting a good face on it, accepting congratulations with an apparently easy grace, dark eyes and handsome, rather florid face appearing to be flushed with happiness and excitement. The night after the invitations arrived, however, Willie found him locked in his room and when he finally prevailed upon him to let him in, found him red-eyed, terribly tense and almost incoherent.

"What have I done?" he kept whispering to himself. "*What have I done?*"

"You've done the right thing," Willie kept responding, gripping his shoulder with an encouraging hand. "*You've done the right thing.*"

"Oh, my God," North whispered, sounding utterly abandoned and gripping Willie's hand in return as though it were something cast to him from a lifeboat. "I hope so. Oh, my God, *I hope so.*"

And an hour later, after Willie had repeated all the arguments, reaffirmed all the reassurances, battered down with sheer will and force of personality all the fears and terrors—or so he thought—North was still whispering from time to time, as though Willie weren't there and hadn't spoken, "Oh, God. Oh, God. I hope so. *I hope so . . .*" Adding sometimes, in a voice hopeless and heartbreaking, "There is no solution . . . *there is no solution . . .*"

Next day when Willie ran into an absolutely radiant B.J. at the post office, his own uncertainties grew.

What had he committed them to, in what he had believed to be good faith and deep concern—but saw now could be construed as a strictly egotistical intervention? What future tragedy might he have been responsible for, if she ever found out—or if North backed out at the last moment? What right had he to be Mr. Fix-It to other people's lives when he couldn't even determine the future course of his own?

Where did Richard Emmett Wilson acquire the commission to play God?

"You're upset about something," Billy said, climbing the stairs once more.

"Is it that obvious?"

"No, but I know. Tell me."

So he had, finding himself more grateful than he had ever been for his brother's earnest, idealistic support.

"It's my fault too," Billy said stoutly. "I told him to get married before you did. You don't have to take it all on yourself. And anyway, who knows how it's going to work out? We just have to think it's going to be all right. At least we've sincerely tried to do what we thought was best. Surely that should be rewarded with *something* good."

"God," Willie said, sounding like North. "I hope so. *I hope so.*"

For the next few days the three of them went around pretending to the house that all was well. And presently, because even emotions as tense as North's have to relax sometime, things did ease off into a calmer and more optimistic mood. North still came close to breaking down privately with both of them, but they refused to let him and after a while he began to sound genuinely reconciled and even excited by the prospect of his approaching wedding. He asked Willie to stay over after graduation and be his best man and Willie said he would. Thus fortified, North appeared outwardly to be as calm as they hoped he was inside.

"Don't bet on it," Willie advised; and Billy smiled and said, "No, but at least there's progress."

They assured each other that they would do all they could to help it continue.

22

Wilson's own problem was not resolved until about six weeks before graduation, when he finally made the decision that he felt in retrospect had been implicit from the start.

For a few days after his visit to Piedmont he made no attempt to contact Marian. He wrote Mary his bread-and-butter letter, cordial, correct—reserved. He wanted to convey to them with reasonable subtlety that if there ever were the possibility of something more lasting between himself and their daughter, it would be cease-fire, not surrender, in his relations with them. Best get the ground rules established early, Unruh had advised when he read him a first draft—"if, that is, you really think you want to carry it any further. Personally, I still think you should dump her and get it over with."

Willie was still far from this, however. He told Guy he was too cynical.

"Not cynical, just been around the track. Like mother, like daughter, I've found, particularly with the piranha type. Scratch the sweet young thing and there's domineering Mama, waiting to be reborn in the next generation as soon as you're signed, sealed and delivered. You don't really want that, do you?"

"I don't know what I want," he confessed with a humorous impatience. Unruh snorted.

"Yes, I've already noticed that. Well, I wash my hands of it. I'll just have to stand by to pick up the pieces, I guess. You know you can always count on that."

"Yes, I know," he said with a smile, unabashedly grateful, that summed up the permanent commitment to friendship they had made almost from the first moment they had met as freshmen. "Don't think it doesn't help. It sure does."

But it didn't help him make up his mind, which seemed about as shaky as one of Dewey's chocolate puddings—which on second thought wasn't a good analogy since they were, as Buff had once remarked "as solid as Alcatraz."

His intentions, he reflected ruefully, were a long way from that. Particularly when Marian called, sounding genuinely pleased to be talking to him, and invited him to a dinner dance friends of her family were hosting for their daughter at the St. Francis.

"Great!" he said. "I'd be delighted."

Which was exactly the sentiment he expressed next day when Donna called to invite him to a formal candlelight dinner at her house. The two events were scheduled for the next weekend, the dance on Friday, the dinner, fortunately, on Saturday.

"Lu-cky, lu-*cky*," Guy observed dryly. "I wish I were that popular."

"It doesn't help me make up my mind," Willie responded with a rueful grin. But, as it turned out, it did.

Marian, in the fashion he was coming to expect and regard as a permanent facet of her nature, greeted him with apparent excitement and pleasure when he pulled up to the Union in Smitty's Cord, the universal—and much-desired—solution when someone didn't have a car. Willie had not seen what he now always thought of with a shiver as his "death car" since the night of the accident. It had been taken away, a total wreck, to the junkyard next morning and there had presumably been destroyed along with its physical evidence of that awful occasion. His father had offered to stake him to another secondhand jalopy but he had said that since he only had one more quarter and then the summer at home before leaving for England, he really wouldn't need it. Smitty was so generous with his Cord and Buff with his Buick that usually no one who really needed transportation was ever left short. He had asked for the Cord deliberately to impress Marian. She seemed to be.

"It isn't a Rolls or a Lincoln," he said with a humor he was sure she wouldn't get, and she said, "Oh, it's *much* nicer. And so uncommon, too. That's what's really fun."

"I know," he said. "So many people have Rollses and Lincolns."

"Quite a few," she said seriously. "It really gets kind of boring."

From there the discussion went on into other aspects of rich versus modest living. He couldn't entirely suppress his irony and by the time they reached the City they had, as usual, failed to see eye to eye on something, she had taken it personally, and they were again traveling in not very amicable silence.

Christ, he thought. Here we go again.

For a time, however, relatively easy companionship was restored by the social necessity of responding to the greetings of their host and hostess, and by the bright if somewhat vapid (he thought) conversational contributions of Marian's society friends. He hadn't quite realized—they didn't talk like that much in "a small farming community in the San Joaquin Valley"—how much verbal mileage could be made from country clubs (who belonged and who didn't)—golf—tennis—parties past and future—the house at Lake Tahoe—the trip to Europe ("Better steer clear, hadn't you?" "Oh, we aren't afraid of the war talk. Who'd be stupid enough to start another war?")—Franklin Roosevelt ("Honestly, that *man!*" "I'll bet he'll get his third term in '40, though. You can fool enough of the people enough of the time") the stock market ("You ought to get into some of these new airline stocks. They don't look like much now, but my broker tells me there's a good future in them")—colleges ("Daddy says *anybody* can go to Stanford. He wants me to go to Vassar and Bob Junior to Yale").

And so on, it seemed to Willie, ad infinitum: an endless buzzing babble that overrode the valiantly striving orchestra and continued unabated through dances, intermissions and, finally, an eleven-o'clock snack and "Good Night, Ladies."

Through it all he and Marian enjoyed their usual on-again-off-again-gone-again-Finnegan relationship: one minute, he thought, relaxed and easy, the next tense and arm's length.

Guy had said, "Promise me you'll give it one more chance, and then knock it off. You aren't going anywhere."

He had shrugged and smiled and said, "Oh, I'm not that pessimistic, yet."

"Be pessimistic," Guy ordered. "Believe me."

And presently, as the evening wore on—and it did wear, he thought at last, it was wearing him to a frazzle—he began to come reluctantly to the conclusion that Guy was right. They weren't going anywhere. Whatever the attraction had been—and looking back he could dimly glimpse something of the original excitement, there must have been *some* reason for it but he couldn't say exactly now—it had gradually been eaten up by her constant shifts of mood.

You just have too many problems, sister, he thought as "Good Night, Ladies" overtook them, surveying her with half-closed eyes through his and everybody else's cigarette smoke. Maybe Mary's fault, maybe Walter's, maybe just your own. Anyway, too much for me. I need a little more stability in my life and in my emotions, thank you. I don't know exactly for what, yet, but I do need it. So, goodbye.

Which he did not in any way convey to her as they danced the farewell dance. The mood then was friendly—or relieved, he thought ironically, I'm not sure which. It remained friendly on the drive back to campus, which he took a little more slowly than usual. The Cord was really a fearsome responsibility, though no one so far had put even the slightest scratch on it. He wasn't about to be the first.

Their conversation down the Bayshore was a continuation of what she had engaged in all evening, mildly gossipy, mildly personal, mildly uninteresting: a barrier, he felt. He fed it with apparently attentive questions about this one and that one, not really interested but keeping it alive because he didn't want one last silence to develop and become uncomfortable.

At the Union he gave her a chaste kiss on the cheek, chastely returned; asked her to give his best to her parents and Cee "and don't forget Dora and Flip," which made her laugh a little; said "See you soon" with a formality to which she responded with an equally formal "Oh, I hope so" . . . and went home to tell Guy, just back from dinner with Maggie at L'Omelette, followed by Charles Laughton and Elsa Lanchester in *The Beachcomber* at the Varsity Theater, "It's all over."

"Big drama?" Guy inquired.

Wilson smiled, a trifle grimly.

"Slow fade-out."

And that was what he made it in the ensuing weeks, stopping to chat when he ran into her accidentally on the Quad or in the Libe, treating her to a Coke at the Cellar a couple of times when they happened to meet there, inquiring politely about her classes, asking after her folks—and not calling her again or varying from an attitude of cordial but completely impersonal friendliness.

"You're so—so *polite*," she said once with a troubled little half-laugh, sounding quite disturbed; but she never went further to try to find out why, or to break through his reserve. He never provided her with an opportunity when she perhaps could have.

"You're pretty formidable when you decide to be remote," Latt had told him once, kiddingly but not so kiddingly; and he guessed he could be, all right. But damn it, he didn't think it was his fault, when everything was balanced out.

He decided that his mind was made up; he would just stick to it.

And, gradually, whatever had been was no more.

And that left Donna.

"Go for it!" Guy advised during what turned out to be their last joint visit to the City.

Beginning with the formal dinner at her house, he found that he was; and suddenly he felt as though a great weight had been lifted from his shoulders. The damned things you could get yourself into just by *thinking*, the knots you could tie yourself up in when you let your mind become obsessed by something, particularly a girl! Starting from a casual glimpse at the Cellar on Reg Day, autumn quarter, he had built this whole superstructure of interest, concern, imagination; expended a fair amount of time, energy and emotion; persuaded himself that what he now recognized as the remotest of possibilities might actually become reality; convinced himself for a while that nothing was something. It had been foolish, really: just plain silly. He could see that now. "Green-gold girl" was a romantic concept but it hadn't worn well. He thanked whatever lucky stars might be for the combination of things that had finally made him recognize its evanescent nature and the problems inherent in it, and pull away.

He only hoped Marian had reached the same conclusion without too much unhappiness. He didn't think she had the capacity to feel anything very deeply, but he didn't want her to be hurt.

Which was damned big of him, he thought wryly.

But there it was.

He arrived a little early at Donna's house for the dinner, and for the first few minutes was entertained by two of the new pledges, looking very young, very fresh, very starry-eyed, absolutely thrilled to death to have the chance for a private talk with the student-body president. If he had been Gulbransen, he thought, he would have had their names and measurements memorized by the time Donn came floating down the stairs five minutes later, looking even fresher, more starry-eyed and, if possible, more youthful than they. But he wasn't, and turned away, smiling benignly, to greet his vice-president with a sudden surge of warmth and pleasure that quite surprised him. Good old Donn! Beautiful old Donn! *Lovely* old Donn! What a difference a day makes, according to one of Haggerty's standards. How true, how true, thought Richard Emmett Wilson.

"Hi," she said, reaching up with a casual possessiveness to straighten the rented bow tie adorning the rented shirt of his rented tuxedo. "I'm really glad you could come. Everybody's thrilled about your being here. What do you think we ought to do about banning cars on Lasuen Street from English Corner to the post office?"

His response was laughter, startled but affectionate.

"Business, business!" he exclaimed. "Always business! This is a social night, Donn."

"Well, I know," she said with a little smile that poked fun at herself, "but I just thought since we have to take it up in Excom next week—"

"Leave it there," he ordered, and surveyed her with approval. "You look great."

"Thank you," she said, blushing. "So do you. And thank you for the orchid. It's beautiful."

"I won't be able to pay my house rent this month, but oh well. If you're happy."

"I am," she said, with a brilliant smile, taking his arm to steer him gently toward the living room. "I've missed you these last few weeks."

"Once a week in Excom," he pointed out, but she shook her head.

"*That* isn't what I mean. As you know very well. Talk about 'business, business'! How is Marian Emerson?"

He stopped, laughed, started to feel a little annoyed, then realized he wasn't at all. It just no longer mattered.

"Fine," he responded casually. "I saw her last night. She seemed to be doing O.K."

"That's good," she said. "I guess," she added brightly, "that I'm lucky to have caught you for this dinner, with your social schedule."

"It's not so fantastic," he said, "Pretty dull, actually."

"But with a lot of Marian," she suggested, giving him a shy but inquisitive glance. He shrugged. "Very little, actually." He hesitated for a second, thinking: Advantage, advantage. But he found he didn't mind giving it to her anymore. "After last night," he added thoughtfully, "I doubt if I'll be seeing her again."

"Oh," she said, trying not to sound pleased. "Did you have a fight?" And added quickly and sincerely, "Forgive me, that's none of my business. I *am* sorry."

He gave her a perfectly friendly and unperturbed smile.

"It's all right. No, we didn't—at least, not exactly. She's a—a rather difficult girl, in some ways. Very pretty—"

"Oh, beautiful."

"—and very bright, but—I don't know. She's very tense, I think, underneath. Difficult. It was a dance at the Frantic given by some East Bay friends of hers. Pretty dull, I'm afraid. We parted friends—I think. But I don't think I'll bother anymore." He squeezed her hand on his arm. "I think I'll stick with more mature women from now on. More fitting." He grinned. "Don't you think?"

"I wouldn't presume to tell you," she said with a rather breathless little laugh as they entered the living room to face the full flood of formal femininity and tuxedoed masculinity, among whom he was surprised to see Bob Godwin, Tony Andrade and Tim Bates.

"You'll be available, though?" he asked under his breath as her house president came forward to greet him.

"Oh!" she said. "Willie!"

"Good," he said comfortably. "I'm counting on that."

And all the rest of the evening, which was done very nicely, tables for eight set up in the dining and living rooms, "candlelight and the works," as he described it to Franky and Guy later, he realized that she was even more conscious of him than usual . . . blushed more . . . laughed more . . . and her somewhat proprietary air where he was concerned seemed to be just a shade more pronounced than usual.

"And you know?" he said thoughtfully. "I didn't seem to mind it at all."

"That's it," Guy said. "You're done for."

He didn't know whether he was or not, but in any event it was a very enjoyable evening, as he told her very sincerely when he said good night and prepared to walk back to the house with Timmy, Bob and Tony through the balmy late-spring darkness.

On a sudden impulse he asked her at the door what she was doing Sunday night, she said nothing, and he arranged on the spot for dinner at Sticky's, to be followed by *Love Affair* with Irene Dunne and Charles Boyer. Not only that, but he found himself adding, "Hold next Saturday open, if you haven't anything else." And arranging to take her to lunch prior to Excom meeting on Tuesday.

"My God," remarked Tim, who had overheard most of this, "you're really going to town with Donn all of a sudden, aren't you?"

"He's a senior," Tony said as they walked along the Row together. "He's getting old. Time is fast a-fleeting. Poor baby!"

"Well," he retorted with unusual mildness, "she *is* a nice girl."

"Did you just find that out now?" Tim demanded. "You've known her for four years."

"I know," he said, "but somehow it's different all of a sudden. I don't know why. Anyway," he concluded with more customary vigor, "you bastards can just eat your hearts out. I'm going to date Donna!"

Tim smiled.

"So you're going to date Donna! Big deal!"

"Keep an eye on him," Bob Godwin suggested with a laugh. "It may be."

And before Willie knew it, it was.

Suddenly it seemed, as Franky remarked a week or two later, "It's Donna, Donna, Donna, all the time!"

"So?" Willie demanded. "That's bad?"

"No, it's not bad," Franky replied cheerfully. "It's great. We're just happy to see you doing what we've all wanted you to do, right along. That noise you hear is your fraternity brothers applauding. Go to it. You've got a lot of catching up to do."

"Oh, I don't know," he said with a grin. "All it takes is to say 'Will you marry me?' and you're all caught up, just like that."

"Ho, ho!" Haggerty exclaimed. "Listen to that arrogant bastard! I hope Donna doesn't let you off that easy. I hope she makes you sweat it out good and plenty!"

"We'll see," he said with a joking complacency. "We'll see."

Actually, as they realized, he wasn't all that confident; which, they agreed, was good for him.

"He needs to be humbled a little," sagely remarked Gulbransen, who never was, never had been and probably never would be. "He's had things his own way with the women on this campus too long."

Which brought raucous laughter, cries of "Look who's talking!"—"Meet Mr. Humble!"—and the like.

"Just the same," Gil said, rising above it, "it won't hurt Willie to have to crawl to her a little bit. I just hope she plays hard to get and doesn't say yes too quickly."

But as it turned out, she did; and as it turned out, no harm was done, because somehow they both seemed at last to be in complete agreement that it was inevitable, so why procrastinate?

He planned for several weeks, during which he saw her frequently both in their official capacities and in more social contexts, the time, the place and the way in which he would go about broaching the subject; and, as often happens with predictable plans involving unpredictable emotions, it didn't happen that way at all.

It happened, as it should have happened, during a walk along the Quad, with the campus quiet, drowsy, half deserted and utterly peaceful, on a beautiful afternoon in mid-May shading gently from spring into summer. It happened, as Donn often said later, "exactly right."

They had seen a lot of each other during the previous month or so—"You're getting as bad as Janie and me," Billy couldn't resist kidding him—but it still hadn't seemed quite right to say anything, just yet. They had studied together the previous night, had a date for dinner and a movie tomorrow night. This particular day he hadn't really expected to see her at all.

He was wandering idly along the Outer Quad after stopping to chat with Ari Katanian and other friends who had congregated around English Corner as students often did on sleepy good-weather afternoons. He had presently said so-long and strolled lazily away with no particular plan, no specific destination: just walking. It was peaceful, it was beautiful, it was great to be young and alive. War and rumors of war were far away, classes were moving well, no crises of any kind loomed to disturb the last weeks of his presidency. Everything was perfect, the world was drifting . . . drifting . . .

He was just about to jump down from the colonnade, stretch out on the grass, put his binder under his head and take a nap, when some distance ahead he saw her come out of one of the classrooms and start off in the opposite direction. She didn't glance his way and he watched her for a moment, finding the sight of her tall, determined figure somehow very touching as she strode along. He couldn't have said why it touched him, it just did. He watched for a moment and then cupped his hands and called. *"Donna!"* echoed down the arches. She stopped abruptly and turned back with a smile that quite literally lit up her face. It was at that moment that he decided, as he told Unruh in some puzzlement later, that "this was it."

"I don't know why," he confessed. "It just was."

"That's the way it happens," Guy said with the wisdom acquired from his one month's lead with Maggie.

"Hi!" he called. "Stay there. I'll join you."

"What are you up to?" she asked as he caught up. She looked very pleased, with that extra excited little glow he had begun to notice lately when they met. And in himself too, he acknowledged: no need to be superior about it. His reaction when he saw her was becoming very special too. Quite emotional, *quite* physical. Rather unsettling and tending to make him feel somewhat removed from reality. Rather as though he had been lifted onto some other plane where his feet didn't quite connect with the ground. And with such a *rightness* about it. He had been in love once or twice before but it had never seemed so *right*.

So comfortable.

So settled.

So all-loose-ends-suddenly-wrapped-up-in-one-perfect-package-with-no-more-worries-about-anything.

"Hey!" she said with a laugh, snapping her fingers in front of his eyes. "Come back, come back, wherever you are! I said, what are you up to?"

He grinned and shook his head, blinking his eyes with exaggerated vigor.

"Just walking. It's too beautiful to stay indoors. Or study. Or do anything serious. Why don't you join me?"

"Well, I was just on my way," she said slowly, "to see Armpits McGee about a special paper I'm going to write for her—" then a happy smile broke out— "but I think that can wait. Where are we going?"

He shrugged.

"Oh, I don't care. Around the Quad, maybe? Governor's Lane? Over to the lake? The golf course? You name it."

"Let's just do the Quad . . . and then maybe to the lake . . . or over to the museum—"

"Or maybe just walk round the Quad and then sit in the sun and get a tan. How's that?"

"Sure. You've got a good one already."

"Lake time. So do you."

"Lake time . . ." Again she started to tuck her hand in his arm but he disengaged himself firmly and instead took her hand in his. She blushed.

"Why, Mr. Wilson! Isn't that rather fresh? In front of God and everybody?"

"To hell with 'em," he said complacently and then grinned. "Not *you*, God, of course, but everybody else. Give me your books."

When she complied he squeezed her hand. She returned the pressure, at first timidly, then with a relaxed confidence.

"I think it's fun to walk along the Quad," she said thoughtfully. "I find I'm doing it quite a lot these days. I realized the other day I was actually going out of my way." She sighed humorously. "Oh, Willie! Why do we have to grow up! *I* don't want to leave this place!"

"You and a thousand others. Including me. It *is* beautiful, isn't it?"

And for several moments as they walked along hand in hand they were silent, contemplating the sweep of lawn away from the Quad to the Ellipse

and on up Palm Drive . . . which still held too many memories. He looked
quickly away, back to the sandstone arches and the long, echoing colonnade.

"I wonder what Oxford is like?" she said. "Have you ever been there?"

"No, never been out of the country except down to Tijuana once, years
ago when we were kids. I doubt if it can be as beautiful as this, but I'm sure
it's got something." He smiled. "Eight hundred years of Englishmen can't
be wrong."

"Are you beginning to get excited about going?"

"Oh, yes. Yes, it's going to be great."

"I just hope there isn't a war," she said, and the pressure of her hand on
his became convulsively stronger.

"I, too," he said soberly.

"Are you going right over after graduation?"

"No, I've about decided to stay on campus for summer quarter. Some of
us have started taking an air reserves training course—"

"I didn't know that!" she said, sounding apprehensive and quite dismayed.

"We haven't told many people because a lot of 'em think it's hysterical—
borrowing trouble—and letting our imaginations run away with us, as Bill
Nagatani told me the other day. He's going to run a story about us next
week, and no doubt one of his amiably put-down editorials. A lot of people
can't understand why we're doing it. We just want to be prepared a little bit,
that's all."

"Who's 'we'?"

"Tim and Hack and Buff and Guy and Duke Offenberg. And me. And
Moose, in the ground crew." He laughed. "Poor old Mooser starts to throw
up the minute he hears the propellers start, but he's game. He'll make it."

"Are you all staying over?"

"We're going to keep the house open for whoever's going to stay. Dewey
will be gone so we'll have to rustle our own breakfasts and eat other meals
out, I guess—otherwise it will be just for sleeping purposes only. It should
be fun. We're getting kind of excited about it."

Her usual cheerful expression clouded over.

"You men like war, don't you? You think it's coming and you think it's
awful but you're 'getting kind of excited about it.' "

"Well," he said honestly, "you may be right. I've never been in one, of
course, but from what I read and from listening to some of the veterans down
home, it's like a separate world. It's like a great game outside reality, where
you can forget all the other cares and responsibilities of the everyday world
and just exist in some other place, with different rules."

"In which grown-up men," she said with a sudden bitterness that was
quite uncharacteristic—he guessed she'd been doing a lot of thinking about
it, too, behind the happy public exterior—"use awful toys to do awful things
to one another in this great game of theirs. I don't like it!" She looked for a

second as though she might cry. "I don't like the thought of you being involved! I'm afraid!"

"You mustn't be," he said as they rounded Engineering Corner and continued their slow stroll along the arcades of their youth. "I'll be all right."

"Maybe," she said bleakly, again clinging to his hand with an almost desperate pressure. "And maybe not. . . ." Then the tension seemed to ease. She glanced at him with a sudden shy little smile. "I may be staying over summer quarter, too."

"Oh?" he said, finding that where a few weeks ago he might have felt a little besieged by this, it now made him genuinely pleased and happy. "Good! How come?"

"Dr. Chalmers asked me. He said he's thinking of establishing a regular public relations office and he said he thought I would be good at it, if I wanted a job." She laughed. "When he got through persuading me, which took about one minute, he said, 'I think perhaps Willie is going to be staying over, too.' I think he may have a job in mind for you, too."

He uttered a startled laugh and shook his head.

"That guy never misses a trick. I did mention it to him a couple of weeks ago. Trust him to work something out. For us both."

"Do you mind?" she asked shyly. She looked very serious. "I mean, it *was* his idea. I didn't—"

He stopped dead and gave her a look of mock indignation.

"No, I don't mind, silly girl! I think it's wonderful. I've been trying to figure out how I could keep you here myself."

"You have?" she said with a disbelief that at first didn't dare yield to happiness, then suddenly dissolved into what Franky called "Donn's sunflower smile." "That's very nice of you, Willie."

"Huh!" he said. "It's more than that, girl. Is *that* all you can say about it, 'very nice'? It's practically a declaration of intent!"

Which, as he told Guy, wasn't exactly what he had meant to say, "but somehow it just popped out."

The result was sensational.

She flung her arms around his neck and squealed, "*Oh! Oh! Oh!*"—half laughing and, it seemed, half crying. Then she stopped abruptly and looked at him with great intensity.

"Do you mean that?" she demanded. "And don't make any of your silly jokes, Willie Wilson! I want a straight answer! *This is important.*"

"Yes, yes, *yes!*" he said, beginning to laugh with a great and wonderful relief. "No joke! I mean it, I mean it! O.K.?"

"*Yes!*" she cried. "It's O.K.!"

"Then you will?"

"*Yes!*" she cried again. "Oh, yes, yes, *yes!*"

And much to their surprise and amusement, fellow students who happened to be walking along the Quad at that moment were treated to the unexpected but obviously genuine spectacle of the president and vice-president of the student body locked in considerably more than official embrace.

After that, for perhaps another hour, they just wandered, hand in hand, through the singing springtime.

Up to the lake. To the golf course beyond. Back down to the Quad. Over to the museum. Back to the Quad. Winding up, finally, seated on the lawn, leaning back against the base of the colonnade. Still holding hands. Not saying much. Just learning to be together quietly, without forced conversation. Not worried about Excom, student problems, student activities, all the other hectic business of hectic days that had always seemed to inhibit such peaceable association before.

The afternoon drew on, shadows began to grow upon the grass.

Finally she sighed and said, "I guess I'd better get back. I have a lot of studying to do."

"Me too."

He unwound his lanky length, stood up, brushed off his pants, held down a hand to help her. Almost without conscious volition, it moved to her hair, where it rested.

"I love you," he said.

She looked up at him steadily.

"And I you," she said quietly.

He realized later that in that moment, given form and substance and articulated at last, it began to be true.

They remained so for several more moments, perfectly still, his hand on her hair, the lovely, singing springtime all around.

"And that," he told a raucously applauding house at dinner that night, "is how it all came about. It was all Dr. Chalmers' fault."

"You ought to call him and tell him so," Buff suggested. So after dinner, he did.

"Yes?" the gravely dignified voice came over from the President's House on the knoll above campus.

"I just wanted you to know, sir," Willie said without introduction, "that your little scheme succeeded."

"What scheme is that?"

"You will be pleased to hear that Miss Donnamaria Van Dyke and I seem to be engaged. And all because you arranged for her to stay over summer quarter to keep me company."

The president chuckled.

"There was more to it than that, Willie. I offered a very bright young lady a job in which I think she can perform excellent service for the University. I may have one for you too, if you care to drop by and see me. But actually your presence was quite coincidental, as far as Donna was concerned."

"And you," Willie demanded, realizing he was being quite daring but carried away by euphoria, "expect me to believe that, sir?"

"Believe what you like," Dr. Chalmers said serenely. "The whole thing is a *magnificent* idea. Congratulations! I can't think of two nicer, brighter, more outstanding—anyway, if you decide to get married in Memorial Church, invite Mrs. Chalmers and me. We'd love to come."

"We'll probably do that," he said, "and we'd be very honored if you do come." He laughed happily, ten feet off the ground. "After all, sir, we've all been through a lot together!"

"That we have," Dr. Chalmers said with a laugh, thinking how many of these boys and girls there had been down the years and how many things they had all been through together. "Give my love to Donna."

Which was such an uncharacteristic unbending that Willie couldn't resist calling Donn immediately to tell her; after which, by Unruh's count, he related it in the house on at least ten separate occasions over the next two days.

So the positives, the in-betweens and the not-just-yets all got fitted into their places in nature's scheme of things as senior year drew ever more quickly to a close. And for them, for the others in the house, for the University, the country, the world, the calendar moved on inexorably toward the somber day in 1939 when September would return again.

23

Before it did, and with it war, Bob Godwin ran for the office of student-body president for the academic year 1940 and was elected by a vote of 1,123 to 1,001—closer than he had anticipated and closer than he liked. But Willie advised that victory was victory, so relax and enjoy it.

Tony Andrade, Loren Davis and Johnny Herbert continued their amicable lopsided camaraderie with "the cousins," Angie D'Alessandro and Louise Gianfalco, making frequent trips up to Napa Valley for pleasant weekends with Lou's father at his house in the vineyard, which he was rapidly expanding with the purchase of one hundred acres on one side and the start of negotiations for another sixty on the other side.

Smitty Carriger, president, working with Ray Baker, supervised a general sprucing-up of the house that included work teams to apply new paint to the exterior; other work teams to dig up and reseed the lawn; the replacement out of his own pocket and Buff's of two floor-dragging sofas in the living room; and strict economies in the kitchen which produced agonized threats from Dewey to "up and quit" but resulted (after he was told politely but firmly, "O.K., go ahead," and thereupon subsided, though with continuing muffled grumbles) in substantial savings and even some recognizable if modest improvements in menu.

Galen Bryce and Renny Suratt, thrown together increasingly by the general disapproval of their brethren, became even more, as North put it, "the two ravens who sit above our door crying, 'Nevermore!' "; but after being on the receiving end of their stinging sarcasms and arch psychological analyses an unbelievable number of times, their tolerantly patient housemates finally gave up and left them to their apparently desired isolation. "They deserve each other," Franky said.

Duke Offenberg, bolstered and supported as always by Shahna, went steadily ahead adding grade points to the high academic average that was taking him straight toward Phi Beta Kappa and the career in academic administration that was his goal—if, as they often agreed apprehensively, the world survived the war they were convinced was coming, and "things" worked out all right for them.

Among the sophomores, Billy Wilson had featured roles in two of the major productions of spring quarter, and wrote his first play, which concerned the happy love affair of a boy and girl at a famous Western university. His brother told him encouragingly that parts of it were very good but that possibly a subject from which he could distance himself a little more—? Billy looked a little shamefaced and agreed. His second effort involved a castle in Europe, a dispossessed heir, a beautiful contessa—Willie said that wasn't quite it, either. Undaunted, Billy started again. Willie told him he was proud of him and he was obviously going to make it one of these days. "I am," Billy said firmly; and neither of them doubted it for a moment.

Jeff Barnett, his cheerfully amiable, puppy-dog personality surviving a bad cold toward the end of winter quarter (a lot of people got them along about that time, Tony and Lor, Rodge Leighton, Hank Moore), bounced back to captain the swim team, moved up the tennis ladder and gradually acquired a well-publicized string of girlfriends that appeared likely in time to challenge Gulbransen's record.

Rodge and Hank, "the diligents" as Franky called them, went soberly and industriously about their days being earnest, hardworking students, steady, reliable citizens, and pleasant, supportive, always dependable friends.

Marc Taylor, returning for spring quarter, was shy and diffident at first but soon relaxed when he realized the warmth of the welcome that awaited him. He reported that he had flown to Albuquerque en route from Pennsylvania and had stopped off to spend two days with Randy at the ranch "because he was awfully nice to me when I—I wasn't—myself, and I wanted to see if I couldn't cheer him up." Randy, he reported, was still in his cast but was looking forward eagerly to getting his brace and coming back fall quarter. "He's really an awful lot better than he was, mentally," Marc said; adding with a shy smile, "So am I." His elders slapped him heartily on the back, assured him that they could see that, and breathed a collective sigh of relief for him and Randy.

Nobody heard from Rudy Krohl. Once in a while they would see him on the Quad but he snubbed their tentative efforts to say hello, so presently they stopped trying. The aura of his uncomfortable presence finally seemed to dissipate from the house, although, as Tim pointed out, the "things" Duke and Shahna worried about, the "things" that Rudy believed in, did not disappear in America but in fact increased steadily and ominously throughout 1939 as Hitler's belligerence grew and war became ever more imminent.

Few saw By Johnson, either. His basketball career continued to be brilliant, he and Guy worked side by side with reasonable cooperation, but the wall was there and after a few lingering attempts Guy, too, gave up trying to breach it. "It's all strictly business now," he told Willie; Willie shrugged, though he looked pained. He too saw By from time to time on the Quad, almost always accompanied by Maryetta. By gave him a shy nod and tentative smile, which he returned as cordially as he could before Maryetta gave him a glare and yanked By along. His eyes said: *You little bitch.* And hers said: *You son of a bitch.* Superior and triumphant, she remained, undeniably and evidently unchallengeably, in charge.

Napoleon developed a bad limp in his right hind leg and for a while began to lose his appetite. Buff and Ray took him to the vet, who didn't have much to offer except a vague "Of course, he *is* getting to be a pretty old dog, you know, and you may have to think eventually about—" But nobody wanted to think about that, so they brought him home, hovered over him with extra milk, ice cream, special steaks, dog food and bones, and presently the appetite seemed to recover and the limp virtually disappeared. Another collective sigh of relief went through the house.

Josephine delivered what must have been, they calculated, her tenth litter, two toms and a female. The DGs took the female, the Betas took the two toms, and everybody, particularly Josephine, who received many strokes, pats, coos and congratulations, was happy.

The wanderer of the Quad, true to his word and the orders of his elders, wandered no more, at least along the Quad. He did not, however, fade away from pining, as Hack and Buff and Wilson noted dryly, so they supposed he must be going elsewhere. But as long as he kept his part of the bargain they kept theirs, and nobody but the four of them, North and Happy Harmon ever had the remotest idea.

The life of the campus, buoyed by music, bracketed by movies, shaken in varying degrees by events of the great world, moved on through that heartbreakingly beautiful, nostalgic spring.

The Dramatists' Alliance held its annual competition. Billy won second prize for his boy-girl romance, after all, and was greatly encouraged.

Something called the "John Steinbeck Committee," chaired by Maryetta, raised a satisfying amount of used clothing for distribution to Okie migrants in the San Joaquin Valley.

The author-journalist John Gunther spoke at the Tuesday-night lecture series and predicted of Great Britain that "with her military might increasing rapidly, we can count on a more cautious Hitler on the Continent."

The author-journalist Vincent Sheean, more prescient, speaking from the same platform a month later, flatly predicted "the outbreak of general European war in the next six months which, if carried on to any extent, will eventually involve the United States."

Under the auspices of the University Speakers' Bureau, forty-four students were furnished to address service clubs in the Bay Area. Tim spoke to the local chamber of commerce, as ominously as Vincent Sheean and with the extra urgency of youth. He received respectful applause but a good many patronizing chuckles and pats on the shoulders. "It isn't coming, boy, and even if it ever does, *we're* not going in! You can get *that* bugaboo out of your mind!"

The Peace Council (Maryetta Bradford, secretary) organized a "Peace Day" in April; offered pamphlets to read, buttons to wear, petitions to sign; drew a couple of hundred; felt good about it.

Excom, meeting every Tuesday, continued to grapple with the problems that faced the campus: traffic beginning to build up a bit—a water fight in one of the dorms that resulted in fines being levied when it was discovered that one of the balloons had been filled with red paint—windows broken in two houses on the Row and one student quite severely injured as the result of food fights after dinner (the house had a couple, but, under strict rules, nobody threw plates, only contents, so it was all right)—too much romancing out near the stadium, which brought new rules about parking after dark and extra work for Happy and his new assistant authorized by the Board—the hotly debated question of whether to expand hours at the post office and the bookstore—"and all those other kinds of monumentally important crap," as the student-body president confided to Unruh. "You asked for it," Guy reminded him.

The U.S. Naval Reserve pilot training program offered special ground and flight training at the Oakland reserve station, to be followed by advanced training in Pensacola, Florida, and a brief tour with the fleet. Tim and the group considered it but decided to stick with the army, particularly in view of Guy's and Willie's commitments to go to England in the fall.

The annual Convalescent Home Drive was held to benefit the eighty-bed children's facility maintained by the University. A hot, dusty, convivial student-faculty "Labor Day" was held to spruce up the grounds. The annual Water Carnival and Masque Ball raised funds.

Each of the classes held dances, picnics, other social affairs. Row and hall entertained. Basketball, baseball, track, swimming, golf, tennis, polo, intramural sports continued their strenuous programs.

Many students drove over the newly opened Golden Gate Bridge to enjoy the unspoiled beauties of Marin County. Many more visited the newly opened Golden Gate Exposition on Treasure Island, jutting into the Bay off Yuerba Buena Island, midpoint of the newly opened Bay Bridge between San Francisco and Oakland. The exposition's columns, spires, gigantic statues and cascading waterfalls created a magic world that for a few pleasant hours exorcised the oncoming demons of war.

Many boys dated many girls. Many romances succeeded. Many failed. The average was maintained.

The busy, self-centered life of the University rolled on.

On May 1 Neville Chamberlain warned Germany that Great Britain would fight if Danzig was invaded or if Hitler otherwise threatened the independence of Poland.

On May 7 Hitler and Mussolini met to formally transform the Axis from "a working agreement with cultural constructions" to a full-fledged military pact.

On May 15 a straw poll conducted by Maryetta and friends found that a majority of the students who responded favored economic (but not military) aid to Great Britain and France "even though they find German-Italian activities unfairly represented in the American press."

Late in the spring Roos Brothers men's store in town announced a sale of complete suits ranging in price from $26.50 to $34.50. Dr. Chalmers and the trustees announced that fall-quarter room rents would go up to $15 for women, $9 for men.

And there were movies: *Campus Confessions*, with Betty Grable . . . *Out West with the Hardys*, with Mickey Rooney and Lewis Stone . . . *Jesse James*, with Tyrone Power, Henry Fonda and Nancy Kelly . . . *The Great Waltz*, with Luise Rainer, Fernand Gravet and Miliza Korjus . . . *Dawn Patrol*, with Errol Flynn, Basil Rathbone and David Niven . . . *Idiot's Delight*, with Norma Shearer and Clark Gable . . . *Gunga Din*, with Cary Grant, Victor McLaglen and Douglas Fairbanks, Jr. . . . *Three Musketeers*, with Don Ameche . . . *Paris Honeymoon*, with Bing Crosby . . . *St. Louis Blues*, with Dorothy Lamour . . . *You Can't Cheat an Honest Man*, with W. C. Fields . . . *The Oklahoma Kid*, with James Cagney . . . *Made for Each Other*, with Carole Lombard and James Stewart . . . Garbo in *Ninotchka* . . . *The Story of Vernon and Irene Castle*, with Fred Astaire and Ginger Rogers . . . *Three Smart Girls*, with Deanna Durbin . . . *The Little Princess*, with Shirley Temple . . . *Dark Victory*, with Bette Davis . . . and with excitement building as the premiere in Atlanta drew near, already part of the legend, part of the dream, Scarlett and the red earth of Tara and *Gone with the Wind* . . .

And there was music, which their children, subjects of a lesser god, would call "the big-band sound," lush and heavy, pouring from a thousand radios, blasting from old-fashioned turntables or the new, expensive high-fidelity record players of such as Smitty, coming from car radios, coming from everywhere, resounding up and down the Row, booming through the halls, constant accompaniment to life except in periods of darkest night just before midterms and finals when SILENCE was enforced, more or less successfully, with suitable emphasis and profanity . . . the sounds of a generation, the favorites of a nation on the edge of—what? Nobody could say for sure, but the songs were familiar as skin, comforting as Mother—

Duke Ellington and "Caravan" . . . Jimmy Dorsey's rendition of "So Rare" . . . Bing Crosby and "Sweet Leilani" . . . Bob Hope and "Thanks for the Memory" . . . the Andrews Sisters and "Bei Mir Bist Du Schoen" . . .

"That Old Feeling" . . . "Where or When" . . . "A Foggy Day in London Town" . . . ever-lovely "Stardust" . . . Ella Fitzgerald and "A-tisket, A-tasket" . . . "Falling in Love with Love" . . . Mary Martin and "My Heart Belongs to Daddy" . . . Walter Huston and "September Song" . . . "Music, Maestro, Please" . . . "You Must Have Been a Beautiful Baby" . . . "Deep Purple" . . . Benny Goodman's rendition of "And the Angels Sing" . . . the Andrews Sisters and "Beer Barrel Polka" . . . Bunny Berrigan and "I Can't Get Started with You" . . . Kate Smith and "God Bless America" . . . "Brazil" . . . "I'll Never Smile Again" . . . Judy Garland and "Over the Rainbow" . . . "Moonlight Serenade" and "Sunrise Serenade" . . . Ray Noble's "The Very Thought of You" . . . Count Basie's "One O'clock Jump" . . . and always and always, ubiquitous, inescapable, universal, Tommy Dorsey's rendition of "Boogie Woogie," Glenn Miller's rendition of "In the Mood," Duke Ellington and "Take the A-Train" . . .

So spring turned ever faster toward summer.

And the days dwindled down, as Walter Huston had it, to a precious few.

24

A certain indefinable bustle about the house. A growing excitement in the air, particularly among the seniors. A happy tension, challenging, stimulating and nostalgic all in one. The phone seeming to ring almost constantly, followed by bellows up the stairs of "Willie!" or whoever. The sound of showers going steadily every afternoon and early evening as members prepared themselves for this or that social occasion. The loud conversations, shouted above the rushing waters, about who had made Phi Bete (Wilson, Unruh, McAllister). The completion of final exams, really final for Moose, Buff, Franky, Tim, still only preliminary to many others for the future Oxonians, Guy and Willie, the pre-meds Guy, North and Gil, the pre-legal Ray and, perhaps, Willie.

The summer plans of the air reserve group: Tim, Willie, Buff and Duke arranging to stay on to complete their preliminary training, Tim taking over Nagatani's stringer jobs for City newspapers when Bill returned to Fresno for the time being to help his ailing father on their truck-garden farm; Buff drawing on family reserves; Willie starting on his duties as part-time file clerk in the president's office; North and Guy still undecided but considering part-time work at the Convalescent Home after their marriages; Duke to work part-time in the office of the dean of education . . . and Moose, looking increasingly forlorn, torn between "I'm going to try to hang on somehow so I can be with you guys" and then, with real dejection, "But I know that's just a crock. I can't find anything. I'll just have to go back to Chicago and get a job with the city, like my dad."

This last situation caused real worry among his housemates until the morning of June 15, day of the senior class picnic and the dinner of house seniors that had been arranged the night Ray made hot chocolate and the air group organized itself in a burst of patriotic apprehension.

510

At about nine-fifteen the bellow came up the stairs, "Moose!" After a few moments of rousing him out of bed, where he and a lot of others were still blissfully sleeping the sleep of exhaustion following the last finals, Rodge successfully got him pointed to the phone booth.

"My God!" Haggerty exclaimed, meeting them in the hall. "What are you carrying in front of you, Moose?"

"Oh, go to hell," Moose said sleepily, brushing his hair out of his eyes and rubbing them with a rolled-up paw. "You'd be lucky to have one-tenth of that. On your best day."

"My good man!" Hack retorted. "Have you ever seen me in the shower?"

"Yes," Moose said. "You were looking for it."

Which Hack had to admit was pretty good for just getting out of bed, and with a sleepily triumphant smile Moose went on to the phone booth. There was attentive silence for about five minutes during which he could be heard saying, "Yeah? . . . Yeah? . . . YEAH?" followed by several loud whoops and a gloriously happy, "Oh, God damn! OH, GOD DAMN!"

"What *is* it?" cried Haggerty, Tony, Jeff, Franky and a half dozen others, bursting out of their rooms in some alarm, which increased when they saw their ex–football hero standing in front of the phone booth bawling like a baby.

"Hey, man!" Hack said, shaking him vigorously by the shoulder. "Hey, *buddy*, what is it?"

"I'm so *happy!*" Moose wailed, and with a sudden intuitive inspiration Hack said, "That was Coach."

Moose nodded helplessly.

"WELL?"

"He wants me—" Moose choked out—"he wants me to—to—"

"Stay at school and join the coaching staff," Hack said in a what-else-would-any-sensible-coach-do sort of voice.

Moose, completely overcome, could only nod and bawl some more.

"Yes," he managed finally. "Yes, he *does!*"

And once again dissolved while they clustered around, mussed his hair, pounded his back and generally helped him celebrate.

So that took care of Moose, and everybody was happy for him, even Suratt, who went out of his way to shake hands and say, "Good going, Moose!" in a voice that sounded quite sincere. Moose shook his head in bafflement but managed to respond with a fair show of gratitude, "Thanks, Renny." It was so nice to have everybody rooting for him again that he almost felt like forgiving the two-bit jerk for all his snot-nosed remarks all year.

At the senior picnic, too, he received congratulations from everyone, because his first move had been to call Suzy, even if he wasn't going to marry her, and tell her the news. He knew she could be counted on to spread it, and she did. The picnic was held over on the ocean at Half Moon Bay and almost the entire class was there, including Willie and Donn, Guy and Maggie, Hack and Fran, North and B.J., Franky and Katie, Gil and Karen Ann. At one point Katie, who had been a cheerleader in high school, led them in an impromptu yell based on "Give 'Em the Axe:" "Give us—our Moose! Give us—our Moose! Give us our Moose, Give us our Moose, Give us our Moose, *where*? Right on the staff, the staff, the staff, right on—" and so forth.

It was a glorious occasion for him and a very pleasant, if increasingly nostalgic, one for them all.

Then it was back to the showers—"*Jesus*, we're clean!" Franky exclaimed—and into the tuxedoes most of them had rented for their dinner that night at L'Omelette. Buff and Gil owned their own but nobody else did in that post-Depression era. Roos Brothers, as always, was the answer to everything.

They had invited Aram Katanian to join them, at the suggestion of Willie and Guy, looking back to freshman dorm. "The Three Musketeers," Guy said and Willie murmured, "Yes, now that fourth is no longer. . . ." His voice trailed away and not for the first time or the last that week, they felt a renewed deep pang for Latt, who, as Franky said, "ought to be here but . . . just . . . *isn't*. . . ."

When Hack arrived, having walked through the balmy afternoon from the halls, they lined up on the front steps in the last of the light and Smitty, who was quite an amateur photographer, took their picture.

The taller, Willie, Guy, North, Ari, Gil, stood on the top step, hands resting casually on the shoulders of the shorter just below, Ray, Moose, Franky, Hack. Tim flanked them on the right, Buff on the left. Young, earnest, some noticeably handsome and all looking noticeably nice ("If people only knew!" Buff joked when Smitty gave them copies), they gazed out upon the world with an amiable, friendly, welcoming glance.

Years and years later, in office, den, hall or bedroom, they would still be looking out from that picture with an appealing goodwill, frozen in time. Some would glance at it with a smile, some with a sigh; some would no longer be there at all and only family and friends would be left to note how young and fine and eager they had all looked in that spring of their world's dissolution . . . on the steps of the house . . . in the last of the light. . . .

After they had paid for the meal at L'Omelette, which was as always very good, the waiters withdrew, the door closed upon the private room they had rented, and they were alone together; suddenly self-conscious but fortified by the drinks they were now all old enough to order legally. They had joked and kidded, reminisced until there hardly seemed anything left to reminisce about. Buff at last rapped spoon on glass.

"No speeches!" Franky cried, feeling no pain.

"No speeches!" Buff agreed, feeling none either. "But you do want Hack to play for us one last time, don't you?"

Cries of approval, wild applause. Hack went to the piano that had been installed for them in one corner of the room and softly began to play his "Suite for Sunny Days," with its subtle intermingling of original themes and the University songs they had sung for years and would always remember. They listened in absolute silence as he went through the first five movements. Then he muted it and nodded to Wilson, who stood up and raised his glass.

"I want to propose," he said, not sure at all whether he could manage this or not, "a toast. To Latt!"

"To Latt!" they all said solemnly and drank, looking studiously at the tablecloth and not at one another.

He cleared his throat several times and said abruptly, "I wrote a poem." And launched, without other preliminary, into the tribute that had come to him in its entirety in about twenty minutes, not long after that awful night. His voice at first trembled and threatened to give out. Then it grew stronger and ended on the note of affirmation he had hoped to achieve:

> "ON YOUR DARK JOURNEYS
> "On your dark journeys down the wind, my friend,
> You go alone. No quick-remembered clasp of
>   friendship's hand,
> No laughter making light your solitary way,
> No good companions on your road to journey's
>   end.
> Naught but the night
> And one clear ray of light,
> Tossed on the passing storm . . ."
>
> It is thus we talk as, sitting snug and warm,
> We ponder on the fate of nations and of men.
> "Dust to dust" and "River to the sea," we say,
> And the puzzle of your death is solved again.
> There lingers here no doubt: all things
>   thus and so,
> Each phrase fitting in the smooth, accustomed
>   way,
> Smug words explaining what we cannot know.
> It is thus we close the blinds against the
>   rain,
> Shut out all sharp regret, all futile pain.
>
> And yet, my friend, we say your name with
>   laughter

Twice ten times for every once we say it sad,
Where we are you live, no matter what comes
after.
Yours is still the well-spoke word, the
perfect phrase,
Yours the strongfelt, deep regard you always
had.
You do not lack rememberers on happy days.
For you we do away with clinging doubt
To satisfy our hearts, which will not keep
you out.

So, when your endless travels take you far
Upon the age-thronged highways of the sky,
Pause for a moment on some outward star
And listen, ere you go for aye.

Whether you hear us still, we cannot tell.
But Godspeed, my friend. We wish you well."

He sat down slowly, and for what seemed like a long time no one attempted speech.

"God damn it," Franky said finally in a choked voice. "God *damn* it."

Hack finished playing on a high, gentle, lingering note and closed the
keyboard with a sharp, decisive sound. They stood up silently and filed out.
Nobody said much of anything on the way back to school, or later, when they
reached the house.

The days—the hours, now—sped on.

They attended class day exercises in Memorial Church on Friday, June
16, witnessed the addition of their metal plaque—"1939"—to the long procession of forty-four that already stretched down the center of the well-worn
tiles; went to the president's reception that night, where Dr. and Mrs.
Chalmers greeted them each by name, a feat that could no longer be duplicated after the war as enrollment swelled by thousands; took the girls to
the senior ball later that night and danced the night away to three in the
morning thanks to special dispensation from Dean Maggie. Those who had
been admitted to Phi Beta Kappa were initiated at a dinner on Saturday the
17th. Sunday was baccalaureate and commencement.

Wilson received the scare of his life Thursday morning when the phone
rang and he was informed that Dr. Stafford wished to see him immediately
in her office.

Oh, no, he kept saying to himself as he walked down the Quad to English Corner. Oh, *no*. That would be too pat. That would be just too much. She wouldn't dare. She just simply wouldn't dare.

But he wasn't at all sure when he mustered the determination to rap, with what he told himself encouragingly was a firm and emphatic hand, on the worn old door. He wasn't sure ay-tall, ay-tall.

"Mr. Wilson?" No scrape of chair, no movement within. She was going to make him crawl for it, all right.

"Yes," he said flatly, beginning to get mad, omitting the "ma'am." Let the old bitch do her damnedest. He wasn't going to give her the satisfaction.

"Come!" she ordered with all the imperious emphasis of the towering Tudor she loved to imitate in dress and manner.

"Yes, ma'am," he said, deciding in a split second that discretion might, after all, be the best part of valor; and opened the door to find her staring at him with what the campus called her "basilisk look"—nostrils flaring, lips drawn severely down, eyes expressionless and cold, gray bun in perfect place with not a hair out of order, red velvet jacket falling in perfect drape from her shoulders, heavily jeweled hands clasped serenely—or apparently serenely—on the desk before her. He perceived that there was the slightest tremor in her fingers, however. She's doing her best to make this an Event for me, he thought with a defensive sarcasm, but she can't quite conceal that it's an Event for her, too.

"Mr. Wilson!" she snapped as he moved instinctively toward the chair in front of the desk. "You will remain standing until I give you permission to sit!"

Sit! Speak! Roll over! he thought crazily. Silly bitch!

"Yes, ma'am," he replied, managing, though with some difficulty, to keep his voice steady. "As you like."

"Do you think you deserve anything better?" she demanded. He started to retort; stopped; reconsidered; tried to reply without emotion.

"That's up to you to decide, Dr. Stafford," he said finally. "I wouldn't presume."

"You do presume, just by—by—"

"Yes?"

"Just by being Willie Wilson, who thinks he's so perfect that ordinary mortals must bow down before him."

"But that isn't fair!" he said. "I don't think I'm so—"

He felt as thrown off-base as he had during their clash at Excom (to which she had not returned; she had resigned, as he had suggested, and hearty C, the snug and securely married Professor, had taken her place). And again he stopped.

What was the use?

"Well, sit down," she said after a moment. "You might as well. Do you think you deserve to receive a passing grade in Shakespeare's Contributions?"

"Yes, ma'am—" taking the chair—"you've given me A's and B's on my papers all quarter. Yes, I do."

"So do I," she said shortly. "But tell me, Mr. Wilson, what would be the result if I decide to fail you in the course? I still could, you know."

"Yes, ma'am. It might be hard to explain to the academic council, but—"

"Are you threatening me?" she demanded with a sudden furious indignation, eyes glaring, nostrils distended. Christ, he thought, what drama.

"No, ma'am. Are you, me?"

"I am not here to debate with you, Mr. Wilson," she said more quietly, "and I did not call you in here to have you debate with me. I am not threatening you. I am simply pointing out that if I should decide to fail you—and I still can—it would be a certain inconvenience, would it not?"

"Yes, ma'am. I'm planning to stay over most of the summer anyway, before I leave for England, but in that case I would have to take something else to make up the final three units I need to graduate. I assume you could give me that 'inconvenience' if you liked. But," he asked with genuine bafflement, "why? I've done the work for you, you've seemed to like it all right, I thought we'd been getting along reasonably well."

"With my forbearance," she said coldly. "I can barely *suffer* your arrogant, superior ways."

"But—" he said blankly. "But I'm *not* arrogant and I'm *not* superior—"

"Sometimes one of the services we can perform for you self-centered youngsters who think you own the world is to help you see yourselves as ithers see you," she said dryly, without humor. "You impress *me* very frequently as being quite insufferable. . . . Perhaps you will remember when you leave us that not everyone at the University has taken you at your own evaluation."

He started to respond; stopped, started again; stopped. As he told Guy later, he was so honestly flabbergasted by what seemed to him her completely unfair analysis and attack that he was temporarily silenced.

"You may go, Mr. Wilson," she said before he could rally himself enough to respond, which was probably just as well, he also told Guy, because it would probably have been something terrible. "You will pass my course, you will graduate *magna cum laude* and no doubt you will go on to greater glories at Oxford, provided you don't get cut down in the war, a prospect I should dislike as I dislike any waste of good human material."

Her face twisted for just a second before she froze it back into place again, and suddenly he remembered that she had told Walter Emerson that she had "lost someone over there" in the World War. Maybe that explained it, some odd, twisted resentment of himself because he was here, and young, and popular—and maybe her friend had been too. Maybe they had been going to be married, or something, and he had been cut down and he *wasn't* here and hadn't been for years and years and she had always treasured his memory and had just been forced to become a fearsome old maid instead of being part of a life that perhaps had been as bright and favored and full of promise as Willie's own—

He told himself that this was probably just romanticizing, but it was the only reason he could think of for her hostility. Maybe, in her mind, it was enough. It didn't seem entirely rational to him, but maybe it was, when you got older.

"Be humble, Mr. Wilson," she said. "It will be difficult, but try. Somewhere under the self-confident arrogance and the overweening assurance there may be a nice boy. Let him out. He may surprise you. Are you going to marry Miss Van Dyke?"

"Yes, ma'am," he said, half bewildered by the apparent change of subject. "I hope to."

"Good. Perhaps she can take you in hand. And now you may go, Mr. Wilson. I believe we have concluded our last conversation."

"I hope so, Dr. Stafford," he said with a rush of mingled relief and anger. "I sure as hell hope so!"

"Close the door behind you," she ordered; adding, in an impersonal tone, "And good luck."

God! he thought as he walked blindly out into the soft sunny day. What an interview! Good God Almighty!

But it stayed with him, as she had certainly intended: it would always stay with him. And for several hours he was off-balance in a way he hadn't been since about third grade when some older boys had knocked him down, trampled on his books, and completely, for a while, destroyed his confidence and self-esteem. He found himself going back over not just the year now concluding but all four of his years at the University, recalling a hundred scenes and incidents, hundreds of friends and acquaintances. Had he really been "arrogant" and "superior"? Thinking he was "so perfect that ordinary mortals must bow down before him"? Guilty of "self-confident arrogance and overweening assurance"? "Self-centered"? "Insufferable"?

His thoughts returned to the year just past: leading the move to force Rudy Krohl out of the house . . . trying to force By Johnson into it . . . introducing By to Maryetta (a big mistake) . . . being perhaps too impatient with Marian, too laggard (though now reprieved) with Donna . . . causing the biggest campus disturbance in many years . . . protecting the wanderer . . . intervening in North's difficult life in a way that could ultimately prove disastrous for him and for B.J. . . . pushing through Excom things unimportant in themselves but things which, he saw now, could well have been considered examples of high-handed arrogance by those whom he had defeated or in essence forced to accede to his ideas . . .

But had all that been deliberate? Had it all been arrogance? Had there been no good motives? Was he that blind to his own character?

He stopped and leaned against one of the sandstone columns of the Quad, the feel of the cold stone through his shirt helping him to control to some degree his whirling emotions. Had he really been like that, when all the time he had thought he was being friendly and decent and considerate and compassionate and constructive—when the last thing in his mind was to be arrogant, or superior, or to try and lord it over anybody?

"It can't be," he said in an agonized half-whisper, oblivious of the few students still hurrying through the Quad on last-minute errands in these final hours of the quarter. "It can't be. I'm just not like that. I'm just *not.*"

But then, being Willie, he finally thought honestly: Well, maybe I have been sometimes, a little bit. Maybe I have been more positive and more domineering than I should have been. Maybe I've forced people to do things my way more times than I've been aware of, just because I've felt that I could see things a little faster and a little clearer and a little farther than most, and have let myself become impatient with those who didn't grasp them quite so quickly . . .

"I hope not," he whispered again in the same bleak way. "Oh, I *hope* not."

It took Guy and Buff and Timmy and Franky and Hack and Moose combined to convince him that no, he really was all right, he really wasn't all those harsh things that old bitch (probably all of fifty then) had told him he was. But even when Guy in some desperation made him go to the phone and call Donna for further reassurance, he still remained troubled and unhappy.

A person shouldn't *do* that to another person, he kept repeating to himself; a person shouldn't destroy another's self-confidence like that. But for all her flamboyant ways and fierce personality, he couldn't deny that Stafford *was* a brain and, in a strange way, full of character, integrity and ethics. And so maybe . . . maybe he should remember what she had said . . . and take to heart whatever he honestly felt did apply . . . and try to do better.

There may be a nice boy here, he thought with a wry wistfulness. Maybe I should let him out. He might surprise me.

He never forgot her; and when he heard, some twenty years later, that she had died suddenly in class in the midst of reading one of the sonnets, he felt a pang of real regret that they couldn't have been friends. They both might have profited. And the lesson might have been delivered more gently.

But gentle or no, and for whatever motivation, it had been delivered.

Time telescoped.
No longer days.
Hours.
Minutes.

The Phi Beta Kappa dinner and initiation came and went on Saturday night, a solemn and impressive affair that saw some seventy seniors, including himself, Donna, Guy, North and Ari Katanian, inducted. Sunday, day of baccalaureate, day of commencement, day of the first of many weddings in Memorial Church, dawned bright, cloudless, warm—verging on hot—as spring at last gave way to summer.

The campus was already more than half deserted. Freshmen, sophomores, juniors had all gone home. Halls, dorms, houses on the Row were all more than half empty. Seniors, their families and family friends comprised most of the population now.

There was no avoiding it: the Class of '39 was about to move on and with few exceptions, and for most only as alumni, never walk these pleasant ways again.

"You face a difficult world," Dr. Chalmers said at baccalaureate, "but you take with you the faith and the certainty we hope you have learned here. We have equipped you as best we can: not perfectly, because none of us is perfect, but with whatever we have learned ourselves of decency, tolerance, sound thinking, good judgment. Whether these will be enough to see you through the desperate days that all too likely lie ahead, we cannot say. That is up to you and to many other factors besides yourselves. We pray for you and hope that this beloved place has given you some small armor with which to fend off the years. If you carry away only a modest portion of the love and care we feel for you, you will possess a strength that is as the strength of thousands: for our concern for you is infinite."

"You face a difficult world," said the famous politician who addressed commencement, "yet your elders know, as your country knows, that you will not falter or fail in whatever challenge lies ahead. Equipped with one of the finest educations available in America, fortified by the traditions and practices of this great, free, democratic society, secure in that faith in ourselves and our future which is so *particularly* American in this happy land, you go forth to face challenges whose nature we cannot now accurately predict. But we know you will surely overcome them with that character, that bravery, that righteousness of cause which is truly and forever *American!*"

Which, as Tim murmured dryly to Willie as they sat in the hot sun in the outdoor amphitheater where the exercises were held, was not quite the in-depth of the Chalmers remarks but seemed to be pretty standard these days for members of the older generation contemplating the terrible possibility that they might have to send their sons off to war again.

Then it was diplomas handed out as they crossed the podium one by one in front of a smiling Dr. Chalmers, who shook each of them by the hand with a personal fondness they suddenly realized they were going to miss a lot.

And then the last they would see of their professors as the departing academic procession marched up the aisle—young, old, middle-aged, elderly—those lined faces and tired eyes—that wispy, flying gray hair—that air of patient stolidity as they trudged along in twos and threes in their brilliant robes past the children to whom they had attempted, with varying degrees of harmony or disharmony, failure or success, to give *at least a little something*—you could see the almost desperate hope that they had succeeded in those dogged, determined glances as they smiled and nodded to some remembered, familiar face that now would go and be forgotten, like the rest.

And then the happy applause from students and parents, the lifting of mortarboards, the handshakes and hugs and congratulations, the shouts and cries and tears and laughter and desperate hugs and goodbyes and promises to keep in touch, and underneath them all the soft, insistent, incessant internal drumbeat of *It's over. It's over. It's over.*

That night at eight they gathered in Memorial Church to watch a Franky who never seemed to stop grinning take a winsomely cute, happily beaming Katie to be his lawful, wedded wife. Next morning at eleven they gathered again to witness a serious but happy Hack marry a serenely smiling Fran. And at three in the afternoon they gathered yet again to witness the marriage of B.J. Letterman and North McAllister.

Shortly before the ceremony, in the chaplain's chamber, North was apparently joking quite naturally and easily with B.J.'s father and brothers. Willie, his best man, was standing in back of them, facing him. The boys burst into laughter at something their father had said, concentrating their amused attention momentarily on him. North suddenly shot Willie a look so absolutely agonized and imploring, as he described it to Guy when he finally told him about it later in the summer, that it sent chills up his spine.

He responded instantly.

"Hey, North!" he called out with jocular swiftness. "Come on out back and walk around with me for a minute! I need some fresh air!"

"Me too!" North said and was at his side and out so quickly that the others, laughing and at first disposed to follow, dropped back.

"Oh, Willie!" North gasped when they reached the protecting shelter of a clump of giant rhododendrons behind the church. "Oh, *Willie!*"

And for a terrible moment Willie thought he was actually going to break down completely. His reaction was instinctive. For a split second the thought crossed his mind: This may be misinterpreted. Then he thought: That's unworthy of me and unfair to him.

He stepped forward, held out his arms and hugged North to him as hard as he could. North responded like a drowning man. Willie held him for a long moment, then stepped back, still holding him, and looked directly into his eyes.

"It's going to be all right," he said slowly and firmly. "It's going to be all right. It's going to be *all right.* Now believe me, buddy. It's going to be *all right.*"

"I know, but—" North said in a harsh whisper. "I know, but—"

"All right," Willie repeated. "*All right.*"

And drew him once more into his arms and held him tight. And then pushed him away.

"Now," he said with a cheerfulness in his voice that he marveled at, "let's get back on in there and give 'em hell, O.K.? Your bride is waiting."

"O.K.," North said shakily and as though he really didn't know where he was. Which, Willie thought, he probably at that moment didn't. "O.K."

"Good," Willie said, taking him by the arm and guiding him firmly in. "Good."

And thought with a sudden bitterness he realized was probably childish but he couldn't seem to help it: How about *that,* Dr. Stafford? Still self-centered? Still insensitive? Still insufferable?

Twenty minutes later they all got through it in perfectly respectable fashion. North looked handsome, if a little pale, and no more than normally nervous; B.J. looked ecstatic; and after it was over, the whole party walked across the Quad through the hot afternoon to the waiting car. With happy cries, a lot of rice and a pillowcase full of loose feathers dumped on them by his fraternity brothers, groom and bride were sped on their way.

Walking slowly back to the house with Guy, in an exhausted slump whose extent Guy could sense but couldn't be told about just then, Willie felt like an absolute, dragged-out dishrag.

Ahead lay summer.

Ahead lay England.

Ahead, quite possibly, lay war.

And, as Guy reminded him when they reached the house, standing silent and deserted in the now-quiet street, all its busy life gone somewhere—somewhere—"Well, buddy? You and Donn haven't set the date yet. How about it?"

Which was true, they hadn't. No particular reason he could think of: they just hadn't. It was as though they were finally so certain of one another that there was no need to hurry.

But of course, with everything that was going on in the world, there was.

He smiled.

"I'll put it on my calendar for three twenty-seven P.M. next Tuesday."

"Wait until Maggie and I get back from New Jersey," Guy suggested. "I want to be best man."

"Billy will be devastated if he isn't."

"Oh, that's right. I'd forgotten him. Well, anyway, wait for me. I won't believe it unless I see it with my own eyes."

"Believe it," he said serenely. "I'm committed now."

Guy grinned, put his arm around his waist and gave him a hug—a different kind of hug, perfectly natural, affectionate and relaxed.

"And it wasn't as bad as we always thought it would be, was it?"

"No," he agreed as they went up the steps and into the house of memories. "Not at all."

Not quite as soon as next Tuesday, but within a couple of weeks, the date was set. It too came about quite naturally. They were together frequently as the early weeks of summer passed, always quite sedately and properly— Donn's upbringing and his own innate sense of what was fitting where she was concerned prevented any attempts on his part at anything else—but somehow making it definite didn't seem to come right until another afternoon when he was walking her to the president's office.

Suddenly he asked, "Isn't your birthday sometime in July?"

"The fifth," she said, an excited little note suddenly in her voice. "Why?"

"Why don't we get married then?"

"Why," she said with a delighted smile, "I think that would be perfect!"

They were near Memorial Church. He swung her around and marched her toward it.

"If Dr. Morris is in, let's set it up right now."

The chaplain was, and they did: eleven A.M., Wednesday, July 5.

"And then," he said, "let's get the hell out and go to the Ahwahnee at Yosemite for our honeymoon."

The word seem to paralyze her for a second. It paralyzed him, too, he had to admit. Then they began to grin at one another.

"It's a marvelous hotel," she said. "Oh, Willie! What a *great* idea!"

"Let's go tell Dr. Chalmers," he suggested. "They want to come."

He seized her hand and they actually skipped across the Inner Quad— from which, fortunately, all the people who might have exclaimed, "Now, what the hell are Willie and Donn doing, skipping across the Quad?" were long gone.

And so it came about.

25

Eight hundred and sixteen students enrolled for summer quarter. Eight hundred and one teaching and administrative staff attended to their needs. Student activities dwindled to a minimum. A series of academic and business conferences brought a few outsiders to campus. Everything shifted to low gear. Quad, Libe, Union, Cellar, halls, dorms, Row—everything was half deserted, peaceful, unhurried. Every hour as always, every ten minutes past the hour as always, the bell jangled through classrooms, offices and Quad. Only a handful responded to its loud, insistent clangor now.

The breezes died away except for the rare and transitory breath from the coast. The air became heavy and still. The heat increased. Trees, bushes, red tiles, sandstone arches, empty colonnades, turned dusty, drab, bedraggled.

Physically, as Willie told Donn when they returned from Yosemite, the University looked exactly as it had on the day four years ago—the day that now seemed so far away—when he had first seen it.

Hot, brown, dusty . . . quiet, peaceful, sleepy.

And he loved it now as he had then.

And always would.

Guy and Maggie took the Santa Fe Chief across country after their wedding, stopped by briefly to say hello, flew on to Hawaii for two weeks to see Guy's parents and then returned to campus for the rest of July and August. "Everything O.K., buddy?" Guy inquired when he and Willie were alone. "Fine," Willie responded. "And you?" "Couldn't be better," Guy said. They poked one another in the ribs and looked so pleased with themselves that it was just as well their wives didn't see it.

North too returned, a week after he and B.J. had spent a week at a horse ranch in Jackson Hole and a week each with her parents and his. Willie didn't go out of his way to be alone with him, didn't go out of his way to avoid him. In due course they found themselves together and he ventured to ask, "You all right?" North nodded, uttered a terse, "Mmmm," and said no more. B.J. seemed serenely happy and Willie didn't press.

Buff lazed through the days when they weren't taking flying lessons, dating a few of the summer girls in his amiable, rather offhand way; played some golf, drank some beer, felt pretty useless, as he confessed to Duke, who was happily busy in the office of the dean of education, though still apprehensive about events in Europe. They were holding down the house with Timmy and Moose: the three marrieds had received permission from the administration to live in the house if they wanted to, but all three had elected to live in graduate students' quarters over near women's dorm. They all dropped in frequently and said wistfully that they wished they could be there, but the girls didn't want to. They said they could understand this— they guessed. It marked, in some unstated but definite way, the start of inevitable separations that came with marriage. It was something they all felt, especially the bachelors: a certain diminishment of camaraderie—a little distancing—things not quite so easy, quite so relaxed, quite so close—a separation, subtle but apparently insurmountable—the loss of a bond not exactly describable but, they recognized in its passing, one which had been precious and meaningful to them. Sad, they thought—they all thought. But what could be done?

Aside from that, which he felt perhaps more than any of them, having been so dependent on their close-knit friendship, Moose was happy as a clam, he confessed freely and frequently, helping Coach plan the fall season. He went about the house singing—a strange sound, as Willie remarked, but an exuberant one—and they all felt good about him. He was so happy with everything, he told them, that he would even volunteer to fly with them once in a while just to show that he could. He couldn't, however. The one time he tried, with Buff, he got so sick immediately that Buff could only circle the field once and then had to put it right down again and let him stagger out.

"Not for me," he said with a wan smile when his insides settled a bit. "I'll be your hero on the ground, if you guys don't mind."

They assured him they didn't.

Tim scrounged the sleepy campus for the occasional news item to send the City papers and for this received a very small weekly retainer that helped to round out his other part-time job as teaching assistant to the journalism department's five summer students. He also worked part-time, for the hell of it, as "honorary associate editor" of the skimpy summer *Daily*. He continued to write letters to the editor "viewing with *increasing* alarm," as Guy kidded him, but with what he felt was complete justification—because, as he pointed out, look what was happening: Hitler stepping up his demands for Danzig and a Polish corridor . . . warnings by the British and French foreign ministers that they expected him to respect the status of Danzig as prescribed by the Versailles Treaty . . . announcement that he had massed an enormous strike force of tanks and cavalry on the Polish border . . . rapidly rising tensions throughout Europe as WAR CRISIS GROWS.

They attended their flying classes, worked at their part-time jobs, joined one another for movies, meals and picnics when Donna, Maggie and B.J. got in the mood for them, which was often.

So passed the sleepy weeks of summer. Ever closer came cruel September.

On August 23, a thunderclap from which many naive souls and wishful thinkers in America, including Maryetta Bradford, would never really recover as long as they lived, it was announced that German Foreign Minister Von Ribbentrop had made a secret trip to Moscow to sign a Soviet-Nazi nonaggression pact—the two death's heads, Stalin and Hitler, symbolically and in fact shaking hands over the body of a dying Europe.

A week later, their beginners' training completed, Buff bade them what was, for him, an emotional farewell—there were actually tears in his eyes, they noted—and took off for Montclair, announcing his intention to enlist in the Army Air Corps as soon as he got home. Guy and Maggie left to make another parental swing to Hawaii and Trenton before leaving—they hoped— for England and the Rhodes scholarship. North took B.J. off to Salt Lake City to see her folks for a week before returning to campus to resume his medical studies. Moose hunkered down and decided to stay on in the house fall quarter "if the guys will let me." Word from Tony, the new house manager, was that there was room, and they would be delighted.

Tim, aghast at what was clearly about to happen in Europe, was greatly pleased to get a favorable response from the Baltimore *Sun* to the inquiries he had sent out right after graduation, and got ready to return east with the hope that he might by some miracle wangle an overseas assignment in the war he now knew was inevitable.

Willie and Donn said goodbye to Guy and Maggie with stout promises to see them in England, although now they, like everyone, no longer had any idea where or when or whether they would meet again.

On Labor Day weekend, just before they were to leave to spend three days with the Wilsons and then on to New York to visit the Van Dykes before sailing for England on September 10, Willie called the house and told Timmy and Moose that Donn wanted to have a farewell picnic on one of their favorite hills near campus.

On September 1, in a car Tim had borrowed from a friend on the summer *Daily*, they set out for it around noon.

It was on that high hill, in the closing days of summer, in a news bulletin transmitted by the portable radio that Tim now took everywhere with him, that the days of their youth came finally and entirely to an end—not unexpected, by that time, but devastating indeed, for all of that.

For a while they did not listen to the radio—"God, Timmy, give it a rest!" Moose beseeched; and for once, perhaps moved by the sentimentality of their final gathering in this so greatly favored part of the world, Tim obeyed.

They ate Donn's good ham sandwiches and consumed the last of Buff's beer, bequeathed to them with the admonition "Drink it for me!"

Then they lay back on the grass for a while and just watched the clouds go by, not saying anything, lost in a replete and happy haze . . . until Willie finally took pity on Tim's obvious restlessness and on a sudden wry impulse suggested, "Let's turn on the radio and see if there's a war on."

And did.

And there was.

"Hitler's armies struck today without warning deep into the heart of Poland," the announcer's tense voice boomed out into the serene quiet of the friendly hills. "In London, Prime Minister Chamberlain will make a radio address shortly to the British people. He is expected to announce that Great Britain and her Empire are once again at war with Germany."

Wilson turned off the radio and, for some reason he could not have explained, stood up.

"Well," he said in a voice that shook more than he knew, "I guess that does it."

They stared at one another blankly. Donn started to cry.

A sudden melancholy touched his heart. He reached down and rested his hand gently on her head.

Forever after part of him would always be standing on the lovely hill above the lovely valley, his hand on the head of his wife, the gentle haze of summer, summer, summer all around.

Tears came into his eyes and all the happy days rushed through his heart, going somewhere, somewhere, lost, gone, irretrievable, leaving him stranded on this distant hill while far below the red-tiled roofs of the University shimmered in the sun.

Ah, you wonderful place, he thought, you good times and dear friends! What will they do to us, in their pride and their anger? Where will they send us drifting, on the darkening flood of the years? Toward what bright glory? Into what far harbor?

He could only wonder, in fear and apprehension, on this golden afternoon while far away the hounds of hell were running free and would, he knew now beyond all escaping, come closer.

Perhaps if he and his friends were lucky they might, in time, achieve a fragile peace and so come home, in a different season.

But of that there was no surety.

His heart was full of dreams, his head was full of schemes.

He was twenty-two years old and the world—if this proved agreeable to Adolf Hitler, Franklin Roosevelt, Winston Churchill, Emperor Hirohito and all the others great and small whose lives would impinge upon his in the years to come—might still . . . perhaps . . . turn out to be his oyster.

That remained to be seen.